WHAT THE FACE REVEALS

SERIES IN AFFECTIVE SCIENCE

SERIES EDITORS
Richard J. Davidson
Paul Ekman
Klaus Scherer

The Nature of Emotion
Fundamental Questions
Edited by Paul Ekman and Richard J. Davidson

Boo!
Culture, Experience, and the Startle Reflex
Ronald Simons

Emotions in Psychopathology
Theory and Research
Edited by William F. Flack Jr. and James D. Laird

Affective Neuroscience
The Foundation of Human and Animal Emotions
Jaak Panksepp

WHAT THE FACE REVEALS

Basic and Applied Studies of
Spontaneous Expression Using the
Facial Action Coding System (FACS)

Edited by
PAUL EKMAN &
ERIKA L. ROSENBERG

New York   Oxford   •   Oxford University Press   1997

Oxford University Press

Oxford   New York
Athens   Auckland   Bangkok   Bogota   Bombay   Buenos Aires
Calcutta   Cape Town   Dar es Salaam   Delhi   Florence   Hong Kong
Istanbul   Karachi   Kuala Lumpur   Madras   Madrid   Melbourne
Mexico City   Nairobi   Paris   Singapore   Taipei   Tokyo   Toronto   Warsaw

and associated companies in
Berlin   Ibadan

Library of Congress Cataloging-in-Publication Data
What the face reveals : basic and applied studies of spontaneous
expression using the facial action coding system (FACS) / edited by
Paul Ekman and Erika Rosenberg.
   p. cm. — (Series in affective science)
Includes bibliographical references.
ISBN 0-19-510446-3 (cloth).; ISBN 0-19-510447-1 (paper)
1. Facial expression. 2. Nonverbal communication (Psychology)
I. Ekman, Paul. II. Rosenberg, Erika. III. Series.
BF592.F33W43 1997
153.6′9—dc21   96-36655

9   8   7   6   5   4   3   2   1
Printed in the United States of America
on acid-free paper

Acknowledgments

Ekman, P., Friesen, W., and Simons, R. (1985). Is the startle reaction an emotion? *Journal of Personality and Social Psychology, 49,* 1416–1426. Copyright 1985 by the American Psychological Association. Reprinted with permission.

Hager, J., & Ekman, P. (1985). The asymmetry of facial actions is inconsistent with models of hemispheric specialization. *Psychophysiology, 22,* 307–318. Copyright 1985 by Cambridge University Press. Reprinted with the permission of the publisher.

Rosenberg, E., & Ekman, P. (1994). Coherence between expressive and experiential systems in emotion. *Cognition & Emotion, 8,* 201–229. Copyright 1994 by Erlbaum (UK) Taylor & Francis. Reprinted with the permission of the publisher.

Ruch, W. (1995). Will the real relationship between facial expression and affective experience please stand up: The case of exhilaration. *Cognition & Emotion, 9,* 33–58. Copyright 1995 by Lawrence Erlbaum Associates Limited. Reprinted with the permission of the publisher.

Ruch, W. (1993). Extraversion, alcohol, and enjoyment. *Personality and Individual Differences, 16,* 89–102. Copyright 1993 Pergamon Press Ltd. Reprinted with kind permission from Elsevier Science Ltd., The Boulevard, Langford Lane, Kidlington OX5 1GB, UK.

Keltner, D. (1995). Signs of appeasement: Evidence for the distinct displays of embarrassment, amusement, and shame. *Journal of Personality and Social Psychology, 68,* 441–454. Copyright 1995 by the American Psychological Association. Reprinted with permission.

Craig, K., Hyde, S., & Patrick, C. (1991). Genuine, suppressed, and faked facial behavior during exacerbation of chronic low back pain. *Pain, 46,* 161–171. Copyright 1991 Elsevier Science Publishers. Reprinted with kind permission from Elsevier Science Ltd.

Prkachin, K. (1992). The consistency of facial expressions of pain: A comparison across modalities. *Pain, 51,* 297–306. Copyright 1992 Elsevier Science Publishers. Reprinted with kind permission from Elsevier Science Ltd.

Ekman, P., Friesen, W., & O'Sullivan, M. (1988). Smiles when lying. *Journal of Personality and Social Psychology, 54*, 414–420. Copyright 1988 by the American Psychological Association. Reprinted with permission.

Frank, M., Ekman, P., & Friesen, W. (1993). Behavioral markers and recognizability of the smile of enjoyment. *Journal of Personality and Social Psychology, 64*, 83–93. Copyright 1993 by the American Psychological Association. Reprinted with permission.

Gosselin, P., Kirouac, G., & Doré, F. (1995). Components and recognition of facial expression in the communication of emotion by actors. *Journal of Personality and Social Psychology, 68*, 83–96. Copyright 1995 by the American Psychological Association. Reprinted with permission.

Hess, U., & Kleck, R. (1990). Differentiating emotion elicited and deliberate emotional facial expressions. *European Journal of Social Psychology, 20*, 369–385. Copyright 1990 by John Wiley & Sons, Ltd. Reprinted with the permission of the publisher.

Camras, L., Oster, H., Campos, J., Miyake, K., & Bradshaw, D. (1992). Japanese and American infants' responses to arm restraint. *Developmental Psychology, 28*, 578–583. Copyright 1992 by the American Psychological Association. Reprinted with permission.

Rosenstein, D., & Oster, H. (1988). Differential facial responses to four basic tastes in newborns. *Child Development, 59*, 1555–1568. Copyright 1988 by the Society for Research in Child Development, Inc. Reprinted with the permission of the publisher.

Berenbaum, H., & Oltmanns, T. (1992). Emotional experience and expression in schizophrenia and depression. *Journal of Abnormal Psychology, 101*, 37–44. Copyright 1992 by the American Psychological Association. Reprinted with permission.

Steimer-Krause, E., Krause, R. & Wagner, G. (1990). Interaction regulations used by schizophrenic and psychosomatic patients: Studies on facial behavior in dyadic interactions. *Psychiatry, 53*, 209–228. Copyright 1990 by the Guilford Press. Reprinted with the permission of the publisher.

Ellgring, H. (1986). Nonverbal expression of psychological states in psychiatric patients. *European Archives of Psychiatry and Neurological Sciences, 236*, 31–34. Copyright 1986 by Springer-Verlag. Reprinted with the permission of the publisher.

Heller, M., & Haynal, V. (1994). Depression and suicide faces. *Cahiers Psychiatriques Genevois, 16*, 107–117. This article originally appeared in the French in *Cahiers Psychiatriques Genevois*. Reprinted with the permission of the publisher.

Bänninger-Huber, E. (1992). Prototypical affective microsequences in psychotherapeutic interaction. *Psychotherapy Research, 2*, 291–306. Copyright 1992 by the Guilford Press. Reprinted with the permission of the publisher.

Keltner, D., Moffitt, T., & Stouthamer-Loeber, M. (1995). Facial expressions of emotion and psychopathology in adolescent boys. *Journal of Abnormal Psychology, 104*,

644–652. Copyright 1995 by the American Psychological Association. Reprinted with permission.

Cheney, M., Ekman, P., Friesen, W., Black, G., & Hecker, M. (1990). Type A behavior Pattern: Facial behavior and speech components. *Psychosomatic Medicine, 53*, 307–319. Reprinted by permission of Williams & Wilkins.

Contents

Foreword

M. BREWSTER SMITH

What the Face Reveals is strong evidence for the fruitfulness of the systematic analysis of facial expression initiated by Paul Ekman and Wallace V. Friesen in 1976 and 1978; it will also become a valuable, even obligatory resource for all investigators who wish to use or understand the Facial Action Coding System (FACS), as Ekman and Friesen's approach is called. This book should also be of interest to a broader constituency than students of the face and of emotion: facial expression carries information about a wide range of phenomena, and findings reported here bear on significant issues in personality, psychopathology, and early development. As an outsider to the tradition in which Ekman works, I have been impressed by the important part he and his colleagues have played in restoring affect and emotion to an appropriately central place in human psychology.

Erika Rosenberg recounts the story in her introductory chapter: how behaviorism not only denigrated the inner experience of emotion but canonized bad data on the supposed cultural arbitrariness of emotional expression. After midcentury, Silvan Tomkins's ideas about the basic affects and their linkage to distinctive facial expression pointed the way, but his presentation and advocacy of these ideas were so idiosyncratic and difficult to penetrate that they became generally known only after Paul Ekman and Carroll Izard had undertaken groundbreaking research under his influence. For the last two decades, Ekman's group has been the principal contributor to this complement and sequel to the "cognitive revolution," bringing affect back into the formulations of general psychology.

The detailed, laborious work with FACS reported in this book is also a substantial part of that contribution. It represents a real breakthrough in the study of facial expression. Virtually all previous research focused on the inferences observers draw from depicted or enacted facial expressions; it did not really examine what was going on in the face itself. This book is the first to bring together research that examines facial behavior directly. It bears strong witness to the fruitfulness of Ekman's approach to the study of spontaneous facial expression.

The articles reprinted in this volume date from 1982 to 1995, with the majority (15 of 22) coming from the 1990s. They include an early paper by Ekman, Matsumoto, and Friesen that had not been previously published because it was editorially rejected. The authors have good grounds by now for their assurance that this was an editorial mistake. The reprinted articles appeared in 13 different journals—as Ekman and Rosenberg note, a range beyond the probable ken of the contributors themselves. They involve principal authors from Europe and Canada, as well as the United States. The enterprise has become worldwide, no longer centered on Ekman's active Human Interaction Laboratory at the University of California, San Francisco.

Assembling as it does major reports of basic research on emotional expression and applied research on a variety of topics ranging from schizophrenia, depression, and suicide to therapeutic interaction and Type A behavior, all approached via FACS or its derivatives, the book provides solid evidence for the value of employing this standardized method for the analysis of facial expression. A further feature, which makes for fascinating reading, is the informal "afterwords" contributed by the authors of each reprinted article in which the authors describe their subsequent work on the topic of their papers, bringing the treatment fully up to date and often speculating more freely about the significant issues than the journal format of their original presentations allowed. In the same vein is the concluding chapter by Ekman, "What We Have Learned by Measuring the Face." This chapter, together with the various afterwords, very effectively brings the reader abreast of the current state of the art. Ekman and Rosenberg obviously intend the book to attract more psychologists to their method. Dozens of researchable problems are identified along the way. Several minor revisions of FACS scoring are also specified: prospective users need to consult the book.

This is a book for reference and selective reading. From my outsider's vantage point, I note that although FACS is a richly fruitful device that enables cumulative research on facial expression, it is no magical "open sesame." It is inherently laborious and expensive and requires thorough training. And the phenomena that it deals with are complex, not reducible to simplistic formulas. A dramatically distinctive finding such as the discovery of the Duchenne felt smile stands out, but not surprisingly, the interconnections of facial expression with the rest of human psychology are mostly complicated and hard to elucidate. But this book records very significant progress. It is encouraging that more than a century after Darwin opened the topic of emotional expression, with good observation and inspired prescience, the research enabled by FACS is finally dealing with it in a careful, empirical way very much in the Darwinian tradition.

Contributors

EVA BÄNNINGER-HUBER, Department of Clinical Psychology, University of Zurich, Switzerland

HOWARD BERENBAUM, Department of Psychology, University of Illinois

GEORGE W. BLACK, Department of Epidemiology and Biostatistics, School of Medicine, University of California, San Francisco

DONNA BRADSHAW, Psychology and Social Relations, Harvard University

JOSEPH J. CAMPOS, Institute for Human Development, University of California, Berkeley

LINDA A. CAMRAS, Department of Psychology, DePaul University

MARGARET CHESNEY, Department of Epidemiology and Biostatistics, School of Medicine, University of California, San Francisco

KENNETH D. CRAIG, Department of Psychology, University of British Columbia

FRANÇOIS Y. DORÉ, Department of Psychology, University of Laval, Québec, Canada

PAUL EKMAN, Department of Psychiatry, University of California, San Francisco

HEINER ELLGRING, Max Planck Institute for Psychiatry, Germany

MARK G. FRANK, School of Communication, Rutgers University

WALLACE V. FRIESEN, Department of Psychiatry, University of California, San Francisco

PIERRE GOSSELIN, Department of Psychology, University of Ottowa, Canada

JOSEPH C. HAGER, Network Information Research Corporation, Salt Lake City, Utah

VÉRONIQUE HAYNAL, Laboratory Affect and Communication, Geneva, Switzerland

MICHAEL H. L. HECKER, SRI International, Menlo Park, California

MICHAEL HELLER, Laboratory Affect and Communication, Geneva, Switzerland

URSULA HESS, Department of Psychology, University of Geneva, Switzerland

SUSAN A. HYDE, Cape Brenton Hospital, Cape Brenton, Canada

DACHER KELTNER, Department of Psychology, University of California, Berkeley

GILLES KIROUAC, Department of Psychology, University of Laval, Québec, Canada

ROBERT E. KLECK, Department of Psychology, Dartmouth College

RAINER KRAUSE, Department of Clinical Psychology, University of the Saarland, Germany

DAVID MATSUMOTO, Department of Psychology, San Francisco State University

KAZUO MIYAKE, Kawamura Gakuen Women's University, Abiko-shi, Chiba-ken, Japan

TERRIE E. MOFFITT, Department of Psychology, University of Wisconsin, Madison

LAURA NISENSON, Department of Psychiatry, University of Michigan

MAUREEN O'SULLIVAN, Department of Psychology, University of San Francisco

THOMAS F. OLTMANNS, Department of Psychology, University of Virginia

HARRIET OSTER, School Psychology Programs, New York University

CHRISTOPHER J. PATRICK, Department of Psychology, Florida State University

KENNETH M. PRKACHIN, Psychology Program, University of Northern British Columbia, Canada

ERIKA L. ROSENBERG, Department of Psychology, College of William and Mary

WILLIBALD RUCH, Department of Psychology, University of Düsseldorf, Germany

DIANA ROSENSTEIN, Department of Psychology, University of Pennsylvania

RONALD C. SIMONS, Department of Psychiatry & Anthropology, Michigan State University, East Lansing, Department of Psychiatry & Behavioral Sciences, University of Washington

EVELYNE STEIMER-KRAUSE, Department of Clinical Psychology, University of the Saarland, Germany

MAGDA STOUTHAMER-LOEBER, Western Psychiatric Institute, University of Pittsburgh

GÜNTER WAGNER, Department of Clinical Psychology, University of the Saarland, Germany

WHAT THE FACE REVEALS

Introduction

The Study of Spontaneous Facial Expressions in Psychology

ERIKA L. ROSENBERG

Much of the research in which facial behavior has been measured and related to other variables is unknown to many psychologists because the work has been published in a wide variety of places. In addition to journals in psychology, many studies have appeared in journals of psychiatry, European journals, and journals of medicine. This unique book presents previously published articles on spontaneous facial expression in a single volume, so that they may be more accessible to interested scholars and practitioners. It also contains afterwords by the authors that offer the reader a glimpse of the researchers' current thinking on the issues addressed in their articles.

This is not a book about people's ability to recognize facial expressions. The current psychological literature is replete with such studies and reviews of studies, especially research on the recognition of facial expressions of emotion. We chose not to include facial recognition research because that research is well known, especially in the general areas of social and personality psychology. The focus of this book is research involving measurement of the face itself. In the research on judgments of posed expressions (which constitutes the majority of facial recognition work), facial measurement procedures have been used, if at all, only as a means for selecting or setting the standards for facial stimuli. The expressions are primarily considered to be independent variables, and their effects on other variables are under study.

In this book we have reprinted a selection of articles in which the face is measured as a *dependent* variable or as a correlate of changes in other bodily systems. Often this is done in an exploratory fashion: What facial behaviors occur when people report feeling embarrassed? or Are there facial expressions that characterize people who have been classified as prone to heart disease? or who are depressed? How do they differ in facial behavior from those who are manic? In these cases the face is seen as a potential new source of information about an important problem or as a diagnostic marker of a certain trait or state. In other cases, facial variables are used in a more proscribed manner, in which the frequency, intensity, or duration of certain types of expressions, such as those associated with particular emotions, are measured. Both approaches, plus other innovative new techniques, are presented in this volume.

The work is varied and rich, and in nearly every case the application of systematic facial measurement has shed light on the understanding of many important questions in psychology and psychiatry that have long been unanswered (or unasked) through the application of other techniques. We hope that bringing these works together in one place will not only increase the visibility of these unique research contributions that utilize facial measurement but also stimulate other researchers to study the face.

Here are the kinds of questions that are answered within this book:

- Are there behavioral signs of deception?
- Is there a facial expression for embarrassment?
- Do infants show facial expressions of emotion, and if so, to what extent does this imply an innate versus culturally learned expressive system?
- Can certain facial behavior changes indicate one's personality or, for that matter, mark the presence of psychopathology?
- Do facial expression asymmetries reveal which part of the brain generates emotion?
- Can the face provide clues about suicidal behavior?
- In what ways do the facial behavior patterns of one person in a conversation influence those of another?
- How well does one's facial expressions of emotion correspond to the emotions one is feeling at that time?
- Are there differences between expressions that occur when someone is truly feeling an emotion from those that occur when someone is feigning the emotion?

The book is divided into two major parts: one on basic research and another on applied research. Part I—"Basic Research on Emotion"—consists mainly of research relevant to the psychology of emotion, but it also includes basic research on related topics—namely, deception and pain. Part II—"Applied Research"—presents studies in which facial measures were examined in relation to mental or physical health variables. Many of the studies in Part II show that facial expression variables prove to be useful in discriminating among diagnostic groups. Within each part, each chapter consists of a reprinted article, followed by a brief afterword by the authors of the original piece. In their afterwords, the authors explain how their work on the topic has progressed since the time of original publication of their article, they reflect on the utility of measuring the face in their research, and they speculate on what they might have done differently in their research in light of what they have subsequently learned.

This book concludes with a chapter by Paul Ekman, in which he integrates what we have learned by measuring the face, comments on the specific contributions to various fields by the studies reprinted in this volume, and offers suggestions for future research. The remainder of this introduction includes an overview of the reprinted research articles, a brief history of the study of the face in modern psychology, and a discussion of facial measurement procedures.

Overview of the Original Research Articles

Basic Research on Emotion

Part I includes studies that can be roughly grouped as relevant to basic research on emotion. These studies cover such topics as expressive or behavioral correlates of emotional experience, the neurological control of facial emotion, and the distinctions between deliberate and spontaneous facial behavior.

Ekman, Friesen, and Simons (chapter 1) studied the startle reaction in order to determine if it behaved like a reflex or an emotion. They measured facial behavior, as well as head, neck, and trunk movements, when subjects were told to expect a very loud noise and when they were not warned about the noise. They also tested whether people could inhibit the startle reaction. They concluded that their findings on morphological and temporal characteristics accompanying each condition suggest that the startle reaction is a reflex, not an emotion.

In another methodologically sophisticated study, Hager and Ekman (chapter 2) examined whether facial expressions of emotion are biased or asymmetrical in ways predicted by theories of hemispheric specialization for emotion-relevant processing. They studied both spontaneous and simulated facial expressions of emotion and startle. They quantitatively measured all facial movement exhibited under these conditions, including the symmetry of facial actions (differences in intensity of muscular contraction for each distinct type of facial action that occurred). Hager and Ekman report that the expressive intricacies of deliberate versus spontaneous facial expressions of emotion are not consistent with some recent neuropsychological theories of hemispheric specialization (e.g., Borod & Koff, 1984).

The article by Rosenberg and Ekman (chapter 3) and the first of two articles by Ruch (chapter 4) both sought to determine whether the application of new methodological or analytical techniques could reveal the extent to which facial expression covaries with emotional experience during spontaneous emotional responses. Rosenberg and Ekman induced emotion by showing subjects emotionally evocative films, and then they employed a new rating technique to obtain momentary reports of emotional experience. Analyses focused on evaluating the coherence between expression and emotional reports at several moments throughout an emotional episode. The findings suggest that facial expression and emotional experience are more often congruent than not, and that response cohesion may be mediated by the intensity of the emotional event. Ruch, however, intercorrelated the facial expression measurements and self-report of cheerfulness in three alcohol conditions. He explored whether the degree of correspondence between these two measures of emotion varied as a function of the type of correlational design. Although the articles employ very different methodologies, they both show that on an intra-individual basis, expression and experience vary together.

The second article by Ruch (chapter 5) examined how the personality dimension of extraversion, one of the major personality dimensions described by Eysenck (1981) and one of the Big-5 trait dimensions (Costa & McCrae, 1985), is manifest in facial expression. Ruch also addressed Eysenck's biopsychological notion that body chemistry and personality are interdependent by examining Eysenck's idea that introverts would show facilitated expressivity during low alcohol consumption. Ruch found that alcohol decreased the facial expressions of "exhilaration" in extraverts, but it did not affect introverts.

Keltner (chapter 6) put exhaustive facial measurement to its ideal use—to uncover a "new" facial expression of emotion. He described the morphological and temporal characteristics of a facial expression of embarrassment, based on the coding of spontaneous facial behavior shown in a context in which people reported feeling this emotion. Keltner described an embarrassment expression in which a set of facial actions unfold over time. He also provided preliminary evidence that this expression has signal value that distinguishes it from other facial expressions.

Several articles in the first part of this book deal with the issue of spontaneous versus deliberate facial expressions of emotion. The Ekman, Friesen, and O'Sullivan (chapter 9) article and the Frank, Ekman, and Friesen (chapter 10) article both reported on studies designed to distinguish the smile of enjoyment from smiles that occur in other contexts. Ekman, Friesen, and O'Sullivan used comprehensive facial measurement procedures to determine whether the types of smiles that occurred during an interview when subjects were encouraged to deceive their interviewer about their feelings differed from the types of smiles shown when they were being honest about their feelings. They reported on the morphological differences between honest-condition smiles and deceptive-condition smiles (the presence or absence of contraction of orbicularis oculi). Frank, Ekman, and Friesen studied videotapes of smiles exhibited during two situations; in particular, they focused on whether temporal characteristics of the contraction of zygomatic major differed between smiles that showed the enjoyment marker (contraction of orbicularis oculi, the muscle surrounding the eyes) and smiles that did not include the enjoyment marker. Zygomatic contraction during enjoyment smiles showed smoother contraction and less variable durations of contraction than nonenjoyment smiles.

Gosselin, Kirouac, and Dore (chapter 11) and Hess and Kleck (chapter 12) also reported work in which temporal dynamics of expressions are useful means by which to distinguish between genuine and deliberate facial expressions. Gosselin et al. asked actors to portray emotions either while feeling them or while not feeling them. They both described the facial components involved in these two classes of performed behavior and examined the recognition of the performed movements. Portrayals of emotion expression during the "feeling" condition were closer to the expression of genuine emotion than expression shown during the "no-feeling" condition. Hess and Kleck examined spontaneous versus deliberate facial expression of happiness and disgust in two experiments. In one they compared the dynamic characteristics of posed expression of happiness and disgust to spontaneous expression of these same emotions, obtained during episodes in a film-viewing task when the subjects reported feeling the target emotions. In the second experiment, subjects viewed emotionally evocative films under two conditions, one in which they believed they were not being observed and could respond spontaneously, and another in which they were instructed to try to conceal their feelings from an unseen observer. Analyses of facial behavior in both experiments suggested that deliberate expression shows more irregularity in timing than spontaneous expression of the same emotions.

Two exemplary applications of facial measurement to the study of infant facial behavior appear in this volume. Rosenstein and Oster (chapter 14) coded infants' facial responses to four taste stimuli. Their findings show that newborn infants discriminate among different taste stimuli, which indicates that such sensory skills are not learned but innate (at least as per 2 hours of age). Camras, Oster, Campos, Miyake, and Bradshaw (chapter 13) reported consistencies, as well as differences, between Japanese and American infants' facial responses to arm restraint at two different ages. Although there were some differences between cultures in terms of how quickly infants showed certain negative emotion expressions, generally the data supported the hypothesis of between-culture consistency in expression.

Kenneth Craig and Kenneth Prkachin were pioneering researchers in the area of facial expression of pain, and their work has had basic and applied significance. Pain has a large subjective component—there is much less than a one-to-one correspondence between tissue damage and pain reports (Beecher, 1946; Loeser, 1990). Thus, finding a means for measuring pain behaviorally would be of great value for diagnosticians. Prkachin (chapter 8) measured facial behavior across a variety of pain contexts and described a set of facial actions consistently associated with pain. Craig and his colleagues (chapter 7) compared spontaneous facial behavior during potentially painful movement exercises in people with chronic low back pain with the behaviors shown when they were asked to "fake" or suppress their expressions during the same painful movement. Their findings suggest that there are great similarities between faked and genuine expressions of pain, although the occurrence of certain behaviors may reveal the fake expression.

Applied Research

The research reported in the second part of this book illustrates how the systematic study of facial expressions can reveal patterns of behavior that mark certain traits or psychological disorders. Implications for the understanding of the etiology of some disorders, as well as the diagnostic utility of facial expressions, are discussed.

This part opens with the one article in this book not published elsewhere.[1] Ekman, Matsumoto, and Friesen (chapter 15) demonstrated the diagnostic capability of facial measurement in the study of psychiatric disorders. They studied videotapes of two samples of psychiatric patients. The tapes were obtained during admission and discharge for one sample and during admissions for the second sample. Analyses included using facial expression of emotion at admission to predict clinical improvement, to distinguish among diagnostic groups, and to differentiated among patients within diagnostic groups. Ekman et al. found that facial expressions of emotions distinguished among diagnostic groups (schizophrenics, depressives, and manics) and offered preliminary evidence that certain behaviors may have value in clinical prognosis. Methodologically, they showed that much the same information about the facial behavior in their sample could be obtained using more expedient methods of facial coding (which scored only emotion-relevant facial actions) as opposed to exhaustive description of facial movement.

Berenbaum and Oltmanns (chapter 16) studied schizophrenics and depressives for evidence of blunted affect, a supposed correlate of depression that also occurs in many schizophrenics. Blunted and nonblunted schizophrenics, depressives, and normal subjects were exposed to emotionally evocative film and taste stimuli, and they were videotaped during exposure to the stimuli. The use of emotion-specific facial coding procedures allowed the authors to explore the types of affect that may be blunted, whether they were the same for schizophrenics and depressives, and whether the amount of affect displayed varied with intensity (or amount) of emotion. They found that affect displayed in certain emotionally evocative situations varied among the different groups (blunted schizophrenics, nonblunted schizophrenics, and depressives), with blunted schizophrenics showing the greatest deficits.

Steimer-Krause, Krause, and Wagner (chapter 17) reported on a series of investigations examining facial behavior in psychotherapeutic interaction. They studied schizophrenics, psychosomatics, and normal subjects in various dyadic interactions (healthy–healthy, schizophrenic inpatient–healthy, schizophrenic outpatient–healthy, and psychosomatic–healthy). Facial expressions of emotion shown during the 20-minute conversations were coded from videotape and were examined in terms of how productive subjects were, how variable their facial behavior was, and how their facial affect related to verbal activity. The results showed how facial behavior may mark the "intensity of cathexis" in psychotherapeutic interaction across diagnostic groups, whereas information about the specific types of affects shown may be features of particular types of psychopathologies.

Ellgring (chapter 18) examined the relationship between verbal communication of emotion and facially expressed emotion during interviews in depressives and normals (as well as schizophrenics, in his second study). He reported evidence for dissociation between these measures of affect in both patient groups (though much stronger in the schizophrenics). Normals showed a tight association between expression and verbal communication of affect. These findings are relevant to the coherence issue raised by Rosenberg and Ekman and Ruch (chapters 3–4) in the first part of this book, in that they show that normally present coherence may become dissociated in certain psychopathologies.

Heller and Haynal (chapter 19), in an English translation (and update) of an article originally published in French, described the facial behavior of suicidal depressed patients. They asked whether depressed suicidal and nonsuicidal patients differ on the types of behavior shown in an interview context. They looked at facial actions singly and in combination, and examined patterns of emotional expressions. They charted differences among the groups in terms of the repertoire of behaviors, the duration of facial events, as well as overall mobility, all of which might be put to important diagnostic use.

Bänninger-Huber's (chapter 20) research was an exhaustive case study of nonverbal behavior in a psychoanalytic therapeutic setting. She examined the facial affect of both the client and the therapist, from individual and interactive perspectives. The findings indicated that sharing of positive affect facilitates a productive therapeutic context. Methodologically, Bänninger-Huber's work epitomized the elegant application of microanalytic facial coding to the study of the temporal dynamics of behavior, as well as the innovative use of facial measurement to uncover behavioral sequences that may have interpersonal affective implications.

Keltner, Moffitt, and Stouthamer-Loeber (chapter 21) examined whether certain styles of psychological adjustment—externalizing and internalizing—are associated with emotional behavior. The adjustment literature suggests that externalizers are more hostile and aggressive, whereas internalizers are more withdrawn, fearful, and depressed. These styles are associated with behavior problems, especially in adolescent boys. Keltner et al. studied the facial expressions exhibited by adolescent boys during a structured social interaction context, and analyzed whether these expressions varied systematically by psychological adjustment group. Their findings support the relationship between externalization and anger, although support for the internalization and fear relationship was not as strong. They also found that nondisordered boys showed more embarrassment than the disordered boys, implying perhaps that they are more aware of social mores or norms for appropriate behavior.

The Type A behavior pattern is not a psychological disorder per se, but it is a recognized risk factor for physical illness, namely heart disease. Chesney, Ekman,

Friesen, Black, and Hecker (chapter 22) used facial coding to describe the facial behavior of men during the Type A Structured Interview. Type A males showed more facial behaviors of disgust and GLARE (a partial anger expression involving upper face muscular actions) than Type B men. These facial behaviors correlated with the speech components of the Type A pattern, especially with the hostility component. These findings indicate that nonverbal behaviors may have utility in marking coronary prone behavior.

Historical Context: The Study of Facial Expression in Modern Psychology

The study of facial expression received little attention in modern psychology until the 1960s, a fact that is attributable to the following factors: (1) early research suggested that the face did not provide accurate information about emotion and psychology, for the most part, trusted these findings; (2) the zeitgeist of behaviorism and its blatant rejection of the study of "unobservables" such as emotion discouraged researchers from pursuing this path; and (3) no tool was available for measurement.

Negative Findings From Flawed Early Research

Results from research conducted in the early part of the 20th century indicated that the face did not provide accurate information about emotion. Landis (1924, 1929) took still photographs of subjects in a wide variety of potentially emotional situations (e.g., looking at decapitated rats, being shocked) and showed the photographs (as well as photographs from posed situations) to a set of observers. The observers' judgments of emotion bore no relationship to the eliciting or posed situations. Landis concluded that the face did not provide accurate information about people's emotional states. (For a detailed review and critique of Landis's work and the critical and empirical responses to it, see Ekman, Friesen, & Ellsworth, 1972.)

Several researchers have described the ways in which Landis's work was methodologically flawed (Coleman, 1949; Davis, 1934; Frois-Wittman, 1930), and reanalyses, as well as modified replications, of Landis's research produced positive findings. Further, well-conducted studies on the perception of facial expressions of emotions indicated that people could consistently recognize emotion in the face (Goodenough & Tinker, 1931; Woodworth, 1938). Nevertheless, the prevailing view in psychology, owing in large part to the misrepresentation of early research in a review by Bruner and Tagiuri (1954), was that the face did not provide accurate information about internal states, especially emotions.

Early research on the face suffered greatly from measurement limitations. In the first part of this century, a few researchers attempted to measure the face directly (e.g., Frois-Wittman, 1930; Landis, 1924), with mixed success. For the most part, however, researchers relied on judges' evaluations or ratings of subjects' expressions, either from still photos, films, or live observation. The development of modern systems for measuring facial behavior will be discussed shortly, but let us first look briefly at how the behavioristic zeitgeist hampered facial research.

An Unfavorable Climate in Psychology

The zeitgeist of behaviorism and its blatant rejection of the study of "unobservables" such as emotion certainly contributed to the dearth of research on facial expressions for several decades. As early psychological research suggested that the face did not provide accurate information about internal states, it was deemed a useless enterprise to study facial expressions. Further, if one pursued studying the face for information about emotion (which is the main domain in which facial expression has been studied within psychology), one risked expulsion by the behavioristic mainstream. Conducting research on internal states was not only looked down upon during the early part of this century, it was a career-ending decision.

Several events occurred in the 60s and 70s that brought facial expression back into the fold of psychological research. Silvan Tomkins (1962) presented a theory of affect that posited a central role for the face as a site of emotion. Tomkins and McCarter (1964) published an impressive and systematic study of facial expression judgments, in which they reported that observers consistently identified facial poses (theoretically determined by Tomkins) as indicative of certain emotions. The seminal and popular cross-cultural work on the recognition of facial expressions of emotion in literate and preliterate cultures done by Ekman (Ekman, Sorenson, & Friesen, 1969; Ekman & Friesen, 1971) and Izard (1971) further legitimized the study of the face. It became clear that measurement of facial expression may indeed be a fruitful research enterprise.

The Need for a Measurement Tool

Although it indirectly suggested that facial expression could reveal information about internal emotional states, the cross-cultural work of the late 60s and early 70s primarily showed that people could recognize emotion in the facial behavior of other people. It also indicated that peoples of diverse and preliterate cultures agreed that a core set of prototypical facial expressions were associated with certain emotions. Spontaneous facial expression had yet to be systematically studied on any widespread basis, however, because adequate measurement systems were not available.

Ekman and Friesen (Ekman, 1972; Friesen, 1972) measured the facial behavior of Japanese and American college students in response to stressful films, and examined whether spontaneous expressions of emotion varied by the social context of the film-viewing condition. Japanese and American males viewed the films in two conditions— alone and then in the presence of an experimenter (of the same ethnicity as the subject). This experiment was the first empirical study on the operation of *display rules*, which are culturally learned rules or norms particular to a culture about when it is appropriate to express an emotion and to whom one can reveal one's feelings. Ekman and Friesen's (1971) neurocultural theory of emotion suggests that display rules may account for observable cultural differences in emotion expression while not refuting the existence of universality. By studying films of the subjects, Ekman and Friesen measured the Japanese and American students' facial behavior using an early observational coding system called the Facial Affect Scoring Technique (FAST; Ekman, Friesen, & Tomkins, 1971). They found evidence for universality and the operation of display rules—when viewing the films alone, Japanese and American students exhibited similar expressions of negative emotions (e.g., disgust, anger, and sadness). When in the presence of the authority figure, however, cultural differences emerged. American students showed negative affect very similar to the alone condition, but Japanese students showed much less negative affect, smiled sometimes, and actually masked negative emotion with smiling behavior.

In the 1970s electromyography was applied to the study of spontaneous facial behavior and activity in muscle groups was examined in relation to a variety of psychological variables, such as diagnosis in psychiatric groups and mood ratings (Schwartz, Fair, Salt, Mandel, & Klerman, 1976) and social cognitive processes (Cacioppo & Petty, 1979). Observational coding schemes were developed as well, the most notable among them being the Facial Action Coding System (FACS; Ekman & Friesen, 1978) and Izard's (1979) maximally discriminative facial movement coding system (MAX). The availability of these systems greatly facilitated work on facial expression and emotion, as did the general interest in the psychology of emotion over the past two decades. Now let us look at facial measurement in more detail.

Systems of Facial Measurement

All of the articles reprinted in this volume use FACS for facial measurement. The decision to limit the book to articles using FACS instead of including all articles measuring spontaneous facial behavior was both practically and theoretically motivated. The practical reason is simple: one volume would be insufficient space to include all articles measuring the face using all measurement approaches. Given the space limitation we decided to focus on articles using one measurement technique, so that the focus of the contributions would be on the diverse findings in substantive areas of research, rather than on variability in measurement approaches. This is not a book about measurement. The purpose of this book is to present research contributions to psychology that derive from taking a systematic approach to measuring spontaneous facial expression. This suggested limiting the articles to one system of measurement.

The choice of measurement system stemmed from our own experience. One of the editors (Ekman) was the senior author of FACS and the other has worked extensively with it. Further, of the observational coding systems, FACS has been used most extensively. There are now over 400 certified FACS coders worldwide.[2] Since the publication of the FACS manual in 1978, dozens of empirical articles have been published using this technique for facial measurement.

There are substantive reasons why the choice of FACS made sense as well. As is described in the section below, FACS is the only comprehensive, anatomically based system, which is less burdened by theoretical notions of what the face ought to do than are some other systems (e.g., MAX). Also, FACS measures all facial movement, not just emotion-relevant movement (to which MAX is limited). This book is not a book about emotion only; it is about facial measurement as related to a variety of psychological variables. What follows is a brief discussion of pros and cons of various measurement approaches in the study of facial behavior, which should illuminate the theoretical and methodological reasons we chose to focus on studies that employed FACS.

What Is FACS?

The Facial Action Coding System (or FACS; Ekman & Friesen, 1978) is a comprehensive, anatomically based system for measuring all visually discernible facial movement. FACS describes all visually distinguishable facial activity on the basis of 44 unique action units (AUs), as well as several categories of head and eye positions and movements. Each AU has a numeric code, the designation of which is fairly arbitrary. Tables 1 and 2 list the AUs coded in FACS, as well as the muscle groups involved in each action (these tables also appear in Ekman & Friesen, 1976, pp. 65 & 69).

It is crucial to point out that while FACS is anatomically based, there is not a 1:1 correspondence between muscle groups and AUs. This is due to the fact that a given muscle may act in different ways—or contract in different regions—to produce visibly different actions. An example of this case is the frontalis muscle. Contraction of the medial portion of the frontalis muscle raises the inner corners of the eyebrow only (producing AU 1), while contract of the lateral portion of frontalis raises outer brow (producing AU 2).

FACS coding procedures also allow for coding of the intensity of each facial ac-

TABLE I.I. Single action units (AU) in the Facial Action Coding System

AU number	Descriptor	Muscular Basis
1.	Inner Brow Raiser	Frontalis, Pars Medialis
2.	Outer Brow Raiser	Frontalis, Pars Lateralis
4.	Brow Lowerer	Depressor Glabellae, Depressor Supercilli; Corrugator
5.	Upper Lid Raiser	Levator Palpebrae Superioris
6.	Cheek Raiser	Orbicularis Oculi, Pars Orbitalis
7.	Lid Tightener	Orbicularis Oculi, Pars Palebralis
9.	Nose Wrinkler	Levator Labii Superioris, Alaeque Nasi
10.	Upper Lip Raiser	Levator Labii Superioris, Caput Infraorbitalis
11.	Nasolabial Fold Deepener	Zygomatic Minor
12.	Lip Corner Puller	Zygomatic Major
13.	Cheek Puffer	Caninus
14.	Dimpler	Buccinator
15.	Lip Corner Depressor	Triangularis
16.	Lower Lip Depressor	Depressor Labii
17.	Chin Raiser	Mentalis
18.	Lip Puckerer	Incisivii Labii Superioris; Incisivii Labii Inferioris
20.	Lip Stretcher	Risorius
22.	Lip Funneler	Orbicularis Oris
23.	Lip Tightener	Orbicularis Oris
24.	Lip Pressor	Orbicularis Oris
25.	Lips Part	Depressor Labii, or Relaxation of Mentalis or Orbicularis Oris
26.	Jaw Drop	Masetter; Temporal and Internal Pterygoid Relaxed
27.	Mouth Stretch	Pterygoids; Digastric
28.	Lip Suck	Orbicularis Oris

TABLE I.2. More grossly defined AUs in
the Facial Action Coding System

AU number	FACS name
19.	Tongue out
21.	Neck Tightener
29.	Jaw Thrust
30.	Jaw Sideways
31.	Jaw Clencher
32.	Lip Bite
33.	Cheek Blow
34.	Cheek Puff
35.	Cheek Suck
36.	Tongue Bulge
37.	Lip Wipe
38.	Nostril Dilator
39.	Nostril Compressor
41.	Lid Droop
42.	Slit
43.	Eyes Closed
44.	Squint
45.	Blink
46.	Wink

tion on a 5-point intensity scale, for the timing of facial actions, and for the coding of facial expressions in terms of events. An *event* is the AU-based description of each facial expression, which may consist of a single AU or many AUs contracted as a single expression.

What are the pros and cons of measuring facial behavior with FACS versus another observational coding scheme, such as Izard's (1979) maximally discriminative facial movement coding system (MAX) or by electrophysiological activity (namely, facial electromyography)?

FACS vs. MAX

FACS and MAX are both observational coding schemes that describe expression in terms of constituent components. Componential coding systems can be classified on the basis of the manner in which they were derived: theoretically or anatomically, and according to whether they code facial behavior selectively or comprehensively (for a thorough discussion of these issues see Ekman, 1981; Ekman, Friesen, & Ellsworth, 1982). Theoretically derived techniques are those that categorize facial components on the basis of ideas about which areas of the face should be involved in certain states (e.g., emotion). Izard's MAX (1979) is theoretically derived because it codes just those facial configurations that Izard theorized correspond to universally recognized facial expressions of emotion.

The problem with theoretically derived systems is that they cannot discover behaviors that were not posited in advance. That is, they were not developed to catalog everything the face *can* do, but rather they describe whether the face does things it *should* do according to a given theory. In this sense, then, MAX and other theoretically based coding schemes (such as Ekman, Friesen, & Tomkins's (1971) Facial Affect Scoring Technique, or FAST) are by definition selective. Selective systems are economical in terms of time and effort because they do not exhaustively code all facial movement. But they are costly if one obtains negative findings. For example, if a researcher uses a selective coding system and fails to find expressions of "fear" in subjects who were exposed to a putatively frightening stimulus, then the researcher would be unable to determine if subjects had not experienced fear or if the coding system simply failed to capture the relevant facial behavior.

FACS, on the other hand, is a comprehensive measurement system. It measures all muscular movements that are observable in the face. In developing FACS, Ekman and Friesen trained themselves to isolate their facial muscles and used needle EMG to ensure that they included every possible facial movement in their system. As a comprehensive rather than selective system, FACS is not limited to measuring only those behaviors that are theoretically related to emotion (as MAX is). FACS allows for the discovery of new configurations of movements that might be relevant to extrinsic variables of interest. Many of the articles in this volume are prime examples of the usefulness of FACS for this purpose.

FACS vs. EMG

Facial electromyography (EMG) involves measuring electrical potentials from facial muscles in order to infer muscular contraction. Typically, surface electrodes are placed on the skin of the face of the subject and changes in potential are measured while the subject undergoes various procedures (e.g., viewing emotional slides or films). The advantages of EMG rest primarily in its ability to detect muscular activity that would not be observable to the naked eye and, therefore, would not be detectable via observation-based coding schemes such as FACS or MAX. This would seem to make facial EMG an ideal measurement system. There are problems with EMG, however—ones that may be more or less serious depending on one's research questions. First, EMG is obtrusive—it calls subjects' attention to the fact that their faces are being measured. This may increase the incidence of self-conscious behavior and potentially interfere with the behavior under investigation in other confounding ways (Kleck et al., 1976). Second, although there have been considerable advances in recent years on refining EMG signals (cf., Tassinary, Cacioppo, & Geen, 1989) there remains a problem with cross-talk—that is, surrounding muscular contraction (potentials) interfering or muddling the signal of a given muscle group. For emotion expressions, when slight changes in muscular contraction of adjacent muscle groups can have very different emotional meanings, such cross-talk may misrepresent the "picture" of the contractions on the face, possibly leading to very different emotional interpretations.

Although we have chosen to include only articles using FACS, the articles vary greatly in how they apply FACS. Some use it very ethologically, by enumerating AUs or AU sequences that occur in certain contexts (e.g., Bänninger-Huber, chap. 20). Others use special procedures for FACS for the study of emotion (e.g., Berenbaum & Oltmanns, chap. 16; Rosenberg & Ekman, chap. 3). This latter approach requires further discussion.

Using FACS for Emotion Measurement

Several of the studies included in this volume use FACS for the measurement of facial expressions of emotion. There are two ways in which FACS had been utilized for this purpose. One is a postcoding procedure, the other involves actual modification in the FACS coding process.

FACS Interpretations (FACS/EMFACS Dictionary and *FACSAID*)

FACS-coded facial events can be classified into emotion and nonemotion categories. The *FACS/EMFACS Emotion Dictionary* is a computer program that determines whether each facial event includes core facial movements that characterize certain facial expressions of emotion. The program's interpretations draw on a rich empirically and theoretically derived database from Ekman's laboratory and others, and it has been used for the classification of spontaneous facial behavior in many previous studies (included here and elsewhere; e.g., Ekman, Davidson, & Friesen, 1990; Rosenberg & Ekman, chap. 3). Recently, FACSAID (FACS Affect Interpretation Database) has been developed to replace the *FACS/EMFACS Dictionary*. FACSAID matches facial events with emotional events coded from previous empirical studies.[3]

EMFACS

Ekman and Friesen developed a selective system based on FACS for scoring expressions of single emotions, called EMFACS (EM = emotion). In EMFACS the coder uses FACS codes but views everything in real time (while regular FACS allows for frame-by-frame or slow-motion viewing). Also, the EMFACS coder describes only those facial events that include AUs or combinations of AUs that are "core" to certain emotion expressions. EMFACS is less time-consuming than FACS. It should be understood that EMFACS is FACS selectively applied.

This book is a testament to the number of rich research programs stimulated by the availability of such measurement systems as FACS. Any facial scientist would admit, however, that the time-intensive process of observational facial measurement limits the rate at which new research can be completed. Currently, experts in computer science and psychology are combining efforts to automate facial measurement. One approach is to teach neural networks the principles of observational, componential facial coding by FACS (Bartlett et al., 1996). Once a network is available that knows all of the possible facial changes—and it can recognize them reliably across a wide variety of faces—the time required to measure the face will be reduced dramatically. Within the next decade such procedures should become available, which should lead to a proliferation of research on spontaneous facial expression.

Notes

1. Ekman reports that he was unable to have this article accepted for publication because it did not use current diagnostic categories. However, we include it because in our judgment it has both methodological relevance and promising substantive leads.

2. A "certified" FACS coder is someone who has completed the full self-instructional

manual and who has received a passing score (reliability of .70 or higher) on the FACS final test.

3. The FACS/EMFACS emotion dictionary has evolved into the FACS Affect Interpretation Database (FACSAID). For information, contact Paul Ekman, Ph.D., Human Interaction Laboratory-UCSF, 401 Parnassus Ave., San Francisco, CA 94143-0984. For information about the prior FACS/EMFACS emotion dictionary, contact Wallace V. Friesen, Ph.D., at 202 Old Mill Rd., Georgetown, KY 40324.

References

Bartlett, M. S., Viola, P. A., Sejnowski, T. J., Golomb, B. A., Larsen, J., Hager, J. C., & Ekman, P. (1996). Classifying facial action. In D. Touretzky, M. Mozer, and M. Hasselmo (Eds.). *Advances in Information Processing Systems 8,* (pp. 823–829). Cambridge, MA: MIT Press.

Beecher, H. K. (1946). Pain of men wounded in battle. *Annals of Surgery, 123,* 96–105.

Borod, J., Koff, E. (1984). Asymmetries in affective facial expression: Behavior and anatomy. In N. Fox & R. J. Davidson (Eds.), *The psychobiology of affective development* (pp. 293–323). Hillsdale, NJ: Erlbaum.

Bruner, J. S., & Tagiuri, R. (1954). The perception of people. In G. Lindzey (Ed.), *Handbook of social psychology (Vol. 2,* pp. 634–654). Reading, MA: Addison-Wesley.

Cacioppo, J. T., & Petty, R. E. (1979). Attitudes and cognitive responses: An electrophysiological approach. *Journal of Personality and Social Psychology, 37,* 2181–2199.

Coleman, J. C. (1949). Facial expressions of emotion. *Psychological Monograph, 63* (1), Whole monograph no. 296.

Costa, P. T., & McCrae, R. R. (1985). *The NEO personality inventory manual.* Odessa, FL: Psychological Assessment Resources.

Davis, R. C. (1934). The specificity of facial expressions. *Journal of General Psychology, 10,* 42–58.

Ekman, P. (1972). Universals and cultural differences in facial expressions of emotion. In J. Cole (Ed.), *Nebraska Symposium on Motivation* (Vol. 9). Lincoln: University of Nebraska Press.

Ekman, P. (1981). Methods for measuring facial action. In K. R. Scherer & P. Ekman (Eds.), *Handbook of methods in nonverbal behavior research* (pp. 45–90). Cambridge, Eng.: Cambridge University Press.

Ekman, P., Davidson, R. J., & Friesen, W. V. (1990). The Duchenne smile: Emotional expression and brain physiology II. *Journal of Personality and Social Psychology, 58,* 342–353.

Ekman, P., & Friesen, W. V. (1971). Constants across cultures in the face and emotion. *Journal of Personality and Social Psychology, 17,* 124–129.

Ekman, P., & Friesen, W. V. (1976). Measuring facial movement. *Environmental Psychology and Nonverbal Behavior, 1,* 56–75.

Ekman, P., & Friesen, W. V. (1978). *The facial action coding system (FACS): A technique for the measurement of facial action.* Palo Alto, CA: Consulting Psychologists Press.

Ekman, P., Friesen, W. V., & Ellsworth, P. (1972). *Emotion in the human face: Guidelines for research and a review of findings.* New York: Pergamon Press.

Ekman, P., Friesen, W. V., & Ellsworth, P. (1982). Methodological decisions. In P. Ekman (Ed.). *Emotion in the human face* (2nd ed.) (pp. 22–38) Cambridge, Eng.: Cambridge University Press.

Ekman, P., Friesen, W. V., & Tomkins, S. S. (1971). Facial affect scoring technique (FAST): A first validity study. *Semiotica, 3,* 37–58.

Ekman, P., Sorenson, E. R., & Friesen, W. V. (1969). Pan-cultural elements in facial displays of emotions. *Science, 164,* 86–88.

Eysenck, H. J. (Ed.). (1981). *A model for personality.* New York: Springer.

Friesen, W. V. (1972). *Cultural differences in facial expression in a social situation: An experimental test of the concept of display rules.* Unpublished doctoral dissertation, University of California, San Francisco.

Frois-Wittman, J. (1930). The judgment of facial expression. *Journal of Experimental Psychology, 13,* 113–151.

Goodenough, F. L. & Tinker, M. A. (1931). The relative potency of facial expression and verbal description of stimulus in the judgment of emotion. *Journal of Comparative Psychology, 12,* 365–370.

Izard, C. E. (1971). *The face of emotion.* New York: Appleton-Century-Crofts.

Izard, C. E. (1979). *The maximally discriminative facial movement coding system (MAX).* Unpublished manuscript, available from Instructional Resource Center, University of Delaware.

Kleck, R. E., Vaughan, R. C., Cartwright-Smith, J., Vaughan, K. B., Colby, C., & Lanzetta, J. T. (1976). Effects of being observed on expressive, subjective and physiological responses to painful stimuli. *Journal of Personality and Social Psychology, 34,* 1211–1218.

Landis, C. (1924). Studies of emotional reactions: II. General behavior and facial expression. *Journal of Comparative Psychology, 4,* 447–509.

Landis, C. (1929). The interpretation of facial expression of emotion. *Journal of General Psychology, 2,* 59–72.

Loeser, J. D. (1990). Pain after amputation: Phantom limb and stump pain. In J. J. Bonica (Ed.), *The management of pain* (2nd ed., pp. 244–256). Malvern, PA: Lea & Febiger.

Schwartz, G. E., Fair, P. L., Salt, P., Mandel, M. K., & Klerman, G. L. (1976). Facial muscle patterning to affective imagery in depressed and non-depressed subjects. *Science, 192,* 489–491.

Tassinary, L. G., Cacioppo, J. T., & Geen, T. R. (1989). A psychometric study of surface electrode placement for facial electromyographic recording: I. The brow and cheek muscle regions. *Psychophysiology, 26,* 1–16.

Tomkins, S. S. (1962). *Affect, imagery, consciousness.* New York: Springer.

Tomkins, S. S., & McCarter, R. (1964). What and where are the primary affects? Some evidence for a theory. *Perceptual and Motor Skills, 18,* 119–158.

Woodworth, R. S. (1938). *Experimental psychology.* New York: Henry Holt.

PART ONE

BASIC RESEARCH ON EMOTION

1

Is the Startle Reaction an Emotion?

PAUL EKMAN, WALLACE V. FRIESEN & RONALD C. SIMONS

Despite the wealth of information provided by Landis and Hunt's (1939) pioneering study, emotion theorists have disagreed about whether the startle reaction is a reflex or an emotion. Bull (1951), Lindsley (1951), Plutchik (1962, later Plutchik, 1980, reserved judgment), Tomkins (1962), Wenger, F. N. Jones, and M. H. Jones (1956), and Woodworth and Schlosberg (1954), all considered startle to be an emotion, related to the emotion of surprise. Kemper (1978), Leventhal (1980), Mandler (1975), and Schacter and Singer (1962) all ignored the startle reaction. Averill (1980) and Lazarus (1982) were explicit about their decision to consider a startle a reflex rather than an emotion because cognition does not play a causal role in eliciting it. Landis and Hunt took an intermediate position, considering it to be "preemotional" because a startle is simpler in organization and expression than "true" emotions.

The issue of whether or not startle should be considered an emotion has drawn renewed interest since Zajonc's (1980) proposal (like Tomkin's before him) that affect does not require prior cognitive appraisal. Lazarus's (1984) recent rebuttal cited the findings reported in this article as supporting his contrary view. Although begun before the Zajonc-Lazarus debate, our study provides data relevant to it, by determining the extent to which the startle reaction is influenced by three cognitive activities. One experimental condition examined the role of expectations by telling subjects exactly when they would be startled. Another condition explored how well the startle expression can be suppressed, and a third condition investigated how well the startle expression can be simulated. We also sought to verify Landis and Hunt's account about the remarkable uniformity and brevity of the startle expression, features that might distinguish a startle from emotions such as anger or fear.

We also remedied some of the methodological defects in Landis and Hunt's study. Although their study was exemplary for its time, Landis and Hunt did not report how they made their behavioral measurements, they did not mention interobserver reliability, and often they omitted the quantitative data and significance tests that presumably were the bases for many of their key findings.

Method

A .22 caliber blank pistol shot was chosen to elicit the startle reaction, because Landis and Hunt reported it to be the most effective stimulus. The pistol was mounted on a tripod and placed 1.5 m behind the subject's chair. An experimenter sat directly facing the subject. A cinematographer was also present in the room, located 3 m from the subject. A 16-mm motion picture camera recorded behavior at 50 frames per second. This faster than usual (24 frames per second) rate of recording was adopted because Landis and Hunt claimed that the startle reaction is so brief that high-speed cinematography is needed to record its component facial and bodily changes.

Experimental Conditions

Unanticipated Startle

Although subjects knew the pistol would be fired sometime within the 1-hour session, they did not know precisely when. After about 15 min the pistol was fired while the experimenter was giving instructions for a memory test.

Anticipated Startle

After a short interview (approximately 5 minutes) about previous startle experiences, the experimenter explained the countdown procedure. Starting with the number 10, he listed numbers at the rate of 1 number per second. When he reached zero he fired the pistol.

Inhibited Startle

Subjects returned on another day to participate in the inhibited and the simulated conditions. The instructions for the inhibited condition were as follows:

> This time I want to see how well you can keep from showing any visible response. See if you can act so that someone seeing the film with the sound off won't know that anything has happened. Try not to let anything show as you wait for the gun to go off, and when it does go off, and afterward, until I sat "cut!" Try to look relaxed all the way through. See if you can fool the person who'll be studying this film. Again I'll count down from 10.

Simulated Startle

After about 5 minutes the experimenter said:

> This time I'll count down from 10, but the gun won't go off. Instead, that little light, which you can see in the mirror will come on, like this. (demonstrates) When it does I'd like you to pretend to be startled, just as though that light was an actual gunshot. See if you can act so that someone seeing the film without sound will think that the gun went off and you were really startled. See if you can fool the person who will be studying this film. During the countdown try to look relaxed. I'll say "cut!" to tell you when to stop pretending.

The unanticipated and anticipated conditions were not counterbalanced because pilot studies suggested that the gunshot lost some of its novel impact in the unanticipated condition if it were to follow an anticipated presentation. The pilot studies and Landis and Hunt's findings both suggested little decrement in response when 5 min separated the unanticipated and anticipated conditions. The simulated startle condition was always placed last so that subjects would have had maximal experience with the startle experience before attempting to imitate it.

Subjects

Seventeen individuals who did not consider themselves especially easily startled and who did not have any history of being tested because they were so, comprised the normal group of subjects. There were 10 women and 7 men in this group. They were paid $4.50 per hour for participating. Three of the subjects participated only in the unanticipated and anticipated startle conditions, before the inhibited and simulated conditions were devised.

Because of a clinical interest in individuals who are startled especially easily and readily (Simons, 1980), a second group of such "hyperstartlers" were also tested. Eleven persons, 9 women and 2 men, responded to a newspaper advertisement seeking such easily startled persons as part of a research project. They participated in only the anticipated and unanticipated conditions. Although the results are reported here, the few differences found between the normal and hyperstartlers are discussed in a separate report, which includes other cross-cultural data on hyperstartlers (Simons, Ekman, & Friesen, 1985).

Measurements

We focused our most detailed measurement on the facial part of the startle response because of recent work on the role of facial expression in emotion (e.g., Ekman & Oster, 1979) and because of the availability of a new technique that allows precise, detailed measurement of facial movement. Facial activity was scored with Ekman and Friesen's Facial Action Coding System (FACS; 1976, 1978), which distinguishes 44 *action units*. These are the minimal units of facial activity that are anatomically separate and visually distinguishable. Scoring involves decomposing a facial movement into the particular action units that produced it, either singly or in combination with other units. In addition, FACS provides for rating the intensity of each action unit on a 5-point scale.

Head, neck, and trunk movements were scored less precisely. The most commonly seen head movement was a small, brief tremor. This and all other head movements were combined into a head activity score. The most frequent neck movement was due to the action of the platysma muscle. This and all other neck movements were combined into a neck activity score. Similarly, a trunk activity score included all trunk movements.

The most exact measurement of the timing of any movement would require specifying the particular frame when any change was observed. Because the film had been exposed at 50 frames per second, specifying the exact frame would provide data in 20-ms units. Such precise measurement is very costly, however, requiring repeated viewing in slowed motion. This precise, micromeasurement (20-ms units) was performed only on a subsample of 6 subjects and only in the unanticipated condition. For these subjects, micromeasurement was made for each element of a movement (for facial action units and for head, neck, or trunk activity scores), recording when it first appeared (onset), when it reached maximum muscular contraction (start of apex), when it began to decay (start of offset), and when it disappeared (end of offset).

A more macromeasurement of latency was made for all subjects, in all four conditions, for each element of a movement that had been identified. To obtain this macrolatency measure, time from the point when the pistol was fired was divided into 100-ms (5-frame) blocks. We determined the 100-ms blocks when each action unit began.

Reliability of Measurement

Two coders who did not know about the controversy regarding startle, nor about Landis and Hunt's findings, performed the FACS scoring. Each coder scored about half of the sample, and both of the coders independently scored a subsample of 28 startle reactions, the responses of 7 subjects across all four experimental conditions. The extent of intercoder agreement was evaluated for three aspects of facial measurement: (1) identification of the elemental muscular units acted to produce a movement, (2) location of when the movement began and when it ended, and (3) judgment of the intensity of the actions that comprised the movement.

Although commonly used reliability indices were applicable to evaluate intercoder agreement for the second and third aspects of facial measurement, they were not applicable to the first aspect of facial measurement. The difficulty occurs because FACS does not limit the coder to a small number of alternatives in identifying the elemental muscular units that might have acted to produce a movement. Instead a coder may decide that anywhere from 1 to 44 elemental actions were involved in any movement. An index of reliability was obtained by calculating ratios of agreement (Wexler, 1972). For each of the 28 startle reactions, the number of elemental units on which the 2 coders agreed was multiplied by 2 and was then divided by the total number of elemental units scored by the 2 coders. Perfect agreement would yield a ratio of 1.0. The mean agreement ratio across all 28 samples was .837. In identifying just those actions that were found to most often characterize startle reactions (see table 1.1), the two coders agreed more than 90% of the time.

In the macromeasurement of latency, the 2 coders agreed 47.7% of the time about the 100-ms block in which an elemental unit began. Agreement within one adjacent time block was obtained 98.2% of the time. The agreement about the more precise microtiming measurements (in 20-ms blocks), was about the same as found in other stud-

TABLE 1.1. Actions evident within 200 milliseconds in the unanticipated startle shown by the majority of subjects

Action	Number of Subjects showing the action (N =27)	Latency of action in ms[a]	
		M	SD
Muscles around the eye			
orbicularis occuli, pars lateralis	19	71.1	41.89
orbicularis occuli, pars medialis ,			
Horizontal lip stretch	19	76.3	45.24
risorius			
Neck muscle activity	26[b]	84.6	48.52
platysma or sternocleidomastoii, or both			
Eyes closed	25[c]	54.0	20.00
blink or other longer closure			
Head movements	26[d]	100.0	50.99
Trunk movements	24	125.0	44.23

[a]Measurement made in 100-ms blocks.
[b]Neck not visible for one subject.
[c]Eyes were already closed when gun was fired for 2 subjects.
[d]One subject showed this action just after the 200 ms cutoff (not included).

ies using FACS (Ekman & Friesen, 1978). The mean discrepancy between the 2 coders in locating the onset of an action ranged from 14 to 28 ms, depending on the particular elemental unit. As in other studies with FACS, there was a greater discrepancy in locating the end of an action, ranging from 22 to 116 ms.

The intensity of each of the action units that had been identified in each of the four experimental conditions was then scored by Ekman and Friesen jointly. To evaluate the reliability of their scoring of intensity, a research assistant also made intensity ratings on all of the elemental units shown by the normal subjects in the unanticipated and anticipated conditions. Spearman rank order correlations between the intensity ratings made by the research assistant and those of Ekman and Friesen were calculated separately for each of the elemental units that were shown by half or more of the subjects. All of these p were .90 or higher. The α coefficient comparing the intensity ratings of the research assistant and Ekman and Friesen across all actions was .83.

Results

Two of the finer distinctions made in FACS scoring were disregarded in the data analyses. Although FACS distinguishes the activity of either the inner or outer portions of the orbicularis oculi muscle, which orbits the eye, these two very similar action units were combined into a single muscles-around-the-eye score. How long the eye remained closed was also disregarded, collapsing the distinction between a blink and longer eye closures to obtain a eyes-closed score.

Unanticipated Startle

The scores on one normal subject in this condition were dropped because he reported noticing when the gun was about to be fired. Because no differences between normals and hyperstartlers were observed either in the specific actions that occurred or in their latencies, the results for normal subjects and for hyperstartlers were combined in this condition.

Without exception, all actions that were shown by more than half of the subjects began within 200 ms after the gun was fired. Table 1.1 shows that four actions were present for virtually all of the subjects—eye closure, neck muscle activity, head movement, and trunk movement. Two other actions—activity of the muscles around the eye and horizontal lip stretch—were shown by most subjects. The next most frequent facial action, the lowering of the brows produced by the corrugator muscle, was shown by only 11 of the 27 subjects.

Recall that the macromeasurement of latency was obtained by specifying the 100-ms time block in which an action was first observed to occur. In order to obtain the absolute latency figures reported in table 1.1, any action that began within the first 100 ms was assigned a latency score of 50, and any action that started in the second block was assigned a score of 150, and the mean was calculated using these latency estimates. Although the differences in the latencies reported in table 1.1 might appear to be so slight as to be unreliable, the sequence of actions duplicates exactly Landis and Hunt's report, which was done more than 40 years ago. The absolute values shown in table 1.1 are also very close to those reported by Landis and Hunt.

The more precise, micromeasurement of the timing of facial actions in 20-ms units

TABLE 1.2. Micromeasurement (in 20-millisecond blocks) of the timing of the unanticipated startle ($N = 6$)

| Action | Latency | Period | | | Total duration |
		Onset	Apex	Offset	
Muscles around the eye	84.00	72.00	44.00	72.00	188.00
Horizontal lip stretch	104.00	72.00	36.00	88.00	196.00
Neck muscle activity	100.00	83.33	103.00	133.33	320.00
Eyes closed	73.33	53.33	123.33	103.33	280.00
Head movements	100.00	113.33	200.00	180.00	493.33
Trunk movements	120.00	110.00	673.33	210.00	993.33

was performed on a subsample of 6 subjects for only the actions listed in table 1.1—those that were shown by the majority of the subjects and that began within the first 200 ms. There is a minor discrepancy between the latencies reported in tables 1.1 and 1.2. Table 1.1 probably contains the better estimates, even though they are less precisely measured, because they are based on a larger sample, and they are in agreement with the values reported in Landis and Hunt. The discrepancies in latency between the two forms of measurement are very small. The actions with the shortest latency (eye closure) and longest latency (trunk) were the same with both types of time measurement. Table 1.2 also shows that the head and trunk movements had the longest onset period and the longest offset period.

As noted by Landis and Hunt, shortly after the offset of the startle reaction another facial expression typically occurs. Although we did not measure this secondary reaction, we noted that it usually occurred within 500 ms after the startle offset. Smiling was the most frequent secondary reaction, although the smiles did not appear to be those of enjoyment but rather of embarrassment. Fear and sad expressions were also seen but much less frequently.

Anticipated Startle

Only the actions identified as comprising the startle response in the unanticipated condition (listed in table 1.1) were examined in the anticipated condition. Behavior in the anticipated and unanticipated conditions were compared for the normals and the hyperstartlers separately in regard to the *frequency*, the *latency*, and the *intensity* of each action.

With respect to frequency, the number of subjects who showed the actions that characterized the unanticipated startle (table 1.1) decreased in the anticipated condition, but the decrease was pronounced for only some of the actions and only among the normal not the hyperstartler subjects. Horizontal lip stretch decreased markedly, by more than 50%, among the normal subjects in the anticipated condition [McNemar test, $\chi^2(1, N = 17) = 6.12, p = .05$]. Similarly, trunk activity decreased markedly among the normal subjects in the anticipated startle condition [McNemar test, $\chi^2 (1, N = 17) = 5.14, p = .05$]. Among the hyperstartlers these actions occurred just as often in the anticipated as in the unanticipated conditions.

With respect to latency, neither normals nor hyperstartlers showed any significant difference between their unanticipated and anticipated startles.

With respect to intensity, all actions were less intense in the anticipated condition for normal subjects, although intensity decreased for only some of the hyperstartlers. A single intensity score was obtained for each subject by summing the intensities of each of the actions listed in table 1.1. Table 1.3 shows the mean of these intensity summary scores for each group of subjects, in the unanticipated and anticipated conditions. The decrease in intensity of facial actions in the anticipated condition was significant for the normals but not for the hyperstartlers. This decrease in the intensity of facial action when the startle was anticipated was found for 15 out of 16 normal subjects. The behavior of the hyperstartlers was much more variable; 5 decreased, 5 increased, and 1 did not change. These differences between normals and hyperstartlers will be discussed in a separate report (Simons et al., 1985).

Inhibited Startle

Behavior in this condition was examined for only 14 of the normal subjects; 3 other normal subjects and the hyperstartlers did not participate in this or in the simulated startle condition. Behavior in the inhibited startle condition was compared with behavior shown in the anticipated startle condition, because in both circumstances the subjects knew exactly when the pistol was to be fired. Despite attempts to inhibit responses to the gunshot, there were no significant differences in either the frequency with which an action was shown or in the latency of facial actions. Although the difference was slight, intensity was weaker in the inhibited, than in the anticipated conditions (mean intensity anticipated = 1.9, inhibited = 1.59, $t = 2.2$, $df = 13$, $p = .05$).

Simulated Startle

Behavior in the simulated condition was compared with the unanticipated startle because subjects attempted to produce the appearance of the unanticipated startle rather than that of the less intense startle that had been shown in the anticipated condition. Although all the analyses reported so far considered only those actions that began within 200 ms after the pistol shot, this analysis included any action evident in the first 600 ms that was shown by one third or more of the subjects, because a less rapid and more varied response was expected when startle was simulated. Table 1.4 shows that almost half of the subjects did a brow raise—an action that is part of a surprise expression—which never appeared in either the unanticipated or anticipated startle conditions (McNemar test, $\chi^2 = 4.16$, $df = 1$, $p = .05$). Most subjects neglected to include tightening the muscle around the eye in their simulation (McNemar test, $\chi^2 = 4.08$, $df = 1$, $p = .05$). Table 1.4 also shows that the latency was much longer for every action in the simulated condition. This difference was tested by comparing the latency of the first ac-

TABLE 1.3. Mean intensity of facial actions beginning in the first 200 milliseconds in the unanticipated startle and anticipated startle conditions

Group	Unanticipated startle	Anticipated startle	t	p
Normal subjects ($n = 16$)	14.76	7.12	5.81	.001
Hyperstartlers ($n = 11$)	16.36	15.64	.55	—

TABLE 1.4. Actions evident in the simulated startle and unanticipated startle reactions ($N = 13$)

	Simulated startle		Real startle	
Action	Subjects	Latency (ms)	Subjects	Latency (ms)
Brow raise	6	366.67	0	0
Muscles around eye	4	400.00	10	70.00
Horizontal lip stretch	6	316.67	11	59.09
Neck muscle activity	11	289.36	13	80.77
Eyes closed	9	272.22	13	50.00
Head movements	10	310.00	13	96.15
Trunk movements	12	316.67	12	116.67

tion to be shown in each condition. As table 1.4 suggests this latency score was much longer in the simulated than in the unanticipated condition ($t = 6.96$, $df = 13$, $p = .001$).

To determine whether untrained observers could discriminate between real or simulated startles, both were shown to groups of college students. Two videotapes were prepared with each subject appearing only once on each. On each videotape, seven real and seven simulated startles were edited in a random order. Pilot data showed that the latency difference alone (much longer for simulated than real) allowed near perfect discrimination. To find out whether observers could detect the simulated startle just from the expression itself, the videotape was edited to eliminate latency clues. Forty-eight students saw one tape; 50 saw the other. Both were asked to judge whether each startle was real or simulated. Across both groups of observers the total accuracy was 60% (binomial test, $p = .01$). Very few students did much better than this slight level of accurate discrimination. Only 11 of the 98 students were accurate on 70% or more of the startles they judged. Brow raising in the simulated condition, which was never found in the real startle, may have been a clue that the performance was false, because none of the six simulations that included a brow raise was judged to be real by a majority of the students.

Discussion

All but one of the actions that we found to characterize the unanticipated startle reaction (table 1.1) were also reported by Landis and Hunt. They missed the action of the orbicularis oculi muscle, which tightens the eyelids and may draw the skin surrounding the eye inwards. Landis and Hunt must have seen the appearance changes produced by this muscle even though they failed to measure it, because the appearance changes produced by orbicularis oculi are included in their line-drawing illustration of the startle. This action was shown by 71% of our subjects in the unanticipated condition.

Landis and Hunt reported that eye closure had the shortest latency, followed by lip stretching, then head and neck movement at about the same time, and finally trunk movement. By scoring in 100-ms units and in 20-ms units, we replicated this temporal sequence with the addition that the action of the muscle around the eye occurred at about the same time as the lip stretching. Eye closure, which involves very small muscles, had not only the shortest latency, but the shortest onset period. The movements of the trunk, which require the involvement of very large muscles, had not only the longest latency, but the longest onset period as well.

Landis and Hunt proposed calling startle a "pattern" because of the uniformity in both the component actions and latencies. "The fact that few such patterns have been found in the realm of emotion increases the value of this one" (Landis & Hunt, 1939, p. 12). Its value as a model of emotion depends on whether the features of the startle are general to other emotions or unique to it. Let us now consider the findings in these terms.

Discontinuity in Expression

Some of those who view startle as an emotion (Plutchik, 1962, 1980; Tomkins, 1962; Woodworth & Schlosberg, 1954) see it as the extreme version of surprise. Although each cited Landis and Hunt's description of the appearance of the startle, none commented on the discontinuity in appearance between the startle and surprise. Table 1.5 contrasts the findings on the appearance of the startle with Ekman and Friesen's (1975, 1978) description of the surprise expression. (The surprise description is based on what they found observers in different cultures would judge as surprise. It includes all the features noted by other researchers who have observed or theorized about the appearance of surprise.)

No emotion theorist has suggested that a radical discontinuity in appearance, like that between startle and surprise, characterizes any emotion. Just the opposite has usually been assumed or asserted: The appearance of the expression of an emotion is said to become stronger, due to increased muscular contraction, as the emotion is felt more strongly. A totally different set of muscular actions has never been described for any emotion when it is felt most strongly. Thus rage resembles anger, as terror resembles fear, revulsion resembles disgust, extreme joy resembles moderate happiness, and extreme distress resembles moderate distress.

There are only two studies (Ekman, Friesen, & Ancoli, 1980; Ekman, 1984) that examined how facial appearance differs with variations in the strength of the feeling reported. Both studies found moderate to high correlations between the intensity of the muscular expression and the intensity of the subjective experience of the emotion.

TABLE 1.5. Differences between surprise and startle expressions

Facial feature	Appearance	Muscular basis
Eyebrows		
Surprise	Raised	Frontalis
Startle	Lowered	Orbicularis oculi, pars lateralis
Eyes		
Surprise	Upper lid raised, eyes widened	Levator palebralis, superioris
Startle	Eyes closed, lids tightened	Orbicularis oculi, pars medialis
Lips		
Surprise	Dropped open jaw, lips relaxed	Relaxation of masseter
Startle	Horizontally stretched	Risorius or platysma, or both
Neck		
Surprise	No activity	
Startle	Tightened, taut	Platysma, sternocleidomastoid, trapezius

And, neither study found a discontinuity in expression between extreme and moderate expressions of an emotion such as the discontinuity we found between startle and surprise.

Easy and Reliable Elicitation

Landis and Hunt recommended the startle response to the scientist wishing to study emotion in the laboratory because it is not only uniform in appearance but easily elicited, appearing reliably in every subject, and indeed this was the case in our study as well. Although no claim can be made that the universe of elicitors has been adequately sampled for any emotion, in more than 50 years of research no elicitor has been found for any emotion that functions like the gunshot does for the startle. No elicitors have been reported that invariably produce the same initial observable emotional reaction in every subject. The closest approximation are some films that show animals engaging in cute behavior (Ekman et al., 1980). These films elicit only zygomatic major muscle smiles, but not in everyone. Although the gunshot never failed to produce at least part of the startle facial expression, we have observed that about 15% of the subjects who watch the film of cute animals show no visible facial expression. Attempts to elicit negative emotions produce even more variability in the initial facial expression of emotion. We have observed that a film of a limb amputation can elicit expressions of fear, surprise, disgust, distress, embarrassment, pain, anger, or blends of these emotions as the initial response. Films of other scenes, stress interviews, or pain stimuli are no more successful in eliciting a single initial facial expression of emotion across all subjects.

This lack of uniformity across persons in the initial emotional response to most events is consistent with those theories of emotion that emphasize the role of appraisal. How an individual appraises an event—the meaning given to the event not the event itself—is said to determine the type of emotional response. Certainly appraisal, which appears to play a minor role in the startle, plays a major role in the generation of emotions. In our view (Ekman, 1977, 1984), appraisal can sometimes operate automatically, with minimal, very brief, cognitive activity preceding the emotional response. Even then, the emotional response may not always be uniform across all people. Differences may occur because of variations in expectations, memories, or in the habits that link one emotion to another. In any case, the events that are most likely to elicit a uniform emotional response, such as the death of a child, can not be readily studied in a laboratory.

Attempts to elicit emotion in a laboratory are often contaminated, if not overwhelmed, by the social psychology of the situation. For example, observable facial expressions often change when the subject knows others are observing, and this has been found to vary with culture. Japanese more than American students masked negative emotional expressions in response to stress films if an authority figure was present (Ekman, 1973; Friesen, 1972). And American students showed different facial expressions in response to pain when they knew they were being observed (Kleck et al., 1976). Although no one has compared startles when subjects are alone (unaware of being observed) with startles that occur in the presence of others, anecdotal observations suggests that they would not differ much as long as the subjects did not know exactly when the pistol shot would occur.

Difficulty in elicitation is probably the rule for emotion. Elicitors of emotion probably typically call forth different initial facial expressions across subjects and different emotional expressions over even a short period of time for any given subject. In the laboratory, emotion elicitors are especially influenced by the social context.

Fixed Timing: Latency and Duration

The startle reaction has a fixed, very brief latency, well within the range of what has been reported for most reflexes (Davis, Gendelman, Tishler, & Gendelman, 1982). Latency did not change with anticipation, nor with the attempt to inhibit the startle response. The response always begins within 100 ms of the eliciting stimulus. Although the latency of other emotional expressions has yet to be systematically measured under a variety of conditions, what work has been done does not suggest, nor has anyone theorized, that latency is fixed nor so brief.

The startle is also unique in the brevity of the entire response. The pattern usually disappears in less than one second, which is, again, well within the range reported for most reflexes (Davis et al., 1982). Surprise is the only emotion that also always has a brief duration, although it is not as short. Even though there has not been study of the duration of all other emotions, what evidence there is shows that the duration of an expression varies and is related to the intensity of emotional feelings (Ekman et al., 1980).

Our findings raise some question about whether signal value was important in the origin of the startle expression. Although theorists disagree about the importance of signaling in the evolution of the facial expressions of emotion, all agree it played some role (Allport, 1924; Andrew, 1963; Bell, 1847; Darwin, 1872/1965; Eibl-Eibesfeldt, 1970; Ekman, 1977; Izard, 1971; Lersch, 1932/1971; Tomkins, 1962; van Hooff, 1972). Signaling may not have played a similar role in the evolution of the startle expression because it is so hard for others to see. It is not only very brief (the facial elements disappear within 1/2 s), but the startle expression is usually obscured by the emotional reaction to being startled, which often follows closely after it and lasts much longer. The vocalization that often occurs with startle, may, of course have signal value.

Not Suppressable

Landis and Hunt mentioned that the startle pattern could not be totally suppressed but did not report systematically studying attempts to inhibit it. We found no difference between inhibited and anticipated startle reaction in either the muscular components or latency and only a very small diminution in intensity. Our own attempts to inhibit the startle expression were no more successful than those of the experimental subjects. Our subjective experience was that the startle expression always burst forth before we would interfere with it. Despite knowing exactly when the pistol shot would occur, the expression was over before we could begin our attempt to inhibit it.

Again, there has not been thorough study of this aspect of expression for the other emotions. What evidence there is suggests that it is at least sometimes possible to suppress deliberately the expression of emotion. In the one study (Ekman & Friesen, 1974) in which extremely strong emotion was elicited (with surgical films) and exacting measurement was performed (with FACS), some subjects were able to inhibit their expressions totally.

Unconvincing Simulations

Deliberately produced startles failed to show the very brief latency that characterizes a genuine startle. It seems as if voluntary direction of the facial musculature can not produce the immediate response that is a hallmark of the startle. Because emotional expressions do not have such a brief latency, the clue that their expression is false, the product of deliberate intention, is not so obvious.

Almost half of the subjects raised their brow as if in surprise when simulating the startle. We believe that if the subjects had not been actually startled just minutes before, many more would have activated the wrong muscle movements. Again, there are no comparable data on other emotions. Although there have been many studies of posing emotions, none precisely measured both the posed and genuine expressions.

Anticipation Diminishes Startle

Surprise is probably the only emotion in which anticipation has a uniform effect. Knowing precisely what unexpected event will happen and when it will occur eliminates surprise. Such anticipation diminished the intensity of the startle reaction for 15 of the 16 normal subjects but did not eliminate the startle response. No emotional theorist has suggested that anticipation would have a uniform influence on the experience or expression of fear, anger, disgust, or distress; but there has been no systematic study of this issue. Anecdotal information suggests that anticipation can heighten or diminish emotional experience and expression, depending on the specifics of the emotional elicitor, the social context, and personal characteristics.

Is Startle an Emotion?

The answer matters in terms of the current controversy about whether cognitive appraisal must always precede emotion. No one doubts that startles are brought on without prior appraisal, in an automatic fashion, much like a reflex. Physiologists agree in considering startle a reflex not an emotion (Davis et al., 1982; Graham, 1975). A decision to consider startle an emotion would support Tomkins's and Zajonc's and contradict Lazarus's claim about whether or not cognitive appraisal is a prerequisite for emotion.

The evidence from our study of the startle is mixed. In two respects startle resembles emotions: (1) uniformity in facial appearance, apart from intensity variations or attempts to control the expression, is a characteristic probably shared with happiness, surprise, and fear; (2) brief latency and duration is a characteristic shared with surprise, although startle is briefer than surprise.

However, startle differs from the emotions, including surprise, in four ways: (1) startle is very easy to elicit; (2) it is shown reliably as the initial response by every subject; (3) the startle response can not be totally inhibited; and (4) no one seems able to simulate it with the correct latency. If startle is considered the extreme state of surprise, as claimed by those who say it is an emotion, then it would differ from emotions in a fifth way, appearing radically different from the supposed less extreme surprise expressions. One important type of evidence is still missing—the subjective experience of how it feels to be startled. Anecdotal evidence suggests that being startled feels very different from being surprised, much more different in kind than the difference in feelings between terror and fear, or between rage and anger.

S. S. Tomkins (personal communication, February, 1982) does not regard our findings as a challenge to his claim that the startle is an emotion. He argues that the differences we documented would be found with other emotions if stimuli as strong as the blank pistol shot were used. There are some data to counter Tomkins's reasoning on two features unique to the startle.

1. There is continuity in emotional expression from moderate to extreme states: Unlike the difference between the startle and surprise expressions, the expression of disgust when someone nearly vomits involves most of the same muscle movements activated in an expression of more moderate disgust (Ekman et al., 1980). Similarly, measurements of the facial expressions in news photographs of severe emotional situations (e.g. response to torture, death of a baby), did not find discontinuity in expression (Ekman, 1984).

2. Even with very strong stimuli, no single emotional expression is initially shown across all subjects: The data for this assertion comes both from Ekman's (1984) study and from Landis's (1924) findings when he used the extreme provocation of twisting off the head of a laboratory rat. There have been no studies relevant to Tomkins's claim that expressions cannot be completely inhibited or simulated when the provoking stimuli are very strong.

The balance of evidence suggests that startle differs sufficiently from what is known to characterize emotions that it should probably not be considered an emotion. We make that judgment independently of the argument about whether appraisal is a precondition for emotion because our position on that matter is that emotion can be aroused either with or without prior appraisal (Ekman, 1977, 1984). Our judgment must, however, be tentative. There is not sufficient information about each of the emotions to know how much each emotion differs from each other emotion. Although the startle does not appear to be a good model for the study of emotions, no other single emotion may prove to be so. If other emotions are examined in as much detail and in as many respects as the startle, each may be found, as Tomkins (1962) has suggested, to be unique in many respects. At present, far more is known about startle than about any of the emotions. It is hoped that it will not long remain so.

References

Allport, F. M. (1924). *Social psychology.* Boston: Houghton Mifflin.
Andrew, R. J. (1963). The origin and evolution of the calls and facial expressions of the primates. *Behaviour, 20,* 1–109.
Averill, J. R. (1980). A constructivist view of emotion. In R. Plutchik & H. Kellerman (Eds.), *Emotion: Theory, research and experience* (pp. 305–340). New York: Academic Press.
Bell, C. (1847). *The Anatomy and Philosophy of Expression as Connected with the Fine Arts* (4th ed.). London: John Murray.
Bull, N. (1951). The attitude theory of emotion. *Nervous and Mental Disease Monographs,* No. 81.
Darwin, C. (1872/1965). *The expression of emotions in man and animals.* Chicago: University of Chicago Press.
Davis, M., Gendelman, D. S., Tishler, M. D., & Gendelman, P. M. (1982). A preliminary acoustic

startle circuit: Lesion and stimulation studies. *The Journal of Neurosciences, 2,* 791–805.

Eibl-Eibesfeldt, I. (1980). *Ethology, the biology of behavior.* New York: Holt, Rinehart & Winston.

Ekman, P. (1973). Cross-cultural studies of facial expression. In P. Ekman (Ed.), *Darwin and facial expression: A century of research in review* (pp. 169–222). New York: Academic Press.

Ekman, P. (1977). Biological and cultural contributions to body and facial movement. In J. Blacking (Ed.), *Anthropology of the body* (pp. 39–84) London: Academic Press.

Ekman, P. (1984). Expression and the nature of emotion. In K. Scherer & P. Ekman (Eds.), *Approaches to emotion* (pp. 319–343). New York: Erlbaum.

Ekman, P., & Friesen, W. V. (1974). Detecting deception from body or face. *Journal of Personality and Social Psychology, 29*(3), 288–298.

Ekman, P., & Friesen, W. V. (1975). *Unmasking the face: A guide to recognizing emotions from facial clues.* Englewood Cliffs, NJ: Prentice-Hall.

Ekman, P., & Friesen, W. V. (1976). Measuring facial movement. *Journal of Environmental Psychology and Nonverbal Behavior, 1*(1), 56–75.

Ekman, P., & Friesen, W. V. (1978). *The Facial Action Coding System (FACS): A technique for the measurement of facial action.* Palo Alto, CA: Consulting Psychologists Press.

Ekman, P., Friesen, W. V., & Ancoli, S. (1980). Facial signs of emotional experience. *Journal of Personality and Social Psychology, 39*(6), 1125–1134.

Ekman, P., & Oster, H. (1979). Facial expressions of emotion. *Annual Review of Psychology, 30,* 527–554.

Friesen, W. V. (1972). *Cultural differences in facial expression in a social situation: An experimental test of the concept of display rules.* Unpublished doctoral dissertation, University of California, San Francisco.

Graham, F. K. (1975). The more or less startling effects of weak prestimulation. *Psychophysiology, 12,* 238–248.

Izard, C. E. (1971). *The face of emotion.* New York: Appleton-Century-Crofts.

Kemper, T. D. (1978). *A social interactional theory of emotions.* New York: Wiley.

Kleck, R. E., Vaughn, R. C., Cartwright-Smith, J., Vaughn, K. B., Colby, C. Z. & Lanzatta, J. T. (1976). Effects of being observed on expressive, subjective, and physiological responses to painful stimuli. *Journal of Personality and Social Psychology, 34,* 1211–1218.

Landis, C. (1924). Studies of emotional reactions: II. General behavior and facial expression. *Journal of Comparative Psychology, 4,* 447–509.

Landis, C., & Hunt, W. A. (1939). *The startle pattern.* New York: Farrar, Straus & Giroux.

Lazarus, R. S. (1982). Thoughts on the relations between emotion and cognition. *American Psychologist, 37*(9), 1019–1024.

Lazarus, R. S. (1984). On the primacy of cognition. *American Psychologist, 39,* 124–129.

Lersch, Ph. (1971). *Gesicht und Selle* [Face and Soul]. Munchen: Ernst Reinhart Verlag. (Original work published 1932).

Leventhal, H. (1980). Toward a comprehensive theory of emotion. *Advances in Experimental Social Psychology, 13,* 139–207.

Lindsley, D. B. (1951). Emotion. In S. S. Stevens (Ed.), *Handbook of experimental psychology* (pp. 473–516). New York: Wiley.

Mandler, G. (1975). *Mind and emotion.* New York: Wiley.

Plutchik, R. (1962). *The emotions: Facts, theories, and a new model.* New York: Random House.

Plutchik, R. (1980). *Emotion: A psychoevolutionary synthesis.* New York: Harper & Row.

Schacter, S., & Singer, J. E. (1962). Cognitive, social, and physiological determinants of emotional state. *Psychological Review, 69,* 379–399.

Simons, R. C. (1980). The resolution of the latah paradox. *Journal of Nervous and Mental Diseases, 148,* 195–206.

Simons, R. C., Ekman, P., & Friesen, W. V. (1985). Manuscript in preparation.

Tomkins, S. S. (1962). *Affect, Imagery, Consciousness: Vol. 1. The Positive Affects.* New York: Springer.

van Hooff, J. A. R. A. M. (1972). A comparative approach to the phylogeny of laughter and smiling. In R. A. Hinde (Ed.), *Non-verbal communication* (pp. 209–238). Cambridge, Eng.: Cambridge University Press.

Wenger, M. A., Jones, F. N., & Jones, M. H. (1956). *Physiological Psychology.* New York: Holt, Rinehart & Winston.

Wexler, D. (1972). Method for unitizing protocols of descriptions of emotional states. *Journal of Supplemental Abstracts Service* (Catalogue of Selected Documents in Psychology, Vol. 2, p. 116). Wash., DC: American Psychological Association.

Woodworth, R. S., & Schlosberg, H. (1954). *Experimental psychology* (rev. ed.). New York: Henry Holt.

Zajonc, R. B. (1980). Feeling and thinking: Preferences need no inferences. *American Psychologist, 35,* 151–175.

The Startle and Emotion

PAUL EKMAN

This is the second paper published using FACS; we omitted the first paper (Ekman, Friesen, & Ancoli, 1980) because of space limitations and because it does not raise as many theoretical issues. I selected this startle paper instead because the findings it reports had a major impact on my own thinking about emotion and about research on emotion. Also, it proved important for my coauthor Ron Simons and for my collaborator in subsequent research, Robert Levenson.

I had not thought before about how to distinguish emotions from bordering states, such as reflexes and moods. Although my first writing about how to make such distinctions was published a year before the startle paper, the startle data had already been analyzed and the results very much influenced my thinking. A chapter (Ekman, 1984) I wrote for a book that Klaus Scherer and I edited described ten characteristics that distinguish emotions from other related phenomena. One characteristic was a distinctive pan-cultural signal. I pointed out that although the startle has a distinctive pattern of facial activity, it could not be considered a signal, since it happens too quickly for those present to see it very well. I add now that, if it is a loud noise that is producing the startle, others present would likely be startled also, and their eyes would also close, making it impossible for them to observe the startle reaction in another person.

Duration also distinguishes emotions from other reflexes and moods. The startle motor response not only has a fixed duration but it is also much briefer than is typical for emotional expressions. Another characteristic I proposed to distinguish emotion from other affective phenomena is whether the timing of the expression—latency, onset time, apex time, and offset time—reflects the specifics of a particular emotional experience. This too was suggested by our startle findings, since the startle latency and onset time seem fixed. Another characteristic of emotional expressions is that they can be totally inhibited, and this was suggested by the startle findings, since the startle pattern cannot be inhibited. I further developed and refined these characteristics for distinguishing emotion from other affective phenomena in a later theoretical paper (Ekman, 1992).

The startle paper also served to arouse my interests in individual differences in the magnitude of facial expressions. We observed large individual differences in the magnitude of the startle response in the unanticipated condition, differences which we had not predicted and had no basis for explaining. Some subjects were nearly knocked out of their chair, while for others one had to look closely to see where the startle response occurred. Although I was thinking of the startle as a motor reflex, not an emotion, it seemed possible that the magnitude of the startle response might be an index of the magnitude of the motor response in emotional expressions.

About four years after the startle paper was published, we (I and Robert Levenson at the University of California, Berkeley, planned and carried out this work) gathered a data set that would allow us to examine this question. A little more than 50 subjects went through both the unanticipated and anticipated startle condition and a variety of other tasks, including two fairly standard emotion-arousing procedures: watching short films that we expected would arouse specific emotions, and remembering and reliving specific emotional experiences. In all of the tasks the facial responses were videotaped, subjective experience reports were obtained, and autonomic nervous system data were recorded. Our progress has been slow, since we lost extramural support for this work after the data set was acquired. However we did find that the magnitude of the startle response is correlated with the magnitude of emotional response while watching films or reliving past emotional experiences, examining this for 4 emotions (anger, fear, sadness, disgust), but not for enjoyment, in examining two response systems—expression and self-report, the autonomic physiology data is not yet analyzed.

In the startle paper we noted that individuals differed also in terms of whether their immediate post-startle response was embarrassment or sadness or fear. The data set just described is also allowing us to determine if the nature of the post-startle emotional response is related to various personality measures.

Robert Levenson and his group have done two startle studies. One study compared anticipated and unanticipated startles in Chinese, American, Hispanic, and European-American undergraduates. There were no differences among ethnic groups in physiology or self-reports (Lee & Levenson, 1992). Anticipation and prior experience lessened the magnitude of the startle response, (physiologically, motor behavior, and self-report) (Sutton, Levenson, Lee, Ketelaar, King, & Lee, 1994). An ongoing project compares European Americans, Chinese Americans, African Americans, and Mexican Americans with anticipated, unanticipated, and inhibited startles.

References

Ekman, P. (1984) Expression and the nature of emotion. In, Scherer, K. and Ekman, P. (Eds.) *Approaches to emotion.* Hillsdale New Jersey: Lawrence Erlbaum, pp. 319–344.

Ekman, P. (1992). An argument for basic emotions. *Cognition and Emotion, 6,* 169–200.

Ekman, P. Friesen, W. V. & Ancoli, S. (1980) Facial signs of emotional experience. *Journal of Personality and Social Psychology, 39*(6), 1125–1134.

Lee, K. J. & Levenson, R. W. (1992, October) *Ethnic differences in emotional reactivity to an unanticipated startle.* Paper presented at the meeting of the Society for Psychophysiological Research, San Diego, CA.

Sutton, S. K., Levenson, R. W., Lee, K. J., Ketelaar, T. J., King, A., & Lee, H. (1994, October) *The physiology, behavior, and subjective experience of acoustic startle.* Paper presented at the meeting for the Society for Psychophysiological Research, Atlanta, GA.

AFTERWORD

FACS in the Study of the *Latah* Syndrome

RONALD C. SIMONS

Although I had been following Paul Ekman and Wally Friesen's work on the emotions from their very first publications, my participation in the work described in the preceding paper stemmed from a practical problem rather than a theoretical interest. I had been studying *latah*, a culture-bound syndrome of Malaysia and Indonesia characterized by ready and violent startling (Simons, 1980, 1983a, 1983b), and I was about to return to Malaysia to study and film persons with the syndrome and to investigate ethnographically the cultural context in which the syndrome occurs. I approached Paul with no more than the question of how one might tell genuine from simulated startles since, for reasons too lengthy and convoluted to explain here, that point had become central to an ongoing controversy in the literature: did *latah* involve a physiological peculiarity exploited in a culture-typical way, or was it merely a custom that included sham startles. I believed (believe) that *latahs* are persons who startle with exceptional ease and readiness (Paul suggested the useful term "hyperstartlers"), and because of this I had identified a population of hyperstartling local American volunteers with whom I was planning some preliminary investigations before heading back to Malaysia to study and film *latahs*. The question posed to Paul was whether FACS could be used to discriminate real from sham startles. As this question fit nicely with Paul's own interest in startle, it led ultimately to the work described in the preceding paper.

As it turned out, it was not hard to discriminate real from sham startles, and after Malaysian *latahs* were filmed, it became possible to demonstrate that the startles of *latahs* were indeed real—often real, that is. Some *latahs* also performed sham startles at certain times, a finding which makes much sense in the ethnographic context (Simons, 1983c, 1992, 1994).

Since we had identified both Michigan hyperstartlers and a control population who agreed to be startled and filmed, an obvious additional question was whether there were *any* consistent differences between these two groups that could be ascertained with the means we had at hand. We found the differences reported in the preceding paper and initially planned to investigate them further, but as my work (and its funding) became increasingly concerned with the interaction between physiological events and culture-typical beliefs and behaviors (Simons & Hughes, 1985, 1992), additional experimental work was never carried out. However the fact that the differences we found between

American hyperstartlers and control "normal" American peers also discriminate Malaysian *latahs* from their non-*latah* peers turned out to be important in understanding the *latah* syndrome and the cultural context in which it is embedded (Simons, 1992, 1994, in press). Interestingly, the wheel has turned full circle. In the next few years I hope to return to Southeast Asia to further investigate the differences between *latahs* and their non-*latah* peers, using some of the tools and data developed by Paul and coworkers in the intervening years, as described in his Afterword to the preceding chapter.

References

Simons, R. C. (1980). The resolution of the latah paradox. *Journal of Nervous and Mental Disease, 168,* 195–206.

Simons, R. C. (1983a). Latah II—Problems with a purely symbolic interpretation. *Journal of Nervous and Mental Disease, 171,* 168–171.

Simons, R. C. (1983b). Latah III—How compelling is the evidence for a psychoanalytic interpretation? *Journal of Nervous and Mental Disease, 171,* 178–181.

Simons, R. C. (Producer and Director). (1983c). *Latah: A culture-specific elaboration of the startle reflex* [Film]. (Available from Indiana University Audiovisual Center, Bloomington, Indiana.)

Simons, R. C. (1992). Further skirmishes in the great latah wars. *Transcultural Psychiatric Research Review, 29,* 250–256.

Simons, R. C. (1994). The interminable debate on the nature of latah. *Journal of Nervous and Mental Disease, 182,* 339–341.

Simons, R. C. (in press). *Boo! Culture, experience, and the startle reflex.* New York: Oxford University Press.

Simons, R. C., & Hughes, C. C. (Eds.) (1985). *The Culture-Bound Syndromes;* Reidel; Dordrecht.

Simons, R. C., & Hughes, C. C. (1992). Culture bound syndromes. In A. C. Gaw (Ed.), *Culture, Ethnicity, and Mental Illness* (pp. 75–93). Washington, DC: *American Psychiatric Press.*

2

The Asymmetry of Facial Actions Is Inconsistent with Models of Hemispheric Specialization

JOSEPH C. HAGER & PAUL EKMAN

Recent reports have suggested that asymmetries in facial expressions result from cerebral hemispheric specialization. A summary of these theoretical models is contained in table 2.1. These models differ in two important respects: whether emotional or nonemotional neural processes are involved, and whether specialization of the right, the left, or both hemispheres underlies asymmetry. This report evaluates these issues.

Facial Asymmetry and Specialization

Facial asymmetry has been attributed to both emotional and nonemotional neural processes. Some researchers (Chaurasia & Goswami, 1975; Heller & Levy, 1981) theorized that specialization in right-handers of the right hemisphere for cognitive, nonverbal processes such as the recognition of faces (see Benton, 1980) produced asymmetry. Others (Sackeim, Gur, & Saucy, 1978; Schwartz, Ahern, & Brown, 1979) referred to the evidence that the right hemisphere has an important function in emotional processes (Ley & Bryden, 1981). They speculated that since facial expressions are an integral part of emotion, it is reasonable to expect the right hemisphere to have a special role in the production of facial expressions. These theories of right hemispheric specialization predict that asymmetries of facial actions should be lateralized with the left side stronger or more active.

Still others have hypothesized that each hemisphere is specialized for different emotions. One model is right hemispheric specializations only for negative emotions, and left specialization for positive emotions (Schwartz et al., 1979; Reuter-Lorenz & Davidson, 1981; Sackeim & Gur, 1978). A variant of this theory, mentioned by Davidson and Fox (1982), is right hemispheric specialization for avoidance emotions and left specialization for approach emotions. These theories explicitly predict or suggest that positive or approach expressions would be stronger or show more activity on the right side of the face, but negative or avoidance expressions would show the opposite.

TABLE 2.1. Summary of hemispheric specialization models for facial asymmetry

Brief Statement of Models for Neural Basis of Facial Asymmetry	Illustrative Citations	Predictions or Implications for Facial Asymmetry	
		Emotional Facial Actions	Nonemotional Facial Actions
Emotional Processes			
Emotion in Right Hemisphere	Sackeim et al. (1978), Moscovitch & Olds (1982)	left stronger	left stronger
Positive Emotion in Left, Negative Emotion in Right Hemisphere	Schwartz et al. (1979), Sackeim & Gur (1978)	positive: right stronger, negative: left stronger	possibly same pattern?
Approach Emotion in Left, Avoidance Emotion in Right Hemisphere	Davidson & Fox (1982)	approach: right stronger, avoidance: left stronger	possibly same pattern?
Nonemotional Processes			
Recognition of Facial Identity and Emotion Expression in Right Hemisphere	Chaurasia & Goswami (1975), Heller & Levy (1981)	left stronger	left stronger
Integration of Bilateral Facial Actions by the Left Hemisphere	Geschwind (1965, 1975)	no prediction	right stronger: possibility for left stronger

Geschwind (1965, 1975) argued that bilateral facial movements are typically integrated by the left hemisphere, particularly in response to verbal requests for movements, but that the right hemisphere can control movements in certain conditions, such as when the request is non-verbal. Geschwind did not indicate that hemispheric specialization would be observed in the expressions of non-patients, but his model allows for both left and right asymmetry.

These models of hemispheric specialization do not make explicit the neural mechanisms that explain why specialization would cause asymmetrical facial actions. There are two theoretical bases for this relationship. First is an analogy to the direction of lateral eye movements that was hypothesized to reflect the differential activation of the cerebral hemispheres (Bakan, 1969; see Ehrlichman & Weinberger, 1978, for a critical review). Kinsbourne (1972) theorized that increased activation of the left hemisphere during language processing "overflows" to left hemispheric orientation and motor centers to shift gaze to the right. Kimura (1973) used a similar explanation to account for her findings that free right-hand movements were more frequent during speech than nonspeech but frequencies of left-hand movements did not differ. A second possible explanation disregards hemispheric activation and instead implicates other consequences of hemispheric specialization. For example, messages created in one hemisphere for integrating bilateral facial movements (e.g., Geschwind, 1965) might be degraded crossing to the contralateral hemisphere, thus inducing motor asymmetry. What mechanism produced facial asymmetry was not clearly specified by models of either emotional or nonemotional hemispheric specialization.

These models also failed to specify whether lateralization was the same for emotional expressions as for deliberate and other types of facial actions. Ekman (1980) pointed out that many experiments did not adequately distinguish emotional from nonemotional movements and hypothesized greater asymmetry for nonemotional movements. Ekman, Hager, and Friesen (1981) confirmed this hypothesis, finding that stronger muscular actions tended to occur more often on the left side of the face, but only for deliberate, requested actions, not for actions related to emotion. They also found smiles more symmetrical when children responded to an experimenter's joke or praise than when they smiled deliberately on request.

Other studies found either left or right laterality in facial expression. In some, asymmetries were lateralized so that the left side had greater electromyographic (EMG) activity (Schwartz et al., 1979), more intense expression (Borod & Caron, 1980; Campbell, 1978; Sackeim et al., 1978), stronger muscular contractions (Ekman et al., 1981), and more frequent unilateral actions during conversation (Moscovitch & Olds, 1982). Other reports showed greater facility in performing deliberate actions on the right side of the face (e.g., Alford & Alford, 1981; Kohara, 1975), or that moving the right side of the face is subjectively more "natural" (Alford, 1983), or that the right side of the mouth is more motile during speech (Graves, Goodglass, & Landis, 1982; Hager & van Gelder, in press).

The implications of these different asymmetries for the models described above are unclear, in part, because of three methodological problems: (1) Some studies did not clearly distinguish whether the asymmetry was temporarily produced by muscular actions or was a more permanent physiognomic cue. Among those which measured muscular action, (2) some failed to specify whether emotional or nonemotional processes generated the expressions, and, (3) most did not employ a sufficiently refined measure which could distinguish exactly which muscles acted.

Considerations for Research on Facial Asymmetry

Relevant Facial Cues

A serious shortcoming of many previous reports is the failure to distinguish adequately which characteristics, such as permanent facial features or muscular actions, were measured. Thus, one cannot know whether the results are due to nervous system activity or to some other factor unrelated to neuromuscular activity. This problem is especially severe when asymmetry is measured by observers' judgments about the intensity of expression in the whole face. It is not possible to ascertain whether observers judged the intensity of muscular actions or some other asymmetrical characteristic (Hager, 1982). Even objective physical measurements of facial asymmetry are vulnerable. EMG measurements, for example, are influenced by the tissue between the electrode and the muscle, tissues that might be asymmetrical and cause measurement problems (Fridlund, 1984).

Here, we measured the symmetry of each muscular action separately to assess differences between the two sides of the face in the strength of contraction of individual muscles. This approach defined the features measured and minimized the influence of extraneous factors on measurements. Distinguishing individual facial actions depended upon Ekman and Friesen's *Facial Action Coding System* (FACS) (1978). FACS measures the visible action of facial muscles with Action Units (AUs) that indicate which muscles contract to produce expressions. Action Units correspond to the anatomy of facial muscles, but rather than measuring every change in muscular action, they differentiate what scorers can reliably discriminate. After identifying an AU with FACS, asymmetry is determined. Table 2.2 describes the Action Units that were measured in this study.

Like EMG, FACS scoring measures the activity of muscles, but it is based on the visible changes in facial tissues produced by the action of muscles rather than the electrical potentials generated by contractions. Both FACS and EMG can locate the beginning, apex, and end of muscular action and variations in the intensity of contraction, but EMG has a much finer, continuous scale. FACS and EMG measures of the intensity of contraction are highly correlated (Ekman, 1982).

EMG may be more sensitive to low level changes in muscular activity and is often used to compute integrated measures of activity over time. FACS, however, is more sensitive to the action of individual muscles than surface EMG, which picks up activity of any muscle in the area of the electrode. Needle EMG can measure the action of individual muscles more precisely than surface EMG, but inserting fine wires into subjects' faces is usually impractical. Because surface EMG is imprecise about what muscles are measured, it is probably not possible for it to discriminate the range of facial expressions that FACS can distinguish.

EMG cannot be used to measure facial action when unobtrusive methods are an important consideration. Attaching electrodes heightens the subject's awareness of what is being measured. Subjects may inhibit large expressions in order not to detach the EMG electrodes. EMG is a more automated method for collecting records and extracting data, whereas FACS scoring relies on the trained discrimination of experts aided by high quality video equipment. Compared to EMG, FACS takes a relatively long time to derive usable data from the record. (For a more complete comparison of facial measurement techniques see Ekman, 1982.)

When measuring asymmetry in the intensity of muscular action, however, both measures may be affected by anatomical factors independent of the strength of muscular

TABLE **2.2.** Action units measured in this study

Action Unit (AU)	Muscles Involved	Description of Action	Conditions Where Elicited
1	Inner frontalis	Raises inner corner of brow	Requested actions Startle simulations Emotion simulations
2	Outer frontalis	Raises outer corner of brow	Same as above
1 + 2	Frontalis	Raises entire brow	Same as above
4	Corrugator Procerus	Lowers and pulls brows together	Requested actions Emotion simulations
6	Orbicularis oculi, outer portion	Squints eyes, makes crowsfeet wrinkles	Requested actions Startle simulations Emotion simulations Startle actions Happy emotion action
7	Orbicularis oculi, inner portion	Squints eyes, raises and straightens lower lid	Requested actions Startle simulations Emotion simulations Startle actions
9	Levator labii superioris, alaque nasi	Wrinkles nose	Requested actions Emotion simulations
10	Levator labii superioris	Raises upper lip	Requested actions
12	Zygomatic major	Common smile	Requested actions Emotion simulations Happy emotion action
14	Buccinator	Dimples cheeks	Emotion simulations
15	Triangularis	Lowers corners of lips	Requested actions Emotion simulations
16	Depressor labii inferioris	Pulls lower lip down	Requested actions
20	Risorius	Stretches lip corners straight to the side	Requested actions Emotion simulations Startle actions
45	Orbicularis oculi	Blink or wink	Requested actions Startle simulations Startle actions

contraction (e.g., thickness, mass, and elasticity of skin). Fridlund (1984) suggests that if these anatomical factors are not the same on the two sides of the face, measurements of symmetry based on either visual observation (FACS) or electrical activity (EMG) may be misleading. Unequal muscular contractions may appear to be symmetrical if compensated by anatomical differences. Conversely, equal muscular contractions may appear asymmetrical because of anatomical asymmetries. Fridlund argued that these anatomical confounds are most problematic when comparing asymmetry between conditions that show large differences in the intensity of muscular contractions. In this study, analyses were performed to control for differences in the intensity of actions across conditions whenever possible.

Deliberate versus Spontaneous Movements

This study distinguished deliberate from spontaneous facial movements and compared their asymmetry. These types of facial movements have neural substrates that are at least partially different (e.g., Tschiassny, 1953; Rinn, 1984). Deliberate facial actions probably have their neural origins in the motor strip of the neocortex, but spontaneous emotional movements are probably initiated in subcortical motor centers of the prosencephalon, such as the basal ganglia.[1] The startle actions measured in this study are another type of spontaneous facial movement having neural pathways different from either deliberate or emotional movements. The reflexes involved in the startle are probably mediated by centers in the brainstorm reticular formation (Hoffman & Ison, 1980).

The description of types of facial movements is complicated further by the independence of the spontaneous-deliberate and emotional-nonemotional dimension. Ekman et al. (1981) in a previous study of asymmetry explained that:

> The voluntary (or deliberate) versus involuntary (or spontaneous) dichotomy is far too simple, glossing over many diverse behaviors which might depend upon different neural pathways. For example, involuntary facial expressions might include actions which are overlearned habits and unlearned reflexes [such as the startle], actions which are modulated by choice or habit and those which cannot be so controlled, and actions which are reported into awareness and those which are not.
>
> Even among expressions which refer only to emotion, the voluntary-involuntary distinction does not capture all of the different types of behavior. *Spontaneous* emotional expressions appear quickly, seemingly without choice, although they may be modulated by choice or habit. Some of these expressions are considered to be innate because of similarities across cultures and among some primates. A *simulated* emotional expression is a deliberate attempt to appear as if an emotion is being experienced. . . . A *gestural* emotional expression resembles actual emotional expression but it differs sufficiently in appearance to make it evident to the beholder that the person does not feel that emotion at this moment; he is just mentioning it. . . . It is important that those interested in the differential role of the two cerebral hemispheres in the production of emotional expressions specify which type of facial expression they have studied. (pp. 101–102)

In our study, a relatively pure sample of spontaneous facial actions was obtained in circumstances in which the likelihood of attempts to control the expression, by habit or choice, would be minimal: (1) The startle expression was elicited by a sudden, loud noise. (2) An enjoyment expression was elicited by a comment presumed to be amusing, without any element of embarrassment.

A relatively pure sample of deliberate actions was obtained by requesting the subject to perform specific facial actions without referring to emotion (e.g., raise your eyebrows up). By asking the subjects to perform these actions singly one at a time, the likelihood of inadvertently obtaining emotional behavior was minimized. Ekman, Levenson, and Friesen (1983) found that voluntarily making facial expressions did *not* generate the autonomic nervous system activity associated with emotion unless the entire facial expression was performed.

A mixture of spontaneous and deliberate actions was produced by requesting subjects to simulate six emotional expressions and a startle expression. Subjects could solve this task by either remembering an emotional experience, attempting to let the expression flow from the remembered experience, or by remembering a picture of a face which they attempt to imitate (Ekman, Roper, & Hager, 1980). The findings from Ekman et al. (1983) suggest that by either method, autonomic nervous system activity may be generated.

Hypotheses

This report distinguishes *asymmetry,* which denotes a difference between the two sides of the face, from *laterality,* which indicates consistent asymmetry or a bias for one side. Spontaneous and deliberate actions were predicted to differ in two ways. First, deliberate actions would show more asymmetry than spontaneous actions. Second, deliberate actions, unlike spontaneous actions, were expected to show lateralization of asymmetries. In conditions where spontaneous and deliberate actions were mixed, actions were predicted to show fewer asymmetries and less laterality than deliberate actions, but more than spontaneous actions.

For deliberate actions, the preponderance of evidence suggested the prediction of left laterality (Hager, 1982) with two exceptions. Evidence from Ekman et al. (1981) suggested that the tendency for asymmetries to manifest laterality varied with the action, but their samples were too small to be conclusive on this point. Some actions may not be lateralized. Second, each of the studies that examined winking (Alford & Alford, 1981; Kohara, 1975) showed greater skill and/or preference for winking the right eye. Actions related to blinking and winking were predicted to show right laterality.

Method

Subjects

Gender might be an important variable affecting the symmetry of facial actions (e.g., Alford & Alford, 1981; Borod & Caron, 1980), but the facial scoring required for this study was too time-consuming to factorially vary subject variables. To make the sample more homogeneous, 33 right-handed Caucasian women, aged 18–53 ($M = 27.5$) yrs, were recruited as subjects. A handedness questionnaire (Johnstone, Galin, & Herron, 1979) screened for right-handed subjects.

Equipment

All of the subjects' facial actions were recorded on videotape for later analysis. The subject always faced directly into the camera lens, producing straight ahead shots that were ideal for asymmetry scoring.

Previous researchers (e.g., Landis & Hunt, 1939; Ekman, Friesen, & Simons, in press) have frequently used acoustic stimuli to elicit startles because they reliably elicit the startle response and are relatively easy to administer. The commonly used starter's pistol was inappropriate for this study because, first, the sound pressure level of shots varied widely and might have endangered subjects' hearing. Second, a pilot study suggested that asymmetry depended upon the direction of the noise, and directional properties of shots could not be controlled easily.

To solve these problems, startle sounds were 80-ms bursts of white noise produced electronically, amplified, and transduced by headphones worn by the subject and an array of six speaker cabinets stacked directly behind her. Sound pressure level was 125dB and was balanced to within 1dB on either side of the subject's head. This arrangement controlled stimulus intensity and minimized directional variation.

All of the equipment for controlling the experiment was placed behind a partition so that the experimenter was hidden from view except when giving general instructions and questionnaires. Thus, the subject could not see any subtle cues that the experimenter might have shown about how to do movements, when the unanticipated startle noise was to occur, etc.

Experimental Procedure

Each subject completed the procedure individually. There were two main parts to the study. The startle part of the experiments was modeled after the procedure of Ekman et al. (in press). The subject simulated a startled expression twice, before and after hearing three separate loud noises.[2] The next part of the experiment was a modified version of Ekman and Friesen's Requested Facial Action Test (REFACT) (1982). For simulations of six emotions, the subject was asked to look happy, sad, angry, fearful, disgusted, and surprised, in this order for every subject. The experimenter then asked "Now that this is done, aren't you glad it's over?" in order to elicit a more spontaneous smile. This comment was expected to produce amusement or enjoyment because it acknowledged the strangeness of having to make expressions devoid of feeling on request and it came when relief at completing this task might be a stimulus for enjoyment (Tomkins, 1962). Demand for deliberate or unfelt social smiles was minimized because the experimenter was behind a curtain and the subject was not in a face-to-face interaction.

Subjects in this study knew they were being videotaped, and this knowledge could have heightened self awareness and altered natural spontaneous expressions (see Hager, 1982). Ideally, videotaping should be as unobtrusive as possible. Only the lens of the camera was in view, but we did not hide the videotaping. Evidence suggests that the startle pattern is relatively invulnerable to attempts at control and alteration (Landis & Hunt, 1939). The spontaneous smile was elicited when the subject's attention shifted away from the task and recording. If any subjects did control or alter their spontaneous actions, in either the startle or smile samples, it would work against our hypothesis, diminishing the differences between the spontaneous and deliberate actions.

Next, the subject deliberately made individual facial actions. Requests for some of the deliberate actions were made in two ways, verbally and visually, to check the possibility that asymmetry might be affected by verbal vs. visual mediation. First, the experimenter verbally instructed the subject to perform eight actions (AUs 12, 1 + 2, 4, 45, 10, 9, 20, 6 + 7, in this order; see table 2.2). Then, the subject viewed an expert in facial movement on videotape and imitated the 17 individual actions shown by the expert with no coaching or comments. Eleven of these actions that were measured in previous studies or in other conditions of this study were scored (AUs 1 + 2, 9, 16, 12, 4, 7, 10, 15, 20, 1, 2, requested and scored in this order). Sometimes a subject could not perform the requested action, and at other times performed the action many times for a given request. A maximum of four repetitions of the action were scored (the first and last two). There was no difference in asymmetry between the seven requests common to both verbal and visual conditions so they were averaged for analysis.[3]

Facial Scoring Procedures

A series of scoring steps began with the startle part of the study. Only actions that were part of the startle response were scored. According to Ekman et al. (1985), startle actions that are either common or universal are tightening the muscles around the eye (AUs 6 and 7), stretching the lips horizontally (AU 20), tightening neck muscles (AU 21), closing the eyes (AU 45), and moving the head and shoulders upwards. Following their scoring procedure, any of these actions that began in the first 1/3 second after the noise were scored because this interval includes the beginning of actions that comprise a characteristic startle response. Other, idiosyncratic actions were also scored if they began before the end of the apex of AUs 6, 7, 20, or 21. In the simulate conditions, every AU that began within 1/3 second of the onset of the first AU in the simulation was scored.

The second scoring step was to score the requested facial actions. Eleven different requested actions were selected for scoring because they appeared in other conditions and were included in previous studies. Subjects typically performed each requested action several times so the scores were averaged.

The third step was scoring the emotion simulations and the spontaneous response to the question: "Aren't you glad it's done?" For simulations, the scorer determined the AUs just before the subject began to announce she was finished and scored them all.

Measurement of Asymmetry

Measurement of asymmetry was similar to the procedure used by Ekman et al. (1981). Each individual muscular action was identified using Ekman and Friesen's Facial Action Coding System (FACS) (1978). The scorer assessed the changes in facial appearance between the action's beginning and apex (a single video frame showing both sides at greatest intensity). The intensity of contraction was measured on a six-point scale separately for each side of the face by blocking off the other side from view. The scorer used a video disk to look repeatedly in slow motion and real time for any differences in intensity between the two sides at the apex. A score between − 5 (extreme left asymmetry) and + 5 (extreme right asymmetry) was assigned to indicate whether the action was symmetrical or asymmetrical. If asymmetrical, the score provided a categorical measure of right vs. left and a continuous measure of how great the difference in intensity was. Determining a facial midline is not as important with this procedure as it is when cutting and pasting still photographs (Sackeim et al., 1978). The changing appearances due to a contracting muscle are gauged from their beginning and ending positions, not their relationship to a midline.

Reliability

Asymmetry scoring was based on the FACS technique, which has substantial reliability evidence (Ekman & Friesen, 1978). Similar asymmetry scoring was shown to be reliable in a previous study (Ekman et al., 1981). The experimenter was the main scorer in this study because of his expertise and ability to spend five man-months scoring. One important issue was whether knowledge of the hypotheses biased scoring because of the experimenter's role as scorer. The potential for bias was minimized by the scoring procedure which, for example, spread the scoring over time so that scores in different conditions were hard to remember. The reliability coefficients indicate that bias was not an important factor. The Pearson correlation between the main coder (who knew the hypotheses) and three reliability coders (who did not know the hypotheses) was .72 ($p<.001$). A Kappa used to assess the reliability of the right vs. left category scores was .88 ($p<.0001$) with 94 percent agreement, indicating that when coders agreed an action was asymmetrical, they usually agreed about whether it was left or right.

Results

Differences in Asymmetry between Types of Movement

Spontaneous versus Deliberate Actions

Absolute values of asymmetry scores were used to index the degree of asymmetry, disregarding whether the right or left side was more intense. Wilcoxon signed-ranks tests on these scores showed that, as predicted, spontaneous actions were more symmetrical than deliberate actions. As shown in table 2.3, smiling (AU 12) in spontaneous happy expressions were more symmetrical than in requested actions. Squinting (AU 6) in spontaneous happy expressions was more symmetrical than in requested actions. Lip stretching (AU 20) in the startle expressions was more symmetrical than in requested actions. The prediction was not confirmed for squinting (AUs 6 and 7) and blinking (AU 45) between the startle and the requested actions, which showed no difference.

These significant differences in asymmetry between conditions cannot be attributed to differences in the intensity of actions between conditions. In a separate analysis to eliminate intensity differences, each action in the spontaneous conditions was matched for intensity with a deliberate action with rules to eliminate biased selection. As table 2.4 shows, the matching produced an average intensity difference between conditions that was less than one scoring interval. The results of this analysis showed the same significant differences except for AU 6, which had too many ties but still showed the same tendency.

Spontaneous Startle versus Startle Simulations

Simulations had more actions that were not common in startles (e.g., AUs 1, 2, 12) and fewer actions that were common in startles (e.g., AUs 6, 7, 20). The only difference in asymmetry between simulations and the real startle can be attributed to chance.

Emotion Simulations versus Spontaneous
or Deliberate Actions

All but one subject smiled to the question "Now that this is done, aren't you glad it's over?" at the end of the emotion simulations. We could not eliminate the possibility that some of these actions were deliberate or controlled rather than spontaneous emotional smiles. This possibility, however, worked against the hypothesis of a difference between spontaneous and deliberate actions. As shown in table 2.5, spontaneous smiles (AU 12) were more symmetrical than these AUs in emotion simulations of happy, which were, in turn, more symmetrical than in deliberate actions. There were no other significant differences between actions in emotion simulations and either spontaneous or deliberate actions.

TABLE 2.3. Differences in asymmetry of deliberate versus spontaneous action units in the spontaneous smile and startle conditions

Condition	Action Unit	Mean Score		Greater Rank			z
		Del.	Spon.	Del.	Spon.	Ties	
Happy vs.	6	.540	.174	13	1	9	2.42*
Deliberate	12	.971	.188	29	2	1	4.53**
Startle vs.	6	.341	.409	9	8	6	0.07
Deliberate	20	1.068	.417	20	6	0	3.19**
	45	.111	.091	7	4	22	0.80

Note: Analyses are Wilcoxon signed-ranks tests on the absolute values of asymmetry scores.
*p < .02, **p < .001.

TABLE 2.4. Differences in asymmetry in table 2.3 controlled for intensity

Action Unit	Mean Intensity		Mean Score		Greater Rank			z
	Del.	Span	Del.	Span	Del.	Span	Ties	
6	2.7	3.3	.500	.182	7	1	14	1.59
12	3.5	3.9	.969	.188	19	2	11	3.63**
20	2.8	1.9	1.182	.409	15	4	3	2.27*

Note: Analyses are Wilcoxon signed-ranks tests on absolute values of asymmetry scores for actions matched on intensity. Intensity scale ranges from 0 to 5.
*p < .05, **p < .001.

TABLE 2.5. Differences in asymmetry for AU 12 between the simulated happy condition and the spontaneous and deliberate conditions

Condition	Mean Score	Greater Rank	Ties	z
Simul.	.658	9	1	6.66**
Del.	.981	23		
Simul.	.641	12	17	2.92*
Spon.	.188	3		

Note: Analyses are Wilcoxon signed-ranks tests on absolute values of asymmetry scores.
*p < .01. **p < .001.

Laterality of Actions

Different Deliberate Actions

Table 2.6 summarizes laterality by individual AUs showing that asymmetries of some actions were lateralized, but others were not Aus 4 (brow lowered) and 12 (smiling) were lateralized stronger on the left as predicted, but AUs 9 (nose wrinkle), and 15 (lip corners down), were lateralized right, disconfirming the prediction of left laterality for these actions. The combination of AUs 1 + 2 in the brow raise was also lateralized right, although the separate scorers for AUs 1 (inner) and 2 (outer) suggested that AU 2 was primarily responsible for this effect. Lateralization was not evident, for AUs 1, 6, 7, 6 + 7, 10, 16, and 45 (all tests were exact binomial, two-tailed).

To test the significance of AU as a variable in determining asymmetry scores, one-way repeated measures analysis of variance with AU as the independent variable was performed on the continuous asymmetry scores. Several ANOVAs of this design were calculated by changing the AUs included because missing data for some difficult to perform AUs lowered the valid N, sometimes to less than half the total N. All analyses included a Greenhouse-Geisser correction using the estimated Epsilon (Winer, 1971). The worst case analysis included all 12 different deliberate actions (AUs 1, 2, 1 + 2, 4, 6 + 7, 9, 10, 12, 15, 16, 20, 45) and was significant, $F(11/154) = 2.55$, $p<.05$ (N = 15). The other analyses showed stronger effects with smaller p levels, confirming that the variation of asymmetry scores across AUs was not chance.

Spontaneous Expressions

More smiles (AU 12) were stronger on the left than the right, but not significantly more, and squinting (AU 6) was largely symmetrical. The startles showed little asymmetry, and the only AU to show laterality was squinting (AU 6), which was stronger on the right.

TABLE 2.6. Summary of laterality by action

Action Unit (AU)	Deliberate Actions	Startles	Spontaneous Smiles	Simulated Startles	Emotion Simulations
1	S	—	—	S	S
2	S	—	—	S	S
1 + 2	R	—	—	—	—
4	L	—	—	S	S
6	S	R	S	S	S
7	S	S	—	S	S
9	R	—	—	—	S
10	S	—	—	—	S
12	L	—	S	S	L
15	R	—	—	—	S
16	S	—	—	—	—
20	S*	S	—	S	S
21	—	S	—	S	—
45	S	S	—	S	—

Note: Letters "R" and "L" denote right and left laterality $p < .05$ (two-tailed binomial). The letter "S" denotes no significant laterality.
* The AU in this condition showed a tendency ($p = .06$) for the right.

Simulations

For startle simulations, the incidence of asymmetry was low, and there was no significant laterality. For actions in the six emotion simulations, the laterality of smiling (AU 12) was in the same direction as requested actions.

Laterality within Subjects across AUs

In addition to examining consistency in asymmetry across subjects for each Action Unit, we looked at the consistency within each subject across the actions measured. This approach addressed the issue of whether any particular subject had a bias for one side of her face. Only 5 of the 33 subjects showed such a consistent tendency, and it was not the same side across subjects.

Discussion

Does Specialization for Emotion Produce Facial Asymmetry?

The results of this study were not entirely consistent with any model of hemispheric specialization. Left lateralization of facial activity has been attributed to specialization of the right hemisphere for emotion (Borod & Caron, 1980; Schwartz et al., 1979). Spontaneous emotional and reflex movements as measured here were generally not found to be lateralized. Only action of orbicularis oculi in the startle showed lateralization, but the direction was opposite to that predicted by right hemispheric specialization for emotion.

This study might not have employed a measure sensitive enough to low levels of asymmetry or measured enough actions to detect significant tendencies for lateralization in the happy, startle, and simulation conditions. The study did, however, replicate the findings of Ekman et al. (1981) that there was less asymmetry in spontaneous than in deliberate actions. These findings indicate that factors producing asymmetry in deliberate movements are not related directly to positive emotional processes involving smiling, nor to processes giving rise to negative, reflex-like startle reactions. The finding that the asymmetry of smiles in simulated happy expressions was intermediate between spontaneous and deliberate smiles supports the hypothesis that asymmetry is a function of the extent to which movements are emotional vs. deliberate. Further research is needed on negative emotional expressions.

Dual specialization for emotion does not account for the opposite laterality of different actions. One dual specialization model is that the right hemisphere is specialized only for negative emotions, and the left, for positive emotions (Reuter-Lorenz & Davidson, 1981; Sackeim & Gur, 1978; Schwartz et al., 1979). It predicts that actions related to positive emotion would be lateralized stronger on the right while actions related to negative emotion would be lateralized left. The finding that deliberate actions of AU 12 (the smile involved in positive emotion) are lateralized stronger on the left is opposite to this theory's prediction for positive expressions, and the finding that spontaneous actions of AU 12 show only the same slight tendency lends no support to this position. The asymmetries of some deliberate actions (AUs 9 and 15), which are elements of negative emotion expressions (disgust and sadness), were significantly stronger on the right, not the left. The right stronger laterality of orbicularis oculis (AUs 6 and 7) in the startle also does not support this model because almost all subjects said it was an unpleasant experience.

Another model of dual specialization for emotion is that the right hemisphere is specialized for avoidance emotions and the left hemisphere, for approach emotions (see Davidson & Fox, 1982). Some deliberate actions often involved in approach emotions (e.g., AU 4 in anger; AU 12 in happiness) were lateralized stronger on the left, and others often involved in avoidance emotions (e.g., AU 9 in disgust) were lateralized right stronger. These relationships are the opposite to those suggested by this theory.

Because the pattern of asymmetry for both the spontaneous and deliberate facial actions studied here does not conform to predictions based on models of cerebral specialization for emotion, we reject hypotheses that attribute each asymmetry to lateralization of emotion. We cannot, however, reject models of cerebral specialization for emotion based on this evidence alone. Many of those concerned with emotional lateralization will not consider these findings a challenge because they have not considered the issue of asymmetry of facial expressions of emotion.

Do Facial Actions Show Right or Left Laterality?

Using a detailed visual measurement procedure, laterality was observed to depend upon the muscle measured. This evidence apparently contradicts reports about only left or only right laterality (e.g., Alford & Alford, 1981; Borod & Caron, 1980; Sackeim et al., 1978). These contradictions could be due to different measurements of asymmetry. For example, Sirota and Schwartz (1982) reported that EMG activity from the "zygomatic placement" of electrodes was greater on the right, but they pointed out that other muscles in the same area might have contributed to the activity recorded from this placement. In the study reported here, the action of the zygomatic major (AU 12) was lateralized stronger on the left, but other actions in this area of the face either were not lateralized or tended to be stronger on the right. Thus, this apparent discrepancy between studies might be explained by the relative imprecision of EMG for measuring specific muscles. Another difference is the practice of averaging EMG activity over many seconds while asymmetry was measured in this study at a particular moment. Despite measurement differences, the finding that deliberate actions of AU 4 (corrugator) were lateralized stronger on the left is consistent with Schwartz et al.'s (1979) finding that EMG from a corrugator placement was greater on the left during voluntary facial expression.

Different measurements might account for some inconsistencies between studies, but Ekman et al. (1981) used the same measure as this study and reported left laterality for deliberate actions. Their subjects, however, were much younger and included males. Alford (1983) reported that males had more facility moving the left side of their face than females. Also, Ekman et al. measured only a subset of the actions measured here, and their sample was too small to permit analysis of each action individually, except for zygomatic major actions (AU 12) which were lateralized stronger on the left. This finding was replicated strongly here.

What Can Explain Asymmetry of Facial Actions?

This study indicates inadequacies in models of hemispheric specialization for explaining asymmetry in facial actions. As discussed above, specialization for emotion cannot explain the results of this study. Since deliberate actions showed more asymmetry than spontaneous actions, the neural processes involved in the directed control of actions might be implicated. This study does not support the hypothesis that one hemisphere alone is specialized to direct facial actions, but Geschwind mentioned the possibility that the hemispheres might sometimes share control. No one neural process specialized in a single hemisphere can explain all asymmetry in facial actions if we assume that this specialization affects all actions the same way. Such specialization predicts consistent laterality, but in this study asymmetries of some actions were lateralized left and others, right. In addition, this specialization implies that individual subjects show consistent asymmetry for all actions, but few subjects did: most showed a mixture of left and right asymmetry.

There are several possible explanations for different laterality among actions. First, the assumption that the specialization of one hemisphere affects the symmetry of all actions equally might be incorrect, perhaps because some actions are subject to different kinds of control. Ekman and Friesen (1975) have pointed out that the control of facial actions has several aspects. Even if control functions were lateralized in one hemisphere, different actions might show different laterality depending upon how they were typically controlled. For example, some actions might be inhibited more often and others might be put-on or intensified more often. Galin suggested (Ekman et al., 1981) that the right hemisphere is specialized for inhibiting or modulating emotional expression, rather than for emotion itself, and indeed, smiling and frowning are actions that appear in emotional expressions that are often controlled (e.g., feigning happiness and suppressing anger). Whether these actions, which showed left laterality, are controlled differently or more frequently than right lateralized actions is an issue for further research.

Other explanations of the differences in laterality between actions were found to be inadequate. The area of the face was not a factor because both left laterality and right laterality were found in the upper and the lower face. The possibility that some kind of emotional process entered into the process of deliberately making actions of smiling and brow lowering was rejected. This explanation implies that spontaneous actions of smiling would be lateralized, but they were not. Different frequencies of actions cannot explain different lateralities. Although there are no norms for the frequency of occurrence of actions, brow raising, which was lateralized right, is probably as common as brow lowering and smiling, which were lateralized left.

Sackeim and Gur (1983) suggested that a perceptual bias to favor one side of the face might influence our asymmetry scoring. Typically, such biases are small and are observed when stimulus presentation is restricted. Our scoring procedure emphasized repeated, intensive viewing of both sides of the face. If perceptual bias were a problem for our scoring, it would be difficult to explain why some actions showed left laterality, and others, right laterality. During training of coders, we used both normal and mirror-reversed video monitors without the scorer's knowledge. Comparisons of scores for normal and mirror-reversed faces did not reveal a perceptual bias effect.

Physical, structural characteristics that were not measured in this study might have affected asymmetry, but this possibility raises questions about the antecedents of lateralized structures. Little is known about the causes of asymmetry in structural tissues, but the action of nerves and muscles is an important factor influencing their size and strength and the growth and shape of bone. Hemispheric specialization might produce asymmetries in structural tissues. Peripheral asymmetries cannot entirely explain the results of this study because they are likely to affect all types of movement equally, but asymmetry of spontaneous actions was different from deliberate actions. These differences remained when intensity of contraction was controlled, one of Fridlund's (1984) "acceptance criteria."

Interpreting this study and others might be easier if we knew more about the neural pathways to facial muscles (see Rinn, 1984, for a review). Models relating hemispheric specialization to facial asymmetry often assume contralateral innervation, but the situation is more complicated for upper face muscles and, perhaps, for non-voluntary movements. How facial motor neurons are related to neural centers for activities that can co-occur with facial movements, such as speech, imagery, or body movements, is unknown; and the effects of alternative processes, such as inhibition, are unexplored. Likewise, the models of hemispheric specialization described here may be too crude to accurately predict facial asymmetry. Evidence for intra-hemispheric inhibition would add complexity to predicting facial asymmetry if, for example, motor centers are inhibited by specialized processes in other parts of the same hemisphere.

In summary, this study has shown that asymmetries of certain individual deliberate actions are lateralized, implying that the subjects have in common some functional asymmetry related to differential use of the hemispheres or some structural, anatomical asymmetry, or both asymmetries. The results, however, are inconsistent, at least in part, with all existing models that attempt to explain laterality in facial actions. Future research should explore the possibility that different methods measure different aspects of facial asymmetry, such as the more extreme excursion vs. the more electrically active. Second, the action of each muscle must be considered separately because muscles may typically serve different functions, such as talking vs. emotional expressions, or be controlled in different ways, such as inhibition vs. intensification, or have different neural innervations, such as the brow vs. the lower face. Finally, the type of facial movement, such as spontaneous emotional vs. deliberate non-emotional, needs to be carefully specified and matched to the neural processes hypothesized to underlie asymmetry. Eliciting conditions that produce ambiguous types of actions will produce inconclusive results. It may be that asymmetry is produced by a complex interaction of different processes and variables or by factors that await discovery.

Notes

1. Historically, deliberate movement has been associated with the pyramidal motor system, and emotional movement with the extrapyramidal system. Recent anatomical viewpoints no longer maintain this division of the motor system (e.g., Barr & Kiernan, 1983), but the distinction between two different neural pathways for deliberate and emotional movements is pronounced for the face and has an established clinical basis (Rinn, 1984).

2. There was no difference between the two startle simulations so their scores were averaged. As in the Ekman et al. study, the three noises were elicited under different conditions. In the first, the noise was unexpected, but in the other two, the subject knew exactly when the noise would occur. To one expected noise, the subject reacted naturally: to the other, the subject tried to act as though nothing happened. Asymmetry of actions in the startles did not differ so their scores were averaged for analysis.

3. Wilcoxon signed-ranks tests on the asymmetry scores for separate AUs showed no significant differences for any of the seven AUs.

References

Alford, R. (1983). Sex differences in lateral facial facility: The effects of habitual emotional concealment. *Neuropsychologia, 21,* 567–570.

Alford, R., & Alford, K. F. (1981). Sex differences in asymmetry in the expression of emotion. *Neuropsychologia, 19,* 605–608.

Bakan, F. (1969). Hypnotizability, laterality of eye movement and functional brain asymmetry. *Perceptual and Motor Skills, 28,* 927–932.

Barr, M. L. & Kiernan, J. A. (1983). *The human nervous system* (4th ed.). Hagerstown, MD: Harper & Row, Inc.

Benton, A. L. (1980). The neuropsychology of facial recognition. *American Psychologist, 35,* 176–186.

Borod, J. C., & Caron, H. S. (1980). Facedness and emotion related to lateral dominance, sex, and expression type. *Neuropsychologia, 18,* 237–241.

Campbell, R. (1978). Asymmetries in interpreting and expressing a posed facial expression. *Cortex, 14,* 327–342.

Chaurasia, B. D., & Goswami, H. K. (1975). Functional asymmetry in the face. *Acta Anatomica, 91,* 154–160.

Davidson, R. J., & Fox, N. A. (1982). Asymmetrical brain activity discriminates between positive and negative stimuli in human infants. *Science, 218,* 1235–1237.

Ehrlichman, H., & Weinberger, A. (1978). Lateral eye movements and hemispheric asymmetry: A critical review. *Psychological Bulletin, 85,* 1080–1101.

Ekman, P. (1980). Asymmetry in facial expression. *Science, 209,* 833–834.

Ekman, P. (1982). Methods for measuring facial action. In K. Scherer & P. Ekman (Eds.), *Handbook of methods in nonverbal behavior research* (pp. 45–90). New York: Cambridge University Press.

Ekman, P., & Friesen, W. V. (1975). *Unmasking the face.* Englewood Cliffs, NJ: Prentice-Hall.

Ekman, P., & Friesen, W. V. (1976). Measuring facial movement. *Environmental Psychology and Nonverbal Behavior, 1,* 56–75.

Ekman, P., & Friesen, W. V. (1978). *The facial action coding system.* Palo Alto, CA: Consulting Psychologists Press.

Ekman, P., & Friesen, W. V. (1982). *The Requested Facial Action Test.* Unpublished material. University of California, Human Interaction Laboratory, San Francisco.

Ekman, P., Friesen, W. V., & Simons, R. C. (1985). Is the startle reaction an emotion? *Journal of Personality and Social Psychology, 49,*1416–1426.

Ekman, P., Hager, J. C., & Friesen, W. V. (1981). Symmetry and the nature of facial action. *Psychophysiology, 18,* 101–106.

Ekman, P., Levenson, R. W., & Friesen, W. V. (1983). Autonomic nervous system activity distinguishes among emotions. *Science, 221,* 1208–1210.

Ekman, P., Roper, G., & Hager, J. C. (1980). Deliberate facial movement. *Child Development, 31,* 267–271.

Fridlund, A. J. (1984). *Facial EMG "lateralization for emotion": Motor-control confounds, acceptance criteria, and implications for lateralization of facial displays.* Manuscript in preparation.

Geschwind, N. (1965). Disconnexion syndromes in animals and man. *Brain, 88,* 585–644.

Geschwind, N. (1975). The apraxias: Neural mechanisms of disorders of learned movement. *American Scientist, 63,* 188–195.

Graves, R., Goodglass, H., & Landis, T. (1982). Mouth asymmetry during spontaneous speech. *Neuropsychologia, 20,* 371–381.

Hager, J. C. (1982). Asymmetries in facial expression. In P. Ekman (Ed.), *Emotion in the human face* (2nd ed., pp. 318–352). Cambridge: Cambridge University Press.

Hager, J. C., & van Gelder, R. S. (in press). Asymmetry of speech actions. *Neuropsychologia.*

Heller, W., & Levy, J. (1981). Perception and expression of emotion in right-handers and left-handers. *Neuropsychologia, 19,* 263–272.

Hoffman, H. S., & Ison, J. R. (1980). Reflex modification in the domain of startle: I. Some empirical findings and their implications for how the nervous system processes sensory input. *Psychological Review, 87,* 175–189.

Johnstone, J., Galin, D., & Herron, J. (1979). Choice of handedness measures in studies of hemispheric specialization. *International Journal of Neuroscience, 9,* 71–80.

Kimura, D. (1973). Manual activity during speaking—I. Right-handers. *Neuropsychologia, 11,* 45–50.

Kinsbourne, M. (1972). Eye and head turning indicates cerebral lateralization. *Science, 176,* 539–541.

Kohara, Y. (1975). *Racial difference of facial expression—unilateral movement.* Unpublished manuscript. Shinshu University, Department of Anatomy, Matsumoto, Japan.

Landis, C., & Hunt, W. A. (1939). *The startle pattern.* New York: Farrar.

Ley, R. G., & Bryden, M. F. (1981). Consciousness, emotion, and the right hemisphere. In R. Stevens & G. Underwood (Eds.), *Aspects of consciousness: Structural issues* (pp. 215–240). New York: Academic Press.

Moscovitch, M., & Olds, J. (1982). Asymmetries in spontaneous facial expressions and their possible relation to hemispheric specialization. *Neuropsychologia, 20,* 71–81.

Reuter-Lorenz, P., & Davidson, R. J. (1981). Differential contributions of the two cerebral hemispheres to the perception of happy and sad faces. *Neuropsychologia, 19,* 609–613.

Rinn, W. E. (1984). The neuropsychology of facial expression: A review of the neurological and psychological mechanisms for producing facial expressions. *Psychological Bulletin, 95,* 52–77.

Sackeim, H. A., & Gur, R. C. (1978). Lateral asymmetry in intensity of emotional expression. *Neuropsychologia, 16,* 473–481.

Sackeim, H. A., & Gur, R. C. (1983). Facial asymmetry and the communication of emotion. In J. T. Cacioppo & R. E. Petty (Eds.), *Social psychophysiology: A sourcebook* (pp. 307–352). New York: Guilford.

Sackeim, H. A., Gur, R. C., & Saucy, M. C. (1978). Emotions are expressed more intensely on the left side of the face. *Science, 202,* 434–436.

Schwartz, G. E., Ahern, G. L., & Brown, S. (1979). Lateralized facial muscle response to positive and negative emotional stimuli. *Psychophysiology, 16,* 561–571.

Sirota, A., & Schwartz, G. E. (1982). Facial muscle patterning and lateralization during elation and depression imagery. *Journal of Abnormal Psychology, 91,* 25–34.

Tomkins, S. S. (1962). *Affect imagery consciousness: Vol. 1. The positive affects.* New York: Springer.

Tschiassny, K. (1953). Eight syndromes of facial paralysis and their significance in locating the lesion. *Annuls of Otology, Rhinology, and Laryngology, 62,* 677–691.

Winer, B. J. (1971). *Statistical principles in experimental design* (2nd ed.). New York: McGraw-Hill.

Asymmetry in Facial Muscular Actions

JOSEPH C. HAGER

The background for the preceding study was the conviction that the phenomenon of asymmetry in facial muscular actions might reflect important aspects of neural action or other factors. The main point of the paper was that no extant theory of a single process involving hemispheric specialization could explain the pattern of results in our study. In the subsequent decade, little occurred to change this conclusion. It will take much more data, as well as more theoretical elaboration, before observed asymmetries of facial actions can be attributed with confidence to specific proposed mechanisms. In this effort, the elimination of known methodological errors would seem essential, and innovations, advisable.

Methodological Issues

Judgments of naive observers about asymmetry are too imprecise for the work remaining in this area. Naive judges cannot specify what it is about the face or facial action that affects their decisions. They are probably not capable of making the fine quantitative distinctions that are necessary to resolve issues in this field, nor of separating the possibly different asymmetries of specific actions that might be found in a combination of actions. Instead, skilled facial scorers who are extensively trained to estimate the symmetry of individual actions, or electromyography, or new machines and methods are required to make the necessary measurements. The finding in our study that symmetry varied across muscular actions underlines the inadequacy of untrained judges making global judgments about whole face expressions.

The use of chimeric faces in judgment studies is an inappropriate technique for measuring asymmetry in facial actions, and those stimuli cannot compensate for the above shortcomings of naive judges. Chimeric faces are formed by splitting normal and mirror images of the face down the midline and recombining the halves to form images that show only the right or only the left side of the face. The main weakness of this technique (Hager, 1982) is that it confounds the signs arising from muscular actions with the signs of static and slow sign vehicles of the face (Ekman, 1978). These static and slow sign vehicles are asymmetrical, e.g., the width of the face from the midline to the left has often been found narrower than from the midline to the right, which makes left chimeric faces generally thinner than right chimerics (Koff, Borod, & Strauss, 1985; Nelson & Horowitz's comments in Ekman, Nelson, Horowitz, & Spinrad, 1980). Conclusions about the symmetry of muscular action drawn from the judgments of chimeric faces simply have no compelling force and should be ignored. Even though some researchers have discounted such asymmetries as confounds (Borod & Koff, 1990; Sackeim, Weiman, & Forman, 1984), it is not possible to disentangle the interactions of the sign vehicles in chimeric faces using post hoc statistical adjustments. For researchers who persists in using chimeric faces, the very least that should be done is to correct their known deficiencies before showing them to judges—for example, by using image-processing techniques to equalize the widths of right and left chimeric faces.

A goal in studies of facial action asymmetry should be to eliminate the oxymoron "posed emotion expressions." If an expression is posed deliberately, it is probably not an emotion expression (although there might be some emotion involved). The increasing number of people studying the face and facial expression who are not aware of this convention have found the terminology very confusing, and it is incumbent on facial expression professionals to be more careful. Our study showed the importance of making fine distinctions about how the actions in the study were obtained. We used the term "actions in emotion simulations" to describe such expressions, but phrases such as "posed expressions depicting emotion" would be acceptable alternatives. The greatest methodological mistake is, of course, to be careless about the nature of the expressions one studies (with consequences described by Ekman in Ekman et al., 1980).

Theoretical Issues

The theoretical explanations of facial asymmetry summarized in our article appear little changed today (see Fridlund, 1988, for another view of these theories). One explanation that should be added to table 2.1 is that left hemispheric control of speech actions, or differential activation during speech, yields greater mouth opening on the right. While there is substantial evidence of greater right mouth opening during speech (Graves, Landis, & Simpson, 1985), Hager and van Gelder (1985) questioned whether evidence on degree of mouth opening alone was sufficient to show greater muscular action on the more open side because it might be that greater action on the left side keeps the lips relatively more closed. Subsequent evidence (Graves & Landis, 1990) including changes in symmetry of mouth opening during singing (Graves & Landis, 1985) and better articulatory movements on the right (Cadalbert, Landis, Regard, & Graves, 1994) advance the interpretation that the right side of the mouth is more involved in making speech movements. Informal observation by this author suggests that tension in muscles such as levator labii superioris and depressor labii may hold the lips more apart on one side, forming a better orifice for the articulatory movements of the lips by individual fibers of orbicularis oris, but such speculation awaits confirming evidence. Evidence on whether other actions beyond the lip area change their symmetry during speech is not available. Nor is there evidence on whether the effect of speech on the symmetry of actions might carry over to other nonspeech tasks such as deliberate requests to raise or lower the lips.

A serious issue for theories that attribute asymmetry in facial action to lateralized emotional processes is that the upper motor neuron pathways for emotion-based facial actions are largely unknown, but are independent of the corticobulbar system mediating deliberate actions (see Rinn, 1984, for a review). Even if facial actions during emotions were highly lateralized—for example, with actions stronger on the left—how could this evidence support right hemispheric specialization for emotion—for example, if one is not certain whether the innervations for emotional actions are crossed, uncrossed, or bilateral? Thompson (1985) in a similar vein questioned whether findings about asymmetry of voluntary upper face actions can clearly reflect which cerebral hemisphere is dominant in this task. In general, lower motor neurons for muscles of the lower face are innervated by the contralateral facial area of the precentral motor cortex, but neurons ending on the upper facial muscles have bilateral connections to motor cortex neurons. Thus, there is no reason to assume that the asymmetry of deliberate actions has any relevance for theories of hemispheric specialization for emotion or emotion expression, nor should one assume that nonpyramidal upper motor neurons in emotion systems have the same contralateral pattern of innervation (or bilateral in the case of the upper face) as the corticobulbar tracts. Theories about right hemispheric specialization for facial expression (e.g., Borod & Koff, 1990) have to be reconciled with evidence that the left hemisphere is more involved in the voluntary production of facial muscular actions (e.g., Dawson, Warrenburg, & Fuller, 1985; Gazzaniga & Smylie, 1990).

In order to clarify the variety of explanations for asymmetry researchers need to be specific about the muscle measured, the condition under which actions are obtained, and the specific neural processes that might affect the symmetry of the muscles studied.

Innovations in Research

Most studies have attempted to observe claimed effects of hemispheric specialization for a single process in the hypothesized asymmetry of facial expression. An alternative is to study multiple processes claimed to affect facial asymmetry in different ways, experimentally accentuating each process in relation to the others, in turn, and observing corresponding shifts in expressive asymmetry. The advantage of this approach is that measuring shifts in asymmetry as predicted reduces the possibility of confounding variables, such as muscle size or facial structures, as explanations because their effect would be constant. The studies of shifts in mouth opening reviewed above and studies of positive versus negative emotion (Brockmeier & Ulrich, 1993) provide examples of this strategy. Several alternative explanations for asymmetry mentioned in our article and by Rinn (1984) could be explored in this fashion, particularly inhibition of emotion and suppression of expression.

Virtually all studies have used facial expression as a dependent variable, randomly assigning subjects, administering a treatment, and measuring asymmetry of expressions. An alternative approach is to select subjects based on their facial expression, then study the variables of interest. For example, if the greater right opening of the mouth during speech is a result of hemispheric activity, then subjects who have greater left opening should have a correspondingly different hemispheric lateralization, with differences possibly measurable by electroencephalogram or a measure of metabolic activity. One advantage of this approach is that reliance on precise facial measurement of subtle differences is reduced because one can select subjects with obvious, extreme differences in asymmetry.

More sensitive and reliable ways to measure the asymmetry of particular actions are very desirable for new research to resolve open issues, especially if they are less expensive. One promising area that may yield such advances is digital image processing, recognition, and measurement by computer (Hager & Ekman, 1995). Optical computation is another potential, though more distant, solution (Halvorson et al., 1994).

Attempts to associate facial asymmetries with other variables besides hemispheric specialization could broaden the relevance of facial asymmetry. For example, expressive asymmetries might be related to asymmetries in posture, such as scoliosis, arm or leg folding preferences, and asymmetries in head pose. Older adults often have marked asymmetries in facial wrinkle patterns, suggesting that asymmetrical patterns of muscular use may increase during aging and may leave permanent traces. Some studies suggest that the very young have different patterns of asymmetry (e.g., Rothbart, Taylor, & Tucker, 1989). Early studies on facial expression asymmetry addressed its relation to personality variables (see Hager, 1982, for a review), but little has been done in follow up (but see Sackheim et al., 1984).

State of the Evidence

Fridlund's (1988) appraisal of the evidence indicated that (1) no one theoretical model fits all the data; (2) asymmetry is more likely in requested, specific facial actions or conversation than in actions responding to jokes or startle; (3) there is a weak tendency for more intense action on the left; and (4) asymmetry depends on the muscle, without consistency within individuals. Skinner and Mullin (1991) conducted a meta-analysis of 14 studies of facial expression asymmetry that used naive judges. They concluded that their "analysis reveals a highly significant but small effect for the left side of the face to be judged more expressive than the right. Additionally it reveals that asymmetry is (a) stronger for emotional than neutral expressions, (b) stronger for posed emotional expressions compared with spontaneous emotional expressions and (c) predicted by some dimensions of emotional experience, notably pleasantness" (p. 113). These conclusions are not inconsistent with our study, and indicate by omission the many issues on which there is no consensus. The study of asymmetry in facial expressions continues to hold the promise of providing insights into neural processes such as hemispheric specialization.

References

Borod, J. C., & Koff, E. (1990). Lateralization for facial emotional behavior: A methodological perspective. Special Issue: Facial asymmetry: Expression and paralysis. *International Journal of Psychology, 25*(2), 157–177.

Brockmeier, B., & Ulrich, G. (1993). Asymmetries of expressive facial movements during experimentally induced positive vs. negative mood states: A video-analytic study. *Cognition & Emotion, 7*(5), 393–405.

Ekman, P. (1978). Facial signs: Facts, Fantasies, and Possibilities. In T. Sebeok (Ed.), *Sight, sound and sense* (pp. 124–156). Bloomington, IN: Indiana University Press.

Ekman, P., Nelson, C. A., Horowitz, F. D., & Spinrad, S. I. (1980). Asymmetry in facial expression. *Science, 209*(4458), 833–836.

Cadalbert, A., Landis, T., Regard, M., & Graves, R. E. (1994). Singing with and without words: Hemispheric asymmetries in motor control. *Journal of Clinical & Experimental Neuropsychology, 16*(5), 664–670.

Dawson, G., Warrenburg, S., & Fuller, P. (1985). Left hemisphere specialization for facial and manual imitation. *Psychophysiology, 22*(2), 237–243.

Fridlund, A. J. (1988). What can asymmetry and laterality in EMG tell us about the face and brain? *International Journal of Neuroscience, 39,* 53–69.

Gazzaniga, M. S., & Smylie, C. S. (1990). Hemispheric mechanisms controlling voluntary and spontaneous facial expressions. *Journal of Cognitive Neuroscience, 2*(3), 239–245.

Graves, R., & Landis, T. (1985). Hemispheric control of speech expression in aphasia: A mouth asymmetry study. *Archives of Neurology, 42*(3), 249–251.

Graves, R., & Landis, T. (1990). Asymmetry in mouth opening during different speech tasks. Special Issue: Facial asymmetry: Expression and paralysis. *International Journal of Psychology, 25*(2), 179–189.

Graves, R., Landis, T., & Simpson, C. (1985). On the interpretation of mouth asymmetry. *Neuropsychologia, 23*(1), 121–122.

Hager, J. C. (1982). Asymmetries in facial expression. In P. Ekman (Ed.), *Emotion in the human face* (2nd ed., pp. 318–352). Cambridge, Eng.: Cambridge University Press.

Hager, J. C., & Ekman, P. (1995). The essential behavioral science of the face and gesture that computer scientists need to know. In M. Bichsel (Ed.), *Preceedings—International Workshop on Automatic Face- and Gesture-Recognition,* June 26–28, 1995, Zurich (pp. 7–11). Multimedia Laboratory, University of Zurich, Winterthurerstrasse 190, CH-8057 Zurich.

Hager, J. C., & van Gelder, R. S. (1985). Asymmetry of speech actions. *Neuropsychologia, 23*(1), 119–120.

Halvorson, C., Hays, A., Kraabel, B., Wu, R., Wudl, F., & Heeger, A. J. (1994). A 160-femtosecond optical image processor based on a conjugated polymer. *Science, 265*(5176), 1215–1216.

Koff, E., Borod, J. C. & Strauss, E. H. (1985). Development of hemiface size asymmetry. *Cortex, 21*(1), 153–156.

Rinn, W. E. (1984). The neuropsychology of facial expression: A review of the neurological and psychological mechanisms for producing facial expressions. *Psychological Bulletin, 95,* 52–77.

Rothbart, M. K., Taylor, S. B., & Tucker, D. M. (1989). Right-sided facial asymmetry in infant emotional expression. *Neuropsychologia, 27*(5), 675–687.

Sackeim, H. A., Weiman, A. L., & Forman, B. D. (1984). Asymmetry of the face at rest: Size, area and emotional expression. *Cortex, 20*(2), 165–178.

Skinner, M., & Mullen, B. (1991). Facial asymmetry in emotional expression: A meta-analysis of research. *British Journal of Social Psychology, 30*(2), 113–124.

Thompson, J. K. (1985). Right brain, left brain; left face, right face: Hemisphericity and the expression of facial emotion. *Cortex, 21*(2), 281–299.

3

Coherence Between Expressive and Experiential Systems in Emotion

ERIKA L. ROSENBERG & PAUL EKMAN

We endorse the view that emotions involve *patterns of responses* that have evolved for their ability to organise disparate bodily systems to respond efficiently to critical environmental events. This position—one version of evolutionary emotion theory—postulates different patterns of responses for each emotion, and implies a coherence among behavioural, physiological, and subjective systems (Darwin, 1872/1965; Ekman, 1977, 1992; Levenson, 1988; Plutchik, 1962; Tomkins, 1962).

Tomkins (1962, pp. 243–244) wrote that affects are sets of organised responses that "are capable when activated of simultaneously capturing such widely distributed organs as the face, the heart, and the endocrines and imposing on them a specific pattern of correlated responses". In the empirical literature on emotion, evidence is just beginning to appear that there is cohesion among different emotion response domains. There has been some evidence of coherence between facial expression and self-report of emotion (Ekman, Friesen, & Ancoli, 1980) and for coherence between expression and physiology (Davidson, Ekman, Saron, Senulis, & Friesen, 1990; Ekman, Davidson, & Friesen, 1990; Levenson, Ekman, & Friesen, 1990). Such research, however, has not looked at correspondences among emotional response systems at specific points in time, but rather has evaluated correspondences among response measures from aggregated occurrences of particular emotions across blocks of time. If Tomkins was right, congruence between systems should be evident also on a more momentary basis. During an emotion, changes in expression, physiology, and experience should correspond temporally and categorically. Facial signs of anger should occur with the subjective experience of anger and anger-specific physiological patterns.

In contrast to previous research that has looked at overall correspondences in emotional response systems, we sought to determine whether facial expression and subjective measures of emotion occur together on a momentary basis during specific emotional episodes. Such congruence between measures is a minimum requirement for the type of coherence presupposed by our view of emotion. By *coherence* we mean integrated, concurrent, emotion-specific changes in different emotion response domains.

Sources of Coherence

Our aim was not to demonstrate *why* coherence should occur between facial and subjective response systems but rather to determine the extent to which coherence does occur. It is important to note, however, that the mechanisms that are potentially responsible for congruence in emotional response systems are a matter of debate. Our view is that coherence is due to the central organisation of emotion in the brain (after Darwin, 1872/1965; Tomkins, 1962). This might be called *internally driven* coherence. Alternatively, observable coherence in emotional responding is consistent with facial-feedback theory (e.g., Laird, 1974). If peripheral stimulation can instantaneously feedback to the brain to cause emotional experience, then facial expression and reports of experience would appear to be congruent. This type of coherence might be called *externally driven*. There is research to partially support both views, but none to distinguish among various explanations for coherence between expression and self-report (cf. Ekman et al., 1990; Davidson et al., 1990, for evidence of internally driven coherence, and Kleck et al., 1976; Lanzetta, Cartwright-Smith, & Kleck, 1976, for evidence for facial-feedback theory).

Another view is that there are inverse relationships among response systems in emotion. Jones's (1950) internalisation-externalisation hypothesis, which posits that affect inhibited overtly will be manifested physiologically and vice versa, is a well-known example of such a perspective. Such negative correspondences have been observed in normal human adults (e.g., Lanzetta & Kleck, 1970). Buck (1980) demonstrated, however, that the observed direction of the relationship between facial and physiological response measures of emotion may depend on analytical approach. Between-subjects analyses tend to reveal negative correlations between behaviour and physiology, whereas within-subjects correlations tend to be positive (although low to moderate in strength). This distinction has recently been further substantiated and developed (Cacioppo et al., 1992). Negative correspondences have *not* been demonstrated at the level of the individual in normal subjects, however.

The debate over the sources or extent of emotional response coherence has not been resolved by studies of the phenomenon, largely because the issue has not been addressed with sufficient methodological rigour. In the next few pages, we outline the major methodological issues that complicate the study of coherence and offer a new technique that addresses some of these problems.

Methodological Problems in the Study of Coherence

Evaluating Coherence at Multiple Points in Time

Although facial behaviour or facial muscle activity has been obtained continuously in previous studies, researchers have summarised or aggregated facial behaviour— whether measured in terms of observable expressions or EMG-recorded muscular activity—over the time period of each emotion episode in order to render it statistically comparable to single, retrospective emotion reports (Brown & Schwartz, 1980; Ekman et al., 1980; 1990). The correlations between summarised facial expression and single self-reports of emotion have ranged from 0.35 to 0.55, indicating congruence between these systems (Ekman et al., 1980). Correspondence between aggregate measures of expression and report does not tell us whether the two response systems cohere at specific points in time, however.

According to Levenson (1988), aggregation across long periods of time may compromise dynamic information about the emotion response. Averaging across a period that may contain "a number of different emotions, as well as periods of no emotion" can obscure "patterning associated with a single emotion" (p. 30). On the other hand, some might argue that the relationship between affective facial behaviour and subjective experience would disappear at the momentary level, if congruence is an emergent property of aggregated episodes. It may be that for any given emotion there is no correspondence between facial and subjective responses, but rather after several distinct emotional events a pattern of congruence appears. Personality research on the stability of behaviour (Epstein, 1980) certainly indicates that intra-individual consistencies between behaviours can best be appreciated on a cumulative basis.

Special Problems of Measuring Subjective Experience

Measures of emotional experience have to be *elicited,* whereas measures of facial behaviour and physiology are *emitted* either continuously or sporadically throughout an emotional episode. This fundamental difference in the experimenter's access to the various emotional response systems entails two potential problems in the measurement of emotional experience: the problem of symbolic representation and the problem of continuity.

1. The Problem of Symbolic Representation. Measures of the subjective experience of emotion are fundamentally different from behavioural and physiological measures, in that they must be filtered through consciousness. Some processes may be truly inaccessible to conscious report, however (Nisbett & Wilson, 1977). Although signs of emotion may be manifest behaviourally or physiologically, people may not always be aware that they are undergoing emotion, or they might be aware of feeling an emotion but not be certain of which emotion it is. Even if people are clearly aware of the emotions they are feeling, they may choose to censor them (cf. Ekman, 1985).

Once people know they are feeling an emotion and choose to reveal their experience, that experience must be symbolically represented. This further reduces the comparability among response systems. Self-ratings of emotional experience may carry with them the baggage of error variance related to self-reports in general, such as acquiescence (Campbell, Siegman, & Rees, 1967), social desirability (Crowne & Marlowe, 1964), and demand characteristics (Orne, 1962).

There are a number of ways to have people symbolically represent their subjective experiences of emotion. Subjects could be asked to choose colours or textures that best represent their emotions (Block, 1957) or to use rating dials or joysticks to quantitatively rate the degree of their positive and negative feelings (Levenson & Gottman, 1983, 1985). Most often, however, experimenters request a verbal report. Although offering more precision, this method imposes language on an experience that may not occur in verbal form. This problem is further complicated by the fact that most researchers do not allow subjects to use words of their own choice; instead they prescribe a specific set of words and/or a set of numbers that subjects must use to describe their emotional experiences (e.g., Ekman et al., 1980, 1990).

Another potential problem in the measurement of emotional experience is memory reconstruction. Usually, in studies of the relationship between facial expressions and/or physiological measures with subjective measures of emotion, single self-reports have been obtained after an emotional episode (Brown & Schwartz, 1980; Ekman et al., 1980, 1990). Several distinct emotions can occur even during a brief stimulus period, but we do not know which aspects of these emotional experiences are captured in single, retrospective reports. They may overemphasise the most recent or the most intense elements in the experience, or they may result from an averaging across the varied experience within a period. Retrospective emotion reports may involve the formation of "global impressions", which are vulnerable to potential influences of selection, recollection, and aggregation (cf. Reis & Wheeler, 1991). Studies of daily emotional experience suggest that relative to momentary reports, retrospective accounts of daily emotion overemphasise the intensities of emotions and show preference for negative over positive emotions (Thomas & Diener, 1990). Similar biases have been observed in research in mood and menstrual symptom reporting (Englander-Golden, Chang, Whitmore, & Dientsbier, 1980). Thus, comparisons of single reports of reconstructed experience with behaviour and/or physiology obtained during a spontaneous experience may yield less than perfect correspondences.

   2. *The Problem of Continuity.* It is rare that a stimulus event calls forth one emotion. More commonly, multiple, brief emotions unfold over time, even over periods lasting for only a minute or two (Ekman, 1984). Therefore, to establish evidence for coherence between emotional response systems, one must examine congruence among measures of specific emotional events at particular points in time. Facial expression and physiological changes can be monitored continuously during an emotional episode. Concealed cameras can be used to videotape spontaneous facial expression of emotion, which can then be systematically scored (using a coding scheme such as the Facial Action Coding System; Ekman & Friesen, 1978) or facial muscle activity can be continuously monitored using electromyography (EMG). Changes in several types of autonomic or central nervous system activity can be recorded online, throughout an emotional episode. There is no way to constantly monitor subjective experience of emotion that is analogous to the methods available for these other response systems.

   The methods that do exist for measuring subjective experience on a relatively continuous basis may introduce artefacts. Thought sampling, wherein subjects report on their experiences while they are undergoing an emotional event, is one option. The spontaneous, online nature of this procedure is advantageous, but the constant demand to report on experience may to an unknown extent interfere with the degree to which the subject becomes emotionally responsive to the stimulus. Additionally, speaking aloud one's feelings may increase self-consciousness and the sense of being observed, which may alter affect as well as expressivity (cf. Kleck et al., 1976).

   Some investigators have had subjects provide continuous ratings of their affect during a video replay of their emotional interactions (Kagan, Krathwohl, & Farquhar, 1965; Levenson and Gottman, 1983, 1985). In Levenson and Gottman's (1983, 1985) video-recall technique, subjects use a dial to rate continuously their recalled affect. Turns in one direction convey the degree to which the interaction evoked positive emotion; turns in the other direction reflect negative emotion. Subjects make these ratings after the emotional event while watching a video of their emotional interaction, although recently investigators have had some success obtaining positive and negative emotion ratings during an affective situation (Fredrickson & Levenson, in press). Dial rating during an interaction, however, may create a demand on subjects to monitor their affect that is disruptive to emotional experience. Also, this procedure cannot be used to obtain information about the possible occurrence of each of a number of specific emotions.

To the best of our knowledge, no research has examined whether coherence between facial expression and self-report is discernible on a moment-by-moment basis. In the present research, we chose to deal with the temporal and memory limitations of self-report of emotion described above by having subjects rate their emotions on a momentary basis and by providing them with a cue to aid them in remembering which emotions they had felt. Additionally, we examined momentary changes in facial expressions of emotion rather than aggregated facial measures, and then looked at the extent to which specific expressions and reports varied together.

Overview of Empirical Strategy

We showed subjects brief, emotionally evocative films, and asked them to report on their emotions using a new, moment-by-moment reporting procedure. This new procedure allows subjects to rate the extent to which they experienced each of several categories of emotion for many locations over a time interval during which a number of emotions may occur, without interrupting the flow of emotional experience. In this method, called *cued-review,* subjects see a replay of the stimulus film and provide emotion reports at points when they remember having felt an emotion during their initial viewing. The cued-review technique provides reports of momentary changes in the subjective experience of emotion for a time period during which more than one emotion may have occurred. Thus, although cued-review is not a continuous measure of subjective experience, it may allow us to study coherence between facial expressions and self-reports of emotions that occur at specific moments during a stimulus period.

We expect that reports of emotion at specific moments should be sensitive to the ebb and flow of subjective experience—variations that may correspond to fluctuations in spontaneous facial expression of emotion. With cued-review we can determine whether there is congruence between reports of experience and facial expressions of emotion at specific points in a time.

Our first set of hypotheses postulate co-occurrence at specific points in time between facial expression and self-report of emotions. First, we will examine co-occurrence at specific moments on a between-subjects basis:

HYPOTHESIS 1A. For film locations where there is a high frequency of facial expression of emotion across subjects, there should also be a high frequency of self-report of emotion.

Our next hypothesis posits that correspondences that appear on a between-subjects basis also occur within-subjects:

HYPOTHESIS 1B. Within-subjects, self-reports of emotion and facial expression of emotion should occur at the same locations during a stimulus period.

It is also possible that the extent to which we observe coherence may depend on the intensity of the event. There are two possible explanations for intensity-dependent coherence in our study: as self-reports of momentary occurrences of emotion are obtained after the initial stimulus period, subjects may remember only their more intense experiences even with the aid of a visual cue; or it could be that before response systems will act in unison, emotional events may have to reach a minimum intensity level, as has been suggested recently by other emotion researchers (Davidson, 1992; Tassinary & Cacioppo, 1992). Co-occurrence between expression and report was examined for each subject's most intense versus least intense facial expression and again for each subject's most intense versus least intense self-report locations:

HYPOTHESIS 1C. People should be more likely to give self-reports of emotions during their most intense facial expressions of emotion than during their least intense facial expressions;

HYPOTHESIS 1D. People should be more likely to show facial expressions of emotions during their most intense self-reports of emotion than during their least intense self-reports of emotion.

The most specific level at which to evaluate coherence is that of categorical agreement—the extent to which co-occurring facial expression and self-report agree as to the type of emotional response. The second set of hypotheses examines coherence at the level of categorical agreement, in order to answer questions such as this one: If a person shows a facial expression of fear did he or she also remember experiencing fear? We expect that this should be true generally, i.e. for all emotional expressions and reports (hypothesis 2a), and more specifically for more intense emotional events. Hypothesis 2b defines intensity on a between-subjects basis (in terms of more emotionally salient portions of the film), whereas 2c and 2d define intensity on a within-subjects basis (in terms of individuals' most intense facial expressions and self-reports, respectively).

HYPOTHESIS 2A. When facial expressions of emotion and self-reports of emotion co-occur in time for any given subject, they should agree as to the type of emotion that occurred;

HYPOTHESIS 2B. For film locations where there is a high incidence of facial expression and self-report of emotion across subjects, those subjects who have facial expressions and self-reports of emotion at these locations will demonstrate categorical agreement between these two measures;

HYPOTHESIS 2C. Where people show their most intense facial expressions of emotion, they should also report having experienced the same type of emotion;

HYPOTHESIS 2D. Where people provide their most intense reports of emotional experience, they should also show facial expressions of the same type of emotion.

Method

Subjects

Twenty female students were recruited from universities in the San Francisco area (Age, $M = 22.6$ years, SD = 4.37). They were paid $10 for the one hour of experimental time.

Design

All conditions were run on a within-subject basis. Each subject viewed several film segments and rated her emotions immediately following each film using two methods: cued-review (CUE) and retrospective report (RETRO).[1] To control for order effects, the presentation sequence of the experimental films was varied between-subjects by a method of incomplete counterbalancing in which each film appeared once in each possible ordinal position. Whether RETRO or CUE ratings were obtained first for each of the experimental films varied by a method of incomplete counterbalancing. There were four possible orders for whether RETRO or CUE came first, five subjects were assigned randomly to each of these orders.

Procedure

Subjects sat at a table facing a 19 inch, colour CRT monitor. On another cart to the right of the large monitor, was a 5 inch, black and white television positioned above a VCR. The lens of the video camera (which was mounted in the adjacent room) was hidden in the glass cabinets behind the monitor. The experimenter sat in another room for the entire experiment following the initial instruction and practice periods, and was able to see the subject's face on a video monitor. The experimenter controlled the playing of the stimulus tapes during the initial viewing (emotion-induction). The tapes used for playback during cued-review were controlled by the subject and played on the VCR in the experimental room.

Emotion Induction Films

Subjects viewed six film segments, four of which had been edited to a length of 1:14–1:18 minutes. These four film clips, which were the experimental induction films, had been selected for their ability to elicit primarily disgust and secondarily fear and other negative emotions, in previous research.[2] Disgust was chosen for the primary emotion, because it has distinct facial expressions that can be reliably elicited in laboratory exposure to films (Ekman et al., 1980). We included only two of the four films for analysis: (RAT), which depicted a scene where a rat approaches a sleeping man, and eventually enters his mouth;[3] and (AMP), which contained scenes of burn patients and an amputation procedure from a medical training film (similar versions of AMP were originally used for emotion induction by Ekman & Friesen, 1974). The other two film segments were omitted from analysis, because they were both scenes from popular horror or science fiction movies that many of the subjects reported having seen already. We were concerned that remembered affect from previous viewings of these films or knowledge of socially consensual reactions to these films could influence affect ratings and reactions in the laboratory.

A fifth and sixth film segment, both of which were 1 to 2 minutes in length and which elicit primarily happiness (a fairy tale ending to a romantic film and a scene of a puppy playing with a flower) were not part of the experimental manipulation, but always appeared as the last segments for each subject to alleviate any unpleasant effects of the first four films (subjects gave ratings for both of these segments as well).

All subjects were tested individually. The experimenter told the subject that she would be seeing a series of short film clips, some of which would be unpleasant, and that we were interested in her emotional reactions to them. The subject then had a practice trial in which she received instructions for and practised each rating technique. The experimenter was in a separate room during the practice trial. The film stimulus used for the practice trial was selected for its ability to elicit mild enjoyment (scenes of monkeys and gorillas playing in a zoo, from Ekman & Friesen, 1974). The order in which each subject performed the rating procedures in the practice trial was counterbalanced across subjects.

Rating Techniques

We derived the cued-review procedure from Kagan et al.'s (1965) interpersonal process recall technique and Levenson and Gottman's (1983, 1985) video-recall technique, but it differs from these methods in that the replayed videotape is not a recording of the subject interacting with a partner. Instead, it is the film that was used for emotion induction. In cued-review, subjects are instructed to stop the video replay at the points where they remember having felt an emotion during their first viewing of the stimulus film. They then use an emotion report form to rate what they remember feeling at that precise location in the film. After completing a given rating, subjects then start the video again and stop the playback whenever they remember having felt a *change in emotion* (in either degree or type) during the first viewing. Subjects then complete another form for that location. Thus, subjects go back through the entire stimulus segment and provide a series of emotion reports about what they remember feeling during the initial viewing period. We call this technique cued-review, because it was designed so that subjects could use the visual cue of the stimulus film to help them remember what they felt the first time they saw the segment. In this study, the experimenter independently recorded the locations of each subject's stopping points from the adjacent room.

For both the CUE and RETRO ratings, each rating form contained eight emotion terms: anger, contempt, disgust, embarrassment, fear, happiness, sadness, and surprise, each of which was rated on a scale from 0 to 8, where "0" represented "not the slightest bit" of the emotion and "8" represented "the most I have ever felt in my life". This method for anchoring the scale in terms of life experience was developed by Ekman and first reported in Levenson et al. (1990).

In the RETRO condition, subjects were told to report what they remembered feeling when they viewed the film on one form, called the "post-film emotion form". Subjects were asked to rate the extent to which they felt each of the eight emotion terms over the entire firm period using the 0 to 8 scale. At each stopping point in the CUE procedure, the subjects completed emotion forms called "review-film emotion forms". The review-film emotion forms included the same terms and scales as those in the RETRO condition. The only difference was that subjects rated what they remembered feeling in the film during the initial viewing *at the point in the film where they had stopped the tape* during the CUE procedure.

In the CUE condition, the video was played back on a small, black and white monitor and with no sound. This was done to reduce the emotion eliciting properties of the stimulus film on re-viewing, because we wanted to minimise the chances of subjects reporting on re-experienced rather than remembered affect in the CUE condition. On debriefing, no subject reported re-experiencing affect during cued-review.

In the practice period, each subject received instructions for the rating techniques. Then they had two practice trials, as described above. Once the subject and experimenter were satisfied that the subject understood the procedures, the experimenter left the room and did not communicate with the subject until all films had been shown and all ratings had been made. For all subjects, each film segment first appeared on the large colour monitor. Then instructions appeared on the screen that told subjects which rating procedure to use.

Each of the following intervals was 30 seconds in length: the interval between the end of the film segment and video replay (for conditions when the CUE ratings were made before the RETRO), the interval between the end of each film segment and RETRO ratings when that condition was first, the interval between the end of one rating procedure and the beginning of the other, and the interval between the end of a rating procedure and the start of the next film.

Video Recordings

Spontaneous facial behaviour exhibited during film viewing was videotaped via concealed camera. Not one subject guessed that she had been videotaped. After the experiment was completed, subjects were informed of the camera, and written consent was requested for the use of the recordings for scientific purposes. Subjects were told that if they did not want their tapes analysed, we would destroy the tapes and they would still receive full payment for their time. No subject denied permission for the use of her videotape.

Facial Data

Facial behaviour was scored using Ekman and Friesen's (1978) Facial Action Coding System (FACS). FACS dissects all observable facial movement into 44 visually distinguishable and anatomically separate units of muscular action. We scored every facial event that occurred in terms of the action units that singly or in combination with other action units produced it. We then grouped combinations of action units into specific emotion and nonemotion categories on the basis of an empirically and theoretically derived computer database of expression patterns for use in the data analyses below.

Intercoder reliability for FACS coding has been well established across several laboratories (Ekman & Friesen, 1976; Ekman, Friesen, & Simons, 1985; Fox & Davidson, 1988; Krause, Steimer, Sanger-Alt, & Wagner, 1989; Steiner, 1986). The two coders for this study each had more than one year's experience as a FACS coder, and their reliability had been established against a standard criterion (Ekman and Friesen's own scoring) prior to scoring. Interrater agreement for this sample was calculated by obtaining a ratio of the number of agreements between the coders divided by the total number of agreements and disagreements. The agreement ratio between coders was 0.81.

In sum, from each subject there were records of facial behaviour exhibited during the film viewing period (which were later FACS coded), a single retrospective report of her subject experience during each film, and multiple CUE reports on the same experience.

Results

Was there sufficient incidence of facial expression and CUE reports to be able to determine whether they co-occurred?

In order to test our hypotheses, it was necessary to establish that there were multiple reports and multiple expressions for each film, and that each film provided a comparable amount of opportunities to test correspondence on a momentary basis. Overall, subjects stopped the film during the cued-review condition an average of 5.51 times (SD = 2.36). The median and modal number of stopping points were five. The mean number of stopping points did not differ significantly between films (paired $t(19)$ = 1.89, $P = 0.074$), but on average, subjects provided more CUE reports for the AMP film than the RAT (AMP M = 5.95, RAT M = 5.10). The mean number of facial expressions of emotion did not differ significantly between films (RAT M = 4.50, AMP M = 6.75, paired $t(19)$ = -1.74, $P = 0.098$), but there tended to be more expression in response to the amputation film. It appears that a sufficient amount of expression and reporting occurred for both films to proceed with analyses of specific emotions at several points in time.

All analyses presented below use all emotions that subjects exhibited. Coherence was always calculated idiographically, in terms of whether a subject's facial expression and self-report of emotion were congruent. Disgust was the emotion exhibited most often by most of the subjects, but other emotions occurred. For each of the films, facial expressions of sadness occurred more than 17% of the time, fear 10% of the time, and expressions of happiness, contempt, anger, and nonspecific negative emotion each between 3% and 5% of the time. Across all facial actions scored on a 5-point intensity scale, the mean level of intensity for RAT = 2.5, SD = 1.9; for AMP, M = 3.34, SD = 5.4.

For the CUE reports for RAT, the majority of the reports listed fear or disgust as the most intense or "peak" emotions, with only a few occurrences of other emotions, such as surprise and sadness, as the most intense reported emotion. For AMP, disgust was the overwhelmingly dominant response in CUE reporting, with only a few reports listing surprise, fear, anger, and sadness as the peak emotion. For RAT, the mean intensity for CUE ratings of disgust was 3.02, SD = 1.34; fear M = 3.19, SD = 1.64. For AMP CUE reports, disgust M = 4.69, SD = 1.81; fear M = 1.62, SD = 1.67.

The remaining analyses are organised according to a series of five analytical questions relevant to the specific hypotheses. Questions 1 and 2 are relevant to Hypotheses 1a–1c. Questions 3–5 concern Hypotheses 2a–2d.

QUESTION 1: *Did facial expressions of emotion and self-reports co-occur in time?*

The first set of hypotheses addressed coherence at the temporal level, and posited that facial expressions and CUE reports of emotion would co-occur in time. Hypothesis 1a predicted that for film locations where there was a high frequency of facial expression across subjects, there would also be a high frequency of self-report of emotion. In order to test this hypothesis, we first needed to determine whether certain locations of the film were more active in terms of expression than others.

Determining Facially Active Locations

For each film, there were certain locations where more than half of the subjects showed facial expressions of emotion. We conducted binomial tests to determine whether the proportion of subjects who exhibited a facial expression of emotion at these "active" locations differed from what would have been expected to occur by chance at any given film location. Chance probabilities were determined by sampling total film time at moving 4sec windows, and then calculating the probability of an emotion expression occurring across subjects at each interval (the number of subjects showing a facial expression of emotion/total number of subjects). We then averaged these multiple probabilities to yield a chance or "expected" probability of an emotion expression occurring at any given 4sec interval in each film. We chose 4sec for the interval length on the basis of previous research that has shown that most facial expressions of emotion last between 0.5sec through 4sec (Ekman, 1984). Chance probabilities were calculated separately for each film. The proportion of subjects showing an emotional expression during each active interval was then compared to the chance level.

Indeed, there were locations within each film where most subjects showed significantly more facial expressions of emotion than at any given 4sec interval of film time. For the RAT film, there was one such "facially active location", for AMP there were two.

Table 3.1 shows that for each of the facially active film locations, the proportion of subjects who showed a facial expression of emotion was significantly greater than the proportion expected by chance to occur at any given 4sec window of film time. This finding held for both of the films, and for both candidate locations within one of the films (AMP). No other locations in either film differed substantially from chance.

Now that we have established that the film locations of peak facial expression of emotion activity were significantly more active than any other given 4sec window of film time—for both films—we can test Hypothesis 1a: There should be a high incidence of self-report of emotion at film locations where facial expressions of emotion were more likely to have occurred. We conducted binomial tests to determine whether the proportion of subjects who provided a CUE report of emotion at the facially active

TABLE 3.1. Observed and chance probabilities of subjects showing a facial expression of emotion at facially active locations

Film	Proportion Observed	Proportion Expected by Chance	P
RAT	0.75	0.20	< 0.001
AMP			
Location 1	0.50	0.25	< 0.01
Location 2	0.70	0.25	< 0.001

Note: Probabilities based on binomial tests, $N = 20$.

locations was significantly greater than would have been predicted by chance. For each film, chance probabilities were calculated by sampling moving 4sec windows of film time, and then calculating the probability of a CUE report occurring across subjects at each interval (the number of subjects who gave a CUE report/total number of subjects). We then took the mean of these multiple probabilities to yield a chance or "expected" probability of a CUE report occurring at any given 4sec interval of film time.

We compared the observed proportions of subjects who provided CUE reports at each facially active location with the chance values. Table 3.2 shows that for each of the facially active locations, significantly more subjects provided a CUE report than would have been expected by chance. This finding held for all facially active locations across both films.

The fact that significantly more subjects provided CUE reports at facially active locations than would have been expected by chance supports Hypothesis 1a. Even more compelling evidence for the coherence question is the fact that the 4sec windows of film time that were peak locations of emotional facial expression activity (i.e. the facially active locations) were also the locations of highest CUE reporting for both films.

Hypothesis 1b framed the question of co-occurrence on a within-subject basis, and predicted that for individual subjects facial expressions of emotion and CUE reports of emotion would tend to occur at the same points in film time. We included facial expressions and CUE reports of all emotions in this analysis. Although the films were selected for their ability to arouse primarily disgust and fear, occasionally they evoked other emotions. As Hypothesis 1b is a question of general co-occurrence that is not asked at the level of specific types of emotions, CUE reports and facial expressions of anger, contempt, disgust, fear, happiness, sadness, and surprise were included in this analysis.

In order to test Hypothesis 1b, we calculated a co-occurrence quotient for each subject: The total number of times a CUE report coincided with a facial expression of emotion/total number of facial expressions of emotion. A CUE report was considered to be "coincident" if it overlapped with a facial expression of emotion within a 4sec window of film time (i.e. plus or minus 2sec). For each film we took the mean of the co-occurrence quotients across subjects. We then compared this mean co-occurrence quotient to a hypothesised chance quotient. The chance values were defined as the probability of a CUE report occurring at any given 4sec interval of film time. They were calculated as follows: For both RAT and AMP, the model number of CUE points equalled 5. Multiplying this by the 4sec sampling window yields 20sec of film time allocated for CUE reports. Total film time for RAT was 78sec, thus 20/78 or 0.26 of film time was allocated to CUE reporting. For AMP, total film time was 74sec, so 20/74 or 0.27 of film time was allocated to CUE reporting. For ease of analysis, we rounded up

TABLE 3.2. Observed and chance probabilities of subjects providing CUE reports of emotion at facially active locations

Film	Proportion Observed	Proportion Expected by Chance	P
RAT	0.95	0.29	< 0.001
AMP			
Location 1	0.80	0.25	< 0.001
Location 2	0.95	0.25	< 0.001

Note: Probabilities based on binomial tests, $N = 20$.

both numbers to yield a chance reporting quotient of 0.30 for both films. Rounding up is a conservative strategy and works against our hypothesis.

To test Hypothesis 1b, we then compared the observed mean co-occurrence quotients with the chance quotients in one sample t-tests. For RAT, the mean co-occurrence quotient across subjects was 0.46 ($SD = 0.28$). This was significantly greater than the chance value of 0.30 ($t(16) = 2.305$, $P < 0.02$). For AMP, the observed co-occurrence quotient was 0.47 ($SD = 0.22$), which was also significantly greater than the chance value of 0.30 ($t(18) = 3.409$, $P < 0.01$).

The question of co-occurrence can be asked from the point of view of the CUE reports as well: To determine whether subjects showed facial expressions at points in each film where CUE reports occurred. When we conducted the same analyses using CUE report locations as the starting point and looked for co-occurring facial expressions, we obtained nearly identical results; therefore, the details of those analyses are omitted.

The above results support Hypothesis 1b, showing that on the average, co-occurrence of any type of emotional facial expression and self-report was greater than would have been expected by chance, whether the question is framed from the perspective of facial expression or CUE report of emotion. The observed co-occurrence quotients, however, did not indicate co-occurrence for all CUE reports and facial expressions of emotion. On the average—for both films—CUE reports occurred during the same film locations as facial expressions of emotion about half of the time. This raises questions about the conditions that influenced whether or not particular expressions and reports co-occurred.

QUESTION 2: Did co-occurrence between expression and report vary as a function of intensity of emotion?

Our next two hypotheses predicted that within-subjects, co-occurrence may be more likely for more intense emotional events. Hypotheses 1c and 1d posited that people would be more likely to give CUE reports at locations of their most intense facial expressions of emotion than of their least intense facial expressions and vice versa: People would be more likely to show emotional expressions at the same locations in film time as their most intense CUE than their least intense CUE reports. To test Hypothesis 1c, we determined the number of subjects who gave a CUE report within a 4sec interval of their *most* intense facial expression of emotion, and how many provided a CUE report at the same locations as their *least* intense facial expressions of emotion. We then conducted McNemar tests of change in related samples (Siegel, 1956) to determine whether co-occurrence was more likely to occur during most intense emotional expressions versus least intense emotional expressions.

Determining Intensity of Facial Expressions of Emotion

In FACS, action units (AUs) that are critical to distinguish among certain emotional expressions are scored on a 5-point intensity scale (Friesen & Ekman, 1992). To determine the intensity of an expression, we summed the intensity scores for each critical AU in the expression to yield a total intensity score. For each subject (for each film) we designated the emotional expression with the highest total intensity score as the most intense facial expression of emotion. If there was a tie on total intensity score, we chose the expression with the longest duration. We designated the expression with the lowest sum intensity score as the least intense facial expression of emotion. If there was a tie for lowest total intensity score, we chose the expression with the shortest duration.

For RAT, 16 of the 20 subjects gave CUE reports at the same points in film time as their most intense facial expressions of emotion; only four did so during their least intense expression. The McNemar test showed that this was a statistically significant difference ($\chi^2 = 10$, $df = 1$, $P < 0.01$). For AMP, 19 subjects gave CUE reports during their most intense facial expressions of emotion, but only seven did so during their least intense emotional expressions. The difference between these proportions was also significant ($\chi^2 = 10$, $df = 1$, $P < 0.01$). These results support Hypothesis 1c.

Hypothesis 1d examined the same question framed from the standpoint of most intense CUE reports, predicting that people would show a facial expression of emotion at the same locations as where they gave their most intense reports of emotional experience.

Determining Intensity of CUE Reports of Emotion

For each report, subjects rated each emotion term on a 9-point intensity scale. We summed the intensity scores for all emotion terms on each report. Then, for each subject, we designated the report with the highest total intensity as the most intense CUE report, and the one with the lowest total intensity as least intense CUE report. Cases of tie were settled by random selection.

Again we conducted McNemar tests. For the RAT film, 16 of the 20 subjects showed a facial expression at the same location as their most intense emotion reports. Only seven subjects showed emotional expressions during their least intense emotion reports. This difference was significant ($\chi^2 = 10$, $df = 1$, $P < 0.01$). For AMP, however, there were no significant differences in the number of subjects who showed facial expressions of emotion during most intense CUE reports versus least intense CUE reports (16 vs. 13, respectively, $\chi^2 = 1.29$, $df = 1$, $P > 0.20$). The results from three tests of Hypotheses 1c and 1d support the intensity hypothesis on a within-subject basis. The one exception will be considered in the discussion section.

QUESTION 3: *Was there categorical agreement between co-occurring facial expressions and self-reports?*

The second set of hypotheses examined coherence in terms of categorical agreement on the type of emotion between co-occurring facial expression and self-report. Hypothesis 2a predicted agreement between expression and CUE report. To test this hypothesis we conducted analyses similar to those for Hypothesis 1b, only this time we compared categorical *agreement* coefficients to the hypothesised chance values. We calculated agreement or "matching" quotients for each subject defined as: The number of times a CUE report that coincided with a facial expression of emotion agreed or matched as to the type of emotion that occurred/total number of facial expression—CUE report co-occurrences. Matching was defined in terms of whether emotional category of facial expression was the same as the category of the emotion rated at highest intensity on the CUE report.

Because the distributions of matching quotients across subjects were extremely non-normal, one sample Wilcoxon signed ranks tests were conducted to compare observed quotients to hypothesised population chance values (Shott, 1990). We used the same chance values that were used in the test of Hypothesis 1b, which reflected the probability of a CUE report occurring at any given 4sec interval of film time. We reasoned that these chance values—as expected values of co-occurrence and not necessarily matching between expression and report—would necessarily be high estimates of matching. Thus, our tests of difference from this chance value would be very conservative. For RAT, the observed median matching quotient was 0.42. This was not significantly different from the chance level of 0.30 ($T(16) = 83$, $P > 0.10$).[4] For AMP, the sample median quotient was 0.50, which was significantly greater than the chance value of 0.30 ($T(19) = 149$, $P < 0.025$). Thus, only results from the AMP film support the hypothesis of overall matching between facial expressions of emotion and co-occurring CUE reports posited in Hypothesis 2a. When we evaluated categorical matching for facial expressions that occurred at the same locations as CUE reports, we obtained results identical to those obtained from the above analyses.

Co-occurring reports and facial expression agreed on category of emotion only for the AMP film. These analyses were conducted across each film, for all locations at which CUE reports and facial expressions co-occurred. Would there be greater evidence of agreement at points in each film that were more emotionally intense? Question 4 examines this by looking at categorical agreement at points during each film at which most subjects showed emotional responses (thereby defining intensity on a between-subjects basis). Question 5 looks at whether categorical agreement is greater at the most intense points during each film at each subject's location of greatest expressivity or report (thereby defining intensity on a within-subjects basis).

QUESTION 4: Was there categorical agreement between co-occurring facial expression and self-reports at emotionally active locations?

Hypothesis 2b predicted categorical agreement between co-occurring facial expression and CUE report of emotion at the emotionally active locations (film locations characterised by a high degree of expression and report). A new set of chance conditional probabilities were computed. For moving 4sec intervals of film time we determined the probability of a match on type of emotion given a co-occurrence between CUE and facial expression, and then took the mean of these to yield chance probabilities of co-occurrence at any given 4sec interval of film time. We then conducted binomial tests to compare the observed and chance probabilities of a subject matching on emotion category given temporal correspondence of facial expression and CUE report.

As seen in table 3.3, the proportion of the subjects whose expression and report

TABLE **3.3.** Observed and chance conditional probabilities of subjects matching on emotion category given that they had shown a co-occurrence of facial expression and CUE report at emotionally active locations

Film	Proportion Observed	Proportion Expected by Chance	P
RAT	0.71 ($n = 14$)	0.20	< 0.001
AMP			
Location 1	0.90 ($n = 10$)	0.25	< 0.001
Location 2	0.83 ($n = 12$)	0.25	< 0.001

Note: Probabilities based on binomial tests.

matched on category for the RAT film—given that they had demonstrated co-occurrence between facial expression and CUE report of emotion at the emotionally active location—was significantly greater than would have been predicted by chance. Similar results occurred for both of the emotionally active locations in the AMP film, where significantly more of the subjects who showed temporal linkage between facial expression of emotion and CUE report at active locations actually matched between measures on emotion category. These findings support Hypothesis 2b.

QUESTION 5: *Was categorical matching a function of intensity?*

Hypothesis 2c predicted that where people show their most intense facial expression of emotion, they will also report experiencing the same type of emotion. In order to test this hypothesis, we calculated the proportion of subjects whose CUE report and facial expression matched on category *given* they had demonstrated co-occurrence between the two measures for the most intense facial expressions of emotion and we compared these to chance values via binomial tests. For RAT, 12 of the 16 subjects who had CUE reports concomitantly with most intense facial expression matched on category. For AMP, 13 of the 19 subjects who demonstrated co-occurrence between most intense facial expression and CUE reporting matched. Each of these proportions was compared to a chance value of 0.30 (derived in the test of Hypothesis 1b) in a binomial test. Both observed proportions were significantly greater than chance (RAT, $P < 0.001$; AMP, $P < 0.001$). We then looked at matching for the least intense facial expression of emotion.[5] For RAT, of the four subjects who demonstrated co-occurrence at their least intense facial expression of emotion, only one matched on category. This proportion was not different from chance ($P > 0.40$). For AMP, of the seven subjects who gave a CUE report at the same location as their least intense facial expression, only two matched on emotion category, which did not differ significantly from chance ($P > 0.30$). These results support Hypothesis 2c.

Hypothesis 2d framed the within-subjects categorical agreement question from the standpoint of most intense CUE report. For each film, we calculated the proportion of subjects who—given they showed a facial expression of emotion at the same film locations as their most intense CUE report—matched on emotion category. This was then compared to chance values. Chance values for these analyses were based on the average number of times subjects showed facial expressions of emotion per film. With one exception (to be discussed later) the result obtained from these analyses were the same as those from the analyses of Hypothesis 2c. For both films, of the subjects who showed facial expressions of emotion at same film locations as their most intense CUE reports (10 out of 16 for both films) a significantly greater than chance proportion matched on emotion category ($P < 0.01$). Again, as in the tests of Hypothesis 2c, this did not hold for least intense CUE reports. Only 1 of the 7 subjects who showed co-occurrence between most intense report and facial expression for RAT matched on category. This was not different from chance ($P > 0.30$). These results support Hypothesis 2d. The one exception occurred for AMP, in which 8 of the 13 subjects for whom co-occurrence for least intense CUE report matched on category. This is different from the chance level of 0.30 ($P < 0.05$). This exception will be considered in the Discussion section.

Although the analyses on categorical agreement included facial expressions and self-reports of any type of emotion, it is possible that the high levels of categorical agreement between co-occurring facial expressions and CUE reports described above were a necessary product of the predominance of one type of emotion being shown facially or reported as the peak emotion within and across subjects. If the films elicited primarily one type of emotion, then any facial expression and self-report that occurred together would have to agree on category. We have already noted that both films elicited primarily disgust. Have we established evidence of specificity, or was categorical agreement just a necessary byproduct of temporally linked expression and report during films that evoked primarily disgust?

The ideal test of this question would be to determine whether categorical agreement of facial expression and CUE report held for nondisgust expressions and reports. Unfortunately, while other emotions occurred in both films, they occurred too infrequently to allow for adequate analysis of nondisgust emotions as a separate group. Also, when other emotions did occur, they were never the most intense instances of expression and report. The confounding of intensity of response with type of emotion would also complicate analysis. Thus, we chose an alternate means of determining whether categorical agreement between expression and report was a necessary byproduct of expressions and reports overlapping in time for films that elicited primarily disgust.

For each subject's most intense facial expression of disgust, we determined whether or not she reported disgust or another negative emotion as the most intense emotion on the corresponding CUE report. We reasoned that if a variety of negative emotions were reported by subjects during their most intense disgust facial expressions—but disgust was reported as most intense significantly more often than other negative emotions—then we would have evidence that categorical agreement was not merely a result of co-occurrence. We conducted χ^2 goodness-of-fit tests to determine whether the distribution of subjects who reported disgust and nondisgust negative emotions as the most intense emotion on the CUE report that corresponded with the most intense facial expression of disgust differed from chance. Probabilities for the chance proportions were calculated as follows: We determined the proportion of each subject's negative emotion reports in which disgust was reported as the most intense or "peak" emotion, and then we took the mean of these proportions across subjects. By this method, for RAT chance distribution of negative emotion report at any film location was: 35% of subjects reported disgust as the peak emotion, and 65% reported other negative emotions as peak. The observed distribution for RAT was: 75% of the subjects who gave a report at the same location as most intense facial expression reported disgust as the peak emotion, and 25% reported experiencing some other negative emotion as peak. This distribution was significantly different from the one expected to occur by chance ($\chi^2 = 8.44$, $df = 1$, $P < 0.005$). For AMP, the chance distribution at any film locations was: 81% of the subjects reported disgust as the most intense, and 19% of the subjects reporting other negative emotions as the most intense. In fact, 80% of the subjects who gave a report at the same location as their most intense facial expression reported disgust as the peak emotion, and 20% reported experiencing some other negative emotion. Not surprisingly, this distribution was not different from the distribution expected by chance for AMP ($\chi^2 = 0.01$, $df = 1$, $P > 0.50$). The same results hold when the question is framed with most intense disgust CUE report as the starting point. Thus, for AMP—in which disgust was the emotion reported and shown facially most of the time—categorical agreement was a necessary consequent of co-occurring expression and report. For RAT, however, as more types of emotions were reported, categorical agreement indicates specificity in coherent emotional responses.

Discussion

Our results provide the first evidence that there is coherence between facial expression and self-report of emotion at specific moments. For emotions that occurred during a brief episode, we obtained evidence linking facial expression and self-report not only in time, but also in type. Thus, we have extended previous findings of correlations between single indices of expression and report of emotion over a period of time (Ekman et al., 1980), and have shown that correspondences exist at specific moments, in particular for intense emotional events.

We found evidence for coherence at several levels of analysis. When we analysed coherence at the level of co-occurrence between facial expression and self-report of emotion at several locations in film time, we found that facial expression and self-report coincided more often than would have been expected by chance. This result held between- and within-subjects, and whether we framed the question with either facial expressions or self-report as the reference from which to evaluate co-occurrence. Overall, the level of within-subjects co-occurrence between self-report and facial expression of emotion was about 50% for each film. This percentage, though significantly greater than the chance values, still suggests quite a bit of nonoverlap. This moderate amount of overlap would be expected, however, when one considers that this value is an index of general co-occurrence between report and facial expression of all intensities and categories. When we asked the question in terms of coherence between expression and report of the same types of emotions, the degree of correspondence improved.

As predicted, we found that co-occurrence was optimal for more intense emotional events, whether we based intensity on facial expression or self-report. The idea that intense emotional responses are more likely than less intense responses to involve linkage between expression and report was substantiated by the fact that in nearly all instances, significantly more subjects demonstrated co-occurrence for their most intense responses than for their least intense responses. The exception to this was that for AMP, both the most intense CUE and least intense CUE showed a high incidence of co-occurrence between face and report. One possible explanation for this is that the AMP film, which elicited more facial expressions of emotion and CUE reports than the RAT film in this sample (though not significantly so), may have elicited more intense emotion overall. Specifically, the least intense CUE reports for AMP might have been more intense than the least intense CUE reports for RAT. A *post hoc* t-test revealed that this was indeed the case ($t(19) = 4.49$, $P < 0.001$).

Our finding that response cohesion may vary as a function of the intensity of the response is consistent with the view that emotions must reach a certain level of intensity before there can be congruence in response systems (Davidson, 1992; Tassinary & Cacioppo, 1992). Although our results are certainly suggestive of the existence of an intensity threshold for congruence in the entire emotional response, there are at least three reasons why this study is not definitive about this matter. First, the self-reports were not made online, but were obtained during a video replay of the stimulus film.

This allows for the possibility that emotions had to reach a minimum level of intensity for their locations in film time to be recalled. Perhaps only the more intense emotions were remembered at the points in each film during which they were actually experienced. The less intense emotions may have been washed out in memory by the more intense ones.

Second, emotional experience may have to reach a minimum level of intensity to overcome problems of symbolic representation in verbal self-report. A person may be consciously experiencing an emotion that is manifest behaviourally and physiologically, but he or she may be unable to expression the experience to others. Subjective experiences can be ineffable.

Third, emotions may have to be sufficiently intense to reach consciousness in the first place, let alone to be reported on. Other aspects of the emotion response—such as the connections between behaviour and physiological change—may not depend on intensity. Information from these systems need not enter consciousness to be measured. Thus, it is possible that the intensity effect is relevant to the entry of an emotion into conscious awareness, and not necessarily relevant to the coherence of other aspects of the emotional response. Physiology and behaviour may cohere at lower intensities of emotion, at which emotional experience is not yet perceived.

We cannot rule out the possibility that memory problems or the problem of symbolic representation of experience accounted for our intensity-dependent findings nor can we disentangle these factors from the possibility that coherence in real-time depends on intensity. The third problem is more complicated. Intensity of an emotion at the behavioural and physiological levels may moderate the entry of the subjective system into a coherent emotional response.[6] The effect of intensity on coherence is a complex question that can be asked at many levels: in terms of coherence with non-conscious responses systems (spontaneous behaviour and physiology), and in terms of coherence between conscious systems and non-conscious systems. The research presented in this paper is only suggestive of an intensity effect that should be explored further.

We obtained evidence for coherence at the most specific level—categorical agreement between concomitant facial expressions and self-reports of emotion. When we looked at film locations where most subjects showed facial expressions and gave CUE reports, a substantial and significant majority of the subjects demonstrated categorical agreement between facial expression and self-report of emotion. When we examined the question of agreement or "matching" between response measures for all emotion expressions and all CUE reports, we obtained evidence for a significant amount of overall categorical agreement between facial expressions that co-occurred with CUE reports in the AMP film only. This is consistent with our notion that the AMP film may elicit more intense emotion overall. When we separated most intense from least intense events for analysis, however, for both films and for both ways of framing the question (from the standpoint of facial expression or CUE report as most intense) there was significantly more matching than would have been predicted by chance for the most intense events only. For AMP only, this held for least intense CUE reports as well, which was consistent with the above findings on the film's intensity.

For both films, subjects' facial expressions and self-reports matched on category—not just valence—for most intense events. This is consistent with findings that relationships between facial expression and self-report of emotion discriminate among different positive and negative emotions. For example, Ekman et al. (1980) found that measures of disgust facial expressions were positively correlated with self-reports of disgust but not with reports of the negative emotions of anger or sadness. In terms of the specificity of positive emotion, smiles involving both raising of the lip corners and contraction of the muscles around the eyes (the Duchenne smile) have been shown to have a specific relationship with reported amusement over and above other positive emotions, such as excitement and happiness (Ekman et al., 1990). Thus, in the study of the relationship between facial expressions and self-report of emotion, it is crucial to obtain ratings on several categories of emotions. The dimensional view that emotional variability can be thoroughly explained by the domains positive and negative affect (Diener & Emmons, 1984; Watson & Tellegen, 1985) may apply to general mood states, but our findings suggest that it is not adequate for the study of momentary emotional response.

One limitation of our findings was that for one of the films (AMP) categorical matching was a necessary consequence of co-occurring expression and report, because this film overwhelmingly elicited one type of emotion—disgust (80% of the emotional responses throughout AMP were disgust). That is, for a film that elicits only disgust expressions and reports, any co-occurring measures would by definition agree on category. For the RAT film, however, enough different emotions were reported to enable us to determine that categorical agreement between co-occurring expression and report was not merely a byproduct of co-occurrence. For RAT, even though subjects reported a variety of negative emotions during their most intense expressions of disgust, a significant majority of them remembered experiencing disgust as their most intense emotion rather than other negative emotions.

An important step in this research programme is to determine how well temporal linkage and agreement between facial expression and self-report generalise to other types of emotion as well as to other subject populations. Our criterion of coherence for the analyses between facial and reported emotion was primarily within-subject, on the basis of whether each subject reported in her CUE report the same emotion that she displayed facially at particular locations in film time. Even though there were some subjects who demonstrated coherence who were reporting and showing anger, fear, surprise, or sadness, most of the time the films elicited disgust. We limited our sample to college-aged women. We believe, however, that coherence between facial expression and self-report observed at specific moments should occur in other populations such as men, older adults, and children.

It may be suggested that the coherence domonstrated in this study was a particular to the stimulus situation; i.e. the viewing of disgust- and fear-eliciting films, and that it might not generalise to other emotional situations. It seems unlikely that humans would have evolved with emotional response systems that behave in one way to films but differently to other emotion elicitors. This possibility seems especially remote in the light of the fact that moderate levels of coherence among behavioural, physiological, and subjective measures have been demonstrated in the very different context of marital interaction research (Levenson & Gottman, 1983, 1985).

We demonstrated that measurement of facial expression and self-report of specific emotions on a momentary basis provides solid evidence of a coherent emotional response, especially for more intense emotional events. The source of this coherence remains unclear. It is possible that the observed coherence was internally driven, externally driven, or both. Our findings are consistent with Tomkins's (1962) notion of emotions as correlated responses, and provide the strongest evidence to date that this is true for facial and subjective measures. Future research should strive to clarify the mechanisms responsible for coherence as well as demonstrate three-way coherence among subjective, behavioural, and physiological measures on a momentary basis.

Notes

1. Retrospective emotions reports in which subjects provided a single report on emotion for each film were collected to examine coherence at a summary level (as has been done in previous research), and to determine which had a stronger relationship with aggregated facial behaviour: retrospective emotion reports or aggregated CUE reports. As the focus of this paper is on momentary correspondences and the aggregate analyses deal with a separate issue, those findings will be presented elsewhere.

2. Previous studies of students' ratings of emotion elicited by some of these films—conducted by James Gross, University of California, Berkeley—were helpful in our selection of stimulus materials.

3. The RAT film was originally used for emotion induction by Richard Davidson, of the University of Wisconsin at Madison.

4. T = the sum of the positive signed ranks, and the number in parentheses refers to the total number of signed ranks.

5. We could not look at the difference in proportions of subjects who matched in the most intense versus least intense condition using the McNemar test, due to the restriction of our sample to those who showed co-occurrence.

6. We thank an anonymous reviewer for suggesting this.

References

Block, J. (1957). Studies in the phenomenology of emotions. *Journal of Abnormal and Social Psychology, 54,* 358–363.

Brown, S., & Schwartz, G. E. (1980). Relationships between facial electromyography and subjective experience during affective imagery. *Biological Psychology, 11,* 49–62.

Buck, R. (1980). Nonverbal behavior and the theory of emotion: The facial feedback hypothesis. *Journal of Personality and Social Psychology, 38,* 811–824.

Cacioppo, J. T., Uchino, B. N., Crites, S. L., Snydersmith, M. A., Smith, G., Berntson, G. G., & Lang, P. J. (1992). Relationship between facial expressiveness and sympathetic activation in emotion: A critical review, with emphasis on modeling underlying mechanisms and individual differences. *Journal of Personality and Social Psychology, 62,* 110–128.

Campbell, D. T., Siegman, C., & Rees, M. B. (1967). Direction-of-wording effects in the relationships between scales. *Psychological Bulletin, 68,* 293–303.

Crowne, D. P., & Marlowe, D. (1964). *The approval motive.* New York: Wiley.

Darwin, C. (1872/1965). *The expression of the emotions in man and animals.* Chicago: University of Chicago Press.

Davidson, R. J. (1992). Prolegomenon to the structure of emotion: Gleanings from neuropsychology. *Cognition and Emotion, 6,* 245–268.

Davidson, R. J., Ekman, P., Saron, C. D., Senulis, J. A., & Friesen, W. V. (1990). Approach-withdrawal and cerebral asymmetry: Emotional expression and brain physiology: I. *Journal of Personality and Social Psychology, 58,* 330–341.

Diener, E., & Emmons, R. A. (1984). The independence of positive and negative affect. *Journal of Personality and Social Psychology, 47*, 1105–1117.

Ekman, P. (1977). Biological and cultural contributions to body and facial movement. In J. Blacking (Ed.), *Anthropology of the body* (pp. 53–84). London: Academic Press.

Ekman, P. (1984). Expression and the nature of emotion. In K. R. Scherer & P. Ekman (Eds.), *Approaches to emotion* (pp. 319–344). Hillsdale, NJ: Erlbaum.

Ekman, P. (1985). *Telling lies.* New York: Norton.

Ekman, P. (1992). An argument for basic emotions. *Cognition and Emotion, 6*, 161–168.

Ekman, P., Davidson, R. J., & Friesen, W. V. (1990). The Duchenne smile: Emotional expression and brain physiology: II. *Journal of Personality and Social Psychology, 58*, 342–353.

Ekman, P., & Friesen, W. V. (1974). Detecting deception from the body or face. *Journal of Personality and Social Psychology, 29*, 288–298.

Ekman, P., & Friesen, W. V. (1976). Measuring facial movement. *Journal of Environmental Psychology and Nonverbal Behavior, 1*, 56–75.

Ekman, P., & Friesen, W. V. (1978). *The Facial Action Coding System.* Palo Alto: Consulting Psychologists Press.

Ekman, P., Friesen, W. V., & Ancoli, S. (1980). Facial signs of emotional experience. *Journal of Personality and Social Psychology, 39*, 1125–1134.

Ekman, P., Friesen, W. V., & Simons, R. C. (1985). Is the startle reaction an emotion? *Journal of Personality and Social Psychology, 49*, 1416–1426.

Englander-Golden, P., Chang, H., Whitmore, M. R., & Dientsbier, R. A. (1980). Female sexual arousal and the menstrual cycle. *Journal of Human Stress, 6*, 42–48.

Epstein, S. (1980). The stability of behavior: II. Implications for psychological research. *American Psychologist, 35*, 790–806.

Fox, N. A., & Davidson, R. J. (1988). Patterns of brain electrical activity during facial signs of emotion in 10-month-old infants. *Developmental Psychology, 24*, 230–236.

Fredrickson, B. L., & Levenson, R. W. (in press). Positive emotion speeds recovery from negative emotional arousal. *Cognition and Emotion.*

Friesen, W. V., & Ekman, P. (1992). *Changes in FACS scoring.* Unpublished instructional document. University of California, San Francisco.

Jones, H. E. (1950). The study of patterns of emotional expression. In M. L. Reymert (Ed.), *Feelings and emotions* (pp. 161–168). New York: McGraw-Hill.

Kagan, N., Krathwohl, D. R., & Farquhar, W. W. (1965). *IPR—Interpersonal Process Recall: Simulated recall by videotape in studies of counseling and teaching-learning.* Michigan State University: East Lansing, MI.

Kleck, R. E., Vaughan, R. C., Cartwright-Smith, J., Vaughan, K. B., Colby, C. Z., & Lanzetta, J. T. (1976). Effects of being observed on expressive, subjective, and physiological responses to painful stimuli. *Journal of Personality and Social Psychology, 34*, 1211–1218.

Krause, R., Steimer, E., Sanger-Alt, C., & Wagner, G. (1989). Facial expression of schizophrenic patients and their interaction partners. *Psychiatry, 52*, 1–12.

Laird, J. D., (1974). Self-attribution of emotion: The effects of expressive behavior on the quality of emotional experience. *Journal of Personality and Social Psychology, 29*, 475–486.

Lanzetta, J. T., Cartwright-Smith, J., & Kleck, R. E. (1976). Effects of nonverbal dissimulation on emotional experience and autonomic arousal. *Journal of Personality and Social Psychology, 33*, 354–370.

Lanzetta, J. T., & Kleck, R. E. (1970). Encoding and decoding of nonverbal affect in humans. *Journal of Personality and Social Psychology, 16*, 12–19.

Levenson, R. W. (1988). Emotion and the autonomic nervous system: a prospectus for research on autonomic specificity. In H. L. Wagner (Ed.), *Social psychophysiology and emotion: Theory and clinical implications* (pp. 17–42). New York: Wiley.

Levenson, R. W., Ekman, P., & Friesen, W. V. (1990). Voluntary facial action generates emotion-specific autonomic nervous system activity. *Psychophysiology, 27,* 363–384.

Levenson, R. W., & Gottman, J. M. (1983). Marital interaction: Physiological linkage and affective exchange. *Journal of Personality and Social Psychology, 45,* 587–597.

Levenson, R. W., & Gottman, J. M. (1985). Physiological and affective predictors of change in relationship satisfaction. *Journal of Personality and Social Psychology, 49,* 85–94.

Nisbett, R. E., & Wilson, T. D. (1977). Telling more than we can know: Verbal reports on mental processes. *Psychological Review, 84,* 231–259.

Orne, M. T. (1962). The social psychology of psychological experiments. *American Psychologist, 17,* 776–783.

Plutchik, R. (1962). *The emotions: Facts, theories, and a new model.* New York: Random House.

Reis, H. T., & Wheeler, L. (1991). Studying social interaction with the Rochester Interaction Record. In *Advances in experimental social psychology.* New York: Academic Press.

Shott, S. (1990). *Statistics for health professionals.* Philadelphia: Saunders.

Siegel, S. (1956). *Nonparametric statistics for the behavioral sciences.* New York: McGraw-Hill.

Steiner, F. (1986). Differentiating smiles. In E. Baenninger-Huber & F. Steiner (Eds.), *FACS in psychotherapy research* (pp. 139–148). Zurich: Department of Clinical Psychology, University of Zurich.

Tassinary, L. G., & Cacioppo, J. T. (1992). Unobservable facial actions and emotion. *Psychological Science, 3,* 28–33.

Thomas, D. L., & Diener, E. (1990). Memory accuracy in the recall of emotions. *Journal of Personality and Social Psychology, 59,* 291–297.

Tomkins, S. S. (1962). *Affect, imagery, consciousness: Vol. 1.* New York: Springer.

Watson, D., & Tellegen, A. (1985). Toward a consensual structure of mood. *Psychological Bulletin, 98,* 219–235.

AFTERWORD

Emotions as Unified Responses

ERIKA L. ROSENBERG

The preceding article addressed a fundamental question in the psychology of emotion: To what extent are emotions *unified* responses? We examined whether the facial expressive system and the subjective, experiential system acted together during specific instances of emotion. The availability of FACS greatly enabled this work. At the outset, we knew we had the means by which to measure specific affective behaviors from the face on a momentary basis. As described in detail in the article, both FACS and facial EMG could have been used for this purpose. We chose FACS for reasons that were discussed in the detail in the article, but a few points bear repeating here. FACS is unobtrusive and allows for differentiation among activity in muscle groups that may be too close to each other to allow for differentiation on the basis of electrical activity (the problem of cross-talk between muscle groups in EMG measurement). FACS offered greater specificity in emotion measurement on a moment-by-moment basis than facial EMG. Frankly, our biggest methodological challenge concerned measuring subjective experience on a similarly momentary yet specific basis, which we resolved by developing the cued-review technique for obtaining self-reports of emotional experience.

Further Work on Coherence

The major finding reported in the preceding article was that facial expressions of emotion and reports of experience acted together most of the time and when they did, they agreed as to the type of emotion the person was experiencing. Such coherence was especially likely during emotion marked by either more intense facial expressions of emotion or more intense subjective reports. One unresolved issue is whether the intensity effect with respect to the momentary subjective reports was mediated by memory effects. The question is this: Does the finding that coherence was greater at moments of more intense subjective report and facial expression tell us that these response systems act in unison only for more intense emotions (which has been theorized by Davidson, 1992; Tassinary & Cacioppo, 1992) or do they tell us that people can only *remember* the temporal location of more intense emotions more accurately? Maybe the fact that coherence was not observed for less intense events is simply a by-product of the fact that cued-review reports are less *temporally accurate* for less intense emotions (i.e., people cannot remember where and even if milder emotions occurred). If this were true, emotion reports for less intense events either would not have been made or would not have correctly corresponded in time with periods of facial expression of emotion. Either way, coherence between face and self-report would not have been observed.

The only way to determine whether coherence is greater for more intense emotions or whether this was merely a function of poor memory for emotion location is to employ a subjective measure that is temporally *on-line* or at least more temporally comparable to facial records obtained *during* an emotional event. Barbara Fredrickson and I are conducting a study aimed at resolving the intensity issue by obtaining on-line subjective data. We are also addressing another drawback of the original study—the fact that we measured only two response systems. Fredrickson and I are looking for three-way coherence among expressive, experiential and physiological systems during emotional responses to films. We have gathered subjective data via an on-line rating dial procedure, thereby eliminating the need for subjects to remember when they felt emotions. Putting the subjective measurement on a more comparable temporal scale with the physiological and facial measures should allow us to determine whether the intensity effect reported in the preceding article was an artifact of memory or if it reflected true intensity-mediated coherence.

Comments on the Use of FACS and Facial Measurement More Generally

Studying spontaneous facial behavior, coding observable movement, and interpreting the movements shown is intensive work. Is it worth it? Do the scientific advances gained outweigh the costs of the work? The answer is yes on both accounts. As reviewed in the article, previous studies using global facial affect measures or specific facial measures averaged over several instances of emotional behavior indicated only a moderate amount of coherence among response systems. Those studies could not reveal whether moments of tight linkage among systems occurred during discrete emotional responses. Our finding that tight linkages *do* occur is a solid piece of evidence for evolutionary views that describe emotions as psychophysiological adaptations—coordinated responses of bodily and mental activity that arise under particular environmental circumstances that were important for human survival in our ancestral past (Tooby & Cosmides, 1990). This view of emotion dictates that normally disparate systems act together for quick, efficient responding to certain critical situations. The preceding study indicates that the face and subjective experience *do* exhibit such coordinated activity. Other studies (e.g., Davidson, Ekman, Saron, Senulis, & Friesen, 1990) indicate physiological responses are part of that coordinated package as well. Without precise facial measurement, such as that offered by FACS, such momentary linkages could not have been uncovered.

Findings of coherence between facial and experiential measures during emotions also shed light on a contentious topic in contemporary social psychology—whether there is any meaningful information about emotion available from the face (cf. Fridlund, 1994; Russell, 1994, as well as Ekman's 1994 rebuttal to Russell). While most of that work has come from the vantage point of whether the face communicates emotional information (Russell, 1994), implicit in Russell's argument and explicit in Fridlund's is the notion that the face has nothing to do with emotion—that it is not a emotional response system per se and it has no meaningful relationship to the experience of emotion. The present report and others (e.g., Davidson et al., 1990; Levenson & Gottman, 1983, 1985; Ruch, chap. 4 in this volume) have demonstrated positive relationships between facial expression and reported experience and/or physiological changes in several different emotional states and scenarios. Such findings of linkage strongly suggest facial expressions of emotion can tell us about the experience of emotion and render null the argument that no meaningful information about emotional experience can be obtained from the face. Further, the joint activation of these two systems attests to the existence of a neurological substrate responsible for such organization during emotional responding, which again brings something to bear on the evolutionary argument. Claims for biology are not in vogue in modern psychology. Rather, it has become increasingly popular to interpret biologically relevant findings as antithetical to cultural influences and therefore not of interest to the social sciences. But biological and psychological adaptations to social variables may have mutually and interdependently evolved, a point that has been argued eloquently by Tooby and Cosmides (1992): "From a perspective that describes the whole integrated system of causation, the distinction between the biologically determined and the nonbiologically determined can be seen to be a nondistinction" (p. 46).

References

Davidson, R. J. (1992). Prolegomenon to the structure of emotion: Gleanings from neuropsychology. *Cognition & Emotion, 6,* 245–268.
Davidson, R. J., Ekman, P., Saron, C., Senulis, J. A., & Friesen, W. V. (1990). Approach-withdrawal and cerebral asymmetry: Emotional expression and brain physiology: I. *Journal of Personality and Social Psychology, 58,* 330–341.
Ekman, P. (1994). Strong evidence for universals in facial expressions: A reply to Russell's mistaken critique. *Psychological Bulletin, 115,* 268–287.
Fridlund, A. J. (1994). *Human facial expression, an evolutionary view.* New York: Academic Press.
Levenson, R. W., & Gottman, J. M. (1983). Marital interaction: Physiological linkage and affective exchange. *Journal of Personality and Social Psychology, 45,* 587–597.
Levenson, R. W., & Gottman, J. M. (1985). Physiological and affective predictors of change in relationship satisfaction. *Journal of Personality and Social Psychology, 49,* 85–94.
Russell, J. A. (1994). Is there universal recognition of emotion from facial expression? A review of cross-cultural studies. *Psychological Bulletin, 115,* 102–141.
Tassinary, L. G., & Cacioppo, J. T. (1992). Unobservable facial actions and emotion. *Psychological Science, 3,* 28–33.
Tooby, J., & Cosmides, L. (1990). The past explains the present: Emotional adaptations and the structure of ancestral environments. *Ethology & Sociobiology, 11,* 375–424.
Tooby, J., & Cosmides, L. (1992). The psychological foundations of culture. In J. H. Barkow, L. Cosmides, & J. Tooby (Eds.), *The adapted mind* (pp. 19–136). New York: Oxford University Press.

4

Will the Real Relationship Between Facial Expression and Affective Experience Please Stand Up

The Case of Exhilaration

WILLIBALD RUCH

Emotions, like other concepts in psychology, are hypothetical constructs which are not directly observable, but are inferred from several indicators. The inference is typically based on behaviour, physiological changes, or reports of subjective experience. Emotions vary in intensity and these intensity differences can be observed at all three levels. At least for the levels behaviour and experience it is commonly assumed that intensity of the emotion is reflected equally well in these domains, e.g. parameters of facial expression and affective experience are expected to show a high positive intercorrelation.

As regards the emotion induced by humour stimuli, however, empirical research has shown that although these manifestations of emotion are, indeed, positively related, the correlations are only low to moderate in strength. McGhee (1977) notes that the correlations between rated funniness and the amount of smiling or laughter typically range from 0.30 to 0.40, seldom exceeding the latter value. These low coefficients may have contributed to the failure of humour researchers to conceptualise the behavioural, physiological, and experiential responses to humour in terms of an emotion construct; rather, funniness ratings and smiling/laughter tend simply to be referred to as intellectual and affective measures of humour appreciation, respectively.

The Emotion of Exhilaration

Ruch (1990) recently proposed that exhilaration is the emotion elicited by humour. He argued that exhilaration satisfactorily accounts for the behavioural, physiological, and experiential changes typically occurring in response to such stimuli as tickling or laughing gas, as well as humour. In addition to describing the three levels of manifestation of exhilaration, and their relationship to one another, he has also described stimuli situations which elicit exhilaration, as well as factors which facilitate or inhibit it. It was proposed that the term "exhilaration" be used according to its Latin root (*hilaris* = cheerful) to denote either the process of making cheerful or the temporary rise in cheerful state (Ruch, 1993). Thus, in contrast to common language, the "excitement" component is de-emphasised in the proposed usage of the term.

Although exhilaration may be seen as a facet of the positive emotion of "happiness" (or "joy"), it is probably the facet most strongly aligned with laughter; whereas empirical studies of happiness/joy rarely report its occurrence, laughter is an inevitable response category in humour studies. The concept of exhilaration fully incorporates, but also goes well beyond, what has traditionally been understood by the so-called "humour response", i.e. the perception of a stimulus as being "funny". Basically, "humour response" is a concept of cognitive experience, regardless of whether it is or is not accompanied by smiling or laughter. Besides explicitly considering the levels of behaviour and physiology, the concept of exhilaration claims with respect to the experiential level, that when people react to humour, their awareness is not restricted to perceiving the joke as funny; they are also aware of changes in feeling state, of physiological changes, and of their actions and action tendencies (Ruch, 1990). In partial support of this claim, it has been demonstrated that the degree of perceived funniness of jokes and cartoons is correlated with the degree of felt exhilaration (Ruch, 1981; Ruch & Rath, 1993). Indeed, the range of the coefficients (from 0.82 to 0.92 with a mean of 0.86) suggests, that these two judgements product practically interchangeable results. However, the question of the extent to which measures of funniness or felt exhilaration correlate with exhilaration behaviour remains to be answered.

Correlation Between Smiling/Laughing and Funniness

McGhee (1977, p. 205) drew attention to the problem of the low inter-correlation between funniness ratings and smiling/laughing and suggested that researchers: ". . . include both measures as dependent variables and report the correlation obtained between them. This will provide a data base from which hypotheses may be drawn and tested regarding factors which influence the relationship between affective and intellectual measures of appreciation. It would also permit a cataloguing of the types of experimental manipulations to which each measure is sensitive."

In response to this suggestion, Ruch (1990) searched the humour literature for those articles which did report correlations between measures of smiling/laughter (using varying measurement approaches, such as observer judgements of degree of smiling or laughter, facial electromyography—EMG, and the Facial Action Coding System by Ekman & Friesen, 1978) and funniness ratings or other self-reports of positive affect. He found that across 25 different studies, the correlations ranged from about −0.30 to a nearly perfect positive relationship. Three studies yielded negative correlations, and about half of the studies produced positive relationships below the 0.40 correlation described by McGhee (1977). The important question, of course, is how can this wide range of correlations be explained?

Authors who obtained low coefficients or coefficients differing in size put forward hypotheses aimed at explaining these effects. For example, Branch, Fine, and Jones

(1973) argued that the content of the humour stimulus makes an important contribution to the strength of this relationship. Among humour films which contained "tendentious" (i.e. sexual) content, they found a 0.63 correlation between funniness ratings and laughter; nontendentious films, however, yielded only a 0.30 correlation. Branch et al. (1973) also found that funniness ratings were more highly correlated with measures of smiling across a sample of subjects than measures of laughter were; low coefficients for laughter (ranging from −0.31 to 0.41) were also found by Porterfield et al. (1988). Weaver, Masland, Kharazmi, and Zillmann (1985) argue that alcohol intoxication might be capable of impairing the correspondence between verbal reports and facial expressiveness, maybe because overt expressive behaviour of the subjects, or the resulting feedback, is reduced or in some way altered by the effect of alcohol intoxications. This argument is based on the observation that the correlations between rated funniness of comedy films and several measures of facial expression were significant for the control group (0.33 to 0.39), but were "substantially lower and nonsignificant" for low and high alcohol conditions. These and related hypotheses are a posteriori explanations and were never examined further.

The low coefficients also led to speculation about potential different meanings of the verbal reports and overt behaviour. For example, it was proposed that smiling represents the intellectual, and smiling/laughing the affective appreciation of humour (Gavanski, 1986; Porterfield et al., 1988). Recently, it was also claimed that amount of smiling reflects not the emotion, but the social context (Fridlund, 1991); this assertion was again based on the observation of a nonsignificant relationship between EMG recordings of the contraction of the zygomatic major (i.e. the smiling muscle) and ratings of happiness.

Ruch (1990) argued that whereas situational and other social or subject factors may have some impact on the relationship between subjective judgements of funniness and the emotional reaction shown, methodological issues may hold the key to understanding the discrepancy generally found between these two aspects of humour appreciation. The size of the coefficients obtained may be influenced by several factors, such as the nature of the assessment method (e.g. spontaneous judgements by an observer vs. use of a videotape for rating, use of psychophysiological measures), validity (e.g. control of method artefacts, separation of types of smiles) and reliability of the coding systems used, or the way the data are coded (e.g. simple judgements of presence or absence of smiling or laughter, discrimination of degree of smiling or laughter, or anatomically based measures of facial activity involved in smiling/laughter). Also, the type of assessment of the affective experience might be crucial; rating scales may be more or less well anchored (e.g. defining the endpoints of the scale vs. defining each scale point clearly), the emotional quality might be more or less adequate (e.g. assessment of global happiness or of exhilaration, or amusement), and the frame for evaluating the stimuli can be stable (e.g. practice items preceding the actual stimuli allow for an emotional warm up and the establishment of a reference point for the funniness of the stimulus material to come) or changing. Further factors relate to the frequency (e.g. single vs. multiple measurements) and timing (e.g. immediate vs. delayed) of the assessment of affective experience and facial expressions.

Although these considerations should influence the *general* level of the correlations obtained, Ruch (1990) argued that the design chosen to compute the correlations is also a major—if not the most important—determinant of the actual size of the coefficients. Thus, it was claimed that for a given set of data, the strength of the relationship between smiling/laughing and funniness judgements will vary in a predictable way depending on what data analysis strategy is applied. In other words, the experimenters' choice of a particular design predetermines the range of coefficients to be obtained, as well as the conclusions drawn about the strength of the relationship between judged funniness and smiling—or more generally—between facial expression and affective experience. Furthermore, it was argued that the inconsistent and low correlations obtained in prior studies are really an artefact based on violations of the requirements for the computation of correlations.

Five Ways to Compute the Correlations between Smiling/Laughing and Judgements of Funniness

Ruch's (1990) review of studies of the relationship between smiling/laughing and judged funniness showed that five different correlational designs—or data analysis strategies—have been used. In general, the computation has been based on two data matrices: one for verbal judgements and one for facial expression. In both matrices, n subjects give responses to m stimuli. The m responses can be added (summed across stimuli) and form an individual's total appreciation score (row total). Conversely, the n responses to a stimulus can be added (summed across subjects) to form a total appreciation score for each stimulus (column total). The five designs differ with respect to whether correlations for data-pairs (e.g. smiling and judgements of funniness) are computed across columns, rows, or columns and rows simultaneously, and whether raw or aggregated data are used. Table 4.1 shows the five different designs.

In Design A (between-subjects design for aggregated data), the correlation between the corresponding row totals (total appreciation scores for a given subject) of the two matrices is computed. One coefficient is obtained expressing the strength of relationship between subjects' perception of funniness of the total set of stimuli presented and the frequency of smiles (or laughter) displayed in response to them. A high coefficient indicates that subjects who smile more often also find the jokes more funny. In Design B (within-subjects design for aggregated data), the correlation between the corresponding column totals (total appreciation scores for a given stimulus) of the two matrices is computed. The resulting coefficient reflects the strength of relationship be-

TABLE 4.1. Designs used to correlate affective experience and overt behaviour

Design	Correlated across	Data used	Aggregated across	No. of Resulting Coefficients
A	n Subjects	Total scores	Stimuli	1
B	m Stimuli	Total scores	Subject	1
C	n Subjects	Raw scores	n.a.	m
D	m Stimuli	Raw scores	n.a.	n
E	n Subjects and m Stimuli	Raw scores	n.a.	1

Note: A = between-subjects design for aggregated data. B = within-subjects design for aggregated data. C = between-subjects design for raw data. D = within-subjects design for raw data. E = across all stimuli and subjects design. n.a. = not applicable.

ween the degree of funniness of the jokes (as perceived by all subjects) and the frequency of smiles induced by them. A high coefficient means that funnier jokes also elicit more smiles.

Designs C and D correspond to Designs A and B, respectively; however, they are based on raw rather than aggregated data. In Design C (between-subjects design for raw data), the correlations between the corresponding columns of the two matrices are computed separately for each joke, and are computed across all subjects. A high coefficient indicates that subjects who tend to find a particular joke funnier also tend to smile more in response to it. One coefficient is obtained for each stimulus, and the median of these m coefficients represents the strength of the relationship. In Design D (within-subjects design for raw data), the correlations between the corresponding rows of the two matrices are computed separately for each subject. They are computed across all stimuli, resulting in n coefficients (one for each subject). Again, the median can be used to represent the average strength of relationship. A high coefficient here shows that the more a particular subject tends to find the jokes funny, the more likely it is that he or she also smiles in response to them. Finally, in Design E (across all stimuli and subjects design) the separation of subjects and stimuli is dissolved and the matrix is treated as a long $(n \times m)$ vector of data points. Thus, the correlation is computed across subjects (rows) *and* stimuli (columns) simultaneously, resulting in only one coefficient. A high coefficient means that in general (regardless of effects associated with subjects or stimuli), higher ratings of funniness are more likely than lower ratings to be accompanied by smiles.

All five designs have been used to analyse humour appreciation data, but a particular study has typically employed only one design; two were occasionally used, but no study has employed all five strategies. Researchers have not given reasons for choosing the particular design used; nor have they discussed the implications associated with them.

The Role of Design in Determining the Size of Coefficients: Two Premises and Four Deductions

What is the basis for assuming that the different designs have an impact on the size of the coefficients obtained? What is the typical rank order of the five designs with respect to the size of the coefficients they produce? Two basic assumptions permit the deduction of statements about the rank order of the designs.

First, *differences between individuals affect the behaviour-experience discrepancy more strongly than differences between stimuli.* Thus, it is assumed that the variability in response patterns to different stimuli is lower than the variability in response patterns which exists among different people. Let us consider three hypothetical response patterns; one which represents the expected level of emotional expression for a given subjective experience, and two which deviate in the direction of hyper- and hypo-expressivity. All three response patterns are equally consistent, however. In the first case, affective experience and overt behaviour are balanced, i.e. with increasing degree of felt emotion, the intensity of facial expression increases. In the case of humour, this means that there is no smiling when no funniness is perceived. With increasing funniness, however, a faint smile appears, then a strong smile, a laugh, and finally a strong laugh. Hyper-expressivity represents one kind of imbalance between behaviour and experience; stronger forms of expression are shown at any given level of affective experience. For example, laughs occur at lower levels of funniness. In hypo-expressivity, there is a shift in the other direction; the intensity of the behaviour is *below* what might be expected from the level of affective experience. In the case of humour, this means that smiling or laughter only occur at very high levels of funniness.

What characteristics of the person can cause deviations from balanced expressivity? They include both temporary and habitual factors. For example, individuals in a cheerful mood smile even at jokes which are not very funny, whereas those in a more serious state produce the same intensity of smile only if the joke is very funny. On the other hand, some individuals habitually smile or laugh more easily than others do, although they do not differ in the intensity of felt affect. For example, one might expect that at comparable levels of judged funniness, extraverts laugh, ambiverts smile, and introverts do not even smile. However, such variations might also be a mere artefact resulting from the inter-individually different use of rating scales.

What factors on the stimulus side may cause deviations from balanced expressivity? There are reasons to assume that different types of humour (e.g. sexual humour vs. puns) judged to have comparable levels of funniness may induce a disproportionately high or low level of overt responses. "Display rules", for example, can influence expressivity without influencing verbal judgements. In the presence of others, it might be appropriate to intensify, reduce, or even suppress smiling or laughter. There is no cause, however, to assume that different jokes will be accompanied by disproportionately stronger or weaker facial expressions if *spontaneous* expressions are not affected by display rules. Although one humour category (e.g. sexual humour) may produce greater laughter than another (e.g. puns), this greater appreciation should be reflected in higher funniness ratings, as well as more laughter. However, it should not yield hyper-expressivity, as defined above. Thus, the first postulate claims that the degree of hypo- or hyper-expressivity which occurs in the case of reactions to humour is more likely the result of differences among people than differences among jokes or cartoons.

Deduction 1, then, is that Design D produces higher coefficients than Design C. For *within*-subjects correlations (Design D) the increasing degree of deviation from balanced expressivity might reduce the size of the coefficient due to floor or ceiling effects. For example, hyper-expressive subjects will not smile until reaching a certain level of affective experience. However, the same amount of imbalance (hyper- *and* hypo-expressivity) in a sample will reduce the coefficient more strongly if the correlation is computed *across* subjects (Design C). In the latter case, for example, a judgement of a joke as moderately funny (e.g. a 4 on a 1–7 scale) could accompany no facial response, a smile, or a laugh in hypo-expressive, balanced, or hyper-expressive subjects, respectively.

The second assumption needs little explanation as it is known from measurement theory: *Aggregation of data may average out other sources of variation, and enhances reliability.* The greater the number of items used to measure a construct, the more reliable the measurement gets. However, different effects can be expected for aggregation of data across *stimuli* and across *subjects.* When summing responses to the stimuli across *subjects,* the effects of differences among subjects average out and the differences between the stimuli get more reliable in both the funniness and the facial expression data. The degree of a person's balance or imbalance is present in all jokes, so it is

kept constant. The differences among stimuli with respect to their exhilarating potential, however, are more reliably measured as an effect of the aggregation. Thus, it follows that Design B yields higher coefficients than Design D (*Deduction 2*), i.e. the aggregation of data for within-subjects designs increases the size of the coefficient (with
the amount of increase being a function of the sample size).

Summing the subject's responses across the *stimuli*, however, has a different effect. On one hand, one can expect the aggregation of data to stabilise the variance due
to different levels of appreciation of humour; i.e. the fact that some people tend to like
humour more than others is more reliably assessed by many items than by one item
only. However, repeated measurement also makes individual differences in the form of
expressivity more reliable; the same degree of judged funniness of the cartoons or jokes
might be associated with few smiles in hypo-expressives but with many facial responses in hyper-expressives. These differences should be more noticeable than in the
case of responses to single stimuli, as—in individual jokes—both types of subject
might fail to smile at low levels of funniness, but laugh at very high levels of funniness.
Thus, one can assume that the aggregation of data in the across-subjects designs will
not yield an increase in the size of the coefficients comparable to the one for the within-
subjects designs. Whether there is an increase at all, no difference, or even a decrease
depends on the relative size of the variance due to the form of expressivity and the variance due to general appreciation of humour. The greater the predominance of the former, the more likely the coefficient for A will be lower than the one for C; conversely,
the more the latter is predominant, the more likely the coefficient for A will be equal to,
or even higher than, the one for C. Thus, no specific prediction about differences between Designs A and C can be made. However, it is clear that Design B will also exceed the coefficients of Design A (*Deduction 3*). Finally, as Design E incorporated both
the effects of subjects and of stimuli, one can expect that the obtained coefficient will
be between the ones for Design D and Design C (*Deduction 4*).

Given that the two postulates are correct, one can expect the deduced rank order of
the designs when analysing a particular data set with the *amount* of difference being affected by several factors, such as the number of data points aggregated, or the amount
individual differences in expressivity present. It should be noted, however, that although the impact of the designs on the size of the coefficients obtained can and will be
empirically *demonstrated,* this is not a case for the involvement of *statistical inference.*
Different data analysis strategies cannot be statistically compared to each other, irrespective of how obviously they yield different results. The validity of the factors involved in the premises (from which the differences among the design are deduced) can
be examined, however, and the present study will examine one basis of the first postulate (assuming that the second postulate will be commonly subscribed to).

It was argued (Ruch, 1990) that the best way to demonstrate the impact of the designs on the size of the coefficients is to apply all data analysis strategies to the same set
of data. Although the 25 studies reviewed provided clear evidence for three of the predictions deduced, this review was limited by the fact that the studies compared differed
not only with respect to the designs employed, but also with respect to other possible
influential factors (e.g. assessment methods used, sample size, number of stimuli). Furthermore, the low number of studies employing Designs E and C, and the wide range of
size of the coefficients (ranging from below zero to higher than 0.80) in Designs A, C,
and D, did not allow for a reliable estimation of an average coefficient.

The Present Experiment

The focus of the present article is the attempt to illuminate some of the mechanisms that gave rise to doubts that facial expression and affective experience are highly inter-related. Generally, the idea advanced in the present paper is that low correlations should not inevitably be interpreted as nonconsistent response patterns or as evidence of a behaviour-experience discrepancy. When low coefficients have been obtained in the past, this might also have been due to the fact that an inappropriate design was employed in the data analysis or that method artefacts were not detected.

Thus, the *main* aim of the present study is to demonstrate using a single data set that the strength of the relationship between facial expression and affective experience varies in the predicted way as a function of the design used to compute the correlations. This phenomenon will be examined for all three experimental groups separately and for the total sample.

The *second* aim of the present study is to replicate the low coefficients reported for three variables and to clarify their causes. Specifically, it will be evaluated whether the effects of alcohol on the size of the coefficients reported by Weaver et al. (1985) is restricted to between-subjects designs. Although it is expected that intake of alcohol significantly reduces the relationship between funniness and overt behaviour in Design A (as found by Weaver et al., 1985), it is assumed that alcohol alters the balance between experience and behaviour differently in different subjects *without* reducing the consistency of the response patterns. In other words, will be demonstrated that the hyper- and hypo-expressive subjects of the high alcohol group who are responsible for reducing the size of the coefficients in Design A, in fact have a highly consistent response patterns (i.e. yield high coefficients in Design D). Assuming that the view that alcohol primarily induces hyper-expressiveness is correct (see Weaver et al., 1985, who note that it is commonly assumed that alcohol makes one "laugh at poorer jokes") the number of hyper-expressive subjects will be higher in the alcohol groups than in the control group, whereas the number of hyper-expressives will not differ. Furthermore, it will be evaluated whether the coefficients are higher for tendentious forms of humour than for nontendentious humour, as found by Branch et al. (1973). Finally, it will be evaluated why laughter results in lower correlations than smiling (Branch et al., 1973; Porterfield et al., 1988).

The *third* aim of the present study is to investigate one of the factors which formed the basis for the postulate that lower coefficients can be expected when the relationship between affective experience and facial expression is studied across subjects as compared to within subjects. It will be examined whether the degree of cheerful mood can account for the subjects' differences in expressivity; i.e. whether subjects low and high in state cheerfulness are characterised by hypo- and hyper-expressiveness, respectively.

Method

Subjects

Sixty-three paid female nonpsychology students volunteered to participate in this experiment. They were screened according to several criteria, such as medication, current health status, history of alcohol problems, possible pregnancy, and quality of vision. The videotapes of two subjects were partly unscoreable, leaving 61 subjects. Their age ranged from 19 to 30 years (M = 22.9; SD = 3.0 years).

Procedure

Overview

A first meeting served to inform subjects about the aim and the course of the experiment. They were told that they were participating in a study examining the effects of alcohol intake on finger dexterity and that depending on which group they were in, they might receive a relatively low dose of alcohol. Their height and weight were determined and subjects were asked to avoid eating during the three hours prior to participating in the main experiment. Approximately one week later subjects returned for the main experiment lasting 90 minutes and were tested individually by a female experimenter. They first completed a mood inventory and a test measuring ability to concentrate. They then received, under double-blind conditions, a beverage which they consumed within five minutes. Subsequently, they completed several dexterity tests and answered the mood scale again. After the period of induction of exhilaration they worked on the dexterity tests again.

Upon completion of the experiment the experimenter opened an envelope which contained the code for the beverages and informed the subject about the content of the beverage. Subjects in the experimental groups were given special attention while the effects of the alcohol wore off. None of the subjects reported any sign of discomfort. When debriefed, they were informed that the main aim of the experiment was to study facial responses to humour, and that the camera served this purpose rather than filming their dexterity. All subjects gave consent to have their tapes analysed.

Consumption of Alcoholic Beverage

Subjects of all three groups consumed a beverage containing a mixture of peppermint water and grapefruit juice prepared by the experimenter of the first session. The subjects of the control group (C) drank this mixture only, but 0.22g and 0.39g alcohol per kg body weight was added for the subjects of the low (E_1) and high (E_2) dose alcohol groups, respectively. For the latter two groups a 90% ethanol was used and was mixed with peppermint water on a 1:1 basis and filled up to 0.21g with grapefruit juice. These manipulations were expected to lead to blood alcohol levels of 0.4‰ and 0.7‰ (Forth, Henschler, & Rummel, 1975). For the sake of clarity, the two experimental groups are referred to as low and high alcohol groups in the present study, although these levels of blood alcohol should be regarded as low and medium doses, respectively; "high dose" is typically reserved for levels from 1.0‰ to 1.5‰ (Pandina, 1982). No high dose was used, as elevation of positive affect can mainly be expected for low and medium doses (Forth et al., 1975). The doses applied can be expected to be effective after 25–35 minutes (Forth et al., 1975; Ideström & Cadenius, 1968; McCollam, Burish, Maisto, & Sobell, 1980; Sidell & Pless, 1971). Hence, the exhilaration-induction procedures began 30 minutes after consumption of the beverage. The application of the dexterity tests not only helped bridge this period of time; it should also have confirmed to subjects that the purpose of the experiment was the examination of dexterity under states of alcohol intoxication.

Assessment of Cheerful Mood

The degree of cheerful mood was assessed by means of the short version of the *Eigen-schaftswörterliste* (EWL-K: Janke & Debus, 1978), a mood questionnaire aimed at providing a comprehensive assessment of mood state. The EWL-K contains a list of 123 mood-descriptive adjectives which are answered in a yes/no format, and provides scores for 14 mood dimensions. There is no separate scale of cheerfulness; however, a measure of cheerful mood was derived by combining the six items of the "elation" scale which directly relate to cheerfulness. The EWL-K was administered twice to subjects; at the beginning of the experiment and immediately before the period of induction of exhilaration. It was expected that only degree of cheerful mood at the second administration would predict the degree of exhilaration induced.

Induction of Exhilaration

Subjects sat in a comfortable chair in a slightly darkened part of the room and were presented one of two permutations of a set 35 black and white slides of jokes and cartoons at an interval of 25 seconds. The selection of humour stimuli was based on a taxonomy of jokes and cartoons (Ruch, 1992). The three categories of incongruity-resolution humour, nonsense humour, and sexual humour were represented by 10 slides each. This set was preceded by five "warming-up" humour stimuli which were not used in any analyses.

Verbal Responses

The subjects were instructed to rate all 35 stimuli according to six criteria. Two 7-point Likert scales assessed perceived *funniness* and *aversiveness*. The degree of funniness served as an indicator of the degree of exhilaration induced. Subjects also indicated in a yes/no format whether they found the humour stimulus *childish, tasteless,* or *boring,* and whether they already had heard or seen the jokes or cartoons before.

Facial Measurement

Measurements were made from colour videotapes, which provided a close-up, head-on view of the subject's face. The camera was visible to subjects, but subjects in a pilot study, as well as in the main experiment, reported not having felt disturbed by the camera and that they believed that the camera was focused on their hand in order to assess dexterity. The measurements were based on the Facial Action Coding System (FACS: Ekman & Friesen, 1978). The FACS is an anatomically based, comprehensive, objective technique for measuring all observable facial movement. It distinguishes 44 action units (AUs). These are the minimal units that are anatomically separate and visually distinguishable. Five AUs were of relevance in the present study and their frequency, intensity (slight, moderate, extreme), symmetry/asymmetry, and duration were coded according to the criteria given in the FACS manual. Three action units, AU12, AU6, and AU7 were expected to occur as part of both smiling and laughter. AU12 refers to the contraction of the zygomatic major, which pulls the lip corner up diagonally toward the cheekbone. AU6 and AU7 describe the actions of the outer and inner part of the orbicularis oculi muscle, respectively. The action of the former raises the cheek and causes crow's feet and wrinkles below the eye; the latter raises and tightens the lower eye lid. "Smiles" which contained AU13 or AU14 (alone or together with AU12) were not considered to represent positive affective responses to humour (Ruch, 1990). AU13 refers to the contraction of the caninus muscle which pulls the lip corner up sharply and puffs up cheeks. AU14 describes the dimple-like wrinkles at lip corners produced by the contraction of the buccinator muscle. Also, if AU12 was asymmetrical and shorter than two-thirds of a second, it was excluded from the analyses.

Additionally, the occurrence of laughter was coded. A laugh was defined as an initial forced exhalation, followed by a more or less sustained sequence of repeated expirations of high frequency and low amplitude, which may or may not be phonated as "ha-ha-ha". Episodes of a single audible forced expiration occurring together with AU12 formed the lower end of the intensity spectrum of events coded as laughter. However, a fully developed laughter pattern was generally observed.

The 1830 responses (30 stimuli x 61 subjects) were coded independently by two coders. In case of disagreement, they watched the relevant responses together until agreement was achieved. The general degree of agreement between the two coders based on 550 responses (composed of the five "warm-up" jokes, as well as tapes of pilot subjects) was 93.1%.

Results

Impact of Design on the Size of the Coefficients

Product-moment correlations between judged funniness and frequency of AU12 were computed for each of the three groups separately, as well as for the total sample. All five correlational designs were used. The results are presented in table 4.2.

Table 4.2 shows that in all three experimental groups (as well as the total sample) the within-subjects designs (D and B) yielded higher coefficients than the between-subjects designs (C and A), both for raw and aggregated data[1] supporting Hypothesis 1 and 3, respectively. Furthermore, the aggregation of data in the within-subjects designs (B and D) yielded an increase of coefficients in all three groups (Hypothesis 2). The fact that the total sample yielded a higher coefficient than the three separate groups for Design B reflects the effect of the aggregation of data; the coefficient is based on the sum of data for 61, rather than 20 or 21 subjects. Accordingly, the difference between B and

TABLE 4.2. Correlations between judged funniness and appearance of AU12

	Design				
	A	B	C	D	E
Total sample	0.55	0.96	0.61	0.71	0.63
No alcohol	0.65	0.86	0.61	0.74	0.62
Low alcohol	0.54	0.92	0.63	0.69	0.64
High alcohol	0.28	0.87	0.62	0.72	0.60

Note: A = between-subjects design for aggregated data. B = within-subjects design for aggregated data. C = between-subjects design for raw data. D = within-subjects design for raw data. E = across all stimuli and subjects design. The results for Designs C and D are median values of several correlations.

D was higher (0.25) for the total sample than for the average (0.17) of the three groups. Finally, in partial support of Hypothesis 4 the coefficient of Design E (across all stimuli and subjects) was between those for C and D, although closer to C in all cases except the high alcohol group.

The aggregation of data for the between-subjects designs (A and C) yielded inconsistent effects. Although in the group of nonintoxicated subjects the coefficient for Design A (aggregated data) was slightly higher than the one for Design C (raw data), the coefficients decreased in the alcohol groups (and in the total sample).

Causes of Negative Coefficients

When computing correlations involving the designs for raw data, a minimum of three occurrences of AU12 was required for jokes (Design C) or subjects (Design D) to be included in the analysis presented in table 4.1. This criterion excluded 11 subjects for Design D, and because three subjects had no response at all, the median coefficient is based on 47 subjects. The range of coefficients was from 0.39 to 0.89. In the case of Design C, each joke elicited more than three responses in the total sample. The coefficients for Design C ranged from 0.33 to 0.77. However, in the separate analyses of the three experimental groups, 6, 7, and 9 (out of 30) humour stimuli were excluded for the control group, low and high alcohol groups,[2] respectively.

Coefficients based on *fewer* responses were computed as well and showed considerable variability, ranging from 0.14 to 0.85 for Design C, and from −0.25 to 0.92 for Design D. Although the low frequency-based coefficients account for *all* of the low and negative coefficients, they do not necessarily have to be low, e.g. the median of the excluded coefficients in Design D was 0.57. When only subjects with five or more responses were considered, no coefficient in Design D was below 0.50. Thus, it may well be that the negative or very low positive coefficients observed by Ruch's (1990) review of studies were derived from similarly skewed binary data.

The Effect of Alcohol

Table 4.1 shows that Weaver et al.'s (1985) findings can be replicated; they used Design A (between-subjects, aggregated data) and found that while rated funniness and facial expression are significantly correlated ($P < 0.01$) among nonintoxicated subjects, the coefficient for the high alcohol group (E_2) was nonsignificant. In the present sample, the difference between the control group and E_2 was very large (0.37) and just failed to reach significance ($P = 0.065$, one-tailed).[3] However, the fact that no such intoxication-based effects can be observed for the other four designs casts doubt on the proposition that alcohol intoxication really generally impairs the correspondence between verbal reports and facial expressiveness.

But why does Design A yield such a low correlation for the high alcohol group? Technically, low and high correlation scatter plots differ from each other by the disproportionate high representation of subjects off the main diagonal in the former. Given the present context, there must be subjects which either rate jokes high in funniness but smile infrequently or smile more often than expectable from the lower ratings. The critical question now is whether these subjects (who reduce the coefficients for Design A in the high alcohol group) do indeed respond inconsistently to the humour stimuli or have a *consistent* response pattern (which is, however, altered in the direction of hypo- or hyper-expressivity).

Figure 4.1 presents the relationship between rated funniness and AU12-frequency for the control group and the high alcohol group. An expressiveness index was computed by dividing the frequency of AU12 by total funniness. This ratio was multiplied by 6 to correct for the differences in range of possible scores. Individuals more than one standard deviation above and below the mean were considered to be hyper- and hypo-expressives, respectively.

Figure 4.1 shows that this index detects four hypo-expressive individuals in each of the two groups; thus, hypo-expressiveness is a factor lowering the coefficients produced by Design A irrespective of alcohol intake. Although the total response rate of these 8 subjects was too low as compared to degree of rated funniness, their individual response patterns were highly co-ordinated. Their few responses were consistently displayed in response to the jokes they judged funniest; hence all hypo-expressives yielded high coefficients in Design D (within-subjects, raw data).

There were 3 and 6 hyper-expressive subjects in the control and high alcohol groups, respectively. The 5 subjects with the lowest funniness ratings (below 30) in the high alcohol group demonstrate the phenomenon of hyper-expressiveness nicely. Although they found the jokes only mildly funny (average of less than "1" on a 0–6 scale) they showed an average frequency of facial responses (i.e. between 3 and 6 AU12 displays, $M = 5.2$), and most of these responses were of higher intensity. Nevertheless, they (like the other hyper-expressives) have a very consistent response pattern. Their coefficients in Design D ranged from 0.71 to 0.92 ($M = 0.81$) and are thus clearly above the average (see table 4.1). Thus, the other type of unbalanced expressivity, namely hyper-expressiveness also does not allow one to draw the conclusion that alcohol impairs the correspondence between affective experience and facial expression. The difference is that while hyper-expressives begin to display smiles at funniness ratings of 0 to 2 (median = 1), the median of these funniness—"thresholds" for hypo-expressives is 5.

Although, without doubt, alcohol does not lower the consistency of individual response patterns, the exact mechanisms causing the low coefficient of Design A in the high alcohol group remain unclear. Compared to the control group there were twice as many hyper-expressive subjects in E_2, but this difference is not statistically significant. Figure 4.1 demonstrates a formal cause; the variability of both AU12-frequency and rated funniness is reduced in E_2 as compared to C [although only the former is significant, $F(19,19) = 2.89$; $P < 0.05$]. Although hyper-expressiveness among subjects who do not judge the jokes to be very funny contributes to the reduction of variability of facial responses, it does not fully account for it.

Does Laughter Really Fail to Reflect Humour Appreciation?

The following pattern of correlations with funniness judgements was obtained for all experimental groups, and for all designs used: the coefficients for AU12 (lip corner puller) were always highest, followed by AU6 (cheek raiser), laughter, and AU7 (lid tightener). The respective coefficients for the total sample for Design E (across all stimuli and subjects) were 0.63, 0.52, 0.29, and 0.19.

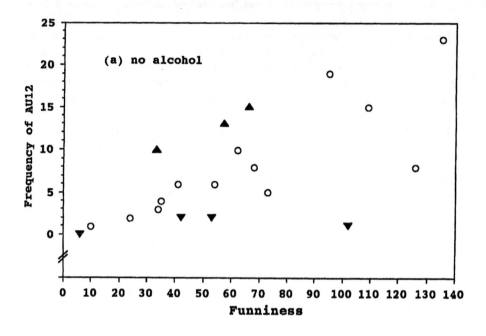

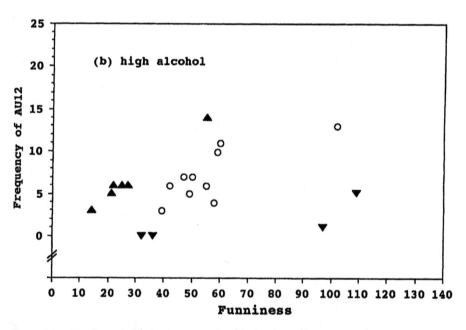

Figure 4.1 Scatterplots of the total scores for judged funniness and AU12-frequency for the control group (a) and the high alcohol group (b). (▲ hyper-; O, normo-; ▼ hypo-expressive subjects.)

Do different elements of exhilaration behaviour indeed differ in their ability to reflect the amount of humour appreciation? Several considerations prohibit this conclusion. First, laughter represents higher intensity levels of exhilaration than does smiling (Ruch, 1990); why should a more intense manifestation of exhilaration be a poorer indicator of the affective experience? Secondly, it is known (Ekman & Friesen, 1982; Ekman, Friesen, & O'Sullivan, 1988) that the presence of the action of the orbicularis oculi marks the felt happy smile; thus, higher coefficients should be expected for the joint action of AU12 and AU6, than for AU12 alone.

Thirdly and most importantly, it has not yet been considered that the maximal coefficient obtainable in point biserial correlations depends on the distribution of the binary variable, i.e. the relative frequency of the AUs. The form of the relationship between relative frequency and maximal coefficients can be described as an inverted-U function: The more the relative frequency deviates (in both directions) from 0.50, the lower the maximal possible size coefficient. Whereas AU12 occurred relatively often (432 cases), the other behaviours were displayed less frequently, the order of occurrence being the same with which the coefficients decrease (AU6 = 258, laughter = 71, and AU7 = 31). In test theory an index has been advanced to allow an evaluation of item-total correlations for items with different endorsement frequency (*Selektionskennwert;* Lienert, 1969). If this index (division of the coefficient by twice the variance of the binary variable) is computed, the resulting values of AU12 (0.75), AU6 (0.74), laughter (0.76), and AU7 (0.73) do not differ from each other. Thus, it is safe to assume that smiling and laughter equally well signify exhilaration.

Effects of Type of Humour?

The use of three humour categories in the present experiment allows for a test of the hypothesis advanced by Branch et al. (1973) that the correlation between judged funniness and overt behaviour will be higher for tendentious than for nontendentious humour. Separate analyses were performed for the humour categories of incongruity-resolution, nonsense, and sexual humour. No systematic effect could be observed. First, the differences in size of correlation were not consistent across the designs, i.e. depending on the design, incongruity-resolution humour (Designs B and E), nonsense (Design C), or sexual humour (Design A) were highest. Secondly, the differences in size of coefficients were generally negligibly small. Thirdly, where differences between the three humour types existed, they were probably due to the different response frequencies, i.e. the order among the humour categories with respect to the size of the coefficients and the size of the means was identical.

Does Cheerfulness Affect Expressiveness?

In order to determine whether the degree of cheerfulness of one's mood can account for individual differences in expressivity, two types of analyses were undertaken. First, the correlations between subjects' degree of cheerfulness (i.e. the score in the subscale of the EWL-K, at the second administration) and funniness "threshold" for facial expression (i.e. the minimal funniness rating which was accompanied by an overt facial response) were computed. The coefficients were computed across the whole sample, because a Kruskal-Wallis analysis showed that the three groups did not differ from each other with respect to degree of cheerfulness ($P = 0.76$) or threshold of AU12 ($P = 0.78$). The rank order correlation between degree of cheerful mood and the funniness threshold for AU12 [$R(58) = -0.27$, $P < 0.05$] confirms that subjects in a more cheerful mood show facial responses at lower minimal levels of rated funniness than do less cheerful subjects.

Second, the ability of cheerfulness to predict degree of judged funniness and facial behaviour was compared. Whereas the coefficient for funniness (0.21, n.s.) was not significant, cheerful mood correlated significantly with the frequency (0.33, $P < 0.01$) and intensity (0.29, $P < 0.05$) of AU12, the maximal response[4] shown (0.41, $P < 0.01$), the joint action of AU12 and AU6 (0.28, $P < 0.05$), and the frequency of laughter (0.40, $P < 0.01$). Thus, subjects who were high and low in cheerfulness differed with respect to the frequency and intensity of facial behaviour shown, but not in terms of their judgements of funniness. Identical conclusion can be drawn from the analysis of nonintoxicated subjects; the coefficients range from 0.33 for judged funniness ($P < 0.15$) to 0.59 for laughter ($P < 0.001$) and 0.61 for the maximal response shown ($P < 0.01$).

Thus, states of high cheerful mood go along with hyper-expressivity, and low cheerful mood goes along with hypo-expressivity. These effects were only found for the assessment of cheerful mood immediately before the beginning of the induction of exhilaration. The degree of cheerfulness at the beginning of the experiment did not significantly predict verbal or facial responses to humour. The average correlation between the two testing times was 0.67 (ranging from 0.29 in E_2 to 0.90 in the control group). Also, although the cheerfulness measure was composed of a subset of the items of the elation scale, the coefficients for the total elation scale were consistently lower than those obtained for the cheerfulness items. This justifies the use of a separate cheerfulness scale, and signifies the importance of this concept in research on exhilaration.

Discussion

The aim of the present study was to draw attention to the fact that the size of the correlation coefficient obtained between measures of facial expression and affective experience is influenced by several methodological factors. Low coefficients might be based on artefacts. The failure to consider them has led to unjustified conclusions about the nature and strength of the relationship between funniness and smiling, and perhaps even about facial expression and affective experience in general. An experiment was conducted which attempted (a) to replicate the empirical basis on which several such conclusions are based, and (b) to demonstrate that these conclusions are not justified.

It was argued that the approach used to compute the correlations constitutes the major neglected factor; even for a given data set it produces systematic variations in the size of the coefficients to be obtained. Starting from two premises, four statements about the relative size of the coefficients produced by the different data analysis strategies were deduced. All three experimental groups as well as the total sample were used to illustrate these predictions. Combining the four deductions (D > C; B > A; B > D; D > E > C) one arrives at B > D > E > C being the typical rank order of the data analysis strategies regarding the size of the coefficients to be obtained for them. Design A cannot be unambiguously located in this sequence. It is certainly below B and most likely below D, but whether it falls below or above C depends on whether—and to what extent—factors which increase the amount of variation on the hypo- versus hyper-expressiveness dimensions are the present in that data set.

Differential alcohol effects seem to be among such sorts of variance. Whereas for the group of nonintoxicated subjects the difference between the highest and lowest coefficient was 0.25, this range increased in 0.59 in the high alcohol group! This was almost exclusively due to the reduction of the coefficients obtained for strategy A. As in the study by Weaver et al. (1985), the coefficient was not significantly different from zero in the high alcohol condition. Additionally, the present study verified a significant decrease as compared to the control group. However, the emergence of this phenomenon seems to be contingent on two factors: Analysis *across* subjects and data *aggregation*. Only the across-subjects analysis is affected by individual differences in type of expressiveness (between-subjects analyses keep them constant) and data aggregation is needed to make this variance more reliable. The importance of the latter can be estimated from the fact that no reduction was observable for strategy C, where the coefficients were also computed across subjects. The nature of this differential[5] alcohol effect could not be substantiated, however. The doubling of the number of hyper-expressives was not significant. It appears that for a verification of this hypothesis a larger sample size is needed, or the same subjects would have to be studied in both intoxicated and nonintoxicated states using parallel sets of humour. The latter strategy would also allow one to study whether alcohol leads to an increase in overt behaviour, or to a decrease in perceived funniness, or both. Whatever the nature of this effect turns out to be, the present study clearly contradicts the postulate that alcohol consumption lowers the *coherence* between facial expression and affective experience.

Thus, the same set of data might suggest quite opposite conclusions, depending on which correlational design is used to analyse the data. Whereas the span of coefficients in the present study can be regarded as extraordinarily high (ranging from 0.28 to 0.96!), a still considerable range can be expected for control group conditions, as was verified in two replication samples (Ruch, 1990). In the replication study most similar to the present one (80 females, 42 jokes and cartoons, EMG-recordings of three facial muscles) the correlations between judged funniness and activity of the zygomatic major were 0.54, 0.89, 0.56, 0.63, and 0.58 for Designs A through E, respectively. Thus, the range of coefficients was 0.35.

Neglecting the impact of the data analysis strategy is not the only way of arriving at incorrect conclusions about the relationship between verbal evaluations and facial reactions to humour on the basis of method artefacts. The present study quite clearly demonstrated another pitfall; namely, the comparison of coefficients for variables of different skewness or response frequency. The analyses showed that is not justified to conclude that the different elements of exhilaration behaviour are correlated with judged funniness to different extents, despite the fact that the uncorrected coefficients suggested such an interpretation.[6] Similarly, the present study shows that it is safe to assume that the type of humour does *not* affect the size of the coefficients obtained. One has to keep in mind, however, that the real strength of the relationship for less frequently occurring responses is not underestimated only in the case of nonaggregated binary data (i.e. strategies C, D, and E) but also for aggregated data. Even after data aggregation, less frequently occurring responses remain less reliable than the more frequent responses, or, in the case of an insufficient number of data points, are more skewed than the latter. For example, the declining size of coefficients for AU12, AU6, laughter, and AU7 could also be observed for strategies A (0.55, 0.42, 0.20, and 0.03) and B (0.96, 0.89, 0.71, and 0.67).

The results obtained from applying the correction formula were supported by the previously mentioned replication study (Ruch, 1990), in which the actions of the zygomatic major and the orbicularis oculi were assessed with the help of facial electromyography. The frequency of actions of the two muscles was about the same, so the coefficients could not have been biased by this factor. Indeed, without any correction, the coefficients obtained for the zygomatic major and orbicularis oculi did not differ substantially in any of the five designs.

However, it is not only *methodological* factors which lower the relationship between judged funniness and smiling/laughing. The present study investigated one of the factors forming the basis for the postulate that lower coefficients can be expected when the relationship between affective experience and facial expression is studied across subjects as compared to within subjects. It was confirmed that degree of cheerful mood is associated with individual differences in expressivity. A cheerful state indeed seems to predispose to hyper-expressiveness, i.e. more cheerful individuals displayed smiling and laughter at lower levels of perceived funniness than less cheerful persons did. Thus, heterogeneity in mood level is a factor selectively affecting the across-subjects analysis. It can be expected that an experimental control of mood variation would elevate the coefficients for strategies A and C.

What is, then, the "real" relationship between affective experience and facial expression of exhilaration? Obviously it is much higher than it has previously been considered to be. First of all, even the lowest coefficient found for the nonintoxicated group (0.61) is far beyond the 0.40 which was considered to be the upper limit of the range of coefficients typically obtained in humour studies (McGhee, 1977). This was mainly due to the fact that the optimal conditions for *generally* enhanced coefficients mentioned above were chosen. Furthermore, the present experiment identified several (method- and content-related) factors which *selectively* cause low coefficients even when the actual coherence of affective experience and facial expression is quite high. It is evident that the different data analysis strategies are likely to underestimate the strength of the relationship in *different* ways. The coefficients yielded by the between-subjects designs A and C are lowered by the presence of variance subsumed under the postulated dimension of hyper- and hypo-expressiveness. The greater the variation of subjects' response pattern on this dimension, the greater the differences between within-subjects and between-subjects designs. Additionally, Design A seems to be more susceptible to such influences than Design C, as aggregation of data enhances the reliability of individual differences in expressivity. While Ruch's (1990) review of studies showed that Design A is the one more frequently used, the present findings suggest that its sole use is not recommended as it suggested an alcohol-induced behaviour experience discrepancy where in fact there was no such discrepancy. The use of strategy A in combination with D (within-subject, raw data), however, would provide a sensitive indicator for the presence of such phenomena. Although the within-subjects designs do take care of a lot of problems, such as differential expressivity, or the fact that some measurements are not comparable across subjects (e.g. absolute EMG amplitudes), they do challenge the assumption of independence of measurements and thus prohibit the use of tests of significance (which are not necessarily needed, however). Coefficients of design D may be lowered for extreme hyper- and hypo-expressive subjects due to the deviation from linearity of the regression[7] (for continuous data) or the reduced maximal size of the coefficients (for binary data). These and other effects appear to be averaged out for Design B (within-subjects, aggregated data), especially for a higher number of subjects. The coefficients obtained for strategy E (across all stimuli and subjects) are lowered by the same factors—albeit to a lower extent—that affect designs C and D. Finally, irrespective of the chosen data analysis strategy, lowered coefficients will be obtained for low frequency behaviour and particularly so in the analysis of binary data (i.e. strategies C, D, and E).

Because researchers have not yet given attention to the factors described in the present article, the conclusion commonly drawn that judgements of funniness show only a low positive relationship to overt expressions of affect is clearly premature, and probably without any foundation at all. On the contrary, it appears to be safer to assume that responses to humour can be described by a single emotion construct; both smiling/laughter and the judged funniness can be considered to indicate the same affective changes in the organism.

It appears recommendable to consider these factors also when applying the relationship between affective experience and facial expression in other emotions. Likewise, it might be of interest to consider the role of correlational designs in other areas of psychology where such dissociation effects are discussed, for example, in research on psychopathology, or effects of psychoactive drugs, or in the study of attitude-behaviour relationships.

Notes

1. It should be noted that this result cannot be explained by a greater degree of variability between stimuli than between subjects. On the subjects' side, there were 3 with no single smile and 5 subjects smiled in more than half of the 30 times. On the variable side, *all* jokes had at least three facial responses and there was only one stimulus eliciting a response in almost half (30 out of 61) of the subjects.

2. The elimination of this larger number of subjects in the high alcohol group is responsible for the discrepant result that the coefficient for C exceeds the one for E.

3. This difference was significant, however, for the intensity of AU12 (C: $r = 0.71$, $P<0.001$; E_2: $r = -0.01$, n.s.; diff $= 0.72$, $P <0.01$) and the frequency of the combined action of AU12 and AU6 (C: $r = 0.69$, $P <0.001$; E_2: $r = 0.12$, n.s.; diff $= 0.57$, $P <0.05$).

4. The maximal response was represented by the highest level of facial enjoyment coded for a subject. This 5-point index covered "no response" ($= 0$), three intensity levels of AU12-smiles, and laughter ($= 4$).

5. A *general* alcohol effect (e.g. if all subjects became equally hyperexpressive) would not reduce the coefficients of strategy A.

6. The results found by Branch et al. (1973) might have been affected by the same factors; smiling was three times more frequent than laughter.

7. Many thanks to the reviewer pointing this out.

References

Branch, A. Y., Fine, G. A., & Jones, J. M. (1973). Laughter, smiling and rating scales: An analysis of responses to tape recorded humour. *Proceedings of the 81st Annual Convention of the American Psychological Association, 8,* 189–190.

Ekman, P., & Friesen, W. V. (1978). *Facial action coding system (FACS)*. Palo Alto, CA: Consulting Psychologists Press.

Ekman, P., & Friesen, W. V. (1982). Felt, false, and miserable smiles. *Journal of Nonverbal Behavior, 6,* 238–252.

Ekman, P., Friesen, W. V., & Ancoli, S. (1980). Facial signs of emotional experience. *Journal of Personality and Social Psychology, 39,* 1125–1134.

Ekman, P., Friesen, W. V., & O'Sullivan, M. (1988). Smiles when lying. *Journal of Personality and Social Psychology, 54,* 414–420.

Forth, W., Henschler, D., & Rummel, W. (1975). *Allgemeine und spezielle Pharmakologie und Toxikologie* [General and special pharmacology and toxicology]. Mannheim: Bibliographisches Institut.

Fridlund, A. J. (1991). Sociality of solitary smiling: Potentiation by an implicit audience. *Journal of Personality and Social Psychology, 60,* 229–240.

Gavanski, I. (1986). Differential sensitivity of humor ratings and mirth responses to cognitive and affective components of the humor response. *Journal of Personality and Social Psychology, 51,* 209–214.

Godkewitsch, M. (1976). Physiological and verbal indices of arousal in rated humour. In A. J. Chapman & H. C. Foot (Eds.), *Humour and laughter: Theory, research and applications* (pp. 117–138). London: Wiley.

Ideström, C. D., & Cadenius, B. (1968). Time relations of the effects of alcohol compared to placebo. *Psychopharmacologia, 13,* 189–200.

Janke, W., & Debus, G. (1978). *Die Eigenschaftswörterliste (EWL)* [The adjective word list]. Göttingen: Hogrefe.

Lienert, G. A. (1969). *Testaufbau und Testanalyse* [Test construction]. Berlin: Beltz.

McCollam, J. B., Burish, T. G., Maisto, S. A., & Sobell, M. B. (1980). Alcohol's effects on physiological arousal and self-reported affect and sensations. *Journal of Abnormal Psychology, 89,* 224–233.

McGhee, P. E. (1977). Children's humour: A review of current research trends. In A. J. Chapman & H. C. Foot (Eds.), *It's a funny thing, humour* (pp. 199–209). Oxford: Pergamon.

Pandina, R. J. (1982). Effects of alcohol on psychological processes. In E. Gomberg, H. White, & J. Carpenter (Eds.), *Alcohol, science, and society revisited.* Ann Arbor: University of Michigan Press.

Porterfield, A. L., Mayer, F. S., Dougherty, K. G., Kredich, K. E., Kronberg, M. M., Marsec, K. M., & Okazaki, Y. (1988). Private self-consciousness, canned laughter, and responses to humorous stimuli. *Journal of Research in Personality, 22,* 409–423.

Ruch, W. (1981). Witzbeurteilung und Persönlichkeit: Eine trimodale Analyse. [Humor and personality: A three-modal analysis]. *Zeitschrift für Differentielle und Diagnostische Psychologie, 2,* 253–273.

Ruch, W. (1990). *Die Emotion Erheiterung: Alusdrucksformen und Bedingungen* [The emotion of exhilaration: Forms of expression and eliciting conditions]. Unpublished habilitations thesis, Department of Psychology, University of Düsseldorf, Germany.

Ruch, W. (1992). Assessment of appreciation of humor: Studies with the 3 WD humor test. In C. D. Spielberger & J. N. Butcher (Eds.), *Advances in personality assessment* (Vol. 9; pp. 34–87). Hillsdale, NJ: Erlbaum.

Ruch, W. (1993). Exhilaration and humor. In M. Lewis & J. M. Haviland (Eds.), *The handbook of emotion* (chap. 42; pp. 605–616). New York: Guilford.

Ruch, W., & Rath, S. (1993). The nature of humor appreciation: Toward an integration of perception of stimulus properties and affective experience. *Humor: International Journal of Humor Research, 6,* 363–384.

Sidell, F. R., & Pless, J. E. (1971). Ethyl alcohol: Blood levels and performance decrements after oral administration to men. *Psychopharmacologia, 19,* 246–261.

Weaver, J. B., Masland, J. L., Kharazmi, S., & Zillmann, D. (1985). Effect of alcoholic intoxication on the appreciation of different types of humor. *Journal of Personality and Social Psychology, 49,* 781–787.

The FACS in Humor Research

WILLIBALD RUCH

The beginning of psychology's renewed interest in humor coincided with the rise of cognitive psychology. Not surprisingly, the analysis of the information processing involved in humor appreciation dominated the models put forward at that time (see Goldstein & McGhee, 1972). Of course, smiling and laughter as very obvious responses to humor could not be overlooked, and hence usually an arrow pointed from the box depicting the successful termination of information processing to "laughter." Nevertheless, the responses to humor were conceptualized at a cognitive-experiential level only, and smiling and laughter were often merely assessed as supplements to the rating of funniness; mainly they served as more "objective" indicators of perceived funniness of a stimulus. Similarly, the first three chapters of the handbook of humor research (McGhee & Goldstein, 1983) were devoted to issues of facial expression, physiology, and cognitive/experiential processes in humor without, however, explicitly combining these three levels and acknowledging the affective nature of the responses to humor.

The causes for reluctance to conceptualize the responses to humor from an emotion psychology perspective most likely can be traced back at least to the First International Conference on Humour and Laughter held in Cardiff, Wales, in 1976 (Chapman & Foot, 1977). There the state of the art in the research of the field was appraised, and the research agenda for the years to come was set. Several authors lamented about the low correlations typically to be found between funniness ratings and smiling and laughter. Obviously, coefficients between .30 and .40 do not suggest a coherent response pattern. The data presented in the article reprinted here show that the application of highly sophisticated assessment tools, like the FACS, generally boosts the size of the coefficients; even the least favourable Design A yields a coefficient of .65 in the control group. Thus, the observed lack of coherence of the response pattern can largely be explained by methodological factors, such as inaccurate measurement or the failure to separate different types of smiles. We could replicate the impact of the correlational design on the rank-order of coefficients in further studies (the reported study actually was carried out in the late 80s) using both FACS and facial-EMG. Since the FACS allows less interindividual variations in intensity than the EMG (owing to, for example, strength of contraction, size and conformation of facial muscles, as well as to artifactual method variance, as caused by imprecise electrode placement), it can be expected that the former is more robust as regards to whether the data were analyzed between or within subjects. Indeed, in a facial-EMG study of 40 subjects and 20 stimuli the between-subject designs ($A = .26$, $C = .36$), but not the within-subject designs ($B = .70$, $D = .56$) gave the impression that intensity of facial expression (mean amplitude for zygomatic major muscle region) and affective experience are not highly intercorrelated (Ruch & van Thriel, 1994).

Further justification to keep smiling and laughter apart from perceived funniness was provided by the fact that both occur in nonhumorous situations as well; i.e., they hardly could be seen as genuine expressions of humor. This point of view was almost inevitable since at that time there was no basis yet for distinguishing types of smiling or laughter on a morphological level. While qualities like "humorous," derisive," or "nervous" were attributed to laughter, after all, it was still "laughter" as an entity. In our lab we began to identify and separate the types of smiling occurring in response to traditional (i.e., jokes and cartoons, funny videos) and nontraditional (i.e., the weight-judging task as a vehicle transporting the incongruity) humor stimuli. While the enjoyment smile definitely is the response occurring when the humor was successful, smiles based on the caninus and buccinator (often asymmetric) occurred as well.

A third issue discussed at the conference related to the relationship between smiling and laughter and their assessment. One position was that the presumably different phylogenetic development of smiling and laughter should be taken as granted; and therefore smiling and laughter are best kept as separate dependent variables (quantified by frequency or duration only). The fact that one can either respond to a humor stimulus with smiling or with laughter (but obviously not with both) has at least three consequences. First, in the sample of responses, smiling and laughter are correlated negatively. Second, potential treatment effects dilute since they are spread over two dependent variables (their mutual exclusive scoring additionally increasing the variances). Third, this view is, of course, maximally different from a postulation of coherent emotional response pattern considering experiential, behavioral, and physiological levels. The other line of thinking considered the whole spectrum of responses as being unidimensional, ranging from negative to positive. This can be best exemplified by the so-called mirth-index (Zigler, Levine, & Gould, 1966), which was scored for negative response (−1), no response (0), half-smile (1), full smile (2), chuckle (3), and laughter (4). This scoring does not allow for blends of emotions (e.g., enjoyment of an embarrassing theme), and it is also unclear into what category masking or phony smiles would be placed by the coders. There is support, however, for the assumption that smiling and laughter indeed represent different levels of intensity of exhilaration (or amusement); laughing occurs at higher levels of exhilaration, and smiling is typical of lower levels. Also, different intensities of smiling reflect different degrees of exhilaration (Ruch, 1990). We currently try to replicate these findings and try to stretch them out to different levels of laughter. Also, we plan to study the type of relationship between smiling and laughing for different emotions as well; for example, there might be a quantitative relationship between the smile and laugh of contempt, both based on the contraction of zygomatic major and buccinator (the contraction of the latter facilitating the articulation position of the vowel typically ascribed to derisive laughter).

All in all, the reprinted study, as well as related ones, gave me corroboration to further pursue the study of humor from an emotion perspective. Also, it made it obvious to me that experimental humor research will profit from adopting the recent advances made in emotion research. This includes the assessment technologies developed (be it facial-EMG or anatomically based coding systems), as well as the theoretical advances such as the identification of different types of smiles and the markers that help to distinguish among them. On the other hand, humor research is an exciting field to study basic emotion phenomena.

References

Chapman, A. J., & Foot, H. C. (Eds.). (1977). *It's a funny thing, humour.* Oxford: Pergamon Press.

Goldstein, J. H., & McGhee, P. E. (Eds.). (1972). *The psychology of humor.* New York: Academic Press.

McGhee, P. E., & Goldstein, J. H. (Eds.). (1983). *Handbook of humor research, Vol. 1: Basic Issues.* New York: Springer.

Ruch, W., & van Thriel, C. (1994). Coherence of facial expression and affective experience of surprise and exhilaration? A facial-EMG study. *International Society for Humor Studies Conference,* Ithaca College, New York, June 22–26.

Ruch, W. (1990). Die emotion erheiterung: Ausdrucksformen und bedingungen. Unpublished habilitation thesis. University of Düsseldorf, Germany.

Zigler, E., Levine, J., & Gould, L. (1966). Cognitive processes in the development of children's appreciation of humor. *Child Development, 37,* 507–518.

5

Extraversion, Alcohol, and Enjoyment

WILLIBALD RUCH

The Eysenckian extraversion superfactor of personality is considered to represent a general disposition for positive affect (Eysenck & Eysenck, 1985). In regards to mood states, extraverts are expected to show variation between positive affect and neutrality whereas the mood states of high neuroticism (N) scorers are expected to vary predominantly between negative affect and neutrality. This hypothesis received support from a variety of studies on mood swings and experimentally-induced mood (e.g., Costa & McCrae, 1980; Hepburn & Eysenck, 1989; Larsen & Ketelaar, 1989).

As regards smiling and laughter, the behavioral indicators of positive affect, the role of extraversion is less clear. There is no study which explicitly tested the postulate that extraverts have a tendency to "laugh and be merry" (Eysenck & Eysenck, 1975, p. 9). However, correlations between smiling/laughter and extraversion were reported in a few studies (see Ruch, 1990, and Ruch & Deckers, in press, for reviews) and these results did not provide much support for the hypothesis. The reasons why these studies failed to verify the hypothesis of a relationship between extraversion and positive affect may be numerous. For example, the assessment of smiling/laughter could lack sophistication or there was no control of the nature of the emotion accompanying the smile or laugh. This is especially the case when smiles or laughs were displayed during a conversation; here the type of associated emotion can vary and they can also represent social signals rather than emotional displays.

Another reason for this lack of findings could have resulted from the failure to discriminate among different types of smiles/laughs according to their morphology. For example, despite a sophisticated assessment of laughter and the use of a homogeneous amusing stimulus, Shimizu, Kawasaki, Azuma, Kawasaki, and Nishimura (1982) did not find a relationship between their "laughing score" and extraversion as assessed by the Maudsley Personality Inventory. In this study of 34 normals and 8 schizophrenic patients, Shimizu et al. (1982) recorded the amount of smiling/laughter induced by a humorous tape on a 0 to 5 step "laughing score." The activity of the zygomatic major (the main smiling/laughing muscle) formed the core of this laughing score. The EMG amplitude was broken down into three intervals yielding 1, 2, or 3 points, respectively. Further points were scored if there were either changes of at least one of the three indicators, i.e., GSR, plethysmogram, and respiration, or if body movement and/or phonation occurred. However, *all* zygomatic activity entered the laughing score, whether or not it was related to amusement. No separation of smiles/laughs reflecting enjoyment of the presented material and other types of smiles/laughs were undertaken. One could argue that the failure to verify the extraversion-laughter relationship in the Shimizu et al. (1982) study might have resulted from the presence of non-enjoyment smiles, which suppressed the expected effects.

Differentiation among Smiles and Laughter

Due to the work of Ekman, Friesen and associates (e.g., Ekman, 1985; Ekman & Friesen, 1982) our understanding of different types of smiles is far advanced. Whereas five muscles (zygomatic major, zygomatic minor, risorius, levator anguli oris, buccinator) insert in the lip corner area and are able to create movements of the lip corners which are interpretable as "smiles," only one of them (the zygomatic major) is active during positive affect. The sole action of this muscle, however, is not sufficient for the creation of a smile of enjoyment. As early as 1862, the French anatomist *Duchenne du Bologne* noted that smiles generated without the involvement of the orbicularis oculi muscle appear to be faked or false. After being neglected for more than a century this hypothesis was picked up again in the last decade and is now substantiated by several studies (for a review, see Ekman, Davidson, & Friesen, 1990). Thus, a genuine smile—as displayed during positive affect—is created by the joint action of the zygomatic major muscle and the lateral part of the orbicularis oculi muscle; the former pulls the lip corner obliquely up and back and deepens the furrow running from the nostril to the lip corner. The latter lifts the cheeks upward and draws the skin toward the eyes from the temple and cheeks; furthermore it narrows the eye opening and may cause crow's feet wrinkles to appear at the outer corner of the eye opening (Ekman & Friesen, 1982).

However, the presence of these two muscles is not a sufficient condition for an enjoyment smile. It is necessary to distinguish between spontaneous (or emotional) and voluntary facial movements as they occur in *felt* and *false* smiles, respectively. Individuals may want to convince somebody that they experience a positive affect although nothing much is felt or even negative emotions are present. Such *false* smiles are usually created without involvement of the orbicularis oculi muscle, however, their identification is not solely dependent on this so-called *Duchenne* marker (Frank & Ekman, 1993). Voluntary smiles are more frequently unilateral (present in one half of the face only) or asymmetrical (stronger in one half of the face); their onset is abrupt or otherwise irregular but not smooth; they are more frequently too short (less than half of a second) or too long (more than 4 sec); and they are more frequently asynchronous (i.e., the zygomatic major and obicularis oculi muscles do not reach their apex at the same time). The validity of these markers for the distinction between enjoyment smiles and false smiles are discussed by Frank and Ekman (1993).

No such differentiation has yet been achieved for laughter. Types of laughter are usually differentiated by the emotion attributed to it but not on a morphological basis. However, the contraction of the zygomatic major and the orbicularis oculi muscles also forms the core of the laughter of positive affect (Ruch, 1990). Several additional muscles are involved in laughing, but their exact number is not yet known (Ruch, 1993). They might be secondary in importance because they largely serve purposes like facilitating the expulsion of air (e.g., the opening of the mouth, throwing backward the head). Also, it is likely that most of the markers distinguishing between voluntary and emotional facial movements will apply to laughs as well. For example, laughter displayed in response to humor has been shown to be exclusively symmetrical (Ruch, 1990). However, the upper time limit of 4 sec can not be applied to laughter; almost half of them last indeed more than 4 sec and the longer lasting episodes of laughter were displayed at funnier jokes than the shorter lasting (Ruch, 1990).

Thus, the joint contraction of the zygomatic major and the orbicularis oculi muscles forms the common link between smiling and laughter as displays of enjoyment. Moreover, smiles and laughs were shown to represent different degrees of enjoyment rather than being displayed at different stimuli (Ruch, 1990), justifying their coding on one common dimension.

Thus, in light of the above considerations, the hypothesis regarding extraversion and positive affect can be refined by restricting the validity to enjoyment smiles and laughs: Extraverts will show enjoyment displays (smiles *and* laughter) more often than introverts. Furthermore, extraverts will show the more intense enjoyment displays (i.e., laughter) more frequently than introverts. Smiles based on other than the zygomatic major muscle, not involving the orbicularis oculi or being otherwise classified as false will not differentiate between extraverts and introverts.

Alcohol, Enjoyment, and Extraversion

Alcohol dampens excitation in the central nervous system (CNS). Its primary depressant activity is not prevalent in the cortex but in lower centers. The reticular formation is especially affected and consequently its integrating role on the cortex, thalamus, and the hypothalamus is impaired. Depending on the dose the effects of alcohol include hilarity and talkativeness, but also loss of motor coordination, amnesia, and narcosis. According to Pandina (1982), alcohol doses yielding blood alcohol levels up to 0.5‰, from 0.5 to 1.0‰, from 1.0 to 1.5‰, and higher than 1.5‰ can be regarded as low, medium, high, and very high doses, respectively. Low doses of alcohol may induce talkativeness, euphoria, or complacency and the effects of medium doses include disinhibition, performance decrements in coordination tests, and the beginning of driving impairment (Forth, Henschler, & Rummel, 1975).

Informal as well as formal evidence suggests that consumption of alcohol changes the individuals' affective state, however, the nature of these changes is not entirely clear (McCollam, Burish, Maisto, & Sobell, 1980). High doses of alcohol seem to facilitate negative affect while the effects of intoxication with low and medium doses includes elevation of positive affect; typically an increase in scales measuring positive mood states (e.g., elation) is reported (Burish, Maisto, & Shirley, 1982; Connors & Maisto, 1979; Vuchinich, Tucker, & Sobell, 1979).

Whereas the mood-elevating effects of low and medium doses of alcohol are well documented, there is no evidence so far for the widespread belief (e.g., Morreall, 1983) that ethanol intoxication lowers the threshold of amusement. Cheerful mood has been shown to represent a state of lowered threshold for facial responses to humor (Ruch, 1990). Given that alcohol is able to elevate the level of positive mood, one could expect that low and medium doses of alcohol would facilitate the elicitation of smiling and laughter in response to humor. However, the studies carried out so far were not able to demonstrate a main effect of alcohol on facial and verbal indicators of amusement (Vuchinich et al., 1979; Weaver, Masland, Kharazmi, & Zillmann, 1985). Several factors may account for this. First, no separation of types of smiling and laughter has been undertaken in these studies. Alcohol might also affect the display of smiles reflecting negative emotions (e.g., contempt) or facilitate other types of smiling. The presence of other types of smiles/laughter in addition to enjoyment displays might level existing effects. Secondly, besides changing the affective state, higher doses of alcohol might also impair the understanding of humor. Thus, a facilitation of positive affects might be restricted to blunt humor and does not occur for subtle humor. Weaver et al. (1985) report such an interaction between intoxication and type of humor, however, it was found only for rated funniness but not for facial expression. Third, most importantly, the differential effects of alcohol were not taken into account. Like for other psychotropic drugs, a response variability also exists for alcohol (Janke, 1983). Differential effects might average out, or at least suppress main effects by enlarging the within group variance. These effects can be studied by investigating the interactions between alcohol consumption and the relevant personality traits.

The role of extraversion in accounting for part of the variability of responses to alcohol has been demonstrated quite early (McDougall, 1929). The drug postulate advanced by Eysenck (1957, 1983) considers extraversion to be a major moderator of the effects of alcohol. Based on the inhibition theory of extraversion it is assumed that "depressant drugs increase cortical inhibition, decrease cortical excitation and thereby produce extraverted behaviour patterns. Stimulant drugs decrease cortical inhibition, increase cortical excitation and thereby produce introverted behaviour patterns" (p. 229).

Thus, depressant drugs and extraversion have broadly comparable effects on behavior. However, interactive effects are expected as well, based on the postulate that extraverts reach the so-called sedation threshold sooner than introverts. The inhibition theory considers extraverts to be near to the maximal point of inhibition, and depressant drugs can not shift the behavior much more in that direction.

Alcohol often served as a means to illustrate the drug postulate. "Alcohol . . . certainly makes many introverts much livelier, more garrulous, and generally more extraverted than normal" (Eysenck & Eysenck, 1985, p. 194). However, only a few of the studies testing the predictions regarding the interaction between extraversion and sedative drugs used alcohol; mainly barbiturates were used (see, for example, Janke, Debus, & Longo, 1979). Those experiments, however, were carried out mainly on performance variables and rarely so in the domain of positive emotion. There is no published study known on the interactive effect of extraversion and alcohol on humor-induced positive effect.

In the present study the effects of alcohol on enjoyment are expected to be different for introverts and extraverts. If frequency and intensity of positive affect go along with extraversion, and depressant drugs make introverts more extraverted, then introverts will display more positive affect under uptake of small and medium doses of alcohol than in a sober condition. Since extraverts are expected to have a lower sedation threshold, one can hypothesize that with increasing doses of alcohol the amount of positive affect decreases for extraverts. Thus, the reduction of positive affect induced by higher doses of alcohol in normals might appear for extraverts at comparably lower doses than for ambiverts (which in turn have a lower threshold than introverts). For extraverts it is therefore expected that they will show less positive affect under uptake of a medium alcohol dose than without alcohol.

Thus, the present experiment examines the role of extraversion and consumption of low and medium doses of alcohol on facial and verbal indicators of humor-induced positive affect. Higher doses will not be applied because they would not facilitate positive affect (Forth et al., 1975). For reasons specified elsewhere (McGhee, 1979; Ruch, 1990, 1993), the term "exhilaration" rather than "amusement" or "mirth" will be used to denote the nature of the elicited emotion. According to its Latin root (hilaris = cheerful) the term "exhilaration" is understood as denoting either the process of making cheerful or the temporary rise in cheerful state. Furthermore, as outlined above, we will examine whether the separation of enjoyment and non-enjoyment displays plays a critical role in verifying the hypothesis that extraversion is a predictor of the frequency and intensity of smiling and laughter.

Method

Subjects

Female non-psychology students were recruited by advertisements on campus and were paid DM 20 for their participation in this experiment. They were screened according to several criteria, such as medication, current health status, history of alcohol problems, pregnancy, German as a native language, and quality of vision. Ss were informed upon arrival that the study was designed to test the effects of alcohol intake on finger dexterity and that the whole experiment would be videotaped. Ss were instructed to avoid eating during the 3 h prior to participating in the experiment. When debriefed, they were informed about the real purpose of the study and that the camera served to film their facial responses to the humorous slides rather than their dexterity. All Ss gave consent to have their tapes analyzed. The videotapes of 2 Ss were partly unscoreable, leaving 61 Ss. Their age ranged from 19 to 30 years, which a mean of 22.9 and a standard deviation of 3.0.

Materials

Eysenck Personality Questionnaire-Revised
(EPQ-R; Eysenck, Eysenck, & Barrett, 1985)

The German version of the EPQ-R is a 102 item questionnaire answered in a yes/no format. It contains four scales: Psychoticism (P: 32 items), Extraversion (E: 23 items), Neuroticism (N: 25 items), and Lie or Social Desirability (L: 22 items). The EPQ-R was administered to the Ss 1 week before the main experiment.

Eigenschaftswörterliste-Kurzform
(EWL-K; Janke & Debus, 1978)

The EWL-K is an adjective list aimed at providing a comprehensive assessment of mood states. The EWL-K contains a list of 123 mood-descriptive adjectives which are answered in a yes/no format, and provides scores for 14 mood dimensions. These dimensions can be combined to form 6 domains of mood, and further combined to form the global dimensions of positive and negative affectivity. For the present study two scales were of special importance: positive affectivity and extraversion/introversion (one of the 6 domains).

Aufmerksamkeits-Belastungstest d2
(d2-concentration-test; Brickenkamp, 1978)

The d2 measures the ability to discriminate visually among 16 different elements quickly and correctly. The 16 elements result from combinations of *p*s or *d*s with 1, 2, 3, or 4 commas arranged on the top and/or the bottom of the letter. The *S*'s task is to mark all *d*s with 2 commas on a page containing 14 rows with 47 symbols each. The d2 was used to assess the capacity for concentration and the number of correctly identified elements (GZ-F) served as a criterion for determining the degree of alcohol-induced impairment of cognitive functions. Both the d2 and the EWL-K were administered to *S*s twice; at the beginning of the experiment and immediately before the period of induction of exhilaration. This allowed for measuring the effects of alcohol on mood state and concentration ability.

Procedure

Overview

The experiment lasted 90 min. *S*s were tested individually by a female experimenter. They first completed the EWL-K and the d2-test. They then received under double blind conditions a beverage which they consumed within 5 min. The doses applied can be expected to be effective after 25 to 35 min (Forth et al., 1975; Ideström & Cadenius, 1968; McCollam et al., 1980; Sidell & Pless, 1971). During this period the *S*s completed several dexterity tests and answered the EWK-L and the d2 again. Subsequently—30 min after consumption of the beverage—they were shown slides with jokes and cartoons. Thereafter, they worked on the dexterity tests again. All *S*s were offered coffee upon completion of the experiment and *S*s in the experimental groups were given special attention while the effects of the alcohol wore off.

Consumption of Alcoholic Beverage

The beverage consumed by *S*s of the control group contained a mixture of peppermint water and grapefruit juice. The low and high alcohol beverage contained this same mixture, plus 0.22 or 0.39 g alcohol per kg body weight, respectively. A 90% ethanol was used and was mixed with peppermint water on a 1:1 basis and filled up to 0.21 with grapefruit juice. These manipulations were expected to lead to blood alcohol levels of 0.4 and 0.7‰ (Forth et al., 1975). For the sake of clarity, the two experimental groups are referred to as low and high alcohol groups in the present study, although these levels of blood alcohol should be regarded as low and medium doses. Neither the *S*s nor the experimenter were aware of the content of the two beverage drinks which were offered to the *S*s after they completed the initial tests. The choice of beverage determined under which of the three experimental conditions the *S*s took part.

Induction of Exhilaration

The exhilaration-induction procedure lasted for 20 min. *S*s were presented 35 black and white slides of jokes and cartoons at an interval of 25 sec while sitting in a comfortable chair in a slightly darkened part of the room. The first five humor stimuli were for "warming up" and were not used in any analyses. The remaining 30 represented equal numbers of the three categories of incongruity-resolution humor, nonsense humor, and sexual humor (Ruch, 1992). The jokes/cartoons of the three categories were brought into a random order, and were presented to Ss in one of two permutations.

Verbal Responses

The Ss were instructed to rate all 35 stimuli according to degree of funniness and aversiveness on two 7-point Likert scales and to indicate in a yes/no format whether or not they found the humor stimulus tasteless. These scales were selected as markers for the orthogonal humor response dimensions of positive and negative affect which are typically obtained in factor analyses of response scales (Ruch & Rath, in press). The former scale represents the intensity of positive responses to humor and has been shown to correlate very highly with judged degree of felt exhilaration (Ruch & Rath, in press). The latter two scales cover the negative responses induced by humor.

Facial Measurement

Measurements were made from color videotapes, which provided a close-up, head-on view of the S's face. The measurements were based on the Facial Action Coding System (FACS; Ekman & Friesen, 1978). The FACS is an anatomically based, comprehensive, objective technique for measuring all observable facial movement. It distinguishes 44 action units (AUs). These are the minimal units that are anatomically separate and visually distinguishable. Facial coding usually requires slowed-motion inspection of recorded behavior. FACS also allows for measurement of the timing of a facial movement, its symmetry and intensity, and its degree of irregularity of onset, apex or offset.

The 1830 potential responses in the present experiment were coded for frequency, intensity, symmetry/asymmetry and duration of 5 AUs by two coders independently from each other. In case of disagreement, they watched the respective responses together until agreement was achieved. Their degree of agreement—estimated on the basis of other material—was 93.1%.

The intensity and symmetry/asymmetry of the AUs were coded during the apex of their occurrence. Three intensity grades (slight, moderate, extreme) were distinguished according to the criteria given in the FACS manual. For statistical treatment of the data the three grades were assigned values from 1 to 3, and the absence of any facial action was coded as 0. The asymmetry was determined by judging whether the appearance changes of the AU were stronger in the left or right half of the face. The duration was defined as the same interval from the first noticeable appearance of the characteristic changes of an AU to their complete disappearance.

On the basis of the coded material several displays were distinguished. The *enjoyment smile* was defined by the presence of 2 AUs, the AU12 and AU6, with no further facial actions present. AU12 ("lip corner puller") refers to the contraction of the zygomatic major. AU6 ("cheek raiser") describes the actions of the outer part of the orbicularis oculi muscle. The AU12 should be symmetrical and last longer than 2/3 of a second. The *enjoyment laugh* was coded when laughter vocalization or audible respiration changes occurred together with a joint symmetric action of AU12 and AU6 which lasted longer than 2/3 sec. Episodes of a single audible forced expiration accompanied by an AU12 and AU6 formed the lower end of the intensity spectrum of events coded as laughter. However, a fully developed laughter pattern was generally observed which typically consisted of an initial forced exhalation, followed by a more or less sustained sequence of repeated expirations of high frequency and low amplitude, which may or may not be phonated as "ha-ha-ha." *Enjoyment smiles* and *enjoyment laughs* were combined to form the category of *enjoyment displays.*

The category of *non-enjoyment displays* consisted of 3 subgroups: (1) AU12-smiles which were not accompanied by an AU6, or asymmetrical and of short duration; (2) smiles involving AU13; (3) smiles involving AU14. AU13 ("cheek puffer") refers to the contraction of the caninus muscle which pulls the lip corner up sharply and puffs up cheeks. AU14 ("dimpler") describes the dimplelike wrinkles at lip corners produced by the contraction of the buccinator muscle. Both types of smiles were observed to appear alone or together with AU12.

The *frequency* of these displays was determined by counting how often they occurred in response to the 30 slides. Two indices for *intensity* of enjoyment displays were computed. Both of them were independent of the frequency and were based on an ordering of the responses on a dimension including the levels "no response" (= 0), three intensity levels of "enjoyment smiles" (1, 2, and 3, representing the three intensity grades of the AU12 in AU12 + AU6 displays) and "laughter" (= 4). The *maximal intensity* was represented by the highest level of facial enjoyment coded for a *S*. This 5-point intensity index ranged from 0 to 4. A score for the *average intensity* was derived as well by adding the 5-point intensity index across all slides and dividing the sum by the frequency of enjoyment displays. For the ANOVAs composite scores were computed which combined both frequency and intensity of facial displays. The *intensity of enjoyment displays* was derived by adding the 5-point intensity index across all enjoyment displays. A similar composite score was obtained for *intensity of non-enjoyment displays;* this score was much lower since the AU13 or AU14 in the individual responses did not exceed the medium intensity-level.

Results

The extraversion in the present sample ($M = 14.9$, SD = 4.5, $\alpha = 0.84$) yields results comparable to the German norms for females of this age range. *S*s were classified into introverts ($n = 20$, score range from 5 to 12 points on the E scale), ambiverts ($n = 20$, from 13 to 17) and extraverts ($n = 21$, from 18 to 22) which were distributed randomly [$\chi^2(4) = 1.632$, $P = 0.803$] over the control group, low, and high alcohol groups with the number of *S*s in the resulting 9 groups ranging from 6 to 9.

For mood and concentrative ability, 3×3 ANOVAs with alcohol consumption as treatment variable (no ethanol, low dose, high dose) and extraversion as classification variable (introverts, ambiverts, extraverts) were computed for difference scores (second minus first administration) in elation, state extraversion/introversion (EWL domain scale), and the d2-test total score (GZ-F). For the facial data, a $3 \times 3 \times 2$ ANOVA (alcohol consumption × extraversion × type of display) with intensity of enjoyment and non-enjoyment displays as a repeated measurement factor was computed. For the verbal data, 3×3 ANOVAs (alcohol consumption × extraversion) with funniness, aversiveness, and tastelessness as dependent variables were performed.

Effects of Extraversion and Alcohol on Mood State and Concentrative Ability

The effect of alcohol on change in the extraversion/introversion-scale of the EWL just failed to reach significance (see table 5.1). Nevertheless, post hoc comparisons revealed the expected alcohol-induced change into a more extraverted state for the high dose group, whereas Ss of the control group appeared more introverted at the second administration of the EWL than at the first administration. This difference was significant.[1]

Elation increased between the low and high alcohol dose (see table 5.1). However, the analysis of the alcohol-extraversion interaction [F (4,52) = 3.905, P = 0.008] revealed that this was true only for introverts [F (1,52) = 9.788, P = 0.003] and extraverts [F (1,52) = 7.323, P = 0.009]; for ambiverts elation tended to decrease [F (1,52) = 3.457, P = 0.069].

The administration of alcohol impaired cognitive ability (see table 5.1). Although all groups yielded higher scores on the second administration of the test of concentrative ability, the increase was lower for the low and high alcohol group as compared to the controls.

Effects of Extraversion and Alcohol on Responses to Humor

First, the effects involving the separation of type of display were evaluated. The trivial main effect on the repeated measurement factor confirmed that the stimuli evoked more enjoyment displays than non-enjoyment displays, F (1,52) = 42.184, P < 0.0001. There was no interaction between alcohol and type of display, F (2,52) = 0.112, P = 0.895.

Extraversion and Enjoyment and Non-Enjoyment Displays

As expected, there was an interaction between extraversion and type of display, F (2,52) = 3.860, P = 0.027. The nature of this interaction is displayed in figure 5.1.

Figure 5.1 shows that the intensity of the non-enjoyment display does not increase as a function of the S's degree of extraversion. For the enjoyment displays, however, the extraverts show more intense displays than the introverts [F (1,52) = 8.785, P = 0.005] and the ambiverts [F (1,52) = 4.526, P = 0.038]. Because of the more frequent occurrence of enjoyment displays, the main effect for extraversion [F (2,52) = 5.007, P = 0.010] becomes significant. Nevertheless, figure 5.1 confirms that it is *not* justified to

TABLE 5.1. Changes in mood and concentration ability (*post-prae*) as a function of alcohol consumption

	No Alcohol	Low Dose	High dose	F (2,52)	P
Extraversion/introversion	-1.100[a]	-0.524	0.85[b]	2.759	0.073
Elation	-0.100	-0.762[a]	0.900[b]	2.570	0.086
GZ-F	82.150[b]	58.238[a]	63.150[a]	3.551	0.036

[a,b] Means of a row with different superscripts differ at P < 0.05 by two-tailed t-tests.

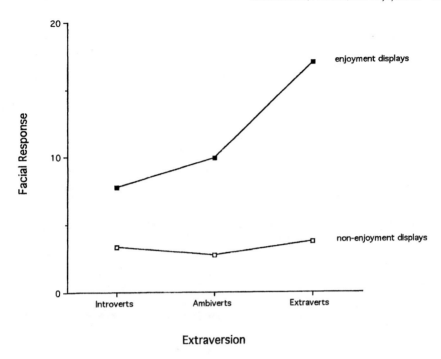

Figure 5.1   Facial responsiveness as a function of type of display and extraversion.

lump enjoyment and non-enjoyment smiles together. For the verbal data no separation of types of response was undertaken; the main effect of extraversion failed to reach significance [funniness: F (2,52) = 2.682, P = 0.078] although extraverts again tended to find the stimuli more funny than the introverts (P = 0.067) and the ambiverts (P = 0.041).

Extraversion, Alcohol, and Enjoyment of Humor

There is an interaction between extraversion and alcohol for both the facial [F (4,52) = 3.611, P = 0.011] and the verbal [F (4,52) = 2.628, P = 0.045] indicator of exhilaration. For the facial data, this interaction seems to be moderated by the type of facial display as indicated by the triple interaction between extraversion, alcohol, and type of enjoyment [F (4,52) = 2.513, P = 0.053], which just fails to be significant. Separate 3 × 3 ANOVAs for enjoyment and non-enjoyment displays confirmed that the interaction between alcohol and extraversion is far from being significant for the non-enjoyment displays [F (4,52) = 1.086, P = 0.373] but significant for the enjoyment displays [F (4,52) = 3.219, P = 0.019]. The nature of this interaction is presented in figure 5.2 (a and b) for the intensity of the enjoyment display and the verbal data, respectively.

Figure 5.2 shows that for introverts there is no different in the magnitude of facial or verbal exhilaration between the control group and the average of the two alcohol groups [F (1,52) = 0.161, P = 0.690; funniness: F (1,52) = 0.531, P = 0.469]. However, extraverts in the high alcohol group do show significantly less facial enjoyment than extraverts in the control group [F (1,52) = 7.098, P = 0.010] and they also rate them

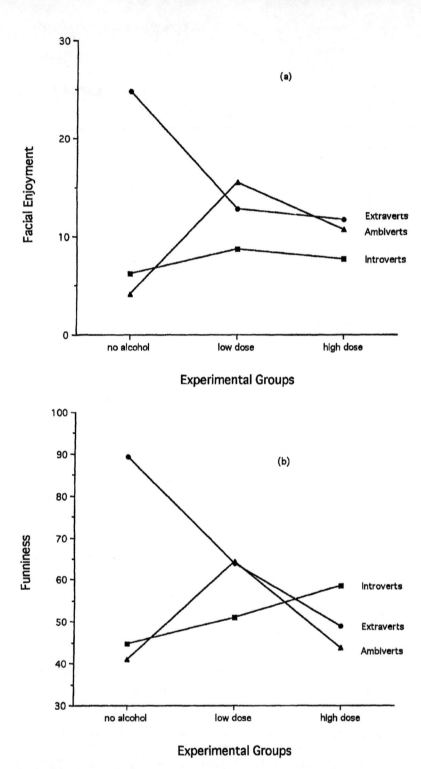

Figure 5.2 Intensity of enjoyment display (a) and judged funniness (b) as a function of alcohol consumption and extraversion.

less funny [F (1,52) = 8.515, P = 0.005]. The reduction of exhilaration in extraverts can already be observed for the low alcohol group [enjoyment display: F (1,52) = 5.447, P = 0.023; funniness: F (1,52) = 3.107, P = 0.084].

Ambiverts were expected to display the same response pattern as the introverts. Post hoc tests revealed that ambiverts indeed showed more facial enjoyment in the low alcohol group than in the control group [enjoyment display: F (1,52) = 4.662, P = 0.036; funniness: F (1,52) = 2.444, P = 0.124]; there is no difference among the two alcohol groups [enjoyment display: F (1,52) = 0.828, P = 0.367; funniness: F (1,52) = 1.908, P = 0.173]. Thus, for ambiverts the facilitative effect of low doses of alcohol can be found in the low alcohol group which was expected to occur for introverts. Thus, there were interactive effects of alcohol on humor-induced exhilaration; this leads to the question whether these effects are mediated by changes in positive affectivity.

Can positive affectivity be seen as a variable mediating the effects of alcohol on humor-induced exhilaration? Individual differences in the EWL-scale positive affectivity correlated with facial (r = 0.326, P = 0.011; control group: r = 0.52, P = 0.023) and verbal (r = 0.276, P = 0.033) enjoyment. Also the rank-order of the cell means of positive affectivity and the intensity of enjoyment displays (r = 0.783, P = 0.027) were correlated. No such correlations appeared for positive affectivity of the first administration. Subsequently, a 3 × 3 ANCOVA (treatment × extraversion) with positive affectivity as covariate was performed for intensity of enjoyment displays and rated funniness as dependent variables. The main effect for extraversion was not significant [enjoyment display: F (2,43) = 0.369, P = 0.694; funniness: F (2,43) = 1.556, P = 0.223] and so was the extraversion alcohol interaction [enjoyment display: F (4,43) = 0.165, P = 0.955; funniness: F (4,43) = 0.824, P = 0.517]. Thus, once the effects due to different degrees of positive affectivity were removed, none of the effects of alcohol on humor-induced exhilaration remained. Neither positive affectivity at the *first* administration of the EWL nor the *difference scores* in positive affectivity were nearly as effective in reducing the explained variance.

Changes in the level of extraverted state can not be seen as mediators. Whereas individual differences in EWL-extraversion/introversion at the second administration did correlate with facial (r = 0.27, P = 0.037; control group: r = 0.536, P = 0.019) and verbal (r = 0.299, P = 0.020) indicators of exhilaration, the pattern of means did not match and it turned out that extraverted state can not account for the effects in the ANCOVA.

Alcohol and Humor-Induced Positive and Negative Affect

There was no main effect of alcohol on humor-induced exhilaration [enjoyment display: F (2,52) = 0.316, P = 0.731; funniness: F (2,52) = 0.528, P = 0.593]. However, there were main effects on intensity of the non-enjoyment displays and on the negative evaluation of the stimuli (see table 5.2).

Pairwise comparisons showed that there were more non-enjoyment displays in the low alcohol group than in the control group and in the high alcohol group whereas the latter two groups did not differ from each other. Inspection of the means showed that this effect was obtained for both forms of non-enjoyment displays: the smiles based on AU13 or AU14, and the AU12-smiles lacking the markers for enjoyment (AU6, symmetry, duration), although it was more pronounced in the former. Similarly, the stimuli were judged more negatively in the low alcohol group than in the control group and in the high alcohol group (for tasteless: P = 0.053) whereas the latter two groups did not differ from each other.

TABLE 5.2. Mean scores of the effect of alcohol consumption on non-enjoyment displays and negative evaluation of the stimuli

	No Alcohol	Low Dose	High dose	F (2,52)	P
Non-enjoyment display	2.850[a]	4.571[b]	2.350[a]	5.043	0.010
Aversive rating	12.450[a]	28.905[b]	15.600[a]	5.971	0.005
Tasteless rating	3.280[a]	3.571[b]	3.395	4.845	0.012

[a,b] Means of a row with different superscripts differ at $P < 0.05$ by two-tailed t-tests.

Thus, the same effects emerged for aversiveness and intensity of the non-enjoyment displays. In fact, there was a significant positive correlation between degree of rated negative affect and intensity of smiles based on AU13 or AU14 (aversive: $r = 0.341$, $P = 0.008$; tasteless: $r = 0.343$, $P = 0.008$) but not with the AU12 without participation of the AU6 ($r = -0.058$, $P = 0.65$; tasteless: $r = 0.107$, $P = 0.407$). The latter correlated highly with rated funniness ($r = 0.561$, $P < 0.001$) but also the former correlated positively ($r = 0.281$, $P = 0.030$).

Extraversion and Frequency and Intensity of Positive Affect

The hypotheses regarding the relationship between extraversion and facial and verbal indicators of positive affect were investigated in more detail. Rank order correlations between the Extraversion scale of the EPQ and the frequency and intensity of several action units are computed for the control group (i.e., sober Ss) and are presented in table 5.3. For purposes of comparison the coefficients obtained for the total sample of 61 Ss are provided as well.

TABLE 5.3. Correlations between extraversion and facial and verbal responses to humor

	Total Sample[1]		Control group[2]	
	r	P	r	P
Frequency				
AU12 + AU6	0.404	0.002	0.553	0.016
Without vocalization	0.388	0.003	0.520	0.023
With vocalization	0.307	0.017	0.567	0.013
Intensity				
Maximal intensity	0.356	0.006	0.407	0.076
Average intensity	0.282	0.029	0.386	0.093
Global measures of exhilaration				
Rated funniness	0.229	0.076	0.458	0.046
Facial enjoyment	0.400	0.002	0.570	0.013
Separation of action units				
All AU12	0.273	0.035	0.474	0.039
AU12 without AU6	0.122	0.344	0.308	0.179
All non-enjoyment displays	0.160	0.215	0.356	0.121
AU13 and AU14	0.141	0.277	0.468	0.041

[1]$n = 61$; [2]$n = 20$.

Table 5.3 shows that extraversion does correlate with both the *frequency* and the *intensity* of facial indicators of exhilaration in the control group as well as in the total sample. As regards the *frequency* of displays, extraverts show all forms of Duchenne-displays (AU12 + AU6) more often than introverts, regardless of whether they were or were not accompanied by vocalizations (i.e., were smiles or laughs). As regards the *intensity* of displays, extraversion correlates with both the maximal intensity displayed and the average intensity. Both indices are logically but not empirically independent of the frequency ($rs = 0.73$ and 0.581, for the Ss showing enjoyment displays); they are also highly intercorrelated ($r = 0.845$, all $Ps < 0.0001$). Not surprisingly, the coefficient obtained for the composite score of facial enjoyment (covering both frequency *and* intensity) is highest in both the control group as well as the total sample. As regards the *verbal* indicators of exhilaration, there appears to be a weaker relationship. The correlation between extraversion and rated funniness is lower and even fails to be significant in the total sample.

The validity of the separation of types of displays is also evident in the comparison of the size of the coefficients obtained for them. The correlation between extraversion and the number of *all* AU12 displayed by a person (i.e., regardless of whether they were or were not accompanied by an AU6) is of medium size and significant. This correlation, however, is low and insignificant when computed for the smiles not involving the eye region, and much higher and significantly so, when computed for responses including the characteristic changes due to contraction of the orbicularis oculi. In the control group, extraverts also tend to display smiles based on AU13 or AU14 more often than introverts.

Finally, whether introverts are agelasts (i.e., non-laughers) was investigated. Of the 61 Ss, 33 did not laugh at all and 9 did not even display one single enjoyment smile (i.e., a joint action of AU12 and AU6 without vocalization). It turns out that introverts are overrepresented among the agelasts; 14 out of 20 (70%) introverts did not laugh, but there were only 8 out of 21 (38.1%) extraverts who did not laugh [$\chi^2(1) = 4.193$, $P = 0.041$]. Similarly, *all* extraverts displayed at least one single enjoyment smile, but 5 (25%) of the introverts failed to do so [$\chi^2(1) = 5.979$, $P = 0.014$]. Thus, the difference between extraverts and introverts relates not only to the question of how often a certain facial expression is displayed or how intense it is but even whether or not it is displayed at all.

Discussion

The present study shows that extraverts tend to exhibit facial signs of positive affect more frequently than introverts. This tendency is restricted to enjoyment displays and cannot be found for other sorts of smiles/laughter. Thus, the verification of this hypothesis is contingent on the separation of smiles according to their morphology. Only responses including a joint action of the zygomatic major muscle and the orbicularis oculi muscler, which are symmetric and last longer than 2/3 sec discriminate among extraverts and introverts. Smiles based on a principal muscle other than the zygomatic major, or false smiles (not including action of the orbicularis oculi; asymmetric smiles, or smiles of short duration) do not vary as a function of the degree of extraversion. Thus, it is possible that the study by Shimizu et al. (1982) did fail to find a difference between extraverts and introverts because of the lack of separation of enjoyment displays and non-enjoyment smiles and laughs. Similarly, a recent study by Jäncke (1993) did not find a significant difference between extraverts and introverts (as measured by the E scale of the EPQ-R) and zygomatic major activity as induced by pictures of positive valence.

The results show that extraversion is associated with both, the frequency and the intensity of positive affect as displayed in the face. Hence, the hypotheses put forward by Eysenck and Eysenck (1985) are supported also outside the domain of self-reported mood. Extraverts did show all types of enjoyment displays more frequently than introverts. Furthermore, the average and the maximal intensity of the enjoyment display increased with increasing degrees of extraversion. The coefficients appear to be lower for intensity than for frequency, however, this might be due to the lower reliability of the former. The *maximal intensity* score is based on one response only, which inevitably lowers the reliability. Besides this, its 5-point format does not provide much discrimination among *S*s. The reliability of the *average intensity* score is lowered by the fact that the base rates of enjoyment-laughs and -smiles were low in the present study (as they are in other laboratory studies as well). Several *S*s did not show laughter at all and some *S*s showed only a few smiles. A higher rate of enjoyment displays would allow for a more reliable estimation of its habitual intensity. This could be achieved by using more and/or funnier stimuli or by providing situational conditions which facilitate the release of exhilaration in an experimental setting. Nevertheless, due to the fact that the intensity indices were logically independent of the frequency, the results of the present study can be regarded as supporting the intensity hypothesis.

The results also show that extraverts do indeed "like to laugh" (Eysenck & Eysenck, 1975). Since laughing occurs at higher levels of positive affect and smiling is typical of lower levels (Ruch, 1990), this result for laughter falls in line with the ones obtained for the intensity hypothesis. In fact, for non-intoxicated *S*s (i.e., in the control group) the correlation between extraversion and laughter was the highest obtained for all individual behavioral indicators of positive affect. The relationship between extraversion and laughter is not restricted to humor-induced laughter, or to laughter induced in the laboratory. Ruch and Deckers (in press) found that extraversion and a questionnaire assessing the propensity to laugh and smile in a variety of everyday situations correlated 0.52 and 0.36 in German and American samples, respectively.

The low size of the correlation between extraversion and judged funniness of the jokes and cartoons deserves separate attention. The results seem to suggest that extraversion does affect facial displays of emotion but less so the affective experience. There might be two reasons for this fact. Firstly, *all* ratings were summed up including those which were accompanied by *no* facial display or even a false smile. It might be that their exclusion would have yielded different results. Such an analysis was not undertaken, however, since this might have artificially duplicated the results found for the facial data. Secondly, there is no reason to assume that extraverts smile and laugh more than introverts when they do not appreciate the stimuli presented. In fact, extraverts can not even be expected to smile if they do not like the material. Thus, the difference between extraverts and introverts with respect to the amount of laughing can be expected to appear only when other factors, like humor preferences, are kept constant. The use of different types of humor reduced the variance with respect to differential humor preference. Nevertheless, there are still tremendous individual differences with respect to the degree of appreciation of canned humor remaining as seen in the variance of the funniness scores. This variance is not considered to reflect only state variance related to individual differences in the easiness of inducing positive affect but seems to contain variance related to humor preference. A more stringent test of the hypothesis would therefore include an elimination of this variance and the analysis of the variance relating only to the threshold of induced positive affect. For example, Ss could be divided into those who appreciate the material and those who do so less. For the group of Ss who do not appreciate the humor very much no difference between extraverts and introverts with respect to the amount of smiling/laughter can be expected. However, among those who appreciate the humor the extraverts will show enjoyment displays more frequently than introverts.

As expected, the effects of alcohol on mood or humor-induced exhilaration were not uniform. The consumption of a moderate dose of alcohol did raise the S's level of state-extraversion. Also, state-extraversion did correlate with the facial and verbal indicators of exhilaration albeit lower so than trait-extraversion. However, the consumption of a moderate dose of alcohol did not generally facilitate the induction of exhilaration; neither facial displays nor verbal judgements of funniness increased as a function of alcohol. This replicates the negative results found in earlier studies on the effects of alcohol on humor-induced laughter (Vuchinich et al., 1979; Weaver et al., 1985).

Alcohol did raise elation and impaired the capacity to concentrate. However, this apparently did not affect responses to humor as inferred from the different pattern of means. A low dose of alcohol did raise the negative evaluations of the humor stimuli and facilitated the release of non-enjoyment displays. Whereas the meaning of the AU13 is still unknown, the joint asymmetric action of the AU14 and AU12 is the facial expression of contempt and hence its association with higher aversiveness ratings is not surprising. The sole action of the AU12 was shown to accompany very low levels of enjoyment of humor (Ruch, 1990). Thus, a low dose of alcohol seems to create a transition state which is characterized by the facilitation of emotionality in the range of negative to mildly positive affect.

The effects of alcohol on humor-induced positive affect are moderated by extraversion. The interactive effects on the verbal and facial indicators of exhilaration are highly comparable. However, the predictions based on the drug postulate did receive only partial support. As predicted, extraverts showed less verbal and facial exhilaration in the high alcohol condition than in the control group. The results indicate that even a low dose reduces the enjoyment of extraverts. However, contrary to the expectations, the introverts' verbal and facial behavior was not affected by alcohol consumption. It was the group of ambiverts which partly displayed the behavioral pattern expected to occur for introverts.

One reason for the failure to find facilitative effects for introverts could be that the doses used were too low to be effective in introverts; doses higher than 0.7‰ would have been needed. This argument is supported by the findings that introverts in the high alcohol group did describe themselves as being more extraverted and in a more positive mood than in the low alcohol group; the behavioral pattern, however, has not yet altered accordingly. Another argument is that the base rate of enjoyment displays among introverts ($M = 2.8$) is too low to reliably reflect the facilitative effects of alcohol. Even if alcohol has facilitating effects on laughter; the threshold for the release of laughter might still be too high for introverts to be exceeded often enough. The application of the suggestions made above might help to rule out this interpretation. So far, the results of the present study seem to be in line with McDougall's (1929) conclusion that the introvert is much more resistant to alcohol than the extravert.

The results are compatible with the view that positive mood states serve as intervening variables accounting for the effects of alcohol and extraversion on humor-induced exhilaration. Individual differences in positive affectivity predicted the differences in degree of exhilaration within and among experimental groups. Once the level of positive mood was kept constant, the effects of extraversion and alcohol diminished almost completely. Positive affectivity seems to represent a state of lowered threshold for the induction of exhilaration just as cheerful mood—which is one segment of positive affectivity—does (Ruch, 1990). Extraversion and alcohol created different levels of positive mood, which, in turn, represented different degrees of preparedness for the release of smiling and laughter. The results also allow for the speculation that the extraverts' higher frequency and intensity of enjoyment displays might be due to the fact that positive affectivity is more strongly prevalent among extraverts than among introverts.

The results of the present experiment underscore the necessity of including extraversion in future studies of the effects of alcohol on humor-induced positive affect. Likewise, the separation of enjoyment displays from other sorts of smiles/laughter appears necessary for the verification of hypotheses.

Acknowledgment

The preparation of this manuscript was facilitated by a Heisenberg grant from the German Research Council (DFG) to the author. The manuscript was written during my stay at the Department of Psychology, University of Bielefeld.

Note

1. An analysis of the non-significant interaction between alcohol and extraversion [$F_{(4,52)}$ = 1.975, $P = 0.129$] showed that for ambiverts the increase in extraverted state occurred between low and no alcohol condition [$F_{(1,52)} = 4.340$, $P = 0.042$] whereas for introverts the increase could be observed between the low and high dose conditions [$F_{(1,52)} = 5.669$, $P = 0.021$].

References

Brickenkamp, R. (1978). *Test d2. Aufmerksamkeits-Belastungs-Test.* Göttingen: Hogrefe.

Burish, T. G., Maisto, S. A., & Shirley, M. C. (1982). Effect of alcohol and stress on emotion and physiological arousal. *Motivation and Emotion, 6,* 149–159.

Connors, G. J., & Maisto, S. A. (1979). Effects of alcohol, instructions, and consumption rate on affect and physiological sensations. *Psychopharmacology, 62,* 261–266.

Costa, P. T., & McCrae, R. R. (1980). Influence of extraversion and neuroticism on subjective well-being: Happy and unhappy people. *Journal of Personality and Social Psychology, 38,* 668–678.

Ekman, P. (1985). *Telling lies.* New York: Berkley Books.

Ekman, P., Davidson, R. J., & Friesen, M. V. (1990). The Duchenne smile: Emotional expression and brain physiology, II. *Journal of Personality and Social Psychology, 58,* 342–353.

Ekman, P., & Friesen, W. V. (1978). *Facial action coding system (FACS)*. Palo Alto, CA: Consulting Psychologists Press.

Ekman, P., & Friesen, W. V. (1982). Felt, false, and miserable smiles. *Journal of Nonverbal Behavior, 6,* 238–252.

Eysenck, H. J. (1957). Drugs and personality, I. Theory and methodology. *Journal of Mental Science, 103,* 119–131.

Eysenck, H. J. (1983). Drugs as research tools in psychology: Experiments with drugs in personality research. *Neuropsychobiology, 10,* 29–43.

Eysenck, H. J., & Eysenck, M. W. (1985). *Personality and individual differences: A natural science approach.* New York: Plenum Press.

Eysenck, H. J., & Eysenck, S. B. G. (1975). *Manual of the Eysenck Personality Questionnaire.* London: Hodder & Stoughton.

Eysenck, S. B. G., Eysenck, H. J., & Barrett, P. (1985). A revised version of the psychoticism scale. *Personality and Individual Differences, 6,* 21–29.

Forth, W., Henschler, D., & Rummel, W. (1975). *Allgemeine und spezielle Pharmakologie und Toxikologie.* Mannheim: Bibliographisches Institut.

Frank, M. G., & Ekman, P. (1993). Not all smiles are created equal: The differences between enjoyment and nonenjoyment smiles. *Humor, 6,* 9–26.

Hepburn, L., & Eysenck, M. W. (1989). Personality, average mood and mood variability. *Personality and Individual Differences, 9,* 975–983.

Ideström, C. D., & Cadenius, B. (1968). Time relations of the effects of alcohol compared to placebo. *Psychopharmacologia, 13,* 189–200.

Jäncke, L. (1993). Different facial EMG-reactions of extraverts and introverts to pictures with positive and negative valence. *Personality and Individual Differences, 14,* 113–118.

Janke, W. (1983). Response variability in psychotropic drugs: Overview of the main approaches to differential pharmacopsychology. In Janke, W. (Ed.), *Response variability in psychotropic drugs.* London: Pergamon Press.

Janke, W., & Debus, G. (1978). *Die Eigenschaftswörterliste (EWL).* Göttingen: Hogrefe.

Janke, W., Debus, G., & Longo, N. (1979). Differential psychopharmacology of tranquilizing and sedating drugs. In Ban, Th. A. et al. (Eds.), *Modern problems of pharmacopsychiatry* (Vol. 14; pp. 13–98). Basel: Karger.

Larsen, R. J., & Ketalaar, T. (1989). Extraversion, neuroticism and susceptibility to positive and negative mood induction procedures. *Personality and Individual Differences, 10,* 1221–1228.

McCollam, J. B., Burish, T. G., Maisto, S. A., & Sobell, M. B. (1980). Alcohol's effects on physiological arousal and self-reported affect and sensations. *Journal of Abnormal Psychology, 89,* 224–233.

McDougall, W. (1929). The chemical theory of temperament applied to introversion and extraversion. *Journal of Abnormal and Social Psychology, 24,* 293–309.

McGhee, P. E. (1979). *Humor: Its origin and development.* New York: Freeman.

Morreall, J. M. (1983). *Taking laughter seriously.* Albany, NY: State University of New York Press.

Pandina, R. J. (1982). Effects of alcohol on psychological processes. In E. Gomberg, H. White, & J. Carpenter (Eds), *Alcohol, science, and society revisited.* Ann Arbor, MI: University of Michigan Press.

Ruch, W. (1990). *Die Emotion Erheiterung: Ausdrucksformen und Bedingungen.* Unpublished Habilitation thesis, University of Düsseldorf, Germany.

Ruch, W. (1992). Assessment of appreciation of humor: Studies with the 3WD humor test. In C. D. Spielberger & J. N. Butcher, (Eds.), *Advances in personality assessment* (Vol. 9; pp. 34–87). Hillsdale, NJ: Erlbaum.

Ruch, W. (1993). Exhilaration and humor. In M. Lewis & J. M. Haviland (Eds.), *The handbook of emotion* (chap. 42; pp. 605–616). New York, NY: Guilford Publications.

Ruch, W., & Deckers, L. (in press). Do extraverts 'like to laugh': An analysis of the Situational Humor Response Questionnaire (SHRQ). *European Journal of Personality.*

Ruch, W., & Rath, S. (in press). The nature of humor appreciation: Toward an integration of perception of stimulus properties and affective experience. *Humor.*

Shimizu, A., Kawasaki, T., Azuma, T., Kawasaki, M., & Nishimura, T. (1982). Polygraphic study on laughing in normals and schizophrenic patients. In M. Namba & H. Kaiya (Eds.), *Psychobiology of schizophrenia* (pp. 115–120). Oxford: Pergamon.

Sidell, F. R., & Pless, J. E. (1971). Ethyl alcohol: Bloodlevels and performance decrements after oral administration to men. *Psychopharmacologia, 19,* 246–261.

Vuchinich, R. E., Tucker, J. A., & Sobell, M. B. (1979). Alcohol, expectancy, cognitive labeling, and mirth. *Journal of Abnormal Psychology, 88,* 641–651.

Weaver, J. B., Masland, J. L., Kharazmi, S., & Zillmann, D. (1985). Effect of alcoholic intoxication on the appreciation of different types of humor. *Journal of Personality and Social Psychology, 49,* 781–787.

Laughter and Temperament

WILLIBALD RUCH

Some experiments may fail because the tremendous interindividual differences in the frequency or intensity of smiling and laughter overpower the effects of treatments. A review of studies that used different elicitors of smiling/laughter (e.g., tickling, laughing gas, humor) yielded that typically between 5 and 39 percent of the subjects show *no* facial response at all to the elicitor (Ruch, 1990). Hence, the search for moderator variables seemed to be of high priority, and the temperamental dimension of extraversion appeared to be the most promising candidate. Indeed, as the target article shows, introverts formed the majority of the nonresponders as regards both smiling and laughter. Moreover, extraverts and introverts differed with respect to the frequency and intensity of enjoyment displays. The study quite clearly showed that obviously the verification of most of the tested hypotheses is contingent on the separation of enjoyment and non-enjoyment displays. Hence, we maintained this separation in further studies on extraversion and laughter where we also differentiated among different intensities of laughter by including type and length of vocalization and movements of the head and the upper part of the body. From these studies, we have learned that it is also necessary to control for the perceived funniness of the stimuli; extraverts obviously only laugh more than introverts when things are funny, but they do not differ much in facial expressiveness when they considered the presented videotapes not funny but dull.

We have gone three ways since the target study. First, we considered that narrower temperamental traits might more powerfully account for individual differences in smiling and laughter than the broad superfactor of extraversion does. Second, we reckoned that *states* might have an impact as well. And third, we wanted to study concepts (states *and* traits) that might be predictive of enhanced thresholds for the release of smiling and laughter; seriousness and bad mood were considered to be qualities antagonistic to the release of smiling and laughter. This led us to the formulation of a state-trait model of cheerfulness, seriousness, and bad mood (Ruch, 1995), to the construction of the State-Trait-Cheerfulness-Inventory (STCI; Ruch, Köhler, & van Thriel, in press), and to a variety of validity studies. State-cheerfulness indeed was predictive in FACS studies of smiling and laughter induced by humorous slides, funny videotapes, or a psychophysical gag. Subjects in a more cheerful mood showed enjoyment smiles at lower minimal levels of rated funniness than did cheerful subjects in a less cheerful mood. This relationship was more pronounced when subjects were tested in the mere presence of the experimenter or a confederate than when tested in physically alone. The hypothesized negative relations with the antagonistic stated emerged as well. We found state-seriousness to be inversely correlated with successful induction of exhilaration in a weight-judging paradigm; subjects in a less serious frame of mind showed more enjoyment-displays when lifting the incongruous weight than subjects in a more serious frame of mind. In another study, all three concepts were correlated with FACS-coded facial behavior in response to six funny videos. Subjects who displayed more facial signs of exhilaration (the index included several levels of smiling to pronounced laughter) were scoring higher in state-cheerfulness and lower in state-seriousness and state-bad mood. Currently, we are trying to alter subjects' mood experimentally along these three dimensions and study the effects on the induction of smiling and laughter using different elicitors.

No further study of alcohol was carried out. However, in a recent pharmacopsychological experiment, we found that trait-cheerfulness moderated the impact of nitrous oxide (i.e., "laughing gas") on state-cheerfulness (Ruch, 1995). Thus, trait-cheerfulness seems indeed to predispose people to react more readily with smiling, laughter, and exhilaration/amusement. The validity of this hypothesis is also tested in the experiments currently carried out.

So far, the inclusion of temperamental traits, such as cheerfulness or extraversion, in the experimental study of smiling and laughter seems to be have been fruitful.

References

Ruch, W. (1990). *Die emotion erheiterung: Ausdrucksformen und bedingungen.* Unpublished Habilitation thesis, University of Düsseldorf, Germany.

Ruch, W. (1995). The "humorous temperament": On the validity of the state-trait model of cheerfulness. *7th Meeting of the International Society for the Study of Individual Differences, ISSID,* Warsaw, July 15–19.

Ruch, W., Köhler, G., & van Thriel (in press). Assessing the temperamental basis of the sense of humor: Construction of the facet and standard trait forms of the State-Trait-Cheerfulness-Inventory—STCI. In W. Ruch (Ed.), *Measurement of the sense of humor* [special issue], *Humor: International Journal of Humor Research.*

6

Signs of Appeasement

Evidence for the Distinct Displays of
Embarrassment, Amusement,
and Shame

DACHER KELTNER

Since universal facial expressions of a limited set of emotions were first documented (Ekman & Friesen, 1971; Ekman, Sorenson, & Friesen, 1969; Izard, 1971), sparse attention has been given to facial expressions of other emotions. The resulting lacuna in the field—that the emotions with identified displays are fewer (7 to 10) than the states that lay people (Fehr & Russell, 1984) and emotion theorists (Ekman, 1992; Izard, 1977; Tomkins, 1963, 1984) label as emotions—presents intriguing possibilities. Displays of other emotions may be blends of other emotional displays, unidentifiable, or may await discovery.

This investigation addressed whether embarrassment has a distinct nonverbal display and, by design, gathered similar evidence for amusement and shame. Embarrassment and the other "self-conscious emotions," which include shame, guilt, and pride, have received considerable attention in recent research aimed at determining the defining characteristics, functions, and distinctiveness of these emotions (see Lewis, 1993; Miller & Leary, 1992). The self-conscious emotions, defined by self-awareness and the comparison of one's action to standards and rules, play central roles in socialization and the adherence to conventions, norms, and morals (Goffman, 1967; Lewis, 1993; Miller & Leary, 1992).

The more internal aspects of the self-conscious emotions, including their perceived antecedents, underlying attributions, and phenomenological experience, are quite distinct (Ausubel, 1955; Babcock & Sabini, 1990; Edelmann, 1987; Lewis, 1993; Lindsay-Hartz, 1984; Miller, 1992; Tangney, 1992). Social communication also plays an important role in the self-conscious emotions. In particular, self-conscious emotions such as guilt and embarrassment motivate individuals to redress preceding transgressions through confession, appeasement, and apology (Baumeister, Stillwell, & Heatherton, 1994; Miller & Leary, 1992). Does the social communication of embarrassment include a distinct nonverbal display?

The Appeasement Function of Embarrassment

Argument for a distinct embarrassment display follows from its hypothesized appease-ment function. According to this view (e.g., Castelfranchi & Poggi, 1990), an indi-vidual who violates a social norm threatens the validity of the norm and potentially incurs the anger and unfavorable evaluation of others. Individuals who show embar-rassment after violating a norm, however, appease others by displaying their submis-sive apology for the transgression and their knowledge of the violated norm. As Goff-man (1967) observed, the embarrassed individual "demonstrates that . . . he is at least disturbed by the fact and may prove worthy at another time" (p. 111).

Previous Observation and Research

The hypothesis that embarrassment has a distinct nonverbal display has produced inconclusive findings. Laboratory studies and naturalistic observation have found that embarrassment is marked by gaze aversion, shifty eyes, speech disturbances, face touches, and a nervous, silly smile that reaches its apex following gaze aversion (Asendorpf, 1990; Edelmann & Hampson, 1979; Eibl-Eibesfeldt, 1989; Goffman, 1967; Modigliani, 1971). Developmental research has shown that failure-related emotion (shame or embarrassment) is marked by gaze and head movements downward and rigid, slouched, forward-leaning posture (Heckhausen, 1984; Stipek, Recchia, & Mc-Clintic, 1992). Finally, the blush, which people report experiencing during embarrass-ment (Edelmann, 1987), also occurs during shame and anger (Lewis, 1993) and there-fore does not uniquely signal embarrassment.

These findings fall short in establishing whether embarrassment has a distinct non-verbal display. The unique facial actions that distinguish embarrassment from other emotions have not been documented. Nor is it known whether embarrassment's actions unfold as the actions of other emotions do (Ekman, 1982). Finally, observers have yet to demonstrate the ability to distinguish displays of embarrassment from those of other emotions (Edelmann & Hampson, 1981).

Overview of this Investigation

To test the hypothesis that the nonverbal display of embarrassment is distinct, this in-vestigation followed two research approaches (Ekman, Friesen, & Ellsworth, 1982). In Study 1, which followed the *components study approach,* the nonverbal behaviors as-sociated with individuals' experiences of embarrassment and amusement were com-pared. Embarrassment was compared with amusement rather than with emotions that do not involve smiling (e.g., fear and anger) because the two emotions are often con-fused (Edelmann & Hampson, 1981; Goffman, 1956). The remaining studies followed the more pervasive *judgment study approach.* Four studies determined whether ob-servers could distinguish between the spontaneous displays of embarrassment and (a) amusement (Studies 2 through 5); (b) shame (Study 5); and (c) other emotions with identified displays, including anger, disgust, and enjoyment (Study 5).

Study 1: Nonverbal Displays of Embarrassment and Amusement

Study 1 compared the nonverbal responses of individuals who had reported feeling embarrassment or amusement in response to carrying out the directed facial action task (DFA), which is noted for its embarrassing qualities (Levenson, Ekman, & Friesen, 1990). In the DFA task, subjects pose and hold awkwardly achieved facial expressions according to the instructions of an experimenter who scrutinizes their behavior and corrects their often numerous mistakes. The DFA task involves several elements of embarrassment: participants are acutely aware of their own performance, observers' judgments of their performance, and the public mistakes they make. Performing the DFA task resembles one prevalent cause of embarrassment, the loss of physical poise (Edelmann, 1987). The study generated three kinds of evidence relevant to the investigation's main hypothesis.

Morphological Distinctions in Embarrassment and Amusement Displays

Behavioral analyses focused on participants' gaze, head, self-touching, and facial activity following their performance of the DFA task. A central aim was to document which actions differentiate the smiles of embarrassment and amusement from each other and from Duchenne, enjoyment smiles and non-Duchenne smiles (Ekman & Friesen, 1982; Frank, Ekman, & Friesen, 1993).

Dynamic Patterns of Embarrassment and Amusement Displays

Temporal analyses documented the differences in the dynamic patterns of the embarrassment and amusement displays. In addition, these analyses addressed whether the embarrassment display, like other displays of emotion, has an abrupt onset and a duration of roughly 4–5 s (Ekman, 1982).

Relations Between Nonverbal Behavior and Self-Reports of Embarrassment and Amusement

Correlations between the self-reported experience of emotion and nonverbal behavior have differentiated facial displays of positive and negative emotion (Ekman, Friesen, & Ancoli, 1980), sympathy and personal distress (Eisenberg et al., 1989), and enjoyment and nonenjoyment smiles (Frank et al., 1993). Analyses examined whether self-reports of embarrassment and amusement were related to different nonverbal behaviors.

Method

Participants

Participants, who attended individual sessions, were drawn from a larger sample of participants who performed the DFA task as a part of a multitask experiment (for complete description, see Levenson et al., 1990).

Procedure

Instructions for the DFA task were given by an experimenter in an adjacent room who could see the participant on a video monitor and communicate over an intercom. The participants were aware of being videotaped, which was accomplished by a partially hidden video camera mounted on the wall in front of the participant and behind a glass partition. The DFA task requires that participants perform several different facial expressions, each one followed by a rest period and a self-report emotion inquiry. Specifically, participants followed muscle-by-muscle instructions to configure their faces into expressions of anger, disgust, enjoyment, fear, sadness, surprise, and a control "effort" face. Participants who were asked to hold each facial configuration, once correctly achieved, for 15 s. Having held the face for 15 s, participants were told to stop and then were given a 12–15 s rest period. Immediately following the rest period, the experimenter began an open-ended inquiry by asking participants if they had "experienced any emotions." Participants first listed the emotions that they experienced during the trial and then rated the intensity of their experiences of only the reported emotions (0 = *no emotion,* 8 = *the most of that emotion ever experienced by the subject*).

Typewritten protocols of all self-report inquiries were reviewed to select terms to identify embarrassed and amused subjects. Reports of feeling embarrassed, silly, stupid, self-conscious, and ridiculous were classified as embarrassment. Reports of feeling amused, funny, goofy, feeling like laughing, and reports of humor were classified as amusement. These synonyms, taken from previous discussions of embarrassment and amusement (Miller & Leary, 1992; Ruch, 1993), were each rated by a group of 12 judges to be more similar to the target emotion than the other emotion. Forty-two percent of participants reported embarrassment or a related term after at least one DFA trial (48% of female participants and 33% of male participants), and 36% of participants reported amusement or a related term (31% of female participants and 38% of male participants). Analyses found no differences in the frequency with which embarrassment and amusement were reported (a) overall, (b) by men or women, and (c) after the different DFA trials, nor in the intensity of self-reported embarrassment ($M = 3.07$) and amusement ($M = 3.60$), all $ps > .10$.

Coding of Nonverbal Behavior

To ensure nonoverlapping samples of embarrassed and amused targets, only the first trial after which a participant reported either emotion was coded and analyzed. This procedure yielded 35 displays of embarrassment (23 female, 12 male) and 28 of amusement (14 female, 14 male). Because inspection of participants' behavior during the actual DFA trials revealed little behavior other than the required facial configuration, only the facial behavior that occurred during the post-DFA, 12–15-s rest period was coded. Facial behavior was coded by using Ekman and Friesen's Facial Action Coding System (FACS: Ekman & Friesen, 1976, 1978), which distinguishes 44 minimal action units of facial activity that are anatomically separate and visually distinguishable. Scoring involves decomposing a facial movement into the particular action units that produced it, either singly or in combination with other units. The intensity (5 levels) of facial activity was scored according to the criteria of the FACS. The duration of facial activity was coded by noting the interval from the first evidence of the facial action (onset time) to the last evidence of its occurrence (offset time). The onset and offset times of hand touches of the face were scored.

Reliability of Measurement

One person coded the behavior of all participants. A second person, who was unaware of participants' reports of emotion and the investigation's aims, coded 10 embarrassed participants and 10 amused participants who were randomly selected from the total sample of participants. Intercoder reliability was evaluated by using a ratio in which the number of action units on which the two coders agreed was multiplied by 2 and then divided by the total number of action units scored by the two persons. This agreement ratio was calculated for each event observed by one or both coders. The mean ratio of agreement was .846.

Results

*Morphological Differences in Embarrassment and
Amusement Displays*

Whereas female participants report more intense and frequent embarrassment than male participants (Miller & Leary, 1992), two-way analyses of variance (ANOVAs) with emotion and sex as between-subjects variables found no significant sex differences on any of the nonverbal measures. All subsequent analyses were collapsed across sex.

The displays of embarrassment and amusement were compared by first examining the frequencies and then the characteristics (latency, duration, and intensity) of the behaviors of interest (gaze shifts, smiles, and other facial actions, head movements, and face touches). Because of the risk of Type I errors, the following strategy was followed (Cohen & Cohen, 1983). For each category of nonverbal behavior, multivariate analyses of variance (MANOVAs) first examined whether embarrassed and amused participants who showed the relevant behavior differed in the characteristics of that behavior. Simple effects analyses followed up on significant multivariate effects. Table 6.1 presents the measures of the nonverbal behavior of embarrassed and amused participants.

Gaze Activity

The MANOVA found that the pattern of gaze activity (latency, duration, number, and intensity of gaze shifts down and to the side) for embarrassed and amused participants differed, $F(5, 34) = 3.00$, $p < .05$. As in previous studies (Asendorpf, 1990; Edelmann & Hampson, 1979; Modigliani, 1971), embarrassed participants looked down more rapidly and for a greater proportion of the rest period and shifted their gaze position more frequently than amused participants (for all noted differences, $p < .05$). The first sideways gaze shifts were typically to the left for embarrassed participants (63%) and to the right for amused participants (76%), $z = 2.32$, $p < .05$.

Smile Controls

Both embarrassed and amused participants showed lower facial actions, deemed *smile controls*, whose muscular action potentially (a) counteracted the upward pull of the *zygomatic major* of the smile, or (b) obscured the smile, or (c) both. Embarrassed participants more frequently showed smile controls and showed them in greater number than amused participants. The MANOVA found that the characteristics of smile controls

TABLE 6.1. Differences in nonverbal behavior of embarrassed and amused targets

Behavior	Embarrassed targets (n = 35)		Amused targets (n = 28)		Statistical comparison
	M	SD	M	SD	
Gaze down					
Frequency (%)	94		72		z = 1.08
Latency	0.71	1.14	3.55	4.42	t = 4.04***
Duration	0.67	0.27	0.34	0.40	t = 4.22***
Gaze shifts					
Frequency (%)	100		85		z = 0.66
Latency	2.53	2.67	2.53	2.53	t = 0.01
Number	4.29	2.72	2.43	2.40	t = 2.83**
Mean intensity	3.05	0.75	2.96	0.89	t = 0.39
Smile controls					
Frequency (%)	83		48		z = 2.20**
Latency	1.46	1.44	3.02	2.94	t = 2.18**
Duration	0.46	0.24	0.62	0.41	t = 1.56*
Number	2.61	1.63	1.61	1.26	t = 2.32**
Mean intensity	2.07	0.66	1.85	0.36	t = 1.10
Smile					
Frequency (%)	57		82		z = 1.92**
Latency	1.95	2.12	2.27	2.23	t = 0.56
Duration	2.23	1.93	2.76	1.72	t = 0.95
Mean intensity	1.62	2.15	2.57	2.57	t = 1.60*
Head movements					
Overall frequency (%)	57		31		z = 2.20**
Head turn to side					
Latency	2.24	1.74	2.34	2.34	t = 0.10
Duration	0.49	0.54	0.37	0.32	t = 1.32
Mean intensity	3.08	1.04	3.22	0.54	t = 0.09
Face touches					
Frequency (%)	26		11		z = 1.47*
Duration	1.02		0.87		

Note: Gaze down and head turn durations refer to the proportion of the rest period during which the action occurred.
*p < .10. **p < .05. ***p < .01.

(latency, intensity, and duration) differed for embarrassed and amused participants $F(3, 33) = 2.77, p < .05$. Simple effects analyses showed that the smile controls of embarrassed participants had a quicker latency than those of amused subjects. Table 6.2 presents the facial actions categorized as smile controls. Embarrassed participants more frequently showed lip presses (82% vs. 54%, $z = 1.74, p < .05$), whereas amused participants more frequently showed tongue protrusions and lip puckers, (38% vs. 13%, $z = 2.51, p < .05$), which some consider approach behavior (Eibl-Eibesfeldt, 1989).

TABLE 6.2. Lower facial actions categorized as smile controls

Action	Embarrassment ($n = 31$)	Amusement ($n = 13$)	z test
AU8: Lips together	6.4	15.4	2.75***
AU14: Dimpler	35.5	23.1	1.30
AU15: Lip corner depress	22.6	15.4	1.18
AU17: Chin raise	12.9	15.4	0.54
AU18: Lip pucker	9.7	23.3	2.74***
AU19: Tongue show	3.2	15.4	5.30***
AU20: Lip stretch	16.1	0.0	—
AU22: Lip funnel	3.2	15.4	5.30***
AU24: Lip press	80.6	53.8	1.74***
AU26: Jaw drop	9.7	15.4	1.43
AU27: Mouth stretch	6.4	0.0	—
AU28: Lip suck	12.9	15.4	0.54
AU29: Jaw thrust	6.4	0.0	—
AU32: Lip bite	3.2	7.7	2.68***
AU34: Cheek puff	3.2	0.0	—
AU36: Tongue bulge	3.2	0.0	—
AU37: Lip wipe	19.4	23.3	0.96

Note: Numbers refer to the percentages of participants of those who showed smile controls who showed each action. The z comparisons were not made when an action was not observed in one of the emotions.
***$p < .01$.

Smiles

Amused participants were more likely to smile than embarrassed participants (82% vs. 57%, $z = 1.92$, $p < .05$), show non-Duchenne smiles (71% vs. 39%, $z = 2.71$, $p < .01$), and tended to more frequently show Duchenne smiles (36% vs. 17%, $z = 1.71$, $p < .10$). The MANOVA of the characteristics of smiles (latency, intensity, and duration) was not significant, $F(3, 40) = 0.58$, $p > .2$.

Head Movements

Embarrassed participants more frequently turned their head away from directly facing the camera than amused participants and were more likely to show head movements down (51% vs. 17%, $z = 3.09$, $p < .01$) and to the left (34% vs. 7%, $z = 2.89$, $p < .05$). Of the 20 embarrassed participants who showed head movements, first movements to the left were more common (50%) than to the right (20%), $z = 2.51$, $p < .05$. The MANOVA of the characteristics of head movements (latency, duration, and intensity) was not significant, $F(4, 23) = 1.19$, $p > .10$.

Face Touches

Embarrassed participants tended to touch their faces more frequently than amused participants (26% vs. 11%, $z = 1.47$, $p < .10$).

A Prototypical Embarrassment Display

A prototypical embarrassment display, presented in figure 6.1, was created by calculating the mean onset and offset times of the actions shown by at least 50%[1] of embarrassed participants. The displays of embarrassment were more likely than those of amusement to follow this prototypical sequence at its first stage: gaze down (81% vs. 24%, $z = 5.77$, $p < .01$); the second stage: gaze down followed by a smile control (70% vs. 14%, $z = 5.66$, $p < .01$); and the third stage: gaze down followed by a smile control followed by a head movement (46% vs. 7%, $z = 4.44$, $p < .01$). This last percentage indicates that 46% of embarrassment displays followed the prototypical pattern. The relations between smiles and smile controls are addressed later. Figure 6.1 also shows that the embarrassment display, like facial expressions of emotion, had an abrupt onset, beginning with gaze down about .7 s after the participants were told to rest, and a duration of about 5 s (only 23% of participants showed behavior other than gaze shifts, such as facial muscle actions or head movements, after the first 5 s of the rest period).

Temporal Aspects of the Embarrassment and Amusement Displays

The temporal patterns of the embarrassment and amusement displays differed in two ways. First, the initial action during embarrassment was gaze down (81% vs. 26% for

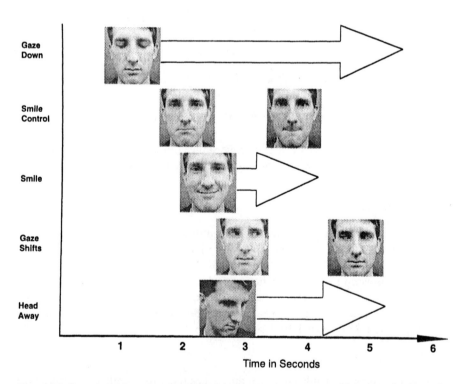

Figure 6.1 Representation of a prototypical embarrassment response. The mean duration of each action is equal to the interval beginning with the leftmost edge of the photograph and ending with the end of the arrow.

amusement, $z = 5.28$, $p < .001$), and, during amusement, a smile (33% vs. 6% for embarrassment, $z = 2.87$, $p < .01$). Second, embarrassed smiles in contrast to amused smiles were more frequently accompanied (70% vs. 32%, $z = 2.71$, $p < .01$) and terminated (55% vs. 14%, $z = 2.32$, $p < .05$) by a smile control. More intense smile controls (the sum of the intensity ratings of their actions) were related to briefer smiles during embarrassment ($r = -.31$, $p < .05$) but not during amusement ($r = .05$, ns).

Correlations Between Nonverbal Behavior and Self-Reports of Emotion

Participants' self-reports of amusement were related to more intense smiles ($r = .67$, $p < .01$), briefer gazes down ($r = -.32$, $p < .05$), and tended to be related to less intense smile controls ($r = -.29$, $p < .10$). Participants' self-reports of embarrassment, in contrast, were related to longer gazes down ($r = .51$, $p < .01$), more intense smile controls ($r = .40$, $p < .05$), briefer smiles ($r = -.35$, $p < .05$), and more frequent gaze shifts ($r = .35$, $p < .05$) with quicker latency ($r = -.29$, $p < .05$).

Discussion

Study 1 produced three lines of evidence consistent with the hypothesis that embarrassment has a distinct nonverbal display. First, the morphology and dynamic unfolding of the embarrassment and amusement displays differed. Embarrassed participants showed more smile controls that obscured the smile, gazes down of longer duration, more head movements down, and first head movements and gaze shifts to the left. Amused participants, on the other hand, smiled more frequently and shifted their gaze to the right. The infrequency of enjoyment (Duchenne) smiles during amusement may have been due to participants' discomfort at having performed the DFA task. Second, the embarrassment display, like other facial expressions of emotion, had a quick onset and tended to last 4–5 s. Finally, self-reports of embarrassment and amusement were correlated with the behaviors that differentiated the two emotions' displays.

It must be borne in mind that the embarrassment display documented in Study 1, which was distinct, was from one situation. Embarrassment is elicited by diverse antecedents, including overpraise, loss of privacy, and loss of physical control (Miller, 1992), which may produce different embarrassment displays than those documented following the DFA task. Furthermore, the context of the DFA task, in which the participant sat alone in a room, communicating with the experimenter over an intercom, certainly influenced the character of the displays documented in Study 1. The tendency to self-touch, for example, was probably reduced by the physiological recording devices attached to the participants' hands. The relatively noninteractive DFA task may also have accentuated certain behaviors, such as gaze and head movements away, that would not be so pronounced in ongoing face-to-face interactions, and may have inhibited the occurrence of socially communicative behaviors, such as head shakes, shoulder shrugs, and eyebrow raises, that would be observed in more social settings. These considerations bear on the generality of the embarrassment display documented in Study 1. Study 5 addresses these concerns by giving observers the task of identifying embarrassment displays identified within a more social interaction. The DFA task, nevertheless, produced an embarrassment display that was distinct in behavioral analyses. The following studies addressed whether observers could accurately identify the embarrassment and amusement displays analyzed in Study 1.

Overview to Studies 2, 3, and 4: Observers' Judgments of Embarrassment and Amusement Displays

If embarrassment displays appease observers, they should be identifiable to others. The following three studies tested this hypothesis. Participants (observers) judged a large sample of embarrassment and amusement displays from Study 1. In Study 2, observers indicated whether each target had reported experiencing embarrassment or amusement. In Study 3, observers judged several emotions and traits that each target displayed. In Study 4, observers generated their own descriptions of targets' emotions.

The following studies also tested the hypothesis that observers' judgments of embarrassment (and shame) displays would be influenced by the target's perceived status. Appeasement displays signal lower status and submissiveness, which deters observers from punitive judgment and action (Castelfranchi & Poggi, 1990; de Waal, 1988). If embarrassment and shame displays signal lower status and submissiveness (e.g., Clark, 1990), they should be more readily perceived when displayed by low-status individuals. Following this reasoning, observers were expected to be more accurate and attribute more emotion in judging the embarrassment and shame displays of women and African Americans, who have historically been associated with lower status, than the same displays of men and Caucasians.

Study 2

Method

Participants

Observers were introductory psychology students (107 women and 45 men) at San Francisco State University who participated in the study before a guest lecture.

Materials

Two videotapes were created for Studies 2, 3, and 4. Only those targets from Study 1 who reported either embarrassment (or a related term) or amusement (or a related term) were considered, to avoid the possibility that other emotions experienced by targets would influence observers' judgments. From this pool of "pure" displays, 16 targets were randomly presented on the first videotape (amused targets: 5 women and 3 men; embarrassed targets: 5 women and 3 men) and 18 different targets were randomly presented on the second videotape (amused targets: 5 women and 4 men; embarrassed targets: 5 women and 4 men). The embarrassed and amused targets on each videotape were matched for the intensity of self-reported emotion. To test the perceived-status hypothesis, within each emotion male and female targets with comparable nonverbal behavior were selected. Specifically, within each emotion male and female targets did not differ statistically in their gaze down latency and duration, smile intensity and duration, smile control frequency and intensity, head movement duration and intensity, and face touch frequency (all $ps > .10$). Each target's post-DFA task behavior was shown for approximately 12s.

Procedure

The videotapes were presented to observers on monitors located on each side of a lecture hall. Eighty-one observers from one class viewed the first videotape, and 71 observers in another class viewed the second videotape. Observers were instructed that they would see a series of individuals who reported feeling either amusement or embarrassment after the period shown on the videotape. After viewing each target, observers were given 30 s to judge (a) whether the target "reported feeling either embarrassment or amusement," (b) "how much emotion the person was showing" (1 = *no emotion, 7 = extreme emotion*), and (c) "how confident you are in your judgment of the target's reported emotion" (1 = *no confidence, 7 = extreme confidence*). Amusement and embarrassment were presented as response alternatives in one of two orders on two randomly distributed forms.

Personality Measures

Following the videotape, observers completed measures of embarrassability (Modigliani, 1968; modified by Edelmann, 1985), propensity to blush (Leary & Meadows, 1991), fear of negative evaluation (Leary, 1983), affective intensity (Affective Intensity Measure [AIM]; Larsen & Diener, 1987), and emotional expressivity (Affective Communication Task [ACT]; Friedman, Prince, Riggio, & DiMatteo, 1980). Participants also rated their current mood (–5 = *very negative*, 0 = *neutral*, +5 = *very positive*).

Results and Discussion

Separate three-way ANOVAs on the dependent measures (overall accuracy, mean attributed emotion, and mean confidence) with videotape, observer ethnicity (African American, Asian, Caucasian, or Hispanic/Chicano), and response form as between-subjects variables found no significant main effects or interactions (all $ps > .15$). In subsequent analyses, data from the two classes (the two videotapes), the different ethnic groups, and the two response forms were combined.

Accuracy in Distinguishing Embarrassment and Amusement Responses

Observers' overall accuracy (.61) was significantly greater than chance (.5) in the binomial test ($p < .01$). Observers were more likely to judge targets as embarrassed ($M = .56$) than amused ($M = .44$), $F(1, 150) = 58.78, p < .001$. Observers' accuracy exceeded their call rates for embarrassed ($Ms = .67$ vs. $.56$), $t(150) = 8.53, p < .001$, and amused targets ($Ms = .54$ vs. $.44$), $t(150) = 7.83, p < .001$.

Influence of Targets' Sex on Observers' Judgments

The perceived-status hypothesis predicted that observers would be more accurate and confident and would attribute more emotion in judging women's displays of embarrassment, a low-status emotion, but show no differences in judging male and female amusement displays. To assess this hypothesis, observers' mean levels of accuracy, attributed emotion, and confidence were examined in separate two-way ANOVAs, with observer sex as a between-subjects variable and target sex and emotion as within-subjects variables. No main effects or interactions were significant in the analysis of overall accuracy (all $ps > .15$). The perceived-status hypothesis did receive support, however, in the analyses of the intensity and confidence judgments. Specifically, although more emotion was attributed to female ($M = 4.27$) than male ($M = 3.80$) targets, $F(1, 146) = 44.80, p < .0001$, this difference was greater for embarrassed (.64) than amused (.30) targets, $F(1, 146) = 7.43, p < .01$. Likewise, although observers were more confident in judging female ($M = 4.60$) than male ($M = 4.42$) targets, $F(1, 146) = 10.92, p < .0001$, this difference was greater for embarrassed (.37) than amused (.02) targets, $F(1, 146) = 7.36, p < .001$. Other main effects showed that male observers were more confident ($M = 4.78$) than female observers ($M = 4.39$), $F(1, 146) = 5.54, p < .05$, that observers attributed more emotion to the amused ($M = 4.14$) than embarrassed ($M = 3.94$) targets, and that observers were more confident in judging amused targets, ($Ms = 4.63$ and 4.38, respectively), $F(1, 146) = 17.11, p < .0001$.

Relation Between Observers' Personality and Judgments

Observers' overall accuracy was correlated with their scores on the AIM ($r = .26, p < .05$), the ACT ($r = .18, p < .05$), positive mood ($r = .22, p < .05$), and their self-rated confidence ($r = .17, p < .05$).

Study 3

Study 2 explicitly directed observers to discriminate between embarrassment and amusement, which may have enhanced their ability to distinguish between the displays of the two emotions. Study 3 avoided priming observers to make such a discrimination by not providing information about targets' self-reported emotion and by gathering observers' judgments of several emotions and trait-like qualities. Observers were expected to attribute (a) more embarrassment, negative emotion (guilt, shame, and disgust), nervousness, and self-consciousness to embarrassed targets and (b) more amusement and self-esteem to amused targets. The perceived-status hypothesis predicted that observers would attribute more embarrassment and shame to female than male embarrassed targets.

Method

Participants

Observers were introductory psychology students at San Jose State University who received extra credit toward their course grade.

Procedure

The videotapes were presented to groups of 10 to 15 observers, each group viewing one videotape. Observers rated how much amusement, disgust, embarrassment, guilt, nervousness, self-consciousness, self-esteem, shame, and surprise each target showed (1 = *none of the feeling shown*, 7 = *extreme amounts of the feelings shown*). The order of the nine items varied on two forms randomly distributed to observers.

Results

An ANOVA with form order and video as between-subjects variables and mean levels of the nine attributes as a within-subjects variable yielded no significant effects. The data for the two forms and videos were combined in subsequent analyses. An ANOVA with target sex, target emotion, and rated emotion or trait as within-subjects variables yielded several significant effects.[2] Observers attributed higher levels of the nine emotions or traits to female ($M = 2.60$) than male ($M = 2.49$) targets, $F(1, 99) = 17.78$, $p < .0001$, and higher levels to embarrassed ($M = 2.58$) than amused ($M = 2.51$) targets, $F(1, 99) = 13.16$, $p < .001$. There was a significant effect for rated emotion, $F(8, 792) = 58.31$, $p < .00001$, and there were significant interactions between target sex and rated emotion, $F(8, 792) = 6.33$, $p < .0001$, target emotion and rated emotion, $F(8, 792) = 67.08$, $p < .0001$, and target emotion, target sex, and rated emotion, $F(8, 792) = 4.88$, $p < .0001$. Table 6.3 presents observers' judgments of the targets, broken down by target gender and emotion.

An ANOVA with target sex, target emotion, and attributed emotion (embarrassment or amusement) yielded a significant interaction consistent with the study's main hypothesis, $F(1, 100) = 147.73$, $p < .0001$. Simple effects analyses showed that observers attributed more embarrassment ($M = 3.11$) than amusement ($M = 1.84$) to embarrassed targets, $F(1, 99) = 118.71$, $p < .0001$, and more amusement ($M = 3.07$) than embarrassment ($M = 2.83$) to amused targets, $F(1, 99) = 5.41$, $p < .001$. Furthermore, observers attributed more embarrassment to embarrassed than amused targets, $F(1, 102) = 8.01$, $p < .01$, and more amusement to amused than embarrassed targets, $F(1, 102) = 244.57$, $p < .00001$.

TABLE 6.3. Attributions of emotion to male and female embarrassed and amused targets

Emotion	Embarrassed targets			Amused targets		
	Female	Male	Combined	Female	Male	Combined
Embarrassment						
M	3.43	2.80	3.11	2.95	2.72	2.83
SD	1.28	1.22	1.13	1.19	1.31	1.05
Amusement						
M	2.09	1.60	1.84	3.00	3.14	3.07
SD	0.86	0.86	0.68	1.11	1.11	0.81
Shame						
M	3.39	3.18	3.29	2.62	2.35	2.58
SD	1.22	1.22	1.10	1.11	0.96	0.88
Guilt						
M	1.86	2.05	1.96	1.64	1.71	1.67
SD	0.90	1.06	0.91	0.84	0.83	0.69
Disgust						
M	3.03	3.06	3.04	2.52	2.83	2.67
SD	1.25	1.35	1.16	1.10	0.87	0.82
Surprise						
M	1.52	1.55	1.53	1.89	1.97	1.93
SD	0.68	0.83	0.64	0.84	0.95	0.75
Self-Esteem						
M	2.49	2.45	2.47	2.80	2.75	2.78
SD	1.04	1.13	0.96	1.15	1.15	1.06
Nervousness						
M	3.71	3.21	3.46	3.29	2.99	3.14
SD	1.31	1.33	1.20	1.26	1.24	1.11
Self-consciousness						
M	2.45	2.59	2.52	2.04	1.99	2.02
SD	1.10	1.25	1.08	0.95	0.89	0.76

Separate two-way ANOVAs with target sex and target emotion as within-subjects variables examined each of the remaining emotions or traits. As hypothesized, observers attributed more shame, guilt, disgust, nervousness, and self-consciousness to the embarrassed targets, and more surprise and self-esteem to amused targets (all $ps < .001$). Finally, in partial support of the perceived-status hypothesis, observers attributed more embarrassment, shame, and nervousness to female than to male targets (all $ps < .01$), although this effect was not qualified by the expected Target Sex × Target Emotion interaction.

Study 4

In Study 4 observers were constrained even less by the response format: They simply wrote down the word that best described each target's emotion.

Method

Participants

Observers were 187 students (126 women and 61 men) at the University of Wisconsin—Madison, who received extra credit toward their course grade.

Procedure

Observers, participating in groups of 10 to 15, judged the targets from both videotapes in one of two randomly assigned orders. For each target, observers wrote down the word that described "the emotion shown by the individual in the videotape" or "no emotion."

Coding of Free-Response Data

A coding system was developed to categorize participants' responses according to their similarity to embarrassment or amusement. After reviewing a subset of the responses who were unaware of the targets' emotion, three coders and I specified four criteria that resembled the defining elements of embarrassment (referred to earlier) to classify all responses as either embarrassment or amusement. These criteria were validated by a group of 19 judges who rated how much "each quality (criterion) characterizes the experience of embarrassment and of amusement" ($1 = $ *not at all*, $7 = $ *extremely characteristic*). The first criterion was whether the response was a positive or negative emotion. Judges rated negative emotion as more characteristic of embarrassment than amusement ($Ms = 5.57$ and 1.27, respectively), $F(1, 18) = 176.43$, $p < .0001$, and positive emotion as more characteristic of amusement than embarrassment ($Ms = 6.73$ and 2.31, respectively), $F(1, 18) = 233.47$, $p < .0001$. Negative terms (e.g., shame or sadness) were classified as embarrassment: positive terms (e.g., happy or pleasant) were classified as amusement. The second criterion was whether the response referred to thought processes. Judges indicated that thought processes were more characteristic of embarrassment than amusement ($Ms = 5.53$ and 3.94, respectively), $F(1, 18) = 8.64$, $p < .01$, whereas the absence of thought processes was more characteristic of amusement than embarrassment ($Ms = 3.79$ and 2.00, respectively), $F(1, 18) = 14.97$, $p < .001$. Terms referring to thought processes (e.g., self-conscious, concentrating, or thinking) were categorized as embarrassment. The third criterion pertained to whether the word expressed concern for others' evaluation. Judges indicated that the concern for others' evaluation was more characteristic of embarrassment than amusement (Ms = 6.05 and 2.42, respectively), $F(1, 18)$ = 101.54, p < .0001, whereas the lack of concern for others' judgments was more characteristic of amusement than embarrassment (Ms = 5.26 and 1.84, respectively), $F(1, 18)$ = 61.93, p < .0001. Terms referring to concern for others' evaluation were categorized as embarrassment; terms denoting a lack of such concern (e.g., indifferent) were categorized as amusement. Finally, judges indicated that physical agitation, the fourth criterion, was more characteristic of embarrassment than amusement (Ms = 4.95 and 1.89, respectively), $F(1, 18)$ = 58.00, p < .001, whereas physical calm was more characteristic of amusement than embarrassment (Ms = 4.00 and 2.21, respectively), $F(1, 18)$ = 20.60, p < .001. Terms that referred to physical agitation were categorized as embarrassment (e.g., heart beating, arousal); terms that referred to low levels of physical agitation (e.g., calm, sleepy) were categorized as amusement. Using these four criteria, the three coders, blind to the experimental hypotheses, categorized each response as either embarrassment or amusement. Coders categorized a third of the responses, each overlapping with the two other coders on 10 participants' responses (340 terms). The average intercoder agreement was 97.6%.

Results

For each target, observers were given an accuracy score based on whether the term they provided was categorized as the same or different from the target's self-reported emotion. An initial ANOVA of observers' overall accuracy with order of video presentation as a between-subjects variable found no significant effects. The data from the two video orders were combined in subsequent analyses. Observers' overall accuracy rate (.57) exceeded chance (.5) in the binomial test (p < .01). An ANOVA with observer sex as a between-subjects variable and target sex and emotion as within-subjects variables yielded one main effect: Embarrassed targets were more accurately judged (.63) than amused targets (.51), $F(1, 185)$ = 33.65, p < .0001.

Further support of the Study 4 main hypothesis is found in the terms that observers most frequently used to label the embarrassed and amused targets. Observers most frequently labeled the embarrassed targets as *sad* (proportion of total responses = .121 vs. .071 for amused targets, z = 1.67, p < .05), and the amused targets as *happy* (.250 vs. .065 for embarrassed targets, z = 5.07, p < .001). Observers more frequently labeled amused targets as *amused* (.057 vs. .024, z = 1.66, p < .05) and embarrassed targets as *nervous* (.054 vs. .021, z = 1.88, p < .05). Observers infrequently used the term *embarrassment* to label the emotions of embarrassed (.035) and amused targets (.035).

Synthesis of Studies 2, 3, and 4: Relations Between Observers' Judgments and Targets' Behavior

Table 6.4 presents the correlations between observers' judgments and targets' behavior across the three judgment studies. Observers' judgments of embarrassment were positively correlated with the duration of gaze down, intensity of smile controls, number of gaze shifts, intensity of head movements down and to the left, and duration of face touching. Observers' judgments of amusement, on the other hand, were correlated with

TABLE **6.4.** Correlations between observers' judgments and targets' nonverbal behavior

Behavior	Study 2 % Emb	Study 3 Emb	Study 3 Amu	Study 3 Sha	Study 4 % Emb	Study 4 % Amu
Gaze down duration	.36**	.33**	−.21	.45***	.26*	−.26*
Smile control intensity	.10	.31*	.14	.10	.37**	−.26*
Smile intensity	−.46***	.06	.58***	−.42**	−.36**	.39**
Gaze shifts	.16	.36**	.04	.05	.23	−.26*
Head down intensity	.55***	.37**	−.32**	.66***	.37**	−.31*
Head to side intensity	.47***	.08	−.37**	.36**	.33**	−.30*
Face touch duration	.39**	.33**	−.13	.41**	.16	−.12

Note: By definition, the correlation between the percentage of observers who judged the target as amused and targets' behavior from Study 2 is the inverse of the correlation represented in the column. Emb = embarrassment; Amu = amusement; Sha = shame
* p < .10. ** p < .05. *** p < .01.

the intensity of the targets' smile and the absence of certain markers of embarrassment (e.g., head down and gaze down). Observers' attributions of shame in Study 3 were related to head and gaze shifts down, consistent with descriptions of shame (Izard, 1977; Lewis, Alessandri, & Sullivan, 1992) and were unrelated to two perceived markers of embarrassment, smile controls and sideways gaze shifts.

Prototypicality of Targets' Behavior and Observers' Judgments

Targets who displayed more emotion-specific behaviors (i.e., targets showing more prototypical displays) were expected to be judged with greater consensus. To examine this notion, we created a scale, presented in figure 6.2, that classified the targets' displays

Scale ranging from protypical amusement to prototypical embarrassment response

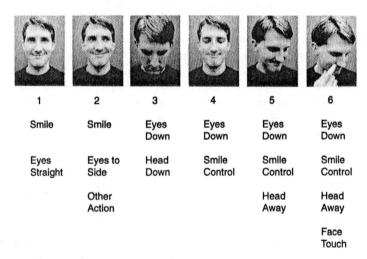

1	2	3	4	5	6
Smile	Smile	Eyes Down	Eyes Down	Eyes Down	Eyes Down
Eyes Straight	Eyes to Side	Head Down	Smile Control	Smile Control	Smile Control
	Other Action			Head Away	Head Away
					Face Touch

Figure 6.2. Scale for categorizing responses according to embarrassment and amusement prototypes.

Judged Emotion of Target Stimuli

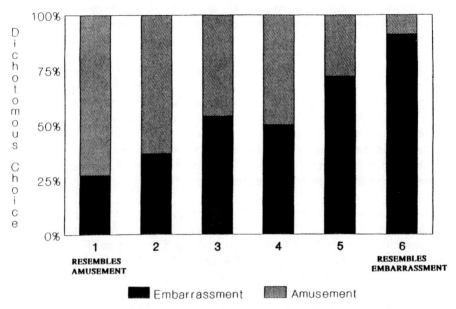

Figure 6.3. Percentages of participants who judged each kind of response as embarrassment and amusement.

according to their resemblance to embarrassment or amusement prototypes. The embarrassment prototype included the behaviors related to targets' self-reports and observers' judgments of embarrassment: gaze down, a smile control, gaze shifts, head turns, and a face touch. The amusement prototype included an uncontrolled laugh or smile (Ruch, 1993) with an onset that preceded gaze aversion. The four scale points in between the embarrassment and amusement prototypes possessed increasing behavioral markers of embarrassment. Each of the 34 displays presented in the judgment studies was placed in one of the six categories represented in the scale. Figure 6.3 presents the mean frequency with which the targets placed into the six different categories were judged as embarrassed and amused in Study 2. Across the judgment studies, and consistent with figure 6.3, observers' judgments were correlated with the prototypicality of the display. The target's scale value ($1 = prototypical\ amusement$, $6 = prototypical\ embarrassment$) was correlated with the percentage of observers who judged the target to be embarrassed in Study 2 ($r = .76, p < .001$) and Study 4 ($r = .67, p < .001$) and with observers' attributions of embarrassment ($r = .36, p < .05$) and amusement ($r = -.51, p < .01$) in Study 3.

Study 5

The primary aim of Study 5 was to address whether the displays of embarrassment and shame are distinct. Many contend that embarrassment and shame share the same nonverbal display and, by implication, are variants of the same emotion (Izard,

1977; Tomkins, 1963). In contrast, the appeasement hypothesis suggests that embarrassment and shame will have distinct displays if they signal apologies for different kinds of transgressions. Indeed, research has shown that shame follows failures to live up to personal ideas of virtue and character (Babcock, 1988; Babcock & Sabini, 1990; Lindsay-Hartz, 1984), whereas embarrassment follows violations of rules regulating social comportment (Edelmann, 1987; Miller, 1992). Furthermore, shameful acts potentially elicit harsher judgments and punishment than embarrassing acts. On the basis of these differences in the content and seriousness of their preceding transgressions, the displays of embarrassment and shame were expected to be distinct to observers.

In Study 5, observers judged the spontaneous displays of two positive emotions (amusement and enjoyment), two negative emotions (anger and disgust), and two self-conscious emotions (embarrassment and shame) shown by adolescent boys during the administration of an interactive IQ test. The perceived status hypothesis was tested by presenting observers with African-American and Caucasian targets' behaviorally equivalent displays of each of the six emotions.

Beyond testing whether embarrassment and shame have distinct displays, Study 5 extended the generality of the embarrassment display documented in Study 1. The embarrassment displays presented to observers in Study 5 were those of adolescents instead of college students. Half of the adolescent targets, furthermore, were African American. Most important, the emotion displays were sampled from a social, interactive situation in which the adolescent target engaged in a face-to-face interaction with an adult. Observers were expected to accurately identify the displays of the six emotions and to be more accurate and attribute more emotion in judging the embarrassment and shame displays of African-American targets.

Method

Participants

Observers were 183 students (97 women and 86 men) at the University of Wisconsin—Madison who received extra credit toward their course grade.

Materials

The targets were 12- to 13-year-old male participants in the Pittsburgh Youth Study (PYS: for details, see Loeber, Stouthamer-Loeber, Van Kammen, & Farrington, 1989). Targets' displays of the six emotions were sampled from a FACS-scored portion (2 1/2 min long) of their participation in the general information subtest of the interactively administered Wechsler Intelligence Scales for Children, reported on elsewhere (Keltner, Caspi, Krueger, & Stouthamer-Loeber, 1993). In the general information test, an adult tester asked the targets a series of questions requiring answers that would be found in an encyclopedia (e.g., "How far is it from New York to Los Angeles?", "Who is Charles Darwin?"). According to script, the tester queried targets when they offered no response or ambiguous responses.

The selected displays of the six emotions satisfied validated behavioral criteria for each emotion. The selected displays of anger, disgust, and enjoyment (Duchenne smiles) corresponded to FACS-based descriptions of those emotions (Ekman, 1984). The selected displays of shame included head and gaze movements down (Izard, 1977;

Lewis et al., 1992). The selected displays of amusement included Duchenne smiles, head movements back, and the mouth opening of laughter. The selected displays of embarrassment included gaze down, a controlled smile, head movements away, and face touching.

The displays of 24 different targets (four for each of the six emotions) were presented in one of two random orders. Two African-American and two Caucasian targets, matched for intensity (within 1 point on the FACS 5-point scale) and duration (within 0.5 s) of the relevant facial, head, and gaze movements, were selected for each of the six emotions. Only the video portion of the target's display from its onset to offset and no other behavior (talking, hand and arm movements except in the embarrassment displays, or other facial movements) was visible. Each target's display was viewed for about 3 s. Each target was visible from the chest up sitting at a table; the tester was not visible.

Procedure

Observers, participating in groups of 5 to 15, first indicated which of the six terms (amusement, anger, disgust, embarrassment, enjoyment, or shame) best matched each target's emotion. Observers then rated the intensity of the target's emotion (0 = *no emotion*, 8 = *extremely intense emotion*).

Results

Overall Accuracy

Observers' overall accuracy (.53) exceeded accuracy levels expected by chance (.167), $p < .001$. Table 6.5 presents observers' two most common categorical judgments and intensity ratings of the targets' displays.

An ANOVA with observer sex as a between-subjects variable and emotion (six levels) and target race as within-subjects variables first examined observers' accuracy levels. Female observers ($M = .55$) were more accurate than male observers ($M = .51$), $F(1, 181) = 6.89$, $p < .01$, and African-American targets were more accurately judged ($M = .55$) than Caucasian targets ($M = .51$), although this effect was qualified by a Race × Emotion interaction, $F(5, 905) = 25.39$, $p < .001$. In partial support of the perceived-status hypothesis, simple effects analyses showed that observers judged African-American targets' displays of embarrassment, shame, and anger more accurately than those of Caucasian targets. Caucasian targets' displays of amusement and disgust were more accurately judged than those of African-American targets (all $ps < .01$). Finally, there was a main effect for emotion, $F(5, 905) = 21.23$, $p < .001$. Although the displays of all emotions were judged with above-chance accuracy, those of embarrassment and shame were the most accurately judged. The displays of all emotions were labeled with the primary emotion term significantly more often than the secondary term (all $ps < .001$), with the exception of enjoyment smiles, which were as likely to be judged as amusement as enjoyment.

An ANOVA of observers' judgments of the intensity of emotion found two main effects. First, there was a main effect for emotion, $F(5, 905) = 188.24$, $p < .00001$. Observers attributed the most intense emotion to the targets displaying shame. Second, observers attributed more emotion to African-American ($M = 4.36$) than Caucasian

TABLE **6.5.** Categorical and intensity judgments of African-American and
Caucasian targets' displays of six emotions

	Race of target				
	African American		Caucasian		
Facial expression	M	SD	M	SD	Combined
Amusement					
Amusement	44.0		61.5		52.3
Enjoyment	29.0		24.0		26.5
Intensity	4.45	1.27	4.20	1.39	4.33
Anger					
Anger	43.5		38.0		40.8
Disgust	15.0		35.0		25.0
Intensity	3.95	1.41	3.25	1.39	3.60
Disgust					
Disgust	51.5		57.5		54.0
Anger	24.4		12.3		18.4
Intensity	3.33	1.44	3.02	1.38	3.12
Embarrassment					
Embarrassment	67.5		53.5		60.5
Shame	10.5		15.1		12.8
Intensity	4.35	1.19	3.93	1.27	4.14
Enjoyment					
Enjoyment	42.5		43.5		43.0
Amusement	40.7		43.2		41.9
Intensity	4.37	1.27	4.02	1.42	4.19
Shame					
Shame	82.0		52.0		67.0
Disgust	05.7		20.1		12.9
Intensity	5.69	1.50	5.46	1.15	5.57

($M = 3.98$) targets, $F(1, 181) = 72.98$, although this effect was qualified by an Emotion × Race interaction, $F(5, 905) = 2.59$, $p < .05$. In partial support of the perceived-status hypothesis, simple effects analyses showed that observers attributed more emotion to African-American targets' displays of each emotion except amusement (all $ps < .01$).

Discussion

In Study 5, observers were presented with a wider array of spontaneous emotion displays than in the preceding judgment studies. Observers were well above chance in identifying the displays of all emotions, which is the first evidence showing that observers can accurately identify spontaneous facial displays of emotion. This is especially impressive when one considers that the displays were only viewed for about 3 s. Consistent with the study's main hypothesis, observers accurately distinguished between the displays of embarrassment and shame, infrequently confusing the two.

Observers' judgments, once again, were swayed considerably by observer and target characteristics. Consistent with previous studies (Hall, 1984), female observers were more accurate than male observers. Although African-American targets' emotion displays were more accurately judged than those of Caucasian targets, the greatest discrepancies were evident in observers' increased accuracy in judging African-American targets' displays of embarrassment and shame. Whereas the accuracy findings were fairly congruent with the perceived-status hypothesis, the emotion attribution findings, for the most part, were not: Observers attributed more emotion to African-American targets' displays of five of the six emotions.

General Discussion

According to the appeasement function of embarrassment, individuals' displays of embarrassment appease observers of social transgressions. This view implies that embarrassment is marked by a distinct display—a hypothesis for which this investigation gathered four kinds of evidence. Because no a priori facial display had been predicted for embarrassment, Study 1 began by examining what nonverbal behavior accompanies the actual experience of embarrassment. Analyses showed that both the morphology and dynamic patterns of the behavior associated with embarrassment and amusement were distinct, differentially related to self-reports of emotion, and emotion-like in their onset and duration.

In the ensuing judgment studies, observers accurately discriminated between the displays of embarrassment and those of emotions most likely to be confused with embarrassment, including amusement, shame, anger, disgust, and enjoyment. Although not as accurate as judges of posed facial expressions (Ekman & Friesen, 1971), observers in our investigation were as accurate as judges of deceptive and nondeceptive behavior (DePaulo, 1992; Ekman, 1985) and enjoyment and nonenjoyment smiles (Frank et al., 1993), and were more accurate than judges of morphologically similar emotions, such as surprise and fear (Ekman & Friesen, 1971). Furthermore, when judging prototypical embarrassment displays, observers were highly accurate (92% in Study 2).

These four lines of evidence support the hypothesis that embarrassment has a distinct facial display. The findings further argue, at least partially, for the distinct displays of shame and amusement, the latter being accurately differentiated from the Duchenne smile of enjoyment. Humans communicate nonverbally both more positive and negative emotions than previously considered (e.g., Ekman, 1992).

Universality and Variants of Embarrassment

In this investigation, targets' self-reports (from Study 1) and observers' judgments converged on a clear embarrassment response, marked by gaze down, controlled smiles, head turns, gaze shifts, and face touches. As previously discussed, these markers of embarrassment are likely to vary according to which of many diverse events has elicited the embarrassment. Accounting for the systematic variation in the embarrassment display is an important line of inquiry, one which will more fully characterize the theme and variants of the embarrassment display.

Knowing the markers of embarrassment makes several research directions possible. To ascertain the cross-cultural constants and variation in embarrassment, still photographs of embarrassment can be constructed and included in more traditional cross-cultural judgment studies. For example, it will be interesting to determine whether people from cultures in which embarrassment and shame are referred to with the same word (e.g., in certain parts of India) can discriminate between the nonverbal displays of embarrassment and shame. Behavioral assessments of individual differences in embarrassment can document both the individual consistency in the embarrassment response and the correlates of embarrassment proneness. Given the themes that are central to embarrassment, one might expect people prone to embarrassment to be more conventional, conforming, and guided by salient personal standards. Pursuing these issues relies first on identifying the nonverbal markers of embarrassment—a building block offered by this investigation.

Appeasement Functions of Embarrassment and Shame

This study has provided evidence for one aspect of the appeasement gestures that allows individuals to "apologize" for transgressions: There are identifiable signals of appeasement-related emotions that are related to the perceived status of the individual displaying the emotion. Subsequent research needs to directly characterize the process by which displays of embarrassment (and shame) appease observers.

A first question concerns whether the embarrassment display reduces the arousal of observers—one component of appeasement (de Waal, 1988). If so, it will be interesting to determine which component of the embarrassment display appeases observers, reducing their tendency toward hostile judgment and action. The candidates include the smile (Ellyson & Dovidio, 1985), the blush (Castelfranchi & Poggi, 1990), and even the neck display that is produced by head turns.

Second, it will be worthwhile to consider the different effects that displays of embarrassment and shame have on observers. Displays of embarrassment and shame may elicit different emotions in observers, such as amusement and sympathy, respectively, which result in different appeasement processes. Observers who experience amusement on observing an embarrassed individual may be inclined to make light of the sender's transgression. Observers who experience sympathy on observing an ashamed individual may instead be inclined to extend a sympathetic gesture to the sender, offering reassurance and comfort. Although so brief in its social manifestation, embarrassment, and its study, offer profound lessons about human relations.

Notes

1. Fifty percent was chosen as the frequency with which an action must occur to be defined as part of the prototype on the basis of previous research on emotion prototypes (Shaver, Schwartz, Kirson, & O'Connor, 1987).

2. All omnibus analyses in Studies 3 through 5 that violated the compound symmetry assumption were carried out with the Greenhouse-Geisser correction and yielded the same p values as those reported in the text.

References

Asendorpf, J. (1990). The expression of shyness and embarrassment. In W. R. Crozier (Ed.), *Shyness and embarrassment: Perspectives from social psychology* (pp. 87–118). Cambridge, England: Cambridge University Press.

Ausubel, D. P. (1955). Relationships between shame and guilt in the socializing process. *Psychological Review, 62,* 378–390.

Babcock, M. (1988). Embarrassment: A window on the self. *Journal for the Theory of Social Behaviour, 18,* 459–483.

Babcock, M. K., & Sabini, J. (1990). On differentiating embarrassment from shame. *European Journal of Social Psychology, 20,* 151–169.

Baumeister, R. F., Stillwell, A. M., & Heatherton, T. F. (1994). Guilt: An interpersonal approach. *Psychological Bulletin, 115,* 243–267.

Castelfranchi, C., & Poggi, I. (1990). Blushing as discourse: Was Darwin wrong? In W. R. Crozier (Ed.), *Shyness and embarrassment: Perspectives from social psychology* (pp. 230–254). Cambridge, England: Cambridge University Press.

Clark, C. (1990). Emotions and the micropolitics in everyday life: Some patterns and paradoxes of "place." In T. D. Kemper (Ed.), *Research agendas in the sociology of emotions* (pp. 305–334). Albany: State University of New York Press.

Cohen, J., & Cohen, P. (1983). *Applied multiple regression/correlational analysis for the behavioral sciences* (2nd ed.). Hillsdale, NJ: Erlbaum.

DePaulo, B. M. (1992). Nonverbal behavior and self-presentation. *Psychological Bulletin, 111,* 203–243.

de Waal, F. B. M. (1988). The reconciled hierarchy. In M. R. A. Chance (Ed.), *Social fabrics of the mind* (pp. 105–136). Hillsdale, NJ: Erlbaum.

Edelmann, R. (1985). Individual differences in embarrassment: Self-consciousness, self-monitoring, and embarrassability. *Personality and Individual Differences, 6,* 223–230.

Edelmann, R. J. (1987). *The psychology of embarrassment.* Chichester, England: Wiley.

Edelmann, R. J., & Hampson, S. E. (1979). Changes in non-verbal behavior during embarrassment. *British Journal of Social and Clinical Psychology, 18,* 385–390.

Edelmann, R. J., & Hampson, S. E. (1981). The recognition of embarrassment. *Personality and Social Psychology Bulletin, 7,* 109–116.

Eibl-Eibesfeldt, I. (1989). *Human ethology.* New York: Aldine de Gruyter.

Eisenberg, N., Fabes, R. A., Miller, P. A., Fultz, J., Shell, R., Mathy, R. M., & Reno, R. R. (1989). Relation of sympathy and personal distress to prosocial behavior: A multimethod study. *Journal of Personality and Social Psychology, 57,* 55–66.

Ekman, P. (1982). *Emotion in the human face.* Cambridge, England: Cambridge University Press.

Ekman, P. (1984). Expression and the nature of emotion. In K. Scherer & P. Ekman (Eds.), *Approaches to emotion* (pp. 319–344). Hillsdale, NJ: Erlbaum.

Ekman, P. (1985). *Telling lies: Clues to deceit in the marketplace, marriage, and politics.* New York: W. W. Norton.

Ekman, P. (1992). An argument for basic emotions. *Cognition and Emotion, 6,* 169–200.

Ekman, P., & Friesen, W. V. (1971). Constants across cultures in the face and emotion. *Journal of Personality and Social Psychology, 17,* 124–129.

Ekman, P., & Friesen, W. V. (1976). Measuring facial movement. *Journal of Environmental Psychology and Nonverbal Behavior, 1,* 56–75.

Ekman, P., & Friesen, W. V. (1978). *Facial action coding system: A technique for the measurement of facial movement.* Palo Alto, CA: Consulting Psychologists Press.

Ekman, P., & Friesen, W. V. (1982). Felt, false and miserable smiles. *Journal of Nonverbal Behavior, 6,* 238–252.

Ekman, P., Friesen, W. V., & Ancoli, S. (1980). Facial signs of emotional experience. *Journal of Personality and Social Psychology, 39,* 1125–1134.

Ekman, P., Friesen, W. V., & Ellsworth, P. C. (1982). *Emotion in the human face.* Cambridge, England: Cambridge University Press.

Ekman, P., Sorenson, E. R., & Friesen, W. V. (1969). Pan-cultural elements in facial displays of emotions. *Science, 164,* 86–88.

Ellyson, S. L., & Dovidio, J. F. (1985). *Power, dominance, and nonverbal behavior.* New York: Springer-Verlag.

Fehr, B., & Russell, J. A. (1984). Concept of emotion viewed from a prototype perspective. *Journal of Experimental Psychology, 113,* 464–486.

Frank, M., Ekman, P., & Friesen, W. V. (1993). Behavioral markers and recognizability of the smile of enjoyment. *Journal of Personality and Social Psychology, 64,* 83–93.

Friedman, H. S., Prince, L. M., Riggio, R. E., DiMatteo, M. R. (1980). Understanding and assessing nonverbal expressiveness: The affective communication test. *Journal of Personality and Social Psychology, 49,* 333–351.

Goffman, E. (1956). Embarrassment and social organization. *American Journal of Sociology, 62,* 264–271.

Goffman, E. (1967). *Interaction ritual: Essays on face-to-face behavior.* Garden City, NY: Anchor.

Hall, J. A. (1984). *Sex differences in nonverbal behavior.* Baltimore, MD: Johns Hopkins University Press.

Heckhausen, H. (1984). Emergent achievement behavior: Some early developments. In J. Nicholls (Ed.), *Advances in motivation and achievement: Vol. 3. The development of achievement motivation* (pp. 1–32). Greenwich, CT: JAI Press.

Izard, C. E. (1971). *The face of emotion.* New York: Appleton-Century-Crofts.

Izard, C. E. (1977). *Human emotions.* New York: Plenum Press.

Keltner, D., Caspi, A., Krueger, R., & Stouthamer-Loeber, M. (1993). *Facial expressions of emotion and personality.* Manuscript in preparation.

Larsen, R. J., & Diener, E. (1987). Affect intensity as an individual difference characteristic: A review. *Journal of Research in Personality, 21,* 1–39.

Leary, M. R. (1983). A brief version of the fear of negative evaluation scale. *Personality and Social Psychology Bulletin, 9,* 371–375.

Leary, M. R., & Meadows, S. (1991). Predictors, elicitors, and concomitants of social blushing. *Journal of Personality and Social Psychology, 60,* 254–262.

Levenson, R. W., Ekman, P., & Friesen, W. V. (1990). Voluntary facial activity generates emotion-specific autonomic nervous system activity. *Psychophysiology, 27,* 363–384.

Lewis, M. (1993). Self-conscious emotions: Embarrassment, pride, shame, and guilt. In M. Lewis & J. M. Haviland (Eds.), *Handbook of emotions* (pp. 353–364). New York: Guilford.

Lewis, M., Allessandri, S. M., & Sullivan, M. W. (1992). Differences in shame and pride as a function of children's gender and task difficulty. *Child Development, 63,* 630–638.

Lindsay-Hartz, J. (1984). Contrasting experiences of shame and guilt. *American Behavioral Scientist, 27,* 689–704.

Loeber, R., Stouthamer-Loeber, M., Van Kammen, W., & Farrington, D. P. (1989). Development of a new measure of self-reported antisocial behavior for young children: Prevalence and reliability. In M. Klein (Ed.), *Cross-national research in self-reported crime and delinquency* (pp. 203–226). Boston, MA: Kluwer-Nijhoff.

Miller, R. S. (1992). The nature and severity of self-reported embarrassing circumstances. *Personality and Social Psychology Bulletin, 18,* 190–198.

Miller, R. S., & Leary, M. R. (1992). Social sources and interactive functions of embarrassment. In M. Clark (Ed.), *Emotion and social behavior* (pp. 202–221). New York: Sage.

Modigliani, A. (1968). Embarrassment and embarrassability. *Sociometry, 31,* 313–326.

Modigliani, A. (1971). Embarrassment, facework, and eye contact: Testing a theory of embarrassment. *Journal of Personality and Social Psychology, 17,* 15–24.

Ruch, W. (1993). Exhilaration and humor. In M. Lewis & J. M. Haviland (Eds.), *The handbook of emotion* (pp. 605–616). New York: Guilford.

Shaver, P., Schwartz, J., Kirson, D., & O'Connor, C. (1987). Emotion knowledge: Further exploration of a prototype approach. *Journal of Personality and Social Psychology, 52,* 1061–1086.

Stipek, D., Recchia, S., & McClintic, S. (1992). Self-evaluation in young children. *Monographs of the Society for Research in Child Development, 57,* 1, 226.

Tangney, J. P. (1992). Situational determinants of shame and guilt in young adulthood. *Personality and Social Psychology Bulletin, 18,* 199–206.

Tomkins, S. S. (1963). *Affect, imagery, consciousness: Vol. 2. The negative affects.* New York: Springer.

Tomkins, S. S. (1984). Affect theory. In K. Scherer & P. Ekman (Eds.), *Approaches to emotion* (pp. 163–196). Hillsdale, NJ: Erlbaum.

The Forms and Functions of Embarrassment

DACHER KELTNER

It is my conviction that embarrassment is a basic emotion, common to humans across cultures, that serves the important social function of appeasing observers of social transgressions. The preceding article provides initial evidence that embarrassment has a distinct nonverbal display that can be reliably coded in the study of spontaneous emotion. My subsequent research has examined the form of the embarrassment display to ascertain whether it is a discrete emotion and its appeasement function to determine whether embarrassment, like other emotions, serves vital social functions.

One question left unanswered by the reprinted article is whether the embarrassment display varies across contexts and, if so, which components of the display are constant and define the theme of the display, and which vary. Establishing the theme and variants of the embarrassment display informs us about likely individual and cross-cultural variations in that emotion (Ekman, 1992). Based on these interests, we observed people in three embarrassing circumstances: following overpraise, a positive induction; while watching someone else make an embarrassing face, a more neutral induction; and following the disclosure of personal feelings about a confederate of the other sex, a more negative induction (Buswell & Keltner, 1995). Although all three inductions reliably produced a prototypical embarrassment display, there was systematic variation in the response. The "theme" of the embarrassment display—that is, the invariant components—included initial gaze down, smile controls, and face touching. Other components of the embarrassment display varied according to the valence of the context: overpraise, the more positive of the inductions, produced more frequent and intense Duchenne smiles, whereas disclosure, the more negative of the inductions, produced longer gaze and head movements down. One might hypothesize that these components of embarrassment will vary according to the individual's or culture's evaluation of embarrassment. Finally, there were interesting gender differences: women smiled and touched their head, in particular their hair, more frequently, which may have been a flirtatious gesture.

A second line of research has addressed whether the embarrassment display can be identified in still photographs, independent of its dynamic movement, and whether its display is interpreted similarly across diverse cultures (Haidt & Keltner, 1995; Keltner

& Buswell, in press). Participants in rural India and the United States were presented with still photographs of prototypical expressions of embarrassment, shame, and amusement (open-mouthed laughter with head cast backwards), along with anger, contempt, disgust, enjoyment, fear, sadness, surprise, sympathy, and 3 nonemotional expressions, and asked to select the word from a list of 14 emotion terms that best matched the expression after describing the expression in their own terms. Participants in both the United States and India accurately differentiated the prototypical display of embarrassment, and had no trouble differentiating it from the display of shame (head down and gaze aversion). Interesting, the second most common response to the embarrassment display in India was romantic love, which we believe relates to the role of embarrassment during flirtation and courtship.

More recently, we have begun to examine the appeasement functions of embarrassment, which include signaling submissiveness, marking the importance of social norms, and increasing social approach (Keltner, Young, & Buswell, in press). Our approach has been to study ritualized social interactions that produce embarrassment, such as teasing and flirtation, that should share its appeasement functions. Following this reasoning, teasing and flirtation should revolve around appeasement-related functions.

One study focused on teasing, a universal social process known to elicit embarrassment (Keltner & Buswell, in press). Studies of people's descriptions of teasing support the contention that teasing revolves around the three appeasement-related functions of embarrassment (for review, see Keltner & Heerey, 1995). First, teasing, like embarrassment, demarcates social status: bullies and the most popular children are the most likely to tease, whereas low-status children and, interesting, popular children were most likely to be teased. Teasing, like embarrassment, revolves around the violation of social norms by encouraging conformity and desired changes in others. Teasing also affords new members to groups the opportunity to demonstrate to others their knowledge of group norms, thus increasing their acceptance within groups. Finally, teasing, like embarrassment, facilitates friendship and intimacy.

To examine these three hypothesized functions of teasing, we brought low- and high-status fraternity members into the laboratory in groups of 4 (2 high- and 2 low-status members per group). In the teasing exercise, participants were given randomly generated initial pairs and 10 minutes to make up nicknames for the other participants and stories justifying those nicknames. They then told their nicknames and stories about each other in strikingly funny, bawdy exchanges. Amid the laughter, taunting, and banter we discerned three patterns of results that supported the hypothesis that teasing, like embarrassment, revolves around appeasement.

First, both in the content of what was said and the emotions displayed, participants demarcated their status differences during the brief interactions. Low-status members praised high-status members in teasing, whereas high-status participants humiliated and expressed their dominance toward low-status participants. Low-status participants more frequently displayed nonverbal markers of lower status, including postural contraction, the nonverbal markers of embarrassment, and submissive smiles, facial expressions of fear, and winces of pain. High-status participants, on the other hand, showed the signs of dominance, including postural expansion and facial expressions of anger and contempt.

Consistent with the second hypothesized function of teasing, the teasing interactions revolved around violations of norms important to fraternity life, including drinking and taking drugs, sexual abnormality, and negative personality traits. Greater deviations of these norms were attributed to the low-status members, encouraging the avoidance of such deviations, whereas low-status members were more likely to explicitly refer to the fraternity guidelines, activities, and power structures, demonstrating their adherence to the group's norms.

Finally, evidence attests to the manner in which teasing increases social approach, and more generally, to the idea that embarrassment-related social practices involve social skill. Participants expressed high levels of contagious positive emotion. Participants rated the personalities of their teasing session partners, in particular their Agreeableness, as higher than that of the fraternity members who they did not tease in the laboratory. The quality of participants' teasing, based on an assessment of how well the tease was told and dramatized, was correlated with the frequency with which participants were nominated as good candidates for fraternity president and how well they were known by others. Finally, the markers of embarrassment displayed by the targets of teasing, the gaze and head movements down and face touching, were positively correlated with the positive emotion reported by the teaser and the audience members. We are taking a similar approach, focusing on the felt and displayed emotion between individuals, to document the role of appeasement related behavior, and embarrassment in particular, in flirtation and cooperation during potential conflict.

References

Buswell, B. N., & Keltner, D. (1995). *The themes and variants of embarrassment: A study of social facial expression across three embarrassing situations.* Manuscript under review.

Ekman, P. (1992). An argument for basic emotions. *Cognition and Emotion, 6,* 169–200.

Haidt, J., & Keltner, D. (1995). *A cross cultural study of the social-moral emotions: Constants and variation in emotion in India and the United States.* Manuscript under review.

Keltner, D., & Buswell, B. N. (in press). Evidence for the distinctness of embarrassment, shame, and guilt: A study of recalled antecedents and facial expressions of emotion. *Cognition and Emotion.*

Keltner, D., & Heerey, E. A. (1995). *The social and moral functions of teasing.* Manuscript under review.

Keltner, D., Young, R., & Buswell, B. N. (in press). Social-emotional processes in human appeasement. *Journal of Aggressive Behaviour.*

7

Genuine, Suppressed, and Faked Facial Behavior during Exacerbation of Chronic Low Back Pain

KENNETH D. CRAIG, SUSAN A. HYDE & CHRISTOPHER J. PATRICK

Facial activity during painful events has attracted attention as a source of diagnostic information in adults (Craig & Prkachin, 1983; Grunau, Johnston, & Craig, 1990; Keefe, Bradley, & Crisson, 1990; LeResche & Dworkin, 1984; Prkachin & Mercer, 1989) and children (Grunau & Craig, 1987; Grunau et al., 1990; Izard, Heubner, Resser, McGinness, & Dougherty, 1980). There also is evidence that facial grimaces of pain determine the reactions of observers in the natural social environment (Craig, Grunau, & Aquan-Assee, 1988; Kleck et al., 1976; Lanzetta, Cartwright-Smith, & Kleck, 1976; Patrick, Craig, & Prkachin, 1986; Prkachin, Currie, & Craig, 1983). Thus, understanding the facial display of pain has considerable importance for understanding both clinical decision making and spontaneous social behavior.

The development of an anatomically based, microscopic system for characterizing discrete facial actions, the Facial Action Coding System (FACS; Ekman & Friesen, 1976, 1978a, 1978b), has led to the description of a relatively consistent set of pain-related facial actions. These have been found to characterize the response to painful events in both the laboratory, using induced pain (Craig & Patrick, 1985; Patrick et al., 1986), and in clinical settings during examination of patients experiencing either exacerbations of persistent pain (LeResche & Dworkin, 1988b; Prkachin & Mercer, 1989) or induced pain (Prkachin & Mercer, 1989). Given a developing consensus concerning the topography of facial activity during pain (Hyde, 1986), the present investigation sought to explore: (1) the pattern of expression in one of the more prevalent clinical pain syndromes, chronic low back pain, (2) whether the display of pain could be suppressed and (3) whether an attempt to fake the display of pain could be discriminated from the genuine reaction.

As conceived, the study provided an opportunity to examine the impact of voluntary control over facial activity on the response to painful events. Clinicians and scientists alike often express interest in whether patients are exaggerating or faking pain (e.g., Cleeland, 1989). Environmental pressures that can lead to purposeful or unwitting dissimulation of pain include financial incentives, release from unpleasant work or social responsibilites, and increased attention from others (Fordyce, 1976). Of less obvious concern in clinical settings, but of great human interest, would be whether people can effectively suppress their non-verbal reaction to painful events, thereby concealing evidence of genuine pain from others. For example, manual labourers and high performance athletes may be motivated to hide or deny pain because to complain could lead to loss of work (Kotarba, 1983). In this study, we were able to examine the relationship between the spontaneous facial reaction of patients during a painful physical manipulation, administered in the course of a standard physiotherapy examination, with the reaction of the same people when they were requested to (1) mask the facial expression during the same painful movement and (2) pose an expression of painful distress.

The extent to which voluntary control of facial displays of pain can be achieved has not been determined, although concerns about the possibility of dissembling pain behavior are pervasive among both clinicians and researchers (Fordyce, 1976; Kremer, Block, & Atkinson, 1983). Lanzetta et al. (1976) found that, when instructed to deceive, subjects were successful in convincing judges that they had received a more or less intense shock than had in fact been delivered. It has been proposed that one of the advantages of non-verbal measures of pain is that they are less subject to conscious deception than verbalizations (Craig & Prkachin, 1980, 1983). However, one cannot expect the non-verbal response to painful events to be exclusively innate or reflexive, despite the prominent sensory component. There is only a moderate relationship between the severity of noxious stimulation and the behavioral response of the individual, given the substantial affective and cognitive contributions to the nature of the response (Craig, 1986). Thus, there is ample room for the possibility of pain being dissembled or purposefully suppressed. Actors and children at play can achieve considerable success in portraying intense states of pain and there are circumstances in which people do not want others to know the presence of severity of pain they are experiencing.

People judging the emotional significance of another's actions appear to assume that non-verbal behavior is less amenable to dissimulation than self-report (Ekman & Friesen, 1969, 1974) and weight it as more important when self-report and non-verbal behavior are discordant (Craig & Prkachin, 1983; DePaulo, Rosenthal, Eisenstat, Rogers, & Finkelstein, 1978; Jacox, 1980). Kraut (1978) has observed that the accuracy of detection of others' attempts to deceive is enhanced when the observers are allowed to observe both non-verbal as well as verbal behavior during the deception. Related to this is the assumption that different components of facial expression are less amenable to voluntary control. When reporting which regions of the face are the most important when making judgments of another's emotional state, observers attached prime importance to the upper face and eyes (Lee & Craig, submitted).

There has been dispute as to the extent to which the expression of emotional states is subject to environmental influence. Darwin (1872/1955) examined the adaptive, evolutionary role of expressive behavior and concluded "that in the case of the chief expressive actions they are not learned but are present from the earliest days and throughout life are quite beyond our control" (p. 352). Presently, the empirical evidence supports the contrary position that social factors influence the non-verbal expression of emotional states both with and without purposeful or voluntary intent. There appear to be cultural conventions concerning stereotypic displays of pain that enable people to enact them with ease. Facial displays of many subjective states are subject to the influence of "display rules" that are internalized in the course of socialization (Ekman & Friesen, 1971). These can serve to enhance or distort communication of the distress felt by the individual (Ekman, 1977; Kleck et al., 1976; Kraut, 1982; Lanzetta et al., 1976). These rules are comparable to those governing self-report of pain. Thus, willingness to complain of pain varies with age, sex, chronicity of the pain complaint, affective status of the individual, perceived professional status of the person soliciting information and other features of the social context (Kremer et al., 1983). In general, one would expect patterns of painful complaint and non-verbal expression that do not have a basis in tissue pathology to be traceable to the individual's distinctive social and psychological origins (Craig & Prkachin, 1980).

This study defined facial reactions of chronic low back pain patients during acute exacerbation of pain. In addition, we explored the relationship between pain-related facial activity anhd clinically relevant variables, including patient self-report, duration of the chronic pain disability and disability status. A methodological issue also was addressed in the design of the study. It has been reported that people attenuate their facial reactions when they know these are the object of another's attention (Kleck et al., 1976). This finding is pertinent because physical examinations are designed implicitly to observe reactions. In the present study, we attempted to influence the tendency to inhibit reactions by purposefully encouraging half of the subjects to be as fully expressive of painful distress as possible.

Method

Subjects

Subjects were an ongoing clinical series of 60 females and 60 males who were undergoing assessment at a tertiary care multidisciplinary back clinic at Shaughnessy Hospital, Vancouver, BC, Canada. Selection criteria for participation in the study included: (1) current pain in the lower back or hips, (2) the ability to understand written and spoken English, (3) no discernible use of alcohol, (4) informed consent to participate in the study. Table 7.1 summarizes demographic characteristics of the sample together with duration of the chronic and current complaint, locus of the complaint, history of back surgery and disability status of the patients. Given the large standard deviation for the duration of the chronic complaint (S.D. = 10.33 years), the median 4 years may be a more representative figure. The broad range of diagnoses and diagnostic opinions, as recorded in the patients' medical charts, is summarized in table 7.2. Each individual received at least one diagnosis, 69 received two and 17 received three, indicating the sample was quite heterogenous, but not atypical of patients referred to back pain clinics.

A multivariate analysis of variance disclosed no differences ($P > 0.05$) between men and women across the following demographic and medical history variables: age, duration of chronic and current complaint, number of back operations. Similarly, chi-square analyses indicated no sex differences ($P > 0.05$) in educational level, ethnic classification, locus of complaint, disposition recommendation, or diagnosis. However, the chi-square analysis for disability status by sex (2×2) revealed an uneven distribution

TABLE 7.1. Demographic variables (male and females combined)

Variable name	M	S.D.	Percentage	Range	n[4]
Age (in years)	42.70	13.71	—	17–78	117
Education					81
Grade school/junior high	—	—	41.40	—	81
High school diploma	—	—	28.70	—	—
Post-secondary education	—	—	16.10	—	—
Technical school or skilled trade	—	—	13.80	—	—
Ethnic group					118
Caucasian, born in Canada or U.S.A., no recent ethnic influence	—	—	77.12	—	—
All other ethnic groups	—	—	22.88	—	—
Duration of complaint chronic (in years)	8.42	10.33	—	0.58–55.0	120
Duration of complaint Current (in years)	2.20	1.52	—	0.25–08.0	120
Locus of complaint					120
Low back pain	—	66.70	—	—	—
Back and leg pain	—	25.00	—	—	—
Back and hip or hip only pain	—	8.30	—	—	—
Prior back surgery	—	—	32.00	—	120
One operation			25.00		
Two operations or more			5.60		
Disability status					115
Receiving or disability claims pending			46.10		
No benefits			53.90		

[4] This figure represents the number of subjects for whom information on the variable was available.

TABLE 7.2. Diagnostic categories

Category	Frequency
Disc degeneration	22
Disc space narrowing	3
Disc protrusion	4
Discogenic low back pain	7
Nerve root irritation	12
Facet joint syndrome	5
Spinal stenosis	2
Spondylolithesis	5
Postoperative pain	7
Soft tissue injury/strain	10
Mechanical low back pain/postural problems	22
Fibrocytis	3
Chronic benign pain syndrome	20
Inactivity	8
Obesity	13
Drug dependency/alcoholism	5
Secondary pain/psychological overlay	15
Other	43

between the 2 groups, $\chi^2 = 9.41$, $P < 0.005$, with the men receiving or having applied for financial benefits more often than the women.

Apparatus and Experimental Setting

The physiotherapy assessments took place in a standard examination room. A video-camera was mounted on a bracket directly above the head of the examination table. An adjacent room contained the videotape recording equipment. The black and white camera captured the shoulders and head of the patient while they were being examined in the supine position.

Self-Report Measures

All patients completed the following self-report measures: (1) the McGill Pain Questionnaire (Patrick et al., 1986), with patients describing on separate forms the "acute" pain they experienced during the course of the examination, approximately 20 min previously, and the "chronic" pain they experience on a typical or average day; (2) verbal descriptor scales of pain developed by Gracely (1979) and Gracely and colleagues (Gracely, McGrath, & Dubner, 1978; Gracely, Dubner, & McGrath, 1979) were used to examine sensory intensity, unpleasantness and painfulness of both the acute and chronic pain. Patients selected the description from the series of adjectives given to them that best described the type of pain being rated.

Procedure

Subjects were approached in the waiting room. The study was described as reviewing physiotherapy procedures, including videotaping reactions but omitting mention of the specific interest in facial expression. Consent to participate was obtained, with the right to withdraw without prejudice specifically mentioned. Of those approached, 10.4% declined the opportunity to participate.

Of prime interest was that component of the physiotherapy examination establishing functional capacities during range of motion tests. After a series of tests conducted while the patient was standing, sitting and lying down with the patient in a supine position, the physiotherapist advised him or her that the study procedure would begin.

Half of the subjects were read instructions designed to enhance non-verbal expressiveness. They were advised that clinicians rely heavily on non-verbal information, including "the expression on your face, any sounds you make like 'ouch' or groaning, and movements of your body," and that they should not cover up such indications when in pain but should freely express as much as possible how they were really feeling. The remaining subjects did not receive any instructions focusing upon expressiveness but were treated identically in all other ways.

The physiotherapist then followed a standardized protocol in accordance with a rehearsed script. She presented a series of 4 activities involving both active and passive movements of the legs: (1) pulling the feet down, with and without resistance, (2) moving each bent knee laterally toward the centre of the table, (3) having the patient pulling the knee towards the chest with his or her hands locked around it and (4) physiotherapist-assisted straight raising of each leg. Each procedure was stopped either when functional range was established or when the patient complained of pain. Patients then were asked to identify which of the movements was most distressing. This movement provided the basis for comparing genuine, faked and suppressed reaction patterns.

The patient was asked to do the following: (1) repeat the movement identified above as inducing the most severe pain, (2) repeat the movement again, but with the therapist requesting, "This time I would like you to try to pretend that it doesn't bother you at all, no matter how much it does. Try to cover up the fact that you find it painful or distressing," and (3) pose pain by repeating one of the movements that did not induce pain at all, with the instruction. "This time I want you to pretend as if the movement is really causing you a lot of pain. Let me know by looking at you that it is painful. Make a 'pain face.'" The genuine reaction was always requested first; the posed and masked reactions were presented in counterbalanced order across subjects to control for order effects.

Subsequently, the patients screened the videotape of their reactions and identified the instant when they had felt the most pain. They then completed the McGill Pain Questionnaire and the verbal descriptor scales to characterize the acute distress experienced during the most painful moment, followed by a second administration of the MPQ to characterize the chronic pain they typically experienced on a daily basis. Only at this time did the experimenter reveal that our primary interest in this study was the facial reactions during painful events.

After the patient had left, the physiotherapist independently viewed the tape and identified that point in time when the patient appeard to be experiencing the most pain. Finally, the experimenter viewed the tape and attempted to identify the periods of greatest facial activity during both the standardized protocol and the test protocol when the most painful movement was being repeated.

Facial Expression Coding

FACS Data

Eight 6 sec segments of each patient's tape were selected for coding purposes with FACS (Ekman & Friesen, 1978a, 1978b). Each continuous 6 sec segment represented a "window" around a particular point in time, i.e., 3 sec preceding and 3 sec succeeding events of interest as follows: (1) a "neutral" segment in which the face was expressionless and the patient was at rest, taken prior to the beginning of the standardized protocol, to provide a comparison reference for coders; (2) a "baseline" segment, the first 6 sec of the patient's videotape, to provide a record of spontaneous facial expression; (3) the instant during the standardized protocol identified by the patient as the time when the most severe discomfort was experienced; (4) the instant during the standardized protocol when the physiotherapist judged the patient to be experiencing the most discomfort; (5) the instant during the standardized protocol when the experimenter believed the patient was displaying the most facial activity; (6) the instant during repetition of the most painful movement when the experimenter judged there to be the greatest facial activity; (7) the instant 3 sec prior to when the physiotherapist instructed the subject to cease attempting to suppress the pain reaction; and (8) that instant when the experimenter judged there to be greatest facial activity when the patient was attempting to pose a pain expression.

Each of the eight 6 sec segments was edited from the original videotape. They were rearranged on a dubbed tape with the "neutral" face (segment 1) appearing first and identified as such, with the other 7 segments appearing in random order without identification as to which event each segment represented.

Three coders certified for their proficiency with FACS (Ekman & Friesen, 1978a) provided the coding. Two each completed 40% and 60% of the primary coding while the third provided the reliability assessment. Each segment was coded for all 44 facial action units (AUs) specified by FACS. Both the incidence and duration of the apex of each AU were recorded. The apex of an AU is defined as "the period during which the movement was held at the highest intensity that it reached" (Ekman & Friesen, 1978a, p. 145).

Global Expressiveness

Two additional research assistants, 1 male and 1 female, judged the degree to which the patients expressed pain using global ratings of inexpressive, somewhat expressive and very expressive. The levels of expression were assigned values of 1, 2 or 3 for quantitative analyses.

Results

Facial Activity

Reliabilities of the FACS and global expressiveness data were determined. For the FACS coding, the reliability coder randomly selected 1 of the 7 segments for each patient (i.e., excluding the neutral segment) or 14% of the complete sample. Percent agreement (Ekman & Friesen, 1978a) was calculated as the proportion of agreements relative to the total number of AUs scored. Agreements were scored only if both coders agreed that an AU had occurred in an overlapping time frame. In the case of blinks, both coders had to agree that a blink had occurred within 0.2 sec of each other. The overall percent agreement was 76%, a figure that coincided with the reliabilities reported by Ekman and Friesen (1978a) and Ekman, Friesen, and Ancoli (1980). It was concluded that satisfactory reliability of the FACS scoring had been demonstrated. To establish the reliability of the global expressiveness scoring, both coders overlapped in the scoring of 50% of the segments. Inter-rater reliability as defined by the Pearson product-moment correlation was 0.87. Using the Haggard (1958) intraclass correlation to establish reliability, the value of R was 0.92. Both indexes of reliability exceeded current standards.

Initial analyses of the FACS data established which AUs were consistently observed during any of the segments. Infrequently occurring AUs were eliminated by restricting analyses to those that occurred on average more than 6 times over all 7 non-neutral segments for all 120 subjects (i.e., more often than 6/840). Fourteen AUs remained for further analyses after this exclusion criterion had been applied. Table 7.3 provides means and standard deviations and table 7.4 briefly defines the 14 recurring facial actions.

We then determined the degree of agreement among the patient, physiotherapist and experimenter as to when the videotaped standard protocol provided the clearest representation of pain. We examined the extent of overlap in the 6 sec frames surround-

TABLE **7.3.** Action unit (AU) categories remaining after application of exclusion criteria. Overall frequency means and standard deviations (in parentheses) for baseline, genuine pain, masked, and posed segments

AU	Baseline		Genuine pain		Masked		Posed	
	M	S.D	M	S.D.	M	S.D.	M	S.D.
1 (inner brow raise)	0.108	(0.338)	0.183	(0.410)	0.050	(0.219)	0.225	(0.493)
2 (outer brow raise)	0.117	(0.371)	0.192	(0.436)	0.050	(0.219)	0.225	(0.476)
4 (brow lower)[a]	0.067	(0.250)	0.292[b]	(0.509)	0.167	(0.417)	0.592[b,c]	(0.642)
6 (cheek raise)[a]	0.075	(0.295)	0.233[b]	(0.463)	0.050	(0.254)	0.475[b,c]	(0.621)
7 (lids tight)[a]	0.008	(0.091)	0.142[b]	(0.416)	0.100	(0.328)	0.158[b]	(0.389)
10 (upper lip raise)[a]	0.000	(0.000)	0.108[b]	(0.384)	0.008	(0.091)	0.150[b]	(0.496)
12 (lip corner pull)[a]	0.133	(0.429)	0.258	(0.572)	0.117	(0.371)	0.725[b,c]	(0.840)
17 (chin raise)	0.042	(0.239)	0.083	(0.180)	0.042	(0.239)	0.830	(0.278)
18 (lip pucker)	0.025	(0.203)	0.075	(0.295)	0.017	(0.129)	0.050	(0.314)
20 (lip stretch)	0.050	(0.219)	0.083	(0.278)	0.008	(0.091)	0.125	(0.401)
25 (lips part)[a]	0.342	(0.667)	0.575[b]	(0.729)	0.208[b]	(0.428)	0.567[b]	(0.753)
26 (jaw drop)[a]	0.292	(0.640)	0.350	(0.617)	0.250	(0.530)	0.350	(0.644)
43 (eyes closed)[a]	0.100	(0.363)	0.358[b]	(0.547)	0.142[b]	(0.373)	0.4750[b]	(0.733)
45 (blink)[a]	4.242	(2.948)	4.033	(3.07)	3.008[b,c]	(2.627)	2.950[b,c]	(2.863)

[a] Consistent with the findings of Craig and Patrick (1985) and/or Patrick et al. (1986).
[b] Mean is significantly different from baseline mean ($P < 0.005$).
[c] Mean is significantly different from mean for genuine pain segment ($P < 0.005$).

TABLE **7.4.** Brief definitions of recurring facial actions[a]

Action	Action unit number	Description
Inner brow raise	1	The inner corner of the eyebrow is pulled up, giving the eyebrows a circular shape.
Outer brow raise	2	The outer corner of the eyebrow is pulled up, stretching the eyelid.
Brow lower	4	The eyebrows are lowered and pulled together, pushing the eyelid down.
Cheek raise	6	The skin around the temples and cheeks are drawn towards the eyes, narrowing the eye opening.
Lids tight	7	The eyelids are tightened, narrowing the eye opening.
Upper lip raise	10	The upper lip is drawn up, with the central portion being raised higher than the lower portions.
Lip corner pull	12	The lip corners are pulled back and upwards.
Chin raise	17	Chin and lower lip are pushed up, causing the lower lip to protrude.
Lip pucker	18	The mouth is pushed forward, causing the lips to pucker.
Lip stretch	20	The lips are pulled back sideways, making the mouth look longer.
Lips part	25	Lips are parted slightly, while the jaw remains closed.
Jaw drop	26	The jaw is opened so that a space between the teeth can be seen.
Eyes closed	43	The eyes are closed, with no apparent tension in the lids.
Blink	45	The eyes are opened and closed quickly.

[a] Coding criteria appear in Ekman and Friesen (1978b).

ing the instant identified by these 3 participants as signifying the most severe discomfort (segments 3, 4, and 5). To assess the incidence of agreements, these were defined as taking place if, having had 1 person conclude pain was expressed at a particular time, the other person agreed that it occurred during the 6 sec frame of time surrounding that instant. The patient, physiotherapist and experimenters' judgments were all compared with each other. Agreement was very high. Only 5% of the time did one disagree with another. At least one of the experimenter or physiotherapist agreed which movement was the most painful 96% of the time. Thus, observers (the physiotherapist and experimenter) very often demonstrated concordance with the patient as to which event best signified pain.

We also assessed whether there were differences in the facial activity associated with the events identified as signifying the most severe pain by the 3 participants (segments 3, 4, and 5) and with the repetition of the most painful experience (segment 6). A one-way MANOVA compared the subject (segment 3), physiotherapist (segment 4) and experimenter identified segments (segment 5) as well as the repeated movement (segment 6) using as dependent variables the 14 AUs that occurred most often. The overall F test was not significant ($P > 0.05$), indicating that the 4 segments did not differ. Given the degree of consistency across the 3 participants and the absence of differences in facial activity among the segments identified by the patient, physiotherapist and experimenter as signifying pain, subsequent analyses were restricted to the segment identified as providing the most pain-related movement identified by the patient (segment 3).

We then examined whether the pattern of facial activity varied with the 3 types of pain expression (genuine, segment 3; masked, segment 7; posed, segment 8) and baseline (segment 2), the instructional set to freely express distress, and the sex of the subject, using MANOVA ($4 \times 2 \times 2$) across the 14 AUs. Instructional set and sex were between subject variables and types of expression provided a within subject variable. The only significant main effect was the contrast among the 3 types of painful expression and baseline, $F (42, 944) = 6.83$, $P < 0.0001$. None of the interactions were significant ($P > 0.05$). Bonferroni adjusted comparisons ($\alpha = 0.01/14$), using univariate analyses of variance across the different types of expression for each of the 14 AUs, revealed significant differences on 9 of the dependent measures: AUs 2, 4, 6, 7, 10, 12, 25, 43, 45.

Post hoc comparisons (Tukey) were conducted across the 3 types of expression and baseline for each of these significant effects, using a conservative Alpha value of 0.005 to control for multiple comparisons. Table 7.3 summarizes the outcome of these analyses and provides mean frequencies and standard deviations for those specific AUs that differed across the different expressions.

Genuine Pain

Relative to the baseline segment, patients displayed the following AUs more frequently: 4, 6, 7, 10, 25, 43.

Masked Pain

The facial expression during this phase could not be discriminated from baseline on the majority of the AUs. Approaching significance was AU 7 ($P < 0.025$). AU 45 displayed less often during the masked experience than during baseline.

Faked Pain

Relative to the baseline segment, patients faking pain displayed the following AUs more frequently: 4, 6, 7, 10, 12, 25, 43. AU 45 was displayed less often during the posed experience than during baseline.

Genuine vs. Masked Pain

Relative to the genuine expression of pain, patients masking pain displayed the following AUs less often: 2, 6, 25, 43, and 45.

Genuine vs. Faked Pain

Relative to the genuine expression of pain, patients faking pain displayed the following AUs more frequently: 4, 6, 12. AU 45 was displayed less often during the posed experience than during the genuine experience.

To examine the possibility of sex differences and the impact of the instructional set to be expressive on the global expressiveness measure, a 2×2 ANOVA was undertaken with these variables as between subject variables. The instruction to be expressive did not have an effect ($P > 0.05$), but there were sex differences ($F (1, 116) = 13.53$, $P < 0.001$). The mean expressiveness rating for men was 1.93 and for women 2.40. An analysis of the proportions (Glass & Stanley, 1970) of men and women judged to fall within the various categories of expressiveness was instructive. Table 7.5 summarizes the findings. More men than women ($Z = 3.47$, $P < 0.01$) were rated as inexpressive, and more women than men ($Z = 2.48$, $P < 0.05$) were rated as very expressive. The numbers of men and women rated as somewhat expressive did not differ significantly.

To establish whether the incidence of specific AUs would predict the global expressiveness ratings, a full step-wise multiple regression was performed. The predictor variables were the 6 AU variables which best distinguished between the genuine expression of pain and baseline (AUs 4, 6, 7, 10, 25 and 43) and the criterion variable was the global expressiveness rating. The regression coefficient was significant up to the second "step" of the analysis, ($F (2, 117) = 21.16$, $P < 0.0001$) at which stage AUs 43 and 6 had entered the equation. Judges' ratings of global expressiveness were greater in the presence of AU 43, AU 6 significantly improved the prediction, but AUs 4, 7, 10 and 25 did not contribute to variations in the ratings of global expressiveness. The multiple R for the relationship between individual pain-related AUs and global judgments of pain expression was 0.52 ($P < 0.0001$).

Self-Report

An initial analysis examined whether sex of the patient and the expressiveness-enhancing instructions affected the self-reports of discomfort. A MANOVA examined whether these variables influenced the following measures of acute (that inflicted during the most painful movement of the standard protocol) and chronic pain (that which was experienced on a typical day): (1) subscales of the McGill Pain Questionnaire, including number of words chosen and the indices of sensory, affective and evaluative qualities of pain (administered separately to reflect acute pain and chronic pain); (2) the 3 Gracely pain descriptor scales measuring sensory intensity, unpleasantness and painfulness, administered to reflect the acute pain. The multiple omnibus F indicated there was

TABLE **7.5.** Facial expressiveness rating frequencies

Sex	Inexpressive	Somewhat expressive	Very expressive	Total
Male	19	26	15	60
Female	4	28	28	60
Total	23	54	43	120

neither a significant effect due to sex of the patient nor an effect due to the expressiveness enhancing instructions ($P > 0.05$).

A further analysis examined whether characterizations of acute pain differed from descriptions of chronic pain. An Hotelling T^2 analysis examined differences between scores on the "acute pain" and the "chronic pain" administrations of the McGill Pain Questionnaire. The overall test was significant ($F (4, 116) = 13.15, P < 0.0001$). Multiple comparisons, using the Bonferroni correction for Alpha level, indicated that for 3 of the dependent variables, the number of words chosen and the sensory and affective scales, the scores were significantly lower for the "acute" ratings as compared to the "chronic" ratings. The mean ratings appear in table 7.6 for the "acute" and "chronic" ratings, along with normative data on chronic ratings from the hospital clinic.

Relationship Between Facial Activity and Self-Report

Full step-wise multiple regressions were performed with the 6 pain-related discriminating AUs serving as predictor variables and the 4 McGill scores and the 3 Gracely pain descriptor scores serving as criterion variables. For the McGill scales, only the regression coefficient for the relationship between AU 6 and the evaluative score was significant ($F (1, 118) = 15.16, P < 0.0005$). The multiple R was 0.34. For the Gracely pain descriptor scales, the regression coefficient was significant (multiple $R = 0.30$) only for the relationship between the painfulness rating and AU 6 ($F (1, 118) = 11.72, P < 0.001$). Thus, there was a marginal relationship between activity in the region of the eye and the self-report of pain.

TABLE **7.6.** Means and standard deviations (in parentheses) for the "acute" and "chronic" MPQ scale scores and for the normative data on chronic pain from the Shaughnessy Hospital Back Pain Clinic

	Acute		Chronic		Back pain clinic ($n = 134$)	
Measure	M	S.D.	M	S.D.	M	S.D.
Number of words chosen (NWC)[a,b]	9.2	(4.40)	11.17	(4.36)	12.37	(4.03)
Sensory[a,b]	13.78	(7.00)	15.54	(7.42)	17.20	(7.50)
Affective[a,b]	1.67	(2.19)	2.60	(2.31)	4.07	(4.30)
Evaluative[b]	2.45	(1.57)	2.51	(1.24)	3.20	(2.00)

[a] The difference between the "acute" and "chronic" administration of this scale was significant at the $P < 0.005$ level.
[b] The difference between the "chronic" score and the Back Pain Clinic normative data of this scale was significant at the $P < 0.01$ level.

Discussion

Facial Activity

The study clearly indicated that facial activity reflected lower back pain exacerbated by physical manipulations of the leg. As well, instructions disposing patients to inhibit the reaction made the pain reaction very difficult to identify and instructions to fake or pose a facial display of pain led to a facial display that tended not to differ qualitatively from the genuine display but was more vivid or intense.

Genuine Pain

A distinctive pattern of spontaneous facial activity was associated with the movement at the time the patients reported the greatest pain. Specifically, an observer could expect to see during the painful moment at least some component of the following facial actions if an individual were in pain: brow lowering, cheek raising, tightening of the eye lids, raising the upper lip, parting of the lips and closing the eyes. However, this entire configuration of facial actions would not be expected to occur in all patients. For example, the most common actions identified in this study were brow lowering and closing the eyes. However, only 45% of the subjects exhibited 1 or both of these 2 actions. These findings were based upon relatively brief samples of chronic pain patients reactions to acute exacerbation of clinical pain. The facial response to ongoing persistent pain has not been described but appears likely to be more subtle. Longer periods of observation in the present study along with a control sample of patients not experiencing back pain might have yielded useful additional information. The response to surgical trauma and prolonged exacerbation of clinical pain also deserve study.

There now are findings on pain-related facial actions from several laboratories using a variety of sources of pain. Only a small subset of the 44 action units coded using the Facial Action Coding System have been found to be responsive to pain. All 7 of the studies, including the present one (Craig & Patrick, 1985; LeResche, 1982; LeResche, Ehrlich, & Dworkin, 1990; Patrick et al., 1986; Prkachin et al., 1983; Swalm & Craig, submitted) identified brow lowering and tightening of the eyelids (thereby narrowing of the eyes) as present. The majority of the studies (4 to 6 of the 7) identified raising of the cheek (again, narrowing the eye) (Craig & Patrick, 1985; LeResche, 1982; LeResche et al., 1990; Patrick et al., 1986; Prkachin et al., 1983; and the present study), eyes closed or blinking (Craig & Patrick, 1985; LeResche, 1982; LeResche et al., 1990; Patrick et al., 1986; Prkachin et al., 1983; Swalm & Craig, submitted), raising the upper lip (Craig & Patrick, 1985; LeResche et al., 1990; Patrick et al., 1986; and the present study), and parting of the lips (Craig & Patrick, 1985; LeResche, 1982; LeResche & Dworkin, 1988a; Swalm & Craig, submitted; and the present study) or dropping the jaw (Craig & Patrick, 1985; LeResche, 1982; LeResche & Dworkin, 1988a; Prkachin & Mercer, 1989) as pain-related facial actions. The following actions were identified as pain-related in only 1 or 2 of the 7 studies: horizontally stretching the lips (LeResche, 1982; LeResche et al., 1990), pulling at the corner of the lips (Craig & Patrick, 1985; Swalm & Craig, submitted), vertically stretching the mouth open (Craig & Patrick, 1985; LeResche, 1982), wrinkling the nose (LeResche & Dworkin, 1988a), deepening of the nasolabial fold (LeResche, 1982), and drooping eyelids (Prkachin & Mercer, 1989).

There is reason to believe that variations on the general theme are systematically related to: (1) the severity of discomfort being experienced (Patrick et al., 1986; Prkachin & Mercer, 1989; Swalm & Craig, submitted), with the lower facial actions more likely to occur during severe pain; (2) the clinical syndrome being investigated, with temporomandibular dysfunction (LeResche & Dworkin, 1988a) differing from painful shoulder pathology (Prkachin & Mercer, 1986) and, as this study indicates, low back pain; (3) age (Grunau & Craig, 1990; Izard, Hembree, Doughterty, & Spizzirri, 1983), and (4) sex (Swalm & Craig, submitted). As well, all studies disclosed substantial individual differences that appeared to be unique to the people being studied.

Some of the variation in facial expression derives from the situation-specific, embarrassed smiling that one often observes in patients or volunteer subjects during pain. Indeed, pulling of the lip corners (AU 12) is often associated with smiling, particularly when cheek raising (AU 6) is present (Ekman & Friesen, 1982; LeResche, Ehrlich, & Dworkin, 1990). Cheek raising actually co-occurred with pulling of the lip corners 16 of the 28 times (57%); the latter appeared during the genuine pain segment. Two of the other studies (Craig & Patrick, 1985; Swalm & Craig, submitted) reported that it was pain related. The presence during pain of a pattern of facial activity often associated with pleasure attests to the complex interpersonal qualities of the experience of pain. Other systematic sources of variation undoubtedly will be identified. Certain facial actions, including raising the eye brows and tightly closing the mouth, appear to contra-indicate pain (Swalm & Craig, submitted).

Masked Pain

The patients were strikingly successful in inhibiting their reactions during repetition of the painful movement. Relative to baseline, all that was discernible to the trained coder was a reduced incidence of blinking and marginal evidence for tension around the eyes, produced by tightening of the eyelid. These residual cues may represent components of what Ekman and Friesen (1984) describe as micro-expressions, those facial behaviors which may be "fragments of a squelched, neutralized or masked display" (p. 90; Ekman & Friesen, 1969) or extremely rapid versions of a macro display. Thus, with the exception of the minor cues mentioned, the patients effectively suppressed the dramatic pattern for genuine pain described above. This provides ample evidence that facial display of pain is under voluntary control. The reduced incidence of blinking may have been related to the purposeful attempt to gain control of facial activity as Holland and Tarlow (1972, 1975) report that people blink less frequently when vigorously pursuing cognitive activities.

LeResche and Dworkin (1984) noted the importance of ascertaining whether individuals can conceal facial behavior. It is clear that substantial concealment is possible, with perhaps complete success attainable if the individual were trained or if there were greater incentives to do so than the mere request to comply with instructions used in this study. This investigation does not exhaust the possibilities for detecting pain when it is being masked or suppressed, given its constructed nature. In other circumstances, certain people may be less or more successful than was observed here (Ekman, 1985).

Faked Pain

There was considerable similarity between the genuine facial display of pain and the expression that was posed during an innocuous movement. When posing, the patients engaged in brow lowering, narrowing of the eyes by cheek raising and tightening of the eye lids, raising the upper lip, pulling the corners of the lips, parting the lips and closing their eyes more often. Blinking occurred less often, perhaps again because of the cognitive activity demanded by the instructions to act as if they were in pain. To some extent the faked expression represented an intensified caricature of the genuine expression as, relative to the genuine facial display, the patients displayed more brow lowering, cheek raising and pulling of the corners of the lips. It is noteworthy that instructions to fake pain did not elicit facial actions other than those that had been associated with genuine pain. Thus, it would appear that one could not look for facial clues to deception other than those identified as markers of pain. The deception appears to represent a vivid prototype of the genuine display. It should be noted that the methodology used in this study does not exhaust the possibilities for identifying deception of pain using facial activity. Other possibilities, extrapolated from Ekman's (1985) work on lying, might include asymmetrical facial displays, timing of the facial activity and the location of the facial expression in the stream of activities.

The greater frequency of AU 12, lip corner pull, during faked in contrast to genuine pain underscores the social complexities of the reaction. As noted, this facial action is often associated with smiling, and the patients may have been experiencing embarrassed reactions or even a sense of amusement at responding to the demand to fake pain in this setting (Ekman & Friesen, 1982).

It is noteworthy that the patients were not provided with a model or explicit instructions for the posed face of pain and, hence, had to rely upon their own experience. Given that they had just endured a painful experience themselves, it is probable that they engaged in self-modeling, but given the influences of social modeling upon pain experience and behavior (Craig, 1986), social customs for displaying pain also probably were present.

Global Expressiveness

While explicit instructions designed to inhibit the facial display of pain worked well, the more general instructions designed to enhance the display of pain did not have an impact. Thus, telling the patients that they should visually let us know how much pain they were experiencing did not affect their behavior during the standard or test protocols. It may have been that these patients were already well motivated to communicate their distress as clearly as possible because treatment and other dispositions in the hospital could depend upon clear messages of distress. Nevertheless, 23 of 120 patients in the present study were characterized as inexpressive by raters, and the intervention clearly did not affect them. Keefe et al. (1990) recently used cluster analyses to identify a subgroup of non-expressive low back pain patients.

The finding that women were judged to be more expressive than men, with almost twice as many women categorized as being very expressive, whereas almost five times as many men were labeled as being very inexpressive, poses a challenge for the analysis of discrete facial actions. It may be that a social stereotype of women being more visibly expressive than men was operating and that there indeed were no differences. Alternatively, the facial coding system we used may have failed to detect differences. We did not code for the intensity of expression as others have done (e.g., Prkachin & Mercer, 1989); hence, we may have missed subtle factors. However, regression analyses, using specific facial actions to predict global expressiveness ratings, revealed that there was a substantial relationship between facial activity and expressiveness ratings (multiple $R = 0.52$), with tension around the eyes and closing the eyes being most predictive. Observed sex differences in global expressiveness ratings are also consistent with findings that judges are more able to correctly categorize slides of emotional expressions exhibited by females (Buck, Miller, & Caul, 1974), and that women manifest more facial electromyographic activity than men while imagining different emotion eliciting situations (Schwartz, Ahern, & Brown, 1980).

Verbal Report

Self-report of pain on the several scales confirmed that the physical manipulations could be described legitimately as painful. It was of interest that the acute pain induced here was characterized as being substantially less severe than chronic clinical pain. Perhaps the lack of surprise attending abrupt onset of pain in the home or workplace would be a key factor. There was only a minimal relationship between the facial activity and self-report of pain with significant multiple Rs ranging between 0.30 and 0.34. This limited relationship is consistent with the argument that different measures assess different features of pain (Patrick, Craig, & Prkachin, 1986). It is not necessary to attribute differences between self-report and non-verbal expression to a lack of candor or truthfulness. As Fordyce (1976) has observed, what people say they do and their actual behavior are subject to different reinforcement effects and will diverge in consequence.

Acknowledgments

Supported by a research grant to Kenneth D. Craig from the Social Sciences and Humanities Research Council of Canada.

The paper is based upon doctoral dissertation research submitted for the Ph.D. degree at The University of British Columbia by Susan A. Hyde. The authors wish to thank Doug Lee, Brenda Gerhard, Cara Zaskow, Joe Klancnik, Rober McMahon, and Ralph Hakstian for assistance with this project and the staff at University Hospital, Shaughnessy Site, whose support and cooperation made the investigation possible.

References

Buck, R., Miller, R., & Caul, W. (1974). Sex, personality and physiological variables in the communication of affect via facial expression. *Journal of Personality and Social Psychology, 30,* 587–596.

Craig, K. D. (1986). Social modeling influences: Pain in context. In R. A. Sternbach (Ed.), *The psychology of pain* (pp. 73–110). New York: Raven Press.

Craig, K. D., Grunau, R. V. E., & Aquan-Assee, J. (1988). Judgment of pain in newborns: Facial activity and cry as determinants. *Canadian Journal of Behavioral Science, 20,* 442–451.

Craig, K. D., & Patrick, C. J. (1985). Facial expression during induced pain. *Journal of Personality and Social Psychology, 48,* 1080–1091.

Craig, K. D., & Prkachin, K. M. (1980). Social influences on public and private components of pain. In I. G. Sarason & C. Speilberger (Eds.), *Stress and anxiety* (Vol. 7; pp. 57–72). New York: Hemisphere.

Craig, K. D., & Prkachin, K. M. (1983). Nonverbal measures of pain. In R. Melzack (Ed.), *Pain measurement and assessment* (pp. 173–182). New York: Raven Press.

Cleeland, C. S. (1989). Measurement of pain by subjective report. In C. R. Chapman & J. D. Loeser (Eds.), *Advances in pain research and therapy. Issues in pain measurement* (pp. 391–404). New York: Raven Press.

Darwin, C. (1872/1955). *The expression of emotion in man and animals*. New York: Philosophical Library.

De Paulo, B. M., Rosenthal, R., Eisenstat, R. A., Rogers, P. C., & Finkelstein, S. (1978). Decoding discrepant nonverbal cues. *J. Pers. Soc. Psychol., 36,* 313–323.

Ekman, P. (1977). Biological and cultural contributions to body and facial movement. In J. Blacking (Ed.), *Anthropology of the body* (pp. 39–84). London: Academic Press.

Ekman, P. (1985). *Telling lies. Clues to deceit in the marketplace. Politics and marriage.* New York: Norton.

Ekman, P., & Friesen, W. (1969). Nonverbal leakage and clues to deception. *Psychiatry, 32,* 88–105.

Ekman, P., & Friesen, W. (1971). Constants across cultures in the face and emotion. *J. Pers. Soc. Psychol., 17,* 124–129.

Ekman, P., & Friesen, W. (1974). Detecting deception from the body or face. *J. Pers. Soc. Psychol., 29,* 288–298.

Ekman, P., & Friesen, W. (1976). Measuring facial movement. *Environmental Psychology and Nonverbal Behavior, 1,* 56–75.

Ekman, P., & Friesen, W. (1978a). *Investigator's guide to the facial action coding system.* Palo Alto: Consulting Psychologists Press.

Ekman, P., & Friesen, W. (1978b). *Manual for the facial action coding system.* Palo Alto: Consulting Psychologists Press.

Ekman, P., & Friesen, W. (1982). Felt, false and miserable smiles. *Journal of Nonverbal Behavior, 6,* 238–249.

Ekman, P., & Friesen, W. (1984). *Unmasking the face.* Palo Alto: Consulting Psychologists Press.

Ekman, P., Friesen, W., & Ancoli, S. (1980). Facial signs of emotional experience. *J. Pers. Soc. Psychol., 39,* 1125–1134.

Fordyce, W. E. (1976). Behavioral methods for chronic pain and illness. St. Louis: C. V. Mosby.

Glass, G., & Stanley, J. (1970). *Statistical methods in education and psychology.* Englewood Cliffs, NJ: Prentice-Hall.

Gracely, R. H. (1979). Psychophysical assessment of human pain. In J. Bonica (Ed.), *Advances in pain research and therapy* (Vol. 3; pp. 805–824). New York: Raven Press.

Gracely, R. P., McGrath, P. A., & Dubner, R. (1978). Validity and sensitivity of ratio scales of sensory and affective verbal pain descriptors: manipulation of affect by diazepam. *Pain, 5,* 19–29.

Gracely, R. P., Dubner, R., & McGrath, P. A. (1979). Narcotic analgesia: fentanyl reduces intensity but not the unpleasantness of painful tooth pulp stimulation. *Science, 203,* 1261–1263.

Grunau, R. V. E., & Craig, K. D. (1987). Pain expression in neonates. *Pain, 28,* 395–410.

Grunau, R. V. E., & Craig, K. D. (1990). Facial activity as a measure of neonatal pain expression. In D. C. Tyler & E. J. Krane (Eds.), *Advances in pain research and therapy.* Proc. of the 1st Int. Symp. on Pediatric Pain (pp. 147–155). New York: Raven Press.

Grunau, R. V. E., Johnston, C. C., & Craig, K. D. (1990). Facial activity and cry to invasive and noninvasive tactile stimulation in neonates. *Pain, 42,* 295–305.

Haggard, E. A. (1958). *Intraclass correlation and the analysis of variance.* New York: Dryden Press.

Holland, M. K., & Tarlow, G. (1972). Blinking and mental load. *Psychological Reports, 323,* 119–127.

Holland, M. K., & Tarlow, G. (1975). Blinking and thinking. *Perceptual and Motor Skills, 41,* 403–406.

Hyde, S. (1986). *Facial expressive behaviour of a chronic low back pain population.* Unpublished doctoral dissertation, University of British Columbia, Vancouver.

Izard, C., Heubner, R. R., Resser, D., McGinness, G. C., & Dougherty, L. M. (1980). The young infant's ability to produce discrete emotional expressions. *Developmental Psychology, 16,* 132–140.

Izard, C. E., Hembree, E. A., Dougherty, L. M., & Spizzirri, C. L. (1983). Changes in facial expressions of 2-to-19-month-old infants following acute pain. *Dev. Psychol., 19,* 418–426.

Jacox, A. K. (1980). The assessment of pain. In L. Smith, H. Merskey & S. Grass (Eds.), *Pain, meaning and management* (pp. 75–88). New York: Spectrum.

Keefe, F. J., Bradley, L. A., & Crisson, J. E. (1990). Behavioral assessment of low back pain: Identification of pain behavior subgroups. *Pain, 40,* 153–160.

Kleck, R. E., Vaughan, R. C., Cartwright-Smith, J., Vaughan, K. B., Colby, C. F., & Lanzetta, J. T. (1976). Effects of being observed on expressive, subjective and physiological responses to painful stimuli. *Journal of Personality and Social Psychology, 34,* 1211–1218.

Kótarba, J. A. (1983). *Chronic pain. Its social dimensions.* Beverley Hills, CA: Sage.

Kraut, R. E., (1978). Verbal and nonverbal cues in the perception of lying. *J. Pers. Soc. Psychol., 36,* 380–391.

Kraut, R. E. (1982). Social presence, facial feedback and emotion. *J. Pers. Soc. Psychol., 42,* 853–863.

Kremer, E. F., Block, A., & Atkinson, J. H. (1983). Assessment of pain behavior: Factors that distort self-report. In R. Melzack (Ed.), *Pain measurement and assessment* (pp. 165–171). New York; Raven Press.

Lanzetta, J. T., Cartwright-Smith, J., & Kleck, R. E. (1976). Effects of nonverbal dissimulation on emotion. *J. Pers. Soc. Psychol., 33,* 354–370.

Lee, D. S., & Craig, K. D. (submitted). *Facial action determinants of observer pain judgments: complexity and configuration.* Unpublished manuscript.

LeResche, L. (1982). Facial expression in pain: A study of candid photographs. *Journal of Nonverbal Behavior, 7,* 46–56.

LeResche, L., & Dworkin, S. (1980). Facial expression accompanying pain. *Social Sciences and Medicine, 19,* 1325–1330.

LeResche, L., & Dworkin, S. F. (1988a). Facial expressions of pain and emotions in chronic TMD patients. *Pain, 35,* 71–78.

LeResche, L., & Dworkin, S. (1988b). Facial expressions of pain and emotion in chronic TMD patients. *Pain, 35,* 71–78.

LeResche, L., Ehrlich, K. J., & Dworkin, S. (1990). Facial expressions of pain and masking smiles: Is "grin and bear it" a pain behavior?. *Pain, Supplement, 5,* S286.

Melzack, R. (1975). The McGill Pain Questionnaire: major properties and scoring methods. *Pain, 1,* 277–299.

Patrick, C. J., Craig, K. D., & Prkachin, K. M. (1986). Observer judgments of acute pain: facial action determinants. *J. Pers. Soc. Psychol., 50,* 1291–1298.

Prkachin, K. M., Currie, N. A., & Craig, K. D. (1983). Judging nonverbal expressions of pain. *Canadian Journal of Behavioral Science, 15,* 43–73.

Prkachin, K. M., & Mercer, S. R. (1989). Pain expression in patients with shoulder pathology: validity, properties and relationship to sickness impact. *Pain, 39,* 257–265.

Schwartz, G., Ahern, G., & Brown, S. (1980). Lateralized facial muscle response to positive versus negative emotional stimuli. *Psychophysiology, 16,* 561–571.

Swalm, D., & Craig, K. D. (submitted). *Differential impact of placebo on verbal and nonverbal measures of pain in men and women.* Unpublished manuscript.

AFTERWORD

On Knowing Another's Pain

KENNETH D. CRAIG

Pain is a private experience with complex and difficult-to-articulate qualities that can only be inferred from overt evidence, a process fraught with risks of errors. An understanding of the communication process, whereby painful experience is encoded in behavior and decoded by clinicians and others, is vital (Prkachin & Craig, in press). Verbal report is often characterized as the "gold standard" for assessment, but there are serious difficulties in translating experience into speech and the likelihood of response biases (Craig, 1992). As well, interpersonal judgments are heavily influenced by non-verbal behavior. The Facial Action Coding System has been an important tool for the study of these psychological and social parameters of pain (Craig, Prkachin, & Grunau, 1992). Some features of studies subsequent to the reprinted paper are described below.

Voluntary Control of Pain Expression

Patients often confront suspicion about the veracity of their complaints. The reprinted study indicated that patients could dissimulate the relatively stereotyped facial display usually associated with pain and that the patients could effectively suppress most features of the spontaneous display of pain. We pursued this further (Hadjistavropoulos & Craig, 1994) with a problematic, but not uncommon, group of chronic pain patients whose signs and symptoms of pain do not correspond to known physiological principles, or "medically incongruent pain." These patients were expected to display exaggerated facial grimaces during exacerbations of clinical pain. Maladaptive cognitive and affective processes did appear to distort pain in these patients, but they did not differ from "congruent" patients in facial activity. We attributed this to the intrusive nature of the demands to dissimulate pain expression and are considering nonobtrusive observation methodologies.

We also have examined whether judges would detect features of deception in deliberately faked or suppressed facial displays of pain (Poole & Craig, 1992). Judges' ratings of the patients' pain experiences corresponded more closely to the severity of distress deliberately posed than to the severity actually experienced. When judges were also provided with self-report of pain, the facial expression was a more important determinant of attributed pain. In addition, judges who had been advised that some patients were attempting to deceive them did not become more discriminating but became more conservative and generally attributed less pain to the patients.

Yet information concerning deception does seem available. In a further study (Hadjistavropoulos, Hadjistavropoulos, & Craig, 1995), judges' classifications of the baseline, exaggerated, suppressed, and nonposed expressions of patients were better than chance, despite many errors. Judges used rules of thumb based on specific action units. For example, when actions not usually associated with pain were evident (Craig et al., 1992), such as inner or outer brow raise, or lip corner pull, judges tended to identify the expression as an exaggerated expression.

These studies had focused on the incidence and intensities of FACS action units, so we culled the literature for additional possible sources of information concerning deception. The more comprehensive coding strategy also examined temporal patterns, contiguity of actions, and specific facial cues thought to be indicative of deception (Hill & Craig, 1995). Findings revealed subtle differences that could improve discriminations. For example, nonpain-related action units, such as inner brow raise, were more likely during faking. As well, the overall duration of pain-related facial actions was longer and facial action asymmetry was more common during the faked pain expression. Thus, intensive FACS analysis led to a greater understanding of the deliberate and spontaneous expressions.

Pain in the Nonverbal Person

FACS has considerable utility for the study of pain suffered by people who cannot provide self-report. Infants; people with intellectually handicaps, brain injuries, and dementia; and patients during postoperative recovery provide prominent examples. Caregivers must rely on nonverbal expression (although judgments invariably reflect other information). Our initial studies focused on infancy because of considerable evidence of undermanagement of children's pain (Craig & Grunau, 1993; Craig, Lilley, & Gilbert, 1996). Our findings applying FACS (Craig, Hadjistavropoulos, Grunau, & Whitfield, 1994) indicated that the facial display in newborns during invasive procedures is stikingly similar to the pattern observed in older children and adults (with interesting differences). Facial expression represents a sensitive and possibly specific measure of infant pain, even in the very prematurely born child (Craig, Whitfield, Grunau, Linton, & Hadjistavropoulos, 1993). Facial actions are also important determinants of adult judgments of pain in children (Hadjistavropoulos, Craig, Grunau, & Johnston, 1994) and provide a criterion measure for infant pain in studies of analgesics (e.g., Scott, Riggs, Ling, Grunau, & Craig, 1994).

Pain is commonplace in elderly persons with cognitive impairments, but it is an inadequately studied problem. We have examined pain during immunization injections in chronic care patients satisfying criteria for dementia or its absence (Hadhjistavropoulos, Craig, Martin, Hadjistavropoulos, & McMurtry, 1995). Contrasts were made of FACS-coded reactions to the needle stick, self-report of pain, and nurses' global judgments of the pain being experienced. Most of the cognitively impaired patients were unable to provide self-report, but facial expressions and nurses' judgments effectively discriminated the injection episode from noninvasive control events. Thus, the FACS provides an important tool for the study of the efficacy of palliative care and analgesics in elderly persons with severe cognitive impairments.

References

Craig, K. D. (1992). The facial expression of pain: Better than a thousand words? *American Pain Society Journal, 1,* 153–162.

Craig, K. D., & Grunau, R. V. E. (1993). Neonatal pain perception and behavioral measurement. In K. J. S. Anand & P. J. McGrath (Eds.), *Neonatal pain and distress* (pp. 67–105). Amsterdam: Elsevier Science.

Craig, K. D., Hadjistavropoulos, H. D., Grunau, R. V. E., & Whitfield, M. F. (1994). A comparison of two measures of facial activity during pain in the newborn child. *Journal of Pediatric Psychology, 19,* 305–318.

Craig, K. D., Lilley, C. M., & Gilbert, C. A. (1996). Social barriers to optimal pain management in infants and children. *Clinical Journal of Pain, 17,* 247–259.

Craig, K. D., Prkachin, K. M., & Grunau, R. V. E. (1992). The facial expression of pain. In D. C. Turk & R. Melzack (Eds.), *Handbook of pain assessment* (pp. 255–274). New York: Guilford.

Craig, K. D., Whitfield, M. F., Grunau, R. V. E., Linton, J., & Hadjistavropoulos, H. (1993). Pain in the pre-term neonate: Behavioural and physiological indices. *Pain, 52,* 287–299.

Hadjistavropoulos, H. D., & Craig, K. D. (1994). Acute and chronic low back pain: Cognitive, affective, and behavioral dimensions. *Journal of Consulting and Clinical Psychology, 62,* 341–349.

Hadjistavropoulos, H. D., Craig, K. D., Grunau, R. V. E., & Johnston, C. C. (1994). Judging pain in newborns: Facial and cry determinants. *Journal of Pediatric Psychology, 19,* 485–491.

Hadjistavropoulos, H. D., Craig, K. D., Hadjistavropoulos, T., & Poole, G. D. (1995). *Subjective judgments of deception in pain expression: Accuracy and errors.* Submitted for publication.

Hadjistavropoulos, T., Craig, K. D., Martin, N., Hadjistavropoulos, H., & McMurtry, B. (1995). *Toward the development of a research outcome measure of pain in elderly persons with cognitive impairments.* Submitted for publication.

Hadjistavropoulos, T., Hadjistavropoulos, H. D., & Craig, K. D. (1995). Appearance-based information about coping with pain: Valid or biased? *Social Science and Medicine, 40,* 537–543.

Hill, M. L., & Craig, K. D. (1995). *Detecting deception in facial expressions of pain: Increasing the comprehensiveness of facial coding.* Presented at the Convention of the Canadian Pain Society, Ottawa, Canada, May 23.

Poole, G. D., & Craig, K. D. (1992). Judgments of genuine, suppressed and faked facial expressions of pain. *Journal of Persoanality and Social Psychology, 63,* 797–805.

Prkachin, K. M., & Craig, K. D. (in press). Expressing pain: The communication and interpretation of facial pain signals. *Journal of Nonverbal Behavior.*

Scott, C., Riggs, W., Ling, E., Grunau, R. V. E., & Craig, K. D. (1994). *Morphine pharmacokinetics and pain assessment in premature neonates.* Paper presented at the Third International Symposium on Pediatric Pain, Philadelphia, PA, June 8.

8

The Consistency of Facial Expressions of Pain

A Comparison Across Modalities

KENNETH M. PRKACHIN

People in pain communicate their experience in many ways (Craig & Prkachin, 1983). These communications, often subsumed by the label 'pain behavior' (Fordyce, 1988), are the basis on which most inferences about pain are drawn in clinical and research settings. Because the consequences of pain are profound, it would be adaptive if the behaviors evoked were consistent and in the service of comparable ends such as survival or the reduction of suffering. It has been suggested that one of the primary functions of pain behavior is to enlist the aid of others (Prkachin, Curry, & Craig, 1983).

Implicit in the use of the single term 'pain behavior' to refer to several events is the assumption that different indicators of pain have similar effects and determinants. However, disparate phenomena called pain behavior may serve multiple functions or be influenced by different variables (Prkachin, 1986). To understand the roles of different pain behaviors, it is necessary to study their properties both separately and in relation to one another.

The present study focused on properties of one specific form of pain behavior: facial expression. People in pain often show changes in facial expression that are readily observable to others. Clinicians and laypeople place great emphasis on the credibility of these behaviors and view them as especially reliable indicators of the quality and intensity of a sufferer's pain (Craig, Prkachin, & Grunau, in press), however, the nature of information about pain carried by facial expression is not comprehensively understood. In order to interpret the meaning of facial changes during pain effectively, clinicians and researchers alike need answers to such questions as whether specific facial actions provide clear clues to pain states, whether cues to pain are common to all pain states or specific to only some, and whether an overt expression of pain relates faithfully to the subjective experience. Answers to these questions are dependent on understanding the function and determinants of pain expression.

The salience of facial changes suggests that they may be especially adapted to a communicative role (Prkachin, 1986). This is consistent with theories of non-verbal communication which suggest that some facial configurations have evolved to serve a 'signal' function (Redican, 1982). If expressions of pain resemble these other forms of facial behavior, they should have similar properties. Of particular interest is whether facial expressions during pain, like expressions of fundamental emotions, are universal (Ekman & Friesen, 1971; Ekman & Oster, 1982). If a universal expression of pain could be identified, clinicians and researchers might then be able to incorporate investigation of facial expression into the assessment of a variety of pain states, an ability that could have advantages in several situations (Craig et al., in press).

The notion of universality implies the existence of a pain signal that is consistent across stimulus conditions and cultures. The present study was addressed to the first of these attributes. Is there a set of facial changes that appears consistently when pain is induced by different methods? Several studies are relevant to this issue.

Facial actions that appear to be correlated with pain have been identified by a number of researchers. Table 8.1 summarizes findings from studies which have employed the Facial Action Coding System (FACS) (Ekman & Friesen, 1978a), a precise measurement technique, to analyze pain expressions. In most studies, a core of actions is likely to occur or to increase in intensity when people are in pain. The core consists of movements of corrugator and orbicularis oculi, which lower the eyebrows, narrow the eye opening and raise the cheeks. Various other movements appear with some frequency, notably actions of levator labii superioris (which raise the upper lip, deepen the nasolabial furrow, or wrinkle the nose), eyelid closing and mouth opening. Other actions (e.g., oblique pulling of the lip corners, opening and horizontal stretching of the mouth) appear with less consistency. Thus, available evidence suggests that a number of facial actions encode pain information. However, previous studies have not determined whether facial actions are consistent during different types of pain because they have employed single stimulus modalities or types of clinical pain.

A second purpose of the present study was to examine the structure of pain expressiveness relative to other measures of pain sensitivity. Interest in pain expression has emerged, in part, because of the need to develop new ways of measuring and assessing pain (Chapman, Casey, Dubner, Foley, Gracely, & Reading, 1985). Measures of pain expression may be valuable because they provide information that is different from that available in other channels. Indeed, several studies have reported that facial expressions during pain are independent of or modestly related to other pain measures, suggesting that they carry unique information (Patrick, Craig, & Prkachin, 1986; LeResche & Dworkin, 1988; Prkachin & Mercer, 1989). In the present study, facial expressions of pain were compared with verbal, pain threshold and pain tolerance measures to determine the degree of overlap among these indices.

The final purpose of the present study was a practical one. In studies of pain expression to date, it has been necessary to employ the FACS in a comprehensive manner to avoid the possibility of overlooking meaningful actions. This is an extremely laborious procedure, often requiring a coding time/real time ratio of 100:1. Consequently, widespread use of facial measurement in the study of pain has been impractical. If a subset of facial actions that occur consistently across a variety of types of pain can be identified, coding time could be reduced thus making application of facial analysis more practical. Even if such a core of actions could be identified, however, it would

TABLE 8.1. Facial actions that have shown significant relationships with pain in previous research with adults

Action		Study
AU4	Brow lower	Craig et al. (1991)
		LeResche (1982)
		LeResche and Dworkin (1988)
		Patrick et al. (1986)
		Prkachin and Mercer (1989)
AU6	Cheek raise	Craig et al. (1991)
		Craig and Patrick (1985)
		LeResche (1982)
		LeResche and Dworkin (1988)
		Patrick et al. (1986)
		Prkachin and Mercer (1989)
AU7	Lid tighten	Craig et al. (1991)
		Craig and Patrick (1985)
		LeResche (1982)
		LeResche and Dworkin (1988)
		Prkachin and Mercer (1989)
AU9	Nose wrinkle	LeResche and Dworkin (1988)
		Prkachin and Mercer (1989)
AU10	Upper lip raise	Craig et al. (1991)
		Craig and Patrick (1985)
		LeResche and Dworkin (1988)
		Patrick et al. (1986)
		Prkachin and Mercer (1989)
AU12	Oblique lip raise	Craig and Patrick (1985)
		Prkachin and Mercer (1989)
AU20	Lip Stretch	LeResche (1982)
		Prkachin and Mercer (1989)
AU25	Mouth open	Craig et al. (1991)
AU26	Jaw drop	Craig and Patrick (1985)
AU27	Mouth stretch	LeResche (1982)
		Prkachin and Mercer (1989)
AU43	Eyes close	Craig et al. (1991)
		LeResche (1982)
		Craig and Patrick (1985)
		Prkachin and Mercer (1989)
AU45	Blink	Craig and Patrick (1985)
		Patrick et al. (1986)
		LeResche and Dworkin (1988)

leave open the question of how best to weigh the information available from different movements to quantify the pain signal. For example, when an expression containing 2 or more pain-related actions takes place, is the information from those movements redundant or unique? Answers to such questions have important implications for the scaling of pain expressions. A final purpose of the present study was to explore the structure of facial movements occurring during pain with multivariate methods in order to determine how optimally to combine the information they provide.

Method

Subjects

Twenty male (mean age: 20.8, S.D.: 2.02) and 21 female (mean age: 19.86, *SD*: 1.28) University of Waterloo undergraduates took part. None had taken any analgesic medication for at least 24 h prior to the test session.

Apparatus and Materials

Subjects were exposed to 4 types of stimulation: electric shock, cold, pressure and muscle ischemia. Isolated, monophasic currents pulsed at 40 Hz were delivered by a Pulsar 6b stimulator (F. Haer and Co., Brunswick, ME) to the volar surface of subjects' right forearms through a pair of silver-silver chloride electrodes 8 mm in diameter. Cold stimulation was produced with the cold pressor test. A styrofoam tank contained water and ice, maintanied at a temperature between 0 and 1°C. An aquarium pump (Aquaclear Power Head 200) placed in the tank circulated the water to prevent local warming during the test. Mechanical pressure was applied with a specially constructed stimulator (Forgione & Barber, 1971). This device applied steady pressure to a plexiglass wedge. The wedge was attached to a lever with a 100-g weight resting on its end. A rubber bandage, a standard mercury sphygmomanometer cuff and a hand dynamometer (Takei Kiki Kogyo) were used to produce ischemic pain.

Procedure

The experiment was conducted in a laboratory room adjacent to a control room. A male and a female experimenter conducted the study. The experimenter responsible for procedures in the experimental room was always the same gender as the subject. During testing this experimenter was isolated from the subject by a curtain. An intercom system allowed audio communication between the control and experimental rooms. Proceedings in the experimental room could be viewed through a 1-way mirror, which was partially obscured using corkboards and notices to allay the subject's potential suspicions about being observed. The face of the subject, seated in a reclining chair facing the mirror, was videotaped in black-and-white on VHS videotape, although the subject was not aware of this.

A box containing 2 buttons, marked 'painful' and 'intolerable' was located at the subject's left side. The buttons were connected to 2 lights in front of the experimenter and to a buzzer in the control room. In this way, the subject could indicate when pain threshold and tolerance had been reached.

Electric stimulation consisted of 3-sec currents delivered to the volar surface of the subject's right forearm. Stimuli were presented in ascending intensity, beginning at 0 mA and increasing in 0.5-mA steps. During cold stimulation, the subject immersed the right arm in water up to the elbow. During pressure stimulation the stimulator was applied to the 1st phalange of the 3rd digit of the right hand. Ischemic pain was produced according to the procedures described by Petrovaara, Nurmikko, and Pontinen (1984) except that the subject squeezed the hand dynamometer at 75% rather than 70% maximal contraction.

The study was described as dealing with subjective responses to electric shock, cold, pressure and ischemia. Subjects were told that the maximum pain they experienced would be up to them and that they were free to terminate stimulation and the experiment at any time. They were also told that the tests would be terminated in any case well before the point at which tissue damage could occur.

Stimuli were presented in 1 of 4 orders. For each modality, the subject pressed a button marked 'painful' when pain was first experienced and a button marked 'intolerable' to indicate the point at which stimulation should cease. At the end of each test, the subject used categorical and ratio scales of affective and sensory descriptors (Heft, Gracely, Dubner, & McGrath, 1980) to describe the maximum pain experienced.

For all modalities, stimulation continued until the subject terminated the test or the cut-off intensity or time was reached. The cut-off points were 14.0 mA for shock, 3 min for cold and pressure pain and 15 min for ischemia.

Before being debriefed, the subject completed a questionnaire indicating the proportion of time during each modality that he/she engaged in catastrophic or coping cognitions. At this point the fact that videotaping had taken place was disclosed, and the subject was given the opportunity to have the tape erased. No one elected this option. Thereafter the subject completed another form giving consent for further use to be made of the videotapes.

Measurement of Facial Action

Facial expressions were measured with the FACS, allowing observers to 'dissect' any facial movement into its muscular bases, thereby determining which of 44 specific actions had taken place. Coding was performed by 3 observers, each of whom had undergone FACS training and passed the test of proficiency devised by the developers of the system.

For each modality, facial actions were scored during a period when subjects were not being exposed to the stimulus (baseline) and immediately prior to pain tolerance. Coding varied slightly, depending on the modality. For tonic pain (cold, pressure, ischemia), actions were scored in 10-sec intervals. Baseline intervals were coded from the 10-sec period that occurred immediately before the stimulus was applied. Pain intervals were coded from the 10-sec period immediately before the subject indicated that pain tolerance had been reached.

The episodic pain of electric shock was scored in 3-sec intervals. Baseline observations consisted of the two 3-sec intervals prior to the 1st shock. Pain intervals were coded from the shock that resulted in a pain tolerance rating and the shock immediately preceding that one. These stimuli were each coded for the 3-sec period during which shock was applied. Data from these 2 intervals were then combined to yield a measure of pain expression during 6 sec of exposure to electric shock-induced pain.

For each modality, if the subject did not request termination by the time the cut-off point had been reached, the maximal level attained was taken as pain tolerance.

Occasionally, technical problems resulted in the baseline segment not being available. In such cases, a segment was selected from portions of the video record that were comparable to the baseline. These intervals were selected only if there was no pain stimulation occurring to the subject at the time, and for the preceding and the following 6 sec.

The time of onset, peak intensity, and offset of each facial action were identified. Only actions with an onset during the interval in question were scored. Thus, if an action began prior to, and was present throughout, the interval, it was not coded, even if it was strong, endured for a substantial time or increased dramatically in intensity during the interval. Ten seconds was set as the maximum duration for any action.

Most actions were rated on a 6-point intensity scale (Friesen, 1988) which varied from 'no action' (0) through 'minimal action' (a 'trace,' coded as (1)) to 'maximal action' (5). Those actions that did not lend themselves to an intensity rating (e.g., AU38—nostril dilate) were coded in a binary format (present/absent).

Three sets of actions were combined, AU6 (cheek raise) and AU7 (lid tighten) were combined into 1 variable (orbit tightening) because the forms and muscular bases of the movements are similar. There is precedent in the FACS literature for performing this combination (Ekman, Friesen, & Simons, 1985). AU9 and AU10, were also combined into 1 action (levator contraction). These actions involve contractions of different strands of the levator labii muscles, resemble each other and have been hypothesized to represent different stages of the same expression (Prkachin & Mercer, 1989). There is also precedent for considering these actions as elements of a unitary expression (Ekman & Friesen, 1978b). AU25, AU26 and AU27, which represent varying degrees of mouth opening, were combined into a 4-point scale consisting of 3 increasing degrees of mouth openness (AU25, AU26 and AU27, coded as 1, 2 and 3) and mouth closure (coded as 0) (cf., Prkachin & Mercer, 1989).

Scoring reliability was assessed by comparing the 2 coders' data to that of the author on 116 intervals. Reliability, assessed by Ekman and Friesen's (1978b) formula was 0.75, which is comparable to that observed in other FACS studies (cf., Craig, Hyde, & Patrick, 1991).

Statistical Analysis

An action was selected for further analysis if (1) it had been reported in previous studies to be associated with pain, or (2) its frequency was greater than 1% of the total sample of actions coded.

The actions selected for further analysis have different properties. Some are binary (present or absent), others vary in frequency, and several vary in intensity. All can be quantified according to their duration. Table 8.2 presents the metric properties of the selected actions.

Because of these variations in metric properties, different analytic strategies were employed as appropriate. Binary variables were analyzed with Cochran's Q test, a nonparametric technique for evaluation differences in related categorical variables. Frequency, intensity or duration measures were analyzed with analysis of variance (ANOVA) procedures. Those actions for which a-priori evidence of an association with pain existed were analyzed in univariate factorial 2 (gender) × 4 (modalities) × 2 (epochs: baseline vs. pain) ANOVAs. When these analyses indicated a significant epochs effect or epochs × modalities interaction, the significance of differences from baseline to pain interval were determined with planned orthogonal t tests (2-tailed; alpha < 0.05) for each modality. Differences between modalities were analyzed with the Tukey *HSD* post-hoc test since there was no prior reason to predict modality differences. Those actions for which a-priori evidence of an association with pain did not

TABLE **8.2.** Facial actions selected for further analysis. Percent
denotes the percentage of all AUs coded in the entire data set.

Action	Description	Percent	Coding
AU1	Inner brow raise	2.0	Intensity
AU2	Outer brow raise	1.9	Intensity
AU4	Brow lower	3.2	Intensity
AU6	Cheek raise	4.5	Intensity
AU7	Lid tighten	5.4	Intensity
AU9	Nose wrinkle	2.2	Intensity
AU10	Upper lip raise	1.6	Intensity
AU12	Oblique lip pull	5.1	Intensity
AU14	Dimple	2.3	Intensity
AU17	Chin raise	4.1	Intensity
AU20	Lip stretch	0.7*	Intensity
AU24	Lip press	2.7	Intensity
AU25	Lips part	2.1	Binary
AU26	Jaw drop	2.9	Binary
AU27	Mouth stretch	0.1*	Binary
AU38	Nostrils flare	1.4	Binary
AU41	Lids droop	2.9	Binary
AU43	Eyes close	2.8	Binary
AU45	Blink	34.5	Frequency

* Action included because of prior evidence of an association with pain.

exist were analyzed in a multivariate analysis of variance (MANOVA) of the same
form. Duration data were analyzed in the same way.

Results

Categorical Analyses

Categorical analyses revealed no significant differences in the likelihood of AU38 (nostril dilation) between baseline and pain states. Eye closing occurred during 20% of pain intervals and 0% of baseline intervals during electric shock, a difference that was significant ($Q(1) = 7.00$, $P < 0.01$). There was also a tendency for eye closing to be more likely during pain than during baseline intervals for cold and pressure pain ($P < 0.10$).

Intensity Analyses

The intensity scores for each action were summed separately for baseline and pain intervals in the 4 modalities. Eight subjects (3 male and 5 female) had missing data on 1 of the variables, either because a trial had not been videotaped or a baseline segment was unavailable. Although this represented only 0.03% of the data, it had the effect of censoring the entire case from repeated measures analyses. Therefore, the data were analyzed in 2 ways. The first employed only subjects with complete data. In the second, a conservative assumption was made that the action in question did not occur at all during the missing intervals and zeros were entered for the missing data. In no case was the outcome of these secondary analyses different from the original, therefore they will not be reported.

In the analyses of AUs for which there was a-priori evidence of a relationship with pain, several actions varied reliably with pain. For brow lowering (AU4), orbital tightening (AU6/AU7), levator contraction (AU9/AU10) and oblique lip pulling (AU12) there were significant epoch effects (Fs (1, 31) ranging from 7.25, $P = 0.01$ to 49.28, $P < 0.001$). For brow lowering and orbital tightening there were also significant stimulus $\times$ epochs interactions (Geisser-Greenhouse Fs (3, 29) = 3.22, $P < 0.05$, and 3.86, $P < 0.01$, respectively). The results of these analyses are presented in figure 8.1. There, it can be seen that the intensity of orbital tightening increased significantly with pain for all, and the intensity of levator contraction increased significantly with 3 of 4 modalities. Although brow lowering increased with pain during all modalities the differences were only significant for shock. Oblique lip pulling and mouth opening increased significantly with shock; however, they were *less* intense during pain for some modalities. Brow lowering, orbit tightening and levator contraction were more intense for electric shock than the other modalities.

Analyses of actions for which there was no a-priori evidence of association with pain yielded no significant effects.

Frequency Analyses

Analysis of blinking frequency revealed a significant epoch effect (F (1, 31) = 16.26, $P < 0.01$). There was no modalities $\times$ epoch interaction. Figure 8.2 reveals that, contrary

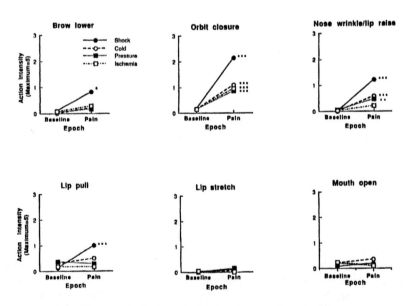

Figure 8.1. Differences in the intensity of facial actions from baseline to pain tolerance.

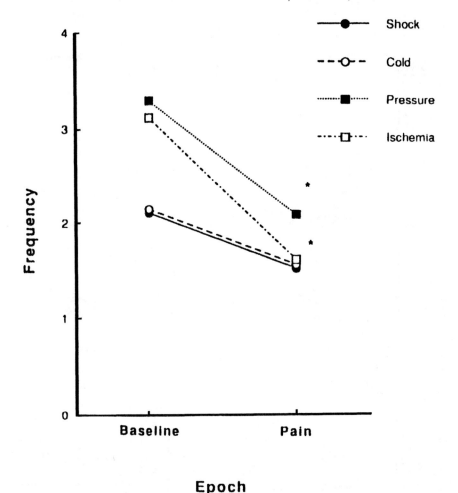

Figure 8.2. Differences in blinking frequency from baseline to pain tolerance.

to expectations, blinking rate *decreased* during pain across modalities, significantly so for pressure and ischemic pain.

Duration Analysis

Comparable analyses of the total durations of facial actions were conducted on all coded AUs. Eye closure (AU43) and blinking (AU45) were analyzed in the univariate data set because of pre-existing evidence that these actions are associated with pain. AU38 was included in the multivariate analyses because it did not meet this criterion.

The results are summarized in figure 8.3. The findings were comparable to those for intensity. The durations of brow lowering (AU4), orbit tightening (AU6/AU7), and levator contraction (AU9/AU10) increased reliably during pain across all modalities. Duration of eye closure (AU43) was greater during pain for all modalities, but

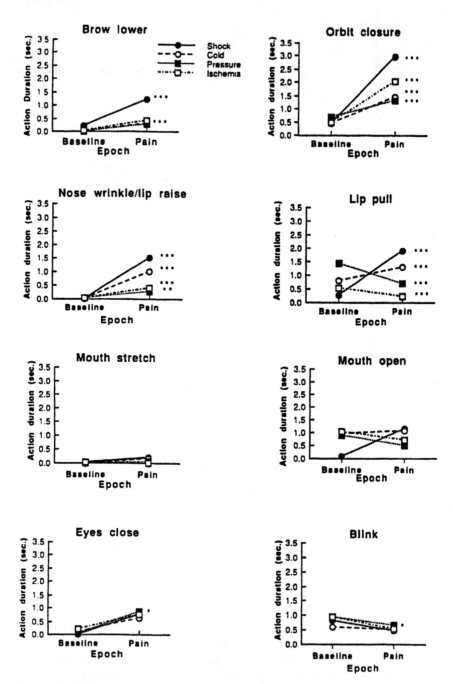

Figure 8.3. Differences in the duration of facial actions from baseline to pain tolerance.

only significantly so for shock and pressure pain. Duration of lip pulling (AU12) varied significantly with pain, but the direction of the relationship varied from one modality to another: for shock and cold it was longer, and for pressure and ischemia it was shorter during pain. For shock and ischemia, the duration of blinking was significantly related to pain, but in the direction opposite to that predicted.

The MANOVA of facial actions for which there was no a-priori evidence of a relationship with pain revealed no further systematic effects.

Combining Facial Actions

Although several studies have examined facial expressions of pain, few have considered the problem of weighting separate actions to most effectively capture the information they provide about the construct they are intended to assess. Factor analysis was employed to ascertain how the separate pain-related actions interrelate empirically and to derive weights that reflect that natural ordering. The foregoing analyses provided evidence that no more than 4 actions were consistently related to pain in categorical, intensity or duration analyses. Intensity scores for brow lowering, orbit tightening, levator contraction and a variable consisting of the number of eye closures (not blinks) were entered into principal component factor analyses.[1] Separate analyses were performed for each modality. An eigen-value greater than 1 was necessary to be retained as a factor. The results are presented in table 8.3. For each modality, the analysis revealed a large 1st factor, accounting for 49–65% of the variance in AU intensities. Analyses for cold and pressure pain also revealed smaller 2nd factors. The structures of the 1st factor in all modalities were generally similar. In each case orbit tightening, levator contraction and eye closure loaded substantially on this factor. Brow lowering also loaded on the 1st factor for all but pressure pain.

These findings imply that the 4 actions reflect a general pain expression factor. Sensitivity of a measure based on such a factor was tested by weighting and combining facial-action intensity scores to reflect the factor structure derived from the foregoing analysis. Since factor analyses yielded structures and factor-score coefficients that were unique to their own distributions, it was necessary to decide on a common metric by

TABLE **8.3**. Results of principal components factor analyses of intensities of four facial actions during shock, cold, pressure and ischemic pain

	Factor loadings					
	Shock	*Cold*		*Pressure*		*Ischemia*
	I	I	II	I	II	I
Brow	0.59	0.52	0.78	0.25	0.96	0.66
Lid/cheek	0.88	0.91	−0.24	0.82	−0.31	0.75
Nose/lip	0.91	0.76	−0.57	0.66	−0.10	0.74
Eyes	0.82	0.83	0.29	0.90	0.09	0.74
Eigenvalue	2.63	2.38	1.08	1.97	1.03	2.09
% variance	65.8	59.5	26.9	49.3	25.8	52.2

Factor-score coefficients: Brow 0.22; Lid/cheek 0.33; Nose/lip 0.35; and Eyes 0.31.

which all modalities could be compared. Because the initial analyses indicated that response to electric shock was the clearest and most intense, the weighting coefficients from the shock factor analysis were used as the basis for conversion. These weights are presented in table 8.3. Intensity scores for each action at baseline and during pain for each modality were then converted to standard scores relative to the shock distribution and multiplied by their factor-score coefficient. The resultant values were then summed to create a weighted composite pain-expression score. Since, due to standardization, the resulting scores could be less than zero, a constant representing the standard score for no action in the shock analyses was added so that a final score of zero represented no action. These values were entered into a 2 (gender) × 4 (modalities) × 2 (epochs) ANOVA. The results are presented in figure 8.4. Significant epoch (F (1, 31) = 34.32, $P < 0.001$), modalities (F (3, 93) = 3.94, $P < 0.05$), and modalities × epochs effects (F (3, 93) = 4.23, $P < 0.01$) were obtained. Planned t tests revealed that factor scores at pain for all modalities were significantly greater than those at baseline. Comparisons across modalities by Tukey *HSD* indicated that the mean factor score during shock pain was greater than that for all other modalities. There were no other significant differences.

Table 8.4 presents the intercorrelations among factor scores for all modalities. With the exception of the relationship between cold and ischemic pain and between shock and pressure pain, these measures tended to be modestly and significantly related. Factor scores for each modality were also correlated with the subject's pain threshold and tolerance scores on that modality, the subjective ratings of maximal pain due to that modality on categorical, sensory and affective scales, and the rating of the amount of coping and catastrophizing engaged in during that modality. Of 28 correlations performed, only 2 were significant, a value that is only marginally greater than that which would be expected by chance. Therefore, it appeared that the pain-expression factor scores were largely unrelated to pain threshold, tolerance, subjective pain ratings and measures of cognitive activity during pain.

Discussion

Although more than 6 facial actions have been reported to occur with pain, there has been some inconsistency in the actions which have been identified. In the present study, brow lowering, orbit tightening and levator contraction were consistently related to pain. The intensity of orbit closure and levator contraction was significantly greater and the duration of both actions longer during pain for all modalities. The duration of brow lowering was significantly longer during pain than at baseline across all modalities, and its intensity was increased during pain, significantly so for electric shock. Eye closure was more likely during pain than baseline for electric shock, marginally more likely during cold and pressure and its duration was greater during pain than baseline for electric shock and pressure.

Consistency of association across different types of pain is a stringent, yet useful, criterion for designating an action pain related. Applying this criterion to the present results suggests that the list of potentially pain-related facial actions can be narrowed. It would appear that the bulk of information about pain conveyed by facial expression is represented by 4 actions: brow lowering, orbit tightening, levator contraction and eye closure. Indeed, the factor-analytic results suggest that, even within this subset, the

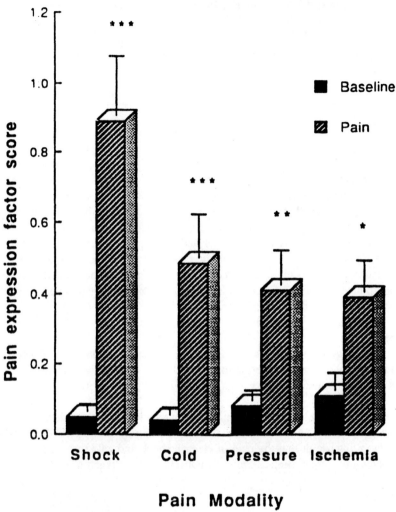

Figure 8.4. Differences in pain expression factor scores from baseline to pain tolerance.

greatest amount of variance is accounted for by orbital and levator action. This suggests that the 4 actions comprise a basic 'signal' (see figure 8.5) that may be universal to different types of pain. Although the present findings were obtained with experimental pain stimuli, the same actions have been associated with pain in most other analyses of facial expression including studies of time-limited, discrete, experimental pain (Craig & Patrick, 1985; Patrick et al., 1986), and of pain patients (LeResche, 1982;

TABLE **8.4.** Intercorrelations among pain expression
factor scores for all modalities

	Cold	Pressure	Ischemia
Shock	0.39*	0.29	0.33*
Cold		0.32*	-0.02
Pressure			0.33*

* $P < 0.05$.

LeResche & Dworkin, 1988; Prkachin & Mercer, 1989; Craig et al., 1991). Thus, the conclusion that this signal is general and common to a variety of states, including clinical pain, appears to be sustainable.

This is not to say that the 4 actions comprise the only pain signal or that other movements may not show a unique and consistent relationship to pain. It is possible that clinical pain states may evoke further actions, especially when pain intensity becomes severe and exceeds the limits that it is possible to impose in experimental studies (LeResche, 1982; Prkachin & Mercer, 1989). For example, horizontal stretching of the lips produced by risorius (AU20) has been reported to be associated with pain in some studies (LeResche, 1982; Prkachin & Mercer, 1989). Nevertheless, available studies would suggest that even in such circumstances the actions identified here would often be present.

Of course, a consistent relationship between facial expressions and appropriate eliciting conditions is only 1 criterion for establishment of universality. Universality also implies cross-cultural consistency (Ekman & Friesen, 1971). Future research should examine this issue.

Three actions that have been associated with pain in previous studies bore peculiar relationships to it in the present study. Oblique pulling of the lips (AU12) was significantly more intense during the pain of electric shock and cold than at baseline, confirming previous observations (Craig & Patrick, 1985; Prkachin & Mercer, 1989).

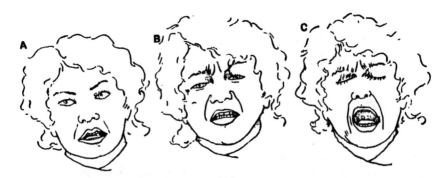

Figure 8.5. A sequence of facial changes showing the emergence of the 4 principal facial actions. A: onset of action. B: brow lowering (AU4), orbit tightening (AU6) and levator contraction (AU10). C: brow lowering, orbit tightening (AU7) and eyelid closing (AU43). Also shown is mouth stretch (AU27) which was not consistently related to pain.

However, during pressure and ischemic pain, this action was less intense and its duration shorter during pain than at baseline. Similarly, mouth opening was more intense during shock and cold but less intense during pressure. Blinking rate and duration actually decreased during all pain modalities, a finding that is in direct contrast to some previous studies (Craig & Patrick, 1985; Patrick et al., 1986), but which is similar to results reported by Craig et al. (1991) and Prkachin and Mercer (1989). Analyses of actions that have not been identified in previous research to bear a relationship to pain uncovered no new candidates to consider as potentially pain related.

That some actions are more likely or more intense during only some pain modalities and not others may be evidence for stimulus specificity. Alternatively, these actions may reflect the occurrence of secondary processes such as coping or self-observation. For example, a parsimonious explanation of why blinking rate is only occasionally associated with pain derives from examining factors confounded with pain in different studies. In studies in which pain has been accompanied by an increased blinking rate, the pain has been of sudden onset (as in electric shock) or in its early stages (as in cold pressor). As noted by Prkachin and Mercer (1989), these conditions are likely to produce the confounded experience of startle which other research has found to produce blinking (Ekman et al., 1985). Thus, it seems likely that those actions which bear an inconsistent relationship with pain across modalities may represent the occurrence of processes that may be confounded with pain.

It would appear that clinicians and investigators interested in assessing pain via facial expression could safely restrict themselves to the investigation of brow lowering, lid tightening/cheek raising, nose wrinkling/lip raising and eye closing. This should simplify the process of measurement in this field considerably. The present data also imply that oblique lip pulling, mouth opening and blinking should *not* be considered actions that carry information specific to pain, and therefore investigators who are uninterested in the potential information that these actions might carry could safely ignore them. The factor analytic results imply, however, that it would be important to measure all the 'core' actions comprehensively. Although data from each modality yielded evidence that the collection of 4 facial changes represented a general reaction in the sense that they were correlated, it was also clear that the information provided by separate actions was not completely redundant. Indeed, each action made substantial contribution to a composite index of pain expression. As shown in figure 8.4, this index provides quite sensitive discrimination of pain and non-pain conditions. Researchers interested in obtaining a measure of pain expression might profitably make use of this index in the future.

Pain expressions were not correlated with pain threshold, pain tolerance or reports of pain intensity. This independence among measures may have been artifactually introduced by the methodology employed, since pain expression and subjective intensity measurements were both taken at the point when subjects were exposed to the maximum pain they would tolerate. With most subjects experiencing substantial pain, and indicating so both verbally and non-verbally, there may not have been enough variation in pain state to effectively determine whether subjective and expressed pain levels were consistent with one another. On the other hand, the outcome is consistent with other findings (LeResche & Dworkin, 1988), indicating that facial expressions provide evidence about pain processes that is different from that available in other measures.

In conclusion, the results of this study support 2 major generalizations. First, a relatively small subset of actions convey the bulk of information about pain that is available in facial expression. Second, the occurrence of those actions is fairly consistent across different types of pain. These findings are consistent with the suggestion that pain expressions may be universal. The present data provide some suggestions for how these phenomena may be profitably quantified in future studies.

Acknowledgments

This research was supported by Grant no. MA-8132 from the Medical Research Council of Canada. The assistance of Farla Kaufman, Steve Symon and Paul McDonald in data collection, of Sharon Thompson and Paul McDonald in facial coding and the artwork of Susan Larrabee is gratefully acknowledged. I am also grateful for the support provided by Linda LeResche and suggestions by Paul Ekman and Gary Rollman.

Note

1. The same analysis of duration data yielded comparable results. These may be obtained by writing the author.

References

Chapman, C. R., Casey, K. L., Dubner, R., Foley, K. M., Gracely, R. H., & Reading, A. E. (1985). Pain measurement: An overview. *Pain, 22,* 1–31.
Craig, K. D., Hyde, S. A., & Patrick, C. J. (1991). Genuine, suppressed and faked facial behavior during exacerbation of chronic low back pain. *Pain, 46,* 153–160.
Craig, K. D., & Patrick, C. J. (1985). Facial expression during induced pain. *Journal of Personality and Social Psychology, 48,* 1080–1091.
Craig, K. D., & Prkachin, K. M. (1983). Nonverbal measures of pain. In R. Melzac (Ed.), *Pain measurement and assessment* (pp. 173–182). New York: Ravin Press.
Craig, K. D., Prkachin, K. M., & Grunau, R. V. E. (in press). The facial expression of pain. In D. Turk & R. Melzack (Eds.), *Handbook of pain assessment.* New York: Guilford.
Ekman, P., & Friesen, W. V. (1971). Constants across cultures in the face and emotion. *J. Pers. Soc. Psychol., 17,* 124–129.
Ekman, P., & Friesen, W. V. (1978a). The facial action coding system. Palo Alto, CA: Consulting Psychologists Press.
Ekman, P., & Friesen, W. V. (1978b). Facial action coding system. Investigator's guide. Palo Alto, CA: Consulting Psychologists Press.
Ekman, P., Friesen, W. V., & Simons, R. C. (1985). Is the startle reaction an emotion? *J. Pers. Soc. Psychol., 49,* 1416–1426.
Ekman, P., & Oster, H. (1982). Review of research, 1970–1980. In P. Ekman (Ed.), *Emotion in the human face* (2nd ed.; pp. 147–177). New York: Cambridge University Press.
Fordyce, W. E. (1988). Pain and suffering: A reappraisal. *Am. Psychol., 43,* 276–283.
Forgione, A. G., & Barber, T. X. (1971). A strain-gauge pain stimulator. *Psychophysiology, 8,* 102–106.
Friesen, W. V. (1988). EMFACS, Human Interaction Laboratory, University of California, San Francisco. Unpublished manuscript.
Heft, M. W., Gracely, R. H., Dubner, R., & McGrath, P. A. (1980). A validation model for verbal descriptor scaling of human clinical pain. *Pain, 6,* 363–373.

LeResche, L. (1982). Facial expression in pain: a study of candid photographs. *J. Nonverb. Behav., 7,* 46–56.

LeResche, L., & Dworkin, S. F. (1988). Facial expressions of pain and emotions in chronic TMD patients. *Pain, 35,* 71–78.

Patrick, C. J., Craig, K. D., & Prkachin, K. M. (1986). Observer judgments of acute pain: Facial action determinants. *J. Pers. Soc. Psychol., 50,* 1291–1298.

Petrovaara, A., Nurmikko, T., & Pontinen, P. J. (1984). Two separate components of pain produced by the submaximal effort tourniquet technique. *Pain, 20,* 53–58.

Prkachin, K. M. (1986). Pain behavior is not unitary. *Behav. Brain Sci., 9,* 754–755.

Prkachin, K. M., Currie, N. A., & Craig, K. D. (1983). Judging nonverbal expressions of pain. *Can. J. Behav. Sci., 15,* 409–421.

Prkachin, K. M., & Mercer, S. R. (1989). Pain expression in patients with shoulder pathology: validity, properties and relationship to sickness impact. *Pain, 39,* 257–265.

Redican, W. K. (1982). An evolutionary perspective on human facial displays. In P. Ekman (Ed.), *Emotion in the human face* (pp. 212–280). New York: Cambridge University Press.

AFTERWORD

The Consistency of
Facial Expressions of Pain

KENNETH M. PRKACHIN

I can't resist telling an ironic story about this article. I first outlined the hypotheses and method for this study in an application for a research grant to the Medical Research Council of Canada in 1983. The intent of that application was to work out, in an experimental model, some of the basic properties of facial behavior during pain. I had conceived of this study as addressing one of the simplest questions one could ask: Is there a consistent set of changes that occur in facial expression when pain occurs, regardless of the nature of the pain involved? Other questions posed in the same application were whether it is possible to discriminate spontaneous from deliberate pain expressions on the basis of facial action, and whether the topography of facial behavior changes when people try to suppress or exaggerate the expression of pain.

The original grant application was unsuccessful on the strength of external reviews that questioned the value of the whole enterprise. Disheartened, I was ready to abandon work in the area, but decided to try one more time to get external support for the project. I was convinced, however, that the issues addressed and the methods outlined in the original proposal were important and adequate, and had received no feedback from the original reviews that would have been helpful in suggesting methodological or conceptual improvements in the studies. I therefore simply resubmitted the application with the sole change of removing the description of this study from the text in order to meet newly imposed page-length regulations. The application fared much better the second time around, with very positive external reviews, and the funds were awarded. Was it the absence of the description of this study that turned the tide? Whatever the answer, this experience has caused me to be highly skeptical about the processes by which we evaluate science.

The field of pain research underwent explosive growth in the 1970s and 80s. Despite this, fundamental questions concerning the properties of the most common ways of assessing pain, particularly their validity and susceptibility to self-presentation biases, had been and to this day remain unresolved (Chapman et al., 1985). One of the reasons for doing this work was to explore the possibility that a new method of evaluating pain, based on facial expression, could be developed. A second impetus was the emergence, during the time of rapid growth in pain research, of influential means of evaluating and treating clinical pain problems that were based on the concept of "pain behavior" (Fordyce, 1976). Although much clinical research and practice was inspired by the elaboration of this concept, its theoretical development was limited. It seemed that an important step toward the development of a more refined theory of pain behavior would be taken by detailed study of the nature (i.e., the topography) and properties (i.e., the determinants and susceptibility to intrinsic and extrinsic influences) of facial expression during pain. Although pain is not ordinarily conceived as an emotion, it does have elements that are described in emotional terms (Craig, 1984). Moreover, viewed from an evolutionary perspective, it seemed eminently reasonable to believe that pain would have a signal that communicates something about the current state of an afflicted individual. For these reasons, parallels in research on emotional expression and the theories of emotion arising out of that work (Ekman, 1977) seemed a compelling model for examining pain communication.

The early work of Linda LeResche (1982), who first employed FACS to describe facial behavior during pain, and Ken Craig and his colleagues (Craig & Patrick, 1985; Patrick, Craig, & Prkachin, 1986) had provided a basis for describing a facial expression of pain, but there were some inconsistencies in the facial actions that changed reliably with pain in those studies, and because of the nature of the stimuli involved in the studies (severe injury, electric shock, and sudden immersion of the arm in ice water), it was possible that some of the actions observed could have been a response to other variables correlated with the stimuli or with pain. A study in which the stimuli producing pain varied seemed an ideal way to separate the actions associated with painful suffering from those associated with such potentially confounded variables.

Perhaps the main contribution of this study is its fairly clear demonstration that, regardless of its source, when pain is expressed some four facial actions are likely to occur. The various analyses reported in the study support the assertion that the actions are cohesive, related to pain experience, and may properly be described as a "pain expression." As is suggested in the article, such information could now profitably be used to simplify the measurement of at least this component of pain behavior in clinical and experimental studies.

In subsequent research, we have explored and found support for the utility of a unitary index, based on the measurement of these four movements. In the first study to do so, we used the FACS measurements of patients suffering from shoulder pain taken from a previous study (Prkachin & Mercer, 1989) to develop an index based on the intensity and the duration of the four actions. We found (Prkachin, Berzins, & Mercer, 1994) that the facial pain index provided good (occasionally remarkable) titration of patients' pain experiences as indexed by their self-reports. Indeed, the facial measurement consistently outperformed naive observers' ratings of pain, suggesting that it may provide especially discriminating information about patients' internal states. These findings further suggest that information on which observers might reasonably base inferences about pain in others is actually available, but that at least naive observers do not make effective use of it. More recently, we have found evidence that difficulties in making use of the available facial information also apply to people who have a stake in being able to make accurate judgments about pain in others, notably professional physiotherapists and occupational therapists (Prkachin, Solomon, Hwang, & Mercer, 1995). Finally, we have begun to explore whether providing individuals with training in the recognition of these four movements can improve their ability to use facial information to evaluate pain in others (Solomon, 1995).

Despite the apparent success of this study, I am convinced that it has not been able to capture some more subtle aspects of pain expression. In order to answer the simple question, "Do some facial actions occur consistently during pain?" it was necessary to make some coarse methodological decisions. The most important of these was to restrict attention to periods of observation during which the subjects were clearly either in pain or not. This was accomplished by contrasting behavior when subjects were not being stimulated with behavior occurring at the time of maximum pain: pain tolerance. Casual observation of the videotapes has shown, however, that the actions identified as pain related also occurred at other times beginning around the subjects' first reports of pain (pain threshold) and occurring at other times in the interval between pain threshold and pain tolerance. It is possible that these actions might be even more informative and provide better predictions about the subjects' pain experiences and other pain-related decisions. Moreover, the method employed was also inadequate to the task of illuminating another interesting and plausible speculation about pain expression: that it emerges in a consistent and sequential order, with some actions being recruited sooner (early signals) and some actions later (late signals). Such knowledge about how a pain expression "unfolds" could add to our understaniding of the structure and neural regulation of pain expression and might be applied profitably in health-care settings.

Finally, as noted in the paper, the findings provide one line of evidence that is consistent with the suggestion that there may be a universal expression of pain. In the absence of cross-cultural evidence, however, a definitive answer to this question is not possible. The pursuit of such cross-cultural information would now seem warranted.

References

Chapman, C. R., Casey, K. L., Dubner, R., Foley, K. M., Gracely, R. H., & Reading, A. E. (1985). Pain measurement: An overview. *Pain, 22,* 1–31.
Craig, K. D. (1984). Emotional aspects of pain. In P. D. Wall & R. Melzack (Eds.), *Textbook of pain* (pp. 156–161). Edinburgh: Churchill Livingstone.
Craig, K. D., & Patrick, C. J. (1985). Facial expression during induced pain. *Journal of Personality and Social Psychology, 48,* 1080–1091.
Ekman, P. (1977). Biological and cultural contributions to body and facial movement. In J. Blacking (Ed.), *The anthropology of the body* (pp. 38–84). London: Academic Press.
Fordyce, W. E. (1976). *Behavioral methods for chronic pain and illness.* St. Louis, MO: C. V. Mosby.
LeResche, L. (1982). Facial expression in pain: A study of candid photographs. *Journal of Nonverbal Behavior, 7,* 46–56.
Patrick, C. J., Craig, K. D., & Prkachin, K. M. (1986). Observer judgments of acute pain: Facial action determinants. *Journal of Personality and Social Psychology, 50,* 1291–1298.
Prkachin, K. M., Berzins, S., & Mercer, S. R. (1994). Encoding and decoding of pain expressions: A judgement study. *Pain, 58,* 253–259.
Prkachin, K. M., & Mercer, S. R. (1989). Pain expression in patients with shoulder pathology: Validity, properties and relationship to sickness impact. *Pain, 39,* 257–265.
Prkachin, K. M., Solomon, P., Hwang, T., & Mercer, S. R. (1995). *Does experience affect judgements of pain behavior? Evidence from relatives of pain patients and health-care providers.* Manuscript submitted for publication.
Solomon, P. E. (1995). *Enhancing sensitivity to pain expression.* Unpublished doctoral dissertation.

9

Smiles When Lying

PAUL EKMAN, WALLACE V. FRIESEN & MAUREEN O'SULLIVAN

Nearly 20 years ago Ekman and Friesen (1969) theorized that because people usually attend more to facial expression than to body movement, a liar would attempt to disguise and censor facial expressions more than hand or foot movement. As they hypothesized, observers were found to be more accurate in detecting deceit when they viewed the liar's body without the face than when they saw the face alone or the face and body together (although the absolute level of accuracy at best was rather meager; Ekman & Friesen, 1969, 1974; Hocking, Miller, & Fontes, 1978; Littlepage & Pineault, 1979; Wilson, 1975; Zuckerman, DePaulo, & Rosenthal, 1981).

Although the face would mislead the untrained eye, Ekman and Friesen (1969) said that involuntary expressions of emotions might leak despite a liar's efforts at disguise. The easy-to-see macroexpressions often would signal the liar's deliberately intended false information, and the more subtle aspects of facial activity, such as microexpressions, would nevertheless reveal true feelings. "In a sense the face is equipped to lie the most and leak the most, and thus can be a very confusing source of information during deception" (Ekman & Friesen, 1969, p. 98). Until now no one has attempted to identify such subtle facial clues to deceit. Those experiments on lying that measured facial behavior considered only the macro category of smiles, laughter, or both. As would be expected, no difference between lying and truthfulness was found in most studies (Finkelstein, 1978; Greene, O'Hair, Cody, & Yen, 1985; Hemsley, 1977; Hocking & Leathers, 1980; Knapp, Hart, & Dennis, 1974; Krauss, Geller, & Olson, 1976; Kraut, 1978; Kraut & Poe, 1980; McClintock & Hunt, 1975; Mehrabian, 1971; O'Hair, Cody, & McLaughlin, 1981; Riggio & Friedman, 1983; and a review by Zuckerman et al., 1981).

In this study we measured more subtle aspects of facial expression, distinguishing among different types of smiling. The materials examined were videotapes in which the subjects first truthfully described enjoyable feelings and then lied, concealing negative emotions and falsely claiming positive feelings. Previous studies of these videotapes have reported clues to deceit in body movements and vocal behavior (Ekman, Friesen, & Scherer, 1976). Viewing the facial expressions in these videotapes convinced Ekman and Friesen that none of the techniques for measuring facial expression available when these videotapes were gathered, in the early 1970s, would succeed in discriminating between the smiles of actual enjoyment and the smiles of feigned enjoyment masking negative emotions. It took Ekman and Friesen 8 years to develop the tool they thought necessary for the task, their fine-grained, comprehensive facial measurement technique, the Facial Action Coding System (FACS) (Ekman & Friesen, 1978). In this article we report the findings from the first use of FACS to measure facial expressions when people deliberately lie.

Most relevant to the particular deceit we studied is Ekman and Friesen's (1982) distinction between felt and false smiles. Felt happy smiles,[1] they said,

> include all smiles in which the person actually experiences, and presumably would report, a positive emotion. These positive emotions include: pleasure from visual, auditory, gustatory, kinesthetic or tactile stimulation; amusement and delight; contentment and satisfaction; beatific experiences; relief from pain, pressure or tension; and enjoyment of another person. We hypothesize that the common-elements in the facial expression of all such positive experiences are the action of two muscles; the zygomatic major pulling the lip corners upwards towards the cheekbone; and the orbicularis oculi which raises the cheek and gathers the skin inwards from around the eye socket. (Ekman & Friesen, 1982, p. 242)

Figure 9.1 shows an example of such a smile. Our first hypothesis is this: Felt happy expressions occurred more often when people frankly described positive feelings (the honest interview) than when people deceptively claimed to be enjoying themselves although they were actually having strong negative feelings (the deceptive interview).

Figure 9.1. An example of the felt happy smile, showing the appearance changes produced by the muscle around the eye, orbicularis oculi, as well as the muscle that pulls the lip corners upwards, zygomatic major.

A false smile is

> deliberately made to convince another person that positive emotion is felt when it isn't. There are two kinds of [such] smiles. In a phony smile nothing much is felt but an attempt is made to appear as if positive feelings are felt. In a masking smile strong negative emotion is felt and an attempt is made to conceal those feelings by appearing to feel positive. (Ekman & Friesen, 1982, p. 244)

We did not consider phony smiles in this study because they are said to occur only when nothing much is felt, and our subjects reported feeling either positive feelings in the honest interview, or negative feelings, which they tried to conceal, in the deceptive interview.

We did measure masking smiles, which Ekman and Friesen said can be detected because "[s]igns of the felt emotions the masking smile is intended to conceal may persist and provide evidence that the smile is false" (Ekman & Friesen, 1982, p. 247). A masking smile thus combines the smiling action (zygomatic major), which is part of the felt smile, with traces of the muscle movements from one or another of the negative emotions. Our second hypothesis is the following: Masking smiles occurred more often when people deceptively claimed to be enjoying themselves although they were actually having strong negative feelings.

These distinctions do not exhaust the repertoire of smiles, but there is no reason to expect that any other type of smiling—which might differ in the muscles recruited, intensity of action, timing, or symmetry—would occur differentially in the honest interview as compared with the deceptive interview. Ekman (1985) described 17 other types of smiling. Almost half of these are conversational signals (Ekman, 1979), regulating the back and forth flow of conversation. The listener response smile is an example of one of the most frequent of these conversational facial signals. This is "a coordination smile used when listening to let the person speaking know that everything is understood and that there is no need to repeat or rephrase. It is the equivalent to the 'mm-hmm,' 'good,' and head nod it often accompanies" (Ekman, 1985, p. 157). (Other forms of listener response were described by Dittmann, 1972, and Duncan, 1974.) Listener response smiles and the other conversational signal smiles were not anaylzed because we believe them to be part of any conversation, whether honest or deceptive.

Method

Deception Scenario

Student nurses were videotaped in each of two standardized interviews. In both interviews, the subject watched a short film and answered an interviewer's questions concerning her feelings about it. The interviewer sat with her back to the screen, unable to see what the subject was watching. The subject sat facing the screen and the interviewer. In the first minute of each interview the subject answered questions concerning her feelings about what she was seeing as she watched the film. Then the film ended, and for the next 2 to 3 min the interviewer continued to ask questions about the experience. The interviews averaged close to 3 min. with a range of from 2 to almost 5 min.

In the honest interview, the subjects were in a relatively unstressful situation. Nature films designed to elicit pleasant feelings were shown, and subjects were instructed to describe their feelings frankly. In the deceptive interview, subjects saw a film showing amputations and burns, intended to elicit strong unpleasant emotions. They were instructed to conceal negative feelings and to convince the interviewer they were watching another pleasant film. The emotional ratings provided immediately after each interview confirmed that the appropriate emotions were aroused. The mean rating on happiness was 7.16 (on a 9-point scale) in the honest interview and 0 in the deceptive interview; the mean ratings on fear, disgust, sadness, and pain were all between 4 and 5 in the deceptive interview and 0 in the honest interview.

This scenario was designed to resemble the lie of the depressed inpatient who, after a few weeks in a mental hospital, conceals anguish with a mask of positive feeling to win release from supervision so as to be able to commit suicide. The scenario required concealing strong negative emotions, felt at the moment of the lie, with a mask of positive feeling. The stakes for success or failure were also high, although not life itself. The dean of the school of nursing invited the student nurses to volunteer to participate in a study of communication skill (100% volunteered). We explained that they would see the type of upsetting material they would soon be confronting in an emergency room. They were told that they would need to conceal any fear, distress, or disgust to obtain cooperation from the patient and family by appearing confident and optimistic. Our experiment was a preview, we said, and a test of how well they could accomplish this. The subjects thought that the measure of how well they did on this test was whether the interviewer would be able to guess when they were lying.[2] We told them about pilot data that showed that experienced, successful nurses did well in our task. Subsequently, we (Ekman & Friesen, 1974) found a correlation between how well subjects misled groups of observers who watched their videotapes and their supervisors' ratings a year later of how well they worked with patients, $p = .62, p < .01$.

In two respects—lying about strong negative emotions aroused at the moment of the lie and the very high stakes for success or failure in lying—our deception scenario differed from virtually all the other experimental deception scenarios devised by other investigators. Also, unlike many other experiments on lying, these subjects did not know they were being videotaped until after the experiment was over.

Verisimilitude dictated that we not attempt to separate the negative emotions aroused by the negative film (the analog to the patient's anguish) from the fear of being caught and any more general stress associated with lying. They were confounded on purpose. Another limitation in our scenario was that there was no control for the order of the honest and deceptive interviews. The honest interview always came before the deceptive interview, because we found in pilot studies that when the order was reversed, the negative impact of the negative films lingered, spilling over into what was intended to be a positive experience in the honest interview. We will consider in the discussion the effects of these features of the deceptive scenario on the results.

Subjects

Forty-seven student nurses were recruited after they had been admitted to but before starting in the School of Nursing. Ten subjects were not able to maintain the deception, admitting in the first minute or two that they were watching a very upsetting film. We found no differences on either the MMPI or Machiavelli test between the subjects who confessed and the subjects who completed the deceptive interview. The confessors did tell us afterwards that their difficulty in lying has been a lifelong characteristic.

Five subjects made mistakes in following the instructions and their records could not be used. One subject refused consent when, after the experiment, she was told it had been recorded on videotape. The mean age of the remaining 31 females subjects was 20.7; the range was from 19 to 26. All of these subjects reported after the experiment that it had been helpful in preparing them for their work as nurses, and all of them volunteered when offered an opportunity to go through the experiment a second time.

Measurement of Facial Expression

Measurements were made from black and white videotapes, which had been focused to show a close-up, head-on view of the subject's face. The camera was concealed although the subjects did know an audiotape was being recorded. The measurements were based on Ekman and Friesen's (1976, 1978) Facial Action Coding System. FACS is the first and only anatomically based, comprehensive, objective technique for measuring all observable facial movement. Measurement requires that a trained scorer "dissect" an observed expression, decomposing it into the elemental facial muscular actions that produced the facial movement. The scores for a particular expression consist of the list of muscular actions that are determined to have produced it.

Although it would have been possible to score all facial movements, we chose to use a modification of Ekman and Friesen's technique (EMFACS) that is more economical, so that scoring required only 10 min for each minute of behavior, rather than the 100:1 ratio if all facial movements were scored. Scorers decomposed an expression into its elemental muscular actions whenever any 1 of 33 predefined combinations of facial actions were observed. These 33 combinations of facial actions include all of the facial configurations that have been established empirically (Ekman & Friesen, 1975, 1978) to signal the seven emotions that have universal expressions: anger, fear, disgust, sadness, happiness, contempt, and surprise.

The scoring, however, was done in descriptive, behavioral terms, not in terms of these emotions. The scorer identified the occurrence of particular facial muscle actions, such as pulling the brows together, brow raising, nose wrinkling, and so forth, rather than making inferences about underlying emotional states such as happiness or anger, or using descriptions that mix inference and description, such as smile, scowl, or frown.

Usually the scorer can easily identify when a facial movement that must be scored has occurred, because the change in appearance is abrupt, changing from an expressionless face or from one expression to another. Similarly, most facial movements disappear in a noticeable fashion. The scorer locates when these readily identifiable facial movements occurred in time and then describes the movements in terms of the muscles that produced them. Occasionally, the same facial configuration is held on the face for a prolonged period and it may be difficult to determine if it should be treated as a single expressive event or as more than one event. We use changes in the intensity of the facial movement to break such prolonged movements into more than one scorable event. Facial muscle movements are scored on a 5-point intensity scale, and increases of 2 points or more in the extent of muscular contraction are treated as new events.

The scorers did not know whether the interviews they scored were honest or deceptive and were unfamiliar with the design or purpose of the experiment. The videotaped interviews were randomly assigned to two highly experienced scorers who had either 1 or 4 years experience measuring facial behavior. Interscorer reliability was evaluated by using a ratio in which the number of facial actions on which the two persons agreed was multiplied by two and then divided by the total number of facial actions scored by the two scorers. This agreement ratio was calculated for all events observed by one or both scorers. Agreements between scorers that no scorable behavior was occurring were not included in the ratio. The mean ratio across all scored events was .77, which is comparable to the level of reliability reported by Ekman and Friesen (1978).

The facial muscular action scores provided by the scorers for each interview were then converted by a computer dictionary into emotion scores. Although the dictionary was originally based on theory, there is now considerable empirical support for the facial action patterns listed in it for each emotion (see review in Ekman, 1984). In addition to providing scores on the frequency of the seven single emotions (anger, fear, disgust, sadness, happiness, contempt, and surprise) and the co-occurrence of two or more of these emotions in blends, the dictionary also allows for subdividing the happiness scores into felt happy expressions, masking smiles, and various other types of smiling activity.

Felt happy expressions are defined as the action of the zygomatic major and orbicularis oculi, pars lateralis muscles, with no muscular activity associated with any of the negative emotions. Masking smiles are defined as the action of the zygomatic major muscle and muscles associated with fear (risorious, or the combination of frontalis and corrugator), disgust (levator labii superioris, alaque nasi or levator labii superioris, caput infraorbitalis), contempt (buccinator), sadness (triangularis, or corrugator and frontalis, pars medialis), or anger (orbicularis oris, or corrugator and levator palpebrae superioris). Figure 9.1 shows a felt happy expression; Figure 9.2 shows examples of the masking smiles. In order to compare our findings with those from previous studies that failed to distinguish different types of smiles, we summed all smiling. This total smiling score included both felt happy smiles and masking smiles and other actions of the zygomatic major muscle. A total negative emotion score also was obtained. It was the sum of all of the instances in which any negative emotion was shown in any part of the face, not accompanied by smiling.

Results

Because the length of the interviews differed across subjects, all scores were converted from raw frequency to frequency per minute. Dependent t-tests showed, as expected, no significant difference in total smiling between the honest and deceptive interviews. Differences in negative emotional expressions could not be compared, because such expressions never occurred in the honest interviews, and virtually never were shown in the deceptive interviews.

A repeated measures MANOVA was computed with interview condition (honest and deceptive) as the independent variable and two dependent variables (felt happy expressions and masking smiles). There was a significant effect for interview condition. $F(2,29) = 4.31$, $p < .023$. Both univariate tests between interview conditions for the dependent variables were significant. As predicted, table 9.1 shows that felt happy expressions decreased and masking smiles increased from the honest to deceptive interviews. Table 9.1 also shows that felt happy smiles do not disappear during deception, but there are fewer of them and more of the masking smiles.

a

b

c

Figure 9.2. All three masking smiles show evidence of negative emotions leaking through the smiling appearance produced by the zygomatic major muscle. The hint of disgust in the top and middle figures is from the action of levator labii superioris, caput infraorbitalis, which raises the upper lip. In the bottom figure a trace of sadness is apparent, caused by the action of the triangularis muscle pulling the lip corners down on the right side of the picture.

Although this analysis supports the conclusion that, on average, felt happy expressions occurred more frequently in honest interviews and masking smiles more frequently in deceptive interviews, it cannot reveal how many individual subjects would be correctly classified using these behavioral indices. Table 9.2 presents this information. In the first two rows, a subject was tallied in the "hit" column if the hypothesized

TABLE 9.1. Smile measures in the two interview conditions

| | Type of smiling expression | | | |
| | Felt happy | | Masking | |
Interview condition	M	SD	M	SD
Honest	2.49	2.0	.80	1.31
Deceptive	1.57	1.08	1.18	1.46
F^a	6.85		5.25	
p	.014		.029	

[a] $df = 1, 30$.

TABLE **9.2.** Number of subjects in which the type of smile differentiated between the honest and deceptive interviews

Type of smile	Hits	Misses	Unclassified	p
Felt happy expressions	10	1	20	.006
Masking smiles	7	1	23	.035
Either measure	13	2	16	.004
Both measures	4	0	27	

difference between honest and deceptive interviews was found on that measure. Small differences were ignored by requiring that differences be greater than twice the standard error of measurement. A subject was considered a "miss" if the difference was counter to the hypothesis; and "unclassified" if there was no score for either interview, if the scores were the same, or if the difference was less than twice the standard error of measurement. In the third row, a hit was tallied if the predicted difference occurred on at least one of the two measures and was not counter to prediction on the other measure. If the difference was counter to prediction on at least one measure and was not as predicted on the other measure, it was considered a miss. If the two measures were in the opposite direction or there was no score on both measures, it was considered unclassified. The last row required that the predicted differences occur on both measures. Binomial tests were computed by comparing the number of hits and misses. Table 9.2 shows that there were many more hits than misses, although about half the subjects could not be classified.

Discussion

Two types of smiles distinguished truthfully describing a pleasant experience from deceptively describing an unpleasant experience. When enjoyment was actually experienced, smiles that included the activity of the outer muscle that orbits the eye (felt happy expressions) occurred more often than when enjoyment was feigned. When subjects attempted to conceal strong negative emotions with a happy mask, smiles that contained traces of the muscular activity associated with negative emotions (masking smiles) occurred more often than when no negative emotions were experienced. These findings confirm Ekman and Friesen's (1969) early prediction that the face may display subtle clues that can provide accurate information about felt emotions despite concealment efforts. These findings contradict nearly all of the studies by other investigators since then that measured smiles. This contradiction arises from two sources.

First, only in this study were different types of smiles distinguished. When we disregarded the type of smile, whether it was a felt happy expression or a masking smile, and like other investigators simply considered smiles as a unitary phenomenon, we too found no difference between the honest and deceptive interviews. Second, our deception scenario was relevant to emotion, whereas most of the scenarios used by prior investigators were not. Smiles will not always provide clues to deceit. Indeed, Ekman (1985) has argued that no behavioral clue is specific to deceit itself, evident only when people lie and absent when they are truthful. Clues to deceit instead must be inferred on the basis of knowledge of the particular deceit one suspects may be occurring. If our subjects had not been experiencing strong negative emotions evoked by the films they were viewing and by their fear of being caught, there would have been no negative emotions to leak through their masking smiles, and that measure would not have differentiated the deceptive interviews from the honest interviews. Similarly, if our subjects had not been experiencing enjoyment evoked by the films they watched in the interview in which they had been told to honestly describe their feelings, there would not necessarily have been more felt happy expressions in that interview than in the deceptive interview.

Facial expressions (and many vocal and bodily clues as well) are most likely to provide clues to deceit when the lie is about emotion, especially emotion felt at the moment of the lie. Even when the lie is not about feelings, Ekman (1985) theorized that feelings about lying—fear of being caught, guilt about lying, or duping delight (the pleasure and excitement of the challenge of fooling someone)—may produce behavioral clues to deceit. Those feelings will not occur in every lie. In our deception scenario, the subjects were not guilty about lying because they had been told to lie and given an acceptable justification for doing so. But they were afraid of being caught because they thought their success in lying was relevant to their chosen career. In none of the previous deception experiments has there been so much at stake.

Although our deception scenario had the virtue of having high stakes, two aspects of its design should be considered as possibly contaminating the findings. First, the order of the interviews was not counterbalanced. We made this decision because we had found in pilot studies that the unpleasant feelings aroused by the amputation-burn film seen in the deceptive interview lingered. We therefore placed the deception session in which the subject had to conceal negative feelings second, always preceded by the honest interview in which the subjects frankly described pleasant feelings aroused by viewing positive films. We can think of no reason, however, why our findings could be attributed simply to order effects, why felt happy smiles might be expected to decrease and masking smiles with traces of fear, disgust, anger, contempt, or sadness to increase simply because of order.

A second feature of the design did affect one of the findings and how it should be interpreted. In the deceptive interview there were two sources for the negative emotions aroused: the amputation-burn film and the fear of being caught lying (detection apprehension). This dual source for the arousal of negative emotions in the deceptive interview causes no problem in interpreting our finding that felt happy smiles occurred less in this interview than when the subjects actually had pleasurable feelings in the honest interview. Nor does it call into question whether the masking smiles seen most often during the deceptive interview were specific to this situation of trying to conceal negative feelings. Such masking smiles do not occur just because someone is watching an amputation-burn film (Ekman, Friesen, & Ancoli, 1980). But there is ambiguity about the source of one of the negative feelings that leaked through the masking smile. We cannot know whether the traces of fear in the smiles were aroused by the film or by fear of being caught lying. The traces of disgust, anger, contempt, or sadness were, however, probably aroused by the film rather than by the task of having to deceive.

It would have been possible to design a deception scenario in which people were not concealing strong negative feelings, as most others have done (cf. Zuckerman et al., 1981). Such deception scenarios, however, have little relevance to the situation we were attempting to model (the patient concealing plans to commit suicide). For such patients, traces of fear in masking smiles might also be due to either the anguish that motivates their self-destructive plan or to detection apprehension. In either case, the clue that they are lying is that the smiles are not felt smiles but masking smiles.

Another factor that may limit our results is the fact that nearly one-fourth of the subjects confessed, unable to maintain their lie throughout the short deceptive interview. Our findings can only be generalized to those people—75% in our study—who can maintain a deception when strong negative feelings are aroused. Not everyone can do this. For those who cannot lie in such a situation, our findings are not relevant. For them there is no issue about how to detect their lie, for they confess it.

Although the decrease in felt smiles and the increase in masking smiles was significant for the subjects as a group, our analysis of each individual's performance revealed that the face provided clues to deceit in fewer than half of the subjects. One explanation might be that such clues were available only among those who felt the most enjoyment in the honest interview and the most negative emotions in the deceptive interview. The subjects' ratings of the emotions they felt during the interviews, which were gathered immediately after each interview, failed to support this hypothesis. Those correctly classified on each measure (hits) did not report, in either the honest or deceptive interviews, emotions that differd significantly (t-tests) in intensity from those who could not be classified on either measure. Research underway suggests that people may differ in which aspect of their behavior provides clues to deceit—face, body, voice, paralanguage, or speech content. If that proves to be so, the cross-situational generality of such differences and their bases will become important issues to explore.

Another issue raised by our findings is whether the felt happy smile and masking smile functon as social signals, recognized by participants during social interaction. The findings from a previous study (Ekman & Friesen, 1974) suggest they might not. Observers who were shown the videotapes used in this experiment did no better than chance in distinguishing the honest from deceptive faces. Did these observers not know what clues to look for, or might the behavioral differences that distinguish felt happy from masking expressions be too subtle to see without slow motion observation?

We believe that the smiles we distinguished are visible. Although we knew what to look for, we found no difficulty in spotting them at real time. Another reason to believe that these subtle facial clues can function as social signals comes from research in progress. We are studying how well different groups within the criminal justice system can detect deceit when viewing the videotapes used in this experiment. Although most did no better than chance, some were accurate; those who were accurate mentioned using facial clues to make their decision.

If we are correct and these facial clues are visible, why do most people not use them in trying to judge who is lying? Ekman (1985) suggested that many people learn through their normal life experience to ignore such clues to deceit, collusively cooperating in being misled so they can avoid dealing with the consequences of uncovering a lie. This speculation, however, is far removed from the present findings. The first empirical step is to determine whether the facial behaviors we found to distinguish the honest and deceptive interviews can be recognized by people who have been told what facial clues to look for and who are motivated to succeed in detecting deceit. If people can learn to do so, then further research could determine the benefits of this knowledge when an observer is exposed to the full range of behavior available in social interaction, which includes much more than the face.

Apart from the specific issue of lying and its detection, the results more generally indicate the value of precise measurement of facial expression and the validity of the distinctions among different types of smiling proposed by Ekman (1985) and Ekman and Friesen (1982). Although there have been no other studies of the masking smile and research is needed to replicate our findings, there have been a number of studies of the felt happy smile. These studies all support Ekman and Friesen's (1982) description of how a felt happy smile differs in appearance and function from other types of smiling.

Four studies used Ekman and Friesen's (1982) specification that felt happy smiles are marked by the action of the zygomatic major and orbicularis oculi muscles. Ekman, Friesen, and Ancoli (1980) found that such felt happy smiles occurred more often than three other types of smiling when people watched pleasant films; and only felt happy smiles correlated with the subjective report of happiness. Fox and Davidson (1987) found that is 10-month-old infants, felt happy smiles occurred more often in response to the mother's approach and other types of smiles occurred more often in response to the approach of a stranger. And only felt happy smiles were associated with left frontal EEG activation, the pattern of cerebral activity repeatedly found in positive affect. Matsumoto (1986) found that depressed patients showed more felt happy smiles in the discharge interview as compared with the admission interview, but there was no difference in the rate of other kinds of smiling. Steiner (1986) found that felt smiles but not other types of smiles increased over the course of psychotherapy in patients who were judged to have improved.

Ekman and Friesen (1982) also proposed the felt happy smiles would differ from other smiles in the amount of time it took for the smile to appear, how long it remained on the face before fading, and in the time required for the smile to disappear. Two studies have shown the utility of these measures of timing, which are, however, much more costly to make than the measurement of which muscles are recruited. Bugental (1986) found that women showed more felt happy smiles with responsive than unresponsive children. Weiss, Blum, and Gleberman (1987) found felt happy smiles occurred more often during posthypnotically induced positive affect than in deliberately posed positive affect.

These studies collectively show that smiles should no longer be considered a single category of behavior. They can be usefully distinguished by measuring different facets of the smile. It remains to be determined how many different smiles may provide different social signals, have different functions in social interaction, and relate to different aspects of subjective experience and concomitant physiology.

Notes

1. A. J. Fridlund (personal communication, May 1986) has raised the question of whether our use of the term *felt* for this class of behavior presumes that subjects are always aware of their subjective feelings of enjoyment. Although this might often be so, it is not the essential characteristic. Instead we posit that felt happy expressions will be found most often in circumstances that people would usually describe as enjoyable; and that felt happy expressions typically occur with simultaneous physiological activity that is distinctive to that expression (for such evidence, see Davidson, Ekman, & Friesen, 1987; Fox & Davidson, 1987).

2. Across all subjects the interviewer did no better than chance, and her accuracy did not improve over the course of the experiment. Because the interviewer could not tell when the sub-

jects were lying, her own behavior would not have provided any useful feedback to the subjects about their performance.

References

Bugental, D. B. (1986). Unmasking the "polite smile:" Situational band personal determinants of managed affect in adult–child interaction. *Personality and Social Psychology Bulletin, 12,* 7–16.

Davidson, R. J., Ekman, P., & Friesen, W. V. (1987). *Frontal brain asymmetry and facial expressions of positive and negative emotions.* Unpublished manuscript.

Dittman, A. T. (1972). Developmental factors in conversational behavior. *Journal of Communication, 22,* 404–423.

Duncan, S. D., Jr. (1974). On the structure of speaker–auditor interaction during speaking turns. *Language in Society, 2,* 161–180.

Ekman, P. (1979). About brows: Emotional and conversational signals. In M. von Cranach, K. Foppa, W. Lepenies, & D. Ploog (Eds.), *Human Ethology* (pp. 169–248). Cambridge Eng.: Cambridge University Press.

Ekman, P. (1984). Expression and the nature of emotion. In K. Scherer & P. Ekman (Eds.), *Approaches to emotion* (pp. 319–343). Hillsdale, NJ: Erlbaum.

Ekman, P. (1985). *Telling lies: Clues to deceit in the marketplace, marriage, and politics.* New York: Norton.

Ekman, P., & Friesen, W. V. (1969). Nonverbal leakage and clues to deception. *Psychiatry, 32,* 88–105.

Ekman, P., & Friesen, W. V. (1974). Detecting deception from body or face. *Journal of Personality and Social Psychology, 29,* 288–298.

Ekman, P., & Friesen, W. V. (1975). *Unmasking the face: A guide to recognizing emotions from facial clues.* Englewood Cliffs, NJ: Prentice-Hall.

Ekman, P., & Friesen, W. V. (1976). Measuring facial movement. *Environmental Psychology and Nonverbal Behavior, 1.* 56–75.

Ekman, P., & Friesen, W. V. (1978). *Facial action coding system.* Palo Alto, CA: Consulting Psychologists Press.

Ekman, P., & Friesen, W. V. (1982). Felt, False and miserable smiles. *Journal of Nonverbal Behavior, 6*(4), 238–252.

Ekman, P., Friesen, W. V., & Ancoli, S. (1980). Facial signs of emotional experience. *Journal of Personality and Social Psychology, 39*(6), 1125–1134.

Ekman, P., Friesen, W. V., & Scherer, K. R. (1976). Body movement and voice pitch in deceptive interaction. *Semiotica, 16,* 23–27.

Finkelstein, S. (1978). *The relationship between physical attractiveness and nonverbal behaviors.* Unpublished honors thesis, Hampshire College, Amherst, MA.

Fox, N. A., & Davidson, R. J. (1987). *Patterns of brain electrical activity during facial signs of emotion in 10-month-old infants.* Manuscript submitted for publication.

Greene, J. O., O'Hair, H. D., Cody, M. J., & Yen, C. (1985). Planning and control of behavior during deception. *Human Communication Research, 11,* 335–364.

Hemsley, G. D. (1977). *Experimental studies in the behavioral incidents of deception.* Unpublished doctoral dissertation, University of Toronto, Toronto.

Hocking, J. E., & Leathers, D. C. (1980). Nonverbal indicators of deception: A new theoretical perspective. *Communication Monographs, 47,* 119–131.

Hocking, J. E., Miller, G. R., & Fontes, N. E. (1978). Videotape in the courtroom. *Trial, 14,* 52–55.

Knapp, M. L., Hart, R. P., & Dennis, H. S. (1974). An exploration of deception as a communication construct. *Human Communication Research, 1,* 15–29.

Krauss, R. M., Geller, V., & Olson C. (1976). *Modalities and cues in the detection of deception.* Paper presented at the 84th Annual Convention of the American Psychological Association, Washington, DC.

Kraut, R. E. (1978). Verbal and nonverbal cues in the perception of lying. *Journal of Personality and Social Psychology, 36,* 380–391.

Kraut, R. E., & Poe, D. (1980). On the line: The deception judgments of customs inspectors and laymen. *Journal of Personality and Social Psychology, 39,* 784–798.

Littlepage, G. E., & Pineault, M. A. (1979). Detection of deceptive factual statements from the body and the face. *Personality and Social Psychology Bulletin, 5,* 325–328.

Matsumoto, D. (1986). *Cross cultural communication of emotion.* Unpublished doctoral dissertation, University of California, Berkeley.

McClintock, C. C., & Hunt, R. C. (1975). Nonverbal indicators of affect and deception in an interview setting. *Journal of Applied Social Psychology, 5,* 54–67.

Mehrabian, A. (1971). Nonverbal betrayal of feeling. *Journal of Experimental Research in Personality, 5,* 64–73.

O'Hair, H. D., Cody, M. J., & McLaughlin, M. L. (1981). Prepared lies, spontaneous lies. Machiavellianism and nonverbal communication. *Human Communication Research, 7,* 325–339.

Riggio, R. E., & Friedman, H. S. (1983). Individual differences and cues to deception. *Journal of Personality and Social Psychology, 45,* 899–915.

Steiner, F. (1986). Differentiating smiles. In E. Branniger-Huber & F. Steiner (Eds.), *FACS in Psychotherapy Research* (pp. 139–148). Zurich: Department of Clinical Psychology, Universität Zuerich.

Weiss, F., Blum, G. S., & Gleberman, L. (1987). Anatomically based measurement of facial expressions in simulated versus hypnotically induced affect. *Motivation and Emotion, 11,* 67–81.

Wilson, S. J. (1975). *Channel differences in the detection of deception.* Unpublished doctoral dissertation, Florida State University, Tallahassee.

Zuckerman, M., DePaulo, B. M., & Rosenthal, R. (1981). Verbal and nonverbal communication of deception. In L. Berkowitz (Ed.), *Advances in experimental social psychology* (Vol. 14; pp. 1–59). New York: Academic Press.

Smiles When Lying

PAUL EKMAN

We now have findings about a number of the issues raised in the discussion. While we had found statistically significant differences in facial behavior that distinguished lying from truthfulness when the data were analyzed across all subjects, when we analyzed the data on a subject-by-subject basis only half (48%) of the subjects could be accurately classified, 16% were mistakenly classified, and the remainder did not differ in facial behavior. Since then we (Ekman, O'Sullivan, Friesen & Scherer, 1991) added measures of voice pitch. Like the face, voice pitch yields very significant differences when the data is reanalyzed across all subjects. Examination of subjects case by case revealed that only 58% were accurately classified, and again 16% were mistakenly classified. Considering both the facial and voice measures raised accuracy to 61%, reduced mistakes to 10%, with the remainder not differing on face and voice. Thus it appears that the combination of these two expressive modalities does reduce errors. Measures of body movement and speech content did not contribute to further success in classification. Work in progress is again attempting to see if the combination of different measures, can yield more accurate identification of lying and truthfulness.

In the discussion we also noted that masking smiles would not always be the type of facial behavior that would betray a lie. We found masking smiles to be a clue to deceit in this study because the subjects were trying to mask strongly felt negative affect with positive affect, but we suggested, that in lies of a different kind, other facial clues would be found. That is indeed the case. In an article in press we (Frank & Ekman, in press) used FACS to measure facial behavior when subjects lied about whether they had taken money and about their political beliefs. FACS was highly successful in distinguishing the liars from the truth-tellers—better than it was for the lie about emotion—but it was not masking smiles, but signs of fear and signs of disgust which betrayed the liars.

The discussion also raised the question as to whether the differences between masking smiles and felt smiles would be detectable at real time by untrained people. In chapter 10 in this book, Frank and I report findings that some people can indeed detect the differences between different kinds of smiles. We still do not know if training can improve accuracy in detecting such differences, and thereby lead to increased accuracy in distinguishing liars from truth-tellers.

We used the phrase "felt smiles" to refer to the smiles in which the outer portion of the muscle orbicularis oculi (in FACS units, AU 6) is involved. More recently we have dropped that phrase in favor of calling them "Duchenne's smile," or smiles with Duchenne's marker, or D-smiles, to honor Duchenne (1862/1990), who first drew attention to the difference between the smile of enjoyment and false smiles.

The discussion of the smiling article ends by saying that this study and other studies reviewed in the discussion show that smiles should no longer be considered a single category of behavior. Unfortunately, some other investigators continue to lump all smiles together. On the other hand, the evidence continues to accumulate that the distinction between Duchenne smiles and other smiles is extraordinarily robust (see reviews in Ekman, 1992, 1993). To mention just one new set of such findings, Ekman, Davidson, and Friesen (1990) examined the pattern of cerebral activity as measured by EEG, when subjects watched films intended to be amusing. Only with D-smiles not with other smiles, was the pattern of cerebral activity manifest which other research has found to be distinctive for enjoyment, and only D-smiles correlated with subjective reports of amusement. Ekman and Davidson (1993) then examined the pattern of EEG activity when subjects were asked to voluntarily produce a D-smile or other smile, and again found that only the distinctive pattern of brain activity found with enjoyment occurred only with the D-smile.

Currently we (with Davidson) are using functional MRI to examine more precisely the brain activity that distinguishes D-smiles from other smiling and other emotional expressions. We are also seeking extramural support to continue to examine face, body, voice, and speech content when people lie, and determine if training enhances accuracy.

References

Duchenne, B. (1990) *The mechanism of human facial expression or an electro-physiological analysis of the expression of the emotions* (A. Cuthbertson, Trans.) New York: Cambridge University Press. (Original work published 1862).

Ekman, P. (1992) Facial Expression of Emotion: New Findings, New Questions. *Psychological Science, 3,* 34–38.

Ekman, P. (1993) Facial expression of emotion. *American Psychologist,* 48, 384–392.

Ekman, P., and Davidson, R. J. (1993) Voluntary smiling changes regional brain activity. *Psychological Science, 4,* 342–345.

Ekman, P., Davidson, R. J., and Friesen, W. V. (1990) The Duchenne smile: Emotional expression and brain physiology II. *Journal of Personality and Social Psychology, 58,* 342–353.

Ekman, P., O'Sullivan, M., Friesen, W. V., and Scherer, K. R. (1991). Face, voice and body in detecting deception. *Journal of Nonverbal Behavior, 15,* 125–135.

Frank, M. G., and Ekman, P. (1997) The ability to detect deceit generalizes across different types of high stakes lies. *Journal of Personality and Social Psychology, 72,* 1429–1439.

10

Behavioral Markers and Recognizability of the Smile of Enjoyment

MARK G. FRANK, PAUL EKMAN & WALLACE V. FRIESEN

The facial expression commonly referred to as "the smile" in fact is not a singular category of facial behavior. As far back as 1862 the French anatomist G. B. Duchenne (1862/1990) noted that the orbicularis oculi muscle, which surrounds the eye, is recruited in smiles that occur with spontaneously experienced enjoyment but not in smiles that are posed (Duchenne, 1862/1990). However, only in the last 10 years have researchers gathered the empirical evidence to confirm Duchenne's observation (Ekman & Friesen, 1982). This particular configuration of the enjoyment smile[1] identified by Duchenne—the orbicularis oculi with zygomatic major—has been called the *Duchenne smile* in honor of Duchenne's original observation (Ekman, 1989).

On the basis of Duchenne's (1862/1990) observation as well as their own empirical observations of a large data set (Ekman, Friesen, & Ancoli, 1980), Ekman and Friesen (1982) predicted that the Duchenne smile would be but one among several morphological and temporal markers of the enjoyment smile. Specifically, they predicted that an enjoyment smile would be marked by (1) The presence of orbicularis oculi, pars lateralis, in conjunction with zygomatic major[2] (Duchenne's smile); (2) synchronization of action between the zygomatic major and orbicularis oculi such that they reach the point of maximal contraction (apex) at the same time; (3) symmetrical changes in zygomatic major action on both sides of the face; (4) onset, apex, offset, and overall zygomatic major actions that are smooth and not as long or short as in other types of smiles; and (5) a duration range of zygomatic major action between 0.5 and 4 s.

Research findings have confirmed the existence of four of these five predicted enjoyment smile markers (the synchrony marker has yet to be systematically explored). The most replicated and best documented of these markers, which has shown the most convergent validity across subject groups and social conditions, is Duchenne's marker—the presence of orbicularis oculi activity. A number of studies have confirmed the presence of this marker in smiles that occur in situations designed to elicit positive emotions compared with in situations designed to elicit negative emotions—even though there was no difference between these situations in the total amount of smiling when smiles were considered as a group without regard for Duchenne's marker (e.g., Davidson, Ekman, Saron, Senulius, & Friesen, 1990; Ekman, Davidson, & Friesen, 1990; Ekman, Friesen, & O'Sullivan, 1988). Similar results have been reported for 10-month-old infants (Fox & Davidson, 1988), children (Schneider, 1987), and German adults (Ruch, 1987). In psychotherapy settings, the Duchenne-marked smiles occurred more often in depressed patients' discharge interviews compared with in their admission interviews (Matsumoto, 1986). Moreover, the number of smiles featuring the Duchenne marker increased when psychotherapy patients were judged to improve (Steiner, 1986).

Smiles with the Duchenne marker have been linked to the emotion of enjoyment not only across a variety of settings but also across a variety of measures. When subjects show smiles with the Duchenne marker, compared with other types of smiles, they (1) report more felt enjoyment (Ekman et al., 1990) and (2) display a different pattern of central nervous system (CNS) activity (Davidson et al., 1990; Ekman et al., 1990). Furthermore, the degree to which the CNS patterns differ between Duchenne-marked smiles and other smiles is significantly correlated with the subject's self-reported enjoyment.

Compared with the amount of research on Duchenne's marker, there have been only a few studies on the symmetry and on the smoothness of onset markers of enjoyment (e.g., Ekman, Hager, & Friesen, 1981; Weiss, Blum, & Gleberman, 1987), and only one study confirmed Ekman and Friesen's (1982) prediction that enjoyment smiles typically last between 0.5 to 4 s, with nonenjoyment smiles either shorter or longer. This duration marker distinguished smiles that spontaneously occur in response to comedy films from smiles that had been deliberately posed (Hess & Kleck, 1990).

Study 1

No prior study has yet examined more than one of the markers that differentiate enjoyment from other types of smiling. The first part of our strategy was to select a sample of smiles on the basis of the best substantiated marker of enjoyment (Duchenne's) and then determine whether such smiles also showed the limited duration marker. The duration marker was selected because it is reliably measured and conceptually straightforward. It involves merely recording the point at which a subject's zygomatic major begins to move from its neutral position and the point at which it returns to neutral. Such ease of measurement is not the case for some of the other enjoyment smile markers; for example, the symmetry marker may be extremely subtle and difficult to measure (see Ekman et al., 1981, for details).

The second part of our strategy was to examine the smoothness of the smiles with Duchenne's marker versus other smiles by measuring the duration relationships among the components of these smiles. Smooth smiles should show a significant positive correlation among the onset, apex, offset, and overall zygomatic major durations; smiles that are not smooth should not show such a pattern. This method is in contrast with facial electromyography (EMG) research, which measured the smoothness of a smile by recording the number of onset and offset periods before a smile returned to a neutral expression (Hess & Kleck, 1990). However, this smoothness criterion assumes that the onset and offset periods were not actually separate smiles or distinctive facial behaviors when in fact they could have been. Our measure of facial behavior did not assume a return to neutral as the end of a given smile and thus eliminated this potential confound.

Our first hypothesis was that smiles with the Duchenne marker will be more consistent, or less variable, in their overall duration than smiles without this marker. This prediction had two sources. First, it is consistent with Ekman and Friesen's (1982) empirical observation that emotional expressions have a more limited duration than do nonemotional expressions, the former usually between 0.5 and 4 s in length, while the latter varies from 0.25 s to considerably longer than 4 s. The second basis for the hypothesis about a more limited duration for emotional compared with nonemotional expressions was Ekman's (1992) theory that emotions are brief, episodic events that last only a few seconds. There is no such constraint on volitional or nonemotional expressions.

Our second hypothesis was that smiles with the Duchenne marker should be smoother and more ballistic than other smiles. This hypothesis was based on evidence of distinct neural substrates for emotional and nonemotional facial activity. It appears that not only do emotional and nonemotional facial activity originate from different areas of the brain (subcortical and cortical motor strip, respectively) and arrive at the face through different motor systems (extraparamidal and pyramidal, respectively), but also the appearances of these actions differ such that extrapyramidally driven emotional facial actions are smoother and more ballisticlike than pyramidally driven nonemotional facial actions (DeMyer, 1980; Meihlke, 1973; Myers, 1976; Tschiassny, 1953; also see review by Rinn, 1984). Thus, emotional facial actions should manifest this smooth, ballisticlike pattern by showing internal consistency among the components of the zygomatic major action such that there will be a positive relationship among the onset, apex, offset, and overall durations of each Duchenne-marked smile. There should be no such coordination among the components of smiles without the Duchenne marker.

Method

Materials

Both the smiles with Duchenne's marker and the smiles that did not evidence Duchenne's marker were drawn from two prior experiments in which subjects' facial behavior was recorded without their knowledge while they watched films designed to elicit emotional responses. These films were shown in the same order in both experiments; the difference was that in one experiment the subjects watched the films alone while their brain activity was measured (quite obtrusively; Davidson et al., 1990), and in the other experiment they described their feelings to an interviewer (Ekman & Friesen, 1974). These two situations are referred to as the *solitary* and *social interaction* situations, respectively. In the solitary situation, the subjects were told that they would be watching the film in private in a darkened room. The only light in this room was the ambient light from the film and a dim red light, which enabled subjects to see and properly use a rating dial. In the social interaction situation, the interviewer sat facing the subject such that the interviewer could not see the film. In both situations the number of smiles with the Duchenne marker correlated significantly with each subject's self-report of enjoyment; in each situation there was no relationship between the total number of all types of smiles and each subject's self-report of enjoyment (Ekman et al., 1990; Ekman et al., 1988).

Both samples of these smiles had been scored previously using the Facial Action Coding System (FACS; Ekman & Friesen, 1978). FACS allows for the measurement of all visible facial behavior and not just actions presumed to be relevant to emotion. FACS scores movement, intensity, and laterality of the facial muscle action. FACS allows for but does not require determining the duration of an action. Facial actions that were FACS scored for both zygomatic major (FACS Action Unit 12) and orbicularis oculi, pars lateralis (FACS Action Unit 6) composed the sample of smiles with the Duchenne marker; facial actions that consisted of FACS-scored zygomatic major (Action Unit 12) without orbicularis oculi composed the sample of smiles without the Duchenne marker. For the purpose of this study, all other facial actions were not considered.

Procedure

For each subject, one smile with the Duchenne marker and one smile without the marker were randomly selected from the first three of each type of smile shown during the course of viewing the films designed to elicit a positive emotion.[3]

This was done to increase the likelihood that the most spontaneous Duchenne-marked smiles would be chosen, as well as to ensure a comparable sample of smiles without the marker. If a subject failed to show at least one smile with and one smile without the Duchenne marker, they were dropped from further analysis. This left a total of 44 subjects who contributed exactly one Duchenne-marked smile and one smile without the Duchenne marker each; 22 subjects were from the social interaction situation, and 22 subjects were from the solitary situation.

Mark G. Frank scored each of the selected smiles for duration. Because he knew the hypothesis, allowing for the possibility that his duration scoring might be biased, one third of this sample was later scored by a FACS-trained scorer who did not know the hypothesis (Erika Rosenberg). The measurements of the two scorers were highly correlated (Pearson $r = +.86$).

Design and Variables

The analysis examined the effect of the type of smile (with Duchenne marker vs. without Duchenne marker) and the situation from which the smiles were drawn (social interaction vs. solitary) on the duration and smoothness of the smiles. The type of smile was a within-subject varible. The hypothesis predicted that the durations of the smiles containing Duchenne's marker will cluster to a greater extent about a mean duration and thus will be less variable than the durations of smiles that do not have Duchenne's marker. This was expected regardless of whether the smiles were shown in the social interaction or solitary situation. Likewise, smiles with the Duchenne marker would be smoother than smiles without; this smoothness would be manifested by a significant correlation among the onset, apex, offset, and overall duration of the smile.

These hypotheses make no prediction about whether there will be a difference in the mean duration of the smiles with Duchenne's marker versus those without; it makes a prediction only about the variance and smoothness of smiles with Duchenne's marker versus smiles without the Duchenne's marker.

Results

Overall Analyses

Table 10.1 shows the means and variances for the duration of smiles with and without Duchenne's marker in both the social interaction and solitary situation.

A test for the equality of variances (Brown & Forsythe, 1974) showed that, as predicted, the variance associated with the duration of smiles with Duchenne's marker was significantly less than the variance associated with the duration of smiles without Duchenne's marker, $F(1, 31) = 8.11$, $p < .005$.[4] This result was obtained in both the social interaction situation, $F(1, 14) = 4.69$, $p < .05$, and the solitary situation, $F(1, 15) = 9.76$, $p < .01$.[5]

This inequality of variances led us to apply a nonparametric Wilcoxon matched-pairs signed-ranks test to the mean duration of the smiles. This test revealed no significant difference between the mean duration of smiles with Duchenne's marker versus smiles without ($Z = -1.02$, *ns*). There was also no significant difference in the mean duration of smiles in the solitary ($Z = -.78$) or the social interaction conditions ($Z = -.94$). A Mann-Whitney test on the overall duration of both types of smiles in the solitary condition versus both types of smiles in the social interaction condition also showed no significant effect of situation on duration of the smile ($Z = -1.74$, $p < .09$).

It should also be noted that the mean duration of the Duchenne smiles in the social interaction situation was between 0.5 and 4 s, as originally predicted by Ekman and Friesen (1982). However, the mean duration of smiles with the Duchenne marker in the solitary situation were considerably longer at 6.18 s, even though these smiles were, as predicted, significantly less variable than the smiles without Duchenne's marker. This finding is considered in more detail later.

Component Analyses

It may be the case that the difference in variability between smiles with Duchenne's marker and smiles without Duchenne's marker is due entirely to a difference in the variability of either the onset, apex, or offset duration (e.g., Bugental, 1986). Thus, the overall duration of a zygomatic major action was broken into its three constituents:

TABLE 10.1. Overall duration of smiles by situation (in seconds)

Type of smile	Situation		
	Social interaction	Solitary	Pooled
With Duchenne marker			
M	3.32	6.18	4.75
Variance	2.04	34.65	20.01
Without Duchenne marker			
M	4.14	10.04	7.09
Variance	7.56	165.53	93.43
N	22	22	44

the onset duration (duration from beginning of action until apex), apex duration (duration from beginning of apex until end of apex), and offset duration (duration from end of apex until the return to neutral). There was strong intercoder reliability in the measurement of the components (all Pearson $rs > +.78$). The statistical tests for equality of variances and mean duration differences applied to the overall durations just discussed were repeated for each of the three components of the smile.

As was the case in the overall smile duration analysis, the onset duration of smiles with Duchenne's marker had considerably less variance (variance = 1.16) than the onset duration of smiles without this marker (variance = 6.63), $F(1, 29) = 8.49$, $p < .007$; this pattern occurred within both the social interaction situation, $F(1, 14) = 8.98$, $p < .02$, and the solitary situation, $F(1, 14) = 4.78$, $p < .05$. There was no significant overall effect for onset duration as well as no significant effect for onset duration within either situation (all $Zs < 0.72$, ns).[6]

A similar pattern of variances occurred for the apex duration; the apex durations for smiles with Duchenne's marker had less variance (variance = 5.36) than did the apex durations of the smiles without Duchenne's marker (variance = 74.13), $F(1, 29) = 8.13$, $p < .009$. This applied marginally to the social interaction situation, $F(1, 13) = 3.48$, $p < .08$, and significantly to the solitary situation, $F(1, 14) = 10.74$, $p < .007$. The mean apex durations did not differ taken together or separated by situation (Wilcoxon $Zs < 1.11$ and < 1.12, respectively).

Contrary to what might be expected, the offset durations of the smiles with Duchenne's marker were not less variable than the offset durations of the smiles without Duchenne's marker, $F(1, 28) = .90$, ns. Whereas there were no differences in variance of the mean offset durations in the solitary situation, $F(1, 13) = 0.02$, ns, there was a significant difference in variance for the social interaction situation, $F(1, 14) = 11.44$, $p < .005$, where the offsets of smiles with Duchenne's marker were less variable. There was no significant effect for mean overall offset duration (Wilcoxon $Z = 0.12$, ns) or for offset duration within each situation (Wilcoxon $Zs < 0.89$, ns).

Our second hypothesis was that smiles with the Duchenne marker are extrapyramidally driven facial actions—that is, consistent, ballistic, and more reflexlike—thus, they also should show a more stable relationship among their smile components than should smiles without the Duchenne marker. One way to measure the stability of this relationship is to examine the intercorrelations among the onsets, apexes, offsets, and overall durations of the different smiles. If smiles with the Duchenne marker are more consistent and smooth in their actions, then within these smiles the components should be significantly correlated with each other.

This was the case with Duchenne-marked smiles, where the overall durations of these smiles correlated significantly with their onset durations (Pearson $r = +.81$, $p < .001$), apex durations (Pearson $r = +.52$, $p < .001$), and offset durations (Pearson $r = +.67$, $p < .001$). Moreover, there was a significant correlation between the smiles' onset durations and their offset durations (Pearson $r = +.47$, $p < .01$). This pattern held in both the social interaction situation and the solitary situation. In contrast, there was only one significant correlation between or among the components of smiles without Duchenne's marker and that was between the overall durations and their apex durations (Pearson $r = +.94$, $p < .001$). This pattern of results strongly suggests that smiles with the Duchenne marker function as a relatively stable unit of behavior; that is, smiles with longer durations have longer onsets, apexes, and offsets, and vice versa. Such was not the case for smiles without Duchenne's marker; for these smiles the overall duration was solely dependent on the duration of the smile's apex.

Discussion

These results are consistent with the proposal that smiles with the Duchenne marker act more like emotional facial actions, as predicted. Smiles with Duchenne's marker manifest significantly less variability than smiles without Duchenne's marker in both overall duration and the duration of their onsets and apexes. Moreover, Duchenne-marked smiles display a regularity and smoothness of action such that the length of any given smile is proportionally spread about its onset, apex, and offset. In contrast, a smile without the Duchenne marker shows no such proportional relationship among its components. It appears as if the sole determinant of the overall duration of these smiles is the duration of their apexes.

These patterns—less variability and more smoothness for smiles with the Duchenne marker than for those without—held regardless of whether the smile was shown in a solitary or social interaction situation. In addition, these results occurred in spite of the finding that there was no mean difference in zygomatic major duration between smiles with or without the Duchenne marker.

Another finding in this study was that the mean duration of the smiles with Duchenne's marker in the social interaction situation supported previous observations that enjoyment smiles are between 0.5 and 4 s in duration (Ekman et al., 1990; Hess & Kleck, 1990). However, the mean duration of this type of smile in the solitary situation was 6.18 s, which seems outside of Ekman and Friesen's (1982) original predicted range. However, there were two outliers in the sample of smiles with the Duchenne marker in the solitary situation: One smile was 25 s long and a second was 17 s long. When these two outliers were dropped, the average length of the Duchenne smiles in the solitary condition was reduced from 6.18 to 4.47 s.[7] This latter figure is quite comparable with one 0.5- to 4-s range proposed earlier (Ekman & Friesen, 1982). However, it should be noted that Ekman and Friesen (1982) based their prediction that enjoyment smiles will range from 0.5 to 4 s in duration on their observations of large data sets that involved social interactions (interviews); this result was replicated in the social interaction situation. Other research has shown that situations can and do have an effect on the duration of zygomatic major actions, depending on the degree of felt presence of other people (Fridlund, 1991). Yet there is no a priori biological or psychological reason why this 0.5- to 4-s duration range is crucial; what is more important in terms of our hypothesis is that the durations of the smiles with the most replicated marker of enjoyment in a given situation clustered around a particular mean, whereas the durations of the smiles without this marker in the same situation were significantly less consistent.

One aspect of this study that makes these results even more compelling is that it used two samples of subjects that were derived from two experiments carried out 15 years apart. Normally, the use of such disparate samples introduces so many possible confounds as to render the results uninterpretable. However, in this study we predicted that there would be no effect of situation on the results. Thus, any other factor that might have differentially impacted the solitary or social interaction situation, such as the presence of electroencephalogram (EEG) caps in the solitary condition, would conspire to work against our hypothesis and against the likelihood that we would obtain evidence for the duration marker in both samples. However, we found virtually the same results in both samples. Thus, this procedure actually adds to the generalizability of our results in a way stronger than a simple replication or two-level manipulation of an independent variable could have.

However, one could still question the solitariness of the solitary situation. Certainly no other person was in the room, the room was darkened, and the subjects were told they would be watching the film in private. Someone committed to the view that despite these conditions, the alone situation was not really solitary could argue that the presence of the EEG lycra skull caps were so obtrusive as to make the subject very aware of her facial expressions. We reject this possibility because it does not seem logical that a cap would make one aware of his or her face. Certainly, EMG electrodes attached to one's face may draw one's attention to his or her face (see Fridlund, Ekman, & Oster, 1987, for a review of issues related to the use of EMG), but it is difficult to imagine how EEG electrodes embedded in a skull cap would do so. It may make a subject become aware of his or her thoughts, but not his or her face.

Finally, enjoyment smiles, manifesting both Duchenne's and the duration markers, occurred in both a social interaction and a solitary situation. These results are incompatible with the view that emotional expressions are solely interactive signals (Kraut, 1982; Smith, 1985) and should not occur when people are alone. Our findings are consistent with the view that the enjoyment smile is one component of an emotion, and emotions can occur when people are alone or in social interaction (Ekman, 1989, 1992). This is not to deny that emotional expressions have social signal value.

Study 2

This study addressed the question of whether the subtle markers of enjoyment can operate as social signals, capable of being distinguished by an untrained, unaided observer. Darwin thought this was possible. Discussing photographs of enjoyment and nonenjoyment smiles that were given to him by Duchenne de Boulogne, Darwin said

> Almost everyone recognized that the one represented a true, and the other a false smile; but I have found it very difficult to decide in what the whole amount of difference consists. It has often struck me as a curious fact that so many shades of expression are instantly recognized without any conscious process of analysis on our part. (Darwin, 1872, p. 359)

Although there have been many studies showing that observers can recognize discrete emotions (cf. review Ekman, 1989), there has been no prior test of whether observers can distinguish a true enjoyment smile from other smiles. Even the studies that examined how well observers could detect deception from facial behavior lumped all forms of smiling into one category and did not determine whether enjoyment smiles could be distinguished from other smiles (see DePaulo, Stone, & Lassiter, 1985; Zuckerman, DePaulo, & Rosenthal, 1981; Zuckerman & Driver, 1985, for reviews).

Only three studies examined the relationship between the type of smiling and observers' inferences about emotion or deception, and they did so only indirectly. One study reported a significant correlation between observers' happiness ratings and a subject's zygomatic major intensity; however, this analysis did not consider different forms of smiling (Hess, Kappas, McHugo, Kleck, & Lanzetta, 1989). A second study found an association between Duchenne-marked smiles and positive attributions by observers; however, it could not be certain that this association was specific to the type of smile observed or some other correlated variable because the observers had watched a videotape that showed diverse facial behavior (O'Sullivan, Ekman, Friesen, & Scherer, 1992). A third study found that children became increasingly unresponsive when interacting with women whose zygomatic major action featured unusual timing features (Bugental, 1986). Again, it is possible that the children's unresponsiveness was due to some other correlated aspect of the womens' behavior.

Not only has there been no study to determine whether observers can detect the difference between an enjoyment and a nonenjoyment smile, but no study has examined which marker of the enjoyment smile—Duchenne or the duration marker—has the clearest signal. We hypothesized that the Duchenne marker would provide a greater social signal than the duration marker for three reasons: (1) Popular lore (e.g., smiling eyes) suggests that the orbicularis oculi action of the Duchenne marker is a recognizable signal, whereas there is no such lore for the duration marker. (2) With the Duchenne marker it is possible to determine for each smile whether the relevant action (orbicularis oculi activity) is present or absent. The duration marker does not specify a feature that can be used to decide about each particular smile, but instead a judgment must be made about the variability in duration shown by a group of smiles. (3) One study reported that the variance associated with a subject's zygomatic major action did not predict observers' ratings of a subject's happiness (Hess et al., 1989).

Any factor that would highlight the Duchenne marker (i.e., orbicularis oculi action) should be associated with increased accuracy. One way to highlight the Duchenne marker is to show a group of observers one person displaying two smiles, one showing the Duchenne marker and one not showing Duchenne's marker, and then ask observers to judge which of the pair of smiles is the enjoyment smile. A second group of observers who see only one smile—either with or without the Duchenne marker—and have to judge whether the smile they saw was an enjoyment or a nonenjoyment smile should not do as well. Having the same person show both types of smiles should control the across-person variability of static facial features (particularly the presence of bagging under and wrinkles around the eyes, which resemble orbicularis oculi action), which would occur when a particular person showed only one type of smile, thus making actual orbicularis oculi action stand out. A second way to highlight Duchenne's marker is to use smiles of low zygomatic major intensity. Smiles of high zygomatic major intensity raise the cheek high enough to create many of the same bulges and wrinkles associated with orbicularis oculi action; this creates many instances in which it appears as if Duchenne's marker is present when it is not. Smiles of low intensity do not change the appearance of the face beyond the lips so the action of the orbicularis oculi muscle should be more readily recognized (see Ekman & Friesen, 1978, for more details).

We showed observers a videotape of subjects showing enjoyment and nonenjoyment smiles and asked them to distinguish between these smiles. We hypothesized that (1) enjoyment smiles have a social signal value and can be distinguished from nonenjoyment smiles at rates greater than chance; (2) the Duchenne marker (orbicularis oculi) will have greater signal strength than the duration marker; and (3) factors that enhance the salience of the Duchenne marker's orbicularis oculi action—enjoyment and nonenjoyment smiles that are shown in pairs and smiles of low zygomatic major intensity—will all be associated with increased accuracy in distinguishing enjoyment from nonenjoyment smiles.

Method

Materials

The smiles shown to observers were selected from the sample of subjects whose smiles were analyzed in Study 1. The current sample consisted of all subjects from the group of 44 who had shown at least one enjoyment smile and one nonenjoyment smile that were of identical zygomatic intensity. Overall, 20 enjoyment-nonenjoyment smile pairs were used, with each member of the pair of smiles equivalent across facial muscle movements (except orbicularis oculis). Within these enjoyment and nonenjoyment smile pairs, half of them featured both the Duchenne marker and the duration marker; the remaining half featured the Duchenne marker without the duration marker; that is, the overall duration of nonenjoyment smile was not more than one standard deviation longer or shorter than the overall duration of the enjoyment smiles as reported in Study 1. Ten of these smile pairs came from subjects in the social interaction sample, and 10 pairs came from subjects in the solitary sample. There were 4 pairs of very slight intensity smiles, 9 pairs of slight intensity smiles, and 7 pairs of moderate intensity smiles (as determined by FACS scoring rules; Ekman & Friesen, 1978).

The smiles from these 20 subjects were edited in the same order onto two silent black-and-white videotapes. The first videotape consisted of a random selection of one of the two smiles of a given subject's enjoyment-nonenjoyment smile pair; the second videotapes consisted of the smile from that smile pair not chosen for the first videotape.

Each of these two videotapes was used for separate single smile judgments. The smile pair judgments were created by alternately playing the first and second videotape. This way, the first subject was viewed showing both enjoyment and nonenjoyment smiles consecutively; the second subject was then viewed displaying both smiles, followed by the third subject, and so on. The presentation order of the videotapes for the smile pair judgments was counterbalanced.

Observers

The observers were 34 male and 46 female Cornell University undergraduates who volunteered for the study in return for course extra credit.

Procedure

The observers were run in a classroom setting, with the group size ranging from 1 to 10. They were given an instruction and response sheet that had the following instructions:

> Today you will see brief videotape clips of persons smiling. You are asked to judge whether each smile is a true, genuine expression of enjoyment (i.e., she is truly happy or enjoying herself) or if in fact this smile is a false or social expression (i.e., she is smiling because it is socially appropriate but she is not necessarily happy herself).

For the single smile judgment condition, the next paragraph read:

After you have made your decision, please circle the word *enjoyment* or the word *social*, depending on which type of smile you believe you saw. You will see 20 people. Exactly half of these smiles are true expressions of enjoyment.

For the smile pair judgment condition, the following was substituted for the previous paragraph:

You will view each person twice. Observe the first smile, but do *not* circle a response. Then observe the second smile, and at that point judge which one of these smiles was the true enjoyment smile. After you have made your decision, please circle the word *First* or the word *Second* corresponding to which smile you believe was the true expression of enjoyment.

At the end of the session, judges were asked to indicate "what cue(s), clue(s), or strategy(ies) did you use to make your judgments?"

We stated that exactly half of the smiles in the single smile condition would be true enjoyment smiles to make it explicit to observers that they had a 50% chance of making a correct judgment if they guessed. Note that in the smile pair condition observers knew they had a 50% chance because only one of the smiles in the pair was the true enjoyment smile. Thus, this instruction had the effect of rendering the chance levels comparable in the minds of both groups of observers.

Design

This design was a $2 \times 2 \times 2$ factorial, with the independent variables type of judgment (single smile judgment vs. the smile pair judgment), presence of the duration marker (smile pairs in which the nonenjoyment smile did not differ significantly from the enjoyment smile in duration vs. smiles where the nonenjoyment smiles were a standard deviation longer or shorter in duration than the enjoyment smiles) and situation (the social interaction situation vs. the solitary situation), with presence or absence of the duration marker and situation being within-subject comparisons. The dependent variable was the proportion of smiles correctly identified. Subsidiary analyses examined the effect of the intensity of the zygomatic major action of the smile and the effect of the observers' reported strategy on the overall proportion of smiles judged correctly.

Results

Overall Analyses

Visual inspection of the data revealed that there were no differences between the ratings made by the 4 subjects who were run alone versus the subjects who were run in groups. Moreover, there were no main or interaction effects for sex of the observer, so these data were collapsed.

Forty observers viewed one of the two single videotapes (single smile judgment), and another 40 observers viewed both videotapes played alternately (smile pair judgment).[8] A 2 x 2 x 2 analysis of variance (ANOVA) revealed, as predicted, that the smile pair comparison condition produced greater accuracy than the single smile comparison. The overall accuracy scores show that the judges who were able to compare a particular subject's enjoyment and nonenjoyment smiles were correct on a mean of 74% of their judgments, compared with 56% for the judges who made single smile comparisons, $F(1, 78) = 42.17, p < .0001$. Both these mean accuracy rates are greater than what would be predicted by chance (chance = .50); smile pairs judgment, $t(39) = 12.47, p < .001$; single smiles judgment, $t(39) = 2.97, p < .01$.

The second hypothesis predicted that the zygomatic major duration marker would not function as a useful clue for distinguishing enjoyment from nonenjoyment smiles; that is, if the duration marker does not have signal value then those smile pairs in which only the enjoyment smile has a mean duration between 0.5 and 4 s will not be more accurately distinguished than smile pairs in which both members are of equivalent duration. The pooled results presented in table 10.2 show that those smile pairs in which the nonenjoyment smile featured a significantly longer or shorter duration than the enjoyment smile (i.e., did not feature the duration marker) were actually less accurately judged than those smile pairs that did not show this duration difference, $F(1, 78) = 5.48, p < .03$.

Because there was no significant main effect or interaction of situation (the social interaction versus the solitary situation), all $Fs(1, 78) < 1.55, p = ns$, the data were collapsed across situation, and the means and standard deviations are presented in table 10.2. There were no significant two-way interactions or a significant three-way interaction among these variables.

Subsidiary Analyses

It was hypothesized that factors that increased the salience of the Duchenne marker would be associated with increased accuracy. Observers' accuracy scores as a function of the zygomatic major intensity of the smile were examined in a 3 (intensity level of the zygomatic major: very slight, slight, or moderate) × 2 (across vs. within-subject comparisons) ANOVA with repeated measures on intensity. The means are shown in table 10.3.

TABLE 10.2. Proportion of correct judgments by type of judgment and by whether both the enjoyment and nonenjoyment smile had the duration marker

	Type of judgment		
Measure	Single smile	Smile pair	Pooled
Only enjoyment smile has duration marker			
M	.54	.71	.63
SD	.19	.16	.19
Both smiles have duration marker			
M	.58	.78	.68
SD	.15	.14	.18
Overall accuracy			
M	.56	.74	.65
SD	.13	.12	.15
N	40	40	80

TABLE 10.3. Proportion of correct judgments of enjoyment
and nonenjoyment smiles by smile intensity and type of
judgment

| | Type of judgment | | |
Smile intensity	Single smile	Smile pair	Pooled
Very slight			
M	.55	.78	.67
SD	.22	.21	.24
Slight			
M	.58	.77	.67
SD	.19	.13	.19
Moderate			
M	.55	.68	.61
SD	.16	.16	.18
Overall accuracy			
M	.56	.74	.65
SD	.13	.12	.15
N	40	40	80

Note: Very slight intensity corresponds to Facial Action Coding System
(FACS) A score, slight intensity corresponds to FACS B score, and moderate
intensity corresponds to FACS C score (Ekman & Friesen, 1978).

In this analysis[9] there was a significant main effect of intensity of the smile, $F(2, 156) = 3.66$, $p < .04$; individual t tests showed that very slight intensity smiles were marginally more accurately detected than moderate intensity smiles, $t(79) = 1.78$, $.10 > p > .05$, and slight intensity smiles were significantly more accurately detected than moderate intensity smiles, $t(79) = 2.04$, $p < .05$. There was no difference in detectability between the very slight and slight intensity smiles, $t(79) < 1$. There was no significant interaction between intensity and type of judgment, $F(2, 156) = 1.89$, $p > .15$.

It is also interesting to note that there was no difference in detectability in moderate intensity smiles between the observers who made smile pair judgments versus those observers who made single smile judgments, $t(78) = 1.55$, *ns*. However, there were significant differences between single smile and smile pair judgments for both very slight intensity smiles, $t(78) = 4.72$, $p < .001$, and slight intensity smiles, $t(78) = 5.15$, $p < .001$. It seems that the smile pair type of judgment further augments the already enhanced orbicularis oculi action created by the lower zygomatic major action of the very slight and slight intensity smiles.

This explanation would be strengthened if there was any evidence that more clearly indicated that the accurate observers were focusing on the orbicularis oculi action. For this reason the observers written responses to the question "what cue(s), clue(s), or strategy(ies) did you use to make your judgments?" was examined.

The judges' strategies were assigned to one of three categories: (a) *no quantifiable strategy* (like "intuition," "guessed," etc.; 27 observers fell into this category), (b) *oculi strategy*—they mentioned the eyes ("sparkling around the eyes," "crinkling around," etc., 35 observers fell into this category); and (c) *zygomatic strategy*—they mentioned the dynamics of the smile action and duration (length, flow, and unnaturalness; 18 observers fell into this category). A second scorer agreed on 90% of the categorizations (72 out of 80).

A correlational analysis showed a relationship between oculi strategy and observers' accuracy. When the observers' reported strategies were coded so that the no quantifiable strategy and zygomatic strategy are coded as 0 and the oculi strategy coded as 1, a significant positive correlation appeared between oculi strategy and overall accuracy (Pearson $r = +.22$, $p < .05$). A closer examination of this correlation shows that the oculi strategy was most strongly related to accuracy at detecting very slight intensity smiles (Pearson $r = +.26$, $p < .02$); there was no significant correlation between oculi strategy and accuracy for either the slight or moderate intensity smiles (Pearson $rs = +.17$ and $+.09$, respectively).

The zygomatic strategy was not associated with increased accuracy. When no quantifiable strategy and oculi strategy are recoded as 0 and zygomatic strategy is recoded as 1, the correlation between zygomatic strategy and accuracy is (Pearson r) $-.12$. Even when examining those smile pairs that differed in duration, the correlation between zygomatic strategy and accuracy for those items is (Pearson r) $-.16$.

Discussion

Enjoyment smiles have social signal value when observers are focused on the task of distinguishing them from other kinds of smiling. Moreover, this signal is amplified as the action of the orbicularis oculi becomes more conspicuous. Three factors that increase the salience of orbicularis oculi action—allowing observers to compare smile pairs versus single smiles, smiles with weaker zygomatic major intensity, and observers who specifically monitored the eye area of the stimulus subjects' faces—were all associated with increased ability to accurately distinguish enjoyment smiles from nonenjoyment smiles. Moreover, under the circumstances in which the orbicularis oculi is most salient—a smile pair judgment, a slight or very slight intensity smile, and for observers who indicated an oculi strategy—accuracy peaked at 81%! However, it should be noted that the lower intensity smiles with the Duchenne marker are more accurately recognized only when they are shown in a comparison situation; there appears to be no differential accuracy effect in the single smile condition.

The duration marker does not appear to have social signal value. The smile pairs in which the duration marker was made salient when the nonenjoyment smile had a significantly longer or shorter duration than the enjoyment smile are actually less accurately distinguished than the enjoyment-nonenjoyment smile pairs that were of comparable duration. A reason for the reduced accuracy might be that the unusually long or short zygomatic major durations of the nonenjoyment smile may have drawn the observers' attention away from the orbicularis oculi area. This can be reasonably construed from the results of Study 2, which demonstrated that factors that decreased the salience of the orbicularis oculi were associated with decreased accuracy.

Although Study 2 has shown that observers can distinguish enjoyment from nonenjoyment smiles, it does not tell us whether each type of smile conveys different information about the emotional state of the person when observers' attention is not focused on just the smile; this was examined in Study 3.

Study 3

The design of Study 2 provided observers with optimal viewing conditions in which to accurately identify enjoyment smiles by (a) eliminating many potential competing behavioral cues, (b) having the same person show both an enjoyment and nonenjoyment smile in one of the conditions, and (c) drawing observers' attention directly to the smiles by asking them simply to pick which smiles were the true enjoyment smiles. By contrast, in more usual interactions, interactants are instructed neither to observe and categorize each other's smiles, nor to specifically compare one smile with the next within an individual. Study 3 was designed to move one step closer to an actual interpersonal situation by asking observers to form an impression of a person without specifically drawing observers' attention to the smile. It was hypothesized that observers would rate stimulus subjects who showed enjoyment smiles as more pleasant and positive than when they showed a nonenjoyment smile.

Method

Materials

The same two videotapes used in Study 2 were used in this study (see Method section of Study 2 for information on the videotapes).

Observers

Thirty undergraduate observers, 14 from Cornell University (8 women and 6 men) and 16 from Cortland State University (8 women and 8 men), participated in this study for course credit. An equal number of Cornell and Cortland State students saw each of the two single smile videotapes.

Procedure

The observers were run in a classroom setting in groups ranging from 1–11. Fifteen observers saw one of the two videotapes, and 15 observers saw the other; thus, observers saw only one type of smile for each person in the videotapes. They were given an instruction and response sheet that asked them to "rate each of the 20 stimulus subjects across the following 15 adjective pairs that you feel most accurately characterizes this person." It should be noted that the observers were not told that these 20 stimulus subjects would be smiling; they were simply asked to record their impressions of each person.

Fifteen bipolar personality–emotion adjective pairs were adopted from a previous study on subjective judgments of nonverbal behavior (Ekman, Friesen, & Scherer, 1976). They were originally selected for their relevance to personality, emotion, and deception. These 15 adjective pairs were as follows: outgoing–inhibited, expressive–unexpressive, sociable–withdrawn, calm–agitated, natural–awkward, stable–unstable, relaxed–tense, honest–dishonest, sincere–insincere, trustworthy–untrustworthy, dominant–submissive, likable–unlikable, felt pleasant–felt unpleasant, act pleasant–act unpleasant, and genuine–sarcastic.

Design

This study consisted of two independent variables (enjoyment smiles vs. nonenjoyment smiles) and the situation from which the smiles were drawn (social interaction vs. solitary) on the 7-point ratings of the dependent variables (the 15 adjective pairs). Both independent variables were within-subject variables.

Results

Rating Analysis

As in Study 2, there were no significant main effects or interactions for sex of observers, or for observers run alone versus observers run in groups, and so these data were collapsed.

The basic assumption of most statistical analyses is that observations remain independent. Because 30 observers made 15 ratings across 20 people, technically each of these 9,000 observations were not independent. Preliminary analyses undertaken to compress the number of observations revealed three findings: (a) combining the observers' impressions of the 20 subjects across the 15 adjective pairs showed that all of the trait term ratings correlated positively ($r > +.17$) with each other at significance levels of $p < .05$ or stronger (Cronbach's alpha across the 15 trait terms = .92); (b) when these ratings were factor analyzed with a varimax rotation, they revealed a strong first factor on which all 15 of the adjective pairs loaded greater than +.48 (the three highest loading traits were felt pleasant, +.94; act pleasant, +.89; and likable, +.86); and (c) this first factor accounted for 53% of the variance. Therefore, for each observer, the 15 adjectives were summed and averaged within each of the 20 stimulus subjects. This created what we called a *general positivity* score for each of the 20 stimulus subjects, within each observer. These were the data analyzed in a 2 (type of smile) × 2 (situation) within-subjects ANOVA.[10]

The means for the general positivity scores were first reflected so that the higher numbers would equal higher positivity; these reflected results are presented in table 10.4. The results of the ANOVA showed a significant main effect such that the videotape clips containing people showing enjoyment smiles were seen as more positive than the videotape clips containing these same people showing nonenjoyment smiles, $F(1, 29) = 11.93$, $p < .001$. There was also a significant main effect for situation, which indicated that subjects in the social interaction situation were seen as generally more positive, independent of smile type, than subjects in the solitary situation, $F(1, 29) = 12.74$, $p < .001$. There was no significant interaction of smile and situation, $F(1, 29) = 0.01$, *ns*, again suggesting that enjoyment smiles have a social signal independent of situation. It seems clear that when the 20 stimulus subjects showed enjoyment smiles they created a distinctly different and more positive impression in the eyes of the observers than when they showed nonenjoyment smiles of equal zygomatic intensity.

Signal Value across Studies 2 and 3

Because both Study 2 and Study 3 used the exact same videotapes (i.e., the same 20 stimulus subjects showing the same facial behavior), the net difference in the general positivity scores between the enjoyment and nonenjoyment smiles for each of the 20

TABLE 10.4. Mean positivity ratings by type of smile and situation

| | Situation | | |
	Social interaction	Solitary	Pooled
Type of smile			
Enjoyment smile			
M	4.75	4.07	4.41
SD	0.62	0.76	0.76
Nonenjoyment smile			
M	4.42	3.49	3.96
SD	0.79	0.34	0.76
Pooled			
M	4.59	3.78	
SD	0.68	0.44	
N	30	30	

Note: Higher numbers equal more positivity.

stimulus subjects were correlated with the average enjoyment smile detection accuracy of these same 20 stimulus subjects reported in Study 2 (the average single smile accuracy). These items correlated (Pearson r at +.56, $p < .025$). This means that for each of the 20 stimulus subjects, the more accurately a given subject's enjoyment smile was distinguished from her nonenjoyment smile by the observers in Study 2, the more positive this same subject's enjoyment smile was rated relative to her nonenjoyment smile by the observers in Study 3. Ultimately, it appears as if the factors that contributed to an observer's ability to distinguish enjoyment smiles from nonenjoyment smiles also contributed to an observer's relatively greater positive impression of people when they display enjoyment smiles compared with when they display nonenjoyment smiles.

Discussion

The social signal value of an enjoyment smile is not limited to explicit judgments (as in Study 2); the results of Study 3 reveal that subjects who show enjoyment smiles are seen as more expressive, natural, outgoing, sociable, relaxed, feel and act more pleasant—generally speaking, as more positive—than when they show nonenjoyment smiles. Observers formed these impressions even though they were not instructed to focus on either the smile or any differences between the types of smiles. When the task was shifted from making explicit distinctions between types of smiles to forming impressions of people based on facial behavior, which is more like the task one faces in everyday life, it appears as if the social signal survives.

One finding in this study was that subjects in the solitary situation were rated as generally less positive than subjects in the social interaction condition. In all likelihood, this result was an artifact attributed to the subjects' unattractive bullethead appearance created by the EEG lycra stretch caps they wore. However, the positivity scores for the different smile types did not interact with the positivity of the situations and therefore does not becloud the main finding that enjoyment smiles create a more positive impression in observers than do nonenjoyment smiles, independent of situation.

One alternative explanation for these results is given that all the positive attributes were on one pole and the negative on the other, it may be the case that the trait positivity of these scales was confounded with an acceptance or rejection set (Bentler, Jackson, & Messick, 1971). We believe that we can reject this explanation because we were not interested in the impressions created by smiles, per se, but by the difference in impressions created by enjoyment smiles versus nonenjoyment smiles. First, if there was no difference in the signal value of enjoyment and nonenjoyment smiles, then any acceptance or rejection set would function equally on the ratings of both types of smiles. Second, this acceptance–rejection set would push the rating toward the positive end of the scale, particularly in light of the finding that people who smile are seen quite positively (e.g., O'Sullivan et al., 1992). This reduced range would work against the hypothesis because it would make it harder to document a difference in ratings for smiles on a scale with a functional size of 5 rating points versus a scale with 7 rating points. Obtaining the results of this study under these conditions again speaks for the robustness of the phenomenon.

General Conclusion

In sum, the results of these three studies show that there are not only multiple physical differences between enjoyment smiles and nonenjoyment smiles, but also these differences are observable and influence subjective impressions. Study 1 showed that enjoyment smiles are marked not only by orbicularis oculi activity as first noted by Duchenne but also by a more limited time duration than nonenjoyment smiles. Moreover, this study also showed that enjoyment smiles feature a more fixed relationship among its components than do nonenjoyment smiles. This pattern of results occurred across situations involving both isolation and social interaction.

Study 2 showed that another difference between enjoyment and nonenjoyment smiles is that enjoyment smiles have distinctive social signals. Even when smile intensity is controlled, they can be explicitly identified across two interpersonal situations. This social signal seems to reside primarily in the orbicularis oculi (Duchenne smile) marker and not in the zygomatic major duration marker. Any factor that resulted in the increased prominence of the orbicularis oculi action resulted in greater accuracy at distinguishing enjoyment smiles from nonenjoyment smiles.

Study 3 showed that even when the observers were not asked to attend to differences in smiling, the different forms of smiling were associated with different subjective impressions. A person is seen as more positive when they display an enjoyment smile compared with when they display a nonenjoyment smile, again independent of the situation in which the smile is elicited. Finally, it appears as if those enjoyment smiles that were more accurately distinguished from their corresponding nonenjoyment smiles were also responsible for creating relatively greater positive impressions in the observers for the enjoyment smile compared with the corresponding nonenjoyment smile.

It seems reasonable to conclude that the enjoyment smile is lawful behavior and that some of the features operate independent of context, as Ekman and Friesen (1982) had predicted. The enjoyment smile behaves in a fashion much more consistent with emotional, extrapyramidally driven facial actions than do other types of nonenjoyment smiles. These other smiles behave in a fashion similar to other forms of volitionally controlled muscle movements. Thus, the enjoyment smile seems to be a facial behavior clearly separate from the category of facial behavior referred to as the smile. Moreover, the enjoyment smile is related to the internal emotional state of the individual in a way that other smiles are not; this is true on the level of self-report ratings (Ekman et al., 1990; Ekman et al., 1980), behavioral observations (Bugental, 1986; Fox & Davidson, 1988; Matsumoto, 1986; etc.) and CNS measures (Davidson et al., 1990; Ekman et al., 1990).

The notion that a smile is not related to an individual's inner state (e.g., Birdwhistell, 1970; Bruner & Taguiri, 1954; Kraut & Johnston, 1979; Landis, 1924; Smith, 1985) was probably based on a failure to observe the morphological and dynamic markers that distinguish enjoyment smiles from other, nonenjoyment smiles. Unfortunately, much research on the smile still fails to embrace markers of the enjoyment smile. For example, a recent study, which did not take into account either the Duchenne marker or the duration marker, reported no relationship between the amount of zygomatic major activity and self-report of happiness (Fridlund, 1991). However, research on Duchenne's marker has demonstrated that it is the amount of zygomatic activity in conjunction with orbicularis oculi that predicts a subject's self-report of happiness or enjoyment and not the total amount of zygomatic activity (Ekman et al., 1990).

Although our studies have shown that enjoyment smiles can have social signal value, they did not show that they typically do have social signal value. We do not know if people will attend to and use this behavioral clue when they are not explicitly asked to do so and when their attention is not focused on just this one piece of behavior, although this is suggested by the studies cited herein. Further research is needed to determine if the signal value will survive when the enjoyment smile is reembedded into its normal day-to-day context, competing for attention with not only other facial expressions, but also tone of voice, word choice, body motions, and so on. However, for now we can conclude that the enjoyment smile differs not only in morphology but also in dynamics and social signal value from the more general category of facial behavior referred to as the smile.

Notes

1. Enjoyment smiles were originally called *felt smiles,* and nonenjoyment smiles were originally called *unfelt smiles* in the Ekman and Friesen (1982) article. Now, given the large amount of evidence across different measures that links smiles with the orbicularis oculi, zygomatic major configuration to positive emotion (reviewed later in this article), we use the term *enjoyment smile* to describe a smile with that particular configuration.

2. On the basis of their observations and their findings that most people can voluntarily produce the action of the inner but not the outer part of the orbicularis oculi muscle (Hager & Ekman, 1985), Ekman and Friesen (1982) differed from Duchenne (1862/1990) in specifying that it is only the outer portion of this muscle that distinguishes enjoyment.

3. Researchers have reported a ratio of seven enjoyment smiles to one nonenjoyment smile in positive emotion situations (Ekman et al., 1990; Ekman et al., 1988). There are a variety of reasons why a nonenjoyment smile would occur in a positive emotion situation: (a) because subjects knew that they would be viewing gruesome films after the positive emotion films, (b) because subjects were displaying or expressing uncertainty, and (c) to maintain the conversational

flow. It may seem more unusual that subjects would show nonenjoyment smiles in the solitary situation; however, subjects do show smiles when they anticipate that something enjoyable may be upcoming on a film but before they experience that emotion (Ekman, 1985, has called these *anticipatory* smiles). In addition, they can imagine the presence of someone, which may cause subjects to show social nonenjoyment smiles (e.g., Fridlund, 1991).

4. All p values reported in this article are two-tailed.

5. Across both situations, this sample contained smiles with the Duchenne marker that were of greater zygomatic intensity than were smiles without it (as scored by FACS intensity ratings ranging from A (*very slight intensity*) to E (*strongest possible intensity*). After we converted these A through E ratings to 5-point ratings, the smiles with the Duchenne marker appeared to be of greater intensity ($M = 3.07$, $SD = 1.17$) than smiles without the Duchenne marker ($M = 1.77$, $SD = .74$), $F(1, 42) = 58.71$, $p < .001$. These zygomatic intensity differences show that the smiles with the Duchenne marker were also more variable in zygomatic intensity than other smiles; this works against the hypothesis that smiles with the Duchenne marker will be less variable in duration than smiles without. The intensity of the zygomatic major action also did not covary either with the duration of the Duchenne-marked smiles ($\beta = .09$), $t(21) = 0.59$, *ns,* or the duration of other smiles ($\beta = -.16$), $t(21) = -1.03$, *ns.*

6. As was the case with the overall mean duration analysis, the intensity of zygomatic major action did not covary with duration for any of the constituent components—onset, apex, and offset—of the smiles (all βs $< .17$), ts(21) < 1.13, *ns.*

7. When the corresponding smile without the Duchenne marker is dropped from the sample, the mean duration for these smiles drops to 9.44 s. However, the removal of both types of smiles for these 2 subjects does not change the significance of the test for equality of variances because that test is based on the variance of observations about the 10% trimmed mean of each group (Brown & Forsythe, 1974). In other words, the Brown and Forsythe (1974) technique requires the exclusion of these two data points when computing the F value.

8. A one-way ANOVA on the accuracy rate revealed that the two single smile videotapes did not significantly differ; likewise, the mean accuracy for the two presentation orders of the smile pair videotapes did not significantly differ. Therefore, the data for the two single smile videotapes were collapsed into one single smile condition, and the data for the two presentation orders for the smile pair videotapes were also collapsed into one smile pair condition.

9. The single smile versus smile pair main effects were reported earlier in table 10.2 and thus will not be repeated here.

10. Given the results of Study 2, as well as the more general focus on the enjoyment smile, the absence or presence of the duration marker was not included in this analysis.

References

Bentler, P. M., Jackson, D. N., & Messick, S. (1971). Identification of content and style: A two-dimensional interpretation of acquiescence. *Psychological Bulletin, 76,* 186–204.

Birdwhistell, R. L. (1970). *Kinesics and context.* Philadelphia: University of Pennsylvania Press.

Brown, M. B., & Forsythe, A. B. (1974). Robust tests for the equality of variances. *Journal of the American Statistical Association, 69,* 364–367.

Bruner, J. S., & Taguiri, R. (1954). The perception of people, in G. Lindzey (Ed.), *Handbook of social psychology* (Vol. 2; pp. 634–654). Reading, MA: Addison-Wesley.

Bugental, D. B. (1986). Unmasking the "polite smile": Situational and personal determinants of managed affect in adult–child interaction. *Personality and Social Psychology Bulletin, 12,* 7–16.

Darwin, C. (1872). *The expression of the emotions in man and animals.* New York: Philosophical Library.

Davidson, R. J., Ekman, P., Saron, C., Senulius, J., & Friesen, W. V. (1990). Approach–withdrawal and cerebral asymmetry: Emotional expression and brain physiology I. *Journal of Personality and Social Psychology, 58,* 330–341.

DeMyer, W. (1980). *Technique of the neurological examination.* New York: McGraw-Hill.

DePaulo, B. M., Stone, J. I., & Lassiter, G. D. (1985). Deceiving and detecting deceit. In B. R. Schlenker (Ed.), *The self and social life* (pp. 323–370). New York: McGraw-Hill.

Duchenne, B. (1862/1990). *The mechanism of human facial expression or an electro-physiological analysis of the expression of the emotions* (A. Cuthbertson Trans.). Cambridge, England: Cambridge University Press.

Ekman, P. (1985). *Telling lies.* New York: Norton.

Ekman, P. (1989). The argument and evidence about universals in facial expressions of emotion. In H. Wagner & A. Manstead (Eds.). *Handbook of psychophysiology: The biological psychology of the emotions and social processes* (pp. 143–164). New York: Wiley.

Ekman, P. (1992). Facial expressions of emotion: New findings, new questions. *Psychological Science, 3,* 34–38.

Ekman, P., Davidson, R. J., & Friesen, W. V. (1990). The Duchenne smile: Emotional expression and brain physiology II. *Journal of Personality and Social Psychology, 58,* 342–353.

Ekman, P., & Friesen, W. V. (1974). Detecting deception from body or face. *journal of Personality and Social Psychology, 29,* 288–298.

Ekman, P., & Friesen, W. V. (1978). *The facial action coding system.* Palo Alto, CA: Consulting Psychologists Press.

Ekman, P., & Friesen, W. V. (1982). Felt, false, and miserable smiles. *Journal of Nonverbal Behavior, 6,* 238–252.

Ekman, P., Friesen, W. V., & Ancoli, S. (1980). Facial signs of emotional experience. *Journal of Personality and Social Psychology, 39,* 1125–1134.

Ekman, P., Friesen, W. V. & O'Sullivan, M. (1988). Smiles when lying. *Journal of Personality and Social Psychology, 54,* 414–420.

Ekman, P., Friesen, W. V., & Scherer, K. (1976). Body movement and voice pitch in deceptive interaction. *Semiotica, 16,* 23–27.

Ekman, P., Hager, J. C., & Friesen, W. V. (1981). The symmetry of emotional and deliberate facial actions. *Psychophysiology, 18,* 101–106.

Fox, N. A., & Davidson, R. J. (1988). Patterns of brain electrical activity during facial signs of emotion in 10-month-old infants. *Developmental Psychology, 24,* 230–236.

Fridlund, A. J. (1991). Sociality of solitary smiling: Potentiation by an implicit audience. *Journal of Personality and Social Psychology, 60,* 229–240.

Fridlund, A. J., Ekman, P., & Oster, H. (1987). Facial expressions of emotion: Review of literature, 1970–1983. In A. Siegman & S. Feldstein (Eds.), *Nonverbal behavior and communication* (pp. 143–224). Hillsdale, NJ: Erlbaum.

Hager, J. C., & Ekman, P. (1985). The asymmetry of facial actions is inconsistent with models of hemispheric specialization. *Psychophysiology, 22,* 307–318.

Hess, U., Kappas, A., McHugo, G. J., Kleck, R. E., & Lanzetta, J. T. (1989). An analysis of the encoding and decoding of spontaneous and posed smiles: The use of facial electromyography. *Journal of Nonverbal Behavior, 13,* 121–137.

Hess, U., & Kleck, R. E. (1990). Differentiating emotion elicited and deliberate emotional facial expressions. *European Journal of Social Psychology, 20,* 369–385.

Kraut, R. E. (1982). Social presence, facial feedback, and emotion. *Journal of Personality and Social Psychology, 42,* 853–863.

Kraut, R. E., & Johnston, R. E. (1979). Social and emotional messages of smiling: An ethological approach. *Journal of Personality and Social Psychology, 37,* 1539–1553.

Landis, C. (1924). Studies of emotional reactions: II. General behavior and facial expression. *Journal of Comparative Psychology, 4,* 447–509.

Matsumoto, D. (1986). *Cross-cultural communication of emotion.* Unpublished doctoral dissertation, University of California, Berkeley.

Meihlke, A. (1973). *Surgery of the facial nerve.* Philadelphia: W. B. Saunders.

Myers, R. E. (1976). Comparative neurology of vocalization and speech: Proof of a dichotomy. *Annals of the New York Academy of Sciences, 280,* 745–757.

O'Sullivan, M., Ekman, P., Friesen, W. V. & Scherer, K. (1992). *Judging honest and deceptive behavior.* Unpublished manuscript.

Rinn, W. E. (1984). The neuropsychology of facial expression: A review of the neurological and psychological mechanisms for producing facial expressions. *Psychological Bulletin, 95,* 52–77.

Ruch, W. (1987). *Personality aspects in the psychobiology of human laughter.* Paper presented at the third meeting of the International Society for the Study of Individual Differences, Toronto, Ontario, Canada, June.

Schneider, K. (1987). Achievement-related emotions in preschoolers. In F. Halisch & J. Kuhl (Eds.), *Motivation, intention, and volition* (pp. 163–177). New York: Springer.

Smith, W. J. (1985). Consistency and change in communication. In G. Zivin (Ed.), *The development of expressive behavior* (pp. 51–75). San Diego, CA: Academic Press.

Steiner, F. (1986). Differentiating smiles. In E. Branniger-Huber & F. Steiner (Eds.), *FACS in psychotherapy research* (pp. 139–148). Zurich, Switzerland: Department of Clinical Psychology, Universitat Zurich.

Tschiassny, K. (1953). Eight syndromes of facial paralysis and their significances in locating the lesion. *Annals of Otology, Rhinology, and Laryngology, 62,* 677–691.

Weiss, F., Blum, G. S., & Gleberman, L. (1987). Anatomically based measurement of facial expressions in simulated versus hypnotically induced affect. *Motivation and Emotion, 11,* 67–81.

Zuckerman, M., DePaulo, B. M., & Rosenthal, R. (1981). Verbal and nonverbal communication of deception. In L. Berkowitz (Ed.), *Advances in experimental social psychology, 14* (pp. 1–59). San Diego, CA: Academic Press.

Zuckerman, M., & Driver, R. E. (1985). Telling lies: Verbal and nonverbal correlates of deception. In A. W. Siegman & S. Feldstein (Eds.), *Multichannel integration of nonverbal behavior* (pp. 129–147). Hillsdale, NJ: Erlbaum.

Some Thoughts on FACS, Dynamic Markers of Emotion, and Baseball

MARK G. FRANK

The Facial Action Coding System (FACS; Ekman & Friesen, 1978) was designed to be a comprehensive system to identify visible facial movements. Moreover, as a bonus it can be adapted to measure the duration of these facial actions, not only the overall duration of any given Action Unit (AU) but also the duration of the components that make up that AU—the onset, apex, and offset durations. In this way FACS is like a baseball pitcher—that is, a pitcher is evaluated solely on his ability to throw a baseball, but if he can hit a baseball too, then it is an unexpected bonus. In the study you just read (Frank, Ekman, & Friesen, 1993), we used FACS to measure not only the overall duration of AU 12 (zygomatic major), but also the onset duration, apex duration, and the offset duration of AU 12. These measures were important because Ekman and Friesen (1982) proposed that smiles that arise from positive emotional states—called *enjoyment smiles*—are both morphologically and dynamically different from smiles that arise for other reasons—called *other smiles*. We tested two of the dynamic markers— the consistency of duration[1] and smoothness of action markers—and found evidence supporting Ekman and Friesen's hypothesis that enjoyment smiles, compared to other smiles, are a more consistent overall duration, and feature smoother actions such that the duration of the onset and apex of any given enjoyment smile correlates to each other and to the overall duration. Thus, analogous to the baseball pitcher above, FACS not only identified the facial actions, but as a bonus was able to measure reliably the component durations of AU 12—in other words, FACS could "bat" as well as "pitch."

These findings, in conjunction with the multifaceted utility of FACS to deal with these issues, have encouraged me to explore whether these dynamic markers of the enjoyment smile also generalize to negative emotion facial expressions such as fear and anger. Moreover, it has also encouraged me to begin examining how these dynamic markers of emotion may be able to assist in distinguishing deceptive from honest accounts of behavior in high emotion-arousing situations. The addition of dynamic markers to the analysis of facial expressions may prove critical in identifying emotional facial expressions because evidence shows, while a significant proportion of subjects can readily feign the morphological markers of emotion (Ekman, Roper, & Hager, 1980), subjects don't seem to be able to readily feign the dynamic markers of emotion, such as smoothness or regularity of onset (Hess & Kleck, 1990). While it is currently easier to identify the morphological markers, ultimately it may be more accurate to rely on multiple markers—both morphological and dynamic—to distinguish a facial expression of emotion from a nonemotion-related facial expression (Frank & Ekman, 1993).

My main reflection on the utility of FACS in our study concerned the scoring of the onset, apex, and offset durations—it was a long and mind-numbing experience. We found that scoring just AU 12 for onset, apex, offset, and overall duration took approximately twice as long to score as a full FACS scoring of materials of the same duration. Our study was bearable in that we scored only AU 12 for 88 different smiles that each averaged about 6 seconds long. In terms of future research this made me think that while FACS would be able to reliably score durations, it might be outside most research budgets to do so. Without a cost-effective way of measuring the components of facial action, one may not be able to explore or to discover phenomena related to the dynamic actions of facial expressions. For example, imagine you decided for exploratory reasons to measure the onset, apex, and offset durations of all the AUs of all the events in a 3-hour sample of facial behaviors. Just twenty seconds of a 5 AU event would take you over an hour to score. I think you get the idea.

I have since been thinking about other, more cost-effective ways in which to explore dynamic markers of facial expressions that do not give up the advantages that FACS has over other techniques such as EMG (e.g., the nonobtrusiveness and comprehensiveness of FACS versus the obtrusiveness and the noncomprehensiveness of EMG measurement of facial muscles; see Fridlund, Ekman, & Oster, 1987, for a more detailed discussion of the advantages and disadvantages associated with EMG). I was not getting very far on solving this problem when I was contacted by Charles Willock. Charles worked for the Australian Radio and Interplanetary Space Service in Sydney, and he phoned me after seeing me talk on Australian TV about facial expressions. He said that he used a technique for tracking changes in the sun's electromagnetic field that might be applicable to tracking changes in facial expression. This technique—called stackplotting (Willock, Thompson, & McIntosh, 1992)—involves using a computer to select a particular slice or segment of a dynamic object, record just this slice over a fixed period of time, and then stacking these slices to produce a visual representation of the ebb and flow of the visible changes in that segment of the object over that time. He felt that this technique could be used to create a visual representation of the ebb and flow of a given facial muscle or muscles over time. Charles has since become a graduate student at UNSW, where we have been working on adapting his computer programs to work on a human face. There are certainly a number of large obstacles that need be overcome before we can apply this program (e.g., lighting, controlling for head position), however it has the potential to save countless hours in scoring the dynamics of facial actions, thus it may make viable the discovery and exploratory work that is needed on dynamic markers of emotion in the face.

It is interesting to note that this system would not eliminate the need for or knowledge of FACS; rather, it would be dependent upon FACS at all levels of the process. One would have to know FACS to know *which* AU to examine, *when* to examine that AU, *where* in the AU to snip out the visual image to stack that would contain the critical FACS scoring criteria—for example, if measuring AU 6, one might look at the changes in a .5 cm wide vertical strip starting from the top of the eyebrow and finishing below the eye; this strip would then include the lateral portion of the eyeball, eyelid, and brow including the "crow's feet" portion of AU 6, and so forth—and finally *how* that AU's movement characteristics are manifested on the face (the furrows, wrinkles, bulges, and dimples associated therein). This technique would still involve a fair amount of labor in locating the segments to be stacked, however the time saving occurs when the computer does the image processing and stacking overnight. The researcher then examines the output images in the morning and notes when changes in the pattern of the image occurs. Then by counting the number of videotape frames between the changes one can determine the onset, apex, and offset durations (to within 1/30th of a second, given that the PAL videotape system in Australia runs at 30 frames per second).

However, this technique, like any technique that claims to measure something using the latest technology, would have to pass what I call the Ed Lynch test. Ed Lynch was a very ordinary ex-Met, Cub, and Red Sox pitcher who was highly touted by a variety of baseball experts on the basis of his uniqueness—he was a right-handed sinkerball pitcher when all other sinkerball pitchers were left-handed. When I mentioned these expert reports of Ed Lynch's pitching prowess to my friend Greg, he simply said, "He may be a right-handed sinkerball pitcher, but he is a *bad* right-handed sinkerball pitcher." In other words, just because a system is unique in using fancy technology to do something, this does not mean that it measures it well or cost-effectively.

The Ed Lynch test will have to be the ultimate standard that we use to judge the utility of this stackplotting technique for the measurement of dynamic markers of facial expressions. We hope it will pass this test and make tractable a number of analyses exploring the nature of dynamic markers of emotion, because until we can come up with a cost-effective way to measure these markers, research on facial expressions will be limited at best.

Acknowledgment

Support when writing this afterward was provided by a grant from the Australian Research Council.

Note

1. While we used the term *duration* marker in the Frank et al. paper (1993), we have decided that this marker may be better thought of as a *consistency* of duration marker—or *consistency* marker for short—because it is not so much the duration of the enjoyment smile that matters as consistency of that duration in relation to other smiles (Frank & Ekman, 1993).

References

Ekman, P., & Friesen, W. V. (1978). *The facial action coding system.* Palo Alto, CA: Consulting Psychologists Press.
Ekman, P., & Friesen, W. V. (1982). Felt, false, and miserable smiles. *Journal of Nonverbal Behavior, 6,* 238–252.

Ekman, P., Roper, G., & Hager, J. C. (1980). Deliberate facial movement. *Child Development, 51,* 886–891.

Frank, M. G., & Ekman, P. (1993). Not all smiles are created equal: The differences between enjoyment and other smiles. *Humor: The International Journal for Research in Humor, 6,* 9–26.

Frank, M. G., Ekman, P., & Friesen, W. V. (1993). Behavioural markers and recognizability of the smile of enjoyment. *Journal of Personality and Social Psychology, 64,* 83–93.

Fridlund, A. J., Ekman, P., & Oster, H. (1987). Facial expression of emotion: Review of literature, 1970–1983. In A. Siegman & S. Feldstein (Eds.), *Nonverbal behavior and communication* (pp. 143–224). Hillsdale, NJ: Lawrance Erlbaum.

Hess, U., & Kleck, R. E. (1990). Differentiating emotion elicited and deliberate emotional facial expressions. *European Journal of Social Psychology, 20,* 369–385.

Willock, E. C., Thompson, R. J., & McIntosh, P. S. (1992). *Stackplotting: An effective technique for visualising image sequences.* Paper presented to the 6th Australasian Remote Sensing Conference, Wellington, New Zealand, November.

11

Components and Recognition of Facial Expression in the Communication of Emotion by Actors

PIERRE GOSSELIN, GILLES KIROUAC & FRANÇOIS Y. DORÉ

According to psychoevolutionist theories (Ekman, 1984, 1993; Izard, 1977; Izard & Malatesta, 1987; Plutchik, 1980), facial expressions play an important role in the communication of emotion and in the regulation of social interactions. The information provided by facial displays allows protagonists involved in social interactions to mutually appraise their emotional states and adjust their behavior in the appropriate way. One phenomenon that contributes to the complexity of the communication of emotion is the control that human beings have of their facial expressions. According to Ekman (1977) and Malatesta and Izard (1984), many control strategies may be used, such as attenuating, amplifying, simulating, or masking the expression of an emotion. The ability of human beings to control their facial expressions raises several issues. One of the main issues is the degree of similarity between facial expressions of genuine emotions and those of simulated emotions. Given that simulation is a strategy commonly used by the encoder to convince the decoder that an emotion is felt, it is justified to assume that facial expressions of simulated emotions are good reproductions of those of genuine emotions.

Studies concerned with this question have revealed three types of differences between facial expressions of genuine and simulated emotions. Facial expressions of simulated emotions are more asymmetric than those of genuine emotions (Ekman, Hager, & Friesen, 1981; Hager & Ekman, 1985), they are characterized by a timing of muscular contraction that is more irregular (Hess, Kappas, McHugo, Kleck, & Lanzetta, 1989; Weiss, Blum, & Gleberman, 1987), and there is some evidence suggesting that they are characterized by missing components. Ekman, Friesen, and O'Sullivan (1988) found that smiles simulated to mask a negative emotion do not include the same facial components involved in the display of a positive emotion. Contractions of the orbicularis oculi, which raise the cheek and gather the skin inward from around the eye socket, occur more frequently in genuine than in simulated happiness.

A second issue raised by the control of facial expression is the ability of human beings to judge the authenticity of emotional expression, especially to discriminate between genuine and simulated emotions. This ability may be very advantageous because deception may sometimes have harmful effects on decoders. The studies concerned with this question have focused on emotional expressions simulated by the encoder to mask a contrary emotional state. In these studies, decoders were presented with short video excerpts showing people expressing their emotions honestly or masking them by simulating the expression of a contrary emotion (Ekman & Friesen, 1974; Ekman & O'Sullivan, 1991; Manstead, Wagner, & MacDonald, 1986; O'Sullivan, Ekman, & Friesen, 1988; Soppe, 1988; Zuckerman, Amidon, Bishop, & Pomerantz, 1982; Zuckerman, Koestner, & Colella, 1985). The results of these studies indicate that the accuracy of decoders in discriminating between honest and deceiving expressions is generally low, particularly when decoders are restricted to the facial channel but also when they are exposed to multichannel cues. Substantial interindividual differences were also found, some individuals being clearly more accurate than others (Ekman & O'Sullivan, 1991). One particularity of the judgment of the authenticity of expressions is the presence of a response bias. Many studies concerned with the detection of deception, particularly for lasting emotional states, have shown that decoders are more prone to judge an expression as being authentic than to judge it as false or deceiving (DePaulo, Stone, & Lassiter, 1985; Zuckerman, Koestner, Colella, & Alton, 1984).

A third issue raised by the control of facial expression is the clarity of the signal with respect to the emotional category. According to previous studies, accuracy in judging the emotional category appears to differ depending on whether the expression is genuine or simulated. Although accuracy in judging the emotional category of simulated (posed) expressions is generally high (Ekman, 1982), decoders do not perform at levels much better than chance when judging genuine (spontaneous) expressions (Motley & Camden, 1988; Wagner, MacDonald, & Manstead, 1986). However, this finding must be interpreted with caution because it may reflect limitations in inducing genuine emotions and not a real difference in facial expressions of genuine and simulated emotions. It is plausible that manipulations made in these studies to induce pure emotions produced, in fact, mixed emotions, decreasing the clarity of the signal.

The two studies that we present in this article examined the encoding and decoding of facial expression of emotions portrayed by actors. In many countries, people spend a significant part of their entertainment time watching dramatic films or series on television. One implication of this phenomenon is that the fictive emotional communication proposed by television, cinema, and theater represents a significant part of the emotional communication experienced by people. For this reason, fictive communication of emotions in dramatic arts is a phenomenon that merits study. Furthermore, the interest shown by people for fictive emotional communication also suggests that there is a relationship between fictive and real communication.

Within the context of their profession, actors frequently must portray the emotions experienced by their characters. The extent to which the portrayals are realistic depends on the repertory, but actors must sometimes be able to perform very convincing emotional portrayals. Dramatic plays, in particular, require that actors achieve a great level of authenticity in portraying emotions so as to produce the expected effect.

The Stanislawski technique was developed at the beginning of the century to improve the authenticity of emotional portrayals (Stanislawski, 1975). With this technique, actors have to retrieve past experiences that are similar to those experienced by their characters. While retrieving these past experiences, they have to reexperience or relive the emotions and express them in the context of the performances. Several months of training are needed to master the Stanislawski technique. Actors must develop the ability to select and retrieve appropriate emotional experiences. They must also learn to portray emotions while taking into account the particularity of the character. This requires an extensive amount of concentration in the context of a public performance.

The extent to which actors feel genuine emotions with the Stanislawski technique is not clear. Although it is possible to verify whether actors feel emotions by asking them for self-reports of their emotional states, self-reports may be influenced by demand characteristic artifacts. Actors may be susceptible to rating their emotional state in agreement with the instructions they receive. Thus, it is difficult in this context to prove that actors really feel emotions. Despite this limit, the Stanislawski technique is of great interest for the study of emotional communication because it is oriented toward realistic expression. The technique differs from what has been asked of actors in previous studies. Actors have usually been asked to portray emotions without specific efforts and preparation so as to produce realistic expressions (see Ekman, 1982). Although the portrayals of emotion produced with this latter method may be somewhat similar to expressions of genuine emotions, we are inclined to think that portrayals produced with the Stanislawski technique would be even more similar.

In Study 1, we examined facial expressions portrayed by actors in two encoding conditions. In the first (encoding felt emotions [EFE]) condition, actors trained with Stanislawski-like techniques were asked to feel and to portray emotions while performing short scenarios. In the second (encoding unfelt emotions [EUE]) condition, actors were asked to portray emotions without feeling them while acting out the same short scenarios.

The first aspect that we examined concerned the occurrence of individual facial movements. Given that actors are well trained in encoding emotion, we predicted that, in both encoding conditions, their portrayals of emotion would more often include facial movements characteristic of genuine emotions than other facial movements. Our criteria for the facial movements characteristic of genuine emotions were the proposals made by Ekman and Friesen (1978b, 1982). On the basis of numerous studies on the encoding and decoding of emotions, these researchers have proposed a list of facial expressions that are representative of genuine emotions.

The second hypothesis was that the characteristic facial movements of genuine emotions would appear more often in the EFE condition than in the EUE condition. This assumption relied on the fact that the Stanislawski technique is specifically oriented toward the reproduction of realistic expressions, whereas the standard procedure is not.

The second aspect that we examined was the simultaneity of facial movements. According to Ekman and Friesen (1978b, 1982), facial expressions of genuine emotions generally include several facial movements that occur simultaneously. Examination of their proposals indicates that the expressions of happiness, fear, anger, surprise, and sadness include at least two facial movements occurring simultaneously. Therefore, we hypothesized that actors' portrayals of these emotions would also manifest this feature of genuine emotions. Specifically, we predicted that the facial movements of genuine emotions would occur more often simultaneously than separately in actors' portrayals. Finally, we hypothesized that the tendency of these facial movements to occur simultaneously would be stronger in the EFE condition than in the EUE condition. This hypothesis was also based on the fact that the Stanislawski technique is specifically oriented toward the production of realistic expressions.

Study 2 was concerned with the decoding of actors' portrayals of emotions from facial behavior. Two types of judgments were examined: the judgment of the emotional category (e.g., happiness, fear, or anger) and that of the authenticity (felt vs. unfelt emotion). First, we hypothesized that decoders would recognize the emotional category in both encoding conditions at a better-than-chance level. On the one hand, several studies have shown that decoders recognize the emotional category in actors' portrayals even when there are no special efforts or preparation on the part of actors to portray genuine emotions. On the other hand, the credibility and the popularity of the Stanislawski technique in dramatic arts strongly suggest that actors' portrayals of emotion produced with this technique are well recognized by spectators.

With respect to the judgment of the encoding condition, we examined whether decoders could discriminate between the portrayals of felt and unfelt emotions from facial behavior. On the basis of previous studies concerned with the detection of deception, we hypothesized that the judgment of the encoding condition would be affected by a response bias toward authenticity. Specifically, it was expected that decoders would be prone to judge emotional portrayals as felt rather than unfelt.

Study I

This study was concerned with the facial components of emotional portrayals produced by actors in two conditions: the EFE condition and the EUE condition. We examined the extent to which the facial components of these portrayals corresponded to those of genuine emotions. We also verified whether the facial components of portrayals produced in the EFE condition were closer to those of genuine emotions than those produced in the EUE condition.

Method

Materials

The facial material used in this study came from a previous study that we undertook (Gosselin, Kirouac, & Doré, 1992). In that study, actors were asked to interpret short scenarios involving the portrayal of various emotions. The following description summarizes how this material was produced and how it was selected for the purpose of the present study.[1]

SCENARIOS.   Material for the interpretations included 24 scenarios. The writing of the scenarios was based on previous studies on the eliciting situations of emotions (Doré & Kirouac, 1986). In these studies, questionnaire methods were used to identify eliciting situations that were judged as being specific to happiness, fear, anger, surprise, sadness, and disgust. A sample of naive participants was asked to write stories for each of the six aforementioned emotions, and another sample of naive participants had to evaluate the intensity of each of the six emotions that could be present in the various situations. These stories were between two and four sentences long. Doré and Kirouac (1986) found that the situations described in the questionnaire were clearly associated with one specific emotion and that the specific emotion was judged as having a fairly high intensity. A test and a retest also revealed an overall correlation of .85 ($p < .05$) over a 4-week period, indicating that intensity judgments remained stable over time.

For the construction of scenarios, we chose four situations for each of the six fundamental emotions of Doré and Kirouac's (1986) questionnaire. These were the situations rated as most specific to the emotion by naive participants. Twenty-four scenarios, each about one page long, were subsequently written on the basis of these situations. Scenario texts were written so as to provide more information about the situations eliciting emotions: these texts specified the ideas, memories, images, actions, and words of the main character as well as the context of the situations. As a means of verifying that the scenarios conveyed the emotion that they were expected to convey, actors were asked to evaluate them about 4 weeks before interpreting them. They were instructed to identify the emotional state of the main character in the scenario by rating each of the six emotions on a 7-point scale. Results showed that all of the 24 scenarios were found to convey very specifically the intended emotion; the mean ratings were 4.76 ($SD = 0.80$) for the intended emotion and 0.21 ($SD = 0.22$) for the unintended emotions.

ENCODING EMOTIONS.   Six actors (5 women and 1 man) from the Conservatory of Dramatic Arts of Quebec were recruited to serve as encoders. The actors ranged in age from 18 to 29 years. They were all in the last year of a 3-year program at the conservatory and had already received intensive training in interpretation. They were trained in various acting techniques developed from the Stanislawski method. These techniques teach the actors to accurately show emotion by learning how to remember and reexperience an emotion. Actors were told that the study was concerned with the expression of felt and unfelt emotions but not specifically with facial expression.

Each actor interpreted individually 2 scenarios per emotional category, for a total of 12. The scenarios were those he or she rated as being the most specific with respect to the intended emotion (i.e., an intensity equal to or greater than 5 for the intended emotion and equal to or less than 1 for unintended emotions). Therefore, the 6 actors did not interpret the same scenarios. Each scenario had to be acted out in two ways. In the EFE condition, actors were instructed to use their training in the Stanislawski technique to feel the emotion they had to portray in the scenario. In the EUE condition, they were instructed to portray the emotion without feeling it. These conditions were defined so as to obtain two types of portrayals: portrayals of felt emotions in the EFE condition and portrayals of unfelt emotions in the EUE condition. In both conditions, actors had to respect the course of events described in the scenario text, as well as the characters' verbalizations. They were also instructed to look at the camera during their interpretations. Actors were given the scenario texts the week before a preliminary encoding session so that they could learn them.

In total, 120 interpretations per actor were performed (6 emotions × 2 conditions × 2 scenarios × 5 repetitions), distributed over ten 90-min sessions. Within each session, actors performed six different scenarios related to the six emotional categories in two encoding conditions. The order of emotion categories was randomly distributed, and the two encoding conditions related to the same emotion followed each other. The order of the two encoding conditions varied according to the preference expressed by each actor. This particularity was introduced after a preliminary session showed that some actors experienced difficulties with the imposed order.

MANIPULATION CHECK.   Four types of measures were used to verify whether actors succeeded in portraying emotions as felt and unfelt. Only video excerpts in which the manipulations were successful (46%) were used in the present study. The manipulation check included ratings made by actors of their emotional state immediately after each interpretation, ratings made by actors of their protrayals from videotapes at the end of each session and 2 months later, and ratings of actors' portrayals made by independent judges from videotapes. We discuss next the implementation of these criteria.

ACTORS' RATINGS.   The first aspect measured was the actor's emotional state immediately after each interpretation. The actors were asked to rate the intensity at which they felt each of the six emotions during the scenario on a 7-point scale ranging from *simulated* (0) to *strongly felt* (6). In the second set of ratings, actors had to rate their own portrayals from tapes showing facial, gestural, and vocal cues. The second set of ratings took place at the end of each encoding session, and the order in which they were presented was the same as the order of interpretation. While viewing videotapes of each of their own interpretations, the actors had to indicate verbally when the intended emotion was portrayed. A time counter display allowed the experimenter to note their responses. Immediately after watching the recording of an interpretation, they were asked to rate the intensity at which they perceived they felt each of the six emotions during the interpretation using the same scales as they had used in the previous stage. The third set of ratings took place 2 months after the actors had performed their interpretations. The procedure was identical to that used for the second set, except that the video excerpts were shown in three or four 60-min sessions in a randon order.

Examination of the ratings revealed that actors generally succeeded in portraying the intended emotion in the appropriate way. The mean ratings for the intended emotion were 4.45, 4.53, and 3.36 for the first, second, and third sets of ratings, respectively, in the EFE condition; the corresponding ratings were 0.53, 0.44, and 0.87 in the EUE condition. In many instances, actors reported that they portrayed the intended emotions in the same interpretation several times. They also gave stable evaluations of the time at which they portrayed the intended emotion. They located the emotion inside a 3-s interval in 58.8% and 57.1% of all instances in the EFE and EUE conditions, respectively.

JUDGES' RATINGS.   Six undergraduate students in psychology, 3 men and 3 women, were recruited to serve as decoders. The sample was small because the length of the judgment task required sixteen 1-hr sessions. Stimuli shown to the judges consisted of a random distribution of 300 neutral excerpts and 1,200 emotional excerpts;[2] excerpts were 10 s in duration and were separated by 20-s intervals. The stimuli showed the faces and bodies of the actors and included their voices. Neutral excerpts were included to allow a variation of participants' responses, that is, to give them the opportunity to report that no emotion was portrayed. The criteria used to select the excerpts were based on the ratings previously made by actors. In the case of emotional stimuli, the purpose of the criteria was to select short excerpts depicting felt emotion or unfelt emotion. The following criteria were used: intensity ratings of actors equal to or greater than 3 for the intended emotion in the EFE condition, intensity ratings of equal to or less than 1 in the EUE condition, and intensity ratings for the unintended emotions equal to or less than 1 for both conditions. We also selected short video excerpts from the aforementioned interpretations on the basis of the two evaluations given by actors when they located the emotion. The agreement between the two evaluations had to be inside a 3-s interval. The beginning and the end of each excerpt were determined by using the mean of the two indicated moments as the midpoint of the excerpt and by subtracting 5 s for the beginning and adding 5 s for the end. We assumed that the mean of the two moments at which the actors reported portraying the emotion was a better indication than one of each. Neutral excerpts were chosen among interpretations that met the criteria described for the emotional stimuli, except that the criterion for time location was that no emotion be reported during a 40-s interval. The beginning and the end of each neutral excerpt were determined by taking the midpoint of those intervals and by subtracting and adding 5 s. The type of ratings the judges were asked to provide was different from the type provided by the actors. Judges were instructed to rate the intensity at which the six fundamental emotions were portrayed on a 7-point scale and to judge whether the emotion or emotions portrayed were felt or unfelt.

Examination of the judges' ratings for emotional excerpts indicated a mean agreement of 96.2% ($Z = 72.27$, $N = 1,200$, $p < .0001$) with respect to the emotion that received the strongest intensity and a mean agreement of 65.2% ($Z = 7.08$, $N = 1,200$, $p < .0001$) with respect to the encoding condition. These ratings allowed a second and final selection of the video excerpts in the present study. The criteria used were as follows: a ratio agreement of 5 of the 6 judges for the emotion being portrayed the most strongly and a ratio agreement of 4 of the 6 judges for the encoding condition. In this way, we kept 513 of the original 1,200 video excerpts, of which 348 were associated with the EFE condition and 165 with the EUE condition.

Procedure

In the present study, the Facial Action Coding System (FACS; Ekman & Friesen, 1978a) was used to score the facial material obtained with the procedure previously described. This system is an anatomically based measurement method that distinguishes 44 facial action units (AUs), the minimum number of action units that are anatomically separate and visually distinguishable. Examples of AUs are the Brow Lowerer, the Upper Lid Raiser, the Nose Wrinkler, and the Lip Corner Puller (see table 11.1). The FACS allows one to describe any facial configuration in terms of the combination of AUs that produced it. In addition, it can be used to specify the point at which each movement begins and ends.

Facial coding required repeated slow-motion inspection of facial behavior. An SVM-1010 video motion analyzer was used on the video excerpts showing only the face. Two coders unaware of emotional category and encoding condition scored the material; these individuals had previously passed the efficiency test designed by Ekman and Friesen (1978b). Each coder scored half of the material. Coders used a list indicating the beginning and the end of video excerpts that had to be coded. These numbers referred to the time code display appearing on the right upper side of the video picture, which corresponded to the evaluations given by actors of the moment at which the intended emotion was communicated. In this way, the codification focused on the

TABLE 11.1. Action units and their appearance change

Facial Action Coding System name	Appearance change
Inner Brow Raiser	Raises only inner part of the eyebrow
Outer Brow Raiser	Raises only outer part of the eyebrow
Brow Lowerer	Lowers eyebrows and pulls them together
Upper Lid Raiser	Raises the upper lid, exposing more of the upper portion of the eyeball
Cheek Raiser	Raises the cheek, causes crow's feet and wrinkles below the eye
Lid Tightener	Raises and tightens the lower eyelid
Nose Wrinkler	Wrinkles and pulls the skin upward along the sides of the nose
Upper Lip Raiser	Raises the upper lip and causes bend in the shape of the upper lip
Nasolabial Furrow Deepener	Deepens the middle portion of the nasolabial furrow
Lip Corner Puller	Pulls lip corner up diagonally toward the cheekbone
Lip Corner Depressor	Pulls the corners of the lips down and produces some pouching, bagging, or wrinkling of skin below the lip corners
Lower Lip Depressor	Pulls the lower lip down, flattens the chin boss
Chin Raiser	Pushes chin boss and lower lip upward
Lip Stretcher	Stretches lips horizontally
Lip Funneler	Funnels lips outward, pulling in medially on the lip corners and turning out at least one lip
Lip Tightener	Tightens the lips, making the lips appear more narrow
Lip Pressor	Presses the lips together, tightens and narrows the lips
Lips Part	Parts lips to a limited extent
Jaw Drop	Parts lips so that space between the teeth can be seen
Mouth Stretch	Stretches mouth open

Note: The indicators listed here provide only a summary of the appearance changes described in the Facial Action Coding System. We included only the action units predicted to signal the six emotions considered in Study 1. Modified and reproduced by special permission of the Publisher, Consulting Psychologists Press, Inc., Palo Alto, CA 94303 from *Facial Action Coding System* by Paul Ekman and Wallace V. Freisen. Copyright 1978 by Consulting Psychologists Press. Inc. All rights reserved. Further reproduction is prohibited without the Publisher's written consent.

moments that were crucial within scenarios. The duration of excerpts to be coded varied from 1 to 3 s, and all AUs that occurred within this interval were coded. However, when a facial configuration was already present at the beginning of the interval, coding had to begin as soon as the configuration appeared. A similar procedure was used when a facial configuration was present at the end of the interval. It was necessary to continue examining the videotape until the end of the facial configuration.

Coders had to classify facial configurations as uncodable in two instances: when the video picture was not clear enough to allow coding and when the actors spoke. Excerpts of actors speaking were not coded so as to avoid bias introduced by the facial muscular activity related to speech rather than emotion. Eighty-seven percent of the facial configurations were codable, and each was described in terms of a series of AUs.

Coding lasted 2 months, and intercoder agreement was calculated four times at equal intervals on the basis of 40 excerpts. As a means of verifying intercoder agreement, each coder coded 20 excerpts taken from the list of the other coder. When disagreements occurred, only the response of the coder to which the excerpt was originally attributed was retained. Intercoder reliability for scoring facial configurations was examined by using a ratio in which the number of AUs on which the two coders agreed was multiplied by 2 and then divided by the total number of AUs scored by the two coders. However, it was necessary to verify, in a previous step, the reliability of the facial configuration location to ensure that the two coders scored the same facial behavior. Given that the FACS provides a formula for locating AUs, we adapted this formula for facial configuration. The reliability facial configuration location was defined as the ratio of the number of times the two coders agreed on the beginning and on the end of the facial configuration (inside a 0.5-s interval) to the total number of scored configurations. The ratios for time locating were .86, .80, .85, .95, and the agreement ratios in scoring facial configurations were .85, .82, .81, .82, respectively.

Results

Analysis of data first focused on the occurrence of individual AUs, and two hypotheses were examined. The first hypothesis was that the mean probability of occurrence of AUs that signal genuine emotions, according to Ekman and Friesen (1978b, 1982) predictions, would be higher than that of the other AUs. The second hypothesis was that the mean probability of occurrence of these AUs would be higher in the EFE condition than in the EUE condition.

Given that Ekman and Friesen (1978b, 1982) made numerous predictions, we used inferential statistics to make a general assessment of them by pooling together AUs predicted to signal a particular emotion and those not predicted to signal it. For example, among the 20 AUs identified as signaling the six emotions, 2 of them, the Cheek Raiser and the Lip Corner Puller, signal happiness. The mean probability of these 2 AUs was compared with that of the remaining 18 in the analysis concerned with happiness. The specific predictions concerning the signal values of individual AUs were verified through a descriptive analysis.

As one can see from table 11.2, the mean probability of occurrence of the predicted AUs was higher than that of the unpredicted AUs. These differences were quite large, especially for happiness, fear, and surprise. However, the mean probability of occurrence of the predicted AUs in the EFE condition did not seem different from that in the EUE condition.

Data were analyzed in a 2×2 randomized block factorial analysis of variance (ANOVA); signal prediction (predicted vs. unpredicted AUs) and encoding condition (EFE vs. EUE) were variables. Confirmation of the second hypothesis required a significant Signal Prediction $\times$ Encoding Condition interaction. The ANOVA was performed separately for each emotion and included the 20 AUs hypothesized by Ekman and Friesen (1978b, 1982) to signal happiness, fear, anger, surprise, sadness, and disgust. Because of the heterogeneity of variances, data were first submitted to a logarithmic transformation. These analyses indicated a significant effect of signal prediction in the case of each of the six emotions: happiness, $F(1, 13) = 360.54$, $p < .0001$; fear, $F(1, 13) = 88.26$, $p < .0001$; anger, $F(1, 13) = 22.40$, $p < .0004$; surprise, $F(1, 10) = 29.42$, $p < .0003$; sadness, $F(1, 11) = 5.65$, $p < .04$; and disgust, $F(1, 11) = 16.76$, $p < .002$. No differences between the two encoding conditions reached significance; also, the Signal Prediction $\times$ Encoding Condition interaction was not significant.

Thus, the results confirmed the first hypothesis: The mean probabilities of occurrence of the AUs predicted to signal each of the six emotions were higher than those of

TABLE 11.2. Means and standard deviations of the probability of occurrence of predicted and unpredicted action units

Action units	Encoding felt emotions condition						Encoding unfelt emotions condition					
	Happiness	Fear	Anger	Surprise	Sadness	Disgust	Happiness	Fear	Anger	Surprise	Sadness	Disgust
Predicted												
M	.93	.25	.18	.36	.14	.17	.84	.28	.18	.34	.07	.27
SD	.11	.05	.03	.22	.09	.11	.22	.11	.08	.19	.05	.07
Unpredicted												
M	.07	.04	.11	.04	.06	.07	.07	.03	.04	.04	.04	.10
SD	.02	.05	.06	.03	.03	.06	.02	.02	.06	.04	.04	.09

the other AUs. The second hypothesis was not confirmed. The mean probabilities of the AUs predicted to signal each of the six emotions were not higher in the EFE condition than in the EUE condition.

Table 11.3 presents the mean probability of occurrence of the 20 AUs predicted by Ekman and Friesen (1978b, 1982) to signal the six emotions. The mean values of the AUs expected to signal a particular emotion are indicated. Inspection of this table reveals that, although AUs predicted to signal particular emotions had a generally higher mean probability of occurrence than the other AUs, not all predictions were confirmed. Moreover, the large values of the standard deviations associated with many AUs indicate important variations between actors in the way they portrayed emotions.

The predictions concerning happiness were supported by the data. The Cheek Raiser and Lip Corner Puller AUs were far more frequent than the other AUs. Their mean probabilities of occurrence were very high: .94 and.92, respectively, in the EFE condition and .77 and .91, respectively, in the EUE condition. Two other AUs that were not predicted to depict happiness were also common: the Lips Part and the Jaw Drop.

As predicted, the Brow Lowerer, the Upper Lid Raiser, and the Jaw Drop were among the most frequent AUs for fear. However, predictions involving the Inner Brow Raiser, the Outer Brow Raiser, and the Lip Stretcher were not strongly supported, and those involving the Mouth Stretch were not supported at all. In the EFE condition, the Lid Tightener, although not predicted, was also common.

Among the 10 AUs predicted to signal anger, 4 were found to occur frequently in both conditions: the Brow Lowerer, the Upper Lid Raiser, the Lip Tightener, and the Jaw Drop. The Chin Raiser was common only in the EUE condition and the Jaw Drop only in the EFE condition. The Lid Tightener, the Upper Lip Raiser, the Lip Funneler, and the Lip Pressor were not observed frequently or were absent. Some AUs that were not predicted to signal anger were also common. The Lower Lip Depressor occurred quite frequently in the EFE condition, and the Lip Stretcher occurred frequently in both conditions.

Most of the predictions regarding surprise were supported by the data. The Upper Lid Raiser and the Jaw Drop were the most frequent AUs in both conditions. The Inner Brow Raiser and the Outer Brow Raiser were also observed quite frequently in both conditions, but the Mouth Stretch was observed only in the EFE condition. Two AUs were also frequent, although they were not predicted: The Lips Part was common in both conditions, and the Lip Stretcher was common in the EUE condition.

Among the eight AUs predicted to signal sadness, only the Lip Corner Depressor, the Chin Raiser, and the Jaw Drop were frequently observed in both conditions. The Inner Brow Raiser, the Brow Lowerer, and the Lips Part were common only in the EFE condition, and no evidence was found indicating the presence of the Cheek Raiser or the Nasolabial Furrow Deepener. Two AUs not predicted to signal sadness were also observed. The Lid Tightener was common in the EFE condition, and the Lip Tightener was common in the EUE condition.

The predictions regarding disgust were supported in both conditions in the case of three of the six AUs: the Upper Lip Raiser, the Lips Part, and the Jaw Drop. Evidence of the presence of the Chin Raiser was found only in the EUE condition. The Nose Wrinkler and the Lower Lip Depressor were not observed frequently. Some other AUs were also observed. The Brow Lowerer was common in both conditions; the Lid Tightener, in the EFE condition, and the Cheek Raiser and the Lip Stretcher, in the EUE condition.

TABLE 11.3. Mean probability of occurrence of action units in the Encoding Felt Emotions (EFE) and Encoding Unfelt Emotions (EUE) conditions

Action units	EFE condition						EUE condition					
	Happiness	Fear	Anger	Surprise	Sadness	Disgust	Happiness	Fear	Anger	Surprise	Sadness	Disgust
Inner Brow Raiser												
M	.07	.12[a]	.17	.15[a]	.22[a]	.01	.06	.20[a]	.04	.28[a]	.01[a]	.08
SD	.06	.14	.14	.29	.26	.03	.12	.24	.09	.19	.02	.12
Outer Brow Raiser												
M	.09	.01[a]	.10	.19[a]	.01	.01	.06	.06[a]	.02	.28[a]	.01	.04
SD	.07	.02	.09	.37	.02	.03	.12	.09	.05	.19	.02	.08
Brow Lowerer												
M	.01	.33[a]	.33[a]	.08	.25[a]	.35	.00	.30[a]	.36[a]	.00	.00[a]	.55
SD	.01	.40	.26	.16	.21	.23	.00	.19	.23	.00	.00	.39
Upper Lid Raiser												
M	.05	.55[a]	.25[a]	.76[a]	.00	.01	.05	.63[a]	.42[a]	.44[a]	.01	.00
SD	.09	.41	.23	.33	.00	.03	.10	.34	.31	.24	.03	.00
Cheek Raiser												
M	.94[a]	.00	.03	.00	.03[a]	.06	.77[a]	.04	.00	.00	.00[a]	.36
SD	.08	.00	.07	.00	.07	.12	.30	.08	.00	.00	.00	.26
Lid Tightener												
M	.01	.29	.05[a]	.02	.39	.36	.03	.08	.06[a]	.00	.12	.08
SD	.03	.45	.08	.04	.25	.38	.07	.17	.14	.00	.08	.10
Nose Wrinkler												
M	.05	.00	.00	.00	.00	.06[a]	.00	.00	.00	.01	.00	.08[a]
SD	.13	.00	.00	.00	.00	.13	.00	.00	.00	.03	.00	.18
Upper Lip Raiser												
M	.00	.03	.10[a]	.10	.05	.21[a]	.04	.02	.00[a]	.00	.00	.33[a]
SD	.00	.06	.16	.21	.10	.20	.06	.06	.00	.00	.00	.21
Nasolabial Furrow Deepener												
M	.00	.00	.00	.00	.02[a]	.02	.00	.00	.00	.00	.00[a]	.00
SD	.00	.00	.00	.00	.03	.04	.00	.00	.00	.00	.00	.00

Action Unit													
Lip Corner Puller													
M	.92[a]	.00	.00	.00	.04	.05	.00	.91[a]	.02	.00	.05	.04	.00
SD	.16	.00	.00	.03	.03	.10	.00	.15	.05	.00	.11	.07	.00
Lip Corner Depressor													
M	.00	.00	.05	.00	.09[a]	.00	.00	.03	.04	.00	.02	.34[a]	.02
SD	.00	.00	.09	.00	.08	.00	.00	.05	.09	.00	.04	.23	.04
Lower Lip Depressor													
M	.00	.04	.28	.00	.02	.05[a]	.00	.01	.08	.04	.00	.00	.00[a]
SD	.00	.07	.09	.00	.03	.11	.00	.03	.08	.10	.00	.00	.00
Chin Raiser													
M	.00	.04	.06[a]	.04	.17[a]	.00	.00	.08	.02	.29[a]	.03	.13[a]	.27[a]
SD	.00	.07	.04	.09	.10	.00	.00	.08	.05	.34	.06	.10	.19
Lip Stretcher													
M	.02	.07[a]	.40	.09	.07	.07	.07	.00	.16[a]	.22	.28	.01	.30
SD	.04	.08	.36	.09	.11	.14	.14	.00	.07	.36	.26	.02	.25
Lip Funneler													
M	.00	.00	.02[a]	.00	.01	.01	.01	.00	.00	.04[a]	.00	.00	.00
SD	.00	.00	.04	.00	.02	.03	.03	.00	.00	.06	.00	.00	.00
Lip Tightener													
M	.01	.00	.21[a]	.02	.02	.01	.01	.05	.02	.18[a]	.00	.26	.00
SD	.03	.00	.14	.04	.04	.03	.03	.09	.05	.24	.00	.28	.00
Lip Pressor													
M	.00	.02	.01[a]	.00	.03	.03	.00	.17	.02	.04[a]	.00	.00	.01
SD	.00	.06	.04	.00	.03	.03	.00	.09	.05	.06	.00	.00	.02
Lips Part													
M	.34	.20[a]	.31[a]	.26	.14[a]	.32[a]	.32[a]	.29	.14[a]	.13[a]	.18	.03[a]	.56[a]
SD	.23	.17	.19	.35	.16	.34	.34	.19	.21	.13	.18	.05	.41
Jaw Drop													
M	.55	.75[a]	.49[a]	.72[a]	.20[a]	.40[a]	.40[a]	.41	.72[a]	.24[a]	.54[a]	.09[a]	.38[a]
SD	.20	.17	.30	.41	.13	.35	.35	.18	.16	.20	.31	.09	.31
Mouth Stretch													
M	.06	.00[a]	.04	.00[a]	.00	.00	.00	.00	.00[a]	.07	.15[a]	.00	.00
SD	.09	.00	.07	.00	.00	.00	.00	.00	.00	.15	.22	.00	.00

[a] Predicted to signal a particular emotion (according to Ekman & Friesen, 1978b, 1982).

The second part of the data analysis was concerned with the tendency of the predicted AUs to occur simultaneously (see table 11.4). By occurring simultaneously, we mean that the predicted AUs were present at the same time at a particular moment, not that they appeared and disappeared at the same time. Two hypotheses were examined. First, it was expected that the AUs predicted by Ekman and Friesen (1978b, 1982) to signal happiness, fear, anger, surprise, and sadness would occur more often simultaneously than separately in both conditions. Second, it was expected that the tendency of these AUs to occur simultaneously would be stronger in the EFE condition than in the EUE condition.

. For each of the six emotions, we conducted a randomized block factorial ANOVA with two variables: simultaneousness (simultaneously vs. separately) and condition (EFE vs. EUE). The simultaneousness variable was examined by comparing the probability of the AUs occurring simultaneously (two or more at the same time) and the probability of the same AUs occurring separately. The second hypothesis implied, for its part, a significant effect of the interaction between the two variables.

The ANOVAs revealed a significant main effect of the simultaneousness variable for happiness, $F(1, 12) = 26.76, p < .0002$, and fear, $F(1, 12) = 40.39, p < .0001$. As expected, the AUs depicting these emotions occurred more frequently simultaneously than separately. Significant Simultaneousness × Condition interactions were found for happiness, $F(1, 12) = 11.33, p < .006$; anger, $F(1, 12) = 13.27, p < .004$; and sadness, $F(1, 9) = 21.17, p < .002$. Tests of simple main effects for simultaneousness indicated that the AUs depicting happiness and anger occurred more often simultaneously than separately in the EFE condition but not in the EUE condition. Tests of simple main effects for condition revealed that the tendency of these AUs to occur simultaneously was also stronger in the EFE condition than in the EUE condition. The AUs depicting sadness occurred more often simultaneously than separately in the EFE condition, whereas the reverse was found in the EUE condition. These AUs also occurred simultaneously more frequently in the EFE condition than in the EUE condition.

In brief, the third hypothesis was well supported in the EFE condition but not in the EUE condition. The expected AUs occurred more often simultaneously than separately in the EFE condition in the case of happiness, fear, anger, and sadness but not in the case of surprise. In the EUE condition, the expected AUs occurred more often simultaneously than separately only in the case of fear. Finally, the fourth hypothesis was partially supported. The expected AUs occurred simultaneously more often in the EFE condition than in the EUE condition in the case of happiness, anger, and sadness but not in the case of fear and surprise.

TABLE 11.4. Mean probability of occurrence of action units appearing simultaneously and separately

Mode of appearance	Encoding felt emotions condition					Encoding unfelt emotions condition				
	Happiness	Fear	Anger	Surprise	Sadness	Happiness	Fear	Anger	Surprise	Sadness
Simultaneous										
M	.92	.79	.75	.74	.74	.59	.80	.37	.41	.22
SD	.10	.16	.16	.32	.22	.25	.20	.24	.09	.16
Separate										
M	.08	.21	.25	.26	.26	.41	.20	.63	.59	.78
SD	.10	.16	.16	.32	.22	.25	.20	.24	.09	.16

Discussion

The results of this study indicate that there is some similarity between the facial components of actors' portrayals and the facial expressions of genuine emotions. When actors are asked to portray emotions, they more often show the AUs characteristic of genuine emotions than other AUs. The descriptive analysis of facial components reveals, for its part, that almost all of the expected AUs of happiness and surprise and about half of the AUs of fear, anger, sadness, and disgust were common in both encoding conditions. In addition, AUs other than those predicted were also common. Thus, although actors generally show the AUs that are characteristic of genuine emotions, they do not show all of them, and they also show other AUs. The fact that the specific predictions were not completely supported by the data is not surprising. Ekman and Friesen's (1978b, 1982) proposals do not claim to cover all of the facial repertory of genuine emotions. Moreover, these authors have pointed out the existence of interindividual differences in facial expressiveness. One implication of interindividual differences is that particular individuals do not necessarily show all of the AUs that can possibly signal emotions. A closer examination of the data for each actor supports this view. In several instances, some predicted AUs were produced by only 1 or 2 of the 6 actors. Although these AUs occurred quite frequently in the portrayals of these actors, their overall mean probability of occurrence was low.

The fact that specific predictions were better supported in the case of happiness and surprise is of particular interest. It suggests that the encoding of negative or unpleasant emotions is harder to achieve than that of positive or neutral emotions. Two factors may be responsible. First, some AUs characteristic of negative emotions may be harder to produce voluntarily than those of happiness and surprise. However, evidence reported by Ekman, Roper, and Hager (1980) does not indicate that this hypothesis is correct, at least for happiness. These researchers found that the Cheek Raiser, one of the two AUs characteristic of genuine happiness, is not easily performed by encoders voluntarily. Second, our results may reflect the effects of social display rules on actors. Although actors are probably more experienced in showing strong negative emotions— and, therefore, in going beyond display rules—than are untrained encoders, it is possible that they do not succeed completely in so doing. Evidence presented by Wallbott (1988) indicates that actors' portrayals of emotions may be affected by display rules. In a study examining portrayals of emotions produced by male and female actors, Wallbott found that male actors were better in portraying anger and that female actors were better in portraying fear and sadness, suggesting that display rules apply not only in real communication but also in fictive communication.

The second conclusion that can be drawn from the results of this study concerns the differences between the two encoding conditions. It was hypothesized that actors' portrayals of emotion in the EFE condition would be closer to those of genuine emotions than the portrayals in the EUE condition. This hypothesis was supported in the case of three of the six emotions: happiness, anger, and sadness. The differences between the two encoding conditions were found in the simultaneity of the expected AUs rather than in their individual mean probability of occurrence. The efforts made by actors to portray felt emotions allowed them to produce better combinations of AUs characterizing genuine emotions. This result is very interesting because it suggests that it is easier for actors to select the appropriate AUs than to combine them in a realistic way. One particular implication of this finding is that it may reflect a hierarchical organization in the production of facial behavior. Our results suggest that the mastering of individual AUs appears to be simpler than the mastering of AU combinations.

The Stanislawski technique appears to have a facilitating effect on the organization of facial behavior. However, this effect does not apply to all of the six emotions considered here. In the case of fear, inspection of the data indicates that the probability that AUs occurred simultaneously was high in both conditions. Thus, without trying to feel the emotion, actors succeeded in combining the AUs characterizing this emotion very well. The case of surprise is different. Inspection of the data shows that, although there were no significant differences between the two conditions, the results leaned toward the hypothesis. The absence of significant differences was related to the large standard deviation in the EFE condition. In conclusion, although the Stanislawski technique has a facilitating effect on the production of realistic expressions, this effect varies according to the emotion.

Study 2

In the second study, we examined the accuracy of judgments made by decoders who had to judge the emotional category and discriminate between the two encoding conditions on the basis of facial portrayals.

Method

Participants

Fifty graduate and undergraduate students (25 women and 25 men), served as decoders. Their ages varied from 18 to 34 years ($M = 22$). The students were paid Can $15 for their participation and were told that the study addressed the issue of emotional expression.

Materials

Materials for the decoding task included a videocassette recorder (Sony SLO-325), a video monitor (Hitachi), videocassettes, and questionnaires. The stimulus material consisted of an edited videotape that first showed excerpts of complete interpretations and then showed 243 short 10-s excerpts that participants had to evaluate. Four excerpts depicting complete interpretation had been previously shown in a familiarization period: two happiness scenarios interpreted by an actor, one for the EFE condition and another for the EUE condition, and two disgust scenarios interpreted by another actor. This was intended to emphasize the difference between the two encoding conditions. These excerpts showed the actors' faces, bodies, and voices.

Stimuli used for the judgment task were 243 video excerpts 10 s in duration randomly taken from those coded with the FACS in Study 1. These video excerpts showed actors' faces but did not include sound. Attempts were made to distribute stimuli equally over emotional categories and encoding conditions. Each excerpt was separated from the next by a 20-s delay period to allow participants to respond.

Procedure

Participants executed the evaluation task in small groups of 2 to 4. The task required two 70-min sessions. First, participants were told that they were to be shown video excerpts of actors' portrayals of emotions. They were also told that actors reported feeling the emotion they portrayed in some episodes and did not report feeling it in other episodes. The familiarization period allowed participants to understand the context from which the short 10-s excerpts that they had subsequently to judge were taken. To emphasize the difference between portrayals of felt and unfelt emotions, we chose two emotions that differ with respect to their valence (pleasant for happiness and unpleasant for disgust). The familiarization period took place at the beginning of the first session and lasted 10 min. For the judgment task, participants were instructed to rate, on a 7-point scale, the intensity at which happiness, fear, anger, surprise, sadness, and disgust were conveyed in the facial portrayals. They also had to judge whether these emotions were felt or unfelt by the actor. These two judgment tasks alternated throughout sessions. Participants were instructed to omit the identification of the encoding condition when they perceived that no emotion was portrayed.

Results

First, we report results pertaining to the question of the extent to which decoders can accurately judge the emotional category. Then we examine the accuracy of decoders in judging the encoding condition.

Judgment of the Emotional Category

Accuracy scores for the judgment of the emotional category were calculated by taking into consideration the emotion that received the highest intensity for each video excerpt. A score of 1 was given when this emotion was the same as the intended emotion in the scenario; otherwise a score of zero was registered. These accuracy scores were subsequently used to compute d', a measure of sensitivity proposed by signal detection theory (Green & Swets, 1966). This index of sensitivity is uncontaminated by response bias (e.g., the tendency of decoders to choose a response category when it is not the appropriate choice).

Table 11.5 indicates that the level of sensitivity in judging the emotional category was fairly high in both conditions. The mean d's were 2.91 for portrayals in the EFE condition and 2.88 for those in the EUE condition, indicating a comparable level of sensitivity. Separate t tests ($p < .005$) for each emotional category and subjective condition revealed that the sensitivity level greatly exceeded the chance level in all instances.

The sensitivity scores were submitted to an ANOVA (Sex × Emotion × Condition) with repeated measures on emotion and condition. This analysis indicated significant differences for emotion, $F(5, 240) = 72.13$, $p < .0001$, and a significant Condition x Emotion interaction, $F(5, 240) = 51.21$, $p < .001$. Tests of simple main effects showed that portrayals in the EFE condition were judged more accurately than those in the EUE condition ($p < .01$) for happiness, $F(1, 240) = 29.13$; fear, $F(1, 240) = 33.00$; and sadness, $F(1, 240) = 14.20$. The reverse was true for disgust, $F(1, 240) = 82.00$, and anger, $F(1, 240) = 25.43$, and no difference was found in the case of surprise. Tukey's test ($p < .01$), computed to examine differences between emotions for each condition, revealed that the patterns of differences were not identical from one condition to the other. In the EFE condition, happiness and surprise were better recognized than the four other emotions, and disgust was recognized to a lesser degree than the others. In the

TABLE 11.5. Sensitivity and intensity ratings in judging the emotional category

| | Encoding felt emotions condition | | | Encoding unfelt emotions condition | | |
| | | Intensity | | | Intensity | |
Emotion	d'	Expected emotion	Unexpected emotion	d'	Expected emotion	Unexpected emotion
Happiness						
M	3.87	4.23	0.78	3.28	3.22	0.73
SD	0.55	0.70	0.67	0.60	0.61	0.58
$t(49)$	49.75*			38.65*		
Fear						
M	2.83	2.58	1.44	2.20	2.16	1.29
SD	0.58	0.77	0.83	0.55	0.62	0.69
$t(49)$	34.50*			28.28*		
Anger						
M	2.80	3.83	0.75	3.35	3.09	0.43
SD	0.53	0.60	0.51	0.62	0.54	0.36
$t(49)$	37.35*			38.20*		
Surprise						
M	3.43	3.18	0.75	3.34	3.28	0.83
SD	0.66	0.77	0.61	0.89	0.83	0.65
$t(49)$	36.75*			26.53*		
Sadness						
M	2.83	2.65	0.42	2.42	2.42	0.61
SD	0.46	0.70	0.37	0.60	0.79	0.44
$t(49)$	43.50*			28.52*		
Disgust						
M	1.71	1.96	1.78	2.71	2.78	1.48
SD	0.64	0.84	0.79	0.40	0.75	0.94
$t(49)$	18.89*			49.90*		
All						
M	2.91	3.07	0.99	2.88	2.78	0.90
SD	0.54	0.69	0.62	0.58	0.65	0.58

Note: Ratings could range from 0 (null) to 6 (very intense)
* $p < .005$.

EUE condition, anger, surprise, and happiness were better recognized than the three other emotions, and fear was recognized to a lesser degree than the others.

For some actors, the facial material shown to decoders did not include expressions for all of the 2 (condition) × 6 (emotion) cells. We therefore computed a separate ANOVA to examine the effect of the actor variable on the overall judgment task. This analysis showed that the accuracy level in judging the emotional category was significantly affected by actor, $F(5, 245) = 77.02$, $p < .0001$. To examine whether these differences between actors were related to the encoding of emotion, we computed the Spearman rank correlation between the probability of occurrence of the predicted AUs and decoding accuracy. A correlation of .67 was found, but this value did not reach significance ($p > .05$).

Although the aforementioned values reveal that decoders accurately judged the emotional category, they do not indicate the extent to which decoders perceived pure emotions.

To address this question, we examined the intensities attributed to the six emotions for each facial stimulus. We computed the mean intensity score for the intended emotion (i.e., the correct response) and the mean intensity score for the unintended emotion that received the highest intensity (table 11.5). Large values for unintended emotions would indicate that decoders perceived emotion blends. The overall mean intensities for intended emotions were 3.07 in the EFE condition and 2.78 in the EUE condition; for unintended emotions, the corresponding intensities were 0.99 and 0.90. The strong contrast between intensities for intended and unintended emotions indicates that, although intended emotions were perceived as moderately intense, there was generally little ambiguity as to the emotion communicated. In all cases, except disgust in the EFE condition, the intensity given to the intended emotion was 2 to 7 times that of the emotion that received the highest intensity among the unintended emotions.

Judgment of the Subjective Condition

Raw accuracy scores in judging the encoding condition were also used to compute the d' index of sensitivity. Table 11.6 shows that the sensitivity was generally low; the mean value for the overall task was only 0.17, with substantial variations from one emotion to another. Data were treated in an ANOVA (Sex × Emotion) with repeated measures on emotion. The analysis revealed a significant effect only for emotion, $F(5, 240) = 11.56, p < .001$. The Tukey test ($p < .01$) indicated that the highest sensitivity was obtained in judging the portrayals of happiness and anger. These portrayals were better judged than those of fear, surprise, sadness, and disgust. Separate analyses performed on each emotional category revealed that the sensitivity was above chance only for happiness, $t(49) = 6.09, p < .005$, and anger, $t(49) = 6.72, p < .005$. Differences between actors were also examined by computing a separate ANOVA on the overall judgment task. A highly significant effect was found, $F(5, 245) = 8.17, p < .0001$, indicating differences between actors.

The presence of response bias in judging the encoding condition was examined by comparing the probability of responding that the emotion was felt with the probability of portrayals from the EFE condition. As shown in table 11.6, the probability of responding that the emotion was felt was generally higher than the probability of viewing

TABLE 11.6. Sensitivity and response bias in judging the encoding condition

Emotion	Sensitivity (d')			Response bias		
	M	SD	t(49)	p(RF)	p(F)	t(49)
Happiness	.56	.65	6.09*	.62	.43	8.95*
Fear	.20	.54	2.62	.55	.54	0.35
Anger	.38	.40	6.72*	.63	.50	5.74*
Surprise	−.11	.57	1.36	.54	.60	2.02
Sadness	−.02	.61	0.23	.67	.64	1.52
Disgust	−.01	.68	0.10	.66	.44	9.15*
All		.17	.55		.61	.55

Note: p(RF) = probability of responding that the emotion was felt; p(F) = probability of a stimulus from the encoding felt emotions condition.
* $p < .005$.

a portrayal from the EFE condition. Inspection of table 11.6 also suggests that the response bias was not uniform from one emotion to another. Given these apparent variations, separate t tests were computed for each emotion. These tests revealed that the response bias reached significance ($p < .005$) in the case of happiness, $t(49) = 8.95$; anger, $t(49) = 5.74$; and disgust, $t(49) = 9.15$.

Discussion

Results of Study 2 confirmed the first hypothesis concerning the judgment of the emotional category. The accuracy level in judging the emotional category was above the level of chance in both encoding conditions. Furthermore, the d' index of sensitivity indicated that the accuracy of judgment was generally high, except for disgust in the EFE condition. Intensity ratings, for their part, showed that actors' portrayals of emotions were judged as being quite specific to the expected emotion.

The high accuracy in the EUE condition is in agreement with what had been found in previous studies. While being asked to portray emotion with no special emphasis on authenticity, actors produce facial expressions that are well recognized by decoders (Ekman, 1982). The high accuracy generally reached by decoders in the EFE condition indicates that the Stanislawski technique allowed actors to produce facial portrayals that clearly signal emotions. The results obtained in this study are in agreement with those obtained in Study 1. The analysis of facial components revealed the similarity between the AUs found in actors' portrayals and those that characterize genuine emotions.

This study also shows that accuracy in judging emotional category varies according to the emotion, the encoding condition, and the actor. The effect of emotion in judging the emotional category is consistent with earlier findings (Wallbott, 1988). We found that happiness and surprise were among the best recognized emotions in both encoding conditions. It is interesting to note that the portrayals produced by actors for these two emotions were closer to the expressions of genuine emotions than the others. As evidenced in table 11.3, the mean probabilities of occurrence of the AUs predicted to signal these emotions were generally higher than those of the other emotions.

The effect found for the condition variable indicates that portrayals produced in the EFE condition were better recognized than those in the EUE condition in the case of happiness, fear, and sadness; the reverse was true for anger and disgust. This pattern of results can only be partially explained from the information gathered in Study 1. We found that portrayals of happiness and sadness in the EFE condition were closer to the expressions of genuine emotions than those produced in the EUE condition. It is possible that the recognition of happiness and sadness reflects this fact. However, this explanation does not account for the recognition of fear, anger, and disgust. Other characteristics of the facial portrayals may have influenced the judgment of the emotional category. For example, differences found between the two conditions might reflect differences in the intensity of AUs or differences in their temporal pattern, such as the duration of the apex. It would be interesting to examine these possible differences in future studies.

The differences we found between the two conditions do not correspond to what has been reported in previous studies regrading the decoding of genuine versus simulated emotions (Motley & Camden, 1988; Wagner et al., 1986). Although facial expressions of simulated emotions are generally well recognized by decoders, those of genuine or felt emotions have been found to generate low recognition accuracy. In the present study, decoders reached high accuracy in judging the emotional category of felt emotions. This discrepancy may reflect the involvement of different processes in the encoding of felt emotions. First, in the present study, actors' encoding of emotion was clearly defined to serve communication. This has not been the case in previous studies concerned with felt emotions. For example, in the study undertaken by Wagner et al. (1986), participants were left alone in a room and instructed to look at pictures designed to induce emotions. Such a setting does not promote communication and may have affected the encoding of emotion. Second, the low accuracy found in previous studies may be related to the fact that the facial stimuli depicted mixed rather than pure emotions. In the present study, facial stimuli were selected by using a manipulation check intended to avoid or reduce this problem.

The significant effect of actor in judging the emotional category replicates the earlier findings of Wallbott and Scherer (1986) and suggests that there are interindividual differences in encoding emotions. Although this aspect was not examined in Study 1, the results of the component analysis support the idea. In many instances, the standard deviations of the probabilities of occurrence of the AUs were large (see table 11.3), indicating substantial differences between actors. The positive correlation we found between the encoding of emotion and the accuracy level in judging the emotional category, although not significant, is interesting. This finding suggests that the decoding of actors' portrayals is related to the ability of actors to produce good approximations of genuine emotions. Our analysis regarding this aspect was severely limited by the number of actors. It would be interesting to explore the question in more detail with a larger sampling of actors.

Results concerning the judgment of the encoding condition show that the accuracy level reached by decoders was generally low and that it varied substantially from one emotion to another. The accuracy was above the level of chance only in the case of happiness and anger. This study did not specify the kind of information used by decoders to distinguish between portrayals of felt and unfelt emotions, but results of Study 1 suggest that the simultaneity of AUs could be a useful source of information. We found that AUs characteristic of genuine happiness and anger tended to occur simultaneously more often in the EFE condition than in the EUE condition. If decoders are sensitive to the simultaneity of AUs, it is possible that they use this kind of information to judge whether the emotion is felt or unfelt. However, this hypothesis does not account for the judgment of the encoding condition in the case of sadness. Although the AUs characterizing sadness occurred simultaneously more often in the EFE condition than in the EUE condition, the accuracy level was not better than chance.

Finally, the results show that there was a response bias in judging the encoding condition. As expected, decoders were prone to judge emotions portrayed by actors as felt rather than unfelt. This bias was found for happiness, anger, and disgust. This result is in agreement with the findings of previous studies concerned with the detection of deception (DePaulo et al., 1985; Zuckerman et al., 1984). Our study suggests that such bias is not limited to lasting emotional states but also applies to the decoding of fundamental emotions, at least for actors' portrayals.

General Discussion

Although actors have often been used as encoders in studies on emotional communication, few of these studies have examined the components of actors' portrayals of emotion. There is some evidence that actors' portrayals of emotions are characterized by gestural and vocal components (Wallbott & Scherer, 1986). Results of Study 1 provide new information with respect to this issue, indicating that the facial components of emotions portrayed by actors correspond, to a certain degree, to those that characterize genuine emotions. These results are particularly interesting because of the lack of component studies concerned with the facial channel. Furthermore, the component analysis presented here included a relatively large sample of emotions.

The fact that portrayals of happiness, anger, and sadness produced in the EFE condition were more similar to the expressions of genuine emotions than those in the EUE condition has implications for the dramatic arts. The first interpretation that can be made of our results is that they support Stanislawski's (1975) claim asserting that attempts made to feel the emotion allow actors to produce portrayals of emotions that are more authentic or realistic. Study 1 did not specify the mechanisms involved in the facilitation of authentic portrayals of emotions, but several hypotheses can be proposed.

According to Stanislawski (1975), actors succeed in feeling genuine emotions while attempting to retrieve and relive past emotional experiences. He claimed that the retrieving of past emotional experiences works as an elicitor of genuine emotions, thus leading to spontaneous-like expressive behavior. Our own data are in agreement with this hypothesis. The ratings that actors made of their emotional state just after each scenario showed that they generally felt the intended emotion. However, as we mentioned earlier, these self-ratings are sensitive to demand characteristic artifacts. Given that actors were asked to feel emotions and that the encoding task was repetitive, they may have rated their emotional state in agreement with what was expected from them. Thus, the hypothesis that actors really felt emotions in the EFE condition is plausible, but more evidence is needed to document this aspect.

A second plausible hypothesis is that attempts to feel emotions have a suggestive effect. While attempting to retrieve and relive past emotional experiences, actors may be more confident in portraying emotions in a realistic way. This increase in confidence may help actors produce better portrayals of emotions. A third hypothesis refers to cognitive representations of emotional expressions. The ability to portray or simulate emotions presupposes that human beings keep in their memory representations of their own emotional expressions, as well as those of others. It is possible that attempts made to retrieve past emotional experiences facilitate the retrieving of expressive representations, leading to better facial portrayals of emotions.

However, there is an alternative explanation for the differences between felt and unfelt emotions. The effect we found for happiness, anger, and sadness may have been caused not by the Stanislawski technique but by the instructions to portray unfelt emotions. According to this second interpretation, the instructions given in the EUE condition may have led actors to decrease the quality of their portrayals. To resolve this issue, it would be necessary to study actors' portrayals with a control condition in which actors would be instructed to portray emotions without specifications regarding the felt versus unfelt dimension.

Study 2 shows that the facial portrayals allowed decoders to judge the emotional category in each encoding condition very well. However, the judgment of the encoding condition was more difficult, the accuracy being above chance only for happiness and anger. Several factors may have contributed to this poor quality of judgment. The first is the response bias that was found in Study 2. This response bias clearly decreased the sensitivity of decoders' judgment for several emotions. Second, the component analysis of facial behavior revealed that the differences between the two encoding conditions were occasional. For example, the mean probabilities that the AUs characterizing genuine happiness occurred simultaneously were .92 and .59 in the EFE and EUE conditions, respectively. This indicates that there were many instances in which the two conditions did not differ with respect to this aspect. Furthermore, we did not find any differences between the two encoding conditions for fear, surprise, or disgust. The fact that the differences found between the two encoding conditions were occasional may, in part, explain the low sensitivity of this kind of judgment.

A third possibility is that the differences between the portrayals of the two encoding conditions were not perceived by decoders. This possibility has been suggested by Ekman, O'Sullivan, Friesen, and Scherer (1991) in their study on the detection of deception. They found that decoders do not use all of the available information when they have to judge the authenticity of emotions from expressive behavior.

The existence of the response bias in judging the encoding condition is an interesting phenomenon. Previous studies on the detection of deception have reported this bias toward authenticity for lasting affective states (e.g., liking or disliking another person). No previous study, to our knowledge, has examined this phenomenon with fundamental emotions. Study 2 brings new information by indicating that the bias toward authenticity might be applied to at least some fundamental emotions.

The fact that the response bias was not found for all of the six emotions suggests that the impact of expressive behavior might vary according to the emotion. This might also mean that the strategy used by decoders to cope with other people's expressive behavior varies according to the emotion. It can be hypothesized that there are probably advantages for decoders to be more prone to believe in the authenticity of certain emotions. For example, taking expressions of anger seriously is probably advantageous because it can allow decoders to be better prepared to stave off potential aggression.

Inasmuch as the bias toward authenticity is not restricted to fictive communication of emotion but also applies to real communication of emotion, it would be interesting to understand in future studies the factors responsible for this bias. It is reasonable to think that decoders' strategies concerning the authenticity of emotional displays play a role in the regulation of their own emotional behavior.

Notes

1. See Gosselin, Kirouac, and Doré (1992) for a detailed description of the stimulus materials used in Study 1.

2. The presentation of 1,200 emotional excerpts results from the fact that actors indicated that they portrayed the intended emotion several times within scenarios.

References

DePaulo, B. M., Stone, J. I., & Lassiter, G. D. (1985). Deceiving and detecting deceit. In B. R. Schlenger (Ed.), *The self and social life* (pp. 323–370). New York: McGraw-Hill.

Doré, F. Y., & Kirouac, G. (1986). Reliability of accuracy and intensity judgments of eliciting situations of emotions. *Canadian Journal of Behavioral Sciences, 18,* 92–103.

Ekman, P. (1977). Biological and cultural contribution to body and facial movement. In J. Blacking (Ed.), *The anthropology of the body* (pp. 34–84). San Diego, CA: Academic Press.

Ekman, P. (1982). *Emotion in the human face.* New York: Pergamon Press.

Ekman, P. (1984). Expression and the nature of emotion. In K. Scherer & P. Ekman (Eds.), *Approaches to emotion* (pp. 319–344). Hillsdale, NJ: Erlbaum.

Ekman, P. (1993). Facial expression and emotion. *American Psychologist, 48,* 384–392.

Ekman, P., & Friesen, W. V. (1974). Detecting deception from the body or face. *Journal of Personality and Social Psychology, 29,* 288–298.

Ekman, P., & Friesen, W. V. (1978a). *Facial Action Coding System (FACS): A technique for the measurement of facial action.* Palo Alto, CA: Consulting Psychologists Press.

Ekman, P., & Friesen, W. V. (1978b). *Facial Action Coding System: Part Two.* Palo Alto, CA: Consulting Psychologists Press.

Ekman, P., & Friesen, W. V. (1982). Felt, false, and miserable smiles. *Journal of Nonverbal Behavior, 6,* 238–252.

Ekman, P., Friesen, W. V., & O'Sullivan, M. (1988). Smiles when lying. *Journal of Personality and Social Psychology, 54,* 414–420.

Ekman, P., Hager, J. C., & Friesen, W. V. (1981). The symmetry of emotional and deliberate facial actions. *Psychophysiology, 18,* 101–106.

Ekman, P., & O'Sullivan, M. (1991). Who can catch a liar? *American Psychologist, 46,* 913–920.

Ekman, P., O'Sullivan, M. B., Friesen, W. V., & Scherer, K. R. (1991). Face, voice and body in detecting deceit. *Journal of Nonverbal Behavior, 15,* 125–135.

Ekman, P., Roper, G., & Hager, J. C. (1980). Deliberate facial movement. *Child Development, 51,* 886–891.

Gosselin, P., Kirouac, G., & Doré, F. Y. (1992). Construction and selection of dynamic facial expressions of six fundamental emotions. *Cahiers de l'École de Psychologie de l'Université Laval, 123,* 1–41.

Green, D. M., & Swets, J. (1966). *Signal detection theory and psychophysics.* New York: Wiley.

Hager, J. C., & Ekman, P. (1985). The asymmetry of facial actions is inconsistent with models of hemispheric specialization. *Psychophysiology, 22,* 307–318.

Hess, U., Kappas, A., McHugo, G. J., Kleck, R. E., & Lanzetta, J. T. (1989). An analysis of the encoding and decoding of spontaneous and posed smiles: The use of facial electromyography. *Journal of Nonverbal Behavior, 13,* 121–137.

Izard, C. E. (1977). *Human emotions.* New York: Plenum Press.

Izard, C. E., & Malatesta, C. Z. (1987). Perspective on emotional development 1: Differential emotions theory of early emotional development. In J. D. Osofsky (Ed.), *Handbook of infant development* (pp. 494–554). New York: Wiley-Interscience.

Malatesta, C. Z., & Izard, C. E. (1984). The facial expression of emotion: Young, middle-aged, and older adult expressions. In C. E. Izard (Ed.), *Emotion in adult development* (pp. 253–273). Beverly Hills, CA: Sage.

Manstead, A. S. R., Wagner, H. L., & MacDonald, C. J. (1986). Deceptive and nondeceptive communication: Sending experience, modality, and individual abilities. *Journal of Nonverbal Behavior, 10,* 147–167.

Motley, M. T., & Camden, C. T. (1988). Facial expressions of emotion: A comparison of posed expressions versus spontaneous expressions in an interpersonal communication setting. *Western Journal of Speech Communication, 52,* 1–22.

O'Sullivan, M., Ekman, P., & Friesen, W. V. (1988). The effect of comparisons on detecting deceit. *Journal of Nonverbal Behavior, 12,* 203–214.

Plutchik, R. (1980). *Emotion: A psychoevolutionary synthesis.* New York: Harper & Row.

Soppe, H. J. G. (1988). Age differences in the decoding of affect authenticity and intensity. *Journal of Nonverbal Behavior, 12,* 107–119.

Stanislawski, K. S. (1975). *La formation de l'acteur.* [Building a character]. Paris: Payot.

Wagner, H. L., MacDonald, C. J., & Manstead, A. S. R. (1986). Communication of individual emotions by spontaneous facial expression. *Journal of Personality and Social Psychology, 50,* 737–743.

Wallbott, H. G. (1988). Big girls don't frown, big boys don't cry—Gender differences of professional actors in communicating emotion via facial expressions. *Journal of Nonverbal Behavior, 12,* 98–106.

Wallbott, H. G., & Scherer, K. R. (1986). Cues and channels in emotion recognition. *Journal of Personality and Social Psychology, 51,* 690–699.

Weiss, F., Blum, G. S., & Gleberman, L. (1987). Anatomically based measurement of facial expressions in simulated versus hypnotically induced affect. *Motivation and Emotion, 11,* 67–81.

Zuckerman, M., Amidon, M. D., Bishop, S. E., & Pomerantz, S. D. (1982). Face and tone of voice in the communication of deception. *Journal of Personality and Social Psychology, 43,* 347–357.

Zuckerman, M., Koestner, R., & Colella, M. J. (1985). Learning to detect deception from three communication channels. *Journal of Nonverbal Behavior, 9,* 188–194.

Zuckerman, M., Koestner, R., Colella, M. J., & Alton, A. O. (1984). Anchoring in the detection of deception and leakage. *Journal of Personality and Social Psychology, 47,* 301–311.

AFTERWORD

Components and Recognition of Facial Expression in the Communication of Emotion by Actors

PIERRE GOSSELIN & GILLES KIROUAC

Since the completion of the studies reported in the above article, our research work has followed two different directions. First, we conducted a series of studies concerned with the recognition of facial emotional prototypes. All of these studies shared a common methodology involving the construction of facial stimuli with specific physical properties. FACS (Ekman & Friesen, 1978a) was used as the measurement tool in constructing these stimuli. The second direction consists of a project we have recently begun concerned with the voluntary production of facial movements. We will focus mainly on this subject in the coming years.

In our judgment studies, we examined recognition of the facial expressions belonging to the repertoire proposed by Ekman and Friesen (1978b). Up to the present time, we have studied about 60 different expressions. In order to appreciate the specificity of facial signals, decoders were asked to rate the intensity of each of the fundamental emotions. The results we obtained indicate that the majority of expressions convey the expected emotion in a very specific way (Gosselin & Kirouac, in press). They also show that the various expressions of the same emotion are not all equivalent, some of them being more specific than others.

Another part of our work has been devoted to ontogenetic questions (Gosselin, 1995; Gosselin, Roberge, & Lavallée, in press; Gosselin & Pélissier, in press). They were primarily aimed at examining the decoding of the above-mentioned repertoire in children. These studies showed that several facial expressions of the same emotion have the same developmental pattern of recognition. They also allowed us to identify the specific discriminations that generate recognition errors during childhood, and their developmental course.

Our second main line of research, which we have just begun, is concerned with the voluntary production of facial movements. In the initial step, we intend to make a detailed description of the various action units and action unit combinations that can be voluntarily produced. In the second step, we plan to study three types of simulation involving different levels of persuasiveness. They are called referential, simple, and affect-imagery-based simulation. Facial activity related to these three conditions will be coded with FACS and will take into account the nature of action units, their symmetry and their temporal dynamics.

The studies we conducted with FACS in the past years have made us sensitive to some problems encountered in constructing and analyzing facial material. In the following paragraphs, we elaborate on these problems, telling how we managed to solve them or how we plan to avoid them in the future.

In our judgment studies, we constructed the facial material with FACS according to theoretical specifications. Encoders were instructed to produce specific facial movements and were photographed while keeping the intended configuration. The material was subsequently coded with FACS by two judges. This strategy is advantageous because it allowed us to relate the recognition of emotion with specific characteristics of facial expression.

In doing these judgment studies, we realized the difficulty experienced by the majority of encoders to voluntarily produce the intended configurations. While some actions units, or action unit combinations, are easily produced, many others are difficult and require extensive practice. In addition, there are noteworthy differences between encoders as to their ability to produce certain action units.

These problems have two consequences. First, constructing facial material with specific characteristics is a demanding enterprise, particularly if several different expressions for an emotion are needed. Second, it is not easy to obtain the same series of expressions for all encoders. This may be a limitation if one wants to include this variable in one's experimental design. We did not succeed in solving these problems. Rather, we decided to examine systematically these questions in the program we are just starting.

One interesting feature of FACS is that it is a comprehensive system allowing researchers to gather detailed information on facial activity. However, it may be problematic to analyze in detail the large amount of information collected in a component study. We encountered this problem in our study with actors when we tried to relate the probability of occurrence of action units with specific emotions and encoding conditions. The number of comparisons was so high that it was difficult to analyze the data with inferential statistics. Furthermore, this problem was exacerbated by the small pool of encoders in our study. Because drama schools only train 5 to 10 students per year, there are not many young actors using the Stanislawski method. We resolved this issue by performing general tests of our hypotheses with inferential statistics. These general tests were followed by descriptive statistics in which we examined the specific relations between the probability of occurrence of action units, emotion, and encoding conditions.

The second problem we encountered in analyzing the data was related to large interindividual differences in facial activity. The variability of the data introduced by idiosyncrasies makes the common patterns shared by encoders more difficult to identify. Again, this problem was aggravated by the small pool of encoders in our study. To reduce the effects of this problem in our current projects on simulation, we chose to increase the power of our research design. First, we increased the number of trials per encoder for each condition. Second, we greatly increased the encoder sample. This was easy to do because our current investigations deal with ordinary people, and not with Stanislawski-method actors.

References

Ekman, P., & Friesen, W. V. (1978a). *Facial Action Coding System (FACS): A technique for the measurement of facial action.* Palo Alto, CA: Consulting Psychologists Press.

Ekman, P., & Friesen, W. V. (1978b). *Facial Action Coding System: Part two.* Palo Alto, CA: Consulting Psychologists Press.

Gosselin, P. (1995). Le développement de la reconnaissance des expressions faciales des émotions chez l'enfant [The development of recognition of facial emotional expression in children]. *Canadian Journal of Behavioural Sciences, 27,* 107–119.

Gosselin, P., & Kirouac, G. (in press). Le décodage de prototypes émotionnels faciaux [Decoding facial emotional prototypes]. *Canadian Journal of Experimental Psychology.*

Gosselin, P., & Pélissier, D. (in press). Effet de l'intensité sur la catégorisation des prototypes émotionels faciaux chex l'enfant et l'adulte [The effect of intensity on categorizing facial emotional prototypes in children and adults]. *International Journal of Psychology.*

Gosselin, P., Roberge, P., & Lavallée, M. F. (in press). Le développement de la reconnaissance des expressions faciales émotionnelles du répertoire humain [The development of recognition of facial emotional expressions in the human repertoire]. *Enfance.*

12

Differentiating Emotion Elicited and Deliberate Emotional Facial Expressions

URSULA HESS & ROBERT E. KLECK

A topic of continuing interest in the field of nonverbal communication regards the nonverbal indicators of deceptive messages (e.g. DePaulo, Stone, & Lassiter, 1985). In most studies in this field the deception consists of the telling of untruthful messages. Less interest has been given to emotional deception; that is, to the attempt to deceive an observer regarding one's emotional state, rather than making an untruthful statement. The present research is concerned with differences between spontaneous, emotion elicited, and deliberate emotional facial expressions; specifically with the dynamic features of the facial expressions that might differentiate the two types of displays. Dynamic aspects of the facial expression are features such as the speed of onset and offset, and the irregularity of the expression that refer to the time course rather than the morphology of the facial display.

The terms 'spontaneous' or 'emotion elicited' emotional facial expression are used to refer to unmodulated emotional facial expressions that are congruent with an underlying emotional state, while 'deliberate' expressions are those intentionally employed by the sender for some purpose. The latter include poses, that is expressions shown in the absence of an underlying emotional state, as well as masking or deceptive expressions, that is, emotional expressions that are incongruent with the underlying emotional state (e.g. smiling when one is angry). Phenomena such as pathological laughter and crying, as well as facial gestures (see Ekman, Hager, & Friesen, 1981; Ekman, 1978) are not included in this definition and will not be part of the present investigation.

The area of inquiry most relevant to the present research is concerned with the nonverbal indicators of deceptive messages. Here, the body of research specifically addressing the qualitative differences between spontaneous and deliberate emotional facial expressions, that is, emotional facial expressions employed to deceive an observer regarding the emotional state of the sender, is small compared to the body of research centred on differences in facial expressions found when the sender is telling the truth or is lying. However, some of the basic considerations regarding the nature of deceptive messages in general are of relevance for deliberate emotional facial expressions as well. Zuckerman, DePaulo, and Rosenthal (1981) point to four different sources of markers of deception. First, the voluntary control involved in deceptive behaviour may in itself produce markers of deception. For instance, senders may try too hard to convey a truthful appearing image and many overdo behaviours they think are important. Since some channels are easier to control than others (e.g. Ekman & Friesen, 1969) discrepancies between channels might occur, or the control effort itself may change the expression (see Campbell, 1986). Secondly, the literature on psychophysiological markers of lying (e.g. Lykken, 1979) shows that deception is usually associated with increases in arousal. Nonverbal indicators of arousal, such as blinking, pupil dilation, pitch, speech errors, and speech hesitations might therefore occur in increased frequency when a sender is lying. A third source of deceptive markers are indicators of affective states such as guilt or shame (Kraut, 1980) or 'duping delight' (Ekman, 1980). Generally, neither guilt and shame nor 'duping delight' are likely to occur in the laboratory to a marked degree, but one might assume that most subjects do not like to deceive and might therefore show some signs of anxiety such as less eye contact, less direct body orientation, and more distance from the communication partner (Mehrabian, 1971), as well as a decrease in the use of illustrators (Ekman, 1980). Lastly, it is generally assumed that producing a deceptive message is cognitively more demanding than telling a simple truth. Senders of deceptive messages should therefore show indicators of cognitive effort such as speech pauses, longer response latencies, pupil dilation, and fewer illustrators (Goldman-Eisler, 1968; Kahneman, 1973; Ekman & Friesen, 1972).

DePaulo et al. (1985) provide an exhaustive meta-analysis of studies on both verbal and nonverbal markers of deception. Indicators of deception that have been reliably detected in the face are pupil dilation, the use of adaptors, and blinking. Gaze, head movements, and smiling, on the other hand, do not appear to distinguish between honest and deceptive messages.

Ekman and Friesen (1982) speculated that the main difference between spontaneous emotional smiles and deceptive smiles lies in some of the topographical and temporal aspects of these expressions. They suggested and provided some preliminary evidence for the notion that smiles that do not reflect an emotional state are (1) more asymmetrical, a notion that has been supported by Hager and Ekman (1985), (2) have 'socially inappropriate' (short) onset[1] and (irregular) offset[2] times, and (3) are shorter than 2/3 second or longer than 4 seconds. Consistent with this notion is Bugenthal's (1986) finding that adults' smiles had faster offsets when directed at unresponsive children and that adults who attributed their success as care-givers to 'luck' instead of 'ability' showed smiles with faster onsets when smiling at children. The study suffers, however, from methodological problems: (1) smiles were the only 'objective' measure of the affective state; (2) only the lower face component of the smiles were measured; and (3) no attempt was made to control for co-occurring facial actions. Similarly, Weiss, Blum, and Gleberman (1987) investigated some of the temporal differences between posed expressions and expressions elicited by hypnotically induced affect. They found shorter onset times and more irregularities (pauses and stepwise intensity changes) for deliberate facial expressions. However, their study, while interesting regarding the variables they investigated, was based on a sample of only three female subjects who were selected for their hypnotic suggestibility.

In summary, findings by Weiss et al. (1987) and by Bugenthal (1986) are consistent with Ekman and Friesen's (1982) notion that spontaneous and deliberate emotional facial expressions should differ in the speed of onset. Further, some evidence is provided by Weiss et al. (1987) that spontaneous expressions are less irregular than are deliberate expressions.

The studies described above raise a number of interesting points, however, they also pose a number of problems. All of Ekman and Friesen's as well as Weiss et al.'s senders were female. While Ekman and Friesen investigated the role of onset, offset and time at apex, they did not measure irregularities; conversely, Weiss et al., measured only onset times and irregularities. The present studies were designed to systematically investigate the differences between spontaneous and deliberate emotional facial expressions regarding their dynamic aspects. To enhance the generalizability of the results obtained, both a positive and a negative emotional expression were employed in the research to be described. An expression of happiness was chosen as the positive emotional expression and an expression of disgust as the negative emotional expression.

Disgust was chosen as the negative emotional expression because it is one of the universal 'basic emotions' for which facial actions, reliably related to specific emotional states, have been identified (Ekman, Friesen, & Ancoli, 1980). Moreover, disgust displays are similar to smiling in that they involve both an upper and a lower face component. Disgust has the additional advantage that it can be reliably and ethically elicited in a laboratory, for instance by using excerpts from educational television programmes on topics like surgery.

Based on the previously discussed findings, it was expected that spontaneous and deliberate expressions both of happiness and of disgust should differ regarding their speed of onset and offset. Further, some evidence suggests that spontaneous expressions might show fewer irregularities of the sort described by Weiss et al. (1987) than deliberate expressions. Two experiments were conducted to investigate the hypotheses at hand.

Experiment I

Subjects were asked to pose expressions of happiness or disgust 'as well as possible' while spontaneous emotional facial expressions were elicited using an emotion induction procedure. The temporal parameters of interest: onset time, offset time, and time at apex, as well as the irregularities (pauses and stepwise intensity changes) within the expressions were measured and compared between conditions. It was felt to be important that the expressive episodes analysed were actual examples of spontaneous and deliberate facial expressions respectively. Therefore, self-reports regarding the emotional state of the subject during the trial were obtained from the stimulus persons and were used as a selection tool. That is, only episodes during which the stimulus persons reported to have felt the relevant emotion during the spontaneous condition were retained as spontaneous episodes; conversely, only episodes during which the subject reported not to have felt any emotion more than slightly were retained as deliberate episodes. This is important for two reasons, firstly, a common problem in emotion research is that not all subjects react in the same manner to an emotion elicitor. Therefore, even when a large majority of subjects finds, for example, a given stimulus highly amusing, some might find it not at all funny, or it might even remind them of a personal problem and induce negative affect. The same might be true for elicitors of negative affect. The surgery videos, for example, tend to elicit high levels of disgust (Kappas, 1989), but some subjects are interested in surgery techniques and therefore tend to report feelings of interest rather than of disgust. Secondly, the literature on the facial feedback hypothesis (e.g. Manstead, 1988), suggests that subjects may feel some emotion during posing.

Method

Subjects

Twenty male and 20 female undergraduates participated individually either for extra course credit or for $5. Data from one subject were later excluded because she was chewing gum during the experiment and from an additional four subjects because of instrument failure, leaving 17 female and 18 male subjects.

Tasks

Facial expressions were elicited during two different types of elicitation conditions (spontaneous and posed) and for two different emotions (happiness and disgust). The spontaneous expressions were elicited by inducing the relevant emotional state. Two elicitation procedures were employed for all subjects, a video elicitation and an imagery procedure. For the first procedure, subjects watched an emotionally evocative video episode. For the second procedure, subjects were asked to relive an emotional experience. To elicit the posed expressions, subjects were asked to pose the expression as well as possible while not attempting to feel the emotion relevant to the expression. To justify the procedure, subjects were told that facial expressions may influence the physiological measures taken (see below); the pose condition was presented as a control condition. Subjects were allowed as many trials as they wished up to a limit of three minutes. They were instructed to press a button when they felt that the last pose was adequate. During all tasks subjects were instructed to look at the video monitor. All subjects were unobtrusively video-taped during the tasks. The tasks were counterbalanced between subjects. Following the completion of the tasks subjects were fully debriefed and permission to use the video record was obtained.

Epidode Selection and Scoring Procedure

Immediately following each task subjects filled out a self-report form regarding the difficulty of the task (7-point scale) and the intensity with which they felt each of the following emotions during the task: peacefulness, fear, anger, happiness, interest, sadness, and disgust (5-point scales).[3] Only expressive episodes that were elicited during one of the 'spontaneous' conditions for which the subject reported a rating of 3 or more on the target scale and a rating of not more than 1 on any of the other emotion scales were retained as spontaneous expressions. Likewise, expressive episodes that were elicited during the posing task for which the subject reported a rating of not more than 1 on any of the scales were retained as deliberate expressions. All other expressive episodes were excluded from further analysis. Ratings on the scale 'interest' were not considered for this selection.

For each subject only one episode per condition was selected. Given that the self-report criteria were fulfilled, the last expression performed by the subjects was analysed for the spontaneous expression from the imagery condition and the posed expressions. For the video episodes the last episode could frequently not be analysed as the expressive behaviour continued until after the end of stimulus presentation and therewith the end of the recording period. Therefore, for the video episodes the first expression was analysed. The selection process resulted in a set of 140 episodes.

Time Scores

Onset time, offset time and time at apex were measured for each expressive episode.[4] An expressive episode was defined as follows: from the first visible change from a neutral face or a background expression (a background expression is an expression held for extended periods of time, while other action units come and go) back to a neutral facial expression or to the background expression. An expression was also considered to be ended when subjects started oral/facial manipulations or when they yawned and or looked away. Onset time was defined as the time from the start of the expressive episode to a peak of intensity. Time at apex was the amount of time the expression is held at the peak and offset time was the time from the first evidence of fading of the expression until it stopped fading. Therefore, if the expression did not return to neutral after a peak, but went through a sequence of fading and intensifying, it might have several onset, offset, and apex times. Namely, if an expression showed disruption or pauses in the onset or offset each step was counted as a separate onset or offset phase, the pause as an apex phase. Also, several onset and offset phases might follow each other directly if the expression was never held for longer than the resolution of the counter employed (1/10th of a second). If more than one onset and offset time, and time at apex occurred, these times were averaged for each expression. That is, the onset and offset times, and the times at apex, employed in the analyses, refer to the average duration of onsets, offsets, and apexes for each expression. The degree of irregularity of the expression is defined by the number of onset, offset, and apex phases the expression contains. Figure 12.1 illustrates these parameters.

Reliability was assessed on a subset of 20 randomly chosen episodes. A second rater established the number of phases within an episode and measured the length of each individual phase. Reliability for the number of onset, offset, and apex phases, that is, irregularities ($r = 0.88$); as well as for length of the phases, that is, onset and offset times, and times at apex ($r = 0.92$) was acceptably high.

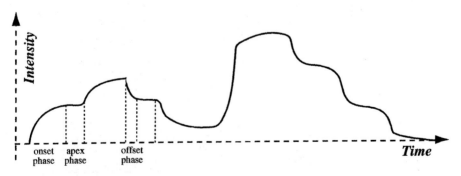

Figure 12.1 Hypothetical example illustrating onset, offset, and apex phases.

Results

Manipulation Check

The spontaneous emotional expressions were elicited by inducing an emotional state using either an emotionally evocative video episode or an imagery procedure. In contrast, subjects were not supposed to feel an emotion during the pose condition. Table 12.1 shows the means and standard deviations as a function of emotion and elicitation condition based on all subjects. The ratings for the two spontaneous conditions were averaged.

The data show that the manipulation was successful. Subjects reported having felt the target emotion during the spontaneous conditions. As expected, they also felt some emotion during the deliberate (pose) condition, but on a considerably lower level.

Multiple Regression Analyses

As mentioned above, the expressive episodes were selected based on the self-report data to ensure that only expressive episodes during which the subject actually felt the relevant emotion were analysed as emotion elicited expressions and only those where the subject did not feel an emotion were analysed as deliberate. Therefore, not all subjects contributed expressions to all conditions. Since this could cause a dependency problem in the following analysis, subject variance was first removed using a multiple regression analysis with dummy coded subject indicator variables as predictors and onset and offset time, and time at apex respectively as the criterion. The same procedure was performed for the irregularities (number of phases). All following analyses are based on the residuals.

In addition, this selection resulted in unequal cell sizes. Therefore, a multiple regression approach was employed with emotion (happy, disgust), condition (emotion elicited, posed) and the interaction term as predictors and onset and offset time, and time at apex as the criterion. The results of this analysis are comparable to the results of a univariate 2×2 ANOVA (Cohen & Cohen, 1983).

Time Data

The analysis of the time data showed no main effects or interactions for average onset and offset time or average time at apex. An analysis of the total length of the expression revealed a main effect for condition, with posed expressions being longer than emotion elicited expressions (*beta:* -0.24; $p < 0.05$). The average phase length over all conditions was (in 10th of seconds) $M = 20.44$ (*S.D.* $= 32.27$, *Md* $= 13.14$).

TABLE 12.1. Means for self-reported emotional state by emotion condition and elicitation condition

Emotional state	Spontaneous		Deliberate	
	Happy	Disgust	Happy	Disgust
Happiness	2.86 (0.58)	0.23(0.52)	1.04(0.68)	0.43(0.82)
Disgust	0.05(0.12)	2.87(0.79)	0.07(0.28)	1.20(1.1)

Note: The standard deviations are given in parentheses.

Irregularity

The analysis of the irregularities (number of phases) of the expression showed a main effect for condition for all frequency of phases measures (onset, offset, and apex; multiple R's: 0.43, $p < 0.05$, 0.35, $p < 0.05$, and 0.35 $p < 0.01$ respectively). The direction was the same for all types of phases; posed expressions had more onset, offset, and apex phases. A main effect for emotion emerged for onset and apex phases, with disgust expressions having more onset and apex phases. A marginal interaction was found for onset phases only. Table 12.2 shows the beta values and significance levels for the phase variables and the mean residuals as a function of emotion and elicitation condition.

Although a significant main effect for condition emerged for the length of the expression, replicating findings by Ekman and Friesen (1982), this cannot be interpreted as indicating differences between posed and spontaneous expressions in the time domain as such. Rather, it is more accurate to see this difference as an artifact of the underlying difference in the number of phases across the conditions. The data are consistent with the view that posed expressions are longer than spontaneous expressions because there are more phases in posed than in spontaneous expressions. A trend emerged suggesting that this effect was more marked for the disgust expressions.

Discussion

The results indicate that posed and spontaneous expressions differ in the time domain insofar as posed expressions are longer and have more phases. No specific differences

TABLE 12.2. (a) Mean residuals for irregularities as a function of emotion and elicitation condition (b) Beta values for number of phases as a function of elicitation condition and emotion

	Spontaneous		Deliberate	
(a) Irregularities	Happy	Disgust	Happy	Disgust
Onset	−0.23(0.51)	−0.06(0.74)	0.02(0.69)	0.86(1.4)
Offset	−0.18(0.63)	−0.27(0.62)	0.20(0.91)	0.61(1.2)
Apex	−0.21(0.58)	−0.15(0.70)	0.11(0.80)	0.73(1.3)
Total	−0.22(0.57) (1.3)	−0.15(0.70)	0.10(0.77)	0.80(1.3)

(b) Variable	Onset	Offset	Apex	Total
Condition	−0.33*	−0.36*	−0.35*	−0.36*
Emotion	−0.28†	n.s.	−0.19‡	−0.21‡
Interaction	0.19‡	n.s.	n.s.	n.s

*$p < 0.01$
† $p < 0.05$
‡ $p < 0.1$.

regarding onset or offset, as suggested by Ekman and Friesen (1982) were found. The predictions by Ekman and Friesen regarding overall length were confirmed, but the data contradict the notion that posed expressions have shorter onsets.

In summary, while the spontaneous, emotion elicited, and deliberate, posed, emotional expressions of happiness and disgust differed significantly regarding the number of irregularities, a difference regarding the time domain was found only for the total length of the expression. However, the latter effect seemed to be driven by a difference in the number of phases. Deliberate expressions contained more phases, that is, more pauses and stepwise intensity changes, than did spontaneous expressions. This finding is consistent with the view that subjects produced the posed expressions by gradually approximating a desired pose. Since subjects were only asked to pose as well as possible and not explicitly to deceive an observer they may have taken less care with the temporal aspects of the expression. While this provides a plausible explanation for the results found in Experiment 1, there is some doubt that these results can be generalized to deceptive expressions in general. Given the number of simultaneous demands on a person engaged in social deception a closed control loop as tightly modulated as the results of this study suggest is unlikely. However, spontaneous expressions are generally considered to be more smooth, reflex-like, and ballistic than voluntary expressions (see Rinn, 1984); thus voluntary expressions used in social deception should also be more irregular than spontaneous expressions, but less irregular than the posed expressions elicited in Experiment 1.

The findings reported above do not confirm earlier findings by Ekman and Friesen (1982) regarding onset and offset times and times at apex, and only partially the findings of Weiss et al. (1987). Hence, it is useful to investigate the specific differences between the present research and the studies of these other investigators. Ekman and Friesen (1982) elicited voluntary smiles by asking subjects to mask their negative emotional state with a positive expression to deceive an interviewer present with them in the same room. Weiss et al. (1987) who likewise found significantly shorter onset times as well as more irregularities for posed than for spontaneous expressions, seated subjects before a one-way mirror and instructed them to convince an observer behind the mirror of the genuineness of the expression. It is possible that the discrepancies in findings regarding the differences between posed and spontaneous expressions are caused by these variations in the posing tasks. Namely, both Ekman and Friesen (1982) and Weiss et al. (1987) instructed their subjects explicitly to deceive an observer. In the present study, however, subjects were only asked to pose the expression as well as possible. On the other hand, both in Weiss et al.'s and in this study significantly more phases were found for voluntary expressions and in both cases the expressions were posed, while the subjects in Ekman and Friesen's study interacted with an interviewer during the deception task. As mentioned before, it is possible that subjects in this study carefully approached an ideal pose, thereby producing the larger number of phases. Subjects received no explicit instructions to deceive an observer and therefore may not have cared to produce a dynamically convincing expression, thereby obscuring some of the temporal differences found by Ekman and Friesen (1982). However, one can assume that differences in the number of phases will still be found between spontaneous and deliberate expressions, even if subjects explicitly attempt to deceive an observer, since these differences are an expression of the closed control loop nature of a deliberate expression.

Experiment 2

To investigate the hypothesis that the findings of Experiment 1, indicating that deliberate facial expressions differ from spontaneous facial expressions, in that they are more irregular, but not with respect to the length of onset and offset times, are *specific* to posed expressions, the general paradigm employed in Experiment 1 was replicated. Again, spontaneous and deliberate facial expressions of happiness and disgust were elicited. As before, the spontaneous and deliberate facial expressions of happiness and disgust were elicited from all subjects. As before in the video condition, the spontaneous expressions were recorded while subjects watched humour- and disgust-provoking video segments under conditions where they presumed themselves to be alone and not under observation. However, in Experiment 2 the deliberate facial expressions were obtained while subjects watched the same video segments under explicit instructions to *deceive* others, who would view them on video-tape, about their emotional state. A cover story was employed to convince subjects that they were video-taped only during specific parts of the experiment.

The deliberate expressions were expected to differ from the spontaneous, emotion elicited, expressions in two ways (a) deliberate expressions should have shorter (average) onset and offset times and should be of longer duration; and (b) deliberate expressions should have more onset, offset, and total phases.

Method

Subjects

Twenty-three male and 25 female undergraduates participated individually in a 45 minute session. They were each paid $6.

Tasks

Subjects were informed at the outset that they would perform three different tasks and were given some information regarding each of the tasks. During the first task, they were to simply watch two brief videos on surgery and comedy. The general purpose of this task was to familiarize subjects with the kind of material they would be viewing. For the second task subjects were instructed to watch a different set of surgery and comedy videos while not attempting to inhibit their facial reactions since they would be video-taped. The intent of this instruction was to lead subjects to believe that the only difference between the first and the second task was the fact that they would be video-taped during the second task, but not the first. In fact, the spontaneous expressions of happiness and disgust were taken from the first task; expressions from the second task were not further analysed. For the third task subjects were told that they would again see happy and disgusting video segments, but this time they were instructed to deceive an observer about their actual emotional state by showing an emotional facial expression congruent not with the emotional state invoked by the video they were seeing but with the other video stimulus. Subjects were reminded that they would be filmed by a video camera hidden in the experimental setup. During this third task subjects saw the same video episodes they had seen during task 1.

Self-report Measures

Following each task subjects completed a self-report form regarding the difficulty of the task (on a 7-point Likert scale) and the intensity with which they felt each of the following emotions during the task (on 5-point Likert scales: 0—not at all; 4—very intense): peacefulness, fear, anger, happiness, interest, sadness, and disgust. They also rated on two 7-point scales how repulsive and how amusing each video episode was.

Stimuli

Two surgery and two comedy sequences were employed. The sequences were edited to be approximately 2:30 minutes in length. The episodes were selected from a larger pool of stimuli that had been rated for funniness and repulsiveness by subjects drawn from the same population as the sample used here. The episodes chosen were of approximately the same degree of funniness and repulsiveness respectively (see Kappas, 1989). All episodes were presented in colour and with the original sound track.

Procedure

Subjects, who participated individually, first read a consent form explaining (1) that they would be video-taped at various times during the experiment, (2) the nature of the deceptive task, and (3) that observers would later watch the video records and try to detect the deception. The form asked for permission to use the video records for this purpose. Subjects then watched one funny and one repulsive video. They were told that they would not be video-taped during this task, but that they should pay careful attention to the videos in preparation for the deception task. Following the completion of this first task, the experimenter reminded the subjects that they would be video-taped from then on.

The second and third tasks were counterbalanced between subjects. All subjects received detailed instructions before each task. The video stimuli were presented in an order counter-balanced between subjects. For subjects 19 through 48 this procedure was amended. Observations by the experimenter and the debriefing interviews suggested that subjects were initially quite nervous, because they did not know precisely what to expect and felt somewhat intimidated by the experimental set-up. To help subjects to relax before the experiment and to acquaint them with the experimental procedure a 2:00-minute nature film was shown, before the instructions for the first task were given. Subjects were told to just relax and to watch the film to 'settle down before the experiment.'

Following the experiment subjects were fully debriefed. Permission to use the video records from task 1 was obtained.

Results

Manipulation Check

Table 12.3 shows the means and standard deviations as a function of emotion and condition for all subjects. The data show that subjects felt moderate happiness and disgust during the spontaneous happy and disgust conditions. Further, they felt moderately disgusted during the episodes during which they were asked to show deliberate

TABLE 12.3. Means for self-reported emotional state by emotion condition and elicitation condition

	Spontaneous		Deliberate*	
Emotional state	Happy	Disgust	Happy	Disgust
Happiness	2.10(1.0)	0.08(0.35)	0.46(0.74)	1.21(1.3)
Disgust	0.08(0.35)	2.46(1.3)	1.90(1.1)	0.46(0.68)

* Note that subjects were supposed to employ a masking deception as the deliberate expression. That is subjects who showed a happy facial expression felt disgust and *vice versa*.

expressions of happiness. However, the mean rating of happiness over all subjects for the condition where subjects were asked to show deliberate expressions of disgust are quite low.

Multiple Regression Analyses

Parallel to Experiment 1, the self-reports were employed to select episodes during which subjects felt the target emotions. For all subjects the first expression during each condition was analysed, if the self-report criterion was fulfilled, resulting in a set of 95 expressions. As again, different subjects contributed differing numbers of expressions, the two-step multiple regression procedure described for Experiment 1 was employed.

Time Data

For all variables except average length of apex phases significant or marginally significant condition and emotion effects were found (onset: multiple R: 0.29, $p < 0.05$; offset: multiple R: 0.36, $p < 0.05$; total phase length: multiple R: 0.34, $p < 0.05$). Inspection of the beta weights showed that posed expressions had significantly shorter average onset, offset, and overall phase lengths and happy expressions had longer average onset, offset, and overall phase lengths. Table 12.4 shows the beta values for the four variables and the mean residuals as a function of emotion and elicitation condition. The average phase length over all conditions was (in 10th of seconds) $M = 13.10$ ($S.D. = 5.62$, $Md = 11.75$).

A parallel analysis was conducted for the four phase variables. Table 12.5 shows the beta weights for the phase variables (multiple R's: onset: 0.44, $p < 0.001$; offset: 0.50, $p < 0.001$; apex: 0.46, $p < 0.001$; total: 0.49, $p < 0.001$) and the mean residuals as a function of emotion and elicitation condition.

For all four variables a significant or marginally significant emotion and condition effect as well as an emotion × condition interaction emerged. Inspection of the beta weights revealed that posed expressions had more onset, offset, apex and total phases and that happy expressions had more onset, offset, apex and total phases than disgust expressions. These effects were modified by an emotion × condition interaction which suggests that while the trend was the same for disgust and happy expressions, a marked difference between posed and spontaneous expressions was found only for happy expressions.

TABLE 12.4. (a) Mean residuals for phase length averages as a function of emotion and elicitation condition. (b) Beta values for phase length averages as a function of elicitation condition and emotion

	Spontaneous		Deliberate	
(a) Emotional state	Happy	Disgust	Happy	Disgust
Onset	0.54(3.1)	0.28(1.9)	0.21(3.3)	−1.77(2.1)
Offset	4.48(11.6)	−2.04(4.7)	1.39(9.0)	−4.11(6.2)
Apex	−0.08(9.7)	0.58(11.4)	0.78(9.7)	−1.83(6.8)
Total	1.38(3.8)	−0.31(3.7)	0.11(3.9)	−2.50(3.1)

(b) Variable	Onset	Offset	Apex	Total
Condition	0.21*	0.21†	n.s	0.22†
Emotion	0.19*	0.24†	n.s.	−0.28†
Interaction	n.s.	n.s.	n.s.	n.s

*$p < 0.01$
† $p < 0.05$

TABLE 12.5. (a) Mean residuals for irregularities as a function of emotion and elicitation condition. (b) Beta values for number of phases as a function of elicitation condition and emotion

	Spontaneous		Deliberate	
(a) Irregularities	Happy	Disgust	Happy	Disgust
Onset	−0.26(1.1)	−0.49(1.1)	1.02(1.6)	−0.35(1.2)
Offset	−0.15(0.99)	−0.54(0.88)	0.96(1.3)	−0.40(0.83)
Apex	−0.11(1.4)	−0.81(1.6)	1.37(2.2)	−0.74(1.3)
Total	−0.52(3.2)	−1.83(3.4)	3.35(4.8)	−1.49(3.0)

(b) Variable	Onset	Offset	Apex	Total
Condition	−0.25*	−0.27†	−0.21*	−0.25*
Emotion	0.28†	0.37‡	0.37‡	0.36†
Interaction	−0.20§	−0.21*	−0.19§	−0.21*

*$p < 0.05$.
† $p < 0.01$.
‡ $p < 0.001$.
§ $p < 0.1$.

Discussion

The results for the phase variables for the disgust expressions differ from the results of Experiment 1. In Experiment 1 the posed disgust expressions had the largest number of onset, offset, apex, and total phases, while in Experiment 2 the largest number of phases was found for the voluntary happy expressions. This difference may be due to the nature of the voluntary disgust expressions in the second experiment. In the first experiment, subjects were asked to pose the expressions while watching a neutral nature film. The choice of expression was left to them and they could concentrate on an ideal pose. In the second experiment, subjects were watching a comedy routine while attempting to deceive an observer that they were actually watching a surgery film. Further, subjects reported difficulty with this task in Experiment 2 and subjects' deliberate disgust expressions in Experiment 1 seemed to model on a vomiting reaction (mouth open, tongue show, etc.) which is highly incongruent with watching a comedy episode. These factors seem to combine to elicit a set of disgust expressions quite different from the ones elicited in Experiment 1.

General Discussion

As expected the results regarding the dynamic parameters predicted to differ between spontaneous and deliberate expressions, onset time and offset time, were different for the two experiments. The results of Experiment 1 were not consistent with the hypotheses. Neither for the happy nor for the disgust expressions were significant differences in onset and offset time found between elicitation conditions. However, deliberate expressions showed more phases or irregularities (pauses and stepwise intensity changes) than spontaneous expressions, a difference suggested by Ekman and Friesen (1982) for which Weiss et al. (1987) reported some evidence.

Experiment 2 is in large part a replication of Experiment 1 and was conducted to investigate whether the failure in Experiment 1 to support Ekman and Friesen's (1982) notions that deliberate emotional facial expressions should have shorter onset and offset times was due to differences in the elicitation of the deliberate expressions between Experiment 1 and their experiment. Therefore, the deliberate expressions in Experiment 2 were elicited by asking subjects to deceive an observer about their emotional state by masking it with an incongruent emotional expression.

Regarding onset and offset times, the results are consistent with the view that differences in onset and offset time should be evident when subjects are explicitly asked to deceive an observer. Regarding the number of irregularities the same main effect for condition was found as in Experiment 1; deliberate expressions were characterized by more onset, offset, apex, and total phases.

In Experiment 2, but not in Experiment 1, an emotion × condition interaction was found; deliberate happy expressions had a larger number of phases than spontaneous happy expressions, but the opposite was the case for the disgust expressions. Because subjects had to mask an underlying positive affect in Experiment 2, but were quite free in choosing an expression in Experiment 1, one might argue that the deliberate disgust expressions might differ for the two experiments. FACS scores obtained in Experiment 1, suggest that subjects were posing a type of disgust associated with vomiting (e.g.

mouth open, tongue show), this type of expression was probably incongruent with watching a comedy film. In addition, there is evidence that a wider range of disgust expressions than of happy expressions exists (Wiggers, 1982). If this is the case, subjects might have chosen a different disgust display as more appropriate for masking in Experiment 2 than the one chosen for posing in Experiment 1.

In summary, Experiment 2 provided evidence in support of the notion that onset and offset times differ between elicitation conditions. Offset times were significantly shorter for deliberate than for spontaneous expressions, for onset times the effect was marginally significant.

Moreover, spontaneous and deliberate happy facial expressions differed in the number of phases; this finding replicated the findings from Experiment 1. In Experiment 2, but not in Experiment 1, an emotion × condition interaction was found for the number of phases. This may be related to the nature of the deceptive disgust expressions chosen by the subjects in the two experiments.

In comparing the results from Experiments 1 and 2 regarding the nature of the facial behaviours displayed, both similarities and differences are present. For the happy expressions the findings regarding the differences between spontaneous and deliberate facial expressions in the number of phases from Experiment 1 were replicated in Experiment 2. For the disgust expressions, on the other hand, the findings differed between Experiments 1 and 2. Namely, only in Experiment 1 were deliberate disgust expressions characterized by a marked increase in the number of phases compared to the spontaneous expressions. As noted earlier, this might be, because subjects in Experiment 1 chose to display a different type of disgust expression (vomiting) than those in Experiment 2. While there are different facial expressions of disgust, there is only one expression, the smile, of happiness, allowing for less choice on the part of the subjects.

Why do spontaneous and deliberate facial expressions differ regarding irregularities or phases? Spontaneous and deliberate facial expressions are mediated by different neurological pathways and spontaneous emotion elicited expressions are believed to be generally more reflex-like, smooth and ballistic than deliberate expressions (see Rinn, 1984). Furthermore, it seems plausible that subjects who are asked to pose an expression have a specific view of an appropriate expression for that pose. In attempting to show that expression they are likely to use a closed-control loop approach, which disrupts the smooth dynamics of the expression. This type of control is likely to result in a 'ratcheting' of the expression.

It is interesting to note that the deliberate facial expressions of happiness were characterized by more irregularities in both Experiment 1 and Experiment 2. This, given the differences between the two experiments regarding the deliberate expressions, shows the finding to be relatively stable. For the first study one might argue that the subjects did not feel observed and therefore only concentrated on what the expression would look like at its apex, without attempting to make the overall expression convincing. In the second experiment, however, subjects were aware that they were video-taped and that at a later time observers would attempt to detect when they were showing the spontaneous expression and when they were showing a deceptive expression.

Following this argument fewer differences in aspects of the time course between spontaneous and deliberate facial expressions should have been found on Experiment

2. On the other hand the subject's task in Experiment 2 was somewhat more difficult than in Experiment 1. Subjects were asked to display an emotional facial expression incongruent to the emotional state elicited by watching a video stimulus at the same time. The complexity of the situation, that is, the necessity to not display the emotion elicited by the video stimulus, while at the same time displaying an incongruent emotional facial expression, might have resulted in subjects neglecting to attempt to control the time course aspects of the expression. However, it is one of the characteristics of deceptive interactions that the deceiver is confronted with a complex situation and one can argue that the findings from this experiment are nevertheless generalizable to social situations outside the laboratory.

It is noteworthy, that the differences between spontaneous and deliberate facial expressions were found for both a negative and a positive emotional expression.[5] This allows the conclusion that the differences in the dynamics of spontaneous and deliberate facial expressions may generalize over emotions and are due to voluntary nature of the expressions more than the valence of the emotions expressed. However, comparing the findings from Experiments 1 and 2 suggests that the dimensions in which the expressions differ as well as the degree of the difference may be moderated by the intent of the deliberate expression (intended to represent a good pose or to deceive) and the emotion expressed.

In summary, the present research provides strong evidence for the notion that the irregularity of the expression differentiates spontaneous and deliberate happy expressions and tentative evidence for this difference in disgust expressions, while addressing some of the methodological concerns regarding previous research. Further, the diverging results concerning onset and offset times between the two studies emphasize the importance of distinctions between different realizations of the construct 'deliberate expression.' The results indicate that poses and 'masking deceptions', while sharing some characteristics, differ in their onset and offset times. Ekman and Friesen (1982) proposed a frame of reference regarding different types of deliberate smiles. The results reported here point to the necessity to extend this frame of reference to other emotional displays to guide future research interested in differences between spontaneous and deliberate facial expressions.

Notes

1. This is defined as time from the first visible facial movement to the apex of that movement.

2. Defined as the time from the end of the apex of the expression until the expression is no longer visible.

3. In Experiment 1 only, heart rate, skin conductance, and skin temperature were also measured; the sensors were attached to the subjects' left hand. Half the subjects employed a continuous self-report measure as well as the retrospective self-report. Results regarding these additional measures will not be discussed in this context.

4. The expressive episodes were identified using the FACS (Ekman & Friesen, 1978) scoring procedures. In addition to the time scores, complete FACS scores were obtained, but will not be discussed in this context.

5. While the difference in phases was not significant for the disgust expressions in the second experiment the means were in the same direction.

References

Bugenthal, D. B. (1986). Unmasking the polite smile: Situational and personal determinants of managed affect in adult–child interaction. *Personality and Social Psychology Bulletin, 12,* 7–16.

Campbell, R. (1986). Asymmetries of facial action: Some facts and fancies of normal face movements. In R. Bruyer (Ed.), *The Neuropsychology of Face Perception and Facial Expression* (pp. 247–267). Hillsdale, NJ: Erlbaum.

Cohen, J., & Cohen, P. (1983). *Applied multiple regression/correlation analysis for the behavioral sciences.* Hillsdale, NJ: Erlbaum.

DePaulo, B. M., Stone, J. I., & Lassiter, G. D. (1985). Deceiving and detecting deceit. In B. R. Schlenker (Ed.), *The self and social life.* New York: McGraw-Hill.

Ekman, P. (1978). Facial signs: Facts, fantasies, and possibilities. In T. Seboek (Ed.), *Sight, sound and sense* (pp. 124–156). Bloomington, IN: Indiana University Press.

Ekman, P. (1980). *Mistakes when deceiving.* Paper presented at the conference on the Clever Hands Phenomenon, New York Academy of Sciences, New York.

Ekman, P., & Friesen, W. V. (1969). Nonverbal leakage and cues to deception. *Psychiatry, 36,* 313–323.

Ekman, P., & Friesen, W. V. (1972). Hand movements. *Journal of Communication, 22,* 353–374.

Ekman, P., & Friesen, W. V. (1978). *Facial Action Coding System.* Palo Alto, CA: Consulting Psychologists Press.

Ekman, P., & Friesen, W. V. (1982). Felt, false, and miserable smiles. *Journal of Nonverbal Behavior, 6,* 238–252.

Ekman, P., Friesen, W. V., & Ancoli, S. (1980). Facial signs of emotional experience. *Journal of Personality and Social Psychology, 39,* 1125–1134.

Ekman, P., Hager, J. C., & Friesen, W. V. (1981). The symmetry of emotional and deliberate facial actions. *Psychophysiology, 18,* 101–106.

Goldman-Eisler, F. (1968). *Psycholinguistics: Experiments in spontaneous speech.* New York: Academic Press.

Hager, J. C., & Ekman, P. (1985). The asymmetry of facial actions is inconsistent with models of hemispheric specialization. *Psychophysiology, 22,* 307–318.

Kahneman, D. (1973). *Attention and effort.* Englewood Cliffs, NJ: Prentice-Hall.

Kappas, A. (1989). *Control of emotion.* Unpublished dissertation.

Kraut, R. E. (1980). Humans as lie detectors: Some second thoughts. *Journal of Communication, 30,* 209–216.

Lykken, D. T. (1979). The detection of deception. *Psychological Bulletin, 86,* 47–53.

Manstead, A. S. R. (1988). The role of facial movement in emotion. In H. L. Wagner (Ed.), *Social psychophysiology: Theory and clinical application* (pp. 105–129). Chichester, England: John Wiley.

Mehrabian, A. (1971). Nonverbal betrayal of feeling. *Journal of Experimental Research in Personality, 5,* 64–73.

Rinn, W. E. (1984). The neuropsychology of facial expression: A review of the neurological and psychological mechanisms for producing facial expressions. *Psychological Bulletin, 95,* 52–77.

Weiss, F., Blum, G. S., & Gleberman, L. (1987). Anatomically based measurement of facial expressions in simulated versus hypnotically induced affect. *Motivation and Emotion, 11,* 67–81.

Wiggers, M. (1982). Judgements of facial expressions of emotion predicted from facial behavior. *Journal of Nonverbal Communication, 7,* 101–116.

Zuckerman, M., DePaulo, B. M., & Rosenthal, R. (1981). Verbal and nonverbal communication of deception. In L. Berkowitz (Ed.), *Advances in experimental social psychology* (Vol. 14; pp. 1–59). New York: Academic Press.

AFTERWORD

Objective Differences versus Observers' Ratings

URSULA HESS

The research presented in the preceding article focused on the objective differences between spontaneous and deliberate emotional facial expressions measured using FACS. The differences found, with regard to both the presence of AU6 for spontaneous but not for deliberate smiles and the differences in the temporal structure, that both types of expressions are potentially observable by a decoder. Thus, the question emerges as to whether these differences serve as cues for observers asked to discriminate between spontaneous and deliberate emotional facial expressions. This question was addressed by Hess and Kleck (1994). For this study, a subset of the expressions analyzed by Hess and Kleck (1990) were presented to observers who were asked to decide whether the expressions were spontaneous or deliberate. The results indicated that the overall decoding accuracy was low and overall not different from chance.

This finding is not surprising. For example, Frank, Ekman, and Friesen (1991), when asking observers to indicate whether an expression is a genuine expression of joy (Duchenne smile) or not, found a mean decoding accuracy of 56%.[1] Further, Ekman and O'Sullivan (1991) assessed the ability to detect smiles that mask a negative expression in people from a variety of professions, such as judges, psychiatrists, and law enforcement personnel, as well as of students. Interestingly, only secret service agents exceeded decoding accuracy around chance level. Similarly, Zuckerman, DePaulo, and Rosenthal (1981), in a review of the literature on a different but related issue, the decoding of deception, found a generally low decoding accuracy.

How can we explain these findings? As mentioned above, the objective differences between spontaneous and deliberate emotional facial expressions, and particularly between emotion elicited and deliberate smiles, are not so subtle as to be invisible. Further, certain groups of individuals, such as the secret service agents mentioned above, have been found to exceed the low decoding accuracy found for most individuals, showing that the distinction can be made.

To address this question, Hess and Kleck (1994) asked their subjects, following the experiment, to list the cues that they found helpful in discriminating emotion elicited and deliberate facial expressions. Path analysis was employed to test whether (1) the cues mentioned by the subjects were related to their judgments and (2) whether they represented valid cues. The results indicate that subjects do indeed tend to base their judgments the cues they claim to use, but also that some of these cues were not valid. The use of invalid cues may thus explain the lack of decoding accuracy. But why do subjects use invalid cues?

I have recently suggested that the use of invalid cues serves the everyday interactional rules (Hess, 1995). Specifically, everyday interactions are guided by social roles and norms. Display rules (Wundt, 1903; Ekman & Friesen, 1971) demand the display of certain emotions in certain situations. Social roles such as gender roles also demand the display or suppression of certain emotions in certain contexts (see Fischer, 1993, for a review).

These rules are usually shared between encoder and decoder. Thus, one may hypothesize that while the encoder strives to display the emotion appropriate to the situation, the decoder strives to decode the emotion display in accord with the same rules. That is, a smooth interaction demands a cooperation between encoder and decoder in accordance with the social norms and rules governing the situation.

Note

1. However, when asked to directly compare an enjoyment and a nonenjoyment expression of the same person, decoding accuracy was markedly higher (74%).

References

Ekman, P., Davidson, R. J., & Friesen, W. V. (1990). The Duchenne smile: Emotional expression and brain physiology II. *Journal of Personality and Social Psychology, 58,* 342–353.

Ekman, P., & Friesen, W. V. (1971). Constants across cultures in the face and emotion. *Journal of Personality and Social Psychology, 17,* 124–129.

Ekman, P., & O'Sullivan, M. (1991). Who can catch a liar? *American Psychologist, 46,* 913–920.

Frank, M. G., Ekman, P., & Friesen, W. V. (1993). Behavioral markers and recognizability of the smile of enjoyment. *Journal of Personality and Social Psychology, 64,* 83–93.

Fischer, A. (1993). Sex differences in emotionality: Fact or stereotype? *Feminism & Psychology, 3,* 303–318.

Hess, U. (1995). *Émotion ressentie et simulée.* Paper presented at the 25th Journées d'études de l'APSLF, Coimbra, Portugal, September 14–16.

Hess, U., & Kleck, R. E. (1990). Differentiating emotion elicited and deliberate emotional facial expressions. *European Journal of Social Psychology, 20,* 369–385.

Hess, U., & Kleck, R. E. (1994). The cues decoders use in attempting to differentiate emotion elicited and posed facial expressions. *European Journal of Social Psychology, 24,* 367–381.

Wundt, W. (1903). *Grundzüge der physiologischen Psychologie.* Leipzig: Wilhelm Engelmann.

Zuckerman, M., DePaulo, B. M., & Rosenthal, R. (1981). Verbal and nonverbal communication of deception. In L. Berkowitz (Ed.), *Advances in experimental social psychology* (pp. 1–59). New York: Academic Press.

13

Japanese and American Infants' Responses to Arm Restraint

LINDA A. CAMRAS, HARRIET OSTER, JOSEPH J. CAMPOS,
KAZUO MIYAKE & DONNA BRADSHAW

To a considerable degree, the recent resurgence of interest in emotion within developmental psychology rests on the striking evidence produced almost a quarter of a century ago which demonstrated that certain basic emotions have universally recognized facial expressions (Ekman & Friesen, 1971; Ekman, Sorenson, & Friesen, 1969; Izard, 1971). The data on recognition are often assumed to entail corresponding universality in the production of these prototypic expressions. However, recent research on concept formation (Strauss, 1979) has shown that prototype recognition may be based on abstraction from exemplars that never exactly correspond to the target itself. Furthermore, evidence for the universality of adult facial expressions does not necessarily imply developmental fixity (Oster & Ekman, 1978; Oster, Hegley, & Nagel, in press). Therefore, despite universality in recognition, individual, cultural, and age differences may exist in the spontaneous production of emotional facial expressions. Direct examination of spontaneous facial behavior is necessary both to confirm the universality of adult expressions of emotion and to explicate their origins and development.

This study represents the first step in a broad cross-cultural investigation designed to clarify some of these issues through the study of infant facial expression. Herein we present an initial comparison of Japanese and American infants' responses to non-painful arm restraint, a powerful emotion elicitor for American infants (Stenberg & Campos, 1990; Stenberg, Campos, & Emde, 1983). Because Japanese and American adults are known to differ in their publicly observable expressive behavior (Ekman, 1972), we believe that a comparison of Japanese and American infants provides a fruitful starting point for cross-cultural investigation.

Several recent studies reported differences in the behavior and experiences of Japanese and American infants that might be relevant to our study. For example, in 1980 Kosawa (cited in Azuma, 1982) found Japanese neonates to be more irritable and less soothable than American infants during administration of the Brazelton Neonatal Behavioral Assessment Scale. In contrast, Lewis (1989; Lewis, Ramsay, & Kawakami, 1991) reported that 3- to 5-month-old Japanese infants exhibited less distress than American infants during pediatric examinations and in response to a diptheria-pertussis-tetanus (DPT) inoculation. However, the cortisol "stress" responses of the Japanese infants were greater than those of the American infants. This latter finding underscores the importance of obtaining multiple measures of emotional response to aid in the interpretation of similarities and differences in facial expression.

Although temperament is often invoked to explain cross-cultural differences in infants' emotional reactivity, the contrast between Kosawa's and Lewis's findings suggests that social experience may also play a critical role, at least in the postneonatal period. Differences in the attitudes and behaviors of Japanese versus American mothers potentially could affect their infants' responses to our arm restraint procedure. In comparison to American mothers, Japanese mothers both assume and desire a closer infant–mother interdependence (Bornstein, Miyake, & Tamis-LeMonda, 1986; Caudill & Weinstein, 1969; Chen & Miyake, 1986; Doi, 1973; Lebra, 1976; Miyake, Campos, Bradshaw, & Kagan, 1986). This cultural difference is reflected in maternal practices such as extensive infant carrying and co-sleeping. Such practices might make physical restraint a less unusual and intrusive stimulus for Japanese infants.

With regard to communication, Japanese and American mothers show similar rates of facial, vocal, and tactile behaviors during face-to-face interactions in the laboratory. However, American mothers contingently respond to their infants' gaze with facial expressions and vocalizations, whereas Japanese mothers respond with facial expressions, leaning close, and touching (Fogel, Toda, & Kawai, 1988). In the home, Japanese mothers are reported to rarely display overt expressions of anger toward their infants, to try to minimize infant crying, and to generally be more emotionally indulgent than American mothers (Doi, 1973; Lebra, 1976; Miyake et al., 1986). Japanese mothers also value a quiet infant more than do American mothers, possibly because the structure of Japanese housing limits auditory privacy. Thus Japanese and American infants might differ in their emotional or expressive responses or both because of their differing histories of social interaction.

Developmental factors might also affect infants' responses to our arm restraint procedure. For example, changes in infants' motor capabilities, in conjunction with their developing appreciation of self as a physical agent, might produce a change in infants' appreciation or appraisal of externally imposed physical restraint. Thus younger infants might appraise physical restraint as less of an impediment than older infants might. Consequently, our procedure might elicit a less negative emotional response in younger infants. At the same time, irrespective of age differences in the elicitation of emotion, we might find age differences in the facial expression of the elicited emotions. This might result from a maturationally determined increase or decrease in expressiveness or from social experience (see Kaye, 1982; Malatesta, Culver, Tesman, & Shepard, 1989; Malatesta & Haviland, 1985; Tronick, Als, & Adamson, 1979).

As implied by the preceding discussion, cross-cultural and developmental investigations of emotional expression must maintain both a conceptual and empirical distinction between expression and emotion. In the present investigation, we accomplished this end by collecting nonfacial as well as facial measures of infant behavior. Our strategy was to compare infants' facial expressions during episodes that elicit comparable emotional responses as indicated by nonfacial measures (body activity and vocalization).

A second strategy was the use of a theoretically nonbiased facial measurement system, Baby FACS (Oster & Rosenstein, 1991). Baby FACS is an anatomically based facial coding system adapted for infants' facial morphology from Ekman and Friesen's

(1978) adult Facial Action Coding System (FACS). In contrast to the widely used MAX (Izard, 1979) and AFFEX (Izard, Dougherty, & Hembree, 1983) coding systems, Baby FACS objectively describes infant facial behavior without making a priori assumptions about the emotions being expressed. Because considerable debate exists as to whether certain infant facial configurations represent discrete negative emotions or less differentiated states of negative affect (Camras, Malatesta, & Izard, 1991; Oster et al., in press), an objective measurement system is necessary to allow for the investigation of similarities and differences in facial behavior independent of this debate. However, we reconsider this controversy in our discussion.

In summary, in the present article we report an initial investigation of Japanese and American infants' emotional and expressive responses to nonpainful arm restraint. We hope to illustrate a productive strategy that uses both facial and nonfacial measures for the investigation of cross-cultural similarities and differences in expressive behavior.

Method

Subjects

The subjects were thirteen 5-month-old American infants (5 boys and 8 girls), seven 12-month-old American infants (3 boys and 4 girls), and 13 Japanese infants (9 boys and 4 girls) who participated in the procedure at both 5 months and 12 months of age. Of the American infants, 3 participated at both 5 and 12 months, whereas the others participated only once in the procedure. The sample included all infants from a larger pilot study whose tapes were available for coding and who met the inclusion criterion described further on.

Procedure

The procedure was conducted in the home for the 5-month-old infants and in the laboratory for the 12-month-olds. The infant was seated in a reclining infant seat (5 months) or a high chair (12 months) with the mother seated on the infant's right side and also facing the camera. The experimenter faced the infant and was positioned in front and slightly to the infant's left so as not to obscure the camera's view.

For the restraint procedure, the experimenter gently grasped the infant's wrists and folded the hands across the infant's stomach. The hands were held until the experimenter judged the infant to show distress or for a maximum of 3 min. The procedure was videotaped using portable videorecording equipment. The tape showed the infant's face, upper body, and hands.

A preliminary viewing of the videotapes revealed that the Japanese and American experimenters differed either in their intuitive judgments of distress or their understanding of the instructions or both; American infants were released sooner than Japanese infants. Therefore, an objective criterion (involving facial measurement as described in the next section) was later established for inclusion of subjects in the data analysis. Only those infants whose arms were held for 3 min or until they met the facial distress criterion were included in the analyses reported here. Thus, 3 American infants (one 5-month-old and two 12-month-olds) were videotaped but were not included in the study because they were released before showing clear signs of distress (after restraint for 77, 36, and 83 s, respectively).

Coding

Facial Behavior

The infants' facial expressions were coded using Ekman and Friesen's (1978) FACS and Oster and Rosenstein's (1991) Baby FACS. FACS is a comprehensive, anatomically based system, the units of which are discrete, minimally distinguishable actions of the facial muscles. FACS describes appearance changes produced by actions of single facial muscles or muscle combinations (termed *action units,* or AUs). Baby FACS is a modification of FACS that specifies critical differences between adults and infants in the appearance changes produced by the actions of the facial muscles. Coding was performed using a Sony 420 videorecorder/player that allows tapes to be played both forward and backward at variable speed. Coders identified the onset and offset of individual AUs and grouped these units into temporally defined "configurations" according to FACS rules.

Because the Japanese and American experimenters differed in the degree of distress they allowed the infants to reach, a coding interval was identified that was comparable for all subjects. The interval began when the infants two wrists were grasped and ended either (1) after the infant displayed an objectively defined negative-affect facial expression lasting for a minimum of 1.5 s or (2) after 3 min of restraint without such an expression being displayed. Criterion negative-affect expressions were defined based on previous research by a variety of investigators of infant "cry faces" and negative emotional expressions (Camras, 1991, in press; Izard, Hembree, & Huebner, 1987; Izard & Malatesta, 1987; Oster, 1982; Oster, Hegley, & Nagel, 1988; Young & Decarie, 1977). These expressions involved lowered, oblique, or raised and drawn together brow movements (AUs 4.1.1 + 4, or 1 + 2 + 4) and an open (AUs 25, 26, or 27) and laterally stretched mouth (AU 20) with or without other accompanying middle or lower face actions, (most commonly AUs 9, 10, 16, or 17). Eyes were narrowed (AU 7), squinted (AU 6), or squeezed closed (AU 43).

Activity

The infants' body movements were rated on a 5-point activity scale that incorporates specific types of body movements in response to arm restraint (e.g., pushing out the elbows, raising the shoulders, arching the back) and qualitative aspects of the infants' movements (e.g., frequency, speed, vigor, diversity, and spatial range). The scale ranged from 1 (*very passive*) to 5 (*extremely active struggling*). A rating of 1 represents very passive behavior; 3 represents mild struggling; and 5 represents extremely active struggling, with vigorous postural movements as well as strong and rapid movements of the head and limbs. For each restraint episode, coders identified the latency to the first struggle (an activity rating of 3 or higher) and the maximum activity level scored during the criterion coding interval.

Vocalizations

Vocalizations were coded using a modification of Thompson and Lamb's (1984) vocalization scale. Vocalizations in the negative range that were different cry types but equivalent in intensity of negative affect were combined, yielding a more equally spaced 8-point scale with vocalizations rated from 1 (*intense delight*) through 4 (*neutral*) to 8 (*intense distress*). Thompson and Lamb's Categories 5 and 6 were combined into our Category 5 (*mild distress*), Categories 8 and 9 into our Category 6 (*moderate distress*), Categories 10 and 11 into our Category 7 (full cry, *clear-cut distress*), and Categories 12–14 into our Category 8 (*intense distress*). Thompson and Lamb's Category 7 was eliminated. For each restraint episode, coders scored latency to first negative vocalization (5 or greater) and maximum vocalization rating within the criterion coding episode.

Training and Reliability

Four facial expression coders were trained and certified to use the FACS and were also trained in the Baby FACS modification. In addition, a conventionally accepted level of facial coding reliability (greater than 70%; Ekman & Friesen, 1978) was established in scoring the specific materials of this study. Reliability was maintained by holding weekly meetings during which coders jointly reviewed samples from the videotapes and discussed problems and ambiguities encountered during the previous week of coding.

Body activity and vocalizations were scored by two coders who were unfamiliar with the facial scoring. Reliabilities represented by correlations between the two coders were as follows: $r(33) = .80$ for latency to negative vocalization (mean difference between coders = 1.69 s); $r(39) = .81$ for vocalization category score (mean difference = 0.39); $r(17) = .98$ for latency to struggle (mean difference = 3.05 s); and $r(39) = .90$ for activity category score (mean difference = 0.29).

Results

To compare infants' nonfacial indicators of negative affect, the maximum body activity and vocalization scores were examined in two Kruskal-Wallace nonparametric analyses of variance (ANOVAs). No significant effects were obtained, indicating that infants in all groups reached similar levels of negative affect within the coding interval. Data inspection showed that 87% of the infants produced a negative vocalization (vocalization score of 5 or greater) and that 52% physically struggled in response to the restraint (activity score of 3 or greater).

Infants' responses were further compared in a 2 (age) × 2 (culture) multivariate analysis of variance (MANOVA) that used three measures of latency to negative affect: latency to criterion negative facial expression, latency to negative vocalization (vocalization score of 5 or greater), and latency to struggle (activity score of 3 or greater).[1] If no criterion negative action occurred, the duration of the coding interval itself was entered as a conservative measure. The analysis yielded a significant overall effect for age, $F(3.40) = 7.44$, $p < .0005$, and significant age effects for all three univariate analyses; $F(1, 42) = 22.8$, $p < .0001$, for facial expression; $F(1, 42) = 9.9$, $p < .003$, for struggle; and $F(1, 42) = 7.08$, $p < .02$, for vocalization. All three measures indicated that 12-month-olds became distressed more quickly than 5-month-olds in both cultures (see table 13.1).

To examine the patterning of facial responses, we identified configurations hypothesized to represent some form of negative affect by both discrete and nondiscrete

TABLE 13.1. Latency (in seconds) to negative-affect behaviors

| | Age × Culture group | | | |
| | 5-month-olds | | 12-month-olds | |
Criterion behavior	Japanese	American	Japanese	American
Facial expression	125.5	63.1	13.4	8.2
Vocalization	51.6	45.0	11.9	5.7
Struggling	84.8	52.5	16.1	7.0

emotion theorists. These included all configurations that qualified as criterion negative-affect expressions and also all configurations that included a criterion-face brow and eye configuration accompanied by a strong upward movement of the lower lip (AU 17) with or without an additional lowering of the mouth corners (AU 15). These latter mouth configurations have been described as components of sadness (Izard et al., 1983) or alternatively as "pouts" and "horseshoe mouth" faces (Oster, 1982; Oster & Ekman, 1978). All identified expressions would be coded in Baby FACS as showing negative affect (variants of cry or precry faces) and in Izard's AFFEX system as distress-pain, anger, sadness, fear, or a blend of these emotions.

Negative configurations produced during more than 3% of the coding interval (see table 13.2, Configurations 1, 3, and 4) were examined in a 2 (age) × 2 (culture)

TABLE 13.2. Proportional duration of facial configurations

Configuration	FACS/Baby FACS action units[a]	% of coding interval
1	4 + 6/7 + 20b + 26/27 ± 9, 10, 11, 16, 17, 23	14.04
2	6 + 12b ± 25/26/27	5.03
3	4 + 6/7 + 20b + 25 ± 9, 10, 11, 16, 17, 23	4.20
4	4 + 43 + 20b + 26/27 ± 9, 10, 11, 16, 17, 23	3.06
5	1 ± 4 + 6/7 + 20b + 26/27 ± 9, 10, 11, 16, 17, 23	1.97
6	1 ± 4 + 6/7 + 20b + 25 ± 9, 10, 11, 16, 17, 23	1.67
7	4 + 43 + 20b + 25 ± 9, 10, 11, 16, 17, 23	1.37
8	1 + 2 + 4 + 5/6/7 + 20b + 26/27 ± 9, 10, 11, 16, 17, 23	0.70
9	1 ± 4 + 6/7 + 17c ± 15	0.17
10	1 + 2 + 4 + 5/6/7 + 17c ± 15	0.17
11	1 + 2 + 4 + 5/6/7 + 20b + 25 ± 9, 10, 11, 16, 17, 23	0.11
12	4 + 6/7 + 17c ± 15	0.03

Note: According to Oster, Hegley, and Nagel (in press) and Camras (in press), tentative interpretations of these configurations are as follows: intense distress or "cry faces" (Configurations 1, 4, 5, and 8), less intense distress or "fuss faces" (Configurations 3, 6, 7, and 11), pouts or horseshoe-mouth faces (Configurations 9, 10, and 12), and enjoyment (Configuration 2). AFFEX interpretations (Izard, Doughterty, & Hembree, 1983) for Configurations 1 through 12 are as follows: (1) anger, (2) enjoyment, (3) anger/fear blend, (4) distress/pain, (5) sad/anger blend, (6) sad/fear blend, (7) distress-pain/fear blend, (8) fear/anger blend, (9) sad, (10) fear/sad blend, (11) fear, and (12) anger/sad blend. FACS = Facial Action Coding System (Ekman & Friesen, 1978); Baby FACS = FACS adapted for infants (Oster & Rosenstein, 1991).

[a] Alternative action units (AUs) are indicated by /. Optional AUs are indicated by ±. Designated intensity levels (i.e., lowercase letters) indicate minimum intensities.

MANOVA which used scores representing the configurations' proportional durations within the coding interval subjected to the arcsine transformation. Because of their theoretical interest, enjoyment smiles (Configuration 2, AU 6 + 12) were also included in the analysis. The analysis yielded a significant overall effect for age, $F(4, 39) = 4.38$, $p < .006$, with significant univariate age effects for the three negative-affect configurations: $F(1, 42) = 6.07$, $p < .02$, for Configuration 1; $F(1, 42) = 5.22$, $p < .03$, for Configuration 3; and $F(1, 42) = 4.96$ for Configuration 4. These results indicate that 12-month-olds displayed more negative facial expressions than 5-month-olds in both cultures.

An additional within-subjects ANOVA compared infants' production of the three negative-affect configurations. A significant effect was yielded, $F(1, 45) = 49.8$, $p < .0001$. Inspection of the data (see table 13.2) showed that Configuration 1 was produced more often than Configurations 3 and 4.

Because the same Japanese infants were tested at both ages, correlations were computed between 5 months' and 12 months' scores for the physical activity, vocalization, and four most frequent facial expression variables. A significant result was obtained only for latency to negative vocalization, $r(11) = .57$, $p < .05$.

Although no significant effect for culture were obtained in these analyses, inspection of the data suggested that some differences might not have been detected owing to the small number of American 12-month-old subjects and the consequently considerable imbalance in cell size. Therefore, we conducted a set of parallel analyses comparing only the 5-month-old infants across cultures. A significant effect for culture was obtained only in the univariate analysis examining latency to criterion negative-affect facial expression, $F(1, 42) = 4.63$, $p < .05$. Although this analysis must serve primarily as a basis for further investigation, it suggests that 5-month-old American infants display negative facial expressions more quickly than 5-month-old Japanese infants (see table 13.1). Inspection of the means for 12-month-old infants further suggests that cultural differences are greatly reduced by that age.

Discussion

In this study we found significant age differences in infants' facial and nonfacial responses to an arm restraint procedure. Regarding cultural differences, Japanese and American infants differed only in their latency to our criterion facial response at 5 months. No cultural differences were found in the types or proportional distribution of facial expressions. Our results thus lend support to the hypothesis that infant facial expressions of emotion are universal.

The cultural difference we found in latency to facial distress at 5 months is consistent with Lewis et al.'s (1991) findings that Japanese infants displayed less overt distress than American infants during DPT inoculations and contrasts with Kosawa's (cited in Azuma, 1982) finding that Japanese neonates are more irritable during the Brazelton examination. However, Lewis et al. also found that Japanese infants showed a greater cortisol "stress" response than American infants, which appears more consistent with Kosawa's results. Taken together, these data suggest that Japanese infants' overt expression of negative affect may begin to be attenuated even during the first few months of life. Consistent with this notion, in our study, Japanese and American

5-month-olds did not differ in latency or intensity of struggling, although they did differ in their latency to facial response. Although we did not find differences in vocal expression in our study, possibly these also would emerge beyond the duration of our coding interval.

As indicated earlier, differences in cultural values and socialization practices are likely to contribute to Japanese versus American differences in infant expressive behavior. Japanese mothers are described as emotionally indulgent and view the minimization of infant distress as an important goal. In response, Japanese infants may initially show a less intense reaction than American infants to an aversive stimulus. However, as we found in our study, Japanese infants may eventually produce the same negative-affect facial expressions as American infants if their distress is not ameliorated.

It is interesting that by 12 months, the cultural difference in facial response latency had largely disappeared and no significant differences between Japanese and American infants were observed. This violates the usual expectation that cultural differences increase rather than decrease with development. Such generalizations thus fail to do justice to the complex interaction of cultural, socialization, temperamental, and developmental factors that underlie infants' responses to an emotion-eliciting event even during the 1st year of life (Barrett & Campos, 1987; Camras, in press; Fogel, Nwokah, & Dedo, in press; Lewis & Michalson, 1983).

More specifically, our study suggests that in some cases the early influence of temperament or socialization or both may be overwhelmed at a later age by the influence of developmental factors that are common across cultures. In our study, older infants reacted more quickly and displayed more negative facial affect than younger infants. This age difference indicates that infants' evaluation of arm restraint is not biologically "fixed" but is tied to developmental status. Because the latency differences were quite substantial (exceeding 30 s on all measures) and because equivalent levels of struggling eventually were reached, we do not believe our findings can be attributed solely to more general age differences in activity level or reaction time. Instead, we tentatively propose that several factors related to the development of goal-oriented behavior underlie infants' changing appreciation of the arm restraint procedure.

Between 5 and 12 months of age, directed reaching and grasping proceed from being newly emergent to highly developed motor skills. Furthermore, major advances in intentional behavior and elaboration of goals take place (Kagan, Kearsley, & Zelazo, 1978; Lewis & Brooks-Gunn, 1979; Piaget, 1952). Thus older infants are more likely than younger infants to have experienced and thus to expect successful goal attainment via controlled arm and hand movements. Such changing expectations with regard to specific arm movements may be facilitated by more generally changing expectations about directed action associated with the development of self-produced locomotion, which also emerges between 5 and 12 months (Bertenthal, Campos, & Barrett, 1984). With regard to our experimental procedure, we propose that because older infants have developed greater expectations as to the goal-contingent effectiveness of their motor actions in comparison to younger infants, they more greatly value control over their own behavior. Consequently, they more quickly respond to arm restraint as an impediment to their agency. This makes restraint an emotionally negative event.

Although we could not examine continuity over age in our American sample, correlational analyses of the Japanese infants' data indicated consistent individual differences in their latency to negative vocalization. This suggests some degree of continuity in expressive behavior similar to that reported by Izard et al. (1987) for a sample of American infants whose facial responses to a DPT inoculation were examined. Further research using larger sample sizes might reveal further consistencies in the facial and vocal response of Japanese and American infants to arm restraint.

Thus far we have described the nature of the infants' emotional response to arm restraint in general terms reflecting widespread agreement that their expressive behaviors reflect some form of negative affect. Beyond this, however, theorists would diverge considerably on the more specific interpretation of the facial configurations we observed. According to differential emotions theory (Izard, 1977; Izard et al., 1983; Malatesta-Magai & Izard, 1991), these configurations represented discrete negative emotions or blends of such discrete emotions (see table 13.2 note), with anger being the most common emotional expression observed. In contrast, several theorists and researchers (Bridges, 1932; Camras, in press; Camras et al., 1991; Matias & Cohn, 1989; Oster et al., 1988, in press; Young & Decarie, 1977) have argued that early in development these expressions are not differentially associated with different negative emotions. Thus, they may be better interpreted as distress or "cry faces." Completely resolving the issue of expression interpretation is beyond the scope of a single elicitor study because it must involve the comparison of facial responses across a range of emotion situations (for further discussions of this issue, see Camras et al., 1991; Fridlund, Ekman, & Oster, 1987; Hiatt, Campos, & Emde, 1979). Our ultimate goal is to examine a wider range of emotion-eliciting situations in order to produce an empirically based description and theory of infant emotional expression.

In conclusion, in this study we provided evidence that infants in two very different cultures show the same facial affect expressions. Strategically, the study represents an initial effort to investigate both universals and cultural differences in emotional facial expression by means of direct measurement of spontaneous infant behavior rather than observer judgments of preselected facial stimuli. We believe this approach is necessary for confirming the universality of facial expression. Furthermore, we believe our study demonstrates that objective facial coding is both feasible and productive in the cross-cultural study of emotional and expressive behavior in infants.

Note

1. Because of the small sample size, gender was not entered as a factor in the data analyses.

References

Azuma, H. (1982). Current trends in studies of behavioral development in Japan. *International Journal of Behavioral Development, 5,* 153–169.

Barrett, K., & Campos, J. (1987). Perspectives on emotional development: II. A functionalist approach to emotions. In J. Osofsky (Ed.), *Handbook of infant development* (2nd ed.; pp. 555–578). New York: Wiley.

Bertenthal, B., Campos, J., & Barrett, K. (1984). Self-produced locomotion: An organizer of emotional, cognitive and social development in infancy. In R. Emde & R. Harmon (Eds.), *Continuities and discontinuities in development* (pp. 175–210). New York: Plenum Press.

Bornstein, M., Miyake, K., & Tamis-LeMonda, C. (1986). A cross-national study of mother–infant activities and interactions. In *Research and Clinical Center for Child Development Annual Report, 1985–86* (pp. 1–12). Sapporo, Japan: Hokkaido University.

Bridges, K. M. B. (1932). Emotional development in early infancy. *Child Development, 3,* 324–341.

Camras, L. A. (1991). Conceptualizing early infant affect: View II and reply. In K. Strongman (Ed.), *International review of studies on emotion* (pp. 16–28, 33–36). New York: Wiley.

Camras, L. A. (in press). Expressive development and basic emotions. *Cognition and Emotion.*

Camras, L. A., Malatesta, C., & Izard, C. (1991). The development of facial expressions in infancy. In R. Feldman & B. Rime (Eds.), *Fundamentals of nonverbal behavior.* Cambridge, England: Cambridge University Press.

Caudill, W., & Weinstein, H. (1969). Maternal care and infant behavior in Japan and America. *Psychiatry, 32,* 12–43.

Chen, S., & Miyake, K. (1986). Japanese studies of child development. In H. Stevenson, H. Asuma, & K. Hakuta (Eds.), *Child development and education in Japan* (pp. 135–146). New York: W. H. Freeman.

Doi, T. (1973). *The anatomy of dependence.* Tokyo: Kodansha International.

Ekman, P. (1972). Universals and cultural differences in facial expressions of emotion. In J. Cole (Ed.), *Nebraska Symposium on Motivation* (Vol. 19; pp. 207–283). Lincoln: University of Nebraska Press.

Ekman, P., & Friesen, W. (1971). Constants across cultures in the face of emotion. *Journal of Personality and Social Psychology, 7,* 124–129.

Ekman, P., & Friesen, W. (1978). *Facial action coding system: A technique for the measurement of facial movement.* Palo Alto, CA: Consulting Psychologists Press.

Ekman, P., Sorenson, E., & Friesen, W. (1969). Pan-cultural elements in facial displays of emotion. *Science, 164,* 86–88.

Fogel, A., Nwokah, E., & Dedo, J. (in press). Social process theory of emotion: A dynamic systems approach. *Social Development.*

Fogel, A., Toda, S., & Kawai, M. (1988). Mother–infant face-to-face interaction in Japan and the United States: A laboratory comparison using 3-month-old infants. *Developmental Psychology, 24,* 398–406.

Fridlund, A., Ekman, P., & Oster, H. (1987). Facial expressions of emotion. In A. Siegman & S. Feldstein (Eds.), *Nonverbal behavior and communication* (2nd ed.; pp. 143–224). Hillsdale, NJ: Erlbaum.

Hiatt, S., Campos, J., & Emde, R. (1979). Facial patterning and infant emotional expression: Happiness, surprise, and fear. *Child Development, 50,* 1020–1035.

Izard, C. E. (1971). *The face of emotion.* New York: Appleton-Century-Crofts.

Izard, C. (1977). *Human emotions.* New York: Plenum Press.

Izard. C. (1979). *The maximally discriminative facial movement coding system (MAX).* Newark: University of Delaware, Instructional Resources Center.

Izard, C., Dougherty, L., & Hembree, E. (1983). *A system for identifying affect expressions by holistic judgments (AFFEX).* Newark: University of Delaware, Instructional Resources Center.

Izard, C., Hembree, E., & Huebner, R. (1987). Infants' emotional expression to acute pain: Developmental changes and stability of individual differences. *Developmental Psychology, 23,* 105–113.

Izard, C., & Malatesta, C. (1987). Perspectives on emotional development I: Differential emotions theory of early emotional development. In J. D. Osofsky (Ed.), *Handbook of infant development* (pp. 494–554). New York: Wiley.

Kagan, J., Kearsley, R., & Zelazo, P. (1978). *Infancy: Its place in human development.* Cambridge, MA: Harvard University Press.

Kaye, K. (1982). *The mental and social life of babies.* Chicago: University of Chicago Press.

Lebra, T. (1976). *Japanese patterns of behavior.* Honolulu: University Press of Hawaii.

Lewis, M. (1989). Culture and biology: The role of temperament. In P. Zelazo & R. Barr (Eds.), *Challenges to developmental paradigms* (pp. 203–223). Hillsdale, NJ: Erlbaum.

Lewis, M., & Brooks-Gunn, J. (1979). *Social cognition and the acquisition of self.* New York: Plenum Press.

Lewis, M., & Michalson, L. (1983). *Children's emotions and moods.* New York: Plenum Press.

Lewis, M., Ramsay, D., & Kawakami, K. (1991). *Affectivity and cortisol response differences beteween Japanese and American infants.* Unpublished manuscript.

Malatesta, C., Culver, C., Tesman, J., & Shepard, B. (1989). The development of emotion expression during the first two years of life. *Monographs of the Society for Research in Child Development, 54* (1–2, Serial No. 219).

Malatesta, C., & Haviland, J. (1985). Signs, symbols, and socialization: The modification of emotional expression in human development. In M. Lewis & C. Saarni (Eds.), *The socialization of emotions* (pp. 89–116). New York: Plenum Press.

Malatesta-Magai, C., & Izard, C. (1991). Conceptualizing early infant affect: View I and reply. In K. Strongman (Ed.), *International review of studies on emotion* (pp. 1–15, 29–32). New York: Wiley.

Matias, R., & Cohn, J. (1989). *Differentiation of positive and negative affect from 2- to 6-months of age.* Paper presented at the meeting of the Society for Research in Child Development, Kansas City, MO, April.

Miyake, K., Campos, J., Bradshaw, D., & Kagan, J. (1986). Issues in socioemotional development. In H. Stevenson, H. O. Azuma, & K. Hakuta (Eds.), *Child development and education in Japan* (pp. 239–261). New York: W. H. Freeman.

Oster, H. (1982). *Pouts and horseshoe-mouth faces: Their determinants, affective meaning and signal value in infants.* Paper presented at the International Conference on Infant Studies, Austin, TX.

Oster, H., & Ekman, P. (1978). Facial behavior in child development. In A. Collins (Ed.), *Minnesota Symposia on Child Psychology* (Vol. 11; pp. 231–276). Hillsdale, NJ: Erlbaum.

Oster, H., Hegley, D., & Nagel, L. (1988). *The differentiation of negative affect expressions in infants.* Paper presented at the International Conference on Infant Studies. Washington, DC, April.

Oster, H., Hegley, D., & Nagel, L. (in press). Adult judgments and fine-grained analysis of infant facial expressions. *Developmental Psychology.*

Oster, H., & Rosenstein, D. (1991). *Baby FACS: Analyzing facial movement in infants.* Unpublished manuscript.

Piaget, J. (1952). *The origins of intelligence in children.* New York: W. W. Norton.

Stenberg, C., & Campos, J. (1990). The development of anger expressions in infancy. In N. Stein, B. Leventhal, & T. Trabasso (Eds.), *Psychological and biological approaches to emotion* (pp. 247–282). Hillsdale, NJ: Erlbaum.

Stenberg, C., Campos, J., & Emde, R. (1983). The facial expression of anger in seven-month-old infants. *Child Development, 54,* 178–184.

Strauss, M. (1979). Abstraction of prototypical information by adults and 10-month-old infants. *Journal of Experimental Psychology: Human Learning and Memory, 5,* 618–632.

Thompson, R. A., & Lamb, M. E. (1984). Assessing qualitative dimensions of emotional responsiveness in infants: Separation reactions in the Strange Situation. *Infant Behavior and Development, 7,* 423–445.

Tronick, E., Als, H., & Adamson, L. (1979). Structure of early face-to-face communicative interactions. In M. Bullowa (Ed.), *Before speech: The beginnings of human communication* (pp. 349–372). Cambridge, England: Cambridge University Press.

Young, G., & Decarie, T. (1977). An ethology-based catalogue of facial/vocal behavior in infancy. *Animal Behavior, 25,* 95–107.

The Cross-Cultural Study of Infant Facial Expressions

LINDA A. CAMRAS

Although cross-cultural universality in emotion recognition has been well established, few investigations have directly examined the production of emotional facial expressions. Our 1992 paper reported pilot data for a larger project on American, Japanese, and Chinese (PRC) infants' facial expressions in response to several different emotion-eliciting procedures. Our project is designed to address three interrelated questions that are currently subject to considerable debate in the developmental literature: (1) Is the production of emotional expressions by infants universal across cultures? (2) Are infant emotional expressions identical in morphology to adult emotional expressions? and (3) Do infants produce emotion-specific negative facial expressions or do they produce a set of generalized negative affect expressions (e.g., "cry faces") in all negative emotion situations?

Until the development of FACS, investigation of these issues was impeded by the lack of a comprehensive anatomically based facial coding system. Such a system is necessary in order to examine fine-grained similarities and differences in facial behavior. However, FACS itself is not completely appropriate for use with infants since the morphology of infant faces differs considerably from adult facial morphology. Therefore, in our project, we are employing BabyFACS, an infant-appropriate version of FACS developed by Oster and Rosenstein.

For our larger project, we are utilizing the arm restraint procedure described in the 1992 paper. We are also utilizing procedures designed to elicit mild fear and surprise as well as anger. For our surprise procedure, we are presenting a small attractive barking toy dog that apparently vanishes from the infant's sight although its barking can still be heard. For our mild fear procedure, we are presenting a grotesquely shaped toy gorilla head that emits a series of unpleasantly loud and rasping growls as it is moved closer and closer to the infant. As before we are videotaping the participating infants. However, we now employ two cameras, one focused on the infant's face and the second capturing the larger situational context (including the experimental stimulus, the mother, and infant's body).

To ensure that our procedures elicit similar emotional responses in all three cultures, we have conducted a rather elaborate manipulation check. We created edited versions of our wide-angle videotapes on which we electronically eliminated the baby's facial expression. Undergraduate observers viewed these tapes and rated the infant's emotional responses on a set of scales, including happiness, surprise, interest, distress, anger, frustration, fear, disgust and sadness. Results verified that our procedures elicited similar levels of anger, frustration, fear and surprise in the American, Japanese, and Chinese infants. However, we did find differences in the judgments for some of the nontarget emotions. For example, the American babies were judged to be happier than the Chinese babies in the vanishing dog procedure and more distressed than the Chinese babies during the arm restraint procedure. Japanese babies were judged to show intermediate levels of happiness and distress. We are hoping this pattern of responses will also be evident in the infants' facial responses.

Currently, we are coding the infants' facial responses using BabyFACS. As described in our pilot study, we will be examining empirically derived facial patterns and comparing them across both cultures and eliciting situations. In addition, we will be examining infants' production of a set of theoretically derived facial patterns. These patterns will include emotion configurations specified in the current version of FACSAID (i.e., the FACS Affect Interpretation Database). In addition, we will examine the configurations specified in Izard's AFFEX system for interpreting infants' facial behavior.

We are predicting that our new study will replicate and extend the findings reported in our earlier article. Related to our first research question, we expect to obtain more evidence supporting the hypothesis that facial expression production by infants is universal across cultures. Related to our second research question, we anticipate that the infants' expressions will differ substantially from the adult full-face configurations for discrete negative emotions. Related to our third research question, we predict that the "cry face" configuration most frequently seen in our anger/frustration situation (arm restraint) will be produced equally often in our fear situation (growling gorilla). This would support our hypothesis that this facial configuration expresses generalized negative affect (i.e., distress) rather than the discrete negative emotion of anger.

Preliminary inspection of the videotapes suggests that infants indeed produce few full-face configurations of fear, anger, or surprise. However, they may produce components of these expressions in the emotionally appropriate situations. For example, the raised and knitted brow movement characteristic of the adult fear expression may be produced by babies more often in the gorilla presentation (i.e., fear) procedure than in the other two procedures. Such differential use of this brow configuration by babies in all three cultures would provide evidence for the universality hypothesis.

Note

1. In interpreting the facial configurations presented in table 13.2, the reader should note that all Aus following the ± are optional. Any subset of this group of Aus (or none at all) may be part of the configuration.

14

Differential Facial Responses to Four Basic Tastes in Newborns

DIANA ROSENSTEIN & HARRIET OSTER

The study of taste-elicited facial expressions in newborns can help to resolve three interrelated questions: (1) How finely can newborns discriminate among various taste stimuli? Do they merely distinguish between sweet and all other substances, or can they also discriminate among sour, salty, and bitter stimuli? Differential facial responses to these stimuli would indicate that they each had a distinctive taste to the infants. (2) Do newborn infants display preferences and aversions indicating innate hedonic responses to particular tastes? Inferences about the hedonics of infants' facial responses can be based on the biologically adaptive functions of particular facial muscle actions (e.g., actions either facilitating or blocking access to stimulation and ingestion) as well as on the presence of facial components seen in adult expressions of pleasure or disgust. (3) Do infants' taste-elicited facial expressions serve as social signals, informing observers about the nature of the substances ingested or about the infant's hedonic responses to them? Such signals would have indirect survival value if adults reliably responded to them in an appropriate fashion, for example, by removing potentially harmful substances from the baby's mouth.

Previous Studies

The morphological structures to perceive different tastes are developed and functional before birth, and the fetal taste receptors are exposed to a variety of chemicals present in amniotic fluid (Arey, 1946; Bradley & Stern, 1967; Mistretta & Bradley, 1977). Animal studies have documented behavioral and electrophysiological evidence of differential responses to taste stimuli as well as hedonic responses to positive versus negative taste stimuli in neonatal rats, sheep, rabbits, orangutans, and other species (Ganchrow, Oppenheimer, & Steiner, 1979; Mistretta & Bradley, 1977, 1985; Nowlis, 1977; Schwartz & Grill, 1985; Steiner & Glaser, 1985).

In human newborns, differential responding to sweet versus nonsweet solutions, including water, has been demonstrated by a variety of physiological and behavioral response measures: pulse and respiration (Canestrini, 1913), heart rate and respiration

(Crook & Lipsitt, 1976; Lipsitt, 1979), brain electrical activity (Fox, 1985), bodily movements (Shirley, 1933), facial expression (Kussmaul, 1859; Peiper, 1963; Preyer, 1970; Steiner, 1973), sucking (Crook, 1978; Engen, Lipsitt, & Peck, 1974; Jensen, 1932), lateral tongue movements (Weiffenbach, 1977; Weiffenbach & Thach, 1973), and ingestion (Beauchamp & Cowart, 1985).

The pattern of hedonic responses shown by newborns clearly indicates an innate preference for sweet solutions. In addition to increasing their consumption of sweeter sugars and of more concentrated sugar solutions (Desor, Maller, & Turner, 1973; Nowlis & Kessen, 1976), infants show a variety of hedonically positive responses to sweet tastes: relaxation and increased sucking (Canestrini, 1913; Steiner, 1973), increased heart rate (Lipsitt, 1979), increased anterior tongue movements, seen as facilitating ingestion (Nowlis, 1977), and longer interburst sucks, interpreted as a savoring of the taste (Crook, 1978). By contrast, in response to sour and bitter tastes, infants show hedonically negative patterns such as facial grimacing (Peiper, 1963; Steiner, 1973), motor restlessness and disruption of sucking (Canestrini, 1913; Shirley, 1933), and tongue movements that block ingestion and push the nipple from the mouth (Nowlis, 1977).

The findings for salt perception in newborns have been less clear-cut. While the results of ingestion studies (Desor, Maller, & Andrews, 1975; Maller & Desor, 1973) suggest that newborns do not discriminate salty solutions from water, other investigators have found evidence that salt is hedonically negative relative to water (Crook, 1978). Nowlis (1973) reported inconsistent responses, with some infants showing a positive (anterior tongue) response pattern and others showing a negative (ejection) pattern. Investigators who have observed facial responses to salt have reported either indifference or nonspecific negative grimaces (Peiper, 1963). Differences in salt thresholds because of differences in the salinity of saliva may account in part for the inconsistent findings (Nowlis, 1973). However, in reviewing studies on salt responses, Beauchamp and Cowart (1985) suggested that newborns may be relatively insensitive to salt and that salt sensitivity develops gradually over the first 2 years of life. Findings from neurophysiological studies of the pre- and postnatal development of the taste system in sheep are consistent with this conclusion (see Mistretta & Bradley, 1983, 1985).

The question of whether human newborns can discriminate among the three basic nonsweet tastes (salty, bitter, and sour) has not been conclusively answered (see reviews by Cowart, 1981; Lipsitt, 1977). Maller and Desor (1973) found that newborns did not suppress ingestion of salty, sour, or bitter solutions relative to distilled water, suggesting that the infants failed to perceive or were indifferent to these tastes. When taste stimuli were added to a sucrose base, infants ingested less of the sour solution but not less of the salty or bitter solutions relative to sucrose alone (Desor et al., 1975). Studies directly comparing ingestion of sour, bitter, and salty solutions are needed to clarify these results. However, because of the newborn's apparent inability to inhibit sucking and ingestion, these behaviors may not reveal the newborn's discriminative capacities. Response measures such as tongue movements, sucking patterns, respiration, autonomic activity, and brain electrical activity have also failed to yield evidence for differential responding to different nonsweet tastes—perhaps because they are not sensitive enough to detect subtle differences in the infants' responses to different hedonically negative tastes.

Facial Responses to Taste Stimuli

Because the facial musculature is highly differentiated even in the newborn (Oster & Ekman, 1978), measures of facial expression can provide a more sensitive measure of differential responses to taste. Facial reactions can be elicited by minute quantities of taste stimuli, and they can be readily observed and measured without intrusive instrumentation. Studies dating back to the nineteenth century have consistently reported that newborns show expressions of "pleasure" in response to sweet-tasting stimuli and facial grimacing in response to sour and bitter stimuli (see reviews by Cowart, 1981; Peiper, 1963). Taste-elicited facial expressions have been observed in full-term and premature newborns and in anencephalic and hydranencephalic infants (see Peiper, 1963; Steiner, 1973, 1979), indicating the innate basis and subcortical origin of the responses.

However, there have been conflicting reports on the discriminability of neonatal facial responses to different nonsweet stimuli. While certain investigators (e.g., Kussmaul, 1859; Preyer, 1970; Steiner, 1973) have reported that infants show distinctive facial expressions for specific nonsweet tastes, others (Peiper, 1963; Stirnimann, 1936 cited in Peiper, 1963) could find only grosser distinctions between "good" (i.e., sweet) versus "bad" (i.e., sour or bitter) tastes. Peiper (1963) cited individual differences in taste thresholds as one reason for the inconsistent findings (see also Chiva, 1979). A more important reason is that the early studies were fraught with methodological shortcomings, including a lack of experimenter and observer bias controls, a lack of standardization of taste stimuli and concentrations, and the use of vaguely defined and often subjective terms for describing the infants' facial reactions.

Steiner (1973, 1979) has conducted the most systematic studies of infants' facial responses to taste. He has reported finding highly stereotyped, taste-specific facial expressions for sweet, sour, and bitter stimuli. However, the data reported in these studies are inconclusive because they do not show how much overlap was present in the facial features shown in response to the three stimuli (e.g., Steiner reports the frequency of lip pursing in response to the sour stimulus but not in response to the sweet and bitter stimuli). Therefore, there is no direct evidence that the "typical" responses to sweet, sour, and bitter tastes were in fact *differentially* elicited by these stimuli. A more recent study by Ganchrow, Steiner, and Daher (1983) does show evidence of differential responding to sweet versus bitter stimuli. However, since bitter was the only nonsweet taste presented in this study, it is not clear that the infants' responses were characteristic of bitter per se, as opposed to negative tastes in general.

Two additional limitations of the studies reported by Steiner et al. contribute to uncertainties about the precise nature of the infant's responses to taste stimuli. First, these investigators have not specified the criteria used for coding expression components, and they have not reported data on interobserver agreement for the scoring of these components. Second, they have not reported the frequency of the full-face expressions described as being typical of each taste stimulus—just the frequency of the separate components of these expressions. Thus, we do not know how many infants actually showed the characteristic sweet, sour, and bitter facial configurations, and we cannot evaluate the claim that the patterning of facial movements for each taste was highly stereotyped and reflex-like.

The two studies reported here were designed to provide a more stringent test of whether newborns show differential facial responses to sour, bitter, and salty solutions as well as a grosser discrimination between sweet and nonsweet tastes. Three additional aims were to specify the patterning of facial responses to each of the four basic tastes, to clarify the nature of the hedonic response to salty solutions, and to examine the communicative value of taste-elicited facial expressions in newborns. The first study involved a detailed and objective coding of infants' facial responses to sweet, sour, salty, and bitter solutions. In the second study, naive observers shown videotapes of the infants' facial responses rated the infants' hedonic responses and attempted to identify the eliciting stimulus.

Experiment 1: Measurement of Infants' Facial Responses to Taste

Method

Subjects

Twelve newborns (six females and six males) born at the Hospital of the University of Pennsylvania (HUP) were selected according to the following criteria: (1) medically uncomplicated full-term pregnancy, (2) medically uncomplicated spontaneous or pitocin-induced vaginal delivery, (3) less than general anesthesia used at delivery, and (4) Apgar score (Apgar, 1953) or at least 8 at 1 and 5 min. All infants were found to be normal and healthy on pediatric examination. The infants' mothers provided written consent prior to testing.

Stimuli

Stimuli consisted of 0.73M (25%) sucrose (sweet), 0.12M (2.5%) citric acid (sour), 0.73M (4.3%) sodium chloride (salt), and 0.003M (.25%) quinine hydrochloride (bitter). Concentrations were from 1.58 to 1.84 log molar units above their respective detection thresholds for adults (Pfaffman, Bartoshuk, & McBurney, 1971). These concentrations were selected because they were comparable with those used in previous studies (e.g., Steiner, 1973) and because small quantities reliably elicit facial responses, thus minimizing exposure to potentially harmful substances. The solutions were presented at room temperature. A 1 cc disposable syringe with the needle removed was used to apply 0.2 cc of each taste solution to the central portion of the dorsal surface of the infant's tongue. Distilled water (0.4 cc), used as a rinse to minimize carry-over effects from one solution to the next, was presented in the same manner as the taste solutions.

Procedure

Infants were tested at approximately 2 hours of age, before their first feeding. Their only prior extrauterine taste experience was briefly sucking from a bottle of distilled water to establish that their sucking abilities were intact. All infants passed this test. Testing occurred in a secluded area of the newborn nursery, when the infants were in a quiet alert state. During testing, the experimenter held the infant upright, facing forward, by loosely supporting the back of its neck and head. This position permitted an unobstructed camera view of the infant's face while helping to maintain an alert state.

The infants' faces were videotaped throughout the session with a portable Sony video-tape recorder and a black-and-white camera with a zoom lens.

Testing sessions consisted of two consecutive 30-sec presentations of each of the four solutions, separated by two 90-sec water rinses. Additional 90-sec water rinses were presented if the infant continued to respond to the previous stimulus. Only two infants received more than two rinses. The order in which the four solutions were presented was determined by a modified Latin square design, insuring that each solution was presented first and was preceded and followed by every other solution at least once. The experimenter and cameraperson were blind to the order of presentation of the solutions, which were prepared in advance and labelled with a code.

Videotape Coding and Analysis

The infants' videotaped facial responses were coded using Baby FACS (Oster & Rosenstein, 1988), a modification for infants' faces of Ekman and Friesen's (1978) Facial Action Coding System. FACS is an objective, anatomically based system whose basic units are minimally distinguishable actions of the facial muscles. Each Action Unit (AU) is designated by a number and scored on the basis of precisely specified changes in the shape and position of facial features and other landmarks such as wrinkles, bulges, and contours of the face. Thus, coding does not involve judgments about the hedonic tone or expressive meaning of the facial responses displayed. Any complex pattern of facial movements can be objectively and unambiguously described in terms of its constituent actions, making it possible to determine empirically whether infants show differentiated patterns of facial activity in response to different tastes. Since Baby FACS is a standardized instrument, results obtained in different laboratories can be compared in terms of a common descriptive language.

Videotape coding and data analysis proceeded in several stages. In the initial stage, one reliably trained FACS coder,[1] blind to stimulus conditions, comprehensively coded all discrete Action Units and AU combinations that occurred during each 30-sec taste trial. Several more grossly defined behaviors were also coded (e.g., spitting, sucking, head turning). The coder made several passes through each trial, viewing the tape in slow motion or frame by frame where necessary. Numbers recorded onto consecutive 1/60th sec fields of the videotapes made it possible to note changes in facial expression and to locate the apex (most intense point) of each facial configuration shown.

Preliminary analyses revealed that the discrete AUs and the more grossly defined behaviors were not highly taste-specific when considered separately. While certain AUs, such as horizontal lip retraction (AU 20), occurred more frequently in response to the three nonsweet stimuli than to sucrose, they did not discriminate among the latter. More important, the analysis of discrete AUs, taken separately, did not provide information about the patterning of facial actions in response to different tastes. Therefore, we turned to an analysis of full-face, apex expressions.

Examination of the two-, three-, and four-AU combinations noted by the first coder suggested that certain facial actions and combinations in the brow/forehead and midface regions were common components of the responses to all three nonsweet stimuli: brow raising (AUs 1 and/or 2), brow lowering (AU 4), cheek raising (AU 6), nose wrinkling (AU 9), upper lip raising (AU 10), and combinations of two or more of these actions. We hypothesized that these components of the infants' facial reactions represented nonspecific negative responses, on several grounds: (1) their presence in defensive responses in the fetus (see Humphrey, 1970) and newborn (Peiper, 1963), (2) their presumed adaptive role in blocking stimulation (tightly closed eyes, nose wrinkling) and ejecting noxious substances (mouth gaping), and (3) their presence in universal adult expressions of disgust (see Ekman, 1982). Two mouth actions, on the other hand, appeared to be more highly taste-specific when they occurred in the context of the negative brow and midface actions; lip puckering (AU 18) and mouth gaping (AU 26 or 27). Based on reports by Steiner and his colleagues (Ganchrow et al., 1983; Steiner, 1973), we expected to find smiling (AU 12) in response to the sweet solution and downturned mouth corners (AU 15) in response to the bitter solution. However, we observed these actions only rarely, and they did not differentiate among taste stimuli, either alone or in combination with other AU's.[2] Therefore, they were not included in further analyses.

On the basis of these preliminary analyses, we constructed a matrix in which the nonspecific, hedonically negative upper- and midface actions were combined with one of the two specific mouth actions or with no distinctive mouth action. The resulting six full-face combinations are shown in table 14.1.[3] A second reliably trained FACS coder, blind to the hypotheses and to the taste stimuli presented in each trial, independently identified all occurrences of these six AU configurations within each trial. Intercoder agreement, defined as mutual identification of the same AU combination at the same location within a trial, ranged from 65% to 85%. All coding disagreements were arbitrated by the two coders until full agreement was reached, and statistical analyses were based on these arbitrated data.

Results

Table 14.1 shows the proportion of infants displaying each of the facial configurations specified in the matrix in response to each of the four taste stimuli. Statistical tests were computed for trials 1 and 2 separately as well as for the proportion of infants who showed each configuration on one or both trials (trials 1 and/or 2). To find out whether the four taste stimuli differentially elicited any of the configurations in the matrix, we used a Cochran's Q statistic for differences among proportions. The results, presented in column A of table 14.1 show significant differences for the full-face set of AU combinations with either lip pursing (AU 18) or mouth gaping (AU 26 or 27).

Distrimination of Sweet versus Nonsweet Stimuli

Cochran's Q tests for differences among proportions also showed strong evidence of differential responding to sucrose versus the other three stimuli. These results are summarized in column B of table 14.1. The sweet versus nonsweet contrast was seen most strongly for responses that involved negative AUs in both the brow/forehead and midface regions as well as one of the two mouth actions (lip pursing or mouth gaping). In response to any of the nonsweet tastes, the cheeks were typically raised and the eyes were narrowed or tightly closed, the nose was wrinkled, and the brows were either raised, lowered, or both raised and pulled together.

The only facial configuration shown more often in response to sucrose, though not significantly so, was one that involved negative AUs only in the midface region, without actions in the brows or mouth. This facial expression was often a transient reaction to the introduction of the syringe into the infant's mouth. It terminated rapidly and was

TABLE 14.1. Facial configurations displayed in response to four taste stiumuli

	Sweet	Sour	Salty	Bitter	A[a]	B[b]
Trial 1:						
No distinctive mouth action:						
With negative midface AUs[c]	.08	0	0	0	...	...
With negative brow and midface AUs[d]	.08	.08	.17	.25	...	**
Lip pursing (AU 18):						
With negative midface AUs	0	.25	.17	.17	...	***
With negative brow and midface AUs	.17	.75	.25	.33	**	***
Mouth gaping (AU 26 or 27):						
With negative midface AUs	0	.08	0	0	...	...
With negative brow and midface AUs	.25	.50	.33	.50	...	***
Trial 2:						
No distinctive mouth action:						
With negative midface AUs	.17	.08	0	.08	...	...
With negative brow and midface AUs	.08	.08	.25	.25	...	***
Lip pursing (AU 18):						
With negative midface AUs	.08	.17	.25	.08	...	***
With negative brow and midface AUs	.08	.58	.17	.17	**	***
Mouth gaping (AU 26 or 27):						
With negative midface AUs	.17	.08	.08	0	...	...
With negative brow and midface AUs	.08	.42	.33	.67	**	***
Trials 1 and/or 2:						
No distinctive mouth action:						
With negative midface AUs	.25	.08	0	.08	...	...
With negative brow and midface AUs	.17	.17	.33	.33	...	***
Lip pursing (AU 18):						
With negative midface AUs	.08	.42	.33	.17	...	***
With negative brow and midface AUs	.25	.83	.33	.33	*	***
Mouth gaping (AU 26 or 27):						
With negative midface AUs	.17	.17	.08	0	...	...
With negative brow and midface AUs	.33	.50	.42	.75	...	***

Note: The values represent the proportion of infants who showed each facial configuration; $n = 12$ infants.
[a] Q tests comparing responses to each of the four stimuli.
[b] Q tests comparing responses to sweet vs. nonsweet tastes.
[c] Midface actions: cheek raising (AU 6) plus nose wrinkling and/or upper lip raising (AUs 9 and/or 10).
[d] Midface actions plus one or more brow actions: brows lowered and pulled together (AU 4) and/or brows raised (AUs 1 and/or 2).
* $p < .05$.
** $p < .01$.
***$p < .005$.

followed by total facial relaxation or sucking (see figure 14.1). Sucking alone, how-ever, was not a distinguishing feature of the response to sucrose, since it was elicited equally often by all four tastes.

Differential Responding to Nonsweet Taste Stimuli

To determine the specificity of the full-face configurations with lip pursing and mouth gaping, we conducted Z tests for correlated proportions (Korin, 1977) based on the proportion of infants who showed each of the two configurations in response to each taste.[4] The results showed that lip pursing combined with negative upper- and midface components was the most frequent response to the sour stimulus and that it was more likely to occur in response to the sour stimulus than to the three other tastes: For trial 1, sour > sweet, $Z = 26.4$, $p < .0001$; sour > bitter, $Z = 2.16$, $p < .03$; sour > salt, $Z = 3.32$, $p < .001$. For trial 2, sour > sweet, $Z = 3.32$, $p < 001$; sour > bitter, $Z = 2.16$, $p < .03$; sour > salt, $Z = 2.80$, $p < .005$. (All tests were two-tailed.) The prototypical response to the sour solution is illustrated in figure 14.2. The full-face configuration with mouth gaping (shown in figure 14.3), the most frequent response to the bitter solution, was shown more often in response to bitter than in response to the three other tastes. As can be seen in table 14.1, the mouth-gaping response was more taste-specific in trial 2 than in trial 1. For trial 2, bitter > sweet, $Z = 26.4$, $p < .0001$; bitter > sour, $Z = 1.91$, $p < .056$; bitter > salt, $Z = 2.3$, $p < .02$. The infants did not show any consistent facial expression to the salty stimulus, which elicited only diffuse mouth and lip movements and occasional negative upper- and midface actions, mouth gaping, and lip pursing.

Discussion

The reported study represents the most rigorous examination to date of taste-elicited facial expressions in infants, both in terms of testing procedures and facial coding and analysis. The findings confirm that newborns with no prior taste experience respond differentially to sour and bitter stimuli, demonstrating that they can discriminate among these taste qualities as well as make a more general sweet versus nonsweet distinction.

Although detailed coding of facial actions with Baby FACS revealed significant differential responding, the differences might not be visible to untrained observers watching the infants in real time. Therefore, the infants' facial responses to taste might not have clearcut communicative value. Experiment 2 was designed to investigate this question.

Experiment 2: Observers' Judgments of Infants' Facial Responses to Taste

To investigate the communicative value of newborn infants' facial responses to taste, we asked whether untrained observers could accurately identify the stimuli eliciting the infants' expressions and whether the facial expressions elicited by the four basic tastes differed in their perceived hedonic tone.

Method

Forty undergraduates viewed one of two composite videotapes of the infants in Experiment 1. Each tape showed the two 30-sec trials of the first taste stimulus presented to each infant, thus eliminating order effects related to stimulus presentations. The full 30-sec trials were presented so that judges could observe the full range of facial responses to each stimulus, including the sequence and timing of the infants' facial movements. The 24 30-sec clips (3 infants × 2 trials × 4 tastes) were arranged in two different randomly determined orders on the two tapes.

Judges were randomly assigned to groups of five to view one of the two tapes dis-

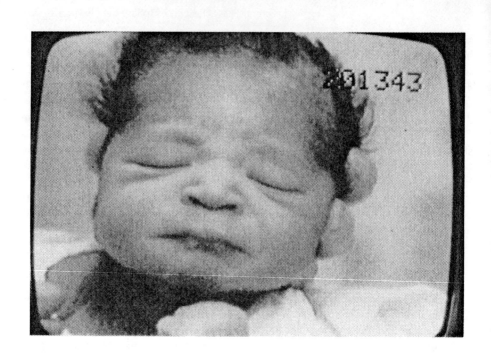

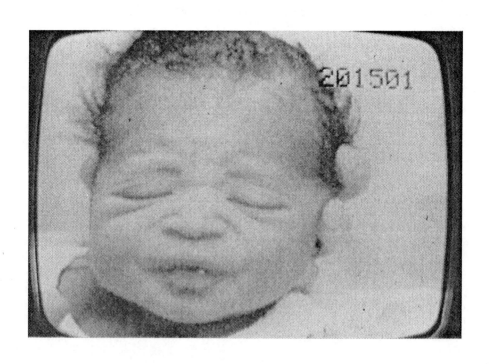

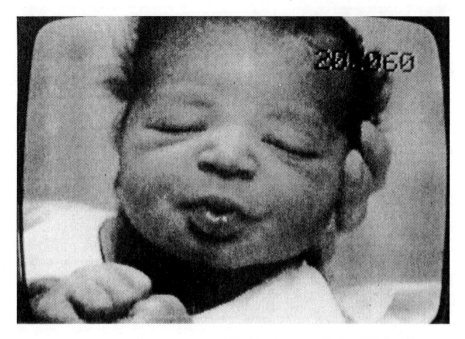

Figure 14.1. Sequence of facial expressions elicited by the sweet solution; initial negative facial actions followed by relaxation and sucking.

played on a black-and-white television monitor. For each clip, they indicated which of the four taste stimuli the infant had received, and they rated the hedonic tone of the infants' facial reactions on a seven-point scale from very negative (1) to very positive (7).

Results

Accuracy of Judgments

Table 14.2 shows the distribution of observers' forced-choice judgments of facial reactions to each of the four taste stimuli. Chi-square tests of actual versus perceived taste stimuli revealed that judges responded in a nonrandom manner. However, inaccurate as well as accurate judgments were made more often than could be expected by chance (25%).

Judges were significantly more accurate than chance in identifying the infants' responses to the sucrose and quinine solutions. They were also significantly less likely than chance to confuse the facial responses to sweet and bitter stimuli with one another or to confuse responses to the sour and salty stimuli. However, the infants' facial responses to sodium chloride and citric acid were most often misjudged as responses to the sweet solution, and their reactions to the quinine solution were misattributed to the sour stimulus more often than could be expected by chance. We suspect that the systematic errors made by the judges were primarily because of inconsistencies and misleading cues in the infants' facial expressions. The judges' hedonic ratings are consistent with this interpretation.

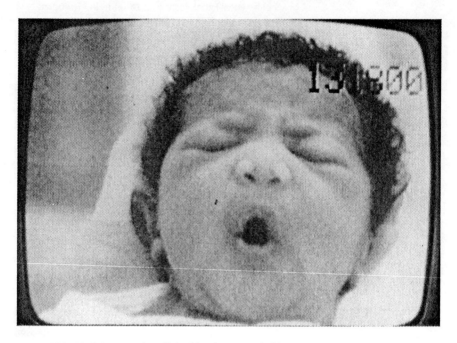

Figure 14.2. Facial expression elicited by the sour solution.

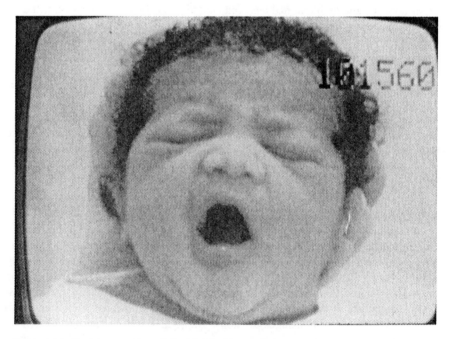

Figure 14.3. Facial expression elicited by the bitter solution.

TABLE 14.2. Forced-choice judgments of taste stimuli presented

| Raters' Judgments | Taste Stimulus Eliciting Facial Response | | | |
	Sweet	Sour	Salty	Bitter
Sweet	**34***	32*	40*	3*
Sour	22	**25**	18*	31*
Salty	30	18*	**20**	28
Bitter	14*	25	23	**37***

Note: The numbers in each cell represent the percentage of total raters' judgments (*n* = 240). Numbers in boldface represent correct choices.
* Chosen significantly more or less often than expected by chance (25%), *p* < .05, two-tailed.

Hedonic Ratings of Infants' Facial Expressions

A one-way ANOVA for the factor taste showed significant differences in mean hedonic ratings of the infants' facial responses to the four taste stimuli, $F(3,956) = 89.42$, $p < .001$. The infants' facial responses to quinine received significantly more negative ratings (2.9 on a seven-point scale from most negative to most positive) than their responses to the other three stimuli, $t = .8$, $p < .05$. However, the facial expressions elicited by the sweet, sour, and salty stimuli (3.7, 3.6, and 3.8, respectively) were not seen as differing significantly from one another in their hedonic value.

Discussion

These findings provide only limited evidence that untrained adults can accurately decode the taste-elicited facial expressions of newborns. The fact that judges made systematic errors in the identification task suggests that consistent cues were present in the infants' facial expressions but that certain cues may have been misleading. For example, judges who mistook the infants' responses to the sour solution for a response to sucrose may have been misled by the high sucking rates elicited by both of these stimuli. In addition, judges may have based their identification of the stimulus largely on the overall perceived hedonics of the infants' facial expressions, rather than on the specific facial cues identified by our direct measurement of facial actions. Thus, facial reactions that appeared more positive (as shown by the judges' hedonic ratings) were attributed to sucrose, and reactions that appeared more negative were attributed to quinine or to citric acid.

General Discussion

The findings from both the direct measurement and judgment studies demonstrate the usefulness of facial expression as a response measure for studying the newborn infant's chemical sensory capacities and hedonic predispositions. The direct measurement of infants' facial responses with Baby FACS (Oster & Rosenstein, 1988) yielded more definitive evidence of the newborn's discriminative abilities than observers' judgments. Using Baby FACS, we demonstrated that at 2 hours of age, infants with no prior taste experience differentiated sour and bitter stimuli as well as sweet versus nonsweet taste stimuli. The responses of the sour, salty, and bitter stimuli were all characterized by hedonically negative facial actions in the brows and midface region. Although some of these actions were also present in the initial 5–10 sec of the infants' responses to the sweet solution, they generally disappeared in the second half of the trial and were followed by facial relaxation and sucking. The facial expressions elicited by the sour and bitter solutions were distinguished from one another—as well as from the sweet- and salt-elicited expressions—by the presence of specific lip and mouth actions in addition to the generalized negative actions.

The facial configuration involving lip pursing (AU 18), typical of responses to the sour solution, was more highly taste-specific than the configuration involving mouth gaping (AU 26/27), which only marginally distinguished between the responses to the bitter and sour tastes. Since many infants showed mouth gaping as well as lip pursing in response to the sour stimulus, it is possible that mouth gaping represents a more general aversive reaction to intense, hedonically negative tastes, possibly reflecting trigeminal as well as gustatory stimulation. The fact that infants showed the mouth-gaping configuration significantly more often in response to quinine HCl than to NaCl is not inconsistent with this interpretation, since the bitter solution may have been perceived as more intense than the saline solution. Further studies comparing responses to a wider range of concentrations of each taste are needed to resolve this issue.

Although untrained observers accurately identified the sweet- and bitter-elicited facial expressions, there were systematic confusions in their judgments of the infants' responses to the sour and salty solutions. The observers' hedonic ratings also failed to differentiate among the responses to the sweet, sour, and salty stimuli. Despite the presence of hedonically negative components in the responses to all three nonsweet stimuli, only the expressions elicited by the bitter solution were seen as highly negative.

One likely reason for the discrepancies between the findings from the direct measurement and judgment studies is that the infants' taste-elicited facial expressions were not as highly stereotyped as earlier reports (cf. Steiner, 1973) had suggested. Although there were statistically significant differences in the distribution of facial configurations elicited by the four taste stimuli, there was also considerable overlap. Like Peiper (1963) and Chiva (1979), we also observed considerable individual differences in the facial responses elicited by the four taste stimuli.

One might ask why newborn infants—whose diet is usually restricted to milk—would show differentiated facial resonses to taste. A consideration of the component actions of the infants' facial expressions suggests that certain actions may represent reflexive responses to gustatory stimulation that serve specific biological functions. For example, sucking and facial actions that facilitate sucking and ingestion predominate in the infants' responses to sweet stimuli, which are likely to be nutritious. As mentioned above, the hedonically negative brow and midface actions elicited by the three nonsweet stimuli are also present in defensive responses to aversive or noxious stimulation in other sensory modalities and serve to protect the sense organs and block stimulation. For example, nose wrinkling—which is characteristic of adult expressions of disgust—may block olfactory stimulation (see Darwin, 1872/1965).

Lip pursing and rapid sucking movements, elicited most frequently by the sour stimulus, have the effect of compressing the cheeks against the gums, thus "milking" the salivary glands. Increased salivation dilutes the sour solution, making it more palatable. (Naturally occurring sour substances, like sweet substances, are likely to be nutritious, not toxic.) The accompanying tightly squeezed eyes and lowered brows may result from a general increase in mucous membrane activity, producing tears and stinging sensations in the eyes (cf. the "spreading reaction" described by Peiper, 1963). The lip pursing component of the response to sour stimuli has been observed in nonhuman primates, but the upper-face actions have not (H. Grill, personal communication).

The distinguishing feature of the facial reaction to the bitter solution was mouth gaping, often accompanied by an elevation of the tongue in the back of the mouth—actions that block swallowing and allow the liquid to drain from the mouth. (We did not observe actual gagging, but these are components of the gag reflex.) Since bitter substances encountered in nature may be poisonous, these responses could be highly adaptive. In addition to its direct effect of preventing ingestion, mouth gaping is a highly conspicuous action that can serve as a communicative signal, informing caregivers that the infant has tasted something potentially harmful. The fact that the infants' responses to the bitter solution received the most negative ratings confirms the signal value of mouth gaping combined with hedonically negative actions in the upper- and midface regions.

Unlike bitter substances, salt is not likely to be noxious to the infant unless it is ingested in large quantities (Finberg, Kiley, & Luttrell, 1963)—quantities which the infant is unlikely to encounter except in accidental circumstances. The absence of a distinctive facial response to salt is consistent with the suggestion that salt sensitivity is poorly developed in the newborn (Beauchamp & Cowart, 1985; Mistretta & Bradley, 1985). Although affectively negative components were more frequent in the salt-elicited than in the sweet-elicited responses, we cannot be certain that salt has a distinctive "taste" to newborns, as compared with distilled water—which may itself elicit mildly negative reactions (see Desor et al., 1975). Additional studies comparing the infants' facial reactions to different concentrations of saline in comparison with distilled water could help to resolve the question of whether infants cannot taste saline or merely lack a well-defined response to salty solutions.

We believe that more detailed analyses of the time course, intensity, and duration of infants' taste-elicited facial responses would yield a more detailed picture of the expressions elicited by each of the four basic tastes. More fine-grained analyses are also needed to trace developmental changes and continuities in taste-elicited facial expressions and to study individual and group differences in taste responses.

Further consideration of the possible biological precursors and communicative value of newborn infants' facial responses to taste may provide insights into the origins and development of human facial expressions of emotion. While some of the facial actions seen in response to the three nonsweet stimuli are components of adult disgust expressions, we cannot at present draw any definite conclusions about the subjective nature of the infants' responses. We do not yet know whether these responses represent the discrete emotion of disgust, as some investigators have assumed (e.g., Fox, 1985; Izard, 1984), or rather relatively peripheral "distaste" responses to gustatory stimulation or more generalized aversive responses. There are two reasons for caution: First, without systematic comparisons of the facial expressions elicited by aversive stimulation in different modalities, we do not know how specific the observed responses are to the chemical senses or to a particular type of stimulation (e.g., noxious but not painful). On the one hand, the infants in our study did not cry or show cry-faces, the most common response to acute pain and distress in newborns. Nor have other investigators reported the full-face, taste-elicited expressions with lip pursing or mouth gaping in response to nontaste stimuli. On the other hand, the component actions observed in the midface and brow regions have been reported in defensive responses to noxious stimulation in several modalities (see Humphrey, 1970; Peiper, 1963). And horizontal lip retraction (AU 20), shown more frequently in response to the three nonsweet tastes, is a component of adult pain expressions. The second reason for caution is that some of the component actions observed (i.e., brow raising, brow knitting, and lip pursing) are usually not part of adult disgust expressions. When they occur in the absence of other facial actions in infants, they appear to reflect interest or puzzlement, rather than negative affect (cf. Izard, 1984; Oster, 1978).

A discussion of the general issue of how best to interpret facial affect displays in young infants is beyond the scope of this paper (cf. Fridlund, Ekman, & Oster, 1987; Izard, 1984; Peiper, 1963; Sroufe, 1979). However, with respect to the development of disgust, detailed studies are needed to trace continuities and changes in taste-elicited facial expressions as well as the extension of these displays to a variety of nonfood substances and objects (including disliked persons and abstract ideas) regarded within a given culture as disgusting (see Darwin, 1872/1965; Oster & Ekman, 1978; Rozin, Hammer, Oster, & Marmora, 1986). Research involving two or more independent response measures (as in Fox, 1985) could prove particularly valuable for understanding developmental changes in the cognitive correlates and subjective experience of disgust expressions.

Notes

1. The FACS Final Test, scored in Ekman and Friesen's laboratory, was passed by the two coders who scored the tapes. In addition, both coders had extensive experience coding infants' facial movements according to the modifications specified in the Baby FACS coding manual (Oster & Rosenstein, 1988).

2. The discrepancies between Steiner's observations and our own may be because of differences in testing procedures or differences in the criteria used for scoring these behaviors. One possibility is that the smiles observed by Steiner (1973) and Ganchrow et al. (1983) were REM (rapid eye movement) smiles occurring as the infants drifted into a drowsy or sleepy state and not responses to the sweet stimulus itself. In the present study, trials were shorter in duration (30 sec vs. 60 sec or longer in Steiner's studies), and infants were maintained in a quiet, alert state by being held upright on the experimenter's lap. Alternatively, the infants in Steiner's studies may not have shown AU 12 (the principal component of smiling) but merely signs of facial relaxation that could be mistaken for smiling (see Oster & Rosenstein, 1988). Similarly, facial actions such as AU 20 (horizontal retraction of the lips) and AU 10 (upper lip raising) produce signs that can be mistaken for the action of AU 15 (pulling down of the lip corners). In fact, we could not see any evidence of AU 12 or of AU 15 in the photographs published by Steiner (1973, 1979) or Ganchrow et al. (1983) to illustrate the typical responses to sweet and bitter stimuli.

3. The configurations shown in table 14.1 are mutually exclusive in the sense that only the full apex configuration was scored for each expression produced by an infant. For example, if the full-face mouth-gaping expression began with nose wrinkling and lowered brows and faded gradually, so that the midface actions persisted after the mouth had closed, only the full-face expression was scored. However, if an infant later showed the lip-pursing expression or a partial expression (mid-face AUs only) within the same trial, that expression was also scored.

4. The use of the Z statistic with a sample of less than 25 is technically inappropriate. How-

ever, since this would be the appropriate statistic for a larger sample, and since there is no other appropriate statistic given the small observed frequencies, we present the results of the Z test to highlight the pattern and direction of results.

References

Apgar, V. (1953). Proposal of a new method of evaluation of newborn infants. *Anesthesiology and Analgesia, 32,* 260–267.

Arey, L. B. (1946). *Developmental anatomy* (5th ed.). Philadelphia: Saunders.

Beauchamp, G., & Cowart, B. (1985). Congenital and experiential factors in the development of human flavor preferences. *Appetite, 6,* 357–372.

Bradley, R. M., & Stern, I. B. (1967). The development of the human taste bud during the foetal period. *Journal of Anatomy, 101,* 743–752.

Canestrini, S. (1913). *Über das sinnesleben des neugeborenen.* Berlin: Springer. (Peiper, A. [1963]. *Cerebral function in infancy and childhood.* [B. Nagler & H. Nagler, Trans.]. New York: Consultants Bureau.)

Chiva, M. (1979). Comment la personne se construit en mangeant. *Extrait de Communications, 31,* 107–113.

Cowart, B. J. (1981). Development of taste perception in humans: Sensitivity and preference throughout the life span. *Psychological Bulletin, 90,* 43–73.

Crook, C. K. (1978). Taste perception in the newborn infant. *Infant Behavior and Development, 1,* 52–69.

Crook, C. K., & Lipsitt, L. P. (1976). Neonatal nutritive sucking: Effect of taste stimulation upon sucking and heart rate. *Child Development, 47,* 518–522.

Darwin, C. (1872/1965). *The expression of the emotions in man and animals.* Chicago: University of Chicago Press.

Desor, J. A., Maller, O., & Andrews, K. (1975). Ingestive responses of human newborns to salty, sour, and bitter stimuli. *Journal of Comparative and Physiological Psychology, 89,* 966–970.

Desor, J. A., Maller, O., & Turner, K. (1973). Taste in acceptance of sugars by human infants. *Journal of Comparative and Physiological Psychology, 84,* 496–501.

Ekman, P. (Ed.). (1982). *Emotion in the human face.* Cambridge: Cambridge University Press.

Ekman, P., & Friesen, W. V. (1978). *Manual for the Facial Action Coding System.* Palo Alto, CA: Consulting Psychologists Press.

Engen, T., Lipsitt, P., & Peck, M. (1974). Ability of newborn infants to discriminate sapid substances. *Developmental Psychology, 5,* 741–744.

Finberg, L., Kiley, J., & Luttrell, C. N. (1963). Mass accidental salt poisoning in infancy. *Journal of the American Medical Association, 184,* 121–125.

Fox, N. A. (1985). Sweet/sour—interest/disgust: The role of approach-withdrawal in the development of emotions. In T. M. Field & N. A. Fox (Eds.), *Social perception in infants* (pp. 53–71). Norwood, NJ: Ablex.

Fridlund, A., Ekman, P., & Oster, H. (1987). Facial expressions of emotion. In A. Siegman & S. Feldstein (Eds.), *Nonverbal communication: A functional perspective* (pp. 143–224). Hillsdale, NJ: Erlbaum.

Ganchrow, J. R., Oppenheimer, M., & Steiner, J. E. (1979). Behavioral displays to gustatory stimuli in newborn rabbit pups. *Chemical Senses and Flavor, 4,* 49–61.

Ganchrow, J. R., Steiner, J. E., & Daher, M. (1983). Neonatal facial expressions in response to different qualities and intensities of gustatory stimuli. *Infant Behavior and Development, 6,* 473–484.

Humphrey, R. (1970). Reflex activity in the oral and facial area of the human fetus. In J. F. Bosma

(Ed.), *Second symposium on oral sensation and perception* (pp. 195–233). Springfield, IL: Thomas.

Izard, C. (1984). Emotion-cognition relationships and human development. In C. Izard, J. Kagan, & R. Zajonc (Eds.), *Emotions, cognition, and behavior* (pp. 17–37. Cambridge: Cambridge University Press.

Jensen, K. (1932). Differential reaction to taste and temperature stimuli in newborn infants. *Genetic Psychology Monographs, 12,* 361–479.

Korin, B. P. (1977). *Introduction to statistical methods.* Cambridge: Winthrop.

Kussmaul, A. (1859). Untersuchungen über das seelenlegen des neugeborenen menschen. (Peiper, A. [1963]. *Cerebral function in infancy and childhood.* (B. Nagler & H. Nagler, Trans.]. New York: Consultants Bureau.)

Lipsitt, L. P. (1977). Taste in human neonates: Its effect on sucking and heart rate. In J. M. Weiffenbach (Ed.), *Taste and development* (pp. 125–140). Bethesda, MD: U.S. Department of Health, Education, and Welfare. (DHEW Publication No. NIH 77-1068).

Lipsitt, L. P. (1979). The pleasures and annoyances of infants: Approach and avoidance behavior. In E. B. Thoman (Ed.), *Origins of the infant's social responsiveness* (pp. 123–153). Hillsdale, NJ: Erlbaum.

Maller, O., & Desor, J. A. (1973). Effects of taste on ingestion by human newborns. In J. F. Bosma (Ed.), *Fourth symposium on oral sensation, and perception* (pp. 279–291). Bethesda, MD: U.S. Department of Health, Education, and Welfare. (DHEW Publication No. NIH 73-546).

Mistretta, C. M., & Bradley, R. M. (1977). Taste in utero: Theoretical considerations. In J. M. Weiffenbach (Ed.), *Taste and development* (pp. 51–63). Bethesda, MD: U.S. Department of Health, Education, and Welfare. (DHEW Publication No. NIH 77-1068).

Mistretta, C. M., & Bradley, R. M. (1983). Neural basis of developing salt taste sensation: Response changes in fetal, postnatal, and adult sheep. *Journal of Comparative Neurology, 215,* 199–210.

Mistretta, C. M., & Bradley, R. M. (1985). Development of the sense of taste. In E. M. Blass (Ed.), *Handbook of behavioral neurobiology* (pp. 205–236). New York: Plenum.

Nowlis, G. H. (1973). Taste-elicited tongue movements in human newborn infants: An approach to palatability. In J. F. Bosma (Ed.), *Fourth symposium on oral sensation and perception* (pp. 292–302). Bethesda, MD: U.S. Department of Health, Education, and Welfare. (DHEW Publication No. NIH 73-546).

Nowlis, G. H. (1977). From reflex to representation: Taste-elicited tongue movements in the human newborn. In J. M. Weiffenbach (Ed.), *Taste and development* (pp. 190–202). Bethesda, MD: U.S. Department of Health, Education, and Welfare. (DHEW Publication No. NIH 77-1068).

Nowlis, G. H., & Kessen, W. (1976). Human newborns differentiate differing concentrations of sucrose and glucose. *Science, 191,* 865–866.

Oster, H. (1978). Facial expression and affect development. In M. Lewis & L. A. Rosenblum (Eds.), *The development of affect* (pp. 43–75). New York: Plenum.

Oster, H. & Ekman, P. (1978). Facial behavior in child development. In A. Collins (Ed.), *Minnesota symposia on child psychology* (pp. 231–276). Hillsdale, NJ: Erlbaum.

Oster, H., & Rosenstein, D. (1988). *Baby FACS: Measuring facial movement in infants and young children.* Unpublished manuscript. (Available from H. Oster, Derner Institute, Adelphi University, Box 701, Garden City, NY 11530.)

Peiper, A. (1963). *Cerebral function in infancy and childhood* (B. Nagler & H. Nagler, Trans.). New York: Consultants Bureau.

Pfaffman, C., Bartoshuk, L. M., & McBurney, D. H. (1971). Taste psychophysics. In L. M. Beidler (Ed.), *Handbook of sensory physiology, chemical senses* (Vol. 4; pp. 75–101). Berlin: Springer-Verlag.

Preyer, W. (1970). *The mind of the child.* (H. W. Brown Trans.). New York: Arno.

Rozin, P., Hammer, L., Oster, H., & Marmora, V. (1986). The child's conception of food: Differentiation of categories of rejected substances in the 1.4–5 year age range. *Appetite, 7,* 141–151.

Schwartz, G. J., & Grill, H. (1985). Comparing taste-elicited behaviors in adult and neonatal rats. *Appetite, 6,* 373–386.

Shirley, M. M. (1933). *The first two years: A study of 25 babies: Vol. 2. Intellectual development.* Minneapolis: University of Minnesota Press.

Sroufe, L. A. (1979). Socioemotional development. In J. Osofsky (Ed.), *Handbook of infant development* (pp. 462–516). New York: Wiley.

Steiner, J. E. (1973). The gustofacial response: Observation on normal and anencephalic newborn infants. In J. F. Bosma (Ed.), *Fourth symposium on oral sensation and perception* (pp. 254–278). Bethesda, MD: U.S. Department of Health, Education, and Welfare. (DHEW Publication No. NIH 73-546)

Steiner, J. E. (1979). Human facial expression in response to taste and smell stimulation. In H. W. Reese & L. P. Lipsitt (Eds.), *Advances in child development and behavior* (pp. 257–293). New York: Academic Press.

Steiner, J. E., & Glaser, D. (1985). Orofacial motor behavior-patterns induced by gustatory stimuli in apes. *Chemical Senses, 10,* 452.

Weiffenbach, J. M. (1977). Sensory mechanisms of the newborn's tongue. In J. M. Weiffenbach (Ed.), *Taste and development* (pp. 205–211). Bethesda, MD: U.S. Department of Health, Education, and Welfare. (DHEW Publication No. NIH 77-1068).

Weiffenbach, J. M., & Thach, B. T. (1973). Elicited tongue movements: Touch and taste in the newborn human. In J. F. Bosma (Ed.), *Fourth symposium on oral sensation and perception* (pp. 232–243). Bethesda, MD: U.S. Department of Health, Education, and Welfare. (DHEW Publication No. NIH 73-546).

Facial Expression as a Window on Sensory Experience and Affect in Newborn Infants

HARRIET OSTER

The Rosenstein and Oster (1988) study nicely illustrates the unique advantages of Baby FACS (Oster & Rosenstein, in press) for investigating the innate sensory capacities and hedonic responses of newborn infants. At the same time, the study addressed more general questions about the differentiation of facial expressions and their relation to emotional feeling states in young infants. A recap of the major findings of this study will thus provide a framework for discussing my ongoing research on these and related issues.

Taste Discrimination in Newborns

Our detailed Baby FACS coding of two-hour-old infants' taste-elicited facial responses revealed differentiated patterns of facial expression in response to sour, bitter, and salty stimuli as well as differential responding to sweet vs. nonsweet tastes. This finding provided the first conclusive evidence that newborn infants with no prior extrauterine taste experience can discriminate among different nonsweet tastes. More generally, because Baby FACS makes it possible to identify finely differentiated patterns of facial expression in infants (Oster & Ekman, 1978), it is ideally suited to studying differential responding to stimuli in any modality, in naturalistic or experimental situations.

Innate Hedonic Responses

The newborns in our study responded to sucrose (the sweet solution) with facial relaxation and sucking, indicating acceptance and suggesting that they experienced the sweet taste as soothing and/or pleasant. They responded to all three nonsweet tastes with hedonically negative facial expressions, involving facial muscle actions and combinations that are components of infant distress expressions and adult expressions of negative affect, indicating that they experienced these tastes as inherently unpleasant. Our objective Baby FACS coding was a more sensitive indicator of the infants' taste discrimination and hedonic responses than judgments by untrained observers (Study 2). Facial expression also proved to be a more sensitive measure of discrimination and he-donic quality than commonly used response measures such as sucking, ingestion, and soothing (for recent reviews, see Blass & Ciaramitaro, 1994; Mennella & Beauchamp, 1993).

The Patterning of Facial Expressions in Newborns

The facial expressions elicited by citric acid and quinine (the sour and bitter solutions) were distinguished from each other—as well as from the sweet- and salt-elicited ex-pressions—by specific lip and mouth actions (lip pursing for citric acid, lower jaw gap-ing for quinine) in combination with more general negative components in the upper face and midface (e.g., lowered and pulled together brows, raised cheeks and tightened lower eyelids, nose wrinkling and/or upper lip raising). The salty solution (sodium chloride) did not elicit a distinctive expression, but it involved more negative compo-nents than the sweet solution.

Our demonstration of significant differential facial responses to sour and bitter tastes confirmed reports from earlier, less rigorous studies. However, our analysis showed that these were not highly stereotyped, invariant expressions, as Steiner (1973) had reported. The infants all showed a range of facial expressions in response to each stimulus, and none of the facial configurations was unique to a given taste quality. Vari-ability is probably the rule rather than the exception in infants' facial responses to posi-tive or negative stimulation in any modality.[1]

It is also important to note that the differential responses to sour and bitter tastes were revealed only by a systematic analysis of full-face configurations. Taken individu-ally, there were no taste-specific Action Units (AUs).[2] As a general rule, individual fa-cial muscle actions are likely to be ambiguous; they do not necessarily signal the same emotion or even the same hedonic quality when they occur in the context of different full-face configurations. For this reason, we need to be extremely cautious in interpret-ing the affective meaning of isolated facial muscle actions or facial configurations that involve the components of two different facial expressions. This is true for adult as well as infant facial expressions. But the designation of negative affect expressions in in-fants as partial or blended expressions of discrete negative emotions (using a priori for-mulas specified in Izard's MAX and Affex coding systems or Ekman & Friesen's EMFACS) is questionable, because it presupposes that infants show clearly differenti-ated *full-face* expressions of discrete negative emotions. As discussed below, the evi-dence for that assumption is weak.[3] The use of a priori formulas to classify the expres-sions observed in the Rosenstein and Oster (1988) study could have resulted in serious misinterpretations of the infants' taste-elicited facial expressions.

For example, AUs 9 and/or 10 (nose wrinkling and upper lip raising) were likely to be present in the responses to all three nonsweet tastes. Because these actions are char-acteristic components of adult disgust expressions, the infants' "distaste" expressions could justifiably be considered as variants of disgust. In some cases, the taste-elicited expressions with AUs 9 and 10 involved facial actions that are not seen in prototypical adult disgust expressions, including horizontally stretched or downturned lip corners or the brow components of adult anger, fear, surprise, and sadness expressions. However, there was no indication that the infants' responses to bad tastes represented blends of disgust with other discrete emotions. Similarly, in other contexts infants' smiles and cry faces may involve AU 9, but there is no justification for coding such expressions as disgust-happiness or disgust-distress blends.

AU 9 is not separately codable in Izard's MAX coding sustem but is described as a possible component of anger, pain, and disgust expressions. According to the MAX formula for disgust (Iward, 1983, p. 33), the mouth is widely opened and angular with the tongue protruding forward beyond the gum line (code 59B) and the lower lip pulled down (code 63). This mouth configuration (corresponding to AUs 16 + 19 + 20 + 26/27 in FACS) was not frequently seen in the infants' responses to any of the negative tastes. A gaping lower jaw (AU 27) without tongue protrusion or marked lateral stretching of the mouth corners—the distinguishing component of the infants' responses to the bitter taste—is identified as an anger component (code 55) in MAX. Therefore, MAX coders would be likely to misclassify the infants' responses to bitter tastes as discrete anger or anger blends, depending on the brow actions present. The prototypical adult disgust expression used in Oster, Hegley, and Nagel's (1992) observer judgment study was in fact misinterpreted as anger by trained MAX coders, although it was identified as a discrete disgust expression by a large majority of untrained judges.

The characteristic response to the sour taste involved lip pursing (AU 18) in combination with negative components in the brows and midface (also seen in adults' responses to sour tastes). According to explicit MAX formulas (Izard, p. 33), this configuration would be coded (or rather miscoded) as a blend of interest (code 65, lips pursed) with anger, fear, or sadness (depending on the accompanying brow configuration). Although lip pursing (AU 18) is a characteristic component of infant expressions signaling interest, concentrated attention, or "puzzlement" (Oster, 1978) when there are no negative components in the brows or midface, there is no evidence that it signals interest in the context of negative brow and midface actions. Nor is there any evidence that the variable negative brow actions seen in the infants' sour-elicited expressions represented anger or fear or sadness signals.

Because the use of a priori coding systems based on prototypical adult expressions can lead to serious misinterpretations as well as unfounded claims about infant facial expressions, I have argued for an empirical approach to studying infants' facial expressions, as discussed further below.

Differentiated Negative Affect Expressions in Newborns

The finding that newborn infants show differentiated patterns of facial muscle activity in response to different hedonically negative taste stimuli represents one of the clearest examples in the literature of a reliable relationship between eliciting stimuli and facial expressions in young infants. In addition, our findings provided at least indirect evidence that the emotional responses of newborn infants are not global and undifferentiated, as Bridges (1932) claimed.

The infants in our study did not cry in response to the taste stimuli, and their "distaste" expressions lacked the defining features of cry faces. As specified in the Baby

FACS manual, cry and pre-cry faces involve moderate to strong lateral stretching of the lip corners (AU 20) in combination with jaw opening (AU 26/27) and negative components in the upper face and midface regions. The negative taste-elicited expressions we observed involved either lip pursing or gaping of the lower jaw with little or no horizontal stretching of the lips (the characteristic sour and bitter responses, respectively), or nonspecific "grimaces" involving horizontally stretched or downturned lip corners with little or no jaw opening. Although nose wrinkling (AU 9) and upper lip raising (AU 10) are often present in intense cry faces, what is most characteristic of distress expressions in infants and adults is a bowing of the nasolabial furrow and flattening of the upper lip (AU 11), which we did not observe in the taste-elicited expressions. Thus, although the facial configurations elicited by the sour, salty, and bitter solutions involved affectively negative facial expression components in all three regions of the face, they did not involve the widely open, "squarish" mouth characteristic of the classic cry face described by Darwin (1872/1965).

What is not clear from this study or from any studies to date is the extent to which the newborn infants' "distaste" expressions are specific to the modality of taste. My own observations suggest that the characteristic, full-face sour and bitter expressions occur rarely, if at all, in response to pain, hunger, or other sources of distress in infants. However, the relatively nonspecific grimaces observed in response to all three negative tastes might represent more general aversive responses. Newborn infants show relativey discrete nose wrinkles or upper lip raises in response to harsh, abrupt, or intrusive (but non-painful) tactile stimulation, such as having their nose wiped or head forcibly turned (as seen in fig. 3 [e] in Oster & Ekman, 1978). It is less clear whether infants show AUs 9 and/or 10 without cry-face components in response to harsh or grating noises or highly discrepant visual stimuli.

A systematic comparison of infants' responses to naturally occurring sources of "displeasure" in several different sensory modalities might help to clarify the early origins of disgust expressions and their distinctiveness from expressions of other negative emotions such as anger, fear, distress, and pain. This question has interesting theoretical implications as well as implications for the identification of infant facial expressions. According to Darwin's (1872/1965) classic view, disgust has its origins in the rejection of bad tastes and foul odors but generalizes to unpleasant stimuli in other modalities, as well as to disliked people, groups, and abstract ideas (see Rozin, Haidt, & McCauley, 1993, for a recent examination of this issue). Detailed observations of infants and children are needed to establish whether disgust-like expressions are in fact specific to the chemical senses or to proximal sensory stimulation at the beginning of life and to establish when and how they generalize to more distal stimulation and cognitive appraisals.

Another important question that was not resolved by our study concerns the precise nature of the infants' subjective feeling states. Did the hedonically negative responses to all three nonsweet tastes reflect the specific emotion of disgust or more inchoate feelings of aversion? Did the distinctive bitter and sour responses reflect qualitatively different feeling states or the same basic feeling state of disgust or aversion along with flavor-specific facial motor responses that serve biologically adaptive functions (ejecting potentially poisonous bitter substances or diluting potentially nutritious sour substances)? In part because the infants showed full-face expressions involving muscle actions seen in other affectively negative expressions, I do not believe that their "distaste" expressions were merely peripherally stimulated, reflexive responses with no correspondence to subjective feelings. These questions are difficult to resolve in preverbal infants. But systematic comparative studies, involving atypical infants and multiple response measures as well as observations in a wide variety of situations, might help to elucidate the relations between facial expressions and emotional feeling states in infants.

An Ontogenetic Perspective on the Development of Facial Expressions

A major focus of my ongoing research in the past five years has been the issue of whether infants show differentiated facial expressions of discrete negative emotions such as anger, fear, and sadness. According to differential emotions theorists (Izard & Malatesta, 1987), the facial expressions of all of the basic emotions are present in their adult-like form from early infancy and are invariant in their form and affective meaning throughout life. Recent findings from my own and other investigators' laboratories have challenged these assumptions (Camras, Malatesta, & Izard, 1991; Matias & Cohn, 1993; Oster et al., 1992). These findings have also raised serious questions about the validity of coding systems such as Izard's MAX and Affex (Izard, 1983; Izard, Dougherty, & Hembree, 1983), which use formulas based on prototypical, universally recognized adult expressions to identify "discrete emotions" in infants.

The results of two observer judgment studies reported by Oster et al. (1992) demonstrated that judges did not identify MAX-specified infant facial expressions of anger, fear, sadness, and disgust as predicted, but rather as distress or blends of different negative emotions. Moreover, a Baby FACS coding of the stimulus expressions (the majority from Izard's slide set) showed that they did not involve the same patterning of facial muscle actions as their presumed universal prototypes. The infants' negative affect expressions involved components of cry faces or distress (e.g., AUs 6, 11, and 44) not present in adult facial expressions of discrete negative emotions; and they lacked some of the distinctive components of the prototypical adult expressions they were meant to represent (e.g., the typical brow configuration of the universal adult fear expression and eye widening in fear and anger expressions). These findings failed to support the claim that infants show adult-like facial expressions of discrete negative emotions and suggested instead that the negative affect expressions of young infants may be less finely differentiated than those of adults. However, only detailed measurement of infants' facial expressions in a variety of emotion-eliciting situations can resolve this issue.

In my own view, emotional expressions are biologically based, evolved behaviors that serve crucial adaptive functions in infancy. Infants show distinctive, highly organized patterns of facial expression from the first hours and days of life, and I believe that these facial expressions can provide reliable information to caregivers about infant's perceptual and cognitive processes, need states, and emotional feeling states. However, a biological perspective on the evolutionary origins and adaptive functions of emotional expressions does not necessarily mean that facial expressions of the basic emotions should be present in their adult-like form from early infancy or that facial expressions are invariant in their morphological form and affective meaning throughout life—as maintained by DET. Instead, I have argued (e.g., Oster & Ekman, 1978; Oster et al., 1992) that infants show distinctive patterns of *infant* facial expression, which signal information to caregivers that is crucial for an *infant's* survival and normal development. One implication of this ontogenetic perspective is that we need a comprehensive, anatomically based coding system to describe the facial expressions actually shown by infants of different ages—whether or not they resemble adult expressions of the basic emotions. We also need an empirical, ethological analysis of the elicitors and behavioral correlates of distinctive infant facial expressions in order to discover their signal value and affective meaning.

Cross-Cultural Studies of Infant Emotional Expression

In an ongoing cross-cultural study discussed in greater detail elsewhere in this volume (commentary on Camras, Oster, Campos, Miyake, & Bradshaw, 1992), my collaborators and I are addressing three questions pertinent to this debate: (1) Do infants less than one year of age show differential facial responses in situations designed to elicit different negative emotions? (2) Do infants show facial expressions resembling prototypical adult expressions of discrete negative emotions such as anger and fear? and (3) Do infants in China, Japan, and the United States show the same patterns of facial expression and the same kinds of emotional responses and emotion-regulatory behaviors? Although we cannot yet draw any firm conclusions, our analyses to date indicate that 11-month-old infants do not show facial expressions that closely resemble full-face, prototypical adult expressions of anger and fear. However, they do appear to show subtly differentiated patterns of facial expression and gaze in the fear- and anger-eliciting situations. As in the taste study, the infants' responses appear to involve both generalized negative components (in this case, components of distress or cry faces) and potentially emotion-specific components (e.g., facial stilling and brow raising and knitting in response to the fear elicitor). The Chinese, Japanese, and American infants in the study showed very similar patterns of facial expression, including complex variants of smiles and cry faces and distinctive infant expressions involving pouting lower lips and jaw thrusts, indicating that these represent pan-cultural infant expressions (see Oster, 1995).

Comparative Studies of Infant Facial Expression

Although this commentary has focused primarily on the question of differential responding in relation to specific eliciting events, Baby FACS is also ideally suited to describing subtle individual differences in the quality and intensity of infant facial expressions—the kinds of differences that can have clinical significance in studies of atypical and at-risk populations. One tool that has proved useful in these studies are 3×3 matrices in the Baby FACS manual for describing variants and intensities of cry-mouth and smile-mouth configurations.[4] For example, in a recently completed study comparing the responses of 7-month-old preterm and full-term black infants in the still-face paradigm, Segal et al. (in press) found significantlly diminished levels of the most intense smiles in the preterm infants.

In my most recent study, I have been investigating the effects of congenital craniofacial anomalies on infant facial expressions and mother-infant interactions (Oster 1995). Because Baby FACS is a comprehensive, anatomically based system, it can take into account the effects of morphological abnormalities on the "mechanics" of facial muscle action. Therefore, an important goal of this study is to provide an objective measure of deficits, distortions, or ambiguities in the facial expressions shown by infants with particular conditions and to provide explicit criteria for coding these actions. Another goal is to specify changes in facial muscle functioning following reconstructive surgery or other medical interventions. Because their faces may be more difficult to read than those of normal infants, our objective Baby FACS coding of the infants' facial expressions will provide a "standard" for assessing maternal sensitivity to the infants' signals. It will also make it possible to tease apart the direct, anatomically definable effects of facial anomalies on infant facial expressions and the more indirect effects of facial disfigurement on the quality of mother-infant interactions and the infant's emotional and social responsiveness.

In summary, Baby FACS has proved to be a sensitive and powerful tool for describing the facial expressions of infants, for discovering systematic relationships between eliciting stimuli and the patterning of facial muscle actions, and for describing subtle individual differences in the intensity and quality of infant facial expressions.

Notes

1. It would be interesting to determine whether preterm infants or infants with no higher brain function (e.g., the anencephalic infants studied by Steiner, 1973) show less variability than normal, full-term infants.

2. A replication with a larger n and more powerful statistical analyses based on duration and percent of time measures might indicate that certain AUs or 2-way AU combinations (e.g., 9 + 18 vs. 9 + 27) are differentially produced in response to different tastes, in combination with more variable negative brow actions. Such measures would also make it possible to do more sophisticated cluster analyses to determine whether there were significant differences in the brow components of responses to the different tastes.

3. Researchers who use Ekman and Friesen's EMFACS in the same way also risk misinterpreting variants of infant distress expressions as emotion blends or partial expressions. The more precisely defined emotion interpretation guidelines in Ekman and Friesen's FACS Interpretation Dictionary (used in the Oster et al., 1992, study), would not be as likely to interpret complex variants of distress as discrete negative emotions or as blends of discrete negative emotions, but rather as unspecified negative expressions or uncodable expressions.

4. The matrices specify three intensity ranges of mouth opening (closed or very slightly open, moderately open, and stretched widely open) and three intensity ranges of either oblique or horizontal lip corner movements (AUs 12 or 20, respectively). Each cell in the matrix corresponds to a distinctive mouth configuration: e.g., "broad" smiles with strong AU 12 action but little or no mouth opening, "gaping" smiles with a widely open lower jaw but low intensity AU 12 action, and big smiles with strong AU 12 action and gaping lower jaw. Researchers can use all nine cells or combine cells into descriptive categories. Other components of the facial expressions, such as brow actions, cheek raising, and orbital actions, are independently coded.

References

Blass, E. M., & Ciaramitaro, V. (1994). *A new look at some old mechanisms in human newborns: Taste and tactile determinants of state, affect, and action.* Monographs of the Society for Research in Child Development, 59 (1, Serial No. 239).

Bridges, K. M. B. (1932). Emotional development in early infancy. *Child Development, 3,* 324–334.

Camras, L. A., Malatesta, C., & Izard, C. E. (1991). The development of facial expression in infancy. In R. Feldman & B. Rime (Eds.), *Fundamentals of nonverbal behavior* (pp. 73–105). New York: Cambridge University Press.

Camras, L. A., Oster, H., Campos, J. J., Miyaki, K., & Bradshaw, D. (1992). Japanese and American infants' response to arm restraint. *Developmental Psychology, 28,* 578–583.

Darwin, C. (1872/1965). *The expression of the emotions in man and animals.* Chicago: University of Chicago Press.

Izard, C. E. (1983). *The maximally discriminative facial movement coding system* (rev. ed.). Newark, DE: Instructional Resource Center.

Izard, C. E., Dougherty, L. M., & Hembree, E. A. (1983). *A system for identifying affect expressions by holistic judgments (Affex)* (rev. ed.). Newark, DE: Instructional Resources Center.

Izard, C. E., & Malatesta, C. Z. (1987). Perspectives on emotional development: I. Differential emotions theory of early emotional development. In J. O. Osofsky (Ed.), *Handbook of infant development* (2nd ed., pp. 494–554). New York: Wiley.

Matias, R., & Cohn, J. F. (1993). Are Max-specified infant facial expressions during face-to-face interactions consistent with Differential Emotions Theory? *Developmental Psychology, 29,* 524–531.

Mennella, J. A., & Beauchamp, G. K. (1993). Early flavor experiences: When do they start? Zero to Three/National Center for Clinical Infant Programs, *14* (No. 2), 1–7.

Oster, H. (1978). Facial expression and affect development. In M. Lewis & L. A. Rosenblum (Eds.), *The development of affect* (pp. 43–75). New York: Plenum Press.

Oster, H. (1995). *The effects of cleft lip and palate and craniofacial anomalies on infant facial expression.* Paper presented at the annual meeting of the Cleft Palate-Craniofacial Association, Tampa, Florida, April 26–29.

Oster, H., Campos, R., Ujiee, T., Zhaolan, M., Lei, W., & Rigney, L. (1995). *Differential responses to anger vs. fear elicitors in American, Japanese, and Chinese infants.* Poster presented at the Biennial meeting of the Society for Research in Child Development, Indianapolis, March 30–April 2.

Oster, H., & Ekman, P. (1978). Facial behavior in child development. *Minnesota Symposia on Child Psychology, 11,* 231–276.

Oster, H., Hegley, D., & Nagel, L. (1992). Adult judgments and fine-grained analysis of infant facial expressions: Testing the validity of *a priori* coding formulas. *Developmental Psychology, 28,* 1115–1131.

Oster, H., & Rosenstein, D. *Baby FACS: Analyzing facial movement in infants.* Monograph and coding manual to be published by Consulting Psychologists Press.

Rosenstein, D., & Oster, H. (1988). Differential facial responses to four basic tastes in newborns. *Child Development, 59,* 1555–1568.

Rozin, P., Haidt, J., & McCauley, C. R. (1993). Disgust. In M. Lewis & J. M. Haviland (Eds.), *Handbook of emotions* (pp. 575–594). New York: Guilford.

Segal, L., Oster, H., Cohen, M., Meyer, M., Caspi, B., & Brown, D. (in press). Smiling and fussing in preterm and full-term 7-month-old preterm and full-term black infants in the Still-Face situation. *Child Development.*

Steiner, J. E. (1973). The gustofacial response: Observation on normal and anencephalic newborn infants. In J. Bosma (Ed.), *Fourth symposium on oral sensation and perception* (pp. 254–278). Bethesda, MD: U.S. Department of Health, Education, and Welfare. (DHEW Publication No. NIH 73-546).

PART TWO

APPLIED RESEARCH

15

Facial Expression in Affective Disorders

PAUL EKMAN, DAVID MATSUMOTO & WALLACE V. FRIESEN

Recent progress in the study of facial expressions of emotion in normal individuals could have relevance to clinical investigations of depression. Universal facial expressions of emotion have been identified (Ekman, 1982a; Izard, 1971; Fridlund, Ekman, & Oster, 1987; Ekman & Friesen, 1986) for seven emotions—anger, contempt, disgust, fear, sadness, surprise, and happiness—that can be objectively and reliably distinguished one from another (Ekman, 1982b). Whether a disturbance in emotion is seen as a symptom (Beck, 1967; Abramson, Garber, Edwards, & Seligman, 1978) or as central in the etiology (Izard, 1977; Tomkins, 1963) of depression, the precise measurement of facial expressions of emotion could be useful in clinical investigations and perhaps also in the treatment of depression and other affective disorders. Specifying which of the seven emotions are evident in facial expressions, their relative strength, and any repetitive sequences of these emotional expressions might help to refine diagnosis, could be of aid in monitoring response to treatment, and might help to predict the likelihood of subsequent improvement or relapse.

The recent spate of studies using electromyographic (EMG) techniques to measure facial activity in depressed patients has shown such a potential (Carney, Hong, O'Connell, & Amado, 1981; Schwartz et al., 1976a, 1976b, 1978; Teasdale & Bancroft, 1977; Teasdale & Rezin, 1978) but there are two inescapable problems in using EMG to measure facial expressions. The first problem is inherent in the attachment of the EMG leads to the surface of the face. Measurement by this means is not only obtrusive but also may inhibit facial expressivity. Second, because many of the muscles active in diverse emotional states lay one on top of the other or are very close to each other, it is not possible to measure with EMG the occurrence of all seven emotions signaled by the face, any of which may be implicated in depression (Ekman, 1982b; Fridlund & Izard, 1983).

An alternative approach to measuring facial expressions of emotion is through systematically examining videotaped or filmed records to identify the muscular movements that constitute the emotional expressions. This approach is totally unobtrusive; the camera even may be hidden. The Facial Action Coding System (FACS) (Ekman & Friesen, 1976, 1978) is the only comprehensive, objective measurement technique using this approach. Measuring facial movement in muscular terms, FACS identifies all seven emotions, the relative strength of each, repetitive sequences, and whether the expression is voluntary or involuntary. We also used an abbreviated, less costly version of FACS, the Emotion Facial Action Coding System (EMFACS) (Friesen & Ekman, 1986), which focuses just on muscular movements relevant to emotion.

In this first attempt to evaluate the potential of these measures of visible facial behavior in studies of affective disorders, we did not gather new interview materials. Instead, to reduce the expense of this exploratory study, we have analyzed archival interview records and a more recent but small sample of interviews. Although methodological limits in these samples constrain the conclusions that can be drawn, the analysis of these two samples illustrates some of the questions that can be asked by precisely measuring facial expressions: Do facial behaviors vary with diagnosis? Are such differences apparent only between depressives and schizophrenics, or do the emotional expressions distinguish major from minor depression? Are there sufficient differences among patients with the same diagnosis to suggest the possibility of using such measures to subclassify or refine diagnoses? Do the facial expressions predict the extent of subsequent clinical improvement, and would predictions based on such measures add information not ordinarily derived from standard clinical ratings of patient behavior?

Methods

Patients

Langley Porter Sample

In 1964, two of us (Ekman and Friesen) filmed all of the patients admitted with depressive symptoms during a six-month period to two wards of the Langley Porter Institute. A short standardized interview was conducted at the time of admission and again near the time of discharge. Seventeen patients had a final diagnosis of depression (8 neurotic, 9 psychotic), based on a consensus of the attending physician and ward head. We had three clinical psychologists independently evaluate these patients on the Brief Psychiatric Rating Scale (BPRS) (Overall & Gorham, 1962) after viewing the first part of the sound film admission interview, and then again after viewing the discharge interview. They also evaluated the extent of general improvement in psychiatric status on a 7-point scale on which 1 indicated regression, 4 no improvement, and 7 maximal improvement. We used the means of their ratings on the BPRS and on improvement in the data analyses.

George Washington Sample

As part of the NIMH Clinical Research Branch Collaborative Program on the Psychobiology of Depression (Katz et al., 1984), we were furnished interviews with 12 patients to study the feasibility of using our measures of facial expression in studies of affective disorders. The interviews were conducted when the patients were admitted to George Washington University Hospital and then again shortly before discharge. Their diagnoses were: 4 major depressive, 3 minor depressive, 2 bipolar disorder manic, and 2 schizophrenic. We selected two portions of the hour-long interviews for measurement: the first eight questions, which largely dealt with how the patient currently felt; and the last five questions, which focused on diverse matters such as hobbies, whether the patient enjoyed life, and feelings about the future. The scores from both portions were combined in the data analyses. Because these patients did not change from admission to discharge—the mean difference in ratings of their pathology was less than half a point on a 7-point scale—we could not use this sample in our analysis of whether facial expressions at admission predict improvement.

Scoring Visible Facial Movement

The two techniques we used—FACS and EMFACS—are both anatomically based objective techniques for measuring facial movement observed on videotape or film. Using either technique, a coder "dissects" an observed expression, decomposing it into the specific facial muscles that produced the movement. The scores for a facial expression consist of the list of muscular actions that produced it. In FACS (but not in EMFACS), the precise duration of each action also is determined, and the intensity of each muscular action and any bilateral asymmetry is rated. EMFACS is more economical to use than FACS, not only because it disregards these aspects of facial movement but also because EMFACS scores only some, not all, observed facial activity. Using EMFACS, a coder decomposes an expression only when one of 33 predefined combinations of muscular actions is observed. These 33 predefined combinations include all of the facial configurations that have been established empirically (Ekman & Friesen, 1975, 1978) to signal the seven emotions that have universal expressions.

The scoring units in both FACS and EMFACS are descriptive, involving no inferences about emotions. For example, the scores for an expression would be that the inner corners of the eyebrows are pulled up and together by the combined action of medial frontalis and corrugator muscles, *not* that the eyebrows are in a sad position. While data analyses can be done on these purely descriptive muscular scores, FACS or EMFACS scores can also be converted by a computer-stored dictionary into emotion scores.

Coders spend approximately 100 hours learning FACS. Self-instructional materials teach the anatomy of facial activity, or how muscles singly and in combination change the appearance of the face. Prior to using FACS all learners are required to score a videotaped test (provided by Ekman and Friesen), to ensure they are measuring facial behavior in agreement with prior learners. To date more than 300 people have achieved high inter-coder agreement on this test in their measurement of facial behavior. Once a coder has learned FACS it takes only a few hours to become familiar with the procedures for using EMFACS.

Felt and Unfelt Happy Expressions

In addition to providing scores on the incidence of anger, disgust, fear, surprise, sadness, and contempt, FACS or EMFACS scores can be interpreted in a way that purportedly distinguishes whether an expression was made involuntarily and therefore is presumably a sign that the emotion displayed was felt, or was made voluntarily, and was not a sign of felt emotion. The idea that voluntary facial expressions could be distinguished from involuntary expressions is consistent with what is known about the neural control of facial expression. Voluntary actions are controlled by corticobulbar pathways that emanate from the precentral motor cortex, while extrapyramidal influences are thought to control involuntary emotional facial movements. This "dual" control of facial expression is shown by the differential consequences of lesions in these two areas, which can impair voluntary but leave involuntary expressions intact, or impair involuntary expressions but leave voluntary expressions intact (Rinn, 1984).

Ekman and Friesen have proposed a number of ways to distinguish voluntary from involuntary expressions. We will consider only their hypotheses about how to make this distinction in regards to smiles, since the evidence to support this distinction for other emotional expressions is still quite sparse.

1. *Asymmetry.* When happiness is not felt but a smile is made voluntarily—to be polite, show agreement, encourage or mislead another—the action of the zygomatic major muscle that pulls the lip corners upwards will be stronger on one side of the face (Ekman, 1980). The smile will not be totally absent on the other side of the face, just weaker, often only slightly weaker. With right-handed persons, the unfelt smile is stronger on the left side of the face (Ekman, Hager, & Friesen, 1981; Hager & Ekman, 1985).

2. *Duration.* Inspection of thousands of spontaneous expressions revealed that nearly all of them last between .5ms and 4 seconds. On this basis unfelt expressions were hypothesized to be either less than .5ms or longer than 4 seconds (Ekman & Friesen, 1982).

3. *Muscles.* Duchenne (1862/1990) suggested that felt happy expressions include not only the activity of the zygomatic major muscle but the action of the orbicularis oculi muscle, which pulls the skin around the eyes inwards toward the eyeball. When happiness is not felt but a smile is assumed voluntarily, the zygomatic major would be active but not the orbicularis oculi.

A number of lines of evidence support this distinction between felt and unfelt smiles. Felt smiles occurred more often when subjects watched pleasant nature films, while unfelt smiles were more frequent when the subjects watched unpleasant surgical scenes (Ekman, Friesen, & Ancoli, 1980; Ekman, Davidson, & Friesen, 1990). Felt smiles occurred more often in response to a joke; unfelt smiles when the same subjects were asked to smile deliberately (Ekman et al., 1981; Hager & Ekman, 1985). There was evidence of differences in the pattern of hemispheric activation asymmetry during the expression of felt versus unfelt smiles (Ekman, Davidson & Friesen, 1990). Ten-month-old infants showed a greater number of felt smiles in response to the mother's approach as compared to a stranger's approach and a greater number of unfelt smiles in response to the stranger as compared to the mother (Fox & Davidson, 1987).

Scoring Procedures

The coders were not told the diagnosis of the patient, nor whether it was an admission or discharge interview. Table 15.1 lists how the scoring was done. Intercoder reliability was evaluated by computing the correlation (Spearman rank order) between the frequencies with which two coders scored the specific facial actions. The correlation between the coder using FACS was .87, and between the coders using EMFACS was .99; both correlations were significant beyond the .01 level of confidence.

TABLE 15.1. How the facial expressions were scored in the two samples

	Samples	
	George Washington $N = 12$	Langley Porter $N = 17$
Scoring procedure	EMFACS FACS	EMFACS
How felt-unfelt smiles were distinguished	Orbicularis Oculi & Duration	Orbicularis Oculi
Number of coders	2	2

Results

Can Facial Behavior at Admission Predict Clinical Improvement?

We begin with this question because it is the only one for which there was sufficient data to compute any statistics. Only the Langley Porter data were considered, as there was virtually no improvement in the George Washington sample. Although EMFACS measures facial behaviors relevant to a range of emotions, only behaviors relevant to sadness, contempt, felt happiness, and unfelt happiness occurred often enough in the interviews to be analyzed. Because of the small samples of neurotics and psychotics, and because this diagnostic distinction is not preserved in *DSM III*, diagnosis was disregarded in the analysis.

The first step was to calculate Pearson product-moment correlations between the EMFACS scores from the admission interview and the clinicians' ratings of improvement by the time of discharge. As a precaution against inflated correlations owing to the undue influence of a few extreme scores, Spearman rank-order correlations and Kendall nonparametric coefficients were also calculated. The confidence levels reported for the Pearson correlations reported below were also obtained with the two nonparametric correlations.

Table 15.2 shows that both contempt and unfelt happiness during the admission

TABLE 15.2. Predicting clinical improvement

Admission Measure	Correlation with Improvement at time of Discharge	
	Correlation	p
Contempt expression	Pearson $r = -.538$	.05
Unfelt happiness expression	Pearson $r = -.600$	.01
BPRS pathology rating	Pearson $r = .458$	.06
Contempt + Unfelt happy	Multiple $R = .794$	.001
Contempt + Unfelt happy + BPRS pathology	Multiple $R = .818$	.001

Note: Correlations are between measures at the time of admission to the hospital and clinical improvement rated at the time of discharge.

interview were negatively correlated with the extent of clinical improvement by the time of the discharge interview. For comparison, the table also shows that the correlation between the BPRS total pathology score at time of admission with later improvement nearly reached significance. The patients who showed more contempt or unfelt happiness, or who were rated on the BPRS as being more pathological, improved less than other patients.

Regression analyses were employed to determine whether the contempt and unfelt happy scores were accounting for the same or independent variance in predicting clinical improvement, and whether the admission BPRS predicted a significant amount of variance in clinical improvement beyond that accounted for by the facial scores. Table 15.2 shows that entering both unfelt happy and contempt scores in the regression equation produced a large increase in the correlation with improvement. Addition of the admission BPRS, however, raised the coefficient from .794 to only .818, an R^2 change of only 3.9% ($F(1,13) = 1.538$, ns). Thus admission BPRS could not predict variance in general improvement ratings beyond that accounted for by facial scores at admission.

Entering the BPRS in the equation first and then adding the contempt and unfelt happiness scores provided an estimate of how much of the variance independent of the BPRS is added by the facial scores. Inclusion of the facial scores accounted for 46% more of the variance in improvement ratings than the BPRS alone, and this change was statistically significant ($F(2, 13) = 36.164$, $p < .001$). Thus facial scores of unfelt happiness and contempt predicted a significant amount of variance in clinical improvement ratings beyond that acccounted for by admission BPRS. We inspected the distribution of emotion scores among the neurotic and psychotic subgroups to see if the scores that predicted improvement—unfelt happiness and contempt—might have been evident in just one of the two groups. That was not the case. Among neurotics and psychotics, some patients showed these two expressions.

Because age differences and length of interview could have confounded the results, correlations were calculated to examine the relationship between these variables and the facial scores. There were no significant correlations for either of these two variables, indicating that the results we report cannot be due to age or length of interview differences.

Problems with both the measure of clinical improvement and the BPRS should be noted. Both measures were based on clinicians' judgments after viewing the first portions of the sound film interviews. Thus, the clinicians making these evaluations were exposed to some of same facial expressions (in addition to the speech, voice, and body movement) that were measured with EMFACS. Such an overlap might have inflated the correlation between EMFACS and the measure of clinical improvement. Two arguments mitigate, at least in part, this criticism. First, we recomputed the correlations utilizing only the facial behavior in the last half of the interviews that had not been seen by the clinicians who had rated improvement, so there would be independence between the behavior measured with EMFACS and the behavior viewed for the global judgment of improvement. The correlations remained at the same level of significance. Second, the lack of independence was even greater between the BPRS and the improvement measures than between either of these and EMFACS, since these two judgments not only were based on viewing the same behavior sample but were made by the very same clinicians at the very same time. Yet EMFACS was more correlated with improvement than was the BPRS. In any case, future studies should employ a more independent measure of clinical improvement, based on judgments made in settings different from the one in which the facial behavior is measured. The same stricture would apply to the sample of behavior on which the BPRS is based. It would be sensible to include also other standard clinical ratings, not just the BPRS.

Does Facial Behavior Differ Between Diagnostic Groups?

To examine this question we utilized the George Washington rather than the Langley Porter interviews. Even though there were very few patients in this sample, the diagnoses were current and there were four diagnostic groups to compare. The correlations among the frequency of an emotional expression, its duration, and mean duration were above .90. We report in figure 15.1 the mean duration for six emotions plus unfelt happiness. (Contempt is not included as a separate category because we did not distinguish it from disgust, as we do now, when this scoring was done.)

Figure 15.1 shows that the major depressives showed more sadness and disgust and less unfelt happiness than minor depressives. The manics showed more felt happiness, unfelt happiness, and less anger, disgust, or sadness than either depression group. The schizophrenics differed from the manics and the depressives in showing more fear and less of all the other emotions.

Does Facial Behavior Differ Within Diagnostic Groups?

Figure 15.2 shows the mean duration scores for the four major depressive patients. Patient 38 stands out from the others in showing no sadness, while Patient 10 differs from the others in showing much more unfelt happiness and disgust. Figure 15.3 shows the mean duration scores for the three minor depressives. Again there appear to be individual differences in emotional expressions among patients with the same diagnosis. While similar in sadness, the patients differ in regard to fear and in regard to the happy expressions.

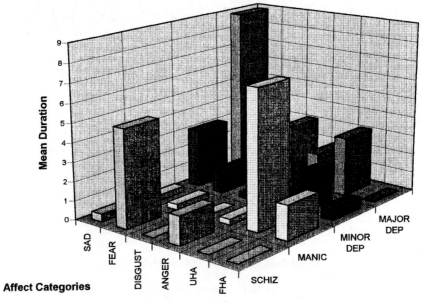

Figure 15.1 Mean duration of affect for psychiatric groups.

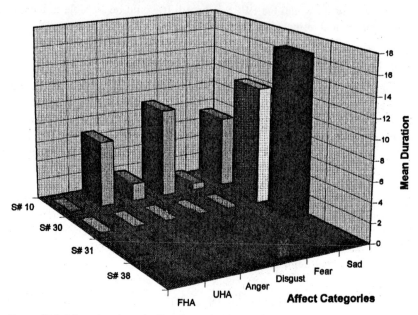

Figure 15.2 Mean duration of affect for major depressives.

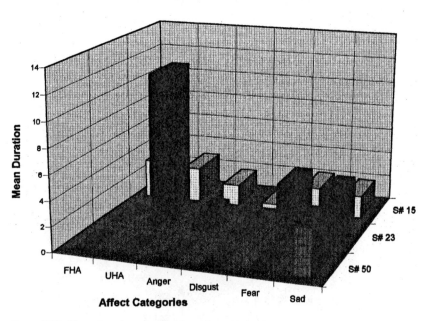

Figure 15.3 Mean duration of affect for minor depressives.

The Relationship Between FACS and EMFACS Scoring

Most clinical investigators would choose to use EMFACS rather than FACS simply because it is less costly, if the two measures produce similar results. FACS scoring, on the level of detail employed here, takes approximately one hour of scoring for each minute scored (a ratio of 60:1, scoring-to-interview time). In the George Washington sample, 20 minutes of facial behavior was scored from each of 12 patients, requiring 240 hours for FACS scoring. In EMFACS scoring, the ratio of scoring to interview time is 6 to 1. Scoring the George Washington sample with EMFACS required 24 hours.

We examined the correlation between FACS and EMFACS scoring to evaluate the similarity in the results obtained with these two measures. Different persons scored the George Washington interview sample with either FACS and with EMFACS. Rank-order correlations were computed for each scoring category in which at least ten instances of that type of behavior was scored. The mean Rho across the ten scoring categories that met this requirement was .656. For nine of the scoring categories, the correlation coefficient was significant beyond the 1% level of confidence. The one scoring category in which the correlation between EMFACS and FACS scores was not significant—the action of risorious muscle—had been the most infrequent, just meeting our requirement of at least ten occurrences, and had not yielded any differences between diagnostic groups.

Examining the number of times a type of facial behavior was scored by FACS and by EMFACS revealed that EMFACS is less sensitive than FACS. EMFACS achieves speed in scoring by not allowing the coder to inspect an expression more than three times, and by prohibiting slowed motion inspection. But this speed is gained at the cost of missing some instances of the behavior to be scored. Whenever it is important to know the absolute number of times a patient showed anger, or fear or sadness, and so forth, or exactly where in an interview each expression was shown, FACS will remain the preferred method. In many clinical studies in which it is important only to make relative differentiations, as in the data reported earlier in table 15.2, EMFACS will be the method of choice because it is less costly. (Ekman & Fridlund, 1987, have more thoroughly contrasted the advantages of each method in studies of affective disorder, and presented other arguments as to why FACS should be used in exploratory studies of affective disorders.)

Discussion

Despite the limits in the samples studied, the results should encourage clinical investigators to consider measuring facial expressions. At the very least, the results argue for repeating these studies with larger samples and better measures of clinical improvement and psychopathology. If the results were to replicate, measures of facial expression could have a variety of uses.

Facial expressions of emotion could be of use in refining diagnosis and in increasing the reliability of diagnostic classification. It would be important, for example, in new studies to determine whether the facial fear scores could help identify those patients in whom anxiety is evident in an otherwise depressed picture. Figures 15.2 and 15.3 suggest that facial measures may be of use also in distinguishing subgroups among patients who share the same diagnosis. Study could then be made of whether those subgroups differ in etiology, length of illness, or response to one or another treatment.

The most exciting finding—that facial expression measures predicted later improvement (table 15.2)—must be regarded with caution. The sample size was small (17 patients) and there were, as discussed earlier, problems with both the improvement measure and the comparison with only one standard psychiatric rating scale. Caution, however, does not require ignoring the encouraging nature of what was found. Facial measures during the acute phase of the disorder did predict the extent of subsequent improvement, and the facial measures were more powerful than the Brief Psychiatric Rating Scale in predicting improvement, accounting for variance not accounted for by the BPRS. In addition to replicating these findings, further research might investigate whether facial measures of emotional state can predict response to different forms of treatment, is of use in monitoring treatment progress not just treatment outcome, the onset of unwanted side effects with the neuroleptics, and in predicting relapse.

References

Abramson, L. Y., Garber, J., Edwards, N. B., & Seligman, M. E. (1978). Expectancy changes in depression and schizophrenia. *Journal of Abnormal Psychology, 87,* 102–109.

Beck, A. T. (1967). *Depression: Clinical, experimental, and theoretical aspects.* New York: Harper and Row.

Carney, R., Hong, B., O'Connell, M., & Amado, H. (1981). Facial electromyography as a predictor of outcome in depression. *British Journal of Psychiatry, 138,* 454–459.

Duchenne, B. (1990). *The mechanism of human facial expression or an electro-physiological analysis of the expression of the emotions* (A. Cuthbertson, Trans.) New York: Cambridge University Press. (Original work published 1862.)

Ekman, P. (1980). Asymmetry in facial expression. *Science, 209,* 833–834.

Ekman, P. (1982a). *Emotion in the human face: Guidelines for research and an integration of findings. 2nd Edition.* New York: Cambridge University Press.

Ekman, P. (1982b). Methods for measuring facial action. In K. R. Scherer & P. Ekman (Eds.), *Handbook of methods in nonverbal behavior research* (pp. 45–135). New York: Cambridge University Press.

Ekman, P., Davidson, R. J., & Friesen, W. V. (1990). The Duchenne smile: Emotional expression and brain physiology II. *Journal of Personality and Social Psychology, 58,* 342–353.

Ekman, P., & Friesen, W. V. (1975). *Unmasking the face: A guide to recognizing emotions from facial clues.* Englewood Cliffs, NJ: Prentice Hall.

Ekman, P., & Friesen, W. V. (1976). Measuring facial movement. *Environmental Psychology and Nonverbal Behavior, 1*(1), 56–75.

Ekman, P., & Friesen, W. V. (1978). *Facial action coding system: A technique for the measurement of facial movement.* Palo Alto, CA: Consulting Psychologists Press.

Ekman, P., & Friesen, W. V. (1982). Felt, false, and miserable smiles. *Journal of Nonverbal Behavior, 6*(4), 238–252.

Ekman, P., and Friesen, W. V. (1986). A new pancultural expression of emotion. *Motivation and Emotion, 10,* 159–168.

Ekman, P., Friesen, W. V., & Ancoli, S. (1980). Facial signs of emotional experience. *Journal of Personality and Social Psychology, 39*(6), 1125–1134.

Ekman, P., & Fridlund, A. J. (1987). Assessment of facial behavior in affective disorders. In J. D. Maser (Ed.), *Depression and Expressive Behavior.* Pp. 37–56. Hillsdale, NJ: Lawrence Erlbaum.

Ekman, P., Hager, J. C., & Friesen, W. V. (1981). The symmetry of emotional and deliberate facial actions. *Psychophysiology*, 18(2), 101–106.

Fox, N. A., & Davidson, R. J. (1987). Electroencephalogram asymmetry in response to the approach of a stranger and maternal separation in 10-month old children. *Developmental Psychology, 23,* 233–240.

Fridlund, A. J., Ekman, P., & Oster, H. (1985). Facial expressions of emotion. In A. Siegman & S. Feldstein (Eds.), *Nonverbal behavior and communicaion.* Pp. 143–224. Hillsdale, NJ: Lawrence Erlbaum.

Fridlund, A. J., & Izard, C. E. (1983). Electromyographic studies of facial expressions of emotions and patterns of emotions. In J. T. Cacioppo & R. E. Petty (Eds.), *Social psychophysiology: A sourcebook.* Pp. 287–306. New York: Guilford Press.

Friesen, W. V., & Ekman, P. (1985). The emotion facial action coding system (EMFACS). Unpublished document.

Hager, J. C., & Ekman, P. (1985). The asymmetry of facial actions is inconsistent with models of hemispheric specialization. *Psychophysiology, 22*(3), 307–318.

Izard, C. E. (1971). *The Face of Emotion.* New York: Appleton-Century-Crofts.

Izard, C. E. (1977). *Human Emotions.* New York: Plenum.

Katz, M. M., Koslow, S. H., Berman, N., Secunda, S., Maas, J. W., Casper, R., Kocsis, J., & Stokes, P. (1984). A multivantaged approach to measurement of behavioral and affect states for clinical and psychobiological research. *Psychological Reports. Monograph Supplements 1-V55.*

Overall, J. E., & Gorham, E. (1962). The brief psychiatric rating scale. *Psychological Reports, 10,* 799–812.

Rinn, W. E. (1984). The neuropsychology of facial expression: a review of the neurological and psychological mechanisms for producing facial expressions. *Psychological Bulletin, 95,* 52–77.

Schwartz, G., Fair, P., Salt, P., Mandel, M., & Klerman, G. (1976a). Facial expression and imagery in depression: An electromyographic study. *Psychosomatic Medicine, 38,* 337–347.

Schwartz, G., Fair, P., Salt, P., Mandel, M., & Klerman, G. (1976b). Facial muscle patterning to affective imagery in depressed and nondepressed subjects, *Science, 192,* 489–491.

Schwartz, G., Fair, P., Mandel, M., Salt, P., Mieske, M., & Klerman, G. (1978). Facial electromyography in the assessment of improvement in depression. *Psychosomatic Medicine, 40,* 355–360.

Teasdale, J., & Bancroft, J. (1977). Manipulation of thought content as a determinant of mood and corrugator activity in depressed patients. *Journal of Abnormal Psychology, 86,* 235–241.

Teasdale, J., & Rezin, V. (1978). Effect of thought stopping on thoughts, mood, and corrugator EMG in depressed patients. *Behavior Research and Therapy, 16,* 97–102.

Tomkins, S. S. (1963). *Affect, imagery, and consciousness,* Vol. 2, *The negative affects.* New York: Springer.

Depression and Expression

PAUL EKMAN

The first version of this article was written in 1982 and was rejected for publication. We revised it and resubmitted it two more times, and it was again rejected. The reviewers complained that the diagnostic categories in sample 1 are no longer relevant, and the size of sample 2 was too small. We were sufficiently discouraged that none of us again did any research on psychopathology and returned instead to basic research on emotion and expression.

I included this article because I am more convinced than ever that it did obtain important findings. The fact that facial measures did better than clinical ratings by expert clinicians (on the BPRS) in predicting improvement is of import and deserves to be replicated. The findings that unfelt happiness (not felt happiness) correlated with improvement adds to the evidence that this distinction is an important one, a fact borne out by many of the articles in this book. The finding on contempt is also a negative predictor of improvement and is also consistent with more recent findings on expression and psychopathology reported in this book. And the discovery of individual differences in expression among patients with the same diagnosis (in sample 2) also suggests the possible value of distinguishing subgroups of patients on the basis of emotional expressions when evaluating treatment effects. (This finding on individual differences in patients with the same diagnosis and the finding reported in the next paragraph were obtained in the middle 1970s.)

This article also reports the only evidence on the relationship between FACS and EMFACS scoring. This is an important methodological issue for anyone who is considering facial measurement, since as the article reports, EMFACS requires only one-tenth the scoring time of FACS. But as the article reports, this benefit is offset by some costs. Some emotional expressions detected by FACS are missed by EMFACS. I will reserve for the last chapter of this book a more general discussion of when to use FACS, EMFACS, or even simpler scoring or rating techniques.

16

Emotional Experience and Expression in Schizophrenia and Depression

HOWARD BERENBAUM & THOMAS F. OLTMANNS

Historically, psychopathologists have placed a great deal of emphasis on the role of emotional disturbance in schizophrenia. Whereas both Bleuler (1911/1950) and Kraepelin (1919/1971) considered affective flatness to be a universal symptom of schizophrenia, the International Pilot Study of Schizophrenia (World Health Organization, 1973) revealed that only 66% of the schizophrenic patients studied exhibited flat affect. People with major depression have also been found to have flat affect (e.g., Andreasen, 1979; Pogue-Geile & Harrow, 1984). Although blunted affect may not be a universal symptom of schizophrenia and is not specific to the disorder, it does appear to have prognostic importance (Carpenter, Bartko, Strauss, & Hawk, 1978; Knight, Roff, Barrnett, & Moss, 1979).

Most of what is known about affective flatness has come from studies in which psychiatric patients were observed during clinical interviews and received unidimensional ratings of emotional expressiveness. Unfortunately, in such studies there is a risk of overlooking several important factors. For example, it is essential to specify which facets of the emotional response are blunted. Neurological evidence indicates that the systems controlling facial expressions and subjective experience can act independently (e.g., Ross & Mesulam, 1979). This suggests the need to systematically examine both the subjective experience and the outward expression of emotion. Another important factor that has generally been overlooked is the distinction between positive and negative emotions. Knowledge concerning how groups of psychiatric patients differ from each other and from normal persons, such as whether the differences are restricted to a particular facet of emotional responding or are limited to positive or negative emotions, has implications beyond its potential diagnostic utility. The answers to these questions can provide clues to the origins of affective disturbances in psychopathologic disorder.

The mechanism that mediates schizophrenics' affective disturbance is unknown. One possible explanation is that emotional disturbances may be secondary to cognitive deficits. This hypothesis was raised by Bleuler (1911/1950), who wrote, "When concepts and ideas are only thought of in fragments, when thinking always loses itself in side issues and irrelevances, when entirely incorrect associational pathways are utilized, then certainly the emotional expressions (taking the normal as standard) cannot be adequate" (p. 365). Cognitive deficits could lead to affective flatness if they interfered with the processing of stimuli that elicit affect. If this is the case, the likelihood that schizophrenics would express emotions would be expected to vary as a function of the amount of reflection or cognitive processing that is required to experience an emotional response to a stimulus. On the other hand, blunted affect may not be a mere epiphenomenon produced by cognitive impairment. For example, blunted affect may be caused by a disturbance in the mechanism responsible for the outward expression associated with emotional responses.

Systematic study of the emotional expression of schizophrenics has only recently begun. Oltmanns, Strauss, Heinrichs, and Driesen (1988) studied the facial action of schizophrenic and normal subjects while the subjects were viewing excerpts from film clips that were expected to elicit emotional reactions. The schizophrenic subjects exhibited fewer emotional reactions than did the normal subjects in response to both amusing and frightening film clips. Oltmanns et al. also found that the schizophrenic subjects who were rated as most emotionally blunted during a clinical interview were the least emotionally responsive in the laboratory situation.

The goal of our study was to replicate and extend the findings of Oltmanns et al. (1988). First, we wanted to know whether the impairment in emotional expression that was seen in the laboratory paradigm was specific to schizophrenia or whether similar deficits in emotional responsivity would also be found among persons with major depression. Second, we wanted to examine whether differences in the emotional responding of normal and different psychopathological groups would depend on how the emotional responses were elicited or measured. In particular, we wished to explore the role of the valence and cognitive demand of the stimuli used to elicit emotional responses. Third, we wanted to explore the relation between deficits in emotional expression and other facets of emotional disturbance such as anhedonia and depressed mood.

Method

Subjects

Four groups of subjects participated in the study: 23 schizophrenics with blunted affect ("blunted schizophrenics"); 20 schizophrenics with nonblunted affect ("nonblunted schizophrenics"); 17 patients with unipolar major depression; and 20 normal control subjects. All of the psychiatric patients were receiving outpatient treatment at the time of the study. Schizophrenics were placed in the blunted group if the staff research psychologist noted that the patient exhibited blunted or flat affect as defined in the *Diagnostic and Statistical Manual of Mental Disorders* (3rd ed.; *DSM-III;* American Psychiatric Association, 1980), and the presence of affective flatness was corroborated by the staff psychiatrist. Schizophrenics who did not meet this criterion were placed in the nonblunted group.

As a further check on the division of schizophrenic patients into blunted and nonblunted groups, the investigator (Howard Berenbaum), who was blind to the subjects' group assignments, gave each subject a global rating of blunted affect after a brief structured interview designed to obtain basic sociodemographic information. The ratings of blunted affect were made on a 7-point scale ranging from *not at all blunted* (1) to *extremely blunted* (7). The investigator focused primarily on facial expressions and vocal inflections when making his blunting rating. Group means are reported in table 16.1. A Group × Sex analysis of variance (ANOVA) revealed a significant group main effect, $F(3, 72) = 38.83$, $p < .0001$. There was no significant main effect for sex, nor was there a significant Group × Sex interaction. A Tukey Honestly Significant Difference (HSD) post hoc test ($p < .05$) indicated that the blunted schizophrenics had significantly more blunted affect than did all three of the other groups, none of which differed significantly from one another. The assignments of schizophrenics to blunted and nonblunted groups were not changed on the basis of the investigator's bluntness ratings. Reclassifying the schizophrenics according to the investigator's blunting ratings did not lead to any changes in the results of the statistical analyses.

Lifetime diagnoses were made by a staff research psychologist according to *DSM-III* criteria. The diagnoses were made after a semistructured diagnostic interview that was conducted for research purposes along with a review of each patient's clinical records. All diagnoses were corroborated by a staff psychiatrist.

The diagnoses of 23 of the 60 psychiatric patients (9 nonblunted schizophrenics, 7 blunted schizophrenics, and 7 depressed patients) were randomly selected to be checked by the investigator after the patients had already completed the experimental procedures and before he had been told the patients' diagnoses. Diagnoses were made

TABLE 16.1. Sociodemographic characteristics, blunting, IQ, and medication status

Item	Blunted schizophrenics	Nonblunted schizophrenics	Depressives	Normal subjects
Age				
M	34.4	32.4	38.9	36.1
SD	10.7	9.5	11.3	10.8
Education				
M	11.0	11.3	11.6	11.5
SD	2.4	3.7	1.2	1.6
Race (% Black)	43.5	55.0	23.5	40.5
Sex (% female)	47.8	50.0	64.7	50.0
Blunting ratings				
M	5.1	2.1	2.1	1.3
SD	1.7	1.4	1.2	0.4
PPVT score				
M	87.7	94.8	106.4	105.6
SD	23.4	20.1	21.9	16.3
Medications taken				
Neuroleptic (%)	100	100	35	0
Antidepressant (%)	4	15	76	0
Lithium (%)	13	10	6	0
Antiparkinsonian (%)	61	55	6	0
No. of hospitalizations				
M	3.4	4.8	2.1	0.00
SD	2.5	5.4	2.7	0.00

Note: PPVT = Peabody Picture Vocabulary Test.

after the investigator reviewed the patient's records and conducted a structured diagnostic interview with the sections of the Diagnostic Interview Schedule (Robins, Helzer, Croughan, & Ratcliff, 1981) that pertained to affective disorders and schizophrenia. Two of the 23 diagnoses made by the investigator disagreed with those of the staff psychiatrist and psychologist: Of the 16 patients given a staff diagnosis of blunted schizophrenia, 1 was given a diagnosis of schizoaffective disorder by the investigator, as was 1 of the 7 patients given a diagnosis of major depression by the staff. Interrater reliability between the investigator's diagnoses and those of the clinical staff, measured by means of kappa, was .81. The 2 patients diagnosed as schizoaffective by the investigator were classified according to the original staff diagnoses in the statistical analyses. The results of the statistical analyses did not change when the data from these 2 patients were excluded.

Normal control subjects were recruited from a variety of sources, including posters placed in laundromats, university nonprofessional staff, and hospital nonprofessional staff. An attempt was made to match subjects in all groups on the bases of age, sex, race, and level of education. Normal control subjects were screened with the sections of the Diagnostic Interview Schedule (Robins et al., 1981) that pertained to affective disorders and schizophrenia. Potential subjects for the normal control group who received lifetime diagnoses of schizophrenia, schizoaffective disorder, or any form of major affective disorder were excluded from the study.

The sociodemographic characteristics of each of the four groups are presented in table 16.1. ANOVAs did not reveal any significant group differences in age or education. Chi-square tests did not reveal any significant group differences in sex or race. A Group × Sex ANOVA (excluding normal subjects) did not reveal any significant main effects or interactions in the number of hospitalizations, which are also reported in table 16.1.

The Peabody Picture Vocabulary Test (PPVT; Dunn, 1959) was used as a measure of verbal intelligence. Group means on the PPVT are reported in table 16.1. A Group × Sex ANOVA revealed a significant group main effect, $F(3, 72) = 4.60, p < .01$. The highest PPVT scores were obtained by depressed subjects, followed by the normal, the nonblunted schizophrenic, and the blunted schizophrenic subjects. A Tukey HSD post hoc test indicated that the blunted schizophrenics had significantly ($p < .05$) lower IQ scores than did both the depressed subjects and the normal subjects.

The percentages of subjects in each of the psychiatric groups who were receiving different types of medication are also reported in table 16.1. All of the schizophrenics were receiving neuroleptic medication.[1] Forty-three percent of the blunted schizophrenics and 55% of the nonblunted schizophrenics were receiving fluphenazine decanoate. The average doses of fluphenazine decanoate were 14.4 (mg per week) ($SD = 9.4$) among the blunted schizophrenics and 15.1 mg per week ($SD = 6.9$) among the nonblunted schizophrenics, $t(17) = 0.18$ (ns). The schizophrenics not receiving fluphenazine decanoate were receiving a variety of orally administered neuroleptic agents. The average daily dosages, calculated according to milligrams of chlorpromazine equivalents (Davis, 1976), were 484 ($SD = 332$) among blunted schizophrenics and 429 ($SD = 267$) among nonblunted schizophrenics, $t(19) = 0.42$ (ns). None of the psychiatric patients showed signs of tardive dyskinesia.

Stimulus Materials

Subjects were presented with a series of stimuli intended to elicit emotional responses. The affect-evoking stimuli varied along two dimensions: (a) positive (e.g., happiness) versus negative (e.g., disgust and contempt) and (b) the level of cognitive demand or reflection that presumably was required on the part of the subject in order to respond emotionally to the stimulus. The stimuli used in this study were selected after pilot testing with college students and were not intended to elicit reactions differing in intensity.

The stimuli involving low cognitive demand were different-tasting drinks. Tastes are capable of eliciting facial responses in anencephalic neonates (Steiner, 1974) and presumably do not require reflection. The drink that was intended to elicit negative responses was composed of one part distilled white vinegar (reduced with water to 4% acidity) and two parts water. The drink that was intended to elicit positive responses was composed of one part extra fine white sugar and five parts water by volume. Artificial food coloring was added to both drinks so that they had the same appearance.

In addition to tasting drinks, subjects were shown brief film clips lasting between 2 min 47 s and 3 min 32 s. The film clips were expected to require greater amounts of reflection and cognitive processing than were the drinks in order to elicit emotional responses. One of the two film clips that was intended to elicit a negative emotional response began with a scene taken from the film *Chinatown* and ended with a scene from the film *Marathon Man;* the other was composed of two scenes taken from the film *The Godfather.* One of the two film clips that was intended to elicit a positive emotional response was taken from the film *Bill Cosby: Himself,* in which Bill Cosby performs a stand-up comedy routine, and the audiological portion was edited so that the audience's laughter was deleted; the other was taken from the cartoon *Ali Baba Bunny* featuring Bugs Bunny and Daffy Duck.

The stimuli intended to elicit negative responses were expected to elicit primarily disgust, contempt, and fear and were not expected to elicit sadness. Sadness-eliciting film clips were not included because in previous work in our laboratory (e.g., Berenbaum, Snowhite, & Oltmanns, 1987) they had been unsuccessful in eliciting facial expressions of sadness.

Procedure

Subjects first completed the Scales for Physical and Social Anhedonia (Chapman, Chapman, & Raulin, 1976) and the Beck Depression Inventory[2] (Beck, Ward, Mendelson, Mock, & Erbaugh, 1961). Subjects then performed a facial mimicry task so that we could determine whether groups differed in the ability to move facial muscles, such as pulling up the corners of the lips in order to form a smile. It was uncommon for subjects to be unable to perform a facial movement, and the success rates of the groups did not differ significantly.

Finally, subjects were shown the four film clips and tasted the drinks. The order of the stimulus presentations was random, except that subjects were always shown at least one film clip between drinks. Subjects viewed the film clips and tasted the drinks while seated alone in a well-lit room. They were not permitted to eat, drink, or smoke during the entire procedure, and they were asked to try to sit still while viewing the film clips. The film clips were shown on a 19-in. (48.3-cm) color video monitor approximately 7 feet (2.13 m) in front of the subject. The drinks were presented to the subjects in clear 7-oz (207-ml) glasses that were approximately one-fourth full. Subjects were asked to take one sip of the drink, using a straw. They were told that they could drink as little or as much as they wished, with the provision that they drink at least enough to know what the drink tasted like. The subjects were videotaped from approximately the shoulders up while they watched the film clips and tasted the drinks.[3] The camera was behind a one-way mirror so that the subjects could not see it, although they had been told when informed consent was obtained that they would be videotaped. Immediately after each film clip and drink, the subjects were asked to fill out a form to indicate how happy or disgusted the movie and the drink had made them feel. The ratings were made on 7-point scales (1 = *not at all;* 3 = *slightly;* 5 = *moderately;* 7 = *extremely*).

Scoring and Interrater Reliability of Facial Measures

Facial expressions were rated by a Facial Action Coding System (FACS; Ekman & Friesen, 1978) accredited rater according to the Emotion Facial Action Coding System (EMFACS) (Friesen, 1986), which is a special version of the FACS. EMFACS ratings provide information concerning which parts of the face are moving as well as which emotion or blend of emotions a person is most likely to be experiencing. The rater, whose only role in the project was to make EMFACS ratings, was blind to the subjects' group memberships. In addition, the rater was unaware of which drinks the subjects were consuming and which films they were watching.

Rather than obtaining EMFACS ratings of the entire video records of each subject watching each film clip, we rated only a preselected portion of each subject's video record. We selected four segments from each film clip for which to obtain EMFACS ratings. The segments were selected after we observed pilot subjects' responses to the film clips. We selected segments that elicited facial expressions from some but not all pilot subjects. The average length of the segments was 11.5 s, and each segment consisted of material from only a single scene. The segment of the drink tasting that was selected to be rated began as soon as the subject started drinking and ended 5 s after the subject stopped drinking.

The EMFACS action unit ratings were converted, through the use of the EMFACS dictionary, into predictions of emotion. The most frequently rated emotion was happiness, and contempt was the second most frequent. Several other emotions were rated, including disgust, anger, and surprise, but none of these were rated very frequently. We developed a new category, the sum of all rated emotions other than happiness, and refer to it as *nonhappy*.

The video records of 15 randomly selected subjects were rated by a second rater, also blind to subjects' groups, in order to assess interrater reliability. The only two emotions rated with reasonably high interrater reliability were happiness ($\kappa = .68$) and contempt ($\kappa = .64$). Interrater reliability for the nonhappy category was also acceptable ($\kappa = .55$). Interrater reliability (measured with kappa) of the other specific emotions, such as surprise, were low because of the very low base rates.

Because only a portion of the video record was rated, group differences in the EMFACS ratings could arise for reasons other than differences in emotional expressiveness. In particular, it seemed plausible that the schizophrenics would respond to portions of the film clips other than those that elicited responses from the pilot subjects.

Group differences could also arise if the schizophrenics responded to the same parts of the film clips as did the normal subjects but the responses were delayed long enough to prevent their being included in the rated video segments. In order to rule out the possibility that group differences on the EMFACS ratings were an artifact of rating only a portion of the video record, we obtained additional facial ratings. A research assistant, who was blind to subjects' group memberships, recorded the number of facial expressions and the length of time during each complete film clip during which 10 randomly selected blunted schizophrenics and 10 randomly selected normal control subjects exhibited facial expressions of emotion. Both groups were divided evenly by sex. In order to examine interrater reliability, 6 of these 20 subjects were randomly selected to be rated in a similar way by a second rater. Interrater reliability, measured with the intraclass correlation (in which raters were treated as random effects and a single rater's ratings was treated as the unit of reliability), was .87.

The number of segments (summed across all four film clips) during which EMFACS ratings of facial expressions were recorded was significantly correlated with the number of expressions recorded during the four complete film clips ($r = .89, p < .001$). This suggests that the number of segments during which expressions were recorded (which is what we used as our primary dependent variable for facial expressiveness) is meaningfully related to how often subjects exhibited facial expressions throughout the entire film clip. Thus even though our primary dependent variable for facial expressiveness is based on ratings of only a portion of the video material, it appears to provide an excellent estimate of how expressive the subjects appeared throughout the entire video record.

Results

To limit the number of variables that we examined, we chose a single subjective emotion score and a single facial expression score for each type of stimulus. We combined scores for the two positive film clips and scores for the two negative film clips. Because it was rare for subjects in both the pilot and the present studies to exhibit or report happiness in response to the negative stimuli or to exhibit or report negative emotions in response to the positive stimuli, we restricted our analyses to examining positive emotional responses to the positive stimuli and negative emotional responses to the negative stimuli. For positive stimuli, we examined the reported and the observed happiness scores;[4] for negative stimuli, we examined reported disgust and the observed nonhappy scores.

The observed emotion scores for the film clips were based on the number of segments during which an emotional expression was exhibited. For example, a subject's observed emotion score for the positive films was based on the number of segments in the two positive film clips during which the subject smiled. Subjects received observed emotion scores of 0 or 1 for each drink, depending on whether they exhibited an emotional expression. For example, subjects who exhibited a nonhappy response to the negative drink received an observed emotion score of 1. Z scores based on the means and standard deviations of the entire sample, rather than on the original raw scores, were used in all ANOVAs in which more than a single dependent variable was examined. This was necessary because of the different ranges and mean scores for the different dependent variables.

Responses to Affect-Eliciting Stimuli

The nonstandardized group means, collapsed across sex, are reported in table 16.2. Standardized group means, averaged across sex and level of cognitive demand, are illustrated in figures 16.1 and 16.2. The size of the bars in figures 16.1 and 16.2 reveal the degree to which group means deviated from the total sample mean. Bars that rise above 0 indicate that the group mean was larger than the total sample mean; bars that fall below 0 indicate that the group mean was smaller than the total sample mean.

The goal of the first analysis was to examine (a) whether there were group differences in emotional responding and (b) whether such differences depended on how emotional responses were elicited or measured. We addressed these questions by conducting a 4 (group) × 2 (sex) × 2 (stimulus valence; positive vs. negative affect-eliciting stimuli) × 2 (level of cognitive demand) × 2 (measurement; reported vs. observed emotions) ANOVA, in which group and sex were the two between-subjects factors and stimulus valence, cognitive demand, and measurement were the three within-subject factors.[5]

Significant main effects for the within-subject factors were impossible because this analysis was conducted with z scores and the entire sample. Our interest in the within-subject factors was limited to whether they interacted with group. A Group × Measure interaction would indicate that the extent of group differences depended on whether emotional responses were measured with self-report or facial expressions. A Group × Valence interaction would indicate that the groups responded differently to the stimuli, depending on whether the stimuli elicited positive or negative responses. A Group × Cognitive Demand interaction would indicate that group differences varied as a function of the cognitive demand of the stimuli.

TABLE 16.2. Emotional responses to affect-eliciting stimuli

Stimuli / response	Blunted schizophrenics		Nonblunted schizophrenics		Depressives		Normal subjects	
	M	SD	M	SD	M	SD	M	SD
Positive drink								
Subjective experience[a]	3.0	2.4	3.9	2.3	1.8	1.7	2.5	1.6
Facial expression[b]	0.6	0.5	0.2	0.4	0.4	0.5	0.1	0.3
Positive film clips								
Subjective experience[c]	8.0	4.3	8.6	3.9	6.4	2.9	8.4	2.8
Facial expression[d]	1.0	1.3	3.4	2.1	1.9	1.8	3.9	2.6
Negative drink								
Subjective experience[c]	3.5	2.8	4.1	2.5	5.3	1.8	5.0	2.1
Facial expression[d]	0.6	0.5	0.7	0.5	0.9	0.3	0.9	0.4
Negative film clips								
Subjective experience[c]	9.2	3.6	7.5	5.0	8.6	4.3	9.1	3.6
Facial expression[d]	0.8	1.2	2.3	2.5	2.2	2.4	2.6	2.2

[a] Scores could range from 1 to 7.
[b] Scores could be either 0 or 1.
[c] Scores could range from 2 to 14.
[d] Scores could range from 0 to 8.

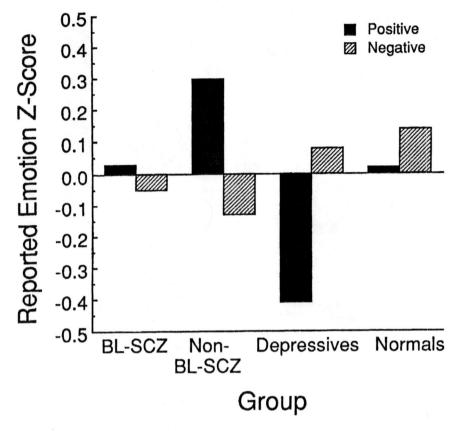

Figure 16.1 Reported emotion *z* scores, averaged across sex and level of cognitive demand. (BL-SCZ = blunted schizophrenics; Non-BL-SCZ = nonblunted schizophrenics.)

The initial ANOVA revealed a significant main effect for group, $F(3, 68) = 6.08$, $p < .005$).[6] In addition to the main effect for group, there were significant interactions between group and measure,[7] $F(3, 68) = 4.63, p < .01$, and between group and valence, $F(3, 68) = 3.96, p < .05$, indicating that group differences were influenced by how emotional responses were elicited and measured. This analysis did not reveal a significant interaction between group and cognitive demand. Thus it appears that although the groups differed in their responses to the affect-eliciting stimuli, these differences did not depend on whether the subjects were responding to drinks or to film clips.

Follow-up ANOVAs conducted separately for observed and reported emotions revealed a significant group main effect for observed emotions, $F(3, 68) = 12.00, p < .001$, whereas the group main effect for reported emotions was not statistically significant. One-way ANOVAs revealed significant group main effects for observed responses to both positive and negative stimuli (in which the sum of *z* scores for positive and negative stimuli was the dependent variable). Tukey HSD post hoc tests indicated that both the normal and the nonblunted schizophrenic subjects exhibited significantly ($p < .05$) more facial expressions in response to the positive stimuli than did either the

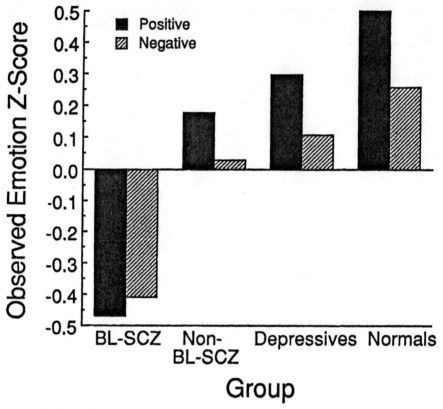

Figure 16.2 Observed emotion z scores, averaged across sex and level of cognitive demand. (BL-SCZ = blunted schizophrenics; Non-BL-SCZ = nonblunted schizophrenics.)

blunted schizophrenic or the depressed subjects and that the normal subjects exhibited significantly ($p < .05$) more facial expressions than did the blunted schizophrenics in response to the negative stimuli.

The facial ratings made on the complete film clips indicated that the difference between the normal and the blunted schizophrenic subjects was not merely an artifact of our choice of film clip segments for which to obtain EMFACS ratings. The sample of normal subjects for whom we obtained ratings of the complete film clips exhibited facial expressions of emotion during an average of 22.3 s per film clip, which was significantly longer than the average of 2.7 s exhibited by the blunted schizophrenics, $t(18) = 2.27$, $p < .05$. The groups also differed in the number of facial expressions that they exhibited. The normal subjects had an average of 3.0 expressions per film clip, which was significantly more than the average of 0.4 exhibited by the blunted schizophrenics, $t(18) = 2.43$, $p < .05$.

The interaction between group and valence appeared to be attributable primarily to the responsiveness of nonblunted schizophrenic and depressed subjects. A separate ANOVA conducted with only these two groups revealed a significant interaction between group and valance, $F(1, 30) = 10.14$, $p < .005$. The nonblunted schizophrenics were significantly more responsive than the depressed subjects to the positive stimuli (responses summed across the positive emotional response z scores), $t(33) = 3.89$, $p < .005$. Although the depressed subjects had higher scores than did the nonblunted schizophrenics in response to the negative stimuli, the difference was not statistically significant.

As noted earlier, there was a significant group effect for scores on the PPVT. Consequently, we conducted a Group × Sex × Stimulus Valence × Cognitive Demand × Measurement analysis of covariance, using IQ as the covariate. As before, there was a significant main effect for group, $F(3, 67) = 6.13$, $p < .005$, and there were significant interactions between group and valence, $F(3, 68) = 3.96$, $p < .05$, and between group and measure, $F(3, 68) = 4.63$, $p < .01$. Although the results of such an analysis must be interpreted with extreme caution (Chapman & Chapman, 1973, pp. 82–83), they are consistent with the hypothesis that the significant effects noted earlier are not artifacts of group differences in intelligence.

Questionnaire Measures

Group means, averaged across sex, on the Beck Depression Inventory and the Scales for Physical and Social Anhedonia are illustrated in figure 16.3. Group × Sex ANOVAs revealed significant group effects[8] for the Beck Depression Inventory, $F(3, 71) = 7.69$, $p < .001$; the Scale for Social Anhedonia, $F(3, 72) = 5.89$, $p < .01$; and the Scale for

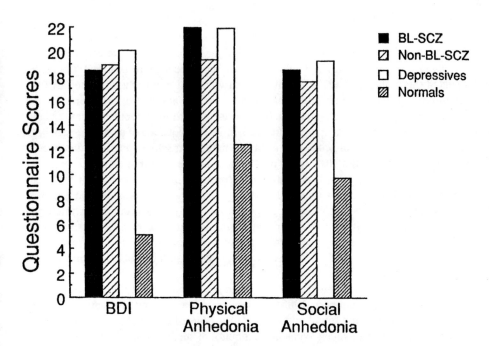

Figure 16.3 Depression and anhedonia questionnaire scores. (BL-SCZ = blunted schizophrenics; Non-BL-SCZ = nonblunted schizophrenics; BDI = Beck Depression Inventory.)

Physical Anhedonia, $F(3, 72) = 4.60, p < .01$. There was a significant sex difference on the Beck Depression Inventory, $F(1, 71) = 4.12), p < .05$: Female subjects had higher scores. There were no significant Group × Sex interactions. Tukey HSD post hoc tests ($p < .05$) revealed that all three of the psychiatric groups differed from the normal subjects, but not from one another, on the Beck Depression Inventory and the Scale for Social Anhedonia. The blunted schizophrenic and the depressed subjects differed significantly from the normal subjects on the Scale for Physical Anhedonia.

Discussion

The blunted schizophrenics were least facially expressive in response to the affect-eliciting stimuli. This finding was consistent with our expectations and suggests that our laboratory procedure tapped some aspect of clinician-rated blunted affect. The results of this study point out the potential utility of laboratory procedures for studying emotional disturbance in schizophrenia and depression.

Perhaps the most interesting result of this study was the significant interaction between group and method of measurement. The blunted schizophrenics differed significantly from other groups in their facial expressions of emotion but not in their reported emotional experiences. These findings suggest that blunted affect in schizophrenia may be primarily a disturbance of expression and not of the ability to feel, or at least report, emotional experiences. This is further supported by the three psychiatric groups' similarities in their self-reports of depression and anhedonia.

In this study we were able to examine several potential explanatory mechanisms for schizophrenics' reduced emotional expressiveness. The stimuli were intentionally chosen so that they would elicit emotional responses in markedly different ways. We hypothesized that our manipulation of the stimulus dimension that we called *cognitive demand* (e.g., drinks vs. films) would have different effects on the different groups. We expected this because of the different ways in which stimuli at the different levels of this dimension would elicit emotional responses. The absence of an interaction between group and cognitive demand is *not* consistent with the hypothesis that the emotional deficit observed in schizophrenia is a simple consequence of cognitive deficit. Of course, our results do not prove that affective flatness in schizophrenia is unrelated to cognitive deficits. In the absence of data validating the cognitive demand manipulations, we cannot be certain of its relation to information processing. Even if the cognitive demand manipulation succeeded in doing what it was intended to, there may be other cognitive deficits that were not tapped in this study. In addition, the stimuli may have differed along dimensions other than cognitive demand, such as a social-nonsocial dimension. Despite these caveats, our results suggest that if a causal relation between cognitive deficits and affective flattening does exist, it is probably more complex than we had originally anticipated.

Although it has been suggested that affective flattening may be caused by neuroleptic agents (e.g., Sommers, 1985), a simple relation between medication and emotional expression was not found in this study. The blunted and nonblunted schizophrenics were receiving equivalent types and amounts of medication, which indicates that the administration of neuroleptic agents is not sufficient to cause affective flatness. Although this study has helped to clarify the nature of the emotional disturbance in schizophrenia, additional research is necessary to elucidate the mechanism responsible for the reduction in emotional expressiveness.

Another important finding was the significant Group × Valence interaction that emerged because the nonblunted schizophrenic and depressed subjects differed in their pattern of responses to the affect-eliciting stimuli. The depressed subjects were significantly less responsive than the nonblunted schizophrenics to the positive stimuli. It is possible that the depressed subjects would have differed significantly from the other groups in response to the negative stimuli if we had used negative stimuli that elicited sadness.

The difference between the depressed and the nonblunted schizophrenic subjects is particularly interesting because the two groups did not differ from each other or from normal subjects on ratings of blunted affect made during a clinical interview. Thus although global ratings of blunted affect can provide an indication of emotional expressiveness, they are not capable of elucidating differences in the types of emotional dysfunctions seen in groups with different psychopathological disorders.

In order to expand the understanding of emotional disturbances, it is important to continue conducting multidimensional assessments of emotional reactivity. In such studies, researchers should examine which specific emotions, such as sadness, anger, and fear, are exaggerated or diminished in different psychopathological disorders. As our findings indicate, measures of emotional reactivity that are based on standard clinical interviews are probably not sufficient for discovering the many ways in which psychiatric groups differ from normal persons and from each other. It is also essential to examine the different facets of emotional responding, such as subjective experience and facial expression. Such a strategy will enable researchers to determine which specific aspects of emotional functioning are disturbed among persons with different psychiatric disorders.

The difference between the depressed subjects' and nonblunted schizophrenics' responses to the affect-eliciting stimuli is also interesting because the levels of depression reported by the two groups did not differ. Our results raise questions about the meaning of reported depression among schizophrenics. The results suggest that the depression reported by schizophrenics may be qualitatively different from the depression experienced by patients with primary diagnoses of major depression. At the very least, our results show that even when schizophrenics report being depressed, they do not share the same pattern of emotional responding exhibited by persons with major depression.

The three psychiatric groups exhibited different patterns of responding to the affect-eliciting stimuli. The blunted schizophrenics were least facially expressive. The nonblunted schizophrenics differed significantly from the depressed subjects in responses to the positive affect-eliciting stimuli. Corresponding differences on the measures of depression and anhedonia were not found, although all three groups differed quite markedly from the normal subjects. These results suggest that schizophrenics and depressed subjects exhibit a variety of disturbances in emotional functioning, each of which may be influenced independently of one another.

Notes

1. The correlations between medication dosage and measures of emotional disturbance were weak. The average correlation between dosage and reported emotions was .02. The average

correlation with observed emotional expressions was –.04. Schizophrenics receiving antiparkinsonian medication did not differ significantly from those who were not. Finally, depressives who were receiving antipsychotic medication did not differ significantly from those who were not. However, calculation of these correlations is not a strong way to evaluate drug effects (Neale & Oltmanns, 1980).

2. One of the subjects (a male nonblunted schizophrenic) omitted one page of the Beck Depression Inventory, and a score was therefore not calculated.

3. Because of mechanical failure, human error, or both, the response of 1 subject (a male nonblunted schizophrenic) to the *Chinatown* film clip was not recorded, as were the complete video records of 2 additional subjects (a depressed female subject and a female blunted schizophrenic). In addition, 1 of the subjects (a depressed female subject) exhibited a continuous chewing movement while viewing the film clips (but not at any other time), and therefore her observed responses to the film clips were treated as missing data.

4. Ekman and Friesen (1982) distinguished between felt and unfelt smiles, the former including action of both the zygomatic major and the orbicularis oculi muscles. Both felt and unfelt smiles were combined to form the observed happiness scores. Separate analyses with only the felt smiles resulted in findings similar to those obtained with the combined smile scores.

5. The dependent variables for this analysis were (a) reported and observed happiness in response to the positive stimuli and (b) reported disgust and observed nonhappy responses to the negative stimuli. It is unconventional to use different dependent measures for different conditions in the same analysis. The analysis was carried out this way because, as mentioned earlier, it was uncommon for subjects to exhibit or report positive emotions in response to the negative stimuli or negative emotions in response to the positive stimuli. Thus although different measures were used for the different conditions, all of the dependent variables were measures of the anticipated emotional responses.

6. When we conducted a parallel set of data analyses in which schizophrenics were divided into blunted and nonblunted groups on the basis of a median split of the experimenter's blunting ratings, the results were identical to those obtained when the original division of schizophrenics into blunted and nonblunted groups was used.

7. Method of measurement (reported vs. observed) was treated as a within-subject factor in the analysis of variance, rather than as multiple dependent measures. The idea of treating different measures as within-subject factors in an analysis of variance was proposed by Block, Levine, and McNemar (1951) as a means of conducting a univariate profile analysis. Because this procedure is somewhat unorthodox, a second analysis was conducted in order to assess the Group × Measurement interaction. Difference scores based on the difference between the reported and observed z scores were computed for each subject in response to each stimulus. A Group × Sex multivariate analysis of variance was then conducted with the six difference scores (one difference score per stimulus) as dependent measures. A main effect for group, $F(18, 178.68) = 2.05$, $p < 0.01$, was significant; this indicates that the differences between reported and observed scores differed significantly across groups and is consistent with the significant Group × Measure interaction obtained in the univariate analysis of variance.

8. Similar results were obtained when subjects with infrequency scores of 3 or higher were excluded from the analyses.

References

American Psychiatric Association (1980). *Diagnostic and statistical manual of mental disorders (3rd ed.)*. Washington, DC: Author.

Andreasen, N. C. (1979). Affective flattening and the criteria for schizophrenia. *American Journal of Psychiatry, 136*, 944–947.

Beck, A. T., Ward, C. H., Mendelson, M., Mock, J. E., & Erbaugh, J. K. (1961). An inventory for measuring depression. *Archives of General Psychiatry, 4,* 561–571.

Berenbaum, H., Snowhite, R., Oltmanns, T. F. (1987). Anhedonia and emotional responses to affect evoking stimuli. *Psychological Medicine, 17,* 677–684.

Bleuler, E. (1950). *Dementia praecox or the group of schizophrenias* (J. Zinkin, Trans.). New York: International Universities Press. (Original work published 1911)

Block, J., Levine, L., & McNemar, Q. (1951). Testing for the existence of psychometric patterns. *Journal of Abnormal and Social Psychology, 46,* 356–359.

Carpenter, W. T., Jr., Bartko, J. J., Strauss, J. S., & Hawk, A. B. (1978). Signs and symptoms as predictors of outcome: A report from the international pilot study of schizophrenia. *American Journal of Psychiatry, 135,* 940–945.

Chapman, L. J., & Chapman, J. P. (1973). *Disordered thought in schizophrenia.* New York: Appleton-Century-Crofts.

Chapman, L. J., Chapman, J. P., & Raulin, M. L. (1976). Scales for physical and social anhedonia. *Journal of Abnormal Psychology, 85,* 374–382.

Davis, J. M. (1976). Comparative doses and costs of antipsychotic medication. *Archives of General Psychiatry, 33,* 858–861.

Dunn, L. M. (1959). *Peabody Picture Vocabulary Test* (manual). Nashville, TN: American Guidance Service.

Ekman, P., & Friesen, W. V. (1978). *The facial action coding system (FACS): A technique for the measurement of facial action.* Palo Alto, CA: Consulting Psychologists Press.

Ekman, P., & Friesen, W. V. (1982). Felt, false, and miserable smiles. *Journal of Nonverbal Behavior, 6,* 238–252.

Friesen, W. (1986). Recent developments in FACS-EMFACS. *Face Value: Facial Measurement Newsletter, 1,* 1–2.

Knight, R. A., Roff, J. D., Barnett, J. & Moss, J. L. (1979). Concurrent and predictive validity of thought disorder and affectivity: A 22 year follow-up of acute schizophrenics. *Journal of Abnormal Psychology, 88,* 1–12.

Kraepelin, E. (1919/1971). *Dementia praecox and paraphrenia* (R. M. Barclay, Trans.). Huntingdon, NY: Krieger.

Neale, J. M., & Oltmanns, T. F. (1980). *Schizophrenia.* New York: Wiley.

Oltmanns, T. F., Strauss, M. E., Heinrichs, D. W., & Driesen, N. (1988). *Social facilitation of emotional expression in schizophrenia.* Paper presented at the meeting of the Society for Research in Psychopathology, Cambridge, MA, November.

Pogue-Geile, M. F., & Harrow, M. (1984). Negative and positive symptoms in schizophrenia and depression: A followup. *Schizophrenia Bulletin, 10,* 371–387.

Robins, L. N., Helzer, J. E., Croughan, J., & Ratcliff, K. S. (1981). The NIMH Diagnostic Interview Schedule: Its history, characteristics, and validity. *Archives of General Psychiatry, 38,* 381–389.

Ross, E. D., & Mesulam, M. M. (1979). Dominant language functions of the right hemisphere? Prosody and emotional gesturing. *Archives of Neurology, 36,* 144–148.

Sommers, A. E. (1985). Negative symptoms: Conceptual and methodological problems. *Schizophrenia Bulletin, 11,* 364–379.

Steiner, J. E. (1974). Innate discriminative human facial expressions to taste and smell stimulation. *Annals of the New York Academy of Science, 237,* 229–233.

World Health Organization. (1973). *The international pilot study of schizophrenia.* Geneva: Author.

Emotion, Facial Expression, and Psychopathology

HOWARD BERENBAUM & LAURA NISENSON

The study reprinted in this volume (Berenbaum & Oltmanns, 1992) attempted to address several issues that had received relatively little prior attention. First, most of the prior research examining affective flattening in schizophrenia used global ratings of affective flattening that were made following a clinical/diagnostic interview. We believed it would be helpful to study emotion in psychiatric patients using strategies similar to those used by researchers studying "basic" emotional processes, namely (1) using a laboratory-type, standardized, affect eliciting procedure; and (2) examining specific types of facial expressions rather than relying on global judgments of facial expressivity. We also wished to compare different diagnostic groups (individuals with schizophrenia and individuals with major depressive disorder) with each other and with nonpsychiatric control participants. Finally, we wished to test the hypothesis that the diminished facial expressiveness often seen in individuals with schizophrenia might be influenced by a reduction in their ability to process affect-eliciting information.

We have conducted several studies examining facial expressions in psychiatric patients since conducting the study reprinted in this volume. In a study conducted with the same group of participants, Berenbaum (1992) examined facial expressions as a means of studying participants' tendencies to experience different types of emotion. Participants were asked to show what they thought their faces would look like if (1) something wonderful happened to them (positive event prompt); and (2) they saw, smelled, or tasted something disgusting (disgust prompt). The participants' initial facial expressions in response to each prompt were rated using EMFACS. The results revealed that in response to the positive event prompt, the schizophrenic, depressed, and nonpsychiatric control participants were equally likely to smile (defined solely on the basis of the raising of the corners of the lips). However, the facial expressions of the depressed individuals were less likely to be considered indicative of happiness than were the facial expressions exhibited by the nonpsychiatric control participants. In response to the disgust prompt, the depressed individuals were more likely than the other groups to exhibit facial expressions of anger or contempt. Thus, this study provided behavioral evidence that individuals with major depressive disorder tend to be less happy and more angry than both schizophrenic and nonpsychiatric individuals.

Stolar, Berenbaum, Banich, and Barch (1994) examined the neuropsychological correlates of affective flattening. Because we were interested in global affective flattening, clinical ratings were made using the affective flattening scale of the Schedule for the Assessment of Negative Symptoms (Andreasen, 1983). We found that higher levels of affective flattening were associated with right hemisphere dysfunction. These results, coupled with the findings by Berenbaum and Rotter (1992) that individuals with poorer volitional control of their facial muscles were less facially expressive when viewing affect-eliciting filmclips, led us to hypothesize that a deficit in the ability to access or utilize mental representations of actions and expressions contributes to affective flattening in schizophrenia.

Nisenson, Berenbaum, Payne, and Resnick (1991) examined the facial expressions of schizophrenic, depressed, and nonpsychiatric individuals in an interpersonal context. We examined the communication of emotion while patients described emotional events in their lives to an interviewer. Facial expressions were measured using EMFACS. We found that the depressed and schizophrenic individuals exhibited significantly fewer felt smiles (i.e., smiles that indicate happiness) than the nonpsychiatric controls. In contrast, the three groups did not differ in how frequently they exhibited unfelt smiles (i.e., smiles that do not reflect felt happiness). These results suggest that the diminished smiling exhibited by schizophrenic and depressed individuals is not due to problems adhering to social display rules but is more likely linked to deficits in spontaneous expression.

Nisenson and Berenbaum (1992) arranged for each of 10 college students to spend 10 minutes interacting with each of 6 hospitalized schizophrenic patients. Our goal was to examine individual differences in the degree to which hospitalized psychiatric patients were liked by their interaction partners. We found that some patients were consistently liked more than others. In this study we also measured how frequently patients smiled. We had hypothesized that patients who smiled more frequently would be better liked than patients who smiled less frequently. However, we found that smiling frequency was not associated with patient likability.

Our experience studying facial expressions in psychiatric patients has taught us how helpful tools such as FACS can be. In particular, FACS can be invaluable when one wishes to examine issues that cannot be adequately addressed using clinical rating scales or even by using global facial ratings made by trained raters. For example, the use of FACS enabled Berenbaum (1992) to find that depressives were less likely to exhibit facial expressions of happiness than nonpsychiatric controls even though they were equally likely to smile. Similarly, the use of FACS enabled Nisenson et al. (1991) to find that schizophrenic and depressed individuals differed from nonpsychiatric controls in the frequency with which they exhibited felt smiles, but not in how frequently they exhibited unfelt smiles.

Although FACS can be extremely useful, it is not without its difficulties. The most complicated problem we have faced is how to utilize all of the detailed information that FACS ratings provide. Even when the information from the individual action units is converted into emotion predictions, the variety and complexity of facial expression categories can be daunting. In our view, FACS is a useful tool, but is not necessarily the right tool for every job. For example, if all one wishes to examine is participants' average amount of facial expressiveness, FACS is, in our opinion, not necessary. In contrast, it has been our experience that FACS can be invaluable when one wishes to test a

specific hypothesis that requires knowing more than how much global, or even va-
lenced, facial expressiveness is exhibited.

References

Andreasen, N. C. (1983). *Scale for the Assessment of Negative Symptoms*. Iowa City: University
of Iowa.

Berenbaum, H. (1992). Posed facial expressions of emotion in schizophrenia and depression.
Psychological Medicine, 22, 929–937.

Berenbaum, H., & Oltmanns, T. F. (1992). Emotional experience and expression in schizophrenia
and depression. *Journal of Abnormal Psychology, 101*, 37–44.

Berenbaum, H., & Rotter, A. (1992). The relationship between spontaneous facial expressions of
emotion and voluntary control of facial muscles. *Journal of Nonverbal Behavior, 16*,
179–190.

Nisenson, L., & Berenbaum, H. (1992). *Individual differences in schizophrenics' impact on their
interaction partners*. Paper presented at the annual meeting of the Society for Research in
Psychopathology, November, Palm Springs, CA.

Nisenson, L., Berenbaum, H., Payne, D., & Resnick, H. (1991). *Felt and unfelt smiles in schizophrenia and depression*. Paper presented at the annual meeting of the Midwestern Psychological Association, May, Chicago, IL.

Stolar, N., & Berenbaum, H., Banich, M. T., & Barch, D. (1994). Neuropsychological correlates
of alogia and affective flattening in schizophrenia. *Biological Psychiatry, 35*, 164–172.

17

Interaction Regulations Used by Schizophrenic and Psychosomatic Patients

Studies on Facial Behavior in Dyadic Interactions

EVELYNE STEIMER-KRAUSE, RAINER KRAUSE & GÜNTER WAGNER

Hypotheses were elaborated on the basis of the therapeutic experience of one author (R.K.) as well as the clinical psychiatric and experimental empirical findings on the patient groups examined. Our approach was guided by statements found in the psychoanalytic literature on conflicts, defense and forms of transference associated with each group of illnesses, and on the corresponding manifestations of countertransference.

Concerning schizophrenic patients, the psychiatric literature (Bleuler, 1969; Schulte & Tölle, 1979) contains accounts, in particular, of reduction phenomena such as emotional shallowness and absence of the ability to modulate emotions and to integrate emotional factors. Concepts such as paramimia and parthymia (Bleuler) and the description of the "expression syndrome of the disintegration of facial activity" have represented attempts to describe these observations (Heimann & Spoerri, 1957). Experimental psychological research on facial expressions of schizophrenics has been concerned either with the decoding ability of schizophrenics (Dougherty, Bartlett, & Izard, 1974; Larusso, 1978; Muzekari & Bates, 1977; Pilowsky & Barnett, 1980; Walker, Marwit, & Emory, 1980; Walker, 1981) or with the extent to which facial "gestalts" of schizophrenics can be evaluated by other test subjects (Gottheil, Paredes, Exline, & Winkelmayer, 1970; Gottheil, Thornton, & Exline, 1976; Winkelmayer, Exline, Gottheil, & Paredo, 1978).

There is, however, no satisfactory explanation for the finding that the facial expressions of schizophrenic patients cannot be decoded as correctly as the expressions of healthy subjects by healthy raters; this refers to qualitative, behaviorally defined particularities of the expressions observed in both groups.

In the psychoanalytic literature, little significance was originally attached to expression phenomena, since the problems of the patients were described in terms of an intrapsychic conflict between the intensive desire for symbiosis, on the one hand, and the simultaneous fear of fusion and dependency, on the other (Frosch, 1983; Rohde-Dachser, 1985). It has been confirmed by various authors (Moser, 1964; Mentzos, 1977), however, that one criterion for the increasing severity of a disturbance is the extent to which the defense mechanisms are shifted from the intrapsychic to the interactive realm. The "cathexis defense" as an intrapsychic mechanism for the regulation of a threatened autonomy has, accordingly, an interactive counterpart in the real avoidance of closeness, a fact that is of great therapeutic significance (Searles, 1984/1985).

On the basis of these considerations and of more detailed considerations presented elsewhere (Krause, Steimer, Sanger-Alt, & Wagner, 1989), it was postulated that in our experimental situation (i.e., conversation with a stranger) the schizophrenics would be primarily intent on maintaining the greatest possible distance during their interactions, and that this would be reflected in reduced facial activity and affectivity.

It was further assumed that the interaction partners of the schizophrenic patients would respond to the postulated desire of these patients for distance by reducing their own facial activity and affectivity to a level below that observed in healthy subjects interacting with each other.

The psychosomatic patients were chosen as the clinical control group for the schizophrenic patients because disturbances in affectivity have been postulated for them as well (von Rad, 1983). Even though the alexithymia theory postulates massive restriction of the affective experience of psychosomatic patients, there have been no studies to date directly measuring and interpreting the facial expressions of adult psychosomatic patients with respect to affective quality. Since we believe, on the basis of clinical experience and theoretical considerations regarding the psychological nature of affects, that psychosomatic illness is not one single clinical entity, we have included patients belonging to two subgroups of so-called psychosomatic illness—namely, ulcerative colitis and functional vertebral complaints—in our study. The suspicion of alexithymia would apply, if at all, only to those groups in which a measurable pathological change in a functional vegetative process can be found. Since it has been postulated, at least by psychoanalytical authors, that this group suffers from structural disturbances, with unresolved problems of individuation, it was expected that the colitis patients would exhibit generally reduced facial activity as one of the indicators of alexithymia, similar to the schizophrenic patients. For patients with pathological changes of the skeletal muscles, e.g., those with functional vertebral complaints, a conversion in the sense of an inhibition of the carrying out of an affect reaction—but not of the signal portion—was postulated.

In summary, the following hypotheses were formulated:

1. The patients differ from the healthy subjects in facial expressiveness.
2. Because of the postulated transference/countertransference processes at work in dyads with patients, the differences evident between patients and the persons in the healthy control group should be greater than those between the patients and their healthy interaction partners.
3. There are specific characteristic values for facial activity associated with each of the different pathologies. Each of the various patient groups exhibits a different deviation from the facial expressions found in the healthy control group, and the various patient groups differ from each other in this respect.
4. As a result of their greater stability, the schizophrenic outpatients are expected

to demonstrate a smaller deviation in their facial expressiveness from the healthy control group than do the schizophrenic inpatients. The same tendency is expected to be shown by the healthy interaction partners of both groups of schizophrenic patients.

5. Nevertheless, inpatient and outpatient schizophrenic subjects are expected to have identical values characterizing them as belonging to one pathological entity.
6. The patients with ulcerative colitis are expected to show greater changes in facial expressiveness in comparison with the control group than the patients suffering from functional vertebral complaints.
7. On the basis of clinical psychiatric descriptions, reductions in facial activity and affectivity are expected to occur in both the colitis patients and the schizophrenic patients.

Methodology

Subjects

Eighty male subjects (20 schizophrenics, 10 psychosomatic patients and 50 healthy subjects) were divided into four types of dyads. Dyad type 1 constituted the control group, in which two healthy subjects per dyad interacted with each other (10 dyads). In dyad type 2, a schizophrenic outpatient and a healthy subject talked to each other (10 dyads). Dyad type 3 consisted of a schizophrenic inpatient and a healthy subject (10 dyads), and dyad type 4 consisted of a psychosomatic patient and a healthy subject (6 patients with ulcerative colitis and 4 with functional vertebral complaints). The interaction partners in each dyad were matched in age and education.

Table 17.1 provides information on the age and education of the subjects. The average age of the group of psychosomatic patients was 7 years greater than the average age of the others, a difference not reaching significance. Nevertheless, this difference will be considered in the interpretation of the data. The schizophrenic patients were requested to participate by the psychiatrists treating them; the schizophrenic inpatients

TABLE 17.1. Average age, range of age, educational level of the subjects*

	Dyad Type 1		Dyad Type 2		Dyad Type 3		Dyad Type 4	
	health A	health B	schiz O	health	schiz I	health	psychosom	health
Age								
Average	27	27.6	28.7	26.6	29.3	29.3	36.2	36.9
Range	19–42	19–42	19–44	19–40	23–41	25–35	22–50	26–57
Education Level†								
I	4	4	5	5	4	5	1	2
II	4	3	2	1	3	—	1	2
III	2	3	3	4	3	5	8	6

* Health = healthy subjects; schiz O = schizophrenic outpatients; schiz I = schizophrenic inpatients; pyschosom = psychosomatic patients.
† I = graduation from a college preparatory high school; II = graduation from a non-college preparatory high school; III = elementary education.

were all patients at a day clinic (patients work at the clinic and are treated during the day; they return home at night). All were undergoing treatment with neuroleptica of various kinds administered in different dosages. The average duration of illness since the first manifestation was 4 (2–13 years) for the outpatients and 6½ years (1–15 years) for the inpatients. On the average, the schizophrenic subjects had three hospital admissions behind them. Of the 20 schizophrenic patients, 18 belonged to the paranoid-hallucinatory subgroup (ICD-9:295.3), one to the hebephrenic subgroup (ICD-9:295.1), and one to the schizophrenia simplex subgroup (ICD-9:295.0). In 6 patients (5 inpatients and 1 outpatient), moreover, residual/deficiency conditions (ICD-9:295.69) had been diagnosed. In consultation with the doctors treating these patients, subjects were recruited only from among those schizophrenic patients who demonstrated a certain ability to communicate and who would not be expected to experience decompensation as a result of the study. In the outpatient group, the last hospital admission had taken place a year before, while the inpatients had spent an average of 10 months in the hospital (on the ward and in the day clinic) prior to the time of admission. None of the patients showed productive symptoms during the experiment.

The patients with psychosomatic illnesses had been undergoing treatment as inpatients at a hospital for psychogenic diseases and had also been chosen by the doctors treating them. Subjects with functional vertebral complaints suffered from vertebral complaints without any organic findings and, according to the case history taken from psychoanalytic interviewing, from a neurotic disturbance.

The healthy subjects were obtained via a newspaper ad. Persons with noticeable clinical symptoms were turned down over the telephone. In addition, the Freiburg Personality Inventory (FPI-R; Fahrenberg, Hampel, & Selg, 1984) was used for selection purposes. All of the subjects were told only that they were to take part in a study on conversational behavior, during which they would be expected to carry on an everyday conversation that would be recorded with video cameras. The subjects each received a fee of DM 20, equivalent to $10.00.

The Experiment

All of the subjects were filmed while carrying on a political conversation with interaction partners they had never met before on the four most important political problems now confronting the Federal Republic of Germany. The experimental set-up, setting and instructions have been described in detail in Krause et al. (1989). The evaluation of the facial expressions was based on the 20-minute discussion period and was made by means of video pictures with time marking. Each interaction partner was videotaped full face with a remote-controlled camera; these separate images were then combined by a trick mixer into a split-screen double image and fed onto video film.

Evaluation

The facial expressions were evaluated by means of the Emotional Facial Action Coding System (EMFACS), which was developed by Friesen and Ekman (1984) on the basis of the Facial-Action-Coding-System (FACS; Ekman & Friesen, 1978). Both FACS and EMFACS are coding systems for recording visible facial movements. Certain muscle innervations are grouped into so-called "action units" (AUs) on the basis of their functional anatomy. Each of these action units is assigned a number; each possible visible change in facial expression can thus be assigned a code number. In this manner inferences about each facial expression are separated from data collection.

In comparison to FACS, EMFACS registers only action units associated with emotions (see figure 17.4 for list of all the action units). In addition, certain action units are rated as to intensity (5-point scale), laterality and asymmetry. Friesen and Ekman (1984) have set down "event rules" for the EMFACS; these rules enable the observer to register those facial expressions within a continuous stream of behavior that are part of one "event," for example, an expression of affect. The decision as to whether two AUs are part of one event or represent two different emotional events can be settled by referring to the hierarchy of conditions; in this context minimum requirements are set with respect to the temporal overlapping of AUs, the maximum intervals between the beginnings of innervations, and fluctuations in innervation intensity (see also Steiner, 1983). In addition, the EMFACS Manual contains a lexicon on the basis of which events can be assigned to the following categories: primary affects (happiness, anger, sadness, disgust, contempt, fear, surprise, interest), blends, masking and various nonspecific negative affects. Blends are forms of facial expressions containing sufficient determinant parts of at least two affects. Masking comprises various forms of "covering up" negative affects with smiling. Nonspecific negative affects are expressions that cannot be clearly assigned to any one negative primary affect. The lexicon contains rules, moreover, for distinguishing between felt and unfelt happiness. One of the most significant distinguishing features in this respect is the synchronous innervation of one of the ocular ring muscles (AU6 or AU7) during smiling (AU12).

A computer program developed by Friesen and Ekman (1984) and Wagner (1986) was used to interpret the codings in accordance with the categories described above. Following several transformation steps, the program supplies a categorization of all codings. Because coding of EMFACS requires perfect knowledge of FACS, all coders were trained in FACS and had to pass the final test with success (reliability over .83). The question of reliability within the EMFACs cannot be automatically deduced from a satisfactory reliability on FACS. EMFACS implies a selection procedure based on the knowledge of FACS, because the coders register only certain AUs and mark them as one event shortly before the expression has its maximum. Our data were coded by one coder, so that even if she was mistaken the likelihood that she made her errors in an unsystematic way is small. Nevertheless, we checked interrater reliability with the help of two or more coders who were trained in the same way. Since the subjects are very different in terms of the difficulty of coding them, we chose one person out of the control group who happened to incorporate all difficulties we might encounter in coding, and one who was rather easy to code. The most difficult was a healthy subject with a large amount of facial expression during speech, which often led to the question of how to code the facial movement. The schizophrenic and the psychosomatic patients are much easier to code, even during speaking.

Retest reliability of the AUs after 4 years for an easy subject, using 28 events within 2 minutes, is 0.85. Retest reliability of the EMFACS categories is 1.00. With the most difficult person's 54 events within 2 minutes retest reliability, on the event level, is 0.7. Retest reliability of the EMFACS categories is .89. Intercoder reliability within two separate 2-minute samples with the most difficult person, comparing the 4-year-old coding with a recent coding by a new coder, is for the affect interpretation of .87 and

.54 respectively. Intercoder reliability with the easy subject mentioned above is .73 on the event level and 1.00 with the EMFACS categories. Intercoder reliability with a third coder with the most difficult subject is .87. Even for rare events such as negative emotions reliability is quite high. The validity of the assignment to categories is based on ethnological and ethological research as well as on the judgment of experienced clinicians and researchers on facial expressions. An up-to-date discussion of this topic is provided by Ekman (1985). As has already been mentioned, the assignment of code numbers to the categories can be regarded as conservative.

Results

First the structure of the available data on facial expression will be presented, on the basis of which the individual results can be assigned a place in the total body of data. A section on the relationship between facial and verbal activity will follow. After this, the hypotheses will be re-examined individually.

Figure 17.1 contains the interpretation categories used for comparing the subjects. The percentages indicate the data distribution in the categories for the control group of 20 healthy subjects. Two evaluation levels are distinguished: firstly, action units; secondly, facial events consisting of one or several action units.

Within the second unit of analysis (facial events), those events which can be interpreted by using the EMFACS lexicon are first separated from those which cannot be interpreted with EMFACS. The latter comprise facial expressions accompanying speech, illustrating and emblematic facial expressions, and a group of facial expressions that cannot be interpreted at the present level of development of the EMFACS lexicon.

The results interpreted with EMFACS can be broken down, in turn, into two main groups: expressions that clearly correspond to a certain primary affect and those for which this is not the case. Events that lent themselves to interpretation but that did not clearly represent any one primary affect were divided in our sampling into three categories: blends and maskings, possible anger, and unfelt happiness/social smiling. The category "possible anger" is based on action units that are components of expressions of anger but that can also occur in other contexts. Tighten one's lips together (AU23), for example, can be a component of "controlled anger" but can also occur during other control intentions and swallowing. Lastly, the primary affects are divided into those with positive and negative hedonistic coloring.

Since we recorded facial expressions within the context of a conversational situation, the relationship between facial and verbal activity has to be taken into account. The exact nature of the relationship between facial expressiveness and talking has hardly been examined at all. Our findings thus far (Krause, 1982a) indicate that more facial expressions are exhibited during talking. It therefore seems reasonable to adjust the production of facial expressions by the amount of talking (number of words spoken per subject or by the talking time of each subject), especially since the patients spoke less than did the healthy control subjects in our sampling (ANOVA; $df = 3$; $F = 2.85$; $p = .051$).

The direction of influence in the positive relationship between speech and facial expressions is by no means clear, however. Our experience, particularly with schizophrenic patients, has been that verbal and facial productivity is regulated in part by a

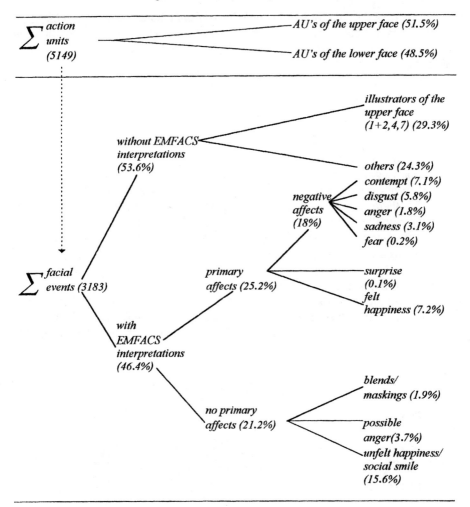

Figure 17.1 Structure of the data.

superordinate control system determining the intensity of "involvement" (Villenave-Cremer, Kettner, & Krause, 1989). It appears, moreover, that there are relationships between language and facial expressions characteristic for specific disorders. The increase in facial activity during talking does not apply to psychosomatic patients, for example. Since facial expressions are made up of qualitatively different phenomena, such as expressions of affect, signals accompanying speech, etc. (see figure 17.1), it can also be assumed that depending on which category is examined, different kinds of relationships will become evident.

On the basis of a detailed analysis of two dyads, moreover, we find evidence that the frequency of facial events depends not only on the number of words spoken by the individuals taking part in the interaction but also on the number of times the conversational ball passes between the two partners (Jablonsky, 1989). For all of these reasons, an adjustment of the data for facial expressions during talking was undertaken only for those facial events that clearly served the function of accompanying speech. These are the raising of eyebrows (AU1 and AU2), which occurred during talking in 80% of the 1656 cases.

Action Units

To begin with, the sum of the action units is to be considered as an operationalization of facial productivity. Since all measures are highly interrelated, only one person from each dyad from the group of 20 healthy subjects talking to each other could be used; because the values of each partner are not only determined by inner processes but also by the partner's values, the degree of freedom is 10 instead of 20. As can be seen from figure 17.2, there are great differences between the random sample taken from the control group and all other subjects, but only slight differences between the patients and their healthy interaction partners. All patient groups—and the interaction partners of the hospitalized schizophrenics—exhibited a significant reduction in facial productivity (see table 17.2) in comparison with the random sample. Within the dyads there is no appreciable difference between the schizophrenic subjects and their partners. There is, however, a significant difference between the psychosomatic patients and their partners (Wilcoxon, $p < .05$). The pronounced discrepancy between the random sample from the control group and the healthy partners of the patients can be interpreted as a first

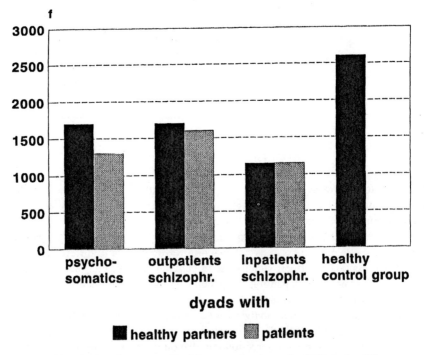

Figure 17.2 Absolute frequency (f) of the sum of action units (AU) in the different groups.

TABLE 17.2. Means (*M*), medians (*Md*), standard deviations (*SD*) and significance values (*p*) for differences with control group concerning total facial productivity (ΣAU), upper face productivity (UF) and lower face productivity (LF)*

		Patients			Healthy Partners			
		so	si	ps	pso	psi	pps	cg
ΣAU	*M*	148.5	108.9	134.5	169.7	111.8	170.1	260.4
	Md	113.5	90	103	155.5	97	137	196
	SD	116.2	69.7	124.1	66.2	60.7	94.9	177.4
	$p^\dagger$	*	**	*		**		
ΣUF	*M*	35.3	15.1	74.7	68.3	44.2	70	140.6
	Md	29.5	11.5	35.5	73.5	29.5	70	95
	SD	28.7	8.3	132.5	29.6	32.7	37.9	135.4
	p	**	***	*		*		
ΣLF	*M*	113.2	93.8	59.8	101.4	67.6	100.1	119.8
	Md	77.5	76.5	53.5	88	67.5	87.5	91.5
	SD	94.6	64.9	29.7	46.5	31.9	69.9	73.5
	p			**		*		

* So = schizophrenic outpatients (*n* = 10), si = schizophrenic inpatients (*n* = 10), ps = psychosomatic patients (*n* =10); pso, psi, pps = healthy interaction partners of the patients; cg = random sample from the healthy control group.
$\dagger p$ values, Mann-Whitney *U*-tests: *$p < .05$, **$p < .01$, ***$p < .001$.

indication that adaptive processes are at work here, with the healthy subjects adjusting to the patients.

Variability of facial expressions, like facial productivity, was reduced in all the patients. This reduction affected the repertoire of facial expressions, i.e., the number of different action units, as well as the number of different facial events recorded per subject. In contrast to facial productivity, however, no reduction in these two variables was exhibited by the partners of the patients, as compared to the random sample—i.e., the partners reduce their expressiveness quantitatively without limiting their repertoire.

In order to determine more precisely which expressions were particularly affected by the reduction in productivity and variability, upper face and lower face productivity were examined separately.

In comparison with the random sample, all other groups of subjects are limited with respect to the productivity of the upper face (see fig. 17.3). The sum of the action units for the lower face differentiates the groups to a lesser extent. In addition, distinct differences appear within the dyads: in dyads with schizophrenic patients, the upper face activity of the patients is also reduced vis-à-vis their partners; in the psychosomatic patients, the sum of lower face innervations is reduced in comparison to both the partners and the control groups.

An examination of the total productivity values—i.e., the sum of the AUs of the upper face and the sum of the AUs of the lower face—reveals important differences between the patient groups. Whereas the schizophrenic patients show less activity in the upper face and unchanged activity in the lower face, the two types of psychosomatic patients exhibited limitations of lower face activity. The interaction partners of the

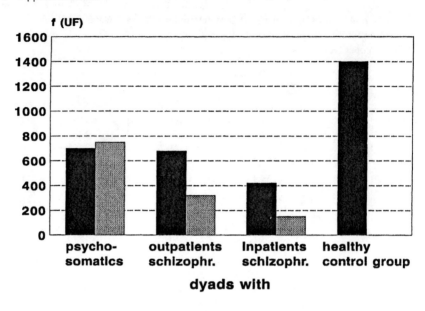

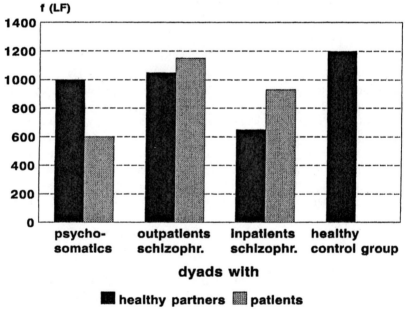

Figure 17.3 Absolute frequency (f) of the total action units (AU) for the upper face (UF) and the lower face (LF) in the different groups.

patients also showed less facial productivity than did the control group; among the partners of the schizophrenic inpatients, this difference was above the significance level.

In the following, we will examine the question of which specific action units are responsible for the reductions of productivity observed in each of the different groups of subjects in comparison with the control group.

The frequency distribution of the action units in the random sample will be described first (figure 17.4). With respect to frequency of occurrence, three groups of action units can be distinguished. The first group comprises three action units in two expression forms—the combination AU1 and AU2 (raising of eyebrows) and AU12 (smile muscle). Taken together, these expressions account for more than 50% of all facial productivity. The second group consists of AUs whose contribution to total productivity amounts to an average of 2.5%–8%. These include expressions of the upper face (AU6, AU7, AU4) and of the lower face (AU10, AU17, AU23, AU14, AU15). The remaining AUs (AU5, AU9, AU11, AU16, AU18, AU20, AU22, AU24) occur infrequently (AU25 and AU26 are different forms of mouth opening and are not of direct interest here).

In the schizophrenic subjects, all expressions of the upper face (AU1, AU2, AU4, AU6, AU7) are reduced in comparison with the control group. There is thus a nonspecific limitation of upper face expressiveness, with the reductions recorded in the schizophrenic inpatients being as a rule more pronounced than those in the schizophrenic outpatients (see table 17.3). In the lower face, both groups of schizophrenic patients exhibited reductions affecting AU12 (smile muscle) and AU17 (lifting of the chin).

The action units in question can occur as components of primary affects but also as

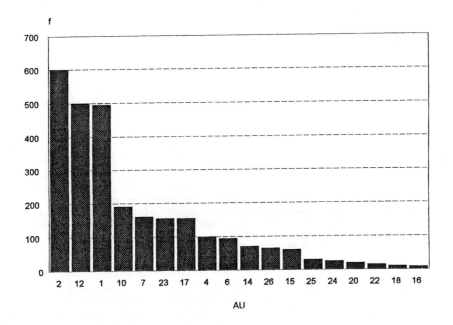

AU1 = Inner Brow Raiser; AU2 = Outer Brow Raiser; AU 4 = Brow Lowerer;
AU 5 = Upper Lid Raiser; AU 6 = Cheek Raiser; AU 7 = Lid Tightener;
AU 9 = Nose Wrinkler; AU 10 = Upper Lip Raiser; AU 11 = Nasolabial Fold Deepener;
AU 12 = Lip Corner Puller; AU 14 = Dimpler; AU 15 = Lip Corner Depressor;
AU 16 = Lower Lip Depressor; AU 17 = Chin Raiser; AU 18 = Lip Puckerer;
AU 20 = Lip Stretcher; AU 22 = Lip Funneler; AU 23 = Lip Tightener; AU24 = Lip Pressor;
AU 25 = Lips Part; AU 26 = Jaw Drop

Figure 17.4 Absolute frequency (f) of the action units (AU) in the random sample ($n = 10$) of the control group.

TABLE 17.3. Means (*M*), medians (*MD*) and standard deviations (*SD*) of action units with significant frequency differences (*p*) from the control group*

Action Units		Patients so (n = 10)	si (n = 10)	co (n = 6)	vc (n = 4)	Healthy Partners pso (n = 10)	psi (n = 10)	pco (n = 6)	pvc (n = 4)	cg (n = 10)
AU 1	M	9.7	3	8.3	42.8	17.2	10.4	17.7	33	48.7
	Md	5.5	3	4	24	17.5	9	16	28.5	23
	SD	13.64	2.26	13.26	49.9	11.92	6.74	15.71	19.61	61.35
	p†	*	**		*		*			
AU 2	M	10.6	5	8.8	78.5	29.4	15.1	26	34.5	59.3
	Md	8	4.5	5.5	36	26.5	9.5	27	30	40
	SD	12.83	3.16	13.08	103.07	20.38	14.48	12.18	16.11	60.09
	p	**	***	**			**			
AU 4	M	1.9	4.3	.8	25.5	4.5	6.6	8	3	9.3
	Md	0	.5	.5	3.5	2.5	4.5	0	3.5	4
	SD	3.84	7.85	1.17	46.38	6.17	6.15	16.83	2.16	14.07
	p	*			*					
AU 6	M	6.5	1.3	1.8	6.3	10.1	5.6	2.7	4.5	8.7
	Md	4.5	1	1.5	1.5	9	1.5	2	3.5	7
	SD	6.92	1.37	1.84	10.53	7.3	7.89	2.5	4.66	7.42
	p		***	**			*	*		
AU 7	M	2	1.5	2.3	.25	6.9	6.3	5.5	10.3	14.6
	Md	.5	0	.5	0	7	5	3	11.5	12
	SD	2.98	2.84	4.32	.5	6.28	6.13	5.13	6.55	12.55
	p	***	***	**	**	*	*	*		
AU 12	M	32.2	17	18.7	20.3	34.6	18.3	24	30.5	49.8
	Md	26.5	14.5	20.5	18.5	32	14.5	18.5	32.5	46.5
	SD	24.1	12.3	10.56	11.67	19.4	13.2	20.02	17.94	22.5
	p	.06	***	**	*		***	*		
AU 17	M	3.7	4.3	6.5	2.8	7.2	9	18.8	11	13.4
	Md	1	1.5	4	2.5	5	9	12	10.5	12.5
	SD	8.6	5.9	7.97	2.5	6.9	6.1	19.83	8.6	8.3
	p	**	**	*	*	*				

* So = schizophrenic outpatients; si = schizophrenic inpatients; co = ulcerative colitis patients; vc = patients with functional vertebral complaints; pso, psi, pco, pvc = healthy interaction partners of the patients; cg = random sample from the healthy control group
† p values, Mann-Whitney *U*-tests: *p < .05, **p <.01, ***p < .001.

culturally defined signs of affect. A raising of eyebrows, for example, can be part of a surprised or fearful face, or it can serve to underline something being said at the same time. A lifting of the lip corners (AU12) can be a component of felt happiness, a conventional sign of polite behavior, or the reflection of unfelt happiness in the sense of happiness simulated but not felt consciously. As additional expression features are added, the specific meaning becomes clearer.

The majority of the registered behavioral segments are either conventionally defined features of this kind, showing nonspecific excitement and/or affectivity. As a result, the reduction of facial expressions found in schizophrenic patients is based to a large extent on the non-utilization of these systems.

The colitis patients exhibit the greatest reduction in their expressiveness in comparison with the control group. Both the upper face ($p < .01$) and lower face ($p < .07$) are affected. All action units of the upper face (AU1 to AU7) are significantly reduced. As with the schizophrenics, the action units AU12 and AU17 are affected in the lower face. Moreover, nearly all other AUs of the lower face are reduced, albeit not significantly (Sänger-Alt, Steimer, Krause, & Wagner, 1989).

In contrast, the patients with functional vertebral complaints showed far less deviation from the control group. The action units affected in this group are AU7 (lid tightener), AU12 (lip corner puller), AU17 (chin raiser) and AU24 (lip pressor). Owing to the small size of our sample, these results have to be replicated; appropriate measures have already been taken to accomplish this objective. The results attained so far point in the expected direction: the subjects suffering from the two different types of psychosomatic disorder differ in their facial expressiveness.

The healthy partners of the patients responded to the facial behavior of the patients with adaptive reactions. All lowered their facial productivity; as a result, the differences between the patient groups and the control group are greater than those between the patients and their healthy partners. Although the healthy partners of the schizophrenic outpatients exhibit few significant deviations from the control group, the partners of the schizophrenic inpatients are almost as limited in the upper face as the patients themselves. In addition, they show a remarkable reduction in smiling. The partners of the colitis patients also showed significant reductions with regard to AU6, AU7 (the two ring muscles around the eyes) and AU12 (smile muscle) in comparison to the control group. The partners of the patients with functional vertebral complaints demonstrated no significant reductions in comparison with the control group.

In order to test the hypothesis that the different groups of subjects varied with respect to the intensity of expression as well, an average intensity of expression was determined for each subject for those action units (AU5, AU10, AU12, AU15, AU17 and AU24) that can be assigned a code number on a 5-point intensity scale according to the EMFACs rules (see table 17.4). The expressions of both the psychosomatic patients and the schizophrenic outpatients were substantially less pronounced in intensity than were those of the subjects in the control group. This was not true for the schizophrenic inpatients, who in fact attained higher values for intensity than did the healthy subjects in the control group.

TABLE 17.4. Means (M), medians (Md), standard deviations (SD) and significant differences from the control group (Mann-Whitney U-test) for the intensity values*

	n	M	Md	SD	U-test
Random sample of the control group	10	2.48	2.57	0.27	
Schizophrenic outpatients	10	2.26	2.18	0.21	$p < .025$
Schizophrenic inpatients	10	2.56	2.69	0.49	
Psychosomatic patients	10	2.14	2.11	0.33	$p < .025$

* Total significance, Kruskal-Wallis ($df = 3$), $p < .025$.

The ensuing discussion will consider the differences between the different groups of subjects for those facial events, amounting to 50% of the total, that can be interpreted with EMFACS.

Interpreted Events

No general "pathological syndrome" pattern is recognizable on the basis of the total sum of the interpreted events and the expression of primary affects. Compared to the control group, however, the psychomatic patients ($p < .05$), and the schizophrenic inpatients ($p < .05$) and their interaction partners ($p < .01$), produced fewer facial events lending themselves to interpretation. This was not true of the schizophrenic outpatients and their partners or of the partners of the psychosomatic patients. Regarding the sum of the expressions of primary affects, the dyad types varied significantly in accordance with Kruskal-Wallis ($p < .01$); limitations in absolute terms were observed in all the patient groups (see table 17.5). In the individual test, however, only the schizophrenic inpatients deviated markedly from the control group with respect to the frequency with which primary affects were employed ($p < .05$).

Expressions of Affect

The varying frequency distribution shown for specific primary affects does appear to be characteristic for individual disorders.

In the control group, the most frequently occurring expression of affect was happiness, followed by contempt, disgust, anger, sadness, fear and surprise. The last two occur extremely seldom. Contempt is the expression of affect most frequently observed in the two schizophrenic groups. Moreover, contempt is the only expression of affect observed more often in the schizophrenic patients than in the healthy random samples. In the schizophrenic outpatients, contempt is followed by happiness, disgust, sadness and anger, an order corresponding to that of the healthy subjects; in the schizophrenic inpatients, on the other hand, contempt is followed by disgust and anger, and only then by happiness. As far as the subjects suffering from psychosomatic disorders are concerned, there are considerable differences between the two subgroups. The expression of affect most frequently encountered in the patients with ulcerative colitis is disgust. In the patients with functional vertebral complaints, it is fear. Owing to the small size of the sample and the wide scattering of results, the patients with functional vertebral complaints were not included in the further affect-specific reflections. The group of inpatient schizophrenics and the colitis patients exhibited significant reductions of felt happiness in comparison with the control groups. The schizophrenic outpatients were just below the significance level. Furthermore, expressions of anger occurred less frequently in the schizophrenic outpatients, and expressions of sadness less frequently in the schizophrenic inpatients, than in the control group. The colitis patients also evidenced significantly less sadness and contempt.

These results give rise to the speculation that there are changes related to the phenomenon of illness per se, irrespective of the particular disorder. All of the patients laughed less "genuinely," for example. Coexisting with these changes, however, are patterns associated with the specific pathologies. The latter changes are responsible for the varying distribution obtained for the expressions of negative affects. Their characteristic feature is that one particular expression predominates in the desolate

TABLE 17.5.   Means (*M*), medians (*Md*) standard deviations (*SD*) and significant differences from the control group for selected EMFACS categories*

| Categories | | Patients | | | | Healthy Subjects | | | | |
		so (n = 10)	si (n = 10)	co (n = 6)	vc (n = 4)	pso (n = 10)	psi (n = 10)	pco (n = 6)	pvc (n = 4)	cg (n = 10)
Σ	M	59.6	51	38.5	45.5	59	37.9	47.5	44.8	72.6
Interpreted	Md	49.5	35	41	31.5	52	33.5	57	46.5	58.5
events	SD	48.8	42.8	22.6	36.2	28.4	17.4	29	20.5	37.4
			*		*		**			
Σ	M	22	17.5	18	29.5	31.7	20	23.3	17	35.2
Primary	Md	23.5	14	20	17.5	29.5	20.5	20	16.5	26
Affects	SD	15	17.9	11.8	37	19.7	11.7	20.9	7	28.1
			*							
Felt	M	6.5	1.7	3.2	6.3	12.2	5.1	5.5	6	11.9
happiness	MD	4.5	1	1.5	1.5	9	4	3	5	12.5
	SD	6.9	1.8	3.5	10.5	9.6	5.2	6.4	5.9	7.9
			**	*			*			
Contempt	M	10.3	10.9	2.5	2	11.8	5.6	5.8	4	9.9
	Md	9.5	4.5	1	1	7.5	5.5	3.5	4.5	9.5
	SD	8.7	17.6	3.2	2.9	14.2	4.2	5.7	3	8
				*	*					
Disgust	M	3.4	2.5	8.7	0	4.6	3.5	5.2	1.8	6.7
	Md	1.5	.5	4.5	0	2	2	1.5	1.5	1
	SD	4.5	3.2	10.4	0	6.8	3.8	7	2.1	11.8
					*					
Anger	M	.6	2.3	4	.5	2.4	4.2	2.7	4	4.1
	Md	0	.5	.5	0	1	1.5	1	3.5	2
	SD	1.3	3.9	8.4	1	3.2	5.4	3.9	4.2	4.9
		*								
Sadness	M	.7	.1	0	2.5	.5	1.2	0	2	2.1
	Md	0	0	0	1.5	0	0	0	1	0
	SD	1.3	3	0	3.1	1.1	2.1	0	2.7	4.4
			*		*					
Unfelt	M	17.7	13.8	14.5	12.5	20.2	9.8	16.5	22.5	27.4
happiness	Md	15	9	14.5	12.5	22.5	8	14	23	26
	SD	12.9	11.7	9.2	6.1	11.2	7	13.3	11	16
		*	*	*			**			

* So = schizophrenic outpatients; si = schizophrenic inpatients; co = ulcerative colitis patients; vc = patients with functional vertebral disturbances; pso, psi, pco, pvc = healthy interaction partners of the patients; cg = random sample of the control group.
*p < .05.
**p < .01.

affective landscape. In the schizophrenic patients it is contempt, in the colitis patients disgust.

The partners adapt to the patients in the narrower sense of facial affectivity as well: here the differences between the patients and the control group were greater than those between the patients and their respective partners. In the dyads containing psychosomatic patients, there was no significant difference between the patients and their healthy partners; in the dyads with schizophrenic patients, the partners expressed more happiness. There was no discrepancy concerning negative expressions of affects. As far as the expression of happiness is concerned, the partners of the colitis patients ($p = .055$) and the partners of the schizophrenic inpatients ($p < .05$)—like their disturbed interaction partners—manifested large reductions in comparison with the control group. This does not apply to the partners of the schizophrenic outpatients. This result can be seen as an indication that the interactions and interpersonal dynamics observed in the dyads with schizophrenic inpatients and in those with schizophrenic outpatients were different in quality. Whereas the partners of the schizophrenic inpatients adapted to a large extent— in particular, with respect to the expression of happiness—the increase in expressions of happiness exhibited by the partners of the schizophrenic outpatients can be seen as an attempt to establish a positive relationship. The analysis of the dialogue between the outpatients and their partners suggests that the partners tended to try to deny the "differentness" of their interaction partners and to compensate for it (see Villenave-Cremer et al., 1989). It was observed that the partners of the schizophrenic outpatients kept trying to get the patients more involved in the conversation and to ignore the language deviations of the schizophrenic patients—thematic preoccupations, concretism, etc.

Expressions Not Corresponding to Primary Affects

There are a number of facial events that cannot be interpreted as non-ambiguous primary affects but can, nevertheless, be interpreted. Two or more affects can thus be activated at the same time (blends), or one affect can cover up another (masking), or vestiges of original forms no longer admitting an interpretation can occur. The employment of smile reactions as polite conventions (social smiling) or for the purpose of self-deception (unfelt happiness) has already been discussed.

Blends and masking occurred only infrequently in the total sample and were used by only a few subjects (1.9% of all events). In a therapy study involving a patient suffering from an anxiety neurosis, smile/anger, smile/contempt blends occurred with extreme frequency. This could represent an additional disturbance-specific sign suggesting that the so-called transference neuroses, in contrast to structural disturbances and healthy states, are associated with ambivalent expressive behavior (Krause & Lütolf, 1988).

Significantly less unfelt happiness was found in the patients with functional vertebral complaints ($p < .05$), the colitis patients ($p < .05$), the schizophrenic inpatients ($p < .05$) and the partners of the schizophrenic inpatients ($p < .01$). The significant level was not reached by the schizophrenic outpatients ($p = .08$). Evidently, a shortage of "felt happiness" cannot be made up for by deliberately produced social smiling, either by the patients or by their partners: within the dyads, this expression occurred with the same frequency in both the ill and healthy interaction partners.

We shall now summarize by presenting some of the individual results in a systematic manner on the basis of the following questions:

1. Are there facial indicators differentiating between the healthy control subjects and the patients?
2. Are there specific facial indicators that, in addition, distinguish schizophrenic patients from psychosomatic patients (in this case, colitis patients)?

3. Do differences exist in this regard between schizophrenic outpatients and schizophrenic inpatients?

The healthy test subjects demonstrate more facial activity, especially in the upper face. This is attributable to their more frequent recourse to facial expressions involving accentuating movements in the upper face (AU1 and AU2), which usually accompany speech. Moreover, they express more felt and unfelt happiness. The 20 schizophrenic patients differ from the colitis patients in the high frequency with which they express contempt, whereas the colitis patients are characterized by numerous expressions of disgust. Schizophrenic outpatients and inpatients can be distinguished by the fact that in the inpatients the expression of anger occurs more frequently, the expressions are more intense, and the reductions experienced in both facial productivity and expressions of affect are more pronounced than in the schizophrenic outpatients.

Interpretation and Discussion

It was possible to confirm the hypotheses regarding the differences in facial expressiveness between the patient groups and the healthy control group and the hypothesis that specific features are characteristic of particular pathologies. However, these are not exclusively reduction phenomena affecting facial productivity and affectivity, as was presumed in Hypothesis 7. Rather, the reduction phenomena appear to affect certain forms of expression irrespective of pathology, whereas the features characteristic of particular pathologies refer to the prominence of specific expressions of affect. On the basis of this result and our intensive study of the facial expressions recorded on 50 video films, we have arrived at a differentiated concept of facial expressiveness in interactions. We believe that two kinds of affectivity can be distinguished in the sector of facial expressions. The first marks the intensity of cathexis, involvement and/or excitement in the interactive relationship. It does not provide any differentiated information on the quality of the affect. This is reflected by the quantity of facial innervation—i.e., facial productivity per se—and in particular by facial signs that have previously been referred to as "conversational signals" (Ekman, 1979). This system is linked in part to the verbal interaction process and proceeds in phase with certain kinetic behavioral patterns, such as head motions and hand gestures. The second kind of expression provides information on the quality of affect in the form of facial events, which can be interpreted as distinctive primary affect-expression. It is difficult, however, to make statements about their intensity, since even a one-time appearance of many of these affective expressions can be extremely important in an interaction.

The groups schizophrenia, ulcerative colitis and stuttering (Krause, 1982a) all exhibit a generalized inhibition syndrome with respect to the first form of affectivity. This also seems to apply to depressive patients (Ellgring, 1989). We do not know how this inhibitory system develops in the different pathologies. We are convinced, however, that the efforts made to control emotions also include control strategies involving a suppression of these behavioral patterns (Buck, 1983).

Consequently, the inhibition of these forms of expression is two-sided, comprising the loss of vitality on the one hand and the attempt to exert control on the other. If we extend our reflections concerning these patients to the decrease in social smiling, an expression that can also be considered a component of this expression system, we find, in addition, a fundamental absence of both charm and the ability to be charmed, especially since both social smiling and "felt happiness" are reduced.

The difficulties encountered in getting along with such persons seem to lie primarily in bearing their non-involvement and the absence of stimulation. After studying the video films, we have the impression that the healthy interaction partners of the patients very quickly demonstrate a kind of unconscious adaptation to the patients, lowering their general level of affectivity, as was evidenced by this reduction of facial productivity and smiling. In particular, the partners of the schizophrenic inpatients showed serious reductions. At present it cannot be determined whether this is a case of startled stiffening caused by the nonverbal "deficits" of the patients or a kind of emotional flattening and boredom due to the shortage of interaction stimuli. Nonetheless, we were able to detect almost no signs of fear in the partners of the patients. In contrast, smiling was the expression found to be increased, in comparison with the control group, in the partners of the schizophrenic outpatients. The different degrees of severity of the illness of the schizophrenic outpatients and the schizophrenic inpatients, as manifested in their behavior during interactions, may account for this discrepancy. Possibly, once the discrepancy between the expectations of the healthy partners and the actual nonverbal affective behavior of the patients has reached a certain level, the healthy subjects cease to make attempts at compensation or normalization.

The second form of differential qualitative affectivity was also greatly limited in the patients with respect to both positive and negative expressions of emotion, whereby one negative expression of emotion predominated. In the schizophrenic patients, the predominant emotion was contempt, in the colitis patients disgust, and in the stutterers observed in an earlier study (Krause, 1982a) anger. The characteristic features of each specific pathology are thus represented in a certain "guiding emotion" of negative quality. A subject meriting further examination is the differential significance of this predominance—for example, of contempt or disgust—for the regulation of interactions (Sandweg, 1989). It cannot be inferred from the facial sign itself what it represents. The expression of contempt on the face of the schizophrenic patient, for example, can represent a kind of self-contempt, reflect the self-contempt of the partner, or reflect the contempt of the interaction partner for the patient. Further investigations will attempt to answer these questions. These studies will attempt, firstly, to establish the relationships between the introspective data and the facial expressions observed, and secondly, to analyze exactly the appearance of facial signs with respect to other channels of communication.

References

Bleuler, E., (1969). *Lehrbuch der Psychiatrie.* Berlin: Springer.
Buck, R. (1983). Emotional development and emotional education. In R. Plutchik & H. Kellermann (Eds.), *Emotion: Theory, research and experience, Vol. 2; Emotions in early development.* New York: Academic Press.
Dougherty, F. E., Bartlett, E. S., & Izard, C. E. (1974). Responses of schizophrenics to expressions of the fundamental emotions. *Journal of Clinical Psychology, 30,* 243–246.
Duncan, S., & Fiske, D. W. (1985). *Interaction Structure and Strategy.* Cambridge, England: Cambridge University Press.
Ekman, P. (1979). About brows: Emotional and conversational signals. In M. von Cranach,

K. Foppa, W. Lepenies & D. Ploog (Eds.), *Human ethology: Claims and limits of a new discipline.* Cambridge, England: Cambridge University Press.

Ekman, P. (1978). *Telling lies: Clues to deceit in the marketplace, politics and marriage.* New York: Norton.

Ekman, P., & Friesen, W. V. (1978). *Manual for the Facial Action Coding System.* Palo Alto, CA: Consulting Psychologists Press.

Ellgring, H. (1989). *Nonverbal communication in depression.* Cambridge, England: Cambridge University Press.

Fahrenberg, J., Hampel, R., & Selg, H. (1984). *Das Freiburger Persónlichreitsinventar.* Göttingen: Hogrefe.

Friesen, W. V., & Ekman, P. (1984). *EMFACS-7,* Unpublished manual.

Frosch, J. (1983). *The psychotic process.* New York: International Universities Press.

Gottheil, E., Paredes, A., Exline, R. V., & Winkelmayer, R. (1970). Communication of affect in schizophrenia. *Archives of General Psychiatry, 22,* 439–444.

Gottheil, E., Thornton, C. C., & Exline, R. V. (1976). Appropriate and background affect in facial displays of emotion. *Archives of General Psychiatry, 33,* 565–568.

Greenson, R. R. (1967). *The technique and practice of psychoanalysis.* (Vol. 1.), New York: International Universities Press.

Hans, G., Krause, R., & Steimer, E. (1986). Interaktionsprozesse bei Schizophrenen. Bericht über die theoretischen und methodischen Grundlagen eines Forschungsprojektes. In E. Nordmann & M. Cierpka (Eds.), *Familienforschung in der Psychiatrie und Psychotherapie.* Heidelberg: Springer, 30–51.

Heimann, H., & Spoerri, T. (1957). Das Ausdruckssyndrom der mimischen Desintegrierung bei chronisch Schizophrenen. *Schweizerische Medizinische Wochenschrift, 35/36,* 1126–1128.

Jablonsky, D. (1989). Zwei Dyadische Interaktionen: Versuch einer differentiellen "multi-kanalen" Analyse. Diplomarbeit. University of the Saarland, Saarbrücken.

Krause, R. (1982a). A social psychological approach to the study of stuttering. In C. Fraser & K. Scherer (Eds.), *Advances in the social psychology of language.* Cambridge, England: Cambridge University Press. 77–122.

Krause, R. (1982b). Kernbereiche psychoanalytischen Handelns. *Der Nervenarzt, 53,* 504–512.

Krause, R. (1988). Eine Taxonomie der Affekte und ihre Anwendung auf das Verständnis der frühen Storungen. *Psychotherapie und med. Psychologie, 38,* 77–86.

Krause, R., & Lutolf, P. (1988). Facial indicators of transference processes within psychoanalytic treatment. In H. Dahl & H. Kächele (Eds.) *Psychoanalytic process research strategies.* Heidelberg: Springer, 258–272.

Krause, R., Steimer, E., Sanger-Alt, C., & Wagner, G. (1989). Facial expression of schizophrenic patients and their interaction partners. *Psychiatry, 52,* 1–12.

LaPlanche, J., & Pontalis, J. B. (1972). *The Language of psychoanalysis.* Hogarth.

Larusso, L. (1978). Sensitivity of paranoid patients to nonverbal cues. *Journal of Abnormal Psychology, 87,* 463–471.

Mentzos, S. (1977). *Interpersonale und institutionalisierte Abwehr.* Frankfurt: Suhrkamp.

Moser, U. (1964). Zur Abwehrlehre. Das Verhältnis von Verdrängung und Projektion. *Jahrbuch der Psychoanalyse.* (Vol. 3). Stuttgart: Huber.

Muzekari, L. H., & Bates, M. E. (1977). Judgement of emotion among chronic schizophrenics. *Journal of Clinical Psychology, 33,* 662–666.

Pilowsky, I., & Barnett, D. (1980). Schizophrenia and the response to facial emotions. *Comprehensive Psychiatry, 21,* 236–244.

Rohde-Dachser, C. (1985). Zum Problem der Näheangst. In U. Rüger, (Ed.), *Neurotische und reale Anst.* Göttingen: Hogrefe. 37–47.

Sandweg, R. (1989). Zur Psychodynamik und Therapie chronisch-entzundlicher Darmerkramkungen. *Praxis der Psychotherapie und Psychosomatik, 34,* 73–81.

Sänger-Alt, C., Steimer, E., Krause, R., & Wagner, G. (1989). Mimisches Verhalten psychosomatischer Patienten. Untersuchungen zur Alexithymie an zwei Krankheitsgruppen. *Zeitschrift für Klinische Psychologie* 243–256.

Schulte W., and Tolle, R. (1979). *Psychiatrie.* Heidelberg: Springer.

Searles, H. F. (1984). The role of the analyst's facial expressions in psychoanalysis and psychoanalytic therapy. *International Journal of Psychoanalytic Therapy, 10,* 47–73.

Steiner, F. (1983). Differentiating smiles. In E. Bänninger-Huber & F. Steiner (Eds.), *Bericht aus der Abteilung für Klinische Psychologie (Nr. 19).* Zurich: University of Zurich. 13–28.

Thoma, H., & Kachele, H. (1988). *Psychoanalytic Practice. Vol. 1: Principles.* Heidelberg: Springer.

Von Rad, M. (1983). *Alexithymie. Empirische Untersuchungen zur Diagnostik und Therapie psychosomatisch Kranker.* Heidelberg: Springer.

Villenave-Cremer, S., Kettner, M., & Krause, R. (1989). Verbale Interaktion von Schizophrenen und ihren Gesprächspartnern. *Zeitschrift für Klinishce Psychologie und Psychotherapie, 37,* 401–424.

Wagner, G. (1986). *Entwicklung eines automatisierten Verfahrens zur Affektinterpretation.* Final thesis (psychology), University of the Saarland. Saarbrücken.

Walker, E., Marwit, S. J., & Emory, E. (1980). A cross-sectional study of emotion recognition in schizophrenics. *Journal of Abnormal Psychology, 89,* 428–436.

Walker, E. (1981). Emotion recognition in disturbed and normal children: A research note. *Journal of Child Psychology and Psychiatry, 22,* 263–68.

Winkelmayer, R., Exline, R. V., Gottheil, E., & Paredes, A. (1978). The relative accuracy of U.S., British and Mexican raters in judging the emotional displays of schizophrenic and normal U.S. women. *Journal of Clinical Psychology, 34,* 600–608.

Interaction Regulations Used by Schizophrenic and Psychosomatic Patients

RAINER KRAUSE

Since the publication of Steimer-Krause, Krause, and Wagner in 1990, our research group has published 20 additional papers on the theme of facial expression. Five have been published in English; the 15 remaining are in German publications. Seven of these are empirical studies, and the rest focus on methodological or clinical issues. At the end of 1996 a book on psychoanalytic theory of mental disturbances will be finished in German (Krause, 1996); it contains core chapters on the therapeutic relationship, on drive, and on affect. This book reflects the basic issues and the results of our research that has been done in the last 20 years. A methodological paper called "*Austruckspsychologische Methoden*" (Methodology of Expression Psychology) is to be published in the methodological part of the *Enzyclopedia of Psychology,* edited by the German Society of Psychology (Krause, 1995).

A main issue of our work was to investigate the dynamics of the affect system within social relationships, especially when one of the interaction partners is mentally ill. We have investigated 120 such dyads. The results of their average affective facial expression are depicted in figure 17.1A. As may be seen, we find highly significant gender differences between men and women, as well as differences between the severely ill people, like the schizophrenics and the psychosomatics, and the neurotic patients, the former showing facial affect very seldom, the latter much more than even the healthy subjects talking to one another. Extensive theoretical and empirical work was required to understand the reasons for these differences in the organization of the facial affective behavior. Even more interesting was the fact that the healthy subjects did adapt very intensively to the sick partners without knowing anything about their illness. The results may be seen in figure 17.2A.

The following basic questions had to be solved to understand our results: How is it that the patients influence their partners? What kind of behavioral strategies did they use on which level of consciousness? How is it that healthy subjects process these influences? And on which level of consciousness does this happen? These questions forced us to include in the investigation more and more context variables of facial

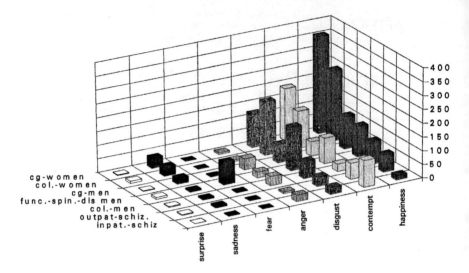

Agenda: cg.: controlgroup;
    col.: patients suffering from colitis ulcerosa;
    schiz.: patients suffering from schizophrenia of the paranoid halluzinatory type;
    func.-spin.-dis.: Patients suffering from functional spine disturbance with a neurotic etiology:
    outpat.: outpatient; inpat.: inpatient

Figure 17.1A

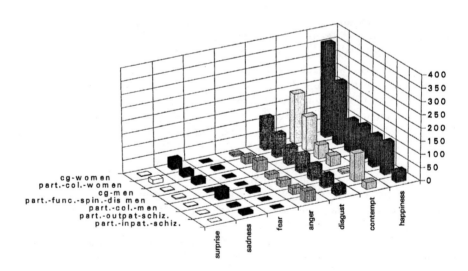

Agenda: cg.: controlgroup;
    part.-col.: partners of the patients suffering from colitis ulcerosa;
    part.-schiz.: partners of the patients suffering from schizophrenia of the paranoid halluzinatory type;
    part.-func.-spin.-dis.: partners of the patients suffering from functional spine disturbance with a neurotic etiology.
    outpat.: outpatient; inpat.: inpatient

Figure 17.2A

affect. We hypothesized it to be important to understand the dynamics of dyadic inter-action and the role of the face within that dynamic.

The first approach was to measure the experience of emotion with affect question-naires after the end of the interaction. We related these measures to the facial expression of both subjects and developed a taxonomy of how to understand the possible relation-ships within the dyad. As we had predicted, the correlation networks between expres-sion and experience within dyads, including a schizophrenic patient, were completely different from those of the healthy subjects or the ones with a psychosomatic patient. Some of these data are published in English (Krause, Steimer-Krause, & Hufnagel, 1992). The basic results were that the attribution rules on how facial affect is to be in-terpreted are different between the groups. Healthy subjects usually attribute negative facial affect to the mental object they are talking about; the schizophrenics "see" it as attached to their self. For them the happiness expression of their partners is unhedonic in nature, since it is interpreted as contempt, or *Schadenfreude,* especially when it is shown during mutual gazing. The schizophrenic's contempt expression during mutual gazing is correlated with an experience of contempt and shame. Shame on the side of the healthy partner is expressed through smiling during mutual gaze avoidance, fear and contempt through smiling and looking at the schizophrenic when he looks away (Merten, 1995). Since group statistics and single-channel analysis did not allow an in-terpretation of the process, Merten (1995) and Steimer-Krause (1995) undertook the very large task of analyzing multichannel patterns of facial affect, gazing behavior, body positions, and paraverbal behavior, as well as their temporal distribution. Patterns found in dyads of schizophrenics talking with healthy interaction partners were com-pared with those found in dyads with both interaction partners being healthy. To handle these highly complex data structures new mathematical and programming algorithms had to be developed.

A major result has been that the nonverbal context, and especially the gazing be-havior, serves as meta-message to distinguish the different possible functions of facial affective signs. So the meta-message can ensure the interaction partner that, for exam-ple, a negative facial affective behavior does not signal a negative wish concerning the ongoing interaction but is meant for the object talked about. Another result concerning interpersonal synchronization of facial behavior is that the healthy partners react less often to the smiles of their schizophrenic interaction partners than can be observed in dyads with two healthy people. Further violations of the dyadic eye-face-speech pat-terns by the patients have been found. Based on single-case analysis of the interaction processes, a scheme of the interactive implementation of projective identification has been proposed.

From that starting point we hope to create together with Paul Ekman and Wally Friesen a new clinical handbook. To broaden our database we cooperated with Tapio Nummenmaa from Tampere in Finland, who has investigated facial expres-sion in couples' interactions using structural analysis. Departing from these pro-jects we decided to scrutinize long-term developments of the afore-mentioned dyadic affective interactions by investigating facial behavior and emotional experi-encing of patients and their therapists in the psychotherapeutic processes. The dia-logues have been transcribed and analyzed using Luborsky's CCRT, which we re-lated to facial affective behavior of patient and therapist (Anstadt, Ulrich, Merten, Buchheim, & Kraus, 1995). Analyzing facial behavior in the first sessions we found facial expression was highly variable. So, for example, 82% percent of the affects of a borderline patient had been disgust; a female agoraphobic patient with panic attack showed 82% felt happiness. Comparing therapists, we found a psycho-analytic-oriented male with 86% of his affects being felt happiness. Two male therapists with cognitive behavioral theoretical orientation showed more than 50% contempt in the first session.

The second result was that 50% of treatment outcome could be predicted from facial behavior in the first session, combining the affect distribution of therapist and patient to a measure that we called "dyadic lead affect." In cases where the most frequent facial affect (lead affect) of both is felt happiness without controlling elements, prognosis is bad. Prognosis is better when both lead affects have anhedonic valence and best when one is negative and the other positive. Another good predictor of treatment outcome has been the relative frequency of the therapist's lead affect, also in the first session. Prognosis is bad if it is high. The therapy of the afore-mentioned psychoanalyst with a relative frequency of 86% ended up as failure.

The next question we had to answer was why a reciprocal dyadic lead affect might be unfavorable. To do that we analyzed the facial affective behavior across the 15 sessions of the treatments and related it to the emotional experiences of patient and therapist and to the patient's CCRT. Comparing the best and the worst treatments, we found that the failures of experienced psychotherapists, independent of treatment techniques, were not related to false handling of the technique, but on some sort of linking of the therapist's affective relationship regulation into that of the patient. This leads to a stabilization of the maladaptive system through an unintended positive affective feedback given by the therapist. The degree of conscious reflection of the behavioral incidents that indicate this linkage might be very different. There are therapists who do not even realize what the patient offers to them. There are some who do realize it and try to fight against it, but without success. And there are those who just give in to the offers of the patient without internal and therapeutic conflicts. In the latter cases the therapist usually finds fitting models about the patient—for example, his ego-weakness.

A behavioral indicator of dyadic stabilizing of the patient's system is the absence of clear-cut phases in affectivity, its temporal distribution, positive facial reciprocity, and a high correlative network of facial affect and emotional experiencing in the dyad. This is an indicator for a dependency, reducing the therapist's freedom (Merten, Ullrich, Anstadt, & Krause, 1995). Departing from that, we proposed to include in the question of indicators not only the fit of the patient's disturbance and symptoms and the treatment technique but also the patient's affective match with the therapist's affect regulation. This might be done relying on the observation of a first session, or even on the observation of affect exchange in the initial interview with a prospective therapist. Furthermore, the separation between working alliance and treatment technique is not very helpful in understanding the psychotherapeutic process because the efficiency of each intervention depends on the actual state of the working relationship. Models correlating the amount of technical interventions with success, disregarding the actual state of the relationship as covariate, cannot claim to describe the psychotherapeutic process (Orlinsky, Grawe, & Parks, 1994). We think that the phases of the relationship regulation can be described lawfully.

References

Anstadt, Th., Ullrich, B., Merten, J., Buchheim, P., & Krause, R. (1995). Affective dyadic behavior, core conflictual relationship themes and treatment outcome. *Psychotherapy Research,* in press.

Krause, R. (1995). Ausdruckspsychologische Methoden. In K. Pawlik & M. Amelang (Eds.), *Enzyklopedie der Psychologie* [Encyclopedia of psychology]. Differentielle Psychologie und Personlichkeitsforschung, Bd.1, Grundlagen und Methoden der differentiellen Psychologie (S.577–608). Gottingen: Hogrefe.

Krause, R. (1996). *Allgemeine psychoanalytische Krankheitslehre.* Stuttgart: Kohlhammer-Verlag.

Krause, R., Steimer-Krause, E., & Hufnagel, H. (1992). Expression and experience of affects in paranoid schizophrenia. *European Review of Applied Psychology,* Special Issue: Cognitive Disorders in Schizophrenia, 42(2), 131–138.

Merten, J. (1995). *Affekte und die Regulation nonverbalen interaktiven Verhaltens.* Strukturelle Aspekte des mimisch-affektiven Verhaltens und die Integration von Affekten in Regulationsmodelle. Peter Lang: Bern.

Merten, J., Anstadt, Th., Ullrich, B., Krause, R., & Buchheim, P. (1996). Emotional experience and facial expression during the therapeutic process and its relation to treatment outcome. *Psychotherapy Research, 6,* 198–212.

Orlinsky, D. E., Grawe, K., & Parks, B. K. (1994). Process and outcome in psychotherapy. Noch einmal. In A. E. Bergin & S. L. Garfield (Eds.), *Handbook of psychotherapy and behavior change* (pp. 270–376). New York: Wiley.

Steimer-Krause, E. (1995). *DCbertragung, Affekt und Beziehung: Untersuchung zum nonverbalen Interaktionsverhalten schizophrener Patienten.* Peter Lang: Bern.

18

Nonverbal Expression of Psychological States in Psychiatric Patients

HEINER ELLGRING

In what way are psychopathological states associated with specific changes in nonverbal behavior and is this behavior organized differently, thus indicating additional functional changes? In order to deal with these questions, observations on nonverbal behavior of schizophrenic patients and their relatives, of endogenous and neurotic depressed patients and of controls will be reported here.

At first, there seems to be an obvious relationship between internal mood states, emotions or affects, and our overt behavior. As socially living individuals, expressive behavior is one of the main sources of information when interpreting the actual motivational state of the other. As has been demonstrated in manifold ways since Darwin (1872/1965), similar principles of expression hold for man and animals (Ploog, 1980).

It may be argued that this means of communication loses its importance when replaced by language. However, numerous situations still exist where the nonverbal expression of affects and emotions are a central part of adult social interaction, not to mention infant-adult communication. For the understanding of an individual suffering from a psychiatric disorder, which nearly always includes emotional disturbances, expressive behavior seems to be relevant for various reasons.

As described by Ploog (1958, 1972), the breakdown of the social communication system in endogenous psychoses can lead to either blocking of motor expression, as is the case in catatonia, or to a disinhibition of drive states and their corresponding behavior. Thus, voluntary control mechanisms active in normal adult expressive behavior may lose their power during psychosis.

On the other hand, expressive behavior may also be regarded as a means whereby the patient can convey his actual states to the environment. Not only is depressive behavior as a "cry for help" (Arieti, 1974) an expression of a mood state but it is also a signal that will elicit behavior from the environment (Coyne, 1976). In this way, nonverbal behavior functions as a means for communicating the altered affective state. This communicative function will, however, be effective only within a range where a person is not impaired too heavily by a psychosis. In order to communicate effectively, there must still be some choice for voluntarily activating parts of the behavioral repertoire. This may be the case for depression—with the exception of extreme severity degrees—but less so in schizophrenic psychosis.

Expressive or nonverbal behavior is treated to some degree as a homogeneous set of signals or signs. Facial behavior, gaze, and gestures are all parts of a coherent repertoire. Together with speech and its accompanying vocal features, it constitutes what appears for an observer to be a coordinated flow of complex communication. It must be remembered, however, that various behavioral elements are controlled by different neural mechanisms. They also represent different cognitive and emotional functions and are under different voluntary control. Gaze behavior, e.g., is closely connected to cognitive and attentional processes (Rutter, Ellgring, 1984; Ellgring, Watson & Clarke, 1980) whereas facial behavior reflects affective processes as well as voluntary display according to socially determined rules (Ekman & Friesen, 1969).

For our understanding of the neural mechanisms underlying facial expression, the behavior of patients suffering from Parkinson's disease deserves some consideration. Similar to depression, these patients exhibit little facial expression during normal conversation. Despite their inability to express feelings in their face, these patients are able to experience emotions and to move their facial muscles on request. Here, there is a dissociation of emotions and their expression. From the cerebral localization of this disease, it can be concluded that expressive behavior is integrated not in the cortex but in the midbrain (Ploog, 1980).

Being aware of the fact that it is always a set of signals and their continuous exchange between individuals that constitutes communication, we will focus our subsequent analysis on a few components of the behavioral repertoire. In order to compare individuals and situations, a quantitative approach has been chosen, i.e., an approach that tries to determine parameters for behavior coded by systematic observation. Behavioral measurements have been taken from video recordings, ensuring observer reliability and registration of fast events like facial actions in slow motion.

Two aspects of nonverbal communication are dealt with. The first addresses the question as to how depression as a homogeneous affective state correlates with changes in behavior of the nonverbal repertoire. The analysis focuses on the individual change of mood and behavior over time. The second aspect investigates the notion of a dissociation of coordinated behavior as a characteristic of psychoses. Various groups are compared with regard to the degree of coordination of nonverbal and verbal communicative behavior.

Individual Specificity of Nonverbal Expression

From intra-individual comparisons it appears that behavior correlates with the varying mood state during depression in an individual-specific way. In a longitudinal study 36 depressed patients (20 endogenous, ICD 296; 16 neurotic, ICD 300; 18 male, 18 female) and 9 controls (5 male, 4 female), with an age ranging from 24 to 64 years were repeatedly videotaped during interviews. For patients, an average period of 60 days (ranging from 25 to 152 days), for controls, periods ranging from 4 to 12 days were covered by observations. Subjective well-being of the patients was assessed by a visual analogue scale.

Various aspects of nonverbal behavior were analyzed for a selection of 120 out of a total of 506 interviews. Facial expression was measured by the Facial Action Coding System (FACS; Ekman & Friesen, 1978) and specific parameters defined: facial repertoire, general facial activity and, as a specific activity, the occurrence of smiles. Speech-related gestures were coded, and assessing on-off patterns only, gaze and speech activities were registered. Gaze and speech were analyzed for all of the interviews available. For neurotic depressed patients these consisted of 5 to 7 interviews, for endogenous patients more than 10, up to 49 interviews. Details of the study have been reported elsewhere (Ellgring, 1984).

In the present situation, two aspects of the results are relevant. Both indicate that the average relationship between subjective well-being and nonverbal behavior may obscure very strong associations on the individual level.

For about 70% of the patients, only 1 or 2 of the total of 6 nonverbal parameters assessed substantially changed along with improvement of the mood state (see figure 18.1).

As can be seen, less than 10% of the patients showed changes in 4, 5, or 6 of these parameters. Only those changes that exceeded variations of the behavior found in repeated observations of normal controls were considered. On the other hand, only 3 of 36 depressed patients (= 8%) showed no substantial change in any of the behavioral parameters.

Generally, the frequency of smile (61%) and the amount of gaze at the other (58%) showed an increase with improvement. For general facial activity (31%) and speech activity (33%), this was the case in about 1/3 of the cases, whereas the facial repertoire (22%) and speech related gestures (14%) rarely changed according to our criteria. There was no clearcut hierarchy amongst these aspects of behavior. From this one has to assume that they are connected to the depressed mood in a way represented by a logical "or" relation. Gaze *or* facial expression *or* other behavior do change in an individual-specific way along with an improvement in subjective well-being. The individual correlations of speech and gaze behavior with subjective well-being strengthen

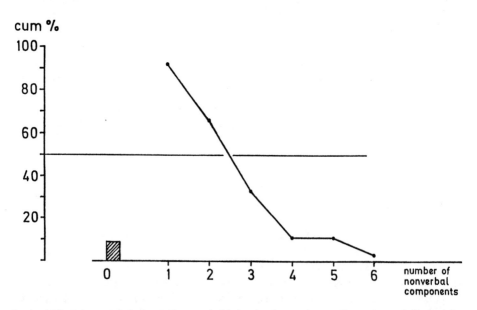

Figure 18.1 Substantial changes of nonverbal behavioral components. Percentage of depressed patients (cum %, *n* = 36), exhibiting substantial change in 0 resp. 1 *or* more components of nonverbal behavior with improvement of subjective well-being.

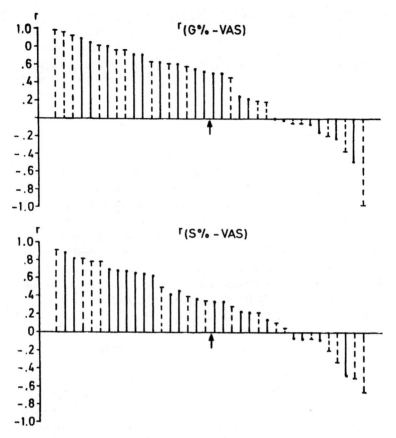

Figure 18.2 Individual correlations between subjective well-being (Visual Analogue Scale, VAS) and relative amount of gaze (G %) resp. speech activity (S %). _____ Endogenous (> 10 interviews), - - - neurotic depressed patients (6–7 interviews).

this argument. As can be seen from figure 18.2, there was a broad range of individual correlations, most of them located on the positive side.

The average correlation between subjective well-being and the relative amount of gaze was $r = 0.58$; the corresponding correlation for the relative amount of speech activity $r = 0.38$. However, these average correlations obscure the finding of very strong individual relationships especially for gaze behavior. Both behavioral aspects correlated independently with subjective well-being ($r = 0.07$).

The general results correspond to those reported in the literature (Jones & Pansa, 1979; Rutter, 1984). When using a group statistic approach only minor changes of nonverbal behavior are found in psychiatric patients. This contradiction to clinical impression dissolves when analyzing at the individual level. Comparable to physiological reactions (Lacey, 1967), there is individual specificity of expressive behavior in depression. This individual-specific "usage" of nonverbal elements as an expression of a depressed state indicates some peculiarities of nonverbal communication.

The fact that various parts of the nonverbal repertoire change during depression in

different individuals seems to contradict the notion of "universality" in nonverbal behavior (see, e.g., Eibl-Eibesfeldt, 1984; Ploog, 1980). However, from a communication
point of view this specificity could be seen as the basis for a "differential" understanding. Persons acquainted with the patient recognize behavioral changes when comparing
the known individual in various situations. The relevant information can then be filtered out, disregarding other elements.

Behavioral Coordination

One of the most fascinating features of nonverbal behavior is the organization of its elements as a highly coordinated behavioral flow, smoothly exchanged between interactants (Cranach, 1971). An obvious example is the coordination of gaze with speech. A
speaker tends to turn the gaze away when starting to speak or when confronted with a
task, and he returns the gaze on completion of the speech or answer (Kendon, 1967;
Ellgring, 1984). For facial behavior, a different coordination is of interest; as facial expression is activated at a high level when one communicates verbally to another person.
It is, however, reduced to a very low level during emotional or nonemotional imagery,
and during observation of emotional films (Ellgring, Hahlweg, Feinstein, & Dose,
1985; Vanger & Ellgring, 1985). It is therefore probable that facial expression is closely
connected to verbal or vocal communication.

During psychosis, a dissolution of otherwise coordinated behavior has been observed by Ploog (1972). The question being investigated empirically, then, is if a dissolution can be found for the verbal-facial coordination reported above.

Again facial behavior was coded from the videotaped interactions. In addition, it
was noted whether facial action took place during an utterance (speaker role) or during
the utterance of the other person (listener role). From the previous experimental results,
a higher proportion of facial expression should occur during those parts of the dialogue
where the person takes the speaker role than when taking the listener role.

For each of 10 endogenous, 10 neurotic patients and 9 controls, three interviews
were examined from the sample mentioned before. In addition, for a group of 10 schizophrenic patients (ICD 295; 4 male, 6 female, age ranging from 17 to 46 years, median
24 years), facial behavior was analyzed when interacting with their relatives at the end
of their clinical stay. Information on relapse within 1 year was available. Relatives' facial behavior was assessed twice: once when interacting with the patient discussing a
point of disagreement and once when being interviewed by a clinician about the patient. The interview took place shortly after admission of the patient and was used to
rate positive and negative attitudes of the relatives towards the patient (Hahlweg, Dürr,
& Müller, 1995, in preparation).

The relative amount of facial expression when in the speaker or the listener role
was the critical variable. If facial expression is independent of the verbal communication, a proportion of 50% would be expected. Figure 18.3 contains average and single
values for the proportion of facial expression being displayed in the speaker role. Values higher than 50% indicated the expected association of facial expression with verbal communication. Values lower than 50% indicated a dissolution of both communication modes.

As can be seen from figure 18.3, there were, on average, substantial differences
between groups with regard to facial-verbal association. Controls and relatives in the

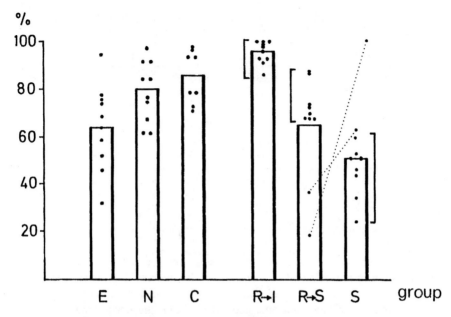

Figure 18.3 Proportion of facial expression when taking the speaker role. Averages and individual data (dotted). E = endogenous, N = neurotic, C = controls, R-I = relatives in interview, R-S = relatives with recovered schizophrenics, S = recovered schizophrenics. Lines connect dyads of patients and relatives (see text).

interview displayed more than 70% of their facial activity in the speaker role. For neurotic depressed patients, this average proportion was slightly lower. Endogenous depressed patients showed a similar proportion as relatives interacting with recovered schizophrenic patients. The clearly lowest average proportion (about 50%) was displayed by schizophrenic patients in this interaction.

Table 18.1 gives the levels of significance for single comparisons between groups using U-tests after a highly significant Kruskal-Wallis analysis ($H = 33.5$, $df = 5$, $P <$ 0.01).

Apart from the group comparisons, the single values, marked in figure 18.3, were examined in more detail. Despite the averages being quite similar for endogenous patients and relatives interacting with schizophrenic patients, there were substantial differences in the kind of variability. Although for endogenous patients there was a broad range of proportion values, only two of the relatives showed exceptional data, the other covering a narrow range. The corresponding values of the patients, on the other hand, were extremes in the opposite direction. Obviously, these cases were complementary but not the remainder. Interestingly enough, in two cases of the three in the sample a high rating of negative attitudes predicted relapse that did not however occur. The third of these cases is indicated by the dotted line in figure 18.3. Again values were located at the extremes of the respective groups though not as dramatically as for the other two. (For further analyses of facial expression, see Ellgring et al., 1985).

TABLE 18.1. Statistical comparisons between groups with regard to their average proportions of facial activity in speaker/listener role

	E	N	C	R-I	R-S	S
E	—	0.07	< 0.01**	< 0.001***	0.91	< 0.11
N		—	0.24	< 0.01**	0.17	< 0.001***
C			—	0.05	< 0.01**	< 0.001***
R-I				—	< 0.001***	< 0.001***
R-S					—	0.06
S						—

P- values from *U*-tests, E = endogenous, N = neurotic depressed patients, C = controls, R-I = relatives in interview, R-S = relatives interacting with recovered schizophrenic patients, S = recovered schizophrenic patients.

So there is the general tendency for coordination of facial expression and verbal communication in normals and also in most of the depressed patients. The only exception was the group of recovered schizophrenics. Here, a random association of facial and verbal communication emerged. In addition, the exceptional data of two dyads indicate compensatory processes between patients and relatives which need further clarification.

Discussion

From the analysis of facial expression we found evidence for a tendency of the non-verbal behavior to dissociate from verbal communication in psychoses. There was a slight tendency for this dissolution in endogenous depressed patients and an even stronger one for recently recovered schizophrenic patients. For normal controls and relatives of patients, there was, in contrast, a very close association of facial expression and verbal communication. One can only speculate on the exceptional data from the group of schizophrenic patients interacting with their relatives. One interpretation would be that a high proportion of facial expression of the relative when listening to the patient (corresponding to a low proportion in the speaker role) may serve as some emotional feedback given to the patient. This could be a protective factor for those interactions where a high degree of rated negative attitude would otherwise predict a relapse. Other explanations are, however, possible and need further empirical investigation.

From the coordination of facial expression to verbal behavior it is clear that under normal conditions both serve communicative functions in an interrelated way (Ploog, 1980). Facial expression complements the verbal content at an emotional level, however they seem to be dissociated in the recovered schizophrenic. It could be that this kind of dissociation may contribute to the perception of disturbed communication in this group.

The individual specificity of behavioral changes found in depressed patients points to an inconsistency with regard to the universality of expressive behavior. In the expression of children and in the perception of emotional expression, cross-cultural universality has been reported (Eibl-Eibesfeldt, 1984). For the patients' behavior, however, this universality seems only to be partly true, with an individual-specific association of behavior and mood changes emerging. It is not known whether this is also the case for other adults in varying emotional states.

When considering an economical way for transmitting emotional information, this individual-specific "usage" of nonverbal behavior has several advantages. Only part of the repertoire has to change during a depressed state. Moreover, since the specific effectors become apparent only for those who are able to observe the individual and compare behavior over the time course, acquaintances have an easier access to this information. From this it follows that the level of transmitting emotional or affective information varies depending on the relationship between interactants. The same behavior, thus, has a different meaning for persons knowing the individual than for strangers. In this way, the same behavior informs on different levels of acuity depending on the closeness of the relationship. Individual-specific expression of mood, therefore, seems to be an effective way of communication.

References

Arieti, S. (1974), Affective disorders: Manic-depressive psychosis and psychotic depression. In S. Arieti, & E. B. Brody (Eds.), *American handbook of psychiatry, Vol. 3. Adult clinical psychiatry* (pp. 449–490). New York: Basic Books.

Coyne, J. C. (1976). Toward an interactional description of depression. *Psychiatry, 39,* 28–40.

Cranach, M. von (1971). Die nichtverbale Kommunikation in Kontext des kommunikativen Verhaltens. In *Jahrbuch der Max-Planck-Gesellschaft zur Förderung der Wissenschaften* (pp. 104–148). Göttengen: Max-Planck-Gesellschaft.

Darwin, C. (1872/1965). *The expression of the emotions in man and animals.* Chicago: University of Chicago Press.

Eibl-Eibesfeldt, I. (1984). *Die Biologie des menschlichen Verhaltens. Grundriß der Humanethologie.* Munich: Piper.

Ekman, P., & Friesen, M. V. (1969). The repertoire of nonverbal behavior—Categories, origins, usage, and coding. *Semiotica, 1,* 49–98.

Ekman, P., & Friesen, W. V. (1978). *Facial Action Coding System.* Palo Alto, CA: Consulting Psychologists Press.

Ellgring, H. (1984). *Nonverbale Kommunikation im Verlauf der Depression—Zum Ausdruck der Stimmung und des Befindens in Mimik, Blickzuwendung, Sprechen und Gestik.* (Habilitationsschrift). Giessen: Justus-Liebig-Universität.

Ellgring, H., Hahlweg, K., Feinstein, E., & Dose, M. (1985). *Affective behaviour of relatives during CFT and family interaction.* Paper presented at the Ringberg Symposium "The Impact of Family Interaction Research on our Understanding of Psychopathology," Schloß Ringberg.

Ellgring, H., Nagel., U., & Ferst, R. (1985). *Facial expression during imagery and communication.* Paper presented at the International Conference on the Meaning of Faces, Cardiff.

Ellgring, H., Wagner, H., & Clarke, A. H. (1980). Psychopathological states and their effects on speech and gaze behaviour. In H. Giles, W. P. Robinson, & P. M. Smith (Eds). *Language—Social psychological perspectives,* Oxford: Pergamon Press. 267–273.

Hahlweg, K., Dürr, H., & Müller, U. (1995). Familienbetreuung bei Schizophrenen. Ein verhaltenstherapeutischer Ansatz zur Rueückfallprophylaxe. Muenchen: Psychologie Verlag Union.

Jones, J. H., Pansa, M. (1979). Some nonverbal aspects of depression and schizophrenia occurring during the interview. *Journal of Nervous and Mental Disease, 167,* 402–409.

Kendon, A. (1967). Some functions of gaze direction in social interaction. *ACTA Psychologica, 26,* 22–63.

Lacey, J. I. (1967). Somatic response patterning and stress: Some revisions of activation theory. In M. H. Applev & R. Trumbull (Eds.), *Psychological stress* (pp. 14–42). New York: Appleton-Century-Crofts.

Ploog, D. (1958). Über das Hervortreten angeborener Verhaltensweisen in akuten schizophrenen Psychosen. *Psychiatrisch Neurologie 136,* 157–164.

Ploog, D. (1972). Breakdown of the social communication system: A key process in the development of schizophrenia? Prospects for Research on schizophrenia, neurosciences. *Neuroscience Research Progress Bulletin, 10,* 394–395.

Ploog, D. (1980). Der Ausdruck der Germütsbewegungen bei Mensch und Tieren. In Max-Planck-Gesellschaft (Ed.), *Jahrbuch 1980* (pp. 66–97). Göttingen: Vanderhöck and Ruprecht.

Rutter, D. R. (1984). *Looking und seeing: The role of visual communication in social interaction.* New York: Wiley.

Vanger, Ph., & Ellgring, H. (1985). *Facial activity and intensity of emotional experience.* Paper presented at the International Conference on the Meaning of Faces. Cardiff, Wales.

AFTERWORD

Nonverbal Expression of Psychological States in Psychiatric Patients

HEINER ELLGRING

Facial Behavior in Psychosis

Many of the changes in nonverbal behavior of psychiatric patients, including facial behavior, still cannot be explicitly described. There is an overwhelming impression of deviance in the "expression of mood states." But individual specificity of effectors, even
in the relatively homogeneous syndrome of depression, makes one wonder how these
heterogeneous patterns of behavior are transformed into a homogeneous impression
(Ellgring, 1989).

On the other hand, when schizophrenic patients are compared to depressed patients, as is being done in a current longitudinal study, no disease specificity of major
facial parameters is shown. A considerable proportion of depressed and schizophrenic
patients show extremely reduced facial activity even at the end of their clinical stay
(Ellgring & Gaebel, in press). Medication seems to have a sedating effect on facial activity (Schneider et al., 1992); nevertheless, even nonmedicated schizophrenic patients
show reduced facial behavior compared with controls.

The question currently studied is whether the reduction still holds for remitted depressed and schizophrenic outpatients who otherwise show no abnormal clinical signs.
Facial expression might then be regarded as a possible vulnerability factor influencing
social interaction even outside periods of disease. In this way, dysfunctional affect regulation during psychosis might be traced to these behavioral deficits (Ellgring & Smith,
in press).

Dissociation of Emotion and Expression in Parkinson's Disease

A line of research that has followed from our study of depression is a search for psychological effects of Parkinson's disease (Ellgring et al., 1993). The goal is to assess
and compare facial behavior in depression, in which an association between behavior
and internal state is assumed, with Parkinson's disease, in which a dissociation of facial
behavior and inner feelings are experienced by patients. Since the primary disturbance

395

in Parkinson's is of motor function, not emotional processes, this disease should allow a clinical test for the facial feedback hypothesis. In a study by Smith, Smith, and Ellgring (in preparation), preliminary results suggest that reduced facial expression is *not* associated with reduced emotional experience.

In another study of Parkinson's, odors were used to elicit emotional reactions, and less facial activity was again observed. However, in this study differences in subjective perception of odor could have been responsible for reduced expressions (Saku & Ellgring, 1992).

Pertinent Problems

Although the FACS is still a necessary tool and cannot easily be exchanged by automatic devices, important problems remain, especially in the clinical field.

Automated Analysis vs. Coding of Behavior

Many medical colleagues are enthusiastic about studying facial behavior. But when it comes to learning FACS and to laboriously coding behavior, this enthusiasm fades. Systematic comparisons of FACS-derived parameters and those derived from automated analyses (Schneider et al., 1992) or from EMG are needed. Then, detailed FACS analyses for selected segments of the behavioral stream can complement automated assessment of facial behavior.

Training Coders

Because new students continually develop interest in the field and researchers need trained coders, it seems worthwhile to improve training in learning FACS. This would include the development of more practice material and definition of different levels of expertise. It also seems that students need personal support when learning FACS. Personally, it was important for me to have the direct support of Paul Ekman and Wally Friesen in their Human Interaction Laboratory.

Parameters of Facial Behavior

The situation is still unsatisfactory with regard to condensing behavioral information. Whereas the description of complex behavioral patterns by means of FACS has a firm basis, the next steps in the process of data analysis still need to be elaborated.

Interpretation of Behavior

The advantage of FACS is that it does not require emotional interpretation. Nevertheless, facial behavior is usually coded because one is interested in "emotional expressions." Although the EMFACS can be used to interpret behavior, this method still needs critical testing. Clinically, certain specific interpretations appear to warrant additional testing, such as the description of a felt or Duchenne smile with cheek raise (AU6); this smile type might not be possible for Parkinson's patients, who nevertheless experience joy or happiness.

Elicitors of Behavior

We still need to know more about stimuli or situations that elicit emotions and/or facial behavior. The obvious independence of emotions and facial behavior in many instances needs to be studied experimentally. Otherwise, ambiguous results contribute to the continuous and sometimes superficial discussion as to whether facial behavior is emotional or social.

What I Would Do Differently?

I would probably analyze facial behavior in basically the same way as before. Describing facial behavior on a functional anatomical basis as it was proposed by Hjortsjoe (1970) and systematically expanded by Ekman and Friesen (1978) still appears to me to be of fundamental importance, even when using other measurements such as facial EMG or automated pattern analyses.

However, if I would be allowed the time, I would try to answer some of the measurement questions beforehand. For example, I would systematically compare facial EMG and FACS-coded observations. This comparison should critically evaluate what kind of information is provided by one method and not (or not as economically) by the other.

Another change I would make, provided the financial means were available, would be to introduce simultaneous measurement of facial behavior, other nonverbal and verbal behaviors, physiological reactions, and continuously monitored subjective experience. This, however, would make the data analysis more complicated. I cannot exclude that it would be even more difficult then to find the general in the ocean of specifics.

References

Ekman, P., & Friesen, W. (1978). *Facial Action Coding System.* Palo Alto, CA: Consulting Psychologists Press.

Ellgring, H. (1989). *Nonverbal communication in depression.* Cambridge, England: Cambridge University Press.

Ellgring, H., & Gaebel, W. (in press). Facial expression in schizophrenic patients. In *Proceedings of the IX World Congress of Psychiatry.* Berlin: Springer.

Ellgring, H., Seiler, S., Perleth, B., Frings, W., Gasser, T., & Oertel, W. (1993). Psychosocial aspects of Parkinson's disease. *Neurology, 43* (Suppl. 6), 41–44.

Ellgring, H., & Smith, M. (in press). Affect regulation during psychosis. In W. F. Flack & J. Laird (Eds.), *Emotions in psychopathology.*

Hjortsjö, C.-H. (1970). *Man's face and mimic language.* Malmö, Sweden: Studentlitteratur.

Saku, M., & Ellgring, H. (1992). Emotional reactions to odours in Parkinson's Disease. A clinical application of ethological methods. *Journal of Ethology, 10,* 47–52.

Schneider, F., Ellgring, H., Friedrich, J., Fus, I., Beyer, T., Heimann, H., & Himer, W. (1992). The effects of neuroleptics on facial action in schizophrenic patients. *Pharmacopsychiatry, 25,* 233–239.

Smith, M., Smith, M., & Ellgring, H. (in preparation). Spontaneous and posed facial expression in Parkinson's disease.

19

Depression and Suicide Faces

MICHAEL HELLER & VÉRONIQUE HAYNAL

As far as psychiatry is concerned, suicide is the major cause of mortality. Unfortunately suicide is difficult to prevent, as its prediction is unreliable. Indeed, neither the categories of "people at risk" as defined by studies ranging from sociology to neurophysiology nor the clinical questionnaires allow to predict satisfactorily an attempt. Therefore, clinicians remain somewhat at a loss when faced with a first attempt or even with a reattempt. Yet clinical practice has shown that some experienced therapists, probably following their intuition, are able to predict suicidal risks with a smaller error margin than their colleagues (Motto, 1991). What do these therapists rely upon? What semiology elements do they perceive even though they are unable to explain them? We propose the hypothesis that most of the cues that subtend this intuition are provided by the suicidal patients' nonverbal behavior.

To our knowledge, studies pertaining to the systematic analysis of suicidal patients' nonverbal behavior are scarce, if nonexistent. In 1976, Ringel described a presuicidal syndrome that has since become well known. He observed in suicidal patients a cognitive and affective restriction that he termed "constriction effect": patients tend to restrict their adaptive capacity until death appears more and more strongly as the only solution. Ringel also showed that the mode of communication in suicidal patients followed a similar evolution.

More recently, Ekman (1985) presented the case study of "Mary." Mary managed to obtain the approbation to leave the hospital by being quite convincing in her lying about her suicide intentions during the interview. This interview was filmed. Later on she admitted the deception. Ekman showed the interview to young psychiatrists and psychologists; most of them were deceived by Mary's behavior—even many of the more experienced clinicians were deceived. In order to evidence the lie, Ekman scanned the film

> for hundreds of hours, going over it again and again, inspecting each gesture and expression in slow motion to uncover any possible clues to deceit. In a moment's pause before replying to her doctor's question about her plans for the future, we saw in slow motion a fleeting facial expression of despair, so quick that we had missed seeing it the first few times we examined the film. Once we had the idea that concealed feelings might be evident in these very brief *micro expressions,* we searched and found many more, typically covered in an instant by a smile. We also found a *micro gesture.* When telling the doctor how well she was handling her problems Mary sometimes showed a fragment of a shrug—not the whole

thing, just a part of it. She would shrug with just one hand, rotating it a bit. Or her hands would be quiet but there would be a momentary lift of one shoulder. (p. 17)

For more than 30 years Ekman and Friesen have studied facial behavior and the emotions expressed on the face. Inspired by Darwin and Duchenne, they have applied the methods of ethology to the study of facial mimics and their emotional signification, as well as on the means used to hide these (cf. where Mary dissimulates her true feelings with a smile, her real emotions only appeared as micro-expressions). Their data confirmed the observation made by Darwin that in order to express emotion, the face uses some elements that are common to all human beings and even to some animal species such as monkeys, cats, and dogs (Ekman, 1980; Grammer, Schiefenhövel, Schleidt, Lorenz, & Eibl-Eibesfeldt, 1988; Preuschoft, 1995). They show that the relationship between these elements and some emotions is relatively independent from behavioral variations owing to different cultural environments. For instance, joy is expressed by the same lengthening of the lips and lifting of the cheeks with a compression of the eyelids in populations as diversified as those in North Africa, New Guinea, or North America. To carry out their research, Ekman and Friesen have developed a system for the coding of facial action (Facial Action Coding System, or FACS; 1978), which has proved to be an invaluable tool since.

The study of facial expressions appeared quite appropriate for our research and the FACS an adequate tool because of the reliability of the coding system (Ekman, & Friesen 1978, 1980; Ellgring, 1989; Krause, Steimer-Krause, & Hufnagel, 1992) and its relative independence from cultural influences. Indeed, the population in Geneva (Switzerland), and therefore the patients we observed, is quite culturally varied.

Studies

Two studies are presented here. The first concerns suicide and the second depression. Both were carried out at the Laboratory of Affect & Communication (LAC).[1]

Study on Suicide

The population was composed of 17 subjects: 10 women and 7 men aged from 19 to 62. They were treated in the psychiatric ward of the Geneva psychiatric institution. All suffered from severe depression as defined by the *DSM III* and presented almost no schizoid or psychotic symptoms.

The patients had attempted to commit suicide within the past two weeks. Each patients was filmed during an interview with a psychiatrist. All patients gave their written consents for being filmed and only their faces were filmed. During the interview the psychiatrist asked 5 questions from the Present State Examination. We analyzed the patients facial behavior during the following question: "Do you still wish to attempt to end your life?" The sampling for the analysis was as follows: from the beginning of the silence that preceded the question, during the question, the following silence, then the first 10 seconds of the patient's answer (mean length: 16.65 seconds). One year after the filmed interview, 5 patients had further reattempted. Thus we defined two groups:

one composed of 5 depressive suicide with further reattempts (FR), the other 12 depressive with no further reattempts (NR).

Study on Depression

The population was composed of 9 subjects: 5 women and 4 men aged from 29 to 59 years old. They were treated in the same institution as the patients of the previous study. All suffered from severe depression as defined by the *DSM III* and presented no schizoid or psychotic symptoms.

The patients were filmed during 5 sessions of semistructured interviews with their psychiatrists, which occurred every two weeks. The interviews addressed the evocation of events that had aroused emotions in the patients (joy, sadness, anger, and neutral.) The sadness topic contained a question on suicide intentions.

We analyzed in each interview, one sample per emotional topic (mean length: 19.33 seconds). After an interview, the patients filled out Beck's Self-Evaluation Questionnaire for depression and the psychiatrists assessed the patients' state using Hamilton's Questionnaire for the evaluation of depression. A comparison of the scores obtained after the first and the last sessions shows that after 10 weeks the state of 3 of the nonsuicidal depressed patients had greatly improved, 1 patient showed moderate improvement, and 5 patients still presented major depression symptoms. In the sadness topic we coded the following question "Have you recently wished to die or to attempt suicide?" We analyzed the facial behavior of the patients from the end of the question until the beginning of the next question or during 20 seconds.

Coding and Analysis

The patients' facial behavior was analyzed using the Facial Action Coding System (FACS). The onset, apex, and offset of the action, as well as its laterality (S if it is symmetrical, L for Left, and R for Right) were coded sequentially. Thus an action of the lips may be coded S12D where S indicates its symmetry, 12 the pull of the lip corner, and D its intensity on a scale ranging from A (minimum) to E (maximum).

After the data collection and analysis for both studies, we obtained a general repertoire of the emotional and facial behavior for the two populations observed. In order to test a common assumption that suicidal risk increases as a function of depression severity, it seemed interesting to compare the results of these two populations of severely depressed patients: suicidal depressives and nonsuicidal depressives. We isolated the results for the situations common to both studies—that is to say, the *suicidal intentions* as collected during the *first interview*.

Results

Three main results are presented here: the first concerns the repertoire for both populations—that is, all the expressions used by each group; the second treats the asymmetrical expressions; and the third measures the duration of the movements in the upper face.

The Repertoire

The repertoire of a given group is composed of all behaviors observed within this group. The 26 depressed patients (17 suicidal and 9 nonsuicidal) were analyzed over a period of approximately 20 seconds. They displayed 60 distinctly different facial expressions, as coded with an EMFACS procedure. Each patient used an average of 2.3 expressions never displayed by another patient. The behavior of depressed patients is finally quite diversified (see table 19.1).

Only 10 expressions are used by at least one suicidal depressive patient and one nonsuicidal depressive patient. The precision of the coding (i.e., intensity) is not the only reason for the high diversity we observe: most expressions are really different when viewed on the tapes.

Most of the facial expressions are used by only one person and only a few expressions are used by several patients of one or both populations. Many of the expressions

TABLE 19.1. Facial repertoire

Expression	Dep	Sui	Expression	Dep	Sui
L02B	0	2	S16B + S25B	0	1
L04B	0	1	S17B + S24B	0	1
L14B	0	2	S18B + S25B	0	1
R02B + L04B	0	1	S22B + S26B	0	1
R10B	0	1	S24A	0	2
R12A	0	1	S01B + S02B	6	3
R14B	0	1	S04B	1	1
R18B	0	1	S12A	1	1
S01B + S02B + S15A	0	1	S14B	1	4
S02B	0	1	S15B	1	2
S04B + S07B	0	1	S17C	2	1
S04B + S07B + S15A	0	1	S18B	1	1
S06B	0	2	S23B	3	1
S06B + S26B	0	1	S23B + S25B	1	1
S07B	0	1	S24B	3	4
S10A	0	1	L01B + L02B + S17B	1	0
S10B	0	1	S01B	1	0
S10B + S15B	0	1	S01B + S02B + S25B	1	0
S10D	0	1	S05C	1	0
S10E	0	1	S06B + S12C	1	0
S12A + S25B	0	1	S10A + S26B	1	0
S12B	0	1	S12A + S17C	1	0
S12D	0	1	S14B + S17B	1	0
S12E	0	1	S14B + S24D	1	0
S14A	0	1	S14B + S26B	1	0
S14B + S17D	0	1	S15C	1	0
S14B + S17D + S24E	0	1	S17A	1	0
S14B + S23B	0	1	S17B	1	0
S15A	0	1	S17D	1	0
S15A + S25B	0	1	S17E	1	0

Expression: EMFACS facial combinations observed. Dep: number of nonsuicidal depressive patients using this combination ($n = 17$). Sui: number of suicidal depressive patients using this combination ($n = 9$).

displayed by suicidal patients were not observed in nonsuicidal patients and vice versa.

Emotional Expressions

Following the hypothesis of the Ekman and Friesen dictionary, the repertoire described in table 19.1 yields the emotional repertoire shown in table 19.2:

Table 19.2 shows that a negative or contempt or disgust hypothesis is attributed to 6 suicidal depressive patients (and 3 out of 6 reattempters) and to only 1 nonsuicidal depressive.

Within the repertoire of our patients, as shown in table 19.3, we coded 9 asymmetrical expressions: one composed of one symmetrical and two asymmetrical AUs, and 8 composed of only 1 or 2 asymmetrical AUs, without symmetrical AUs—for example, only the left eye brow is lifted in an otherwise impassive face or the left corner of the lips freezes into a small nearly permanent smile.

The totality of these 8 asymmetrical expressions were present in 7 of the depressive suicidal patients. Among these, 4 reattempted to commit suicide. Only 1 of these asymmetrical expressions, more complex and mixed with symmetrical AUs, was observed in the population of nonsuicidal depressive patients.

Among these 8 expressions observed, 4 belong to the emotional expressions associated by Ekman and Friesen to "contempt." They are displayed by 5 of the 17 suicidal depressive patients, 3 of these having reattempted suicide. No expression related to contempt, be it asymmetrical or not, was observed in our population of depressive nonsuicidal patients during this topic.

Upper Face Activity

Suicidal depressive patients show a reduced activity in the upper face compared with nonsuicidal depressed patients. Figure 19.1 shows the duration (in percent) during which each upper face unit (around the eyes) was used.[2] The patients are represented on the X-axis divided into two groups: the first 9 patients are the nonsuicidal depressives and ordered according to the severity of their depression after 10 weeks: the first 3 improved within 10 weeks (D1 to D3), the last 5 did not (D5 to D9). The next 17 patients are suicidal depressive patients: the first 12 patients (S10 to S21) did not reattempt to

TABLE 19.2. Number of patients who used each emotional category

	ha-f	ha-u	sa	an	neg	di	co	np	neg + co + di
Dep	1	1	2	4	0	1	0	7	1
Sui	0	4	0	3	1	2	5	15	6
Snr	0	2	0	2	1	2	2	10	3
Sr	0	2	0	1	0	0	3	5	3

ha-f: felt happiness, ha-u: unfelt hapiness, sa: sad, an: anger, neg: unspecific negative feelings, di: disgust, co: contempt; np: no prediction, neg + co + di: either of these emotions. Dep: number of nonsuicidal depressive patients (n = 17). Sui: number of suicidal depressive patients (n = 9). Snr: non reattempter suicidal depressive patients (n = 12), Sr: reattempter suicidal depressive patients (n = 5).

TABLE 19.3. Asymmetric expressions

EMO	AU Combination	TOT	Dep	Sui
No prediction	L01B + L02B + 17B	1	1	0
No prediction	L02B	2	0	2
No prediction	L04B	1	0	1
Contempt	L14B	2	0	2
No prediction	R02B + L04B	1	0	1
Contempt	R10B	1	0	1
Contempt	R12A	1	0	1
Contempt	R14B	1	0	1
No prediction	R18B	1	0	1

EMO: emotional hypothesis proposed by Ekman and Friesen's dictionary. TOT: number of subjects using this combination. Dep: number of nonsuicidal depressive patients ($n = 17$). Sui: number of suicidal depressive patients ($n = 9$).

commit suicide within the following year, the next 4 patients (S1 to S4) reattempted to commit suicide and the last one (S5) succeeded in committing suicide four weeks after the interview. For instance, Patient D7 is a depressive nonsuicidal patient who is very depressed at the first interview (Hamilton score 36) and will not be better after 10 weeks (Hamilton 35); he moves his upper face during 87% of the sample duration. Patient D2 is depressed during the first interview (Hamilton score 29) but will feel much better after 10 weeks (Hamilton score 4); he activates his upper face during 23% of the coded sample.

The Y-axis indicates the percentage of observation time during which each upperface Action Unit was activated (each unit was analyzed separately). Upperface Action Units are: lifting the eye brows (AUs 1 + 2), brow lowerer (AU 4), upper lid raiser (AU 5), cheek raiser and lid compressor (AU 6) (included only when not coded with AU

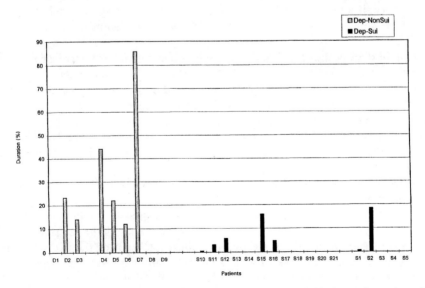

Figure 19.1 Duration of upper face activity for nonsuicide and suicide depressive patients (%).

12), lid tightener (AU 7). We did not consider lid droop (AU 41), slit (AU 42), eyes closed (AU 43), squint (AU 44), blink (AU 45), or wink (AU 46).

A more detailed analysis of the data evidences that it is mainly the duration of the mobilization of the brow raise (1 + 2) that is responsible for the difference, but this combination alone does not really yield a systematic difference. Looking at this graph, we can see that the two populations differ as far as the mean and standard deviation: (1) suicidal depressive patients show relatively low inter-individual variations with a small mean: their duration ratio ranges between 0 and 19%; and (2) nonsuicidal depressive patients display an important interindividual variation with a high mean as their duration ratio ranges from 0 to 87%. Unlike our expectations, our data show no relationship between the scores obtained on the Hamilton scales and the duration ratios for the nonsuicidal depressive patients. Nor was there a relationship for the suicidal patients between the fact that they belonged or not to the reattempt group. That is to say, the reduced activity observed in suicidal patients is not related to a more severe depression than for the nonsuicidal depressive patients.

Discussion

Quantitatively, the repertoire of each population is quite diversified. Indeed, each patient uses at least one Action Unit displayed by no other patient. This diversity alone explains the little overlapping observed between the two repertoires. But behavioral imagination is not the sole variable that must be taken into account. It should be noted though that these results are rather complex because facial behavior also involves the duration and complexity of each movement.

A sign typical of suicide seems difficult to evidence. Evidently, as noted by Frey, Hirsbrunner, Florin, Daw, and Crawford, (1983), the mere counting of the movements is not sufficient to measure activity. In our sample, the difference in activity between our two populations involves mobility, duration, and diversity of repertoire. For instance, if a face shows AU 4 (brow lowerer) only, during the whole time window, its meaning will be different from AU 4 appearing 3 short times or combined with AU 1.

Our third result shows a clear difference in the activity in the upper face measured as a ratio of duration of the Action Units. The difference has two aspects: (1) there is a significant difference between the two averages; and (2) it is also a clear difference of variance between the two groups. This pattern is frequently observed in nonverbal communication as for most of the signs the nonactivation of the muscles is always possible. This has also been observed for postural behavior (Heller, 1991). The decreased activity in the upper face is mainly associated to a limited duration of eye brow mobilization in suicidal patients.

How can we understand such phenomena? According to Ekman and Friesen's "dictionary of emotions" the muscles surrounding the eyes are involved in the expression of several emotions (fear, surprise, joy, sadness), but the eyebrows are often mobilized with the purpose of capturing or maintaining the interlocutor's attention. In other words, there are two meanings (at least) of the eye brow raise (AUs 1+2). One is the conversational sign, culturally expressed to sustain or get the partner's attention or to encourage him to talk. The other, mostly when AU

1+2 is combined with other Action Units, may be an emotional expression (Grammer et al., 1988). Suicide patients filmed several days after their attempt showed a certain inhibition to communicate while they were talking about their suicide intentions. Some of these patients make little attempt to initiate or maintain contact with their psychiatrist. They seem to have constructed a blank mask. Nonsuicidal depressive patients do not display this kind of inhibition. With them, the interaction looks easier. For us, then, both inhibitions are linked: the emotional as well as the conversational.

As Krause and Lütolf (1988) remarked, it is interesting to note what is missing in the facial activity. Indeed, although variability of expressions is quite high among suicides it remains nevertheless restricted to certain areas of the face (lower face, the mouth . . .). Also, the behavior of a given group may exclude some types of expressions.

Besides movement occurrences, duration, and diversity, we also have more qualitative data. Our second result, asymmetric expressions being only observed among suicides, particularly in reattempter patients, may give us clues about meaning. These patients, who displayed few relevant emotions (no sadness nor disgust for reattempters) seem to show mostly contempt. It may be interpreted as contempt for the interview situation, but also probably as contempt of oneself and maybe of one's own life. We were struck by this observation, as it corroborates the hypothesis found in clinical research such as in some psychoanalytical schools (Klein, 1933).

Our results are in accordance with the observations reported by Ringel (1976) in which he defines a "suicidal syndrome" as a relatively differentiated and independent clinical entity. Shneidman (1993) also has developed this direction of analysis.

The scope of this pilot study is, of course, restricted by the limited number of patients observed and by the relatively small duration of the samples analyzed. Yet we believe that our first observations are encouraged enough to be presented. We are now engaged in a larger investigation on nonverbal communication in this field, filming the physician as well as the patient. In studying the interaction we wish, among other things, to improve our data on a qualitative level.

Conclusion

The results of these studies show that a population of nonsuicidal depressive patients behave differently from a population of depressive suicidal patients as far as the expression of emotions on the face is concerned. Analysis reveals that suicidal depressive patients do not suffer from more severe depression than the other patients, as the variable "depression severity" is not associated to the difference between the two populations. Therefore, we believe that suicidal risk is related to factors other than depression. We also believe that such factors may be evidenced in the patient's nonverbal behavior. The inhibition revealed by the analysis of suicidal patients' expressions suggests that the problem could be related to impulsiveness and to violence. In a larger research project that we are currently carrying out, analyzing the doctor's and the patient's facial behavior, we hope to shed further light on the processes involved in suicidal risk.

Notes

1. This work was directed by Michel Heller, with the participation of Pat Claus, Véronique Haynal, and Christine Lessko, within the Clinque de psychiatrie II under the responsibility of Pr. André Haynal. Part of the data we published in France in *Les Cahiers Psychiatriques Genevois, 16* (1994).

2. Means for Dep. and Dep-Sui.: 22.33; 2.88. SD for D.N.S. and D.S: 770.87; 32.26. Mann-Whitney W test: $U = 158, p < = .01$ (two-tailed).

References

American Psychiatric Association. *Diagnostic and Statistical Manual of Mental Disorders,* Third Edition. Washington, DC: APA, 1980.

Darwin, C. (1872/1965). The expression of the emotions in man and in animals. Chicago: University of Chicago Press.

Ekman, P. (1980). L'expression des émotions. *La Recherche 11,* 1408–1415.

Ekman, P. (1985). *Telling lies.* New York: Norton.

Ekman, P. (1989). The argument and evidence about universals in facial expressions of emotions. In H. Wagner & A. Manstead (Eds.), *Handbook of psychophysiology: The biological psychology of the emotions and social processes* (pp. 143–164). New York: Wiley.

Ekman, P. (1992). An argument for basic emotions. *Cognition and Emotion, 6*(3/4), 169–200.

Ekman, P., & Friesen, W. V. (1969). Nonverbal leakage and clues to deception. *Psychiatry, 32,* 88–105.

Ekman, P., & Friesen, W. V. (1978). *Facial Action Coding System.* Palo Alto: Consulting Psychologists Press.

Ellgring, H. (1989). Nonverbal communication in depression. Cambridge, England: Cambridge University Press.

Frey, S., Hirsbrunner, H.-P., Florin, A., Daw, W., & Crawford, R. (1983). A Unified Approach to the Investigation of Nonverbal and Verbal Behavior in Communication Research. In W. Doise & S. Moscovici (Eds.), *Current issues in European social psychology* (Vol 1; pp. 143–198). Cambridge, England: Cambridge University Press.

Fridlund, A. J. (1991). Sociality of solitary smiling: Potentiation by an implicit audience. *Journal of Personality and Social Psychology, 60*(2), 229–241.

Grammer, K. Schiefenhövel, W., Schleidt, M., Lorenz, B., Eibl-Eibesfeldt, I. (1988). Patterns on the face: The eyebrow flash in crosscultural comparison. *Ethology, 77,* 279–299.

Haynal, A. (1993). *Psychoanalysis and the sciences: Epistemology and history.* London: Karnac.

Heller, M. (1991). *Postural dynamics and social status.* Doctoral dissertation, Psychology Faculty, University of Duisburg, Germany.

Heller, M. (1992a). Corps et évaluation de psychothérapies: Un rêve à réaliser. *Psychothérapies, 2,* 111–121.

Heller, M. (1992b). Les émotions: Un parcours littéraire. In J. Besson (Ed.), *Manuel d'enseignement de l'Ecole Française d'Analyse Psycho-Organique.* Toulouse: Ecole Française d'Analyse Psycho-Organique.

Heller, M. (1993). Unconscious communication. In B. Maul (Ed.), *Bodypsychotherapy or the art of contact* (pp. 155–179). Berlin: Verlag Bernhard Maul.

Klein, M. (1940). Mourning and its relation to manic-depressive states. *International Journal of Psychoanalysis, 21,* 125–153.

Klein, M. (1993). Contribution to the psychoanalysis of manic-depressive states. *International Journal of Psychoanalysis, 16,* 145–174.

Krause, R., & Lütolf, P. (1988). Facial indicators of transference processes within psychoanalytic treatment. In Dahl, H. Kächele, & H. Thomä (Eds.), *Psychoanalytic process research strategies,* (pp. 257–273). Heidelberg: Springer.

Krause, R., Steimer, E., Sänger-Alt, C., & Wagner, G. (1989). Facial expression of schizophrenic patients and their interaction partners. *Psychiatry, 52,* 1–11.

Krause, R., Steimer-Krause, E., & Hufnagel, H. (1992). Expression and experience of affects in paranoid schizophrenia. *European Review of Applied Psychology, 42,* 131–138.

Ladame, F. (1981). *Les tentatives de suicide des adolescents.* Paris: Masson.

Ladame, F. (1993). Les paradoxes du suicide. *Adolescence, 11,* 125–136.

Levenson, R. W. (1992). Autonomic nervous system differences among emotions. *Psychological Science, 3,* 23–27.

Motto, J. A. (1991). An integrated approach to estimating suicide risk. *Suicide & Life Threatening Behavior, 21,* 74–89.

Preuschoft, S. (1995). 'Laughter' and 'smiling' in macaques. Doctoral dissertation of the Faculteit Biologie Rijksuniversiteit Utrecht.

Ringel, E. (1976). The presuicidal syndrome. *Suicide and Life Threatening Behavior, 6,* 131–149.

Scherer, K. R., Summerfield, W. B., Wallbott, H. G. (1983). Cross-national research on antecedents and components of emotion: A progress report. *Social Science Information, 22,* 355–385.

Schneidman, E. (1993). *Suicide as psychache.* Northvale: Jason Aronson.

Perspectives for Studies of Psychopathology and Psychotherapy

MICHAEL HELLER & VÉRONIQUE HAYNAL

Beyond the specific analysis described in the preceding article, we share a dream. We hope that fairly soon a psychotherapist may come to see us with a film of his interaction with a patient. After analyzing a sample of this film, we could provide our colleague with a reliable diagnosis and an evaluation of the therapeutic relationship, based on their nonverbal communication. This dream is based on our experience, which has convinced us that what a therapist may know of a patient cannot be acquired experimentally, and that what we can teach a therapist on how he interacts with a patient cannot be acquired through experience and clinical knowledge alone. By combining thus experimental and clinical approaches, we hope to gain new insights into human psychology and interpersonal interaction (Haynal, 1993; Heller, 1992).

What we need to transform this dream into reality is not beyond the scope of what can be done today: (1) funds and support, of course; (2) setting up of a database that includes all the data colleagues and ourselves have collected through samples of behavior filmed in a given test situation; (3) a reliable coding procedure—several already exist, such as FACS for facial behavior and Siegfried Frey's Time Bernese System for gestures; and (4) good software allowing us speedy and relevant comparisons between the newly coded data and our database, producing outputs we can show to a psychotherapist. Although several laboratories are working on such programs, this is where we still need to invest the biggest effort. We will focus the following discussion on some of the problems that need to be solved before such programs can be written.

How Much Information Is Processed While Communicating?

When we analyze a film, we first code behavior. Just using FACS implies using a system that can distinguish on a face approximately 40 units with an average of 4 intensities:

0: non active
1: occurs slightly
2: occurs with a medium intensity
3: occurs at maximum intensity

With such a procedure we must deal with 160 (4*40) possible items when we analyze a photographed face and 320 for two faces. This computation supposes that knowing that a unit is not active may be just as important as knowing what is active. Assuming that the scale found by movie makers is relevant, we suppose that precise coding requires the analysis of 25 frames per second. Thus, one minute of coded psychotherapy involves 480,000 items, and one hour 28,800,000 (Heller, 1993).

The information we have then informs us on visible muscular facial behavior. It does not account for gaze or skin texture, which are also important sources of information. Furthermore, our own limits and our due respect for reliability prevents us from noting down some subtle facial expressions, which we nevertheless perceive as having a powerful impact. This rapid survey of our database provides us with a glimpse of how complex current human behavior really is, and of how much information we will eventually need to deal with. It also leads to two related questions: (1) How can research deal with such a mass of information collected on a *single* interaction? (2) How does a person's brain manage such a huge amount of perceived information, sometimes in only a few seconds?

Well, human beings manage, and research is slowly managing. Finding ways of dealing with such a huge amount of data may lead to interesting thoughts on which algorithms the brain may use. In our laboratory, as in many others, we write down the initial state of the face, and then only what changes and when it changes. We thus have much less than 28,800,000 items *written* on our hard disk for one hour of psychotherapy. We then have programs. Programs don't take much space, but they can use the database to generate huge tables. These tables provide lists of the data that are *implicitly* coded: for example, the state of each Action Unit at any moment or the dynamics of facial configuration from the point of view of time (differentiating chronic smiles from fast ones, or smiles with a fast onset and offset from smiles with a slow offset, etc.). Other tables provide us with statistical analysis of our data. Such tables can be very large. For our nonsuicidal depression study, a listing of *significant differences* for a given variable (e.g., duration of activity) often occupied more than 20 megabytes on the hard disk. When you try to find interesting results in these huge files really, you become aware of the enormous amount of computation the brain must generate before it can go *beyond reflex reactions.*

The advantage of a data-programs-tables strategy is that the basic information does not require much space. Furthermore, programs can be reused with several databases. We only generate all the tables simultaneously when we are trying to understand our data. Later, we may erase all the large tables, and generate more focused tables that will take much less space. When the study ends the tables are erased from our hard disk with the security that they can be generated once again when needed—provided we remember how to use our programs.

Managing all this and understanding what programs and films provide the researcher with still takes a few years, instead of a few seconds, like the brain. We mostly miss not having a theory capable of guiding the creation of such programs.

Emotional and Current Behavior

As analyzing other people's behavior is a daily task, we may have a tendency to think nonverbal communication should be fairly easy to understand. But every time we think we have found a tool allowing us to describe it better, we end up with a way of discovering a new land of complexity. A first key allowing us to penetrate the vast world of facial behavior was forged by Tomkins and Ekman, who used Darwin's model to describe certain well-known emotional expressions. These expressions probably cover only a few percent of the total repertoire used by a person during his daily life and maybe are a bit too quickly described as "the" repertoire of emotional interaction (Heller, 1992b). It nevertheless is one of the few angles that allow us to grasp some behaviors in a coherent way.

The scarcity of "basic emotional expressions" becomes evident as soon as we try to collect films in which these are numerous. To obtain such films researchers need to expose subjects to highly provocative stimuli (gun shots, horror or surgery films, etc.) (Fridlund, 1991; see also Grammer et al., 1988). The facial behaviors of subjects exposed to such events can reasonably be thought of as being emotional. It is interesting to note that in the realm of body psychotherapy, people who think in terms of a Darwinian emotional model also recommend extremely strong emotional stimuli to operationalize their methods. For example, Alexander Lowen will elicit basic emotions of the same type as those described by Ekman, by asking patients to pound, or shout, to use stressful posture or deep massage, to breath extremely fast and deeply, and so on.

To study people suffering from depression, or people who come to see us just after a suicide attempt, we cannot confront them with such overwhelming stimulation. On the contrary, our interviews are designed to provide some support for our patient's attempt to preserve a behavior as compatible as possible with his or her self-esteem. These patients are asked to sign a consent form, which states that the experimental situation may be useful to their own process as well as to a better understanding of similar patients.

Research on psychopathology and nonverbal behavior is thus often carried out through films of semistructured interviews. It is in such a setting that our own studies have been carried out. These situations are fairly formal. We tend to make such interviews as short and unintrusive as possible. Patients nevertheless often express a certain gratitude in being able to talk about various aspects of their difficult life, and may show disappointment when they realize that we stop the interview after 10 to 20 minutes. When they are also included in our films, therapists tend to be the source of our difficulties. For the nonsuicidal depression study, the doctors of our clinic had shown some enthusiasm when we told them that we would like to study the *interaction* between psychiatrists and depressive patients. Nevertheless, patients suddenly received all sorts of diagnoses, but seldom that of major depression! Getting films with patients only was fairly easy; getting films with patients and therapists is a project in itself.

Although some very emotional contents may be conveyed in such interviews, other mechanisms—related to social (cultural?) rules of interaction—are also explicitly activated. Our material thus confronts us with the variety of behaviors that is usually displayed in everyday life. There are two types of problems:

Control Groups

One is the issue of how to manage control groups. Just putting "normal" people in the same situation does not necessarily generate an adequate control group because our interviews were designed to analyze a certain problem (suicide, depression), and would have a completely artificial relevance for a "normal" population. The data shown in this paper raise this issue in a particularly sharp way: one could surmise that part of the difference observed between suicidal depressive patients and nonsuicidal depressive patients may be due to the difference of *relevance* of our suicide topic for the two populations. For suicides, mentioning to a doctor that one would still want to commit suicide may be critical, as it is part of a psychiatrist's duty to react in certain coercive ways to such a statement. On the other hand, nonsuicidal depressive patients may take the question as yet another moment to communicate on deep personal questions. Krause tried to avoid this problem by choosing a situation relevant for any citizen, with or without psychopathology (Krause & Lütolf, 1988).

Classifying Any Type of Behavior Observed on Films

As our situations do not induce a certain type of behavior, we do not know what sort of behavior our subjects produce. Some publications have proposed certain subgroups of behavior (emotional, emblematic, cognitive, cultural, etc.), but the relevance of these components, and knowing how to "classify" a coded behavior, still remains largely a question of personal choice, although some research is attempting to address this issue.

Analyzing Current Behavior

We shall illustrate our arguments by listing some concrete unanswered questions we have currently found in our attempts to analyze data.

Activity Measures

We have tried to write programs that could perform a preliminary analysis of our data automatically. One obvious variable for such programs is that of facial activity, which seems to be related to 5 dimensions: (1) number of times events *occur;* (2) number of *changes;* (3) the *length of time* a unit is activated; (4) mean *intensities* of units; and (5) *variety* of repertoire. This last variable allows us to differentiate moving ten times the same unit, from moving ten times ten different units. These two types of activity are identical from the point of view of occurrences, but not from the point of view of repertoire or of the perceiver.

Although such variables are fairly easy to define, and generally thought of as relevant, it is more difficult to find a way to combine them so as to produce a measure of activity. It is, for example, difficult to combine duration and occurrence in an activity measure. If a person activates a unit during a whole sample, the unit occurs once. A duration measure will thus suggest that the person has been very active, while an occurrence measure will suggest that the person has not been very active.

Time and Emotional Expressions: Signal/Regulation

Several FACS studies have concentrated on photographs or on a short sample per patient. If in this context a "typical" emotional expression is coded, it can be described as the expression of an inner feeling. In our nonsuicidal depression study we saw each patient five times in ten weeks; and for each interview we coded 4 emotional topics. In other words we had 20 samples per patient. Each sample, being fairly short, yielded few expressions. By looking at one sample we may take certain facial configurations to be discrete emotional expressions. But what sometimes happened was that we observed the same "emotional signal" in 18 or 20 of the samples coded for a single patient. It became difficult to go on using the notion of emotional expression, if we define an expression as a specific semiological event closely related to a content and a given moment (a few minutes at the most). If these 18 similar expressions observed at 18 different moments are not an expression, what are they?

Any decision on the subject really depends on the researcher's imagination rather than on theory. One answer is that these expressions are like the tip of an iceberg— something like random recurrent expressions of a continuous mood. Such an explanation makes good sense for a study on depression. But other plausible explanations also exist, without even being contradictory. For example, what some Americans call a "pacifier smile" can be understood as part of a recurrent strategy to diminish an other person's potential aggressivity.

To summarize, as soon as coded samples cover more than a minute, we are faced with a polarity within which we need to situate an expression: (1) at one extreme we have facial configurations that can reasonably be related to a psycho-physiological state (Levenson, 1992); (2) at the other extreme, we have a series of facial configurations that have to be treated as a series of events probably related to regulation mechanisms rather than expressive ones. Thus adding time to our experimental plan clearly adds dimensions in our data and raises new concrete questions.

Applying the Dictionary to any Expressions?

Recently, looking at a tennis match on television, we observed how often players displayed AU10 (upper lip raise). One could easily accept the idea that they were expressing some sort of disgust or contempt for either/or their opponent and themselves. But we could also associate this activity with something like pain and effort. Scherer et al. (1983) followed a similar trend of thought when he suggested that the elements of an emotional expression may have independent functions that can be constructed around an affect to express it. For example, disgust or contempt could be used to convey how painful the other's behavior may be to us.

Slips of the Face

We use "slip of the face" in association with the Freudian slip of the tongue. This notion was suggested to us by Ekman and Friesen (1969), and Krause & Lütolf (1988). In one of our visits at Saarbr‚cken, we saw a patient displaying AUs 6 + 10 + 12 (cheek raise, upper lip raise, and lip corner pull). The perceiver, at first glance, mostly perceives a clear broad smile (AU 6 + AU 12). But coding the psychotherapist of this patient revealed that the psychotherapist did not react the same way when the smile contained or did not contain AU 10. AU 10 is often associated with a gorilla or a dog displaying the upper teeth—an obviously hostile expression. The interviews of this patient analyzed by Krause, as well as the personal reactions reported by the therapist, supported the idea that the therapist had reacted to an apparently hostile expression (AU 10) hidden by a smile (AU 6 + AU 12).

In Krause's example, the relevance of a slip of the face is supported by the protagonist's reaction. For the studies discussed in this article, we filmed only the patient's facial behavior. Attributing an emotional hypothesis to a very short facial dynamic was more tricky. In some cases they really did look like a "slip of the face" when looked at at normal speed. But others seem to convey an emotional content only when they are maintained artificially as a still image. Looking at them at normal speed, we mostly have the impression of a quasi-meaningless transition between two mimics.

Finding rules allowing us to associate meaning with a facial dynamic is a general preoccupation in the field (e.g., Ekman, 1992). But looking at current behavior in detail clearly shows that the algorithms regulating such associations, even when only considering affect regulation systems, are probably sufficiently complex to allow misunderstanding as well as understanding.

References

Ekman, P. (1992). An argument for basic emotions. *Cognition & Emotion, 6,* 169–200.

Ekman, P., & Friesen, W. V. (1969). Nonverbal leakage and clues to deception. *Psychiatry, 32,* 88–105.

Fridlund, A. J. (1991). Sociality and solitary smiling: potentiation by an implicit audience. *Journal of Personality and Social Psychology, 60,* 229–241.

Grammer, K., Schiefenhövel, W., Schleidt, M., Lorenz, B., & Eibl-Eibesfeldt, I. (1988). Patterns of the face: the eyebrow flash in cross-cultural comparison. *Ethology, 77,* 279–299.

Haynal, A. (1993). *Psychoanalysis and the sciences: Epistemology and history.* London: Karnac.

Heller, M. (1992a). Corps et évaluation de psychothérapies: un reve a réaliser. *Psychothérapies, 2,* 111–121.

Heller, M. (1992b). Les émotions: un parcours littéraire. In J. Bresson (Ed.). *Manuel d'enseignement de l'Ecole Française d'Analyse Psycho-Organique, vol. 2.* (pp. 125–175). Toulouse: Ecole Française d'Analyse Psycho-Organique.

Heller, M. (1993). Unconscious communication. In B. Maul (Ed.). *Bodypsychotherapy or the art of contact* (pp. 155–179). Berlin: Verlag.

Krause, R., & Lütolf, P. (1988). Facial indicators of transference processes within psychoanalytic treatment. In H. Dahl, H. Kächele, & H. Thoma (Eds.). *Psychoanalytic process research strategies* (pp. 257–273). Heidelberg: Springer.

Levenson, R. W. (1992). Autonomic nervous system differences among emotions. *Psychological Science, 3,* 23–27.

Scherer, K. R., Summerfield, W. B., & Wallbott, H. G. (1983). Cross-national research on antecedent and components of emotion: A progress report. *Social Science information, 22,* 355–385.

20

Prototypical Affective Microsequences in Psychotherapeutic Interaction

EVA BÄNNINGER-HUBER

In the following article I shall present a new approach to the microanalytic study of cognitive-affective regulatory processes in psychotherapeutic interaction. In this approach the examination of the expressive component of emotions communicated through facial expressions is of central importance. The approach is based on the assumption, shared by many psychotherapists, that the interaction between client and therapist contributes essentially to therapeutic change (Caspar & Grawe, 1989; Elliott, 1984; Gill & Hoffman, 1982; Grawe, 1987; Greenberg & Safran, 1987; Horowitz, 1979; Krause, 1982, 1984; Moser, 1985; Rice & Greenberg, 1984; Safran, 1990a, 1990b; Schneider, 1989; Stern, 1985; Strupp, 1987; Sullivan, 1953; Thomä & Kächele, 1985, 1988; Weiss, Sampson et al., 1986). However, little is known about how these processes of change work. It is true that there is a considerable amount of clinical knowledge about emotions in therapeutic interactions at a macrolevel, but we still know too little about what is happening at a microlevel of affective processes within therapy. It is thus important to develop methods to examine the therapeutic interaction, along with the cognitive–affective processes involved.

The approach to the detailed description of interaction sequences was developed in a research project in which, for methodological reasons, no therapeutic only spontaneous, interactions of longstanding couples were examined (Bänninger-Huber, Moser, & Steiner, 1990; Bänninger-Huber, & Steiner, 1992; Moser, Bänninger-Huber, & Steiner, 1989). The method developed in this project makes it possible to relate objectively assessed observations (especially facial expressions, recorded with the Facial Action Coding System [FACS] by Ekman & Friesen, 1978) to models of affective regulatory processes. Thus, affective regulation in a selected temporal sequence may be described in detail in terms of a process model. In other words, this method makes it possible to correlate and to interpret the facial behavior of two interacting partners coded with FACS, taking the emotional context into consideration.

Using this method it was possible to identify short interactive sequences of the two partners in which common strategies to cope with affective conflict situations could be observed. Such strategies are considered to be typical for the affective relationship of the couples involved. They are, therefore, defined as prototypical affective microsequences.

In the study presented here in part, the concepts and methods developed in the "couples project" were transferred to the therapeutic situation. In particular, the question as to whether comparable prototypical affective microsequences also occur in therapies and what role they play in affective regulation was examined.

Empirical and Theoretical Background

Face-to-face interactions in psychotherapies were studied. The focus was on facial expressions because, compared with other nonverbal communication channels, specific indicators of different emotional processes are most likely to be identified in this channel (Ekman, 1965; Ekman & Friesen, 1974, 1975; Scherer & Wallbott, 1990). Furthermore, facial behavior reflects not only the individual's intrapsychic regulation, but has at the same time communicative meaning for the partner. The expressive–communicative component of emotional processes is a signal to the interactive partner about how one wants the other to behave and what behavior can be expected in turn. Thus, facial behavior is important for the regulation of interaction, as it is, for example, a medium to attract attention from, or to elicit friendliness in, the interacting partner (De Rivera, 1977; Frijda, 1986; Izard, 1971, 1977; Krause, 1988, 1990; Moser, 1985, 1989; Scherer & Wallbott, 1990; Stern, 1985; Tomkins, 1975; von Salisch, 1991). Facial behavior occurs, as a rule, unconsciously and automatically. It is therefore neither immediately accessible to subjective perception nor recordable directly by a questionnaire approach (Moser et al., 1989). However, by means of microanalysis of video recordings, facial behavior may be identified even if it is not observable to the naked eye. We consider this behavior to be highly relevant (cf. the concept of so-called micromomentary expressions by Haggard & Isaacs, 1966; see also Ekman, 1985; Ekman & Friesen, 1975).

There are also pragmatic reasons for focusing on facial behavior. Because we are primarily interested in the study of therapeutic interaction certain traditional methods of measurement in emotional research cannot be used, as they seriously disturb the emotional interchange and course of interaction. This is true, for example, of physiological methods of measurement as well as of electromyographic measurements. By contrast, video equipment suffices to record facial expressions, which can subsequently be analyzed in detail. In addition, FACS is a method for the objective and highly differentiated recording of facial behavior.

As an important theoretical basis a psychoanalytic model of the regulation of object relations developed by Moser (1985) as well as Moser, von Zeppelin, and Schneider (1991) was used. In dyadic interactions this model differentiates between two domains of regulation: that of the self and that of the relationship. Both domains are linked in the sense that success in self-regulation is a prerequisite for high emotional involvement in an object-relation.

Central to our approach is the assumption that during the course of ontogenetic development internalized object relation structures develop (Fairbairn, 1952; Kohut, 1971, 1977). These structures involve specific affect regulation repertoires in the nonverbal channel. An individual's repertoire of affect regulation is expressed in the type of relationship he or she offers others. In other words, an individual evokes through his or her behavior specific reactions, emotions, and fantasies in the partner. Accordingly, such relationship-offers also occur in therapeutic interactions: a client may use his or her specific form of affective regulation in his or her relationship with the therapist (Krause & Lütolf, 1989).

In this approach knowledge and methods from different, traditionally separate fields of research are connected. Work done in the fields of interaction and emotion research has produced important models of the function of facial behavior in terms of the regulation of interaction. Furthermore, important procedures in the systematic observation of interactive behavior have been developed. In the therapeutic field, however, sophisticated models of intrapsychic processes exist. An integration of these approaches has the advantage of facilitating understanding of therapeutic interaction with the aid of concepts from emotion research. Yet, therapeutic knowledge of intrapsychic events can contribute to a more differentiated understanding of emotional reactions.

Coding and Graphical Representation of Facial Behavior

FACS is an anatomically based system for recording reliably all visually distinguishable facial movements. Each muscle innervation corresponds to a so-called action unit (AU). The AUs are given numbers. Thus, with FACS the measurement can be made in noninferential terms that describe the facial behavior objectively. Suggestive implications of linguistic labels such as a "friendly" or a "squeezed" smile may be avoided. The interpretation of the data takes place in a second step, independent of the recording. Specific AU combinations are assigned to certain psychological concepts which allow validation by external criteria. For a number of basic emotions, say, anger, joy, or sadness, such assignments already exist in the "tables of emotion prediction" (Ekman & Friesen, 1978, 1982a).

The use of a differentiated system for recording facial expressions is important, because affective regulatory processes usually occur very rapidly (Moser et al., 1991; Pfeifer & Leuzinger-Bohleber, 1989; Scherer, 1988). It is therefore necessary to study these processes at a microlevel with a high resolution. With FACS, precise coding is possible up to .02 seconds.

All AUs described in the original manual (Ekman & Friesen, 1978) are recorded. Head position and blinks are coded, too. Additionally, a code for "gazing toward the partner" (AU 66) and "audible laughter" (03) is used. These data, including the verbatim text, are represented graphically in the form of a microplot, produced by the computer program FACSER[1] (Steiner, 1987, 1990).

A microplot has the following features (see figure 20.1): a temporal scale divided into units of .1 sec; the corresponding FACS codings (combinations are summarized); the head positions represented analogically by pictograms; and mutual gaze represented by a line, blinks by a bar, and the verbatim protocol. In the upper part of the plot the interactive behavior of the client is presented, and in the lower part that of the therapist. In addition the apexes of the facial events are photographed and are indicated on the plot by an arrow.

Development of the Model of the Affective Regulation Process

When developing a process model of the affective regulation in a selected sequence we aim at the description and theoretical interpretation of all recorded nonverbal

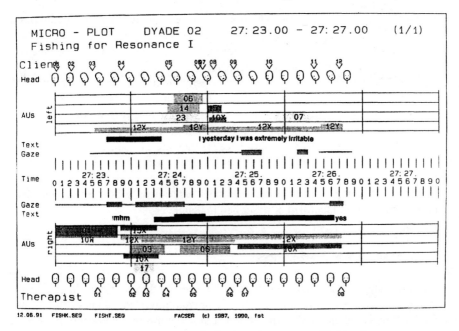

Figure 20.1   Microplot of the prototypical affective microsequence "fishing-for-resonance scene."

phenomena. When doing this, we always try to understand the facial expressions with respect to their intrapsychic as well as their interactive meaning. Verbal data are used for the psychological understanding of the interactive situation.

The model of the affective regulation process involves information from the following four hierarchically arranged levels. Models at the top level, or *high-level concepts,* include concepts such as self-regulation, relationship-regulation, affective relatedness, resonance, response, or dialogue regulation. This theoretical background is provided by a model of relationship-regulation (Moser, 1985; Moser et al., 1991; von Zeppelin & Moser, 1987). At the next lower level, that of *low-level concepts,* affective processes are differentiated on the basis of emotion-theory considerations, for example, different basic emotions, communicative affects versus self-feelings, and state versus trigger affects (De Rivera, 1977; Ekman, 1984; Frijda, 1986; Moser, 1983, 1985; Ortony, 1988; Scherer, 1984, 1988). We assume that these affective processes are expressed in a specific manner at the level of verbal and nonverbal data, especially in facial expression. Included are phenomena such as facial expressions, laughing, turning away, and synchronicity. These are designated *high-level data,* and are dependent to a greater or lesser degree on the observer's concepts. At the lowest level, we deal with verbal and nonverbal data that can be assessed objectively (action units, blinks, head position, gaze direction, temporal parameters of the different indicators).

Low- and high-level data are connected by operationalizations. Here we refer primarily to research done by Ekman and Friesen (1978, 1982a), as well as research on different types of smile (e.g., Bänninger-Huber & Rauber-Kaiser, 1989; Bänninger-Huber & Steiner, 1987; Ekman, 1985; Ekman & Friesen, 1982b; Ekman, Friesen, & O'Sullivan, 1988; Stettner, Ivery, & Haynes, 1986; Wicki, Bänninger-Huber, & Steiner,

1989). Further, connections between high-level data and theoretical concepts are postulated in the form of working hypotheses. The process of hypothesis generation takes place in an iterative manner, in that one repeatedly moves back and forth between observational data and concepts at the model level.

It must be noted that empirically proved operationalizations are not yet available for all connections between low- and high-level data. This is true in particular for those emotions that are relevant for the domain of self-regulation, such as shame, guilt, or narcissistic injuries. These emotions are not listed on the tables of emotion predictions (Ekman & Friesen, 1978, 1982a), because they are not considered to belong to the basic emotions (e.g., Ekman, 1984; Ekman & Friesen, 1969, 1978; Izard, 1977; Tomkins, 1962, 1963). Also, little is known about phenomena such as the contagious effect of emotions, empathic reactions, or facial synchronization processes, which have so far very rarely been identified or described in detail.

Prototypical Affective Microsequences

We examined client–therapist interactions with respect to the question: Which affective processes result when disturbances in affective-regulation of the client occur? In psychotherapy one is dealing with difficult and conflictive topics. The resulting emotions (e.g., confusion, anxiety, shame, hurt) represent a greater than usual strain for the client's self-regulation. Frequent disturbances in the client's self-regulation can be expected. In order to maintain the therapeutic relationship the therapist has to diminish these disturbances. He or she must regulate the interaction in such a way that sufficient positive emotions result to balance out the disturbances in the client's self-regulation (Moser et al., 1991).

The concept we used for the description of these regulatory processes was that of prototypical affective microsequences (Bänninger-Huber et al., 1990; Moser et al., 1989). Prototypical affective microsequences are short sequences of the affective relationship regulation (lasting 5 to 30 sec). They are a product of both persons involved in the interaction and can be viewed as mutual structural coupling, co-ontogenesis in the sense that each partner maintains his or her own adaptation and organization (Maturana & Varela, 1987). They occur primarily when the relationship regulation experiences a disturbance. In therapeutic interaction, disturbances in the relationship regulation occur, for example, when the discussion of a difficult topic reactivates or threatens to reactivate an intrapsychic conflict in the client. In general, disturbances refer to occasions where something occurs that the individual cannot master with his or her current cognitive "ad hoc model"[2] (Moser, 1985; Moser et al., 1991). Whereas in the relationship regulation cognitive and affective processes are involved, a falling back on affective regulatory mechanisms occurs in prototypical affective microsequences.

The communicative situation in therapies is characterized by an asymmetric role distribution between patient and therapist. The regulation of the dialogue is usually left to the client, and his or her affective experience is the focus of attention. The therapist's task is to register emotions as they arise and to share them empathically with the client while controlling his or her own reactions (Krause & Lütolf, 1989). Given the therapist's relative interactional abstinence the affective regulation of the client becomes particularly apparent in therapies.

It may be assumed that different types of affective microsequences will occur in a client. They will differ according to the significance assigned to the therapist by the schema activated in the therapeutical situation, that is, according to what is called the "transference situation" in psychoanalytic terms. In this article a specific type of affective microsequence is described, it being a specific form of manifestation of the specific object relation structure of the client examined. We assume that this type of affective microsequence is used to reestablish positive self-feelings after a disturbance. We differentiate between successful and unsuccessful prototypical affective microsequences.

Successful microsequences are characterized by the fact that the client succeeds, by smiling and/or laughing, in establishing a resonant affective state with the therapist. Our assumption is that this mutually experienced resonance helps the client to overcome disturbances in self-regulation, in that it gives a sense of security. This is a precondition for the client to be able to go on working on conflictive topics.

In unsuccessful prototypical affective microsequences, however, the client does not succeed in establishing a resonant state with the therapist by means of a smile and/or laughter. Instead, the therapist may respond with a verbal intervention in which he or she refers to the negative emotions mentioned by the client before the latter smiles. Thus, in such a case, the disturbance is not overcome together with the therapist but is given back to the client's domain of self-regulation.

Smiling and Laughing as Regulatory Phenomena

In balancing out a disturbance, the two nonverbal phenomena of smiling and laughing are of special importance. Both play an important role as nonverbal phenomena in the establishment and maintenance of the relationship between two persons. Smiling and laughing serve the function of strengthening the emotional bond between two individuals by means of the expression of positive emotions (Moser, 1989; Moser et al., 1989). Smiling and laughing are highly inductive processes that are used to establish affective resonance.

Smiling and laughing are also important in the context of negative emotional reactions. Smiling can be used as a "damage control strategy" (Bänninger-Huber et al., 1990) in that it communicates basic relatedness in spite of the expressed negative emotions. Smiling can be viewed as a thread of resonance running through the whole interaction in that it repeatedly communicates an emotional bond to the partner. Smiling can also contribute to the increase of affective relatedness, even if it has already disappeared from the face, in that the partner subsequently cognitively evaluates and stores the signal. Laughing can interrupt one's own negative affective states as well as the partner's (Bänninger-Huber et al., 1990). The brief interruption of the dialogue permits internal affective reorganization. Laughter results in a new affective state in the partners.

The Therapy Examined

The therapy described in the following example was a psychoanalytic therapy conducted by the author over 52 hours, videorecorded in its entirety. The split-screen recordings alternate every 5 minutes between a close-up of the face and a whole-body image. At the time of the therapy the client, Mr. A., was in his mid-30s. After several years in his profession he had chosen to pursue university studies. After failing an important exam he changed his major. However, he did not pass his exams in this area either. At this time he chose to enter therapy, giving as the reason the upcoming repetition of the exams.

The Selection of the Microsequences from the Interactive Process

The selection of microsequences from the continuous flow of behavior requires an intensive inspection of the videotapes in real time and in slow motion and at present is made on the basis of a search heuristic that has not been fully operationalized. Because the development of a disturbance in the affective-regulation of the client in a therapy is primarily an intrapsychic process, the elicitation of a disturbance cannot be assessed objectively but has to be inferred from the understanding of the emotional situation. Possible indicators for a disturbance are observable, however; different types of smile and laughter, intensive facial micromomentary expressions, especially indicators of negative emotions, pauses in speech, and the frequent occurrence of adaptors.

Successful and Unsuccessful Prototypical Affective Microsequences

In Mr. A.'s therapy a successful affective microsequence prototypically developed in the following way: He spoke about personal problems (e.g., learning disturbances, problems in the relationship with his girlfriend, with his parents, etc.). Speaking on these topics led to a disturbance in the client's domain of self-regulation. In this phase indicators of a disturbance could be observed; slips of the tongue, ruptures of sentences, pauses, frequent occurrence of adaptors as well as indicators of negative emotions.

Now, the typical strategy of the client consisted in taking up, at the dialogue level, a topic that increased the affective relatedness between therapist and client. Most often this would be a kind of a joke expressed by the client, with his head turned away. Then he would peep toward the therapist in order to evaluate the impact of his verbalization. On the face of the therapist weak indicators of negative emotions became observable, changing her expression to "concerned."

The client would start smiling, sometimes even audibly laughing, and turn his face toward the therapist. The therapist, at the beginning, defended herself against the client's affect induction by producing extended blinks. The therapist reciprocated the smile while indicators of negative emotions were also visible on her face. Then she would start laughing audibly. This resulted in a mutual gaze in a resonant state. The termination of the resonance occurred, for example, by the client's turning away from the therapist, by a repeated extended blink of the therapist, or by an intervention.

Unsuccessful microsequences consist in the client's failure to establish resonance by means of smiling and/or laughing. At the beginning the course at the interactive level of this type of affective microsequence is much like that of successful microsequences. The client tries to establish a resonant state with the therapist by means of a verbal statement or of a smile or laughter. The therapist, however, does not show the facial expression wished by the client, that is, she does not smile (or laugh). Instead, she responds shortly after with a verbal intervention referring to the negative emotions mentioned by the client before he smiled. In such cases the therapist does not seem to give the smiling and laughing of the client the significance of a resonance offer that would be necessary to overcome the disturbance of the client's self-regulation, but seems to interpret the smiling and laughing as a defense against negative affects to be worked on.

An Example: The "Fishing-for-Resonance Scene"

The microsequence, for which the process model was worked out in detail, presented here comes from the third therapy session. Successful affective microsequences could be identified in several sessions of Mr. A.'s therapy. They occurred at the beginning, in the middle as well as toward the end of the therapy. In the following a particularly clear-cut example of this type of microsequence will be presented. On the basis of the interactive behavior shown by the client, as outlined above, this microsequence is called the "fishing-for-resonance scene." It lasted about 4 sec and occurred 27 min after the beginning of the session.

The fishing-for-resonance scene was preceded by a verbalization of Mr. A's, to which the therapist reacted with an intervention. In this sequence several indicators of a disturbance in the domain of his affective regulation can be observed. He said he noticed that there were many issues about which he was in doubt and somehow was hampered by not considering enough positive aspects. He spoke with much hesitation (repeating and correcting words, using filling sounds as well), pausing for 5 sec in the middle of the sentence. During this pause he held his head turned away from the therapist and showed mouth movements that may be interpreted as signs of tension (Moser et al., 1989). He pressed his lips together, wiped his lips with his tongue several times and breathed audibly. After finishing his sentence he looked toward the therapist, shook his head and again pressed his lips together.

The therapist reacted by saying that even being in doubt was unpleasant and negative for him. Mr. A interrupted the therapist, saying that this was depressing. He accompanied this statement with facial indicators of negative emotions (AUs 7 and 15).

The affective microsequence started with Mr. A. giving an example of a recent situation that had evoked negative emotions in him. He referred to the outcome of federal elections that had taken place the day before, saying, "Just thinking about the outcome of the elections. . . ." With this broken-off statement, he introduced a topic about which the therapist was likely to have the same opinion. This may be viewed as an attempt, at the dialogue level, to increase the affective relatedness between client and therapist.

During the verbalization his head was turned away from the therapist, and in a downward position (figure 20.2, K1). At time marker 27:23.46, he peeped at the therapist, but did not yet turn his head toward her (figure 20.2, K2). His looking at the therapist may have been to check the impact of this statement about the elections.

When the client looked at her, the therapist showed some very weak indicators of negative emotions on her face, namely AU combination $1 + 10x$ (figure 20.2, T1). AU 1 is a component of the facial expression "sadness." AU 10 cannot be assigned unam-

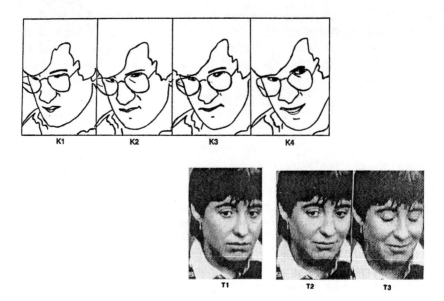

Figure 20.2 Pictures of the facial events described in the prototypical affective microsequence "fishing-for-resonance scene," part 1.

biguously to a basic emotion, but, according to the tables of emotion predictions (Ekman & Friesen, 1978, 1982a), can be an expression of anger, disgust, or contempt. We assume that this is an expression of the therapist empathizing with the client's negative affects expressed before this sequence.

Only one tenth of a sec later the client responded with a smile (AU 12x) (figure 20.2, K3, K4). This type of smile can be classified as a "phoney smile" (Bänninger-Huber & Rauber-Kaiser, 1989; Bänninger-Huber & Steiner, 1987; Ekman & Friesen, 1982b). Phoney smiles are deliberate smiles but are often produced automatically and unconsciously. They are shown when a friendly attitude is to be communicated to the partner. The therapist looks toward the client and thus may have seen the onset of his smiling.

The therapist reacted initially with a listener response ("mhm") to the client's statement. Half a second after he began to smile the therapist reciprocated, innervating AU 12x. Her smile, however, was accompanied by the AU combination 10x + 15x + AU 17 (figure 20.2, T2). On the basis of the facial appearance this smile could be classified as a miserable smile. According to Ekman and Friesen (1982b), "The miserable person acknowledges feeling unhappy, making clear to the self and to others that the misery is, at least for the moment, contained" (p. 248).

In the case of the therapist this function was modified. We assume that the negative emotions expressed in this particular smile occur, on the one hand, because the therapist agreed with the client's negative evaluation of the elections, and thus reflected the way she feels, and on the other hand, because she was empathizing with the client's negative feelings. By expressing these affects while smiling, she communicated to the client, "I know that this situation is awful, but I am with you." So the therapist's miserable smile confirmed the existence of negative emotions and at the same time signaled emotional attachment.

Furthermore, it may be assumed that the indicators of negative emotions contained in the miserable smile are, at the same time, an expression of defense by the therapist against the affect induction coming from the client. Evidence for this hypothesis comes from the fact that immediately after the reciprocation of the smile (.06 sec) the therapist produced a blink of extraordinary duration (.64 sec) (figure 20.2, T3; figure 20.3, T4). On the basis of repeated observation of the data we assume that the therapist produces these extended blinks when she intends to avoid the establishment of a resonant state that would lead the client away from his negative emotions. By a short interruption of gazing toward the client, the danger of another "undeliberate" affect induction may be averted and the forced emotional involvement may be reduced (Bänninger-Huber et al., 1990). At the same time as her miserable smile the therapist produced a short, audible laugh. This probably served the function of helping her cope with her own negative emotions in this situation. At the same time she communicated to the client that his statement had an emotional impact on her.

During the therapist's blinking the client turned his head toward her (figure 20.3, K5). At time marker 27:24.56, he intensified his smile with the innervation of orbicularis occuli (6 + 12y) (figure 20.3, K6). The relatively intensive smile was modified by a simultaneous innervation of AU 23 and tightening of the lip corners (AU 14). This resulted in a blended smile (Ekman, 1985). In these blends two or more emotions are experienced simultaneously and registered in the same facial expression. In this case one

Figure 20.3 Pictures of the facial events described in the prototypical affective microsequence "fishing-for-resonance scene," part 2.

dealt with nonspecific indicators of negative emotions that can be viewed as signs of tension. Whether these were due to the therapist responding too slowly to the client's attempt to induce a smile remains an open question.

Only .2 sec later the therapist intensified her smile (at time marker 27:24.60). She innervated the AU combination 6 + 12y + 25, a "felt smile" (figure 20.3, T5). This placed them in a state of resonance for a short time, increasing their affective related-ness (figure 20.3, K7). This made it possible for the client to continue with the dia-logue. He described his feelings of anger with reference to the outcome of the elections, saying, "Yesterday I was extremely irritable." During the verbalization Mr. A. contin-ued to smile, although less intensively. The thread of resonance did not break. In addi-tion to his smile he produced the AU combinations 10x + 15y (figure 20.3, K8, K9) as well as AU 7, indicators of negative emotions that corresponded to his verbalization. As soon as the therapist realized that Mr. A. was turning back to his negative emotions she also reduced her smile and empathically adopted the client's negative emotions (AU 10x) (figure 20.3, T6; figure 20.4, T7, T8).[3]

At time marker 27:26.44 the client turned his head back toward the therapist after having turned it away for about a second (figure 20.4, K10), he looked at her and inten-sified his smile (figure 20.4, C11, K12). The therapist reacted at the dialogue level with a listener response, saying, "Yes," and then blinked again. Was she trying to prevent the whole situation from beginning again?

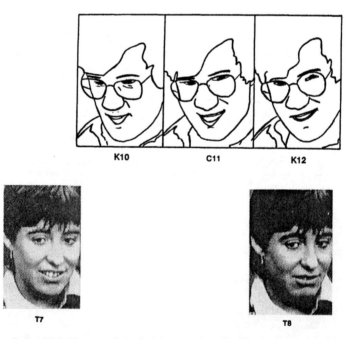

Figure 20.4 Pictures of the facial events described in the prototypical affective microsequence "fishing-for-resonance scene," part 3.

The Significance of the Fishing-for-Resonance Scene for the Affective Regulation of the Client

I assume that establishing resonance during this scene had a positive influence on the client's self-regulation. His own smiling helped him overcome the negative emotions elicited by the conflictive nature of what he was talking about. The therapist showed with her smile that she went along with him. In this way the client saw that he was in control of the situation, which gave him a needed sense of autonomy. The fact that he was able to make the therapist smile and laugh also increased his self-esteem.

The client's regulatory disturbance was thus overcome, and the client was able to continue talking. (He reported about how he heard about the results of the elections and how he reacted.) This topic was, however, not very personal and proved within a short period of time (35 sec) to be a dead end. An interruption occurred at the dialogue level, and a "flirtation scene" began. The flirtation scene lasted 20 sec in all. It was characterized by frequent smiling and laughing on the part of both the therapist and the client. After the interruption, the client said, "Now I don't know what I should say any more." The onset of the client's intensive smile was abrupt. The therapist looked at the client and instantly began to smile, although the client was not looking at her. She intensified her smile, laughed audibly, and said, "You can also remain silent." The client responded with laughter, and said, "Sure, why not, we could sit here and look at each other." The client and therapist then actually did this, smiling at each other intensively for a relatively long time.

The assumption is that the client continues repeating microsequences such as the fishing-for-resonance scene until the desired level of security, autonomy, and self-esteem (see Moser et al., 1991) is attained. In this particular instance this may only be true after the flirtation scene, which, in fact, provided a major clue to the detection of the type of affective microsequence specific for the client. The frequency with which the client enacts such fishing-for-resonance scenes[4] could be related to great regulatory strain on the part of the client.

Based on several clues contained in the therapy material it may be assumed that the therapeutic situation as such represents to the client a conflictive situation that is due to his or her problems with self-esteem. In order to maintain self-esteem, he or she must present him- or herself as a competent person without flaws. However, in order to receive help from the therapist, the client is forced to reveal to the therapist his or her incompetence and problems. This conflict causes topics of little emotional relevance to disturb affective-regulation.

Because of this it is of special importance with Mr. A. in particular that disturbances in the therapeutic interaction be overcome immediately. If the therapist were not willing to accept the particular relationship the client offers, there would be a great danger of the client breaking off the therapy. Thus, fishing-for-resonance scenes play an important role in the maintenance of the therapeutic relationship. Additionally, they gave a client a basic sense of security, thus enabling him or her to work productively later on (Schneider, 1990).

Discussion

Using a method that correlates objectively recorded observations and models of emotional processes affective-regulatory processes in therapist–client interaction can be described in detail in terms of a process model. Such descriptions are a necessary precondition for studying the question as to which function specific affective exchange processes between client and therapist may serve in terms of therapeutic changes in the client.

Therapeutic interactions were studied with regard to the question: Which affective processes result when disturbances in the affective regulation of the client occur? For this purpose the concept of prototypical affective microsequences was introduced and proved to be significant, in a preparatory study, for the description of affective regulatory processes in couples' interactions.

The evaluation has shown that prototypical microsequences may be identified not only in couples' interactions but in the therapeutic setting as well. It was possible to identify affective microsequences in several sessions of Mr. A.'s therapy. They occur at the beginning, in the middle, and toward the end of therapy. Thus, we have here regulatory phenomena that manifest themselves repeatedly at the level of interactive behavior. Two types of prototypical affective microsequence may be differentiated; successful and unsuccessful.

Successful prototypical microsequences help the client by establishing a resonant affective state with the therapist to overcome disturbances in the domain of self-regulation. Facial phenomena, such as smiling and laughter, are important to giving the client a basic sense of security. This is a precondition for the client to work repeatedly on difficult and conflictive topics.

By contrast, unsuccessful prototypical microsequences may have as a consequence that the negative emotions elicited by the discussion of a conflictive topic persist and possibly become an object of immediate processing. At present, however, it is not yet clear which type of microsequence (successful, unsuccessful) in which therapeutic situation contributes to a productive process of change. Neither is it clear yet what role disturbances at the microlevel of affective behavior play in long-term therapeutic processes of change. It is probably precisely the repetitive experience that it is possible to overcome a disturbance with the help of, and together with, an object that has a particular therapeutic effect (cf. the concepts "optimum frustration" [Kohut, 1984; Terman, 1988] as well as "optimal responsiveness" [Bacal, 1985, 1988]).

Successful and unsuccessful prototypical affective microsequences are a specific form of manifestation of the specific object-relation structure of the client examined here. In addition, there are other forms of affective regulatory processes in which the object-relation structure of the client expresses itself. Whether it is possible to identify prototypical microsequences as well in these enactments of object relations has still to be studied. The observations made so far suggest that the enacted object relation structures do not all show the same temporal characteristics but that certain processes need longer time periods.

Using a methodological approach allowing a microanalytic examination of affective processes it is possible not only to describe the phenomena at a higher level of resolution, but also to develop more differentiated theoretical concepts. This is particularly useful with regard to therapy. If interactive change processes are perceived as the essential aspects of the therapeutic process, it is necessary to make models available to the practitioner that enable him or her to perceive and conceptualize such processes.

Notes

1. FACSER includes procedures for interactive data input, data manipulation, statistical evaluations, printing of reports, and drawing of process plots.

2. The term "ad hoc model" is meant to designate the way in which an individual represents a situation he or she experiences with another person, that is, a situation that has to be regulated with respect to emotional wishes, the maintenance of self-esteem, and so forth.

3. Little research has been carried out on the process of empathically taking over affects in one's facial expression. Is the facial expression of affects adopted empathically usually less intensive than those experienced immediately? Does the therapist imitate the client's facial expressions directly, or is the therapist's facial expression due to his or her empathic experience of the respective emotional situation?

4. During the 4 min leading up to the fishing-for-resonance scene described above, three similar scenes occurred.

References

Bacal, H. (1985). Optimal responsiveness and the therapeutic process. In A. Goldberg (Ed.), *Progress in Self Psychology* (Vol. 1; pp. 202–226). New York: Guilford.

Bacal, H. (1988). Reflections on "optimum frustration." In A. Goldberg (Ed.), *Learning from Kohut: Progress in self psychology* (Vol. 4; pp. 127–131). Hillsdale, NJ: Analytic.

Bänninger-Huber, E. (1991). *Identifizierung und Beschreibung affektiver Mikrosequenzen.* Schlussbericht an den Schweizerischen Nationalfonds, NF-Projekt 11-26636.89.

Bänninger-Huber, E., Moser, U., & Steiner, F. (1990). Mikroanalytische Untersuchung affektiver Regulierungsprozesse in Paar-Interaktionen. *Zeitschrift für Klinische Psychologie, 19,* 123–143.

Bänninger-Huber, E., & Rauber-Kaiser, S. (1989). Die Differenzierung verschiedener Lächeltypen: FACS-Codierung und Einschätzungen. Eine Untersuchung zur Eindrucksbildung. *Schweizerische Zeitschrift für Psychologie, 48,* 21–34.

Bänninger-Huber, E., & Steiner, F. (1987). *Comparing different facial indicators within a psychotherapy study.* Paper presented at the 18th Annual Meeting of the Society for Psychotherapy Research, Ulm.

Bänninger-Huber, E., & Steiner, F. (1992). Identifying microsequences: A new methodological approach to the analysis of affective regulatory processes. In M. Leuzinger-Bohleber, H. Schneider, & R. Pfeifer (Eds.), *"Two butterflies on my head": Psychoanalysis in the interdisciplinary scientific dialogue.* Heidelberg: Springer.

Caspar, F., & Grawe, K. (1989). Weg vom Methoden-Monismus in der Psychotherapie. *Bulletin der Schweizer Psychologen, 11,* 6–19.

De Rivera, J. A. (1977). *A structural theory of emotion* (Psychological Issues Monograph 40). New York: International Universities.

Ekman, P. (1965). Differential communication of affect by head and body cues. *Journal of Personality and Social Psychology, 2,* 725–735.

Ekman, P. (1984). Expression and the nature of emotion. In K. R. Scherer & P. Ekman (Eds.), *Approaches to emotion* (pp. 319–443). Hillsdale, NJ: Erlbaum.

Ekman, P. (1985). *Telling lies.* New York: Norton.

Ekman, P., & Friesen, W. V. (1969). Nonverbal leakage and clues to deception. *Psychiatry, 32,* 88–105.

Ekman, P., & Friesen, W. V. (1974). Detecting deception from the body or face. *Journal of Personality and Social Psychology, 29,* 288–298.

Ekman, P., & Friesen, W. V. (1975). *Unmasking the face.* Englewood Cliffs, NJ: Prentice-Hall.

Ekman, P., & Friesen, W. V. (1978). *Facial Action Coding System (FACS) Manual.* Palo Alto: Consulting Psychologists Press.

Ekman, P., & Friesen, W. V. (1982a). *EMFACS coder's guide.* Unpublished manuscript.

Ekman, P., & Friesen, W. V. (1982b). Felt, false, and miserable smiles. *Journal of Nonverbal Behavior, 6,* 238–252.

Ekman, P., Friesen, M. V., & O'Sullivan, M. (1988). Smiles when lying. *Journal of Personality and Social Psychology, 54,* 414–420.

Elliott, R. (1984). A discovery-oriented approach to significant change events in psychotherapy: Interpersonal process recall and comprehensive process analysis. In L. N. Rice & L. S. Greenberg (Eds.), *Patterns of change. Intensive analysis of psychotherapy process* (pp. 249–286). New York: Guilford.

Fairbairn, W. R. D. (1952). *Psychoanalytic studies of personality.* London: Routledge & Kegan.

Frijda, N. H. (1986). *The emotions.* Cambridge, UK: Cambridge University Press.

Gill, M. M., & Hoffman, I. Z. (1982). A method for studying the analysis of aspects of the patient's experience of the relationship in psychoanalysis and psychotherapy. *Journal of the American Psychoanalytic Association, 30,* 137–167.

Grawe, K. (1987). *Schema-Theorie und heuristische Psychotherapie.* Forschungsbericht aus dem Psychologischen Institut der Universität Bern.

Greenberg, L. S., & Safran, J. D. (1987). *Emotion in psychotherapy: Affect, cognition, and the process of change.* New York: Guilford.

Haggard, E. A., & Isaacs, K. S. (1966). Micro-momentary facial expressions as indicators for ego mechanisms in psychotherapy. In L. A. Gottschalk & A. H. Auerbach (Eds.), *Methods of research in psychotherapy* (pp. 154–165). New York: Appleton-Century-Crofts.

Horowitz, M. J. (1979). *States of mind: Analysis of change in psychotherapy.* New York: Plenum.

Izard, C. E. (1971). *The face of emotion.* New York: Appleton-Century-Crofts.

Izard, C. E. (1977). *Human emotions.* New York: Plenum.

Kohut, H. (1971). *The analysis of the self.* New York: International Universities.

Kohut, H. (1977). *The restoration of the self.* New York: International Universities.

Kohut, H. (1984). *How does analysis cure?* Chicago: University of Chicago Press.

Krause, R. (1982). Kernbereiche psychoanalytischen Handelns. *Der Nervenarzt, 53,* 504–512.

Krause, R. (1984). Psychoanalyse als interaktives Geschehen. In U. Baumann (Ed.), *Psychotherapie: Mikro- und Makroperspektiven* (pp. 146–158). Göttingen, Germany: Hogrefe.

Krause, R. (1988). Eine Taxonomie der Affekte und ihre Anwendung auf das Verständnis der 'frühen' Störungen. *Psychotherapie Psychosomatik Medizinische Psychologie, 38,* 77–112.

Krause, R. (1990). Psychodynamik der Emotionsstörungen. In K. R. Scherer (Ed.), *Enzyklopädie der Psychologie* (pp. 630–705). Göttingen: Hogrefe.

Krause, R., & Lütolf, P. (1989). Mimische Indikatoren von Übertragungsvorgängen: Erste Untersuchungen. *Zeitschrift für Klinische Psychologie, 18,* 55–67.

Maturana, H., & Vareta, F. (1987). *Der Baum der Erkenntnis: Die biologischen Wurzeln des menschlichen Erkennens.* Bern: Scherz.

Moser, U. (1983). *Beiträge zu einer psychoanalytischen Theorie der Affekte* (part 1). Berichte aus der Interdisziplinären Konfliktforschungsstelle, Nr. 10. Soziologisches und Psychologisches Institut der Universität Züroch.

Moser, U. (1985). *Beiträge zu einer psychoanalytischen Theorie der Affekte: Ein Interaktionsmodell* (part 2). Berichte aus der Interdisziplinären Konfliktforschungstelle, Nr. 14. Psychologisches Institut der Universität Zürich, Abteilung Klinische Psychologie.

Moser, U. (1989). *Die Funktion der Grundaffekte in der Regulierung von Objektbeziehungen: Ontogenetische Gesichtspunkte.* Berichte aus der Abteilung Klinische Psychologie, Nr. 25. Psychologisches Institut der Universität Zürich.

Moser, U., Bänninger-Huber, E., & Steiner, F. (1989). *Mikroanalytische Untersuchung von Affek-*

tverläufen in interaktiven Situationen. Schlussbericht an den Schweizerischen Nationalfonds, NF-Projekt 1.453–0.86.

Moser, U., von Zeppelin, I., & Schneider, W. (1991). The regulation of cognitive affective
processes: A new psychoanalytic model. In U. Moser & I. von Zeppelin (Eds.), *Cognitive-
affective processes: New ways of psychoanalytic modelling.* Berlin: Springer.

Ortony, A. (1988). Subjective importance and computational models of emotions. In V. Hamilton, G. H. Bower, & N. H. Frijda (Eds.), *Cognitive perspectives on emotion and motivation*
(pp. 321–343). Dordrecht, Holland: Kluwer.

Pfeifer, R., & Leuzinger-Bohleber, M. (1989). Motivations- und Emotionsstörungen: Ein Cognitive Science Ansatz. Part 1. Grundlagen, Klassifikation und Diagnose. *Zeitschrift für Klinische Psychologie, Psychopathologie und Psychotherapie, 37,* 40–73.

Rice, L. N., & Greenberg, L. S. (1984). The new research paradigm. In L. N. Rice & L. S. Greenberg (Eds.), *Patterns of change* (pp. 7–25). New York: Guilford.

Safran, J. D. (1990a). Towards a refinement of cognitive therapy in light of interpersonal theory:
I. Theory. *Clinical Psychology Review, 10,* 87–105.

Safran, J. D. (1990b). Towards a refinement of cognitive therapy in light of interpersonal theory:
II. Practice. *Clinical Psychology Review, 10,* 107–121.

Scherer, K. R. (1984). On the nature and function of emotion: A component process approach. In
K. R. Scherer & P. Ekman (Eds.), *Approaches to emotion* (pp. 293–317). Hillsdale, NJ: Erlbaum.

Scherer, K. R. (1988). Criteria for emotion-antecedent appraisal: A review. In V. Hamilton,
G. H. Bower, & N. H. Frijda (Eds.), *Cognitive perspectives on emotion and motivation*
(pp. 89–126). Dordrecht: Kluwer.

Scherer, K. R., & Wallbott, H. G. (1990). Ausdruck von Emotionen. In K. R. Scherer (Hrsg.), Enzyklopädie der Psychologie (S. 345–422). Göttingen: Hogrefe.

Schneider, H. (1989). Toward a more detailed understanding of self-organizing processes in psychotherapy. In A. L. Goudsmit (Ed.), *Self-organization in psychotherapy: Demarcations of a
new perspective* (pp. 72–99). Berlin: Springer.

Schneider, H. (1990). *How does change start in the client? A model based on theories of self-organizing processes.* Paper presented at the 21st Annual Meeting of the Society for Psychotherapy Research at Wintergreen, VA, June 26–30.

Steiner, F. (1987, 1990). *FACSER.* Programm-Paket zur Erfassung und Auswertung von Daten,
codiert nach den Vorschriften des Facial Action Coding System (FACS). Unveröffentlichtes
Benutzer-Manual.

Stern, D. N. (1985). *The interpersonal world of the infant: A view from psychoanalysis and developmental psychology.* New York: Basic.

Stettner, L. J., Ivery, E., & Haynes, O. M. (1986). *The human smile: Analysis of structural features and perceived meanings.* Paper presented at the meeting of the International Society
for Human Ethology. Tutzing, FRG.

Strupp, H. (1987). Response to "a countertheory of transference" by John M. Shlien. *Person-
Centered Review, 2,* 196–202.

Sullivan, H. S. (1953). *The interpersonal theory of psychiatry.* New York: Norton.

Terman, D. M. (1988). Optimum frustration: Structuralization and the therapeutic process. In
A. Goldberg (Ed.), *Learning from Kohut: Progress in self psychology* (vol. 4; pp. 113–125).
Hillsdale, NJ: Analytic.

Thomä, H., & Kächele, H. (1985). *Lehrbuch der psychoanalytischen Therapie: 1. Grundlagen.*
Berlin: Springer.

Thomä, H., & Kächele, H. (1988). *Lehrbuch der psychoanalytischen Therapie: 2. Praxis.* Berlin:
Springer.

Tomkins, S. S. (1962). *Affect, imagery, consciousness; Vol. 1. The positive affects.* New York:
Springer.

Tomkins, S. S. (1963). *Affect, imagery, conciousness; Vol. 2. The negative affects.* New York: Springer.

Tomkins, S. S. (1975). The phantasy behind the face. *Journal of Personality Assessment, 39,* 550–562.

von Salisch, M. (1991). *Kinderfreundschaften.* Göttingen, Germany: Hogrefe.

von Zeppelin, I., & Moser, U. (1987). Träumen wir Affekte? Affektive Kommunikation im Traumprozess: Part 1. Affekte und manifester Traum. *Forum der Psychoanalyse, 3,* 143–152.

Weiss, J., Sampson, H., & the Mount Zion Psychotherapy Research Group. (1986). *The psychoanalytic process.* New York: Guilford.

Wicki, W., Bänninger-Huber, E., & Steiner, F. (1989). *Smiling at a process variable in psychotherapy research.* Paper presented at the Third European Conference of the Society for Psychotherapy Research, Bern, Switzerland, September.

From PAMS to TRAPS: Investigating Guilt Feelings with FACS

EVA BÄNNINGER-HUBER

Using a microanalytic approach, we were able to identify successful and unsuccessful prototypical affective microsequences (= PAMS) of affective regulation. PAMS are characterized by the frequent occurrence of smiling and laughing of both the client and the therapist. They have the function to overcome disturbances in the client's self-regulation in order to maintain the psychotherapeutic working alliance. These findings raise the question of what role successful and unsuccessful PAMs play in terms of therapeutic change. For instance, in which moments can the therapist risk not to react with a smile? How often does the therapist have to join a smile until it is possible to confront the client with unpleasant things? What happens afterwards?

To answer these questions it is important not only to focus on facial behavior but also to include verbal aspects of psychotherapeutic interaction. Up to now, most studies of therapeutic relationship focus either on verbal or nonverbal behavior. Therefore, in a follow-up project a new approach has been developed that allows to relate verbal and nonverbal aspects of psychotherapeutic interaction (Bänninger-Huber, 1995; Bänninger-Huber & Widmer, 1994). Using a single case approach, we elaborated on correspondence between the client's reported relationship patterns and specific observable patterns enacted with the therapist. Specifically, we focused on the question of which interactive relationship patterns occur in the context of guilt feelings and which role guilt feelings may play in intraindividual and interactive regulation of emotion. These questions are of therapeutic relevance because such enacted relationship patterns have recently been conceptualized as important elements of the therapeutic relationship that are viewed as crucial for therapeutic change. However, these conceptualizations of the therapeutic process rely only on reconstruction from the therapist's memory. Thus, our approach emphasizes the relation between the level of observable affective interaction and therapeutic concepts.

The empirical material consisted of selected videotaped sessions of a psychoanalytic therapy of a young depressive woman. During these sessions the client as well as the therapist reported or experienced guilt feelings repeatedly. The guilt feelings verbally reported by the client were identified and systematically described by a model-oriented structure. This structure contains all elements that can belong to guilt feeling eliciting situations and is represented by means of *frame* (Minsky, 1975; Lüthy & Widmer, 1992). The frame method captures narrative episodes exclusively; interactive elements of the therapeutic dialogue—for example, the client's comments on her stories, the therapist's interventions, and the client's reactions—are not taken into account. Thus, these sequences have been further analyzed using the method described in Bänninger-Huber (this volume), because we suppose that these sequences are characteristic for the therapeutic relationship and especially relevant for therapeutic change.

Applying these methods, different patterns of interaction were observed that repeatedly occur in the context of reported guilt feelings. A particular kind of such relationship patterns are the so-called traps. In these traps, the client attempts to "seduce" the therapist to take on the role of an authority figure with respect to the actions that causes the client's guilt feelings. These interactive sequences are characterized by specific verbal and nonverbal behavior. On the level of verbal behavior, direct and indirect questions are frequent on the side of the client. The client gives her interpretation of the reported situation and (indirectly) urges the therapist to give her opinion ("I for myself don't think this is so bad, it doesn't harm anybody"; "I think this is legitimate, isn't it?"). Simultaneously, specific patterns including PAMS can be observed on the nonverbal level. While traps last between 15 seconds and some minutes, PAMS usually last only some seconds.

Successful and unsuccessful traps can be distinguished according to their interactive course—that is, the reaction of the therapist. A *successful* trap occurs when the therapist follows the offer of the client and takes on the role of an authority figure by commenting the client's action verbally. In *unsuccessful* traps, however, she omits a verbal reaction. Our hypothesis is that the nonverbal reactions of the therapist in PAMS (e.g., smiling, listener-response) serve the function of maintaining the affective relatedness with the client. This is one basis for the continuous functioning of the (intrapsychic) affective regulation of the client and prevents interruption in the relationship regulation. Owing to the fact that the therapist does not take on the desired role of an authority figure in unsuccessful traps in terms of the reported conflicting scene (e.g., by saying: "it's your husband's fault"), the (intrapsychic) conflict remains. This noncompliant behavior is a precondition for client and therapist to be able to continue work on this guilt conflict. How far and under which circumstances successful or unsuccessful traps can be productive for psychotherapeutic change needs further investigation.

The investigation of interactive processes of affective regulation in the context of guilt feelings is also of interest for emotion psychology. For example, hardly anything is known about the facial expression of guilt feelings. By remembering, fantasizing, or reporting a specific situation that earlier led to guilt feelings, the same emotion may be reactivated in the "here and now" of the psychotherapeutic interaction. To cope with this reactivated emotion, the client shows specific interactive behavior that in turn can evoke specific reactions of the therapist. In contrast to basic emotions (Ekman, 1992), structural emotions (Moser, 1983) such as guilt feelings do not lead to emotion-specific facial expression, but can be observed as interactively enacted coping strategies such as traps.

There are several good reasons for using FACS as an instrument for recording and describing facial behavior in our approach. The main advantage of FACS is the possibility to measure facial behavior objectively. The interpretation of the data takes place in a second step, independent of the recording. Thus, interpretations may be reevaluated after changes in the theoretical framework. Especially important is an objective, observation-based behavior description in the context of psychotherapy research. Only this will help to overcome the unreliable, subjective rating techniques that are used nowadays to judge the complex therapeutic processes.

As we are interested in observing authentic therapy sessions, certain traditional methods of measurement in emotion research cannot be used because they seriously disturb the emotional interchange and course of interaction (e.g., physiological measurement or EMG). FACS is differentiated enough to allow the reliable coding of affective regulatory processes from videotapes. Using the FACS or EMFACS emotion prediction tables, it would be possible to analyze the data in terms of their emotional meaning. However, as facial behavior is very complex and may serve different functions, not all of these predictions are empirically tested (Bänninger-Huber & von Salisch, 1994). Considering the present state of research, it seems useful to interpret FACS data not only with the emotion prediction tables but also taking the situative context, especially the interactive and the temporal aspects, into consideration. This approach becomes even more fruitful if top-down processes of operationalizations of preconceived theoretical notions are combined with bottom-up processes of exact observation and description of expressive behavior.

References

Bänninger-Huber, E. (1995). Die Untersuchung von Schuldgefühlen in der psychotherapeutischen Interaktion. In G. Koch (Hrsg.), *Auge und Affekt* (S. 39–56), Frankfurt: Fischer Taschenbuch.

Bänninger-Huber, E., & v. Salisch, M. (1994). Die Untersuchung des mimischen Affektausdrucks in face-to-face Interaktionen, *Psychologische Rundschau, 45,* 79–98.

Bänninger-Huber, E., & Widmer, C. (1994). Guilt feelings in psychotherapeutic interaction. In N. H. Frijda (Ed.), *Proceedings of the VIIIth Conference of the International Society for Research on Emotions* (pp. 139–143). Cambridge, July 14–17.

Ekman, P. (1992). An argument for basic emotions. *Cognition and Emotion, 6,* 169–200.

Lüthy, A.-M., & Widmer, C. (1992). A model-oriented representation of superego rules. In M. Leuzinger-Bohleber, H. Schneider, & R. Pfeifer (Eds.), *"Two butterflies on my head"— Psychoanalysis in the interdisciplinary scientific dialogue* (pp. 197–214). Heidelberg: Springer.

Minsky, M. (1975). A framework for representing knowledge. In P. H. Winston (Ed.), *The psychology of computer vision* (pp. 211–280). New York: McGraw-Hill.

Moser, U. (1983). *Beiträge zu einer psychoanalytischen Theorie der Affekte.* Berichte aus der Interdisziplinären Konfliktforschungsstelle, Nr. 10, Soziologisches und Psychologisches Institut der Universität Zürich.

21

Facial Expressions of Emotion and Psychopathology in Adolescent Boys

DACHER KELTNER, TERRIE E. MOFFITT & MAGDA STOUTHAMER-LOEBER

It is widely believed that emotions serve adaptive functions (e.g., Ekman, 1992; Izard, 1977; Lazarus, 1991). Each emotion motivates cognitive processes, physiological responses, and expressive behavior that help the individual respond adaptively to specific problems of survival, such as fleeing from danger, developing and maintaining close social bonds, and avoiding or apologizing for social and moral transgressions.

Emotions also figure prominently in psychological maladjustment. In certain cases, the absence of emotion contributes to psychological dysfunction: Schizophrenic individuals suffer from flat affect (Bleuler, 1911/1950) or the reduced outward expression of affect (Kring, Kerr, Smith, & Neale, 1993), and psychopathic individuals experience reduced punishment-related emotion (Hare, 1978; Newman, 1987). Certain pathologies are associated with extreme levels of emotion: Anxious people experience high levels of fear (Izard, 1972); antisocial children experience and act on inappropriate anger (Cole & Zahn-Waxler, 1992). The link between psychopathology and emotion, in fact, is so pervasive that 45% of the diagnoses listed in the *Diagnostic and Statistical Manual of Mental Disorders* (3rd ed.; *DSM-III;* American Psychiatric Association, 1980) referred to abnormal emotional response of one kind or another (Thoits, 1985).

In the current study, we tested three hypotheses concerning the relations between facial expressions of emotion and adolescent psychopathology. First, we expected externalizing adolescents, who are prone to aggressive and delinquent behavior, to show more anger. Second, we expected internalizing adolescents, who are prone to anxiety, depression, withdrawn behavior, and somatic complaints, to show more fear and sadness. Our final hypothesis pertained to embarrassment, which is believed to contribute to psychological adjustment by motivating people to avoid social–moral transgressions and to apologize for transgressions that have occurred (Miller & Leary, 1992). This reasoning led us to expect the nondisordered adolescents to show the most embarrassment and the externalizing adolescents to show the least embarrassment.

434

Benefits to the Study of Discrete Facial Expressions

Facial expressions are a remarkable indicator of emotion. Facial expressions correlate with the self-reported experience of emotion (Ekman, Friesen, & Ancoli, 1980; Keltner, 1995) as well as with patterns of autonomic nervous system (Levenson, Ekman, & Friesen, 1990) and central nervous system activity (Davidson, Ekman, Saron, Senulius, & Friesen, 1990). The study of facial expression offers researchers a window into complex emotional processes as they unfold dynamically.

The specific benefits to the use of facial expression in studies of psychopathology and emotion are several. First, the study of facial expressions of emotion allows researchers to test very specific hypotheses regarding emotion and psychopathology. Whereas studies using standard autonomic nervous system measures, such as heart rate and skin conductance, for example, permit tests of global hypotheses concerning levels of arousal or the valence of emotion, studies relying on facial expression can test hypotheses related to the discrete emotions. This, in turn, allows researchers to differentiate closely related, often comorbid psychopathologies (in the current study, internalizing and externalizing problems).

Second, by studying facial expression, we avoid the problem of the considerable predictor-criterion overlap between self-report scales that measure psychopathology, personality, and emotion (see Tennenbaum, 1977; Watson & Clark, 1992). For example, the Internalizing cluster of the often used Child Behavior Checklist (Achenbach & Edelbrock, 1983; Achenbach, Howell, Quay, & Conners, 1991) contains items such as "is fearful, anxious." The Positive and Negative Affect Scale (Watson, Clark, & Tellegen, 1988), a widely used self-report measure of emotion, includes items such as "I often feel anxious, worried." If one were to study the relationship between the Achenbach measure of internalization, or other pathology scales for that matter, and widely used self-report measures of emotion, one would expect positive correlations on purely semantic grounds. Facial expression, in contrast, occurs in a different medium than self-report and avoids the predictor-criterion overlap problem.

Externalizing Problems and Anger

The evidence for the hypothesized relation between externalizing problems and anger is twofold. First, anger in part defines externalizing problems (e.g., in the Child Behavior Checklist) and emerges as an important component of conduct disorder in factor-analytic studies (Hinshaw, 1987). Empirical studies have also documented relations between anger and externalizing problems. The self-reported tendency to experience and express anger correlates with acting out behavior in a normal population (Finch & Rogers, 1984) and in children in psychiatric care (Finch & Eastman, 1983), and it was higher in externalizing than internalizing children (Mabe, Treiber, & Riley, 1992). Children who engage in antisocial behavior are rated by parents, teachers, and peers as more hostile and angry (Cole & Zahn-Waxler, 1992). Young men and women who rated themselves as prone to aggression were more likely to engage in a variety of delinquent behaviors (Krueger et al., 1994).

Internalizing Problems and Fear and Sadness

The argument for a link between internalizing problems and fear and sadness is likewise both definitional and empirical. Most definitions of internalizing problems include symptoms of anxiety and depression, which are related to fear and sadness (e.g., Izard, 1972). Empirical studies also point to a link between internalizing problems and fear and sadness. Children clinically diagnosed with depression, one component of internalizing problems, report higher scores on self-report depression inventories, of which anxiety and sadness are components (Asarnow & Carlson, 1985; Kazdin, Colbus, & Rodgers, 1986). Measures of childhood depression in fifth graders were most strongly related to self-reports of sadness, and in the case of boys, to anger as well (Blumberg & Izard, 1985). Socially withdrawn children are often rated as sad, anxious, or depressed (Rubin, Hymel, Mills, & Rose-Krasnor, 1991). Of course, fear plays a defining role in anxiety disorders (e.g., Izard, 1972). These findings, then, point to the second hypothesis tested in the current investigation: Adolescent boys with internalizing problems will display a higher ratio of more intense facial expressions of fear and sadness than nondisordered and externalizing adolescent boys.

Psychological Adjustment and the Social–Moral Emotions

Beginning at least with Freud, scholars have proposed that moral behavior, socialization, and adaptive assimilation into society are founded on the social–moral emotions, which include embarrassment, shame, and guilt (Lewis, 1993; Miller & Leary, 1992; Tangney, 1991). The social–moral emotions involve self-consciousness, taking other people's perspectives on one's own behavior, and comparing personal actions to standards of morality and conventionality. The social–moral emotions serve at least two vital functions. First, the experience of embarrassment, shame, and guilt, in response to past and anticipated events, motivates people to avoid social transgressions (R. H. Frank, 1988; Miller & Leary, 1992). Second, the display of social–moral emotions, in particular embarrassment, serves as an apology for committed transgressions, thus restoring social relations disturbed by the transgression (Castelfranchi & Poggi, 1990; Keltner, 1995; Semin & Manstead, 1982).

One prevalent hypothesis holds that the absence of the social–moral emotions predicts antisocial behavior (e.g., Cleckley, 1955; Hare, 1978). Externalizing problems are in part defined as the absence of guilt (Achenbach & Edelbrock, 1983). Empirical evidence supports this definition of externalizing problems. Low scores on guilt-proneness measures were negatively correlated with measures of antisocial behavior (Ruma, 1967) and drug use (Schill & Althoff, 1975) and positively correlated with measures of moral development (Ruma & Mosher, 1967). In synthesizing the literature on antisocial behavior and emotion, Kochanska (1993) proposed that the feeling of discomfort at having committed a transgression is one of two components of conscience that predict psychosocial adjustment.

Recent research that has identified the nonverbal displays of embarrassment, one of the social–moral emotions (Edelmann & Hampson, 1979; Keltner, 1995), has made it possible to test the hypothesized relation between facial displays of social–moral emotion and antisocial behavior. Our third hypothesis, which is based on the previous argument linking psychological adjustment to social–moral emotion, posited the following relationship: Symptomalogical adolescent boys, and especially externalizing adolescents, will show a lower ratio of less intense embarrassment than nondisordered adolescents.

Present Investigation

To test the hypotheses outlined above, we examined the facial expressions of emotion shown by adolescent boys during an individually administered IQ test. The interactive IQ test was selected as the emotional situation because it (a) evokes different emotions, including those relevant to our hypotheses; (b) evokes individual variation in emotional response; and (c) is similar to a central socializing context of adolescents—educational performance and evaluation. Adolescents were categorized into one of four diagnostic categories (internalizer, externalizer, nondisordered, and mixed) according to their teachers' ratings on the Child Behavior Checklist (Achenbach & Edelbrock, 1983).

Method

Participants

The materials used in this study include teachers' ratings of behavior problems and videotapes of 12- and 13-year-old boys collected in 1990. These data are archived as part of the Pittsburgh Youth Study (PYS; for details about the study, see Loeber, Stouthamer-Loeber, Van Kammen, & Farrington, 1989).

The boys in the sample had been previously divided into four groups on the basis of their teachers' reports using the Achenbach Child Behavior Checklist (Kreuger, Caspi, Moffitt, White, & Stouthamer-Loeber, in press). Checklist items comprise two factors corresponding to the dichotomy between "internalizing" and "externalizing" syndromes (Achenbach et al., 1991). The four groups constructed from teachers' ratings allowed comparison of boys who represented cases of "pure" externalizing problems, boys who represented cases of "pure" internalizing problems, boys who simultaneously exhibited features of both externalizing and internalizing problems (mixed), and boys who were deemed nondisordered.

Previous validation research has demonstrated that boys falling at or above the 80th percentile in the population on these measures of childhood behavior problems are likely to have difficulties severe enough to warrant referral for treatment (Achenbach et al., 1991). Hence, we used the 80th percentile from the population norm as a cutoff in determining psychopathology group membership. Boys who fell at or above the 80th percentile on the population distributions of teacher-reported externalizing scores and below the 80th percentile on the teacher-reported internalizing scores were deemed pure externalizers. Boys who fell at or above the 80th percentile on the teacher-reported internalizing scores and below the 80th percentile on the teacher-reported externalizing scores were deemed pure internalizers. Boys who fell at or above the 80th percentile on the teacher-reported externalizing scores and at or above the 80th percentile on the teacher-reported internalizing scores were deemed mixed cases. Boys who fell below the mean on both the teacher-reported externalizing scores and the teacher-reported internalizing scores were deemed relatively nondisordered. The high ratio of mixed cases found in our sample (see table 21.1) is not unusual: Epidemiological surveys typically observe high levels of comorbodity between externalizing and internalizing problems (Anderson, Williams, McGee, & Silva, 1987: Bird, Gould, & Staghezza, 1993; Fergusson, Hornwood, & Lynskey, 1993).

From the original sample of 508 boys, we coded the behavior of all those boys who were classified into one of the four groups and whose facial behavior was codable. The videotapes collected in 1990 were not designed for the kind of coding carried out in the present study; for example, most boys were videotaped from the side or at too great a distance to allow for the resolution necessary to code facial expression. Thus, we included in our study only those boys whose facial behavior was codable and who were classified into one of the four groups. This left 70 boys for the current study. The original sample was drawn in 1986 to represent the population distribution of risk factors for further violent crime among fourth-grade boys in the Pittsburgh public school system (girls were not sampled because physical violence was the target outcome for the longitudinal study). The 70 boys used for the present research did not differ from the remaining 438 participants on measures of race, IQ as measured by the Wechsler Intelligence Scale for Children—Revised (WISC-R; Wechsler, 1974), father's or mother's socioeconomic status (SES), or any behavior problem scale from the Child Behavior Checklist (all $ps > .3$). The four groups of participants' scores on the internalization and externalization scales are presented in table 21.1, which shows that the classification procedure did yield distinct groups.

Measures

WISC-R

The adolescents were administered an abbreviated version (Yudin, 1966) of the WISC-R. The WISC-R is a standardized test of intelligence consisting of a series of questions and puzzles presented by a trained examiner positioned across a table from an examinee. Each adolescent was videotaped while completing this test. The video camera was in plain view during the entire testing session and was positioned to record only the adolescent's behavior. The examiner was off-camera.

TABLE 21.1. Means on teacher-reported CBCL externalizing and internalizing factor scales for four comparison groups of boys

	Diagnostic group				
Scale from CBCL	INTERN (*n* = 9)	EXTERN (*n* = 9)	MIXED (*n* = 12)	NON-DIS (*n* = 40)	$F(3.66)$
Externalization	18.76	40.69	45.17	2.83	146.95****
Internalization	17.35	5.52	22.11	2.01	106.20****

Note: CBCL = Child Behavior Checklist (Achenbach & Edelbrock, 1983). INTERN = internalizers; EXTERN = externalizers; NON-DIS = nondisordered.
****$p < .0001$.

Of the different components of the WISC-R, we elected to code adolescents' facial behavior while taking one component known as the Information subtest. During the Information subtest adolescents attempted to provide answers to a series of questions ("How many days make a week?", "How far is it from New York to Los Angeles?", "What is a barometer?") asked by the tester. According to instructions, adolescents were probed by the tester when they offered ambiguous answers. This general information task elicited frequent emotion because adolescents succeeded and failed in front of an authority figure at a task relevant to their school performance. Furthermore, because adolescents were engaged in a face-to-face interaction, their facial behavior was clearly visible and unconstrained by other demands such as writing.

Coding of Facial Behavior

Adolescents' facial behavior was coded by Dacher Keltner, who was blind to the behavior problem scores of the adolescents. A version of the Facial Action Coding System (FACS; Ekman & Friesen, 1976, 1978) was used (EMFACS) to code adolescents' facial behavior. EMFACS concentrates on coding only the emotion-relevant facial muscle movements that have been derived from previous theory and research (reviewed in Ekman, 1984). Although EMFACS is not as laborious as FACS, approximately 1 hr was required to code each adolescent's 2-min episode of behavior. In the current study, EMFACS criteria were used to code the facial expressions of anger, contempt, disgust, enjoyment (Duchenne smile), fear, sadness, and surprise (which was not observed), as well as smiles of amusement, defined as Duchenne smiles accompanied by audible laughter and an open mouth (Keltner, 1995; Ruch, 1993). Facial expressions of embarrassment were identified when the adolescent showed a controlled smile, gaze down, and head movement away and down (Keltner, 1995). Each facial muscle movement was scored on a 5-point scale (1 = *minimum intensity,* 3 = *moderate intensity,* 5 = *extreme intensity*). Intensity and duration scores for each category of facial expression were derived by finding the mean of the intensity and duration scores of the emotion-relevant facial actions.

Reliability of Measurement

Dacher Keltner coded the behavior of all 70 adolescents. A second person, who had passed the FACS reliability test and was blind to the investigation's aims and hypotheses, coded five randomly selected adolescents. Intercoder reliability was evaluated by using a ratio in which the number of action units on which the two coders agreed was multiplied by two and then divided by the total number of action units scored by the two persons. This agreement ratio was calculated for each event observed by one or both coders. The mean ratio of agreement was .78.

Results

Table 21.2 presents the frequency, intensity, and duration of the facial expressions that adolescents showed during the information portion of the WISC-R (Wechsler, 1974) test.

Table 21.2 shows that the adolescents displayed frequent negative emotion and embarrassment during the IQ test. Tests of the hypotheses focused on two measures of facial expression of each emotion. First, emotion-ratio scores were calculated by

TABLE 21.2. Characteristics of facial expressions of emotion shown during 2 min of an IQ test

Emotion	Participants showing expression	Average frequency	Average intensity	Average duration (s)
Negative				
Anger	25	1.64	2.78	1.68
Fear	29	2.28	2.34	2.65
Sadness	27	2.52	2.38	2.47
Social-moral				
Embarrassment	45	2.07	4.08	2.71

Note: Mean intensity scores for all expressions equal the mean of the intensity codes of the relevant facial actions, except in the case of embarrassment, which is the sum of the markers of embarrassment (gaze down, smile, smile control, head movement, face touch).

dividing the number of facial expressions of each emotion shown by the adolescent by the total number of facial expressions of emotion shown by that adolescent. The ratio scores estimate the extent to which each emotion constituted each adolescent's distribution of expressed emotions. The overall expression magnitude scores were based on the intensity and duration as well as the frequency of facial expressions of emotion. Both intensity and duration of facial expression of emotion predict self-reports of emotion (e.g., Ekman et al., 1980), and in combination, provide a more reliable assessment of facial expression than simple frequency counts. Thus, for each category of emotion, magnitude composite scores were equal to the sum of the number, intensity, and duration z scores for that emotion. Table 21.3 presents the means for the ratio and z-score composite measures for each of the negative emotions relevant to our hypotheses.

Our hypotheses were tested with planned comparisons with weights that are represented in table 21.4. For hypotheses relevant to anger, fear, and sadness, we used planned contrasts to test whether the "pure" groups (externalizers and internalizers) were different from the relevant comparison groups and then whether groups with a disorder (externalizers and mixed, internalizers and mixed) differed from the relevant comparison groups. For the hypotheses concerning embarrassment, we used planned contrasts to test whether nondisordered boys showed more embarrassment than the three groups and than the externalizing boys in particular.

Externalizing Problems and Anger

Our first hypothesis predicted that adolescents with externalizing problems (both pure and mixed boys) would show more anger than both the nondisordered and the internalizing adolescents. On the anger ratio measure, analyses showed that "pure" externalizing adolescents showed an anger ratio score ($M = .23$) ($M = .07$), $t(47) = 2.30$, $p < .03$. The comparison of the anger ratio scores of "pure" externalizing and mixed adolescents (overall $M = .16$) and nondisordered adolescents ($M = .06$) also approached significance, $t(59) = 1.87$, $p = .066$. Analyses of the composite z-score

TABLE **21.3.** Distribution of emotions across four comparison groups

	Diagnostic group			
Emotion	INTERN (n = 9)	EXTERN (n = 9)	MIXED (n = 12)	NON-DIS (n = 40)
		Negative		
Anger				
Ratio	0.10	0.23	0.11	0.07
z score	0.43	1.31	−0.41	0.05
Fear				
Ratio	0.15	0.05	0.05	0.17
z score	1.07	−1.35	−1.04	0.39
Sadness				
Ratio	0.10	0.04	0.17	0.15
z score	0.13	−0.57	0.12	0.06
		Social-moral		
Embarrassment				
Ratio	0.14	0.16	0.08	0.22
z score	0.05	−0.63	−1.43	0.56

Note: INTERN = internalizers; EXTERN = externalizers; NON-DIS = nondisordered.

TABLE **21.4.** Contrast weights usd in planned comparisons to test hypotheses

	Diagnostic group			
Emotion	INTERN (n = 9)	EXTERN (n = 9)	MIXED (n = 12)	NON-DIS (n = 40)
Anger	−1	1		
		1		−1
	−2	1	1	
		1	1	−2
Fear and sadness	1	−1		
	1			−1
	1	−2	1	
	1		1	−2
Embarrassment	−1	−1	−1	3
	−1			1
		−1	−1	2

Note: INTERN = internalizers; EXTERN = externalizers; NON-DIS = nondisordered.

measure found one marginally significant effect: "Pure" externalizing adolescents had larger anger z scores ($M = 1.31$) than nondisordered adolescents ($M = -0.41$), $t(47) = 1.69$, $p < .10$.

Internalizing Problems, Fear, and Sadness

Our second hypothesis predicted that adolescents with internalizing problems (both "pure" and mixed) would display more fear and sadness than both the nondisordered and externalizing adolescents. One contrast analyzing facial expressions of fear proved to be significant: "Pure" internalizing adolescents' fear z scores ($M = 1.07$) were greater than those of externalizing adolescents ($M = -1.35$), $t(16) = 1.99$, $p = .05$. No differences were found in comparing the relevant groups' displays of sadness on either the ratio or z-score composite measures.

Nondisordered Adolescents and Social–Moral Emotions

Our final hypothesis predicted a relation between the absence of social–moral emotion (embarrassment) and the presence of psychological disorder. The most general form of this hypothesis predicted that nondisordered adolescents would show more embarrassment than the other three groups. Consistent with our hypothesis, nondisordered adolescents' embarrassment ratio scores ($M = .22$) were higher than those of the three disorder groups (overall $M = .12$), $t(68) = 2.20$, $p < .05$, as were their z scores ($M = 0.56$ vs. overall $M = -0.16$), $t(68) = 1.95$, $p = 0.54$. Our more specific prediction was that adolescents with externalizing problems in particular would show less embarrassment than nondisordered adolescents. Consistent with this hypothesis, externalizing and mixed adolescents showed less embarrassment than nondisordered adolescents on both the ratio score (overall $M = 0.11$ vs. 0.22), $t(59) = 1.91$, $p = .06$ and the z score (overall $M = -1.09$ vs. 0.56), $t(59) = 2.25$, $p < .03$.

Correlations Between Achenbach Subscales and Facial Expressions of Emotion

In subsequent analyses, we examined the correlations between the two facial expression measures for each emotion and the subscales of the measures of externalizing problems (Delinquent behavior and Aggressive behavior) and internalizing problems (Anxiety/Depression, Withdrawn, and Somatic Complaints). These correlations addressed two issues. First, we examined whether the across-subject correlations would replicate the findings from the between-group comparisons. Second, as a more focused test of the hypothesized relation between fear and sadness and internalizing problems, we examined the relations between the measures of fear and sadness and the most relevant internalization subscale (i.e., anxious–depressed).

The correlations in table 21.5 both replicate and extend the findings observed in the previous analyses. Consistent with our first hypothesis, both the ratio and z-score measures of anger were significantly and positively correlated with teacher reports of delinquent ($rs = .39$ and $.31$, $ps < .01$) and aggressive ($r_{ratio} = .28$, $p < .01$) behavior. The ratio and z-score measures of embarrassment, consistent with our hypothesis, were significantly and negatively correlated with teacher reports of aggressive behavior ($rs = -.22$ and $-.29$, $p < .01$ and $p < .05$, respectively).

TABLE 21.5. Correlations between teacher-reported subscales of Achenbach
Child Behavior Checklist (CBCL) and facial expressions of emotion

	CBCL subscale				
Emotion	Anxious-depressed	Withdrawn behavior	Somatic complaints	Delinquent behavior	Aggressive behavior
Anger					
Ratio	.10	.17	.20*	.39***	.28**
z score	.06	.10	.19	.31***	.19
Fear					
Ratio	−.08	−.06	−.08	−.20*	−.25**
z score	−.06	−.01	.00	−.20*	−.27**
Sadness					
Ratio	−.01	−.05	−.10	−.13	−.09
z score	.02	−.10	−.14	−.06	−.06
Embarr.					
Ratio	−.20*	−.31**	−.18	−.18	−.22*
z score	−.19	−.35***	−.13	−.16	−.29**

Note: Embarr. = embarrassment.
* $p < .05$. ** $p < .01$. *** $p < .001$ (all ps are two-tailed).

Several correlations in table 21.5 also pertain to other claims concerning psychopathology and emotion. First, the ratio and z-score measures of fear were negatively and significantly correlated with teacher reports of delinquent ($r_{ratio} = -.20$, $p < .05$) and aggressive behavior (rs $= -.25$ and $-.27$, ps $< .05$, respectively), consistent with the hypothesis that fear inhibits antisocial behavior (e.g., Hare, 1978; Newman, 1987). Second, the ratio and z-score measures of embarrassment were negatively and significantly correlated with teacher reports of anxiety–depression ($r_{ratio} = -.20$, $p < .05$) and withdrawn behavior (rs $= -.31$ and $-.35$, ps $< .01$), suggesting that embarrassment reflects social approach (Castelfranchi & Poggi, 1990).

Discussion

In the current study, we tested hypotheses concerning the relations between externalizing problems and anger, internalizing problems and fear and sadness, and the absence of externalizing problems and social–moral emotion (embarrassment). The discrete facial expressions of emotion shown by adolescents classified into one of four groups were coded during their participation in an interactive IQ test. The IQ test is an ideal situation for testing these hypotheses because it is fairly ambiguous, elicits individual variation in emotion, and is part of a central socializing context in which adolescents are evaluated.

Adolescents with externalizing problems (both pure and mixed) did show a higher ratio of anger expressions than nondisordered adolescents, a finding that provided partial support for the first hypothesis. Pure externalizing adolescents also showed anger expressions of greater magnitude (i.e., of greater duration and intensity) than nondisordered adolescents. Subsequent correlational analyses replicated and extended these findings, showing that adolescents who were reported by their teachers to be more prone to delinquent and aggressive behavior expressed a higher ratio of facial expressions of anger that were of greater magnitude.

The hypothesis that internalizing adolescents would show more fear and sadness received weaker support than the other hypotheses. On one measure, the overall magnitude of fear, "pure" internalizing adolescents did indeed show more fear than "pure" externalizing adolescents. Internalizing adolescents did not show more fear, however, than the nondisordered adolescents, and they did not show more sadness than the externalizing and nondisordered adolescents, as we had hypothesized they would.

The hypothesis that nondisordered adolescents would show more social–moral emotion (embarrassment) than adolescents with externalizing or internalizing problems was also supported. Nondisordered adolescents did show more embarrassment than the adolescents in the three pathology groups, especially compared to adolescents with externalizing problems. Correlations were also consistent with this hypothesis, demonstrating that adolescents who showed increased embarrassment during the IQ test were reported by their teachers as less prone to aggressive behavior.

These findings provide the first evidence for the claim that different adolescent disorders are manifest in distinct facial expressions of emotion. Furthermore, the current study documented links between adolescent psychopathology and emotional expression even though the measures of emotion and psychopathology came from two sources (the child's teacher and the child) rather than one, and emotional responses were assessed in one brief situation.

The failure to observe consistent facial correlates of internalization has several possible explanations. It may be that emotional expression is not related to internalizing problems. Rather, disorders of anxiety and depression may best be defined by particular cognitive biases, beliefs, and phenomenologies that are not manifest in the face. Alternatively, it may be that the emotions underlying internalizing problems are not reliably displayed socially in the face, but rather are most poignant and pronounced in private, internal experience. Consistent with this claim, interrater agreement is usually weaker between reporters of children's depression and anxiety than for other disorders (Achenbach, McConaughy, & Howell, 1987).

The nature of the experimental situation—the IQ test—may have shaped the pattern of results observed in the current study. First, of the three hypotheses tested in the current study, that concerning the relation between social–moral emotion and adolescent psychopathology may have received the most legitimate test. The conditions of the IQ test most clearly resemble the conditions that produce embarrassment: Students make several mistakes in front of an authority who closely scrutinizes their performance. Consistent with this observation, embarrassment was the most commonly observed emotion during the information subtest of the IQ. Had we studied adolescents in situations that are more evocative of sadness and fear, such as a social loss or a physical threat to safety, we might have observed relations between the facial expressions of these emotions and internalizing problems.

One must also exercise caution in generalizing broadly about the capacity (or, as the current findings suggest, incapacity) for externalizing adolescents to display the social–moral emotions. The current study only showed that externalizing adolescents did not show much embarrassment in a school-related context, which may reflect the unimportance of school to externalizing adolescents. No doubt this is a consequential finding when one considers the significance of school performance to socialization. Yet in other contexts, for example in status negotiations among peers or in more social contexts outside of the classroom, externalizing adolescents may show more embarrassment than during an IQ test.

Emotional Correlates of Impulse Control

The current findings dovetail with recent conceptualizations of the relation between antisocial behavior and deficits in the ability to inhibit or control impulses (Block & Block, 1980; Moffitt, 1993). Across a variety of measures, externalizing adolescents who are prone to aggressive and delinquent behavior demonstrate the inability to inhibit impulses (e.g., White et al., 1994). This inability to inhibit impulsive behavior may be the overarching construct that accounts for the emotional correlates of externalization that were observed in the current study.

First, adolescents with externalizing problems showed a higher ratio of anger than nondisordered adolescents. They were the least likely to inhibit this antisocial emotion while interacting with the adult examiner. Certainly, one norm of emotional expression is the inhibition and control of anger in front of authority figures. Externalizing adolescents were not inclined to follow this norm.

Second, adolescents who showed more fear were, according to their teachers, less inclined to engage in delinquent and aggressive behavior. Several theorists posit that fear is part of an inhibitory system that enables people to respond to punishment, internalize moral standards, and control antisocial impulses (Hare, 1978; Kochanska, 1993; Newman, 1987).

Finally, externalizing adolescents showed the least embarrassment, an emotion that reflects inhibitory processes. The origins of embarrassment are alleged to be in the inhibition of prohibited pleasure (Tomkins, 1984). Anticipated embarrassment inhibits antisocial behavior (R. H. Frank, 1988; Miller & Leary, 1992). Inhibited behavior is part and parcel of the characteristic facial expression of embarrassment, which includes the gaze aversion (which is thought to sever current social interaction) and the inhibited smile (Keltner, 1995). Construed in this way, the relative absence of embarrassment observed in externalizing adolescents may mark their distinction to inhibit their emotions and actions according to social morals and conventions. In summary, the three emotional correlates of antisocial behavior observed in the current study—increased anger and decreased fear and embarrassment—may reflect a more general deficit in inhibiting impulses that characterizes individuals prone to antisocial behavior. Follow-up research should examine the relation between emotion and emotion regulation.

Social Display of Adolescent Psychopathology

Because of the social nature of facial expression, we close by offering a few speculations regarding the potential social consequences of the tendencies to display certain emotions. Facial expressions convey information to others about the individual's emotion (Ekman, Sorenson, & Friesen, 1969; Izard, 1977), personality (M. Frank, Ekman, & Friesen, 1993; Keltner, 1995), and likely behavior (Ekman, 1993; Fridlund, 1992), which influences the inferences and actions of others. We believe that the responses that facial expressions evoke in others mediate the social relationships that externalizing, internalizing, and nondisordered adolescents develop. Certainly one can readily imagine the consequences of frequently displaying intense anger, a tendency observed in externalizing adolescents. Displays of anger, brief and fleeting as they may be, evoke negative emotions in others (Ohman, Dimberg, & Esteves, 1989). People's negative emotional responses to externalizers' frequent anger, in turn, are likely to contribute to the social rejection and hostile relations that define the lives of aggressive children and adults (e.g., Coie, Dodge, Terry, & Wright, 1991).

The appropriate display of social–moral emotions such as embarrassment, especially after social transgressions, is likely to have equally profound social consequences. Displays of embarrassment elicit liking, sympathy, and social acceptance in others (Semin & Manstead, 1982). Displaying embarrassment, we would argue, stimulates and maintains the kinds of rewarding, secure social bonds that contribute to psychological adjustment. In the absence of expressing embarrassment, less sympathy, liking, and social acceptance are likely to be the responses of others, which may profoundly shape the course of adolescent psychopathology.

References

Achenbach, T. M., & Edelbrock, C. S. (1983). *Manual for the Child Behavior Checklist and Revised Child Behavior Profile.* Burlington, VT: Authors. (Available from T. M. Achenbach, Department of Psychiatry, 1 South Prospect Street, University of Vermont, Burlington, VT 05401).

Achenbach, T. M., Howell, C. T., Quay, H. C., & Connors, C. K. (1991). National survey of problems and competencies among four- to sixteen-year olds: Parents' reports for normative and clinical samples. *Monographs of the Society for Research in Child Development, 56*(3, Serial No. 225).

Achenbach, T. M., McConaughy, S. H., & Howell, C. T. (1987). Child/adolescent behavioral and emotional problems: Implications of cross-informant correlations for situational specificity. *Psychological Bulletin, 101,* 213–222.

American Psychiatric Association. (1980). *Diagnostic and statistical manual of mental disorders* (3rd ed.).Washington, DC: Author.

Anderson, J. C., Williams, S., McGee, R., & Silva, P. A. (1987). DSM-III disorders in preadolescent children: Prevalence in a large sample from the general population. *Archives of General Psychiatry, 44,* 69–76.

Asarnow, J. R., & Carlson, G. A. (1985). Depression self-rating scale: Utility with child psychiatric inpatients. *Journal of Consulting and Clinical Psychology, 53,* 491–499.

Bird, H. R., Gould, M. S., & Staghezza, B. M. (1993). Patterns of diagnostic comorbidity in a community sample of children aged 9 through 16 years. *Journal of the American Academy of Child and Adolescent Psychiatry, 32,* 361–368.

Bleuler, E. (1950). *Dementia praecox or the group of schizophrenias* (J. Zinkin, Trans.). New York: International Universities Press. (Original work published 1911)

Block, J. H., & Block, J. (1980). The role of ego-resiliency and ego-control in the organization of behavior. In W. A. Collins (Ed.), *Minnesota Symposium on Child Psychology* (Vol. 13; pp. 39–101). Hillsdale, NJ: Erlbaum.

Blumberg, S. H., & Izard, C. E. (1985). Affective and cognitive characteristics of depression in 10- and 11-year-old children. *Journal of Personality and Social Psychology, 49,* 194–202.

Castelfranchi, C., & Poggi, I. (1990). Blushing as discourse: Was Darwin wrong? In W. R. Crozier (Ed.), *Shyness and embarrassment: Perspectives from social psychology* (pp. 230–254). Cambridge, England: Cambridge University Press.

Cleckley, H. (1955). *The mask of sanity* (3rd ed.). St. Louis, MO: Mosby.

Coie, J. D., Dodge, K. A., Terry, R., & Wright, V. (1991). The role of aggression in peer relations: An analysis of aggression episodes in boys' peer relations. *Child Development, 62,* 812–826.

Cole, P. M., & Zahn-Waxler, C. (1992). Emotional dysregulation in disruptive behavior disorders. In D. Cicchetti & S. L. Toth (Eds.), *Rochester Symposium on Developmental Psychopathology: Vol. 4. Developmental perspectives on depression* (pp. 173–210). Rochester, NY: University of Rochester Press.

Davidson, R. J., Ekman, P., Saron, C., Senulius, J., & Friesen,. W. J. (1990). Emotional expression and brain physiology. I: Approach/withdrawal and cerebral asymmetry, *Journal of Personality and Social Psychology, 58,* 330–341.

Edelmann, R. J., & Hampson, S. E. (1979). Changes in non-verbal behavior during embarrassment. *British Journal of Social and Clinical Psychology, 18,* 385–390.

Ekman, P. (1984). Expression and the nature of emotion. In K. Scherer & P. Ekman (Eds.), *Approaches to emotion* (pp. 319–344). Hillsdale, NJ: Erlbaum.

Ekman, P. (1992). An argument for basic emotions. *Cognition and Emotion, 6,* 169–200.

Ekman, P. (1993). Facial expression and emotion. *American Psychologist, 48,* 384–392.

Ekman, P., & Friesen, W. V. (1976). Measuring facial movement. *Journal of Environmental Psychology and Nonverbal Behavior, 1,* 56–75.

Ekman, P., & Friesen, W. V. (1978). *Facial action coding system: A technique for the measurement of facial movement.* Palo Alto, CA: Consulting Psychologists Press.

Ekman, P., Friesen, W. V., & Ancoli, S. (1980). Facial signs of emotional experience. *Journal of Personality and Social Psychology, 39,* 1125–1134.

Ekman, P., Sorenson, E. R., & Friesen, W. V. (1969). Pan-cultural elements in facial displays of emotions. *Science, 16,* 86–88.

Fergusson, D. M., Hornwood, J., & Lynskey, M. T. (1993). Prevalence and comorbidity of DSM-III-R diagnoses in a birth cohort of 15 year olds. *Journal of the American Academy of Child and Adolescent Psychiatry, 32,* 1127–1134.

Finch, A. J., & Eastman, E. S. (1983). Multimethod approach to measuring anger in children. *Journal of Psychology, 115,* 55–60.

Finch, A. J., & Rogers, T. (1984). Self-report 4 instruments. In T. Ollendick & M. Hersen (Eds.), *Child behavioral assessment principles and procedures* (pp. 106–123). New York: Pergamon Press.

Frank, M., Ekman, P., & Friesen, W. V. (1993). Behavioral markers and recognizability of the smile of enjoyment. *Journal of Personality and Social Psychology, 64,* 83–93.

Frank, R. H. (1988). *Passions within reason.* New York: Norton.

Fridlund, A. J. (1992). The behavioral ecology and sociality of human faces. In M. S. Clark (Ed.), *Emotion: Review of personality and social psychology* (pp. 90–121). Newbury Park, CA: Sage.

Hare, R. D. (1978). Electrodermal and cardiovascular correlates of psychopathy. In R. D. Hare & D. Schalling (Eds.), *Psychopathic behavior: Approaches to research* (pp. 107–143). Chichester, England: Wiley.

Hinshaw, S. P. (1987). On the distinction between attentional deficits/hyperactivity and conduct problems/aggression in child psychopathology. *Psychological Bulletin, 101,* 443–463.

Izard, C. E. (1972). *Patterns of emotions: A new analysis of anxiety and depression.* New York: Academic Press.

Izard, C. E. (1977). *Human emotions.* New York: Plenum Press.

Kazdin, A. E., Colbus, D., & Rodgers, A. (1986). Assessment of depression and diagnosis of depressive disorder among psychiatrically disturbed children. *Journal of Abnormal Child Psychology, 14,* 499–515.

Keltner, D. (1995). The signs of appeasement: Evidence for distinct displays of embarrassment, amusement, and shame. *Journal of Personality and Social Psychology, 68,* 441–454.

Kochanska, G. (1993). Toward a synthesis of parental socialization and child temperament in early development of conscience. *Child Development, 64,* 325–347.

Kring, A. M., Kerr, S. L., Smith, D. A., & Neale, J. M. (1993). Flat affect in schizophrenia does not reflect diminished subjective experience of emotion. *Journal of Abnormal Psychology, 102,* 507–517.

Krueger, R. F., Caspi, A., Moffitt, T. E., White, J., & Stouthamer-Loeber, M. (in press). Delay of gratification, psychopathology and personality: Is low self-control specific to externalizing problems? *Journal of Personality.*

Krueger, R. F., Schmutte, P. S., Caspi, A., Moffitt, T. E., Campbell, K., & Silva, P. A., (1994). Personality traits are linked to crime among men and women: Evidence from a birth cohort. *Journal of Abnormal Psychology, 103,* 328–338.

Lazarus, R. S. (1991). *Emotion and adaptation.* New York: Oxford University Press.

Levenson, R. W., Ekman, P., & Friesen, W. V. (1990). Voluntary facial activity generates emotion-specific autonomic nervous system activity. *Psychophysiology, 27,* 363–384.

Lewis, M. (1993). Self-consciousness emotions: Embarrassment, pride, shame, and guilt. In M. Lewis & J. M. Haviland (Eds.), *Handbook of emotions* (pp. 353–364). New York: Guilford Press.

Loeber, R., Stouthamer-Loeber, M., Van Kammen, W., & Farrington, D. (1989). Development of a new measure for self-reported antisocial behavior for young children: Prevalence and reliability. In M. W. Klein (Ed.), *Cross-national research in self-reported crime and delinquency* (pp. 203–226). Dordrecht, The Netherlands: Kluwer.

Mabe, P. A., Treiber, F. A., & Riley, W. T. (1992). The relationship of anger to child psychopathology. *Child Psychiatry and Human Development, 22,* 151–164.

Miller, R. S., & Leary, M. R. (1992). Social sources and interactive functions of embarrassment. In M. Clark (Ed.), *Emotion and social behavior* (pp. 202–221). New York: Sage.

Moffitt, T. (1993). Adolescence-limited and life-course-persistent antisocial behavior: A developmental taxonomy. *Psychological Review, 100,* 674–701.

Newman, J. P. (1987). Reaction to punishment in extraverts and psychopaths: Implications for the impulsive behavior of disinhibited individuals. *Journal of Research in Personality, 21,* 464–480.

Ohman, A., Dimberg, U., & Esteves, F. (1989). Preattentive activation of aversive emotions. In T. Archer & L. G. Nilsson (Eds.), *Aversion, avoidance and anxiety: Perspectives on aversively motivated behavior.* Hillsdale, NJ: Erlbaum.

Rubin, K. H., Hymel, S., Mills, R. S. L., & Rose-Krasnor, L. (1991). Conceptualizing different developmental pathways to and from social isolation in childhood. In D. Cicchetti & S. L. Toth (Eds.), *Rochester Symposium on Developmental Psychopathology: Vol. 4. Developmental perspectives on depression* (pp. 91–122). Rochester, NY: University of Rochester Press.

Ruch, W. (1993). Exhilaration and humor. In M. Lewis & J. M. Haviland (Eds.), *The handbook of emotion* (pp. 605–616). New York: Guilford Press.

Ruma, E. H. (1967). *Conscience development in delinquents and nondelinquents: The relationship between moral judgment, guilt, and behavior.* Unpublished doctoral dissertation. Ohio State University, Columbus.

Ruma, E. H., & Mosher, D. L. (1967). Relationship between moral judgment and guilt in delinquent boys. *Journal of Abnormal Psychology, 72,* 122–127.

Schill, T. R., & Althoff, M. (1975). Drug experiences, knowledge, and attitudes of high and low guilty individuals. *Journal of Consulting and Clinical Psychology, 43,* 106–107.

Semin, G. R., & Manstead, A. S. R. (1982). The social implications of embarrassment displays and restitution behavior. *European Journal of Social Psychology, 12,* 367–377.

Tangney, J. P. (1991). Moral affect: The good, the bad, and the ugly. *Journal of Personality and Social Psychology, 61,* 598–607.

Tennenbaum, D. (1977). Personality and criminality: A summary and implications of the literature. *Journal of Criminal Justice, 5,* 225–235.

Thoits, P. A. (1985). Self-labeling processes in mental illness: The role of emotional deviance. *American Journal of Sociology, 91,* 221–249.

Tomkins, S. S. (1984). Affect theory. In K. Scherer & P. Ekman (Eds.), *Approaches to emotion* (pp. 163–195). Hillsdale, NJ: Erlbaum.

Watson, D., & Clark, L. A. (1992). On traits and temperaments: General and specific factors of emotional experience and their relation to the five factor model. *Journal of Personality, 60,* 441–476.

Watson, D., Clark, L. A., & Tellegen, A. (1988). Development and validation of brief measures of Positive and Negative Affect: The PANAS scales. *Journal of Personality and Social Psychology, 54,* 1063–1070.

Wechsler, D. (1974). *Manual for the Wechsler Intelligence Scale for Children—Revised.* New York: Psychological Corporation.

White, J. L., Moffitt, T. E., Caspi, A., Bartusch, D. J., Needles, D. J., & Stouthamer-Loeber, M. (1994). Measuring impulsivity and examining its relationship to delinquency. *Journal of Abnormal Psychology, 103,* 192–205.

Yudin, L. W. (1966). An abbreviated form of the WISC for use with emotionally disturbed children. *Journal of Consulting Psychology, 30,* 272–275.

AFTERWORD

Facial Expression, Personality, and Psychopathology

DACHER KELTNER

The article on adolescent psychopathology was motivated by the longstanding hypothesis that psychological disorders and personality traits are related to discrete emotion tendencies (e.g., Ekman, 1984; Goldsmith, 1993; Izard, 1972; Keltner, in press; Malatesta, 1990). According to this view, beginning early in life, individuals tend to experience and express certain emotions, which over the course of development become associated with habitual styles of social perception, communication, and interaction that define individuals' personalities and potential psychopathologies.

Establishing the links between personality, psychopathology, and facial expressions of emotion illuminates how traits and disorders are perceived by others, are responded to by others, and more generally, how personality and psychopathology shape the social environment (Keltner, in press). Based on this interest, we have examined the relations between facial expressions of emotion and the Five Factor Model of personality (FFM), which includes Extraversion (active, enthusiastic, sociable), Agreeableness (kind, sympathetic, friendly), Conscientiousness (dependable, reliable, thorough), Neuroticism, (unstable, anxious, self-pitying), and Openness to Experience (artistic, creative, imaginative). These five traits have been derived from extensive factor analytic studies of people's descriptions of their own and others' personalities and demonstrate impressive stability and heritability (John, 1990).

Previous studies yielded consistent correlations between Extraversion, Agreeableness, Conscientiousness, and Openness to Experience and *self-reports* of increased positive emotion, and between Neuroticism and *self-reports* of increased negative emotion (for review, see Keltner, in press). Our own research examined the relations between the FFM and facial expressions of emotion in different populations, ranging from adolescents to middle-aged adults, in different contexts, and using different measures of the FFM (Buswell & Keltner, 1995; Keltner, in press; Keltner & Bonanno, 1995; Keltner, Caspi, Krueger, & Stouthamer-Loeber, 1995).

Extraversion has consistently predicted facial expressions associated with social approach. Extraversion was positively correlated with increased Duchenne smiles of enjoyment and amusement, and in two studies with increased facial expressions of sadness, which we view as a signal of increased social approach. Consistent with this interpretation of sadness, bereaved adults' facial expressions of sadness were positively correlated with the size of their social networks ($r = .30$, $p < .05$), indicating that displays of sadness, much like Extraversion, are related to increased social contact (Keltner & Bonanno, 1995).

Neuroticism relates to three expressive tendencies that illuminate potential social problems associated with this trait. Summarizing across studies, Neuroticism was correlated with increased facial expressions of anger, contempt, and fear. In a study in which participants watched another person make an embarrassing face, Neurotic individuals showed increased facial expressions of distress, which predict avoidance of the distressed individual (Eisenberg et al., 1989). Finally, following an overpraise induction, Neuroticism was negatively correlated with participants' Duchenne smiles—the dominant response in the situation.

Agreeableness was positively correlated with facial expressions of emotion that would encourage cooperative, friendly social interactions consistent with the defining attributes of this trait. In two studies, Agreeableness was positively correlated with Duchenne laughter, which reduces social tension and increases social approach (Ruch, 1993). In another study, Agreeableness was negatively correlated with facial expressions of anger and disgust. Finally, in the empathic embarrassment study, more Agreeable participants were more likely to display sympathy for the embarrassed person, as indicated in increased oblique eyebrows of sadness, head movement forwards, and concerned gaze (Eisenberg et al., 1989).

The final findings regarding links between personality and emotion pertain to Conscientiousness, which was correlated with reduced facial expressions of negative emotion, increased Duchenne laughter, and with increased embarrassment, defined as a controlled smile, gaze aversion, head movements down and away and face touching (Keltner, 1995). These facial correlates of Conscientiousness are consistent with the defining attributes of the trait, which include impulse control, conventionality, and adherence to social norms.

These findings establish that certain traits are defined by tendencies towards discrete emotions: Extraversion predicts facial expressions of social approach; Neuroticism predicts facial expressions of negative emotion; Agreeableness predicts sympathy; and Conscientiousness predicts embarrassment. The studies also show that traits are often robustly related to the absence or inhibition of emotion: Neuroticism was related to reduced positive emotion, and Agreeableness and Conscientiousness were related to reduced negative emotion. Theories accounting for trait-related expressive behavior must account for occasions in which traits predict the absence of socially significant behavior. Finally, other analyses indicated that personality traits were most likely to predict the atypical, uncommon emotions within situations, and less likely to predict or be negatively related to the typical, common emotional responses to situations.

A second line of research has examined whether facial expressions of negative emotion predict poor psychological adjustment to trauma, consistent with the health and psychological correlates of the disposition to experience negative affect (Watson & Clark, 1984). We addressed this question in a study of mid-life conjugal bereavement, examining whether the emotions expressed in the face and self-report following a bereavement interview 6 months post loss predict grief symptoms 14 months following the loss of the spouse (Bonanno & Keltner, 1995; Bonanno, Keltner, Holen, &

Horowitz, in press). Directly contradicting the widely accepted cartharsis hypothesis of grief, bereaved adults' facial expressions of negative emotion shown during the 6 month interview predicted *increased* grief severity at 14 months ($r = .64, p < .0001$). In contrast, participants' facial expressions of Duchenne laughter and smiles of enjoyment predicted reduced grief severity at 14 months ($r = .38, p < .001$). We are currently exploring the hypothesis that high levels of expressed negative emotion disrupt inter- and intrapersonal functioning, thus aggravating grief symptoms.

References

Bonanno, G., & Keltner, D. (1995). *The negative consequences of expressing negative emotion during bereavement.* Unpublished manuscript.

Bonanno, G. A., Keltner, D., Holen, A., Horowitz, M. J. (in press). When avoiding unpleasant emotions might not be such a bad thing: Verbal-autonomic response dissociation and midlife conjugal bereavement. *Journal of Personality and Social Psychology.*

Buswell, B. N., & Keltner, D. (1995). *The themes and variants of embarrassment: A study of social facial expression across three embarrassing situations.* Manuscript under review.

Eisenberg, N., Fabes, R. A., Miller, P. A., Fultz, J., Shell, R., Mathy, R. M., & Reno, R. R. (1989). Relation of sympathy and personal distress to prosocial behavior: A multimethod study. *Journal of Personality and Social Psychology, 57,* 55–66.

Ekman, P. (1984). Expression and the nature of emotion. In K. Scherer & P. Ekman (Eds.), *Approaches to emotion* (pp. 319–344). Hillsdale, NJ: Erlbaum.

Goldsmith, H. H. (1993). Temperament: variability in developing emotion systems. In M. Lewis & J. Haviland (Eds.), *The handbook of emotions* (pp. 353–364). New York: Guilford.

Izard, C. E. (1972). *Patterns of emotions: A new analysis of anxiety and depression.* New York: Academic Press.

John, O. P. (1990). The "big five" factor taxonomy: Dimensions of personality in the natural language and in questionnaires. In L. Pervin (Ed.), *Handbook of personality theory and research.* New York: Guilford.

Keltner, D. (in press). Facial expressions of emotion and personality. In C. Malatesta-Magai and S. H. McFadden (Eds.), *Handbook of emotion, aging, and the lifecourse.* New York: Academic Press.

Keltner, D., & Bonanno, G. (1995). *Facial expressions of emotion, personality and bereavement.* Manuscript under review.

Keltner, D., Caspi, A., Krueger, R. F., & Stouthamer-Loeber, M. (1995). *Personality and facial expressions of emotion.* Manuscript under review.

Malatesta, C. Z. (1990). The role of emotions in the development and organization of personality. In R. A. Thompson (Ed.), *Nebraska Symposium on Motivation: Vol. 36. Socioemotional development* (pp. 1–56). Lincoln: University of Nebraska Press.

Ruch, W. (1993). Exhilaration and humor. In M. Lewis & J. M. Haviland (Eds.), *The handbook of emotion* (pp. 605–616). New York: Guilford.

Tellegen, A. (1985). Structures of mood and personality and their relevance to assessing anxiety, with an emphasis on self-report. In A. H. Tuma & J. Mason (Eds.), *Anxiety and the anxiety disorders* (pp. 681–707). Hillsdale, NJ: Erlbaum.

Watson, D., & Clark, L. A. (1984). Negative affectivity: The disposition to experience aversive arousal states. *Psychological Bulletin, 96,* 465–490.

Watson, D., & Clark, L. A. (1992). On traits and temperament: General and specific factors of emotional experience and their relation to the five factor model. *Journal of Personality, 60,* 441–476.

22

Type A Behavior Pattern

Facial Behavior and Speech Components

MARGARET A. CHESNEY, PAUL EKMAN, WALLACE V. FRIESEN,
GEORGE W. BLACK & MICHAEL H. L. HECKER

The behavioral components comprising the Type A coronary-prone pattern have been receiving increased attention in recent years. For the most part, these studies have concentrated on such components conveyed in speech reflecting competitive, aggressive, or hostile attitudes, and a sense of time urgency. However, as originally described by Rosenman et al. (1964), Type A behavior is also marked by nonverbal or motoric signs including "facial grimaces, scowls, teeth-clenching, and tic in which teeth are clenched and masseter muscles are tensed" (p. 2). The purpose of this study was to examine facial behaviors as components of the Type A behavior pattern.

The leading procedure for assessing Type A behavior is the Structured Interview (SI), which consists of 26 questions about the subject's characteristic responses to a variety of common situations that have the potential to elicit competitiveness, irritation, and impatience (Rosenman, 1978; Chesney, Eagleston, & Rosenman, 1981). Typically, judges classify subjects as Type A or Type B based on the content and speech stylistics of the subjects' interview responses (Rosenman, 1978). However, in describing the use of the SI to assess Type A behavior, Rosenman (1978) also drew attention to the facial characteristics of the Type A as being "extraordinarily alert; that is, his eyes are very much alive, more quickly seeking to take in the situation at a glance. He may employ a tense, teeth-clenching and jaw-grinding posture. His smile has a lateral extension rather than an oval . . . one senses that there is a set type of hostility in the face, mostly evidenced by the eyes." Consistent with this description, ratings of the behavior pattern in the Western Collaborative Group Study (WCGS), (the primary study demonstrating the relationship of Type A behavior to coronary heart disease incidence) were based on both a checklist of interviewer's observations of each subject's nonverbal behaviors, including facial tension and lateral smiling, and the audiotape-recorded speech behavior (Rosenman et al., 1964). Thus, while facial and other nonverbal behaviors were considered originally to be an integral part of the behavior pattern, they have not been included in rating the global behavior pattern since the WCGS.

The evidence that Type A behavior is a coronary heart disease (CHD) risk factor derives from prospective, population-based studies showing that, controlling for standard risk factors, subjects exhibiting Type A behavior are more likely to develop clinical CHD than subjects exhibiting the converse, Type B behavior pattern (Rosenman, Brand, Sholtz, & Friedman, 1976; Haynes, Feinleib, Levine, Scotch, & Kennel, 1982; French-Belgian Group, 1962). Additional evidence is provided by studies examining the relationship of Type A behavior to severity of coronary artery disease determined by autopsy (Friedman, Rosenman, Straus, Wurm, Kositchek, 1968) and angiography (Blumenthal, Williams, Kong, Schanberg, & Thompson, 1978; Frank, Heller, Kornfeld, Sporn, & Weiss, 1978; Williams et al., 1980). Not all studies of the association between Type A behavior and CHD endpoints have been confirmatory (Cohen & Reed, 1985; Shekelle, Gale, & Norusis, 1985; Shekelle et al., 1985; Dimsdale, Block, Catanzano, Hackett, & Hutter, 1978; Dimsdale et al., 1979). One of the explanations of the failure to observe a relationship is that the assessment of the behavior pattern lacks precision (Dembroski, MacDougall, Williams, Haney, & Blumenthal, 1985). This has prompted recommendations that studies "measure individual Type A behaviors, particularly hostility and anger-expression, as well as global Type A." (p. 956) (Matthews & Haynes, 1986; Haynes & Matthews, 1988).

Investigators have attempted to provide more objective measurements of Type A behavior by coding components of the behavior pattern based on speech stylistics (Matthews, Glass, Rosenman, & Bortner, 1977; Dembroski, MacDougall, Herd, & Shield, 1983; Chesney, Hecker, & Black, 1988; Carmelli, Swan, Rosenman, Hecker, & Ragland, 1989; Hecker, Chesney, Black, & Frautschi, 1988). In a component reassessment of the interviews from the WCGS, hostility, competitiveness, speaking rate, immediateness, and Type A content were found to be significantly related to CHD incidence at the 8.5-year follow-up (Chesney, Hecker, & Black, 1988), and both CHD and cancer mortality at a 22-year follow-up (Carmelli et al., 1989). Among these predictive components, only hostility remained a significant risk factor when all the other Type A components scored were included in a multivariate analysis (Hecker, Chesney, & Black, 1988). In the Multiple Risk Factor Intervention Trial, ratings of stylistic hostility in Type A interviews have been found to be independently associated with increased CHD incidence, while global Type A behavior failed to show such a relationship (Dembroski, MacDougall, Costa, & Grandits, 1989).

Efforts to develop objective measurements of Type A behavior have also included nonverbal behaviors. Blumenthal et al. (Blumenthal, O'Toole, & Haney, 1984) scored movement of the arms, legs, hands, and feet or positional changes during Structured Interviews given on two occasions 4 months apart. Although this summary measurement of movement was found to be stable, it did not distinguish between Type A and Type B subjects. Heller (1980) scored hand movement during the SI and found significant differences between Type As and Type Bs in the frequency per minute of those hand movements that accompany speech. However, when the effect of speaking rate was taken into account, the differences were no longer significant. Friedman, Harris, and Hall (1964) proposed subgrouping Type As and Type Bs on the basis of verbal and nonverbal behaviors, and certain personality characteristics. They found that Type As who had high scores on a defensive-hostility factor (based on such nonverbal behaviors as fist making, postural shifts, and emphatic gestures) had more missing peripheral pulses than Type As who had low scores on this factor. This difference was discussed as a possible indication of peripheral vascular disease in the former group of Type As.

Facial behaviors received particular attention in a prospective study of postmyocardial-infarction patients. For that study, Friedman and Powell (1984) developed a protocol for scoring the SI which included seven facial behaviors: eye contact breaks; eye blinks; eyebrow lifts; brow knits; mouth corner back grimace, head emphasis movements; facial tautness suggesting emotions, as indicated by horizontal forehead furrows; facial tautness suggesting hostility as indicated by vertical furrows between the brows and/or tight lip muscles. Powell and Thoresen (1985) found that head emphasis movements, muscle tension in the eyes and eyebrow lifts were significant predictors of recurrent CHD in univariate analyses. However, when these nonverbal indices were examined in multivariate analyses with other behavioral variables, the nonverbal behaviors were no longer significant.

The rationale for measuring facial behavior in the study of Type A behavior goes beyond these observations about specific, facial behavior. Aggressiveness (Rosenman & Friedman, 1961), hostile feelings (Rosenman et al., 1964), potential for hostility (Dembroski et al., 1989), and anger (Powell & Thoresen, 1985) are central affective qualities said to characterize Type A individuals. While these qualities are manifest in a variety of behavioral modes, facial expression is considered by many theorists to be the central signal system for emotion (Tomkins, 1962; Plutchik, 1962; Ekman, Friesen, & Ellsworth, 1972; Izard, 1972). Moreover, cross cultural research has established biologically based, universal facial expressions relevant to these affective states (see Ekman, 1989, for a recent review of the evidence). Type A research would suggest that anger expressions should be more frequent in Type A individuals but so also might disgust and contempt facial expressions, which are considered by most emotion theorists (e.g., Tomkins, 1962; Plutchik, 1962; Izard, 1972) to be related to aggressiveness and hostility.

Despite this rationale for examining facial behavior, no study of Type A individuals has systematically measured all of the possible signs noted in the literature, let alone all of the facial expressions related to hostility. One impediment for such work is that some of the hypothesized facial signs are described too vaguely to allow objective measurement. Perhaps more importantly, precise techniques for comprehensively and objectively measuring observable facial behavior have become available only in the last 10 years (see Ekman, 1982 for a review), and their use requires highly specialized training. The rationale for our collaboration was to combine strategies in facial measurement of Ekman and Friesen (Ekman & Friesen, 1976, 1978) with the assessment of Type A behavior of Chesney et al. (1988), thereby allowing comprehensive study of the range of facial expressions which might be diagnostic of the Type A behavior pattern.

The present study evaluated whether there are facial behaviors characteristic of the Type A behavior pattern. Facial movements during the SI were measured using techniques based on Ekman and Friesen's Facial Action Coding System (1976, 1978). In addition, the SI was coded for speech components so that the relationship between facial behavior and speech could be examined. Finally, heart rate during the SI was assessed so that relationships among facial behaviors, Type A behavior pattern, and cardiac activity could be examined.

Method

Subjects

Subjects were 48 male salaried employees in predominantly managerial positions at an aerospace firm in the San Francisco Bay Area (mean age 50.6 years). These subjects had participated in a study of work-related stress 4 years before the present study and none had a history of heart disease. They were selected from a larger sample of 85 males on the basis of their classifications as Type A or Type B according to the SI, which was administered following the procedure described below. These interviews were rated independently by three judges using the five-point scale (A1, A2, X, B3, and B4). The ratings were performed using audiotape recordings of the SI by judges who were blind to the facial and heart rate data. Using these ratings, the subjects were rank-ordered from subjects rated by all three judges as A1 to those rated by all three judges as B4. The upper 24 were designated Type A and the lower 24, Type B. In addition to this ranking procedure, subjects were assigned Type A or Type B ratings based on a majority rule, i.e., two of the three judges in agreement that the subject was Type A (A1 or A2) or Type B (B3 or B4). In cases where there was no majority rating, the three judges met and arrived at a consensus. These majority or consensus ratings were compared with the rankings. All of the upper 24 subjects had been rated Type A and all of the lower 24 subjects had been rated Type B.

Procedure

After a resting baseline period of 6 minutes, subjects were administered the SI by an interviewer trained in administration of the Type A interview. Electrocardiographic (ECG) data were collected throughout the interview by ECG electrodes taped over the subjects' right clavicle and lowest left rib. ECG data were recorded on a Beckman polygraph Model R-511A and an Ampex FM recorder.

Subjects' interviews were audiotaped using a Nakamichi Model 550 recorder with a remote Sony ECM-50 microphone, and videotaped using a Sony Model SL0323 recorder. All recordings were given time designations for later correspondence by a Systron-Donner time code generator Model 8152.

Heart rate was scored by a MINC DECLAB computer using interbeat intervals on the ECG. Baseline heart rate was scored as the mean heart rate during the 6th minute of the baseline period. Heart rate responsivity was calculated as the difference between the mean heart rate during the SI and the mean heart rate during the baseline period. The cumulative frequency distribution of heart rate during the SI was derived for each subject and heart rate variability computed as the difference between the 90th- and 50th-percentile heart rates.

Facial Measurement

Facial movements were measured from the videotaped SI recordings for each subject using Ekman and Friesen's Facial Action Coding System (FACS) (1976, 1978). This is an anatomically based, comprehensive, objective technique for measuring all observable facial movement. With this system, trained scorers decomposed all facial expressions occurring during the SI into their elemental muscular actions when any one of 33 predefined combinations of facial actions are observed. These 33 combinations of facial actions include all of the facial configurations that have been established empirically (Ekman, 1989; Ekman & Friesen, 1978) to signal the seven emotions that have universal expressions: anger, fear, disgust, sadness, happiness, contempt, and surprise. FACS scoring is performed, however, in descriptive behavioral terms, rather than making inferences about these underlying emotional states. The scores for a particular expression consist of the list of muscular actions that are determined to have produced it. Repeated viewing of the videotaped record is necessary for scoring and to evaluate interscorer agreement.

The facial muscular scores obtained are then converted by a computer dictionary into emotion scores. While the dictionary was originally based on empirical theory, research has since provided evidence for the validity of the facial action patterns. This includes cross-cultural studies (Ekman, 1989), correlations with reports of subjective experience and differentiation of specific patterns of physiological activity co-occurring with specific expressions (Ekman, Levenson, & Friesen, 1983; Ekman, Davidson, & Friesen, in press).

For the present study, the videotaped SIs were randomly assigned to two experienced scorers who had either 1 or 4 years of experience measuring facial behavior and who had shown interscorer reliability estimates exceeding 0.80 for FACS scores prior to their scoring the videotapes for this study. These scorers did not know whether the subjects had been classified as Type A or Type B, and were unfamiliar with the literature about Type A behavior. The scoring was performed on the videotapes without sound.

Scores were obtained on the frequency of seven single emotions (anger, fear, disgust, sadness, happiness, contempt, and surprise) and the co-occurrence of two or more of these emotions in blends. Because the incidence of Fear and Sad scores was quite low, these two nonhostile, negative emotions were also combined into a single category of Fear plus Sad, in addition to considering them separately. The dictionary also provides a distinction between enjoyment smiles and other smiles not related to feelings of enjoyment. Enjoyment smiles are presumed to have been made involuntarily and have been found to be associated with the subjective experience of positive affect and associated physiological changes (Ekman, 1989; Ekman, Davidson, & Friesen, 1990). Alternatively, other smiles are presumed to have been made voluntarily, and have been found not to be associated with positive affect nor with physiological changes unique to enjoyment.

Specific combinations of facial actions that were suggested by the literature on facial expression and Type A behavior were also scored. Table 22.1 lists the observations about facial expressions found in the literature on Type A behavior, the relevant facial behavior that was scored, and how that behavior is interpreted by FACS, based on facial expression literature. Items 1 through 4 in table 22.1 are separate elements of what together comprise an anger expression (Ekman, 1989; Ekman & Friesen, 1978). Singly they are ambiguous: they may be signals of anger that is being inhibited or censored; or they may be quite unrelated to anger. For example, teeth clenching (item 3) occurs as a mannerism or when a person is attempting to inhibit the vocal expression of any emotion, whether it be fear, distress, disgust, or anger. The lowered brow (item 1) and the tightened lower eyelid (item 2) may occur when a person is thinking or concentrating, or if the person is having difficulty understanding what someone else is saying or having difficulty determining what to say next (Ekman, 1979). Usually when these actions signal such cognitive activity, the person also gazes away from the interviewer. To focus on actions that might be more relevant to hostility and not signs of cognitive activity, only those instances of items 1 and 2 in which the subject was looking toward the interviewer were considered. Since they involve actions in the same region of the face

TABLE 22.1. Correspondence between facial signs from the Type A literature and FACS

Facial Sign from Type A Literature	Relevant Facial Activity Scored	Interpretation from Facial Expression Literature
1. Scowl, brow knit, vertical furrows between brows	Brow lowered and pulled together by corrugator muscle	Anger, if accompanied by upper eyelid raise and/or tightened lower eyelid and/or pressed or tightened lips
2. Hostility in the eyes	Upper lid raised by upper lid levator and lower lid tightened by orbicularis oculi pars palebralis muscles	Anger, if brow lowered and/or lips pressed or tightened
3. Teeth-clenched, masseter muscle tensed	Bulge at mandible produced by masseter muscle	Can occur with anger, or attempts to control any emotion
4. Tight lips	Tightened lips by inner strands of orbicularis oris muscle	Possible anger
5. Lateral smile, mouth corner back, grimace	Lip corners pulled up and/or stretched horizontally by zygomatic major and/or risorious muscles	Happy and/or possible fear
6. Brow raise or lift horizontal forehead	Brow raise and horizontal forehead furrows are produced by the frontalis muscle	Surprise only if accompanied by upper eyelid raise and/or jaw dropped open

and subject to the same interpretation, we combined items 1 and 2 into a single score which we refer to as Glare in which the brows are lowered, the upper eyelid is raised and/or the lower eyes are tensed, and the gaze is directed at the other person.

Speech Component Measurement

A component scoring procedure was used to assess Type A components from subjects speech stylistics and content during the audiotaped interviews. A detailed description of this procedure is presented elsewhere (Chesney et al., 1988). This procedure involves the division of the SI into 20 segments. Each segment begins with one of 20 key questions in the interview and includes all of the subjects' responses to the key question and all subsequent dialogue until the next key question is asked. In this manner, all of the subjects' speech during the interview were scored, including speech that coincided with that of the interviewer. The subjects' speech stylistics and content were scored in terms of 12 operationally defined components. Previously described facets of the Type A behavior pattern (Rosenman et al., 1964), as well as other variables thought to be related to CHD risk comprised the behaviors that were measured using this procedure.

The recorded interviews were played back three times in order to complete an assessment of the components. Each component was given a score on a five-point scale for each interview segment or set of segments (from 0 to 4). This score indicated the extent to which a given component behavior was present during the SI. Scores were summed for each component across the interview segments and the total score was used in analyses. The speech components of the SIs were coded by one of the authors (MHLH) and originators of the speech component scoring procedure. This scoring was done without knowledge of the subject's classification as Type A or Type B.

Statistical Analysis

Preliminary examination of the data revealed that the distributions of FACS scores were highly skewed and that the variance of FACS scores within Type A and Type B groups was related to the means for those groups. For this reason it was decided to use nonparametric statistical tests in the data analysis instead of the classical methods. In particular, the Wilcoxon-Mann-Whitney test based on the ranks of the data was used to compare Type As and Type Bs on FACS scores. The Wilcoxon-Mann-Whitney test was also used to compare Type As and Type Bs on speech component scores. This test provides a t-statistic which then was used in conjunction with the usual published tables for the t-distribution. Residuals from a regression of FACS scores on speech component scores were used for a Wilcoxon-Mann Whitney test to compare Type As and Type Bs on FACS scores adjusted for speech component scores. Spearman rank-order correlations were used to assess the association of cardiovascular measures with FACS and speech component scores.

Results

Means for the FACS scores for Type As and Type Bs are shown in table 22.2. Type A subjects were found to have significantly higher scores on Glare and Disgust than Type Bs. Means on the speech components for Type As and Type Bs are presented in table 22.3. Significant differences were found between the two behavior types on each of the components with the exception of Exactingness (i.e., attention to detail). The significant differences observed were in the expected direction, i.e., Type As expressed more of every component except Despondency, which is more characteristic of Type B speech behavior (Chesney et al., 1988). It is important to note that the classification of subjects as Type A or Type B is based on global clinical ratings of the speech stylistics and content on audiotape recordings of the SI. Thus, the correlation between the speech components and global ratings are likely to be inflated due to common method variance. The largest differences between Type As and Type Bs were observed for Syllabic Emphasis, Loudness of Voice, Hostility, and Speaking Rate.

The correlations between FACS scores and the speech components were examined in order to provide further information on the constructs assessed by FACS. The correlations among the FACS scores for Glare, Disgust, Contempt, and Anger were also examined since, as mentioned in the Introduction, Disgust, Anger, and Contempt are presumed to be related to hostility or aggressive reactions. As shown in table 22.4, there are significant relationships between a number of these measures. In particular, the Glare facial score correlated significantly with Hostility and Competitiveness, two of the speech components that have been previously shown to be associated with CHD incidence (Chesney et al., 1988). Disgust, another facial behavior on which Type As and

TABLE **22.2.** FACS percentile Scores for Type As and Type Bs

Behavior Type	Type A		Type B			
	X	SD	X	SD	t	p*
Facial components						
Disgust	59.9	27.8	40.1	25.3	2.57	0.01
Fear & Sad	56.4	27.9	43.6	22.1	1.77	
Sad	55.3	27.2	44.7	20.7	1.52	
Smile-Nonenjoyment	55.7	25.9	44.3	31.6	1.37	
Smile-Enjoyment	50.3	26.2	49.7	32.4	0.06	
Anger	45.0	28.6	55.0	29.4	-1.20	
Contempt	50.3	29.4	49.7	29.0	0.08	
Fear	52.8	24.7	47.2	19.5	0.88	
Surprise	52.4	25.7	47.6	19.8	0.73	
Glare	62.8	27.4	37.2	25.1	3.38	0.001
Teeth clench	50.2	17.5	49.8	16.3	0.09	
Tight lips	52.1	27.3	47.9	31.4	0.49	
Lateral smile	49.6	21.6	50.4	23.2	-0.13	
Brow raise	52.4	29.9	47.6	28.8	0.57	

* *p* values are two-tailed.

Bs were found to differ, was significantly associated with the following Speech components: Hostility and Competitiveness. Unlike Glare, the Anger facial components did not show a positive association with any of the speech components. Contempt was significantly related to Despondency (r = 0.34, p < 0.01). There were several significant correlations observed among the FACS scores. The correlation between Glare and Dis-

TABLE **22.3.** Speech component percentile scores for Type As and Type Bs

Behavior Type	Type A		Type B			
	X	SD	X	SD	t	p*
Speech Components						
Hostility	67.7	25.0	32.3	20.7	5.35	0.001
Competitiveness	63.8	26.6	36.2	25.1	3.70	0.001
Immediateness	63.8	22.6	36.2	28.6	3.72	0.001
Speaking Rate	65.3	16.9	34.7	23.8	5.15	0.001
Type A Content	59.9	31.1	40.1	23.7	2.47	0.01
Anger-Out	61.2	28.3	38.8	25.6	2.89	0.005
Self-Aggrandizement	61.4	26.2	38.6	27.3	2.95	0.004
Exactingness	53.1	29.7	46.9	28.8	0.74	
Despondency	43.0	26.4	57.0	28.7	-1.75	
Loudness	67.5	24.3	32.5	20.2	5.44	0.001
Syllabic Emphasis	70.1	22.4	29.9	16.8	7.02	0.001
Acceleration	57.5	30.4	42.5	25.4	1.85	
Hard Voice	61.4	21.1	38.6	21.2	3.74	0.001

* *p* values are two-tailed.

TABLE 22.4. Correlations between FAC scores and speech components

FACS Components	Glare	Disgust	Anger	Contempt
Speech Components				
Hostility	0.411**	0.339**	−0.167	0.035
Competitiveness	0.367**	0.317*	−0.110	0.039
Immediateness	0.100	0.156	−0.258	−0.206
Speaking Rate	0.1512	0.180	−0.342	−0.092
Type A Content	0.144	0.062	0.024	−0.204
Anger-Out	0.292*	0.235	0.054	0.047
Self-Aggrandizement	−0.002	0.064	−0.077	−0.151
Exactingness	0.143	0.167	−0.061	0.040
Despondency	0.229	0.167	0.120	0.335**
Loudness	0.423**	0.248	−0.082	0.023
Syllabic Emphasis	0.339**	0.241	−0.120	−0.107
Acceleration	0.303*	0.253	0.233	0.108
Hard Voice	0.135	0.143	0.063	−0.234
FACS Components				
Contempt	0.180	0.308*	0.303*	
Anger	−0.117	0.130		
Disgust	0.390**			

$*p < .05$, $**p < .01$; p values are two-tailed.

gust was significant ($r = 0.39$, $p < 0.01$). Contempt was significant related to both Anger and Disgust but not Glare.

The extent to which the relationship of Type A to Glare and Disgust was due to the Hostility and Competitive components of Type A behavior was examined using Glare and Disgust scores adjusted for the two speech components. No significant differences between Type As and Type Bs on these two facial behaviors were observed when these scores were adjusted.

The strength of the association between FACS scores and the cardiovascular reactivity measures was assessed by testing the Spearman rank correlation coefficient for each pairing of FACS score and the two cardiac measures. Heart rate variability was positively associated with Nonenjoyment Smiles, and heart rate responsivity was negatively associated with this same facial behavior. This indicates that those subjects showing more Nonenjoyment Smiles had more heart rate variability ($p < 0.02$) but less magnitude of overall change in heart rate ($p < 0.04$) during the SI. None of the other relationships between FACS scores and the cardiac reactivity measures was significant. Subjects were also divided into high and low groups based on their FACS scores on Glare and Disgust. Similar analyses of variance for heart rate measures showed no significant differences among the Type A/B-FACS score subgroups.

The relationship between the speech component scores and the cardiovascular reactivity measures as well as the extent of differences between Type As and Bs in cardiovascular reactivity were also examined. None of the relationships between the speech component scores and cardiac reactivity measures was significant. Also, there were no significant differences between the two behavior types for either heart rate responsivity or heart rate variability.

Discussion

Facial behavior—Disgust and Glare—differentiated Type As from Bs. None of the other facial behaviors studied, including those noted in the clinical literature describing Type A behavior (see table 22.1), showed significant differences between Type As and Bs. With regard to the facial behaviors originally described as characteristic of Type As, it is possible that the early Type A researchers noted differences between Type As and Bs in facial behaviors but, without the benefit of the precise FACS scoring, were unable to adequately define or assess these facial expressions. Since Type As have been described as hostile and aggressive, it might seem surprising that the Type As did not show more anger or contempt facial expressions than did the Bs. Understanding this finding and reconciling it with the positive finding on the Glare score and Disgust requires drawing some theoretical distinctions among affective phenomena.

Emotional traits, such as hostility, can be distinguished from moods, such as irritability, as well as from the emotions such as anger (Ekman, 1984). An emotion involves, from this perspective, a momentary and patterned set of changes in physiology, cognitive activity, subjective feelings, and facial expression. Moods involve much more extended periods of time, hours, or even days, as compared with the second or minutes for emotions. Each mood is saturated with frequent occurrences of a particular emotion(s). When someone is in an irritable mood, he/she is ready to become angry, likely to construe matters in such a way so as to have the opportunity to become angry, and his/her anger when it occurs is likely to be more intense and of greater duration than it would be when he/she is are not in an irritable mood. A trait refers to an even longer span of time than a mood. A trait is considered to be a characteristic style of behavior which predominates at least during a life epoch or phase, and perhaps across more than one epoch in the life span. A hostile trait may be manifested by frequent bouts of irritability, by an aggressive behavioral style, or in impatience, abruptness, and related behaviors.

The Anger facial expression assessed in the present study reflects the emotion of anger. It was rarely displayed by the subjects during the interviews examined in this study, and did not differ in occurrence for Type As or Bs. The salaried, predominantly management, people who were our subjects may have learned, we presume, to monitor and suppress anger expression. This might be especially so for Type A individuals holding such jobs who may have learned the negative consequences of not inhibiting expressions of their anger.

The brows/lowered eyelids tense activity, a category of facial behavior that we developed on the basis of observations in the clinical literature about the appearance of Type A individuals, is open to three interpretations: (1) Glare might be the result of attempts to inhibit the full expression of the anger emotion. The Type A who becomes angry may have attempted to suppress the anger, managing to block its appearance in the lips, with only a fragment of the full anger expression escaping censorship, manifest in the brows and/or eyes. (2) This registration of anger in the upper part of the face might reflect a low intensity of anger elicited by the SI which, though challenging, does not typically provoke anger. (3) The Glare facial expression may mark the trait of hostility not the emotion of anger. With this latter interpretation, Glare represents the aggressive or hostile stance one person takes toward others.

While we have no definitive data to allow a choice between these three interpretations, the lack of a significant relationship between the Glare and Anger scores is consistent with the second and third interpretation. Recent research by others (Suarez & Williams, 1989) also provides support for these two interpretations. This research showed that only when a challenging laboratory task was administered in a manner involving harassment of the subject by the experimenter did subjects who had scored high on a personality trait measure of hostility show increases in anger. The same task administered without harassment failed to elicit such anger increases (Suarez & Williams, 1989). Similarly, in the present study, the SI was not presented in a harassing manner and thus may have not been sufficiently challenging to provide the emotions of anger or contempt. It is of interest that in the previously described laboratory experiment (Suarez & Williams, 1989), those high in hostility showed enhanced cardiovascular arousal only in response to the harassment condition. This finding may also explain the failure in the present study to observe relationships between hostility and cardiovascular reactivity.

The relationship between the Glare score and the Hostility speech component provides further support for the third interpretation. The speech components are conceptualized as measuring a style of speaking associated with the enduring behavioral pattern not with a momentary emotion. Indeed these speech components, which show the highest correlation with Glare score, predicted CHD (Chesney et al., 1988; Carmelli et al., 1989; Hecker et al., 1988). The facial score of the emotion anger was inversely (but not significantly) correlated with these speech component measures.

Questions might be raised about why the Type A subjects showed more Disgust than the Bs, especially since they did not differ on Anger. Although Disgust is an emotion like anger, it may not be the emotion that the Type A subjects are vigilantly monitoring and suppressing. The expression of Disgust might reflect, at least in part, the shifting of angry feelings to this less censored but related emotion. As was the case with Glare, a different but not contradictory explanation for the difference between Type As and Bs in Disgust is that the expression of this emotion reflects an underlying trait of hostility. In conjunction with this interpretation, it is relevant that research has shown a relationship of emotions related to Disgust—cynicism and hostility—to the severity of atherosclerosis (Blumenthal et al., 1978; Williams et al., 1980; Dembroski et al., 1985).

The findings on facial behavior raise the question as to whether these measures would add to more conventionally used approaches to identifying individuals at increased risk for CHD. The results of the analysis using the adjusted facial behavior scores indicated that the higher Glare and Disgust scores in the Type As compared with the Type Bs are accounted for by the strong relationship of hostility to Glare and Disgust. These results suggest that the Glare and Disgust facial behaviors are an expression of the increased hostility of Type A individuals. Given that the Hostility speech component was found in prospective research to be the strongest predictor of CHD (Chesney et al., 1988; Carmelli et al., 1989; Hecker et al., 1988), and that Glare and Disgust correlated significantly with this component in the present study, there is the possibility that these facial expressions may add new dimensions to the assessment of coronary-prone behavior.

The question for further research is to explore how these measures of facial and speech behavioral components interrelate in predicting CHD. To what extent does adding facial behavior scores such as Glare assist in identifying individuals who are coronary-prone? Might it be that those who manifest both hostile facial and speech components are at the greatest risk? Among those whose facial and speech components are not consonant, is one or another set of components more successful in predicting CHD, or are these people not at risk?

Acknowledgments

We wish to express our appreciation to Dr. Marcia Ward for her assistance with the assessment of the cardiovascular reactivity and to thank Drs. David Keegan and Gary Schwartz for suggesting this worthwhile collaboration.

This research was supported by grants HL25990 and HL26042 from the National Heart Lung and Blood Institute. Dr. Paul Ekman was also supported by Research Scientist Award MH06092 from the National Institute of Mental Health. This research was conducted when the first author was at SRI International.

References

Blumenthal, J. A., O'Toole, L. C., & Haney, T. (1984). Behavioral assessment of the Type A behavior pattern. *Psychosomatic Medicine, 46,* 415–423.

Blumenthal, J. A., Williams, R., Kong, Y., Schanberg, S. M., & Thompson, L. W. (1978). Type A behavior and angiographically documented coronary disease. *Circulation, 58,* 634–639.

Carmelli, D., Swan, G. E., Rosenman, R. H., Hecker, M. H., & Ragland, D. R. (1989). *Behavioral components and total mortality in the Western Collaborative Group Study.* Paper presented at the Society of Behavioral Medicine, San Francisco, California.

Chesney, M. A., Eagleston, J. E., & Rosenman, R. H. (1981). Type A behavior: Definition, assessment and intervention. In C. K. Prokop & L. A. Bradley (Eds.), *Medical psychology: A new perspective* (pp. 2–36). New York. Academic Press.

Chesney, M. A., Hecker, M. H. L., & Black, G. W. (1988). Coronary-prone components of Type A behavior in the WCGS: A new methodology. In B. K. Houston, & C. R. Snyder (Eds.), *Type A behavior pattern: Research, theory and intervention* (pp. 165–188). New York: Wiley.

Cohen, J. B., & Reed, D. (1985). Type A behavior and coronary heart disease among Japanese men in Hawaii. *Journal of Behavioral Medicine, 8,* 343–352.

Dembroski, T. M., MacDougall, J. M., Costa, P. T., & Grandits, G. A. (1989). Components of hostility as predictors of sudden death and myocardial infarction in the Multiple Risk Factor Intervention Trial. *Psychosomatic Medicine, 51,* 514–522.

Dembroski, T. M., MacDougall, J. M., Herd, J. A., & Shields, J. L. (1983). Perspectives on coronary-prone behavior. In D. S. Krantz, A. Baum, & J. E. Singer (Eds.), *Cardiovascular disorders and behavior* (pp. 57–83). Hillsdale, NJ: Erlbaum.

Dembroski, T. M., MacDougall, J. M., Williams, R. B., Haney, T., & Blumenthal, T. A. (1985). Components of Type A hostility and anger in relationship to angiographic findings. *Psychosomatic Medicine, 47,* 219–233.

Dimsdale, T. E., Block, R. C., Catanzano, D. M., Hackett, T. P., & Hutter, A. M. (1978). Type A personality and extent of coronary atherosclerosis. *American Journal of Cardiology, 42,* 583–586.

Dimsdale, J. E., Hackett, T. P., Hutter, A. M., et al. (1979). Type A behavior and angiographic findings. *Journal of Psychosomatic Research, 23,* 273–276.

Ekman, P. (1979). About brows: Emotional and conversational signals. In M. von Cranach,

K. Foppa, W. Lepenies, & D. Ploog (Eds.), *Human Ethology* (pp. 169–248). Cambridge, England: Cambridge University Press.

Ekman, P. (1982). Methods for measuring facial action. In K. R. Scherer & P. Ekman (Eds.), *Handbook of methods in nonverbal behavior research* (pp. 25–90). New York: Cambridge University Press.

Ekman, P. (1984). Expression and the nature of emotion. In K. Scherer & P. Ekman (Eds.), *Approaches to emotion* (pp. 319–344). Hillsdale, NJ: Erlbaum.

Ekman, P. (1989). The argument and evidence about universals in facial expressions of emotions. In H. Wagner & A. Manstead (Eds.), *Handbook of social psychophysiology* (pp. 143–163). New York: Wiley.

Ekman, P., Davidson, R. J., & Friesen, W. V. (1990). The Duchenne Smile: Emotional expression and brain physiology II. *Journal of Personality and Social Psychology, 58,* 342–353.

Ekman, P., & Friesen, W. V. (1976). Measuring facial movement. *Environ Psychol Nonverbal Behav, 1,* 56–75.

Ekman, P., & Friesen, W. V. (1978). *Facial Action Coding System. A Technique for the measurement of facial movement.* Palo Alto, CA: Consulting Psychologists Press.

Ekman, P., Friesen, W. V. & Ellsworth, P. (1972). *Emotion in the human face: Guidelines for research and an integration of findings.* New York: Pergamon.

Ekman, P., Levenson, R. W., & Friesen, W. V. (1983). Autonomic nervous system activity distinguishes between emotions. *Science, 221,* 1208–1210.

French-Belgian Collaborative Group. (1982). Ischemic heart disease and psychological patterns: Prevalence and incidence studies in Belgium and France. *Advances in Cardiology, 29,* 25–31.

Frank, K. A., Heller, S. S., Kornfeld, D. S., Sporn, A. A., & Weiss, M. B. (1978). Type A behavior and coronary angiographic findings. *JAMA, 240,* 761–763.

Friedman, H. S., Harris, M. I., & Hall, I. A. (1984). Nonverbal expression of emotion: Healthy charisma or coronary-prone behavior. In C. VanDyke, L. Temoshok, & L. S. Zegans (Eds.), *Emotions in health and illness: Applications to clinical practice* (pp. 151–165). San Diego. Grune and Stratton.

Friedman, M., & Powell, L. H. (1984). The diagnosis and quantitative assessment of Type A behavior: Introduction and description of the Videotaped Structured Interview. *Integrative Psychology, 1,* 123–129.

Friedman, M., Rosenman, R. H., Straus, R., Wurm, M., & Kositchek, R. (1968). The relationship of behavior pattern A to the state of coronary vasculature. *American Journal of Medicine, 44,* 525–537.

Haynes, S. C., Feinleib, M., Levine, S., Scotch, N., & Kennel, W. B. (1982). The relationship of psychological factors to coronary disease in the Framingham Heart Study. *Advances in Cardiology, 29,* 85–95.

Haynes, S. C., & Matthews, K. A. (1968). Type A behavior and cardiovascular disease. *Annals of Behavioral Medicine, 10,* 47–59.

Hecker, M. H. L., Chesney, M. A., Black, G. W., & Frautschi, N. (1988). Coronary-prone behaviors in the Western Collaborative Group Study. *Psychosomatic Medicine, 50,* 153–164.

Heller, B. W. (1980). *Nonverbal behavior and coronary-prone behavior.* Unpublished doctoral dissertation, University of California, Davis.

Izard, C. E. (1972). *Patterns of emotions: A new analysis of anxiety and depression.* New York: Academic Press.

Matthews, K. A., Glass, D. C., Rosenmann, R. H., & Bortner, R. W. (1977). Competitive drive, Pattern A, and coronary heart disease: A further analysis of some data from the Western Collaborative Group Study. *Journal of Chronic Disease, 30,* 489–498.

Matthews, K. A., & Haynes, S. C. (1986). Type A behavior pattern and coronary disease risk. *American Journal of Epidemiology, 123,* 923–960.

Powell, L. H., & Thoresen, C. E., (1985). Behavioral and physiologic determinants of long-term prognosis after myocardial infarction. *Journal of Chronic Disease, 38,* 253–263.

Plutchik, R. (1962). *The emotions: Factors, theories, and a new model.* New York: Random House.

Rosenman, R. H. (1978). The interview method of assessment of the coronary-prone behavior pattern. In T. M. Dembroski, S. M. Weiss, J. Shields, S. G. Haynes, & M. Feinleib (Eds.): *Coronary-prone behavior* (pp. 55–70). New York: Springer-Verlag.

Rosenman, R. H., Brand, R. J., Scholtz, R. I., & Friedman, M. (1976). Multivariate prediction of coronary heart disease during 8.5 year follow-up in the Western Collaborative Group Study. *American Journal of Cardiology, 37,* 903–910.

Rosenman, R. H., & Friedman, M. (1961). Association of specific behavior pattern in women with blood and cardiovascular findings. *Circulation, 24,* 1173–1184.

Rosenman, R. H., Friedman, M., Straus, R., Wurm, M., Kositchek, R., Hahn, W., & Werthessen, N. T. (1964). A predictive study of coronary heart disease: The Western Collaborative Group Study: Appendix. *JAMA, 189,* 113–120. Appendix, 1–16.

Shekelle, R. B., Billings, J. H., Borhani, N. O., et al. (1985). The MRFIT behavior pattern study. II: Type A behavior and incidence of coronary heart disease. *American Journal of Epidemiology, 122,* 559–570.

Shekelle, R. B., Gale, M., & Norusis, M. (1985). Type A score (Jenkins Activity Survey) and risk of recurrent coronary heart disease in the Aspirin Myocardial Infarction Study. *American Journal of Cardiology, 56,* 221–225.

Suarez, E. C., & Williams, R. B. (1989). Situational determinants of cardiovascular and emotional reactivity in high and low hostile men. *Psychosomatic Medicine, 51,* 404–418.

Tomkins, S. S. (1962). *Affect, imagery, consciousness, Vol. 1: The Positive Affects.* New York: Springer.

Williams, R. B., Haney, T. L., Lee, K., Kong, Y., Blumenthal, J., & Whalen, R. (1980). Type A behavior, hostility, and coronary heart disease. *Psychosomatic Medicine, 42,* 53–549.

Type A and Facial Behavior

PAUL EKMAN, ERIKA L. ROSENBERG & MARGARET CHESNEY

The three questions asked at the end of the previous article are still not answered: (1) Does adding facial behavior scores help in identifying those who are coronary-prone? (2) Are those who show both hostile facial and speech behavior the most at risk? and (3) Among those whose facial and speech component measures are discrepant, which is the best predictor of CHD, or are these people not at risk?

Addressing these questions would have required another study of individuals who are potentially at risk for CHD and then following them over a period of time, and that is not the research we did next. Our failure to follow up on these questions was not because these are unimportant matters. Instead, it was due to limited opportunity to do that type of research—long-term follow-up to determine who is at risk is difficult to arrange and expensive. Also, Chesney switched her research focus, and the next opportunity for collaboration that arose was not to study people at risk, but to study those who already had coronary heart disease. Before turning to that study, however, we want to emphasize again that these are important questions that still deserve attention in the study of CHD.

Ekman and Rosenberg have recently completed a collaborative study with Blumenthal (Duke University), in which they examined the facial behavior shown by coronary patients during the standardized Type A interview. In specific, they used FACS to measure patients' facial expressions during their responses to questions about how they deal with anger. During that time period a physiological measure of the functioning of the left ventricle (determined by multigated coronary angiographic images) revealed whether the patients exhibited transient myocardial ischemia, a coronary artery disease manifestation in which there is a reduction in the oxygen supply to their heart muscle. This type of ischemia is a predictor of fatal and nonfatal coronary events. The question posed was whether facial behavior shown at that moment would differentiate those who did and did not become ischemic. The findings—now submitted for publication—showed that the presence of anger expressions differentiated those who were ischemic from those who were not, when answering the question about how they deal with anger. Disgust, contempt, and glare facial movements did not differentiate the ischemic from nonischemic patients.

There is no reason to expect the findings from this study to replicate the study reported in this book, for they examined quite different populations—people who might be at risk and people who have coronary heart disease. And each study asked a different question; it is the glare and disgust that differentiated who was classified as Type A and who as Type B, and it was anger that differentiated who became ischemic when asked to describe how they handle anger.

Putting together this new study and the Type A study strongly suggests that the measurement of facial behavior may be of use in predicting among normal individuals those who are at risk for CHD, as well as in those with CHD, predicting when their risk is maximal. Clearly both the study in this book and the study with Blumenthal need to be replicated.

There are two ongoing projects in which FACS is being used in the study of coronary-prone behavior in normal adults, although coronary disease endpoints have not been evaluated. Thomas Haney of Duke University and his colleagues, including John Barefoot, Kimberly Maynard, and Barbara Fredrickson, are using FACS to code facial behavior shown during both the Type A Structured Interview and an anger recall task. In the latter task, faces are scored during both the retrieval of an anger memory and the prompted "reliving" of the memory. In this research, the investigators are interested in whether facial displays of emotion, particularly negative emotion, differ from middle to later life or between gender groups. In addition, this research will explore possible relationships between verbal displays and facial displays of positive and negative emotions. In a related project, Barbara Fredrickson (in collaboration with Kimberly Maynard, Tom Buhrman, Thomas Haney, Ilene Siegler, and John Barefoot) videotaped male and female subjects during a nonprovocative interview and during an anger recall task. A vocal indicator of hostility, referred to as "hostile interaction," and a facial indicator of hostility involving FACS-coded corrugator activity exhibited during the interview predicted the duration of sustained diastolic blood pressure elevation during the anger recall task. These findings support the growing evidence that hostility is associated with markers of cardiovascular risk and extend these findings to facial as well as verbal, self-report indicators of hostility.

Conclusion

What We Have Learned by Measuring Facial Behavior

PAUL EKMAN

This extraordinary collection of articles vividly illustrates how rich and diverse is the information that can be obtained by measuring facial behavior. Because measurement of facial behavior provides information about so many different phenomena, these chapters have appeared in many journals: 13 different journals are represented. It would be unusual for anyone to know all of these articles. I suspect that even the authors in this book are not familiar with all of the other articles published here. It was important, therefore, to collect in one place examples of the very diverse kinds of research that can benefit from measuring the face.

One might question why a personality psychologist needs to read about infant facial expression or a pain researcher should read about facial expression in psychotherapy. There are two answers. First, the face itself is a legitimate focus of study, and if one wants to learn what information can be derived from this multisignal system, then it is important to determine all the different kinds of information—messages—these signals can provide. It is not just students of the face who need to know the diverse literature represented here, but also students of emotion. It is no accident that each of these studies that measured facial behavior provides information relevant to students of emotion, for the face is a major source of information about emotion.

Unlike the research reported in this book, most of the psychological literature on facial expression did not measure the face but instead relied on observers' inferential judgments about what emotion is shown in facial behavior. Many of those studies focused on still photographs, most often posed still photographs. A reader of the psychological literature might well think that is all that has been done. But this book shows how much can be learned by actually measuring the face itself, not the inferences observers make when they see the face and by examining spontaneous facial behavior.

It is much more time-consuming to measure facial behavior itself—with FACS or any other technique (such as EMG, or Izard's MAX (1979)—than to obtain inferences about emotion from observers. However, none of the questions asked by these investigators could have been answered except by measuring the facial behavior. In my discussion of their work, I will point out why this is so using specific examples from this book.

I have organized by discussion by considering groups of articles, following the organization of the book. First, I will consider the substantive matters raised by the basic research chapters, and then the substantive issues raised by the applied research chapters. Then I will discuss methodological issues raised by various chapters.

Basic Research Issues

A number of very interesting theoretical issues are raised by the studies presented in this section. Three of the chapters considered individual differences in the magnitude of facial responses. Ekman, Friesen, and Simons wrote about hyper-startlers in response to a loud noise, and Ruch in one of his articles described hypo- and hyper-expressers in relation to humor, and in his other article reported individual differences in enjoyment smiles in relation to personality and mood measures. It is important to determine whether there are hypo- and hyper-expressers for each of the emotions, if such individual differences in the magnitude of facial responses are emotion specific or generalize across emotions, and whether such individual differences in the magnitude of expression are manifest also in the magnitude of subjective responses and physiological activity.

I mentioned in my Afterword to the startle paper that my current research with Robert Levenson is focusing on just these questions. My hunch is that *some* individuals are consistent across emotions in the magnitude of their expressive behavior, and some people are not. I expect also we will find that there are *some* individuals who are consistent in the magnitude of their expressive behavior for just one emotion. We already know from our research in progress that some individuals show coherence in the magnitude of response expressively and subjectively (and I expect physiologically) and others do not show such coherence.

Ruch reported that what he considers a mood—cheerfulness—determines whether one is a hypo- or hyper-expresser in response to humor stimuli. He also found that extroverts showed enjoyment smiling more than introverts, and in his Afterword he reported other work that found three state measures (cheerfulness, low serious, and low bad mood) were related to facial signs of enjoyment. It is not certain from his findings whether these individual differences in enjoyment smiling are due to a trait or state phenomenon. It might be that extroverts more than introverts are in a cheerful, low-serious, low-bad-mood state. It is also possible that even when both introverts and extroverts are cheerful, not serious, and not in a bad mood, the extroverts would show more smiling. Clearly more research is necessary examining subjects with one or another personality configuration when they are in one or another mood state.

I believe that in addition to transient determinants of the magnitude of expressivity such as mood, there may be more enduring individual differences that have a constitutional basis, but that only some individuals will manifest such enduring consistency in the magnitude of emotional expressivity. But we are far from having relevant evidence as yet. (I return to some of these same issues later in the section on applied research, when considering Keltner and Moffit's findings on adolescents who show a high incidence of anger.)

Quite apart from the issue of individual differences, it has been uncertain, from previous literature, whether there ever is, for anyone, a very strong relationship between what emotion is shown on the face and what emotion is reported. Two chapters make clear that we have underestimated the strength of the relationship between expression and subjective experience. Ruch (chapter 4) showed that a number of artifacts may produce an underestimate of the correlation between expression and self-report. Within subject designs, with aggregated data, yield quite high correlations. Rosenberg and Ekman found the typical procedure of asking people to report on their emotional experience some time after that experience occurred led to an underestimate of the correlation between expression and reported emotion, especially if more than one emotion had been experienced. The procedure they employed, which provided a means to help subjects retrieve memories for their specific emotional experience at specific points in time, yielded strong relationships between expression and subjective report. It remains to be determined whether substantial individual differences in the coherence between expression and report will still be found when the procedures used by either Ruch or Rosenberg and Ekman are adopted.

Keltner's paper strongly suggests that there is a distinctive signal for embarrassment. Although he describes what he terms "smile controls" early in his chapter as including a variety of behaviors (table 6.2), it is clear from that table that most of those facial actions were not unique to embarrassment as compared to amusement. In fact, many of them were more common in amusement than embarrassment. In correspondence, Keltner made clear that he considers only lip pressing (AU 24) as a smile control in embarrassment expressions. Our correspondence also made clear that he agrees with my supposition that observers will call an expression shame as compared to embarrassment if the head and eyes are down, with no visible facial activity (AUs). (In recently reviewing the films I took in 1967 of a preliterate culture in New Guinea, I found that when I asked them to pose shame they all put their heads and eyes down. I did not report this finding before now because it did not involve facial expression per se.) Keltner also agrees with my hunch that if he had allowed his observers in Study 5 the choice of sadness, in addition to shame, they might well have not showed such high agreement about identifying a shame expression.

We have strong evidence that head and gaze downwards is not required for observers to label an expression sadness if the face shows some variation of the facial actions we have proposed for this emotion: inner corners of the brows drawn together and upwards, cheeks raised, slight deepening of the nasolabial fold, and slight depression of the lip corners (AUs 1+4+6+11+15). We don't know what would happen if observers were given a choice among sadness, guilt, and shame when judging such as expression. If the gaze was down and the eyes directed down, but the 1+4+6+11+15 expression was visible, would observers call it sadness, guilt, or shame? It would be best in such a study to allow the subjects to give their own response, rather than to provide them with fixed alternatives. My hunch is that sadness will be the predominant response to such a stimulus, but that needs to be determined.

The embarrassment signal that Keltner has identified differs in kind from all the other facial expressions of emotion. Unlike happiness, anger, fear, sadness, surprise, disgust, and contempt, all of which can be signaled just by facial muscular actions, embarrassment requires changes in gaze direction and head movement and, perhaps also, face touching. Gaze direction and head movement can certainly contribute to the other emotional expressions (gaze and head pointed down contribute to sadness, head turned to the side in disgust, backwards head movement in fear, looking down the nose in comtempt), but they are not required as they seem to be for the embarrassment signal. Embarrassment also seems to require a sequence of actions, while the other emotional expressions are more like snapshots rather than sequences over time. Another way to consider Keltner's embarrassment findings are to consider this a compound signal, both in the sense of requiring behaviors in additon to facial expression (gaze and head position) and in not having one apex in which all the actions are shown at the same time, but a flow or sequence of actions. It is conceivable that there may be other emotional states that could be constructed in this fashion.

Prkachin also mentioned the importance of examining the sequence of actions in the pain expression, explaining his impression that some actions typically appear early and others late in the expression. It would be important to determine whether these sequential features, in either embarrassment or pain, are in highly overlapping time—for example, with all actions occurring within the same apex period or nonoverlapping time, with some actons beginning after other actions have started their offset or completely offset.

Can one be embarrassed without being either amused or ashamed? If so, it would likely differ from the signal described by Keltner, either not having a smile, or perhaps having one of the nonenjoyment smiles. Craig interprets the smiling activity that occurs in simulated pain displays as embarrassment, but he does not mention any of the other signs that Keltner has observed for embarrassment.

Keltner suggested that mouth opening (either AU 26 or AU 27) is part of the amusement facial expression. I doubt that this is so. Instead, I believe that as positive emotions increase in intensity the mouth opening will increase, just as AU 12 (zygomatic major) increases. (Ruch, in personal communication, 1995, agrees with me.) Laughter can occur in response to a variety of different positive emotions, not just humor, although I suspect the sound of laughter in response to humor is different from the laughter in response to tickling, for example. Laughter, too, can vary in intensity from a chuckle to peals of laughter, and the extent of mouth opening will also vary. Thus, I suggest that one could not tell from the facial expression itself whether the positive response being shown was in response to something humorous, something involving sensory pleasure, strokes to the ego, and so on. The research to determine whether my conjectures are correct has yet to be done.

Craig et al. and Prkachin reported evidence, from their own work and that of others, of a unique facial expression for pain. While no one considers pain to be an emotion, it is important occasion for emotion (in that sense akin to the startle facial expression) and it is noteworthy that it has its own distinctive facial marking. Prkachin accomplished for pain what we have yet to extablish for any of the emotions, but instead presume: the same four actions occur across four very different types of pain stimulation. This is exactly the type of research that is needed to establish firmly the existence of any signal. His findings— generality in the facial pattern across different types of evocations—with Craig et al.'s findings on the ability to simulate and inhibit this expression delineate some of the most important steps that need to be taken in research on emotional expressions. Of course, it is much easier to specify reliable stimuli to elicit either pain or the startle than it is for the emotions, and easier to do so in a laboratory situation. Prkachin speculated that the pain expression may be universal, and emphasizes the need for cross-cultural research. I have never reported my observations of pain in the preliterate culture in New Guinea that I studied in 1967, but I did observe the very configuration that these authors describe when I saw people experience pain.

Craig et al. pointed out in their Afterword the importance of such a signal for people who cannot verbally report on their pain, such as infants, people with intellectual handicaps, brain injuries, and the like. Consistent with this, Prkachin described the primary function of pain behavior in enlisting the aid of others. Paradoxically, such a signal so vital for survival can be, as Craig has shown, very convincingly simulated and inhibited (the pain expression differs from the startle which cannot be either totally supressed or well simulated).

Craig et al. described the pain display in terms I have used to characterize emotional expressions, constituting not one expression, but a theme and variations. Importantly, Craig provided us with some of the determinants of the variations, something which has not been specified for the emotional expressions.

Ruch suggested that exhilaration is the best term to describe the response to humor, tickling, and laughing gas. Would he think amusement is the low end of that state? Exhilaration seems to be on the same intensity level as the emotion terms used to designate other states (anger, fear, sadness, etc.), while amusement appears by definition to be low in intensity, more akin to being annoyed than being angry. While these are semantic matters, they become relevant to research on facial expression in designating what state is being examined, and in how one deals with the self-report of emotion.

Seven of the 11 chapters in this part dealt with the differences between two forms of expression. In five studies the contrast was between expressions that were emotional or not. In the startle and pain studies, it was between the expressions of those states and attempts to inhibit and attempts to simulate those states. Despite this commonality, it is difficult to integrate the findings from all seven studies because each examined facial behavior elicited in a different way. Ekman, Friesen and O'Sullivan dealt only with behavior during an interaction, and that was the situation in Craig et al., and in one of Frank et al.'s conditions, but he also had a condition in which the behavior had been emitted when alone, which was the condition in Ekman, Friesen, and Simons; Gosselin et al.; Hager and Ekman; and Hess and Kleck.

It might seem as if all seven studies examined false or deceptive behavior, but there were differences among them in how this was done. Ekman, Friesen, and O'Sullivan measured masking smiles—smiles in which there is evidence of negative emotions. Frank examined nonmasking, nonenjoymemt smiles. Ekman, Friesen, and Simons and Craig et al. examined a genuine expression (startle or pain), attempts to inhibit that expression, and attempts to simulate it. Hager and Ekman examined simulated startles, posed emotions, and deliberately made single facial actions. Gosselin et al. had actors show emotions without feeling the emotion, and Hess and Kleck had their subjects pose in one study and attempt to deceive in another. Despite these variations everyone found evidence of differences in the facial behavior that occurs when an emotion is presumably experienced and when it is not. There were some consistent differences in the morphology and in the timing or the expressions.

No one dichotomy is sufficient to capture the differences in the two kinds of behavior examined in studies. The distinctions between voluntary-involuntary, deliberate-spontaneous, emotional-simulated emotional, emotional-posed, frank-deceptive, and alone-social are each useful but more than one of them must be considered in specifying just what is being studied.

The condition that I find of least interest is posing an emotional expression on request. It is uninteresting both because this never happens in ordinary life, only in the psychological laboratory, and because we don't know how people perform this task. It certainly can be done by various means, including, for example, remembering or imagining an emotional situation or remembering an emotional face and imitating it. Posing may sometimes actually generate the emotional experience, and some investigators have used self report as a way to identify whether that did or did not happen.[1] Acting, of course, does occur in real life, but we do not know the extent to which actors do the same things that nonactors do when they are trying to convince others that they feel an emotion they do not feel. When nonactors try to convincingly simulate an emotion, I call this lying, not acting. The crucial difference is that the actor notifies his target that it is performance, while the liar does not (Ekman, 1985).

Looking across these seven studies, and adding some speculations to fill in a few gaps, we find that there are some promising findings on how to distinguish between two types of facial movement, most of which fit Ekman and Friesen's (1982) and Ekman's (1985) forecast. I will compare what occurs on the face when a person (1) spontaneously shows an emotional expression or a pain or startle expression, when there is independent evidence (subjective report or physiology) that either an emotion(s) or startle or pain is being experienced; and (2) deliberately makes a facial movement for the purpose of intentionally misleading another person into believing an emotion or pain or a startle is being experienced when it is not, without giving notification of that intention. I don't think it should matter whether the person is alone or with another person in either of these conditions. Also, I believe that the characteristics I am about to describe for category 1 would also be manifest in other (beyond the startle) reflexive facial actions, or for nonemotional facial movements that are highly learned habits, occurring involuntarily (e.g., agreement signs and other conversational signals).

Category 1 can be distinguished from category 2 in terms of the following characteristics.

1. *Morphology*. This is, so far, best documented for enjoyment, but I have described (Ekman, 1985/1992, 1993) how the absence of muscle movements that are difficult to make voluntarily could differentiate category 1 from category 2 facial movements. This does not appear to be the case for the simulated pain face that does not differ in morphology from the actual pain face.
2. *Symmetry*. While difficult to measure, this is potentially a very valuable differentiator, with symmetry being more common in category 1 than in category 2.
3. *Total duration*. The very brief (under 2 seconds) and very long (more than 5 seconds) should occur more with category 2 than category 1. Micro expressions (those that last 1/3 sec. or less) are excluded, since they are spontaneous, suppressed, or repressed emotions (Ekman, 1985). There also will be some long-duration expressions that fit category 1, but these will be exceptions.
4. *Speed of onset*. Although this will vary with social circumstance, in comparable circumstances, onsets will be shorter in category 1 than in category 2.
5. *Coordination in apexes*. The apexes of each of the actions involved in the expression will be more likely to overlap in category 1 than in category 2.
6. *Ballistic trajectory*. The expression will appear smooth over its course in category 1, rather than jagged or stepped in category 2, as was found by Hess an Kleck.

We do not know how accurately expressions can be classified as category 1 versus category 2 when all six of these indices are used, but I suspect it will be quite high.

Nor do we know whether some of these indices are more powerful discriminators than others, for all people or for some people. (I suspect that no. 2 and no. 3 will prove less powerful than the others in distinguishing category 1 and category 2.) Again, a profitable area for further research.

The research findings reported in this section and in other sections of this book (see especially chapters 15, 16, 17, and 21) strongly suggest that those studying facial expression need to measure at least some of the six parameters listed above if they want to ensure that they are studying emotional rather than nonemotional expressions. The simple fact that people will say that they felt an emotion does not mean that every expression that preceded it was emotional. And because of demand characteristics, sometimes people will report feeling an emotion when in fact they did not. While I am not suggesting that the face is the "gold standard" for knowing when an emotion occurs, one can increase the likelihood that an emotion is being examined if one utilizes at least some of the six parameters of facial movement described above to distinguish the emotional from the nonemotional facial activity.

The evidence reported in this book and other studies summarized by Frank et al. on smiling make overwhelming the need to apply at least some of these six parameters in the study of smiling. Regrettably some investigators ignore this work and continue to simply measure zygomatic major activity without regard for any of the other six parameters listed here (e.g., Fridlund, 1991).

A number of the authors interpreted their findings—emotional expressions occurring when their subjects thought they were alone—as contradicting Fridlund's (1992) claim that emotional expressions do not occur except in the presence of others. Of course, Fridlund would likely reply that people who show facial expressions when alone are imagining that other people are present. That line of reasoning makes Fridlund's position not subject to disconfirmation and therefore of little use. Fridlund (1994) more recently has argued that facial expressions are unrelated to emotion, that they tell us about motivations and intentions, not internal states. I (Ekman, 1989; in press) have argued that this if a false and misleading dichotomy. An evolutionary view of emotion regards the internal changes during emotion as preparation for responses, most often to others, that have been adaptive and messages about motivations and action intentions to be among the kinds of information that can be conveyed to others by an emotional expression.

Elsewhere (Ekman, 1972, 1989, 1992, in press) I have suggested that the presence of others can act to either amplify or deamplify facial expressions of emotion, depending on the role relationship between the people, the emotions being felt, and other aspects of the social context. It is far too simple to maintain that the presence of others will have but one uniform effect on expressiveness. The fact that people experience emotions when alone (e.g., in response to a sunset, lightning, etc.) does not diminish my claim, and that of other theorists who operate from an evolutionary perspective, that emotions evolved to deal with fundamental life tasks that involve other people, such as mating, fighting, or caring for children.

The two developmental studies in this section contribute important information on fundamental issues about emotion and expression. Both studies show that there is differentiation in facial response, in Rosenstein and Oster, in the first two hours of life, and in Carmas et al., in both 5- and 12-month-old infants. To show that expressions are differentiated does not mean that the specific facial expressions that signal emotion in adults are evident so early in life. Both papers report evidence that strongly suggests that is not so, that there may well be infant facial expressions of emotion that are different from adult facial expressions of emotion. Studying their results, it does not appear that these infant facial expressions of emotion are unique, bearing no relationship to their adult counterparts, but they are far from identical.

Camras et al. provided evidence on another fundamental issue—the universality of facial expression. Their comparison of Japanese and American infants provides uniquely important evidence for universality. It is important because it is the first evidence on infants and also because it adds to the small amount of evidence on universality for the display of emotions, not just their recognition. We now know that Japanese and American *infants* do display the same emotional expressions to the same situation. The first evidence of comparable universal facial expressions in Japanese and American *adults* was obtained 25 years ago in our (Friesen and my study, reported in Ekman, 1972) study of college students. That work used the predecessor of FACS, the Facial Affect Scoring Technique (FAST), and found that when Japanese and Americans were each alone watching a slightly pleasant and a very unpleasant film, very similar facial activity occurred.

Camras et al. did find a cultural difference in the latency of negative emotional expressions, with Americans responding more quickly than Japanese to the arm-restraint procedure. They pointed out that, contrary to most theories that cultural differences would increase over time, it was just the opposite. This difference was apparent only in the 5-month-old infants, not the 1-year-old infants. Their explanation seems sensible, and presumably they will be able to replicate this finding in the study described in their Afterword.

Rosenstein and Oster raised the question of why the infant shows a particular expression in response to particular stimuli—what they call the mouth gaping in response to a bitter taste and lip pursing in response to a sour taste. Few investigators since Darwin have raised such questions, and their explanation is quite consistent with how Darwin reasoned, although Darwin did not know of this expression. They show that detailed measurement with Baby FACS, using an empirical approach (as opposed to an approach based on a priori emotion classifications, found in Izard's work), reveals information about the sensory capacities and hedonic responses of newborns that other response measures failed to find (and other facial coding systems would have misinterpreted or missed).

Oster, in her Afterword, raises a very important point about the hazards of using a priori formulas, particularly in infants, to interpret what appear to be "blends," in which one might want to presume that there are two different emotions occurring at once. Oster raises the question of whether elements of AU 9 and AU 12 should, in the infant, be interpreted as disgust and enjoyment. She has instances that suggest that this is not the case, and I have reason to believe she is right not only about infants but about adults as well. Part of the problem is that certain AUs may have different meaning in different contexts, or when shown by infants as compared to adults. Part of the problem is being sufficiently careful to ensure that an AU is actually present, when only one of the appearance changes associated with that AU occurs, rather than all of those changes.[2]

Rosenstein and Oster also note that AU 18 occurs with interest or puzzlement. I have observed this same action in some adults as a mark of these same states.

Applied Research Issues

Six of the eight chapters in this part dealt with depression and/or schizophrenia. The results are not entirely consistent, but that would not be expected given the disagreements about diagnosis that are likely when research is done in three different countries and over a 20-year period. To further complicate comparisons across the studies, some studies made subdistinctions (blunted and nonblunted schizophrenics; in or outpatients; suicidal or nonsuicidal), which other studies did not.

There were differences in the occurrence of enjoyment smiles and nonenjoyment smiles for depressed and schizophrenic patients as compared to controls (Berenbaum and Oltmanns; chapter 16), for schizophrenics as compared to controls (Steimer-Krause et al., chapter 17), and in relationship to clinical improvement for depressed patients (Ekman et al.; chapter 15). Contempt expressions were more evident in schizophrenics than controls (Steimer-Krause et al.; chapter 17), in depressed patients who do not show clinical improvement (Ekman et al.; chapter 15), and in suicidal as compared to nonsuicidal patients (Heller and Haynal; chapter 19). Two studies suggest that patients show less use of the face to illustrate speech—what I termed (Ekman, 1979) *conversational signals,* than controls (Steimer-Krause et al., for schizophrenics as compared to controls; Ellgring for depressed as compared to controls). Heller and Haynal's finding of a diminution of upperface activity for suicidal as compared to nonsuicidal patients may also reflect a decrease in conversational signals. There was also evidence that measures of facial expression can predict subsequent behavior, (ratings of clinical improvement, Ekman et al.) and outcome of psychotherapy.

It is difficult to integrate Ellgring's report with the findings of the others who have studied psychopathology, because Ellgring's use of FACS is so different. His was a very early study, done before Friesen and myself had told those using FACS how to integrate separate facial actions into combinations or "events" when the different facial actions occur in overlapping time. Facial expressions often involve the actions of two, three, four, or five actions, which may start at slightly different moments and time, but merge together into a configuration that is held for a few moments before fading off the face. FACS provides the investigator with a means to identify each of those separate actions (AUs) that produce any configuration, but proper analysis requires that the investigator reassemble them in the original configurations. Ellgring did not do so. He treated each AU as a separate event, except for combining the two actions that combine to raise the entire eyebrow (1+2). The failure to reassemble the separate AUs into configurations, and then analyze those configurations, is responsible, I believe, for why Ellgring found primarily individual differences rather than many common features in what expressions changed over the course of depressive illness. Another problem is that Ellgring did not have available the "emotion dictionary" that Friesen and I had developed to interpret those configurations, translating them into emotion scores. There are many different configurations for any single emotion. If Ellgring had reassembled the separate AUs and then used the interpretative dictionary to convert those AU scores into emotions, I expect he would have found much more commonality across patients, as did the other investigators who studied psychopathology and who took those steps. Ellgring's work also was done before the distinction between enjoyment and nonenjoyment smiles was published. ans so we cannot know if the increase he noted was in one or both forms of smiling.

Berenbaum and Oltmanns demonstrated that facial expression measurement provided information not available from other sources. Blunted-affect schizophrenic patients were less facially responsive that nonblunted schizophrenics, but there was no difference in reported emotional expreience. They interpreted this as showing that blunted affect is a disturbance of expression but not of feeling. Of course, it is possible that the self-reports were not valid, but reflected demand characteristics. While it is difficult to know whether or not that is so, their study does tell us that facial measurement provides information not available in self-report: facial behavior differentiated blunted affect from nonblunted-affect patients, self-report did not. Their study also showed that measures of emotional reactivity based on standard clinical interviews were not sufficient to discover the ways in which psychiatric groups differ from each other and from normals, while measures of facial behavior made those distinctions. This is consistent with Ekman et al.'s finding that clinical ratings on the Brief Psychiatric Rating Scale (BPRS) did not improve predictions of inprovement made on the basis of facial behavior. (Later, in discussing methodological issues, I describe other studies that found that facial measurement provided information not available from observers judgments; see chapters 10, 14, and 21.)

Steimer-Krause et al. found more facial activity during talking, except for the psychosomatic patients. Ellgring reported more facial activity during speaking for normal subjects. Presumably these findings are due to the fact that most of the conversational signals occur when speaking to emphasize speech as it is spoken. Although there are also listener facial responses, these typically do not occur as often as the conversational signals used by the speaker. In addition to conversational signals, I expect that in general there are more facial expressions of emotion when speaking than when listening, although there will be exceptions—for example, when someone is telling you terrible or wonderful news.

Steimer-Krause et al. also make the very important point what when we see an emotion on the face we do not know from the expression itself who is the target of the emotion. For example, the contempt they found that differentiated schizophrenics from other patients or controls may have been directed at themselves, at others not present, or at the person with whom they are interacting. To discover the target of the emotion shown on the face one must examine what is being said and gaze direction. Krause, in his Afterword, cited another study by their group that found that schizophrenics misinterpret who is the target of the emotions shown by others. The schizophrenics interpreted the enjoyment smiles shown by others as a sign that the other person is enjoying the schizophrenic's misfortune. Baenninger-Huber (who has worked with the Krause group) made a similar point, adding that not only do we need to consider what is said or not said when a facial expresion of emotion occurs, but we also need to attend to the sound quality, in terms of what emotion is being signaled vocally.

Baenninger-Huber described a number of very intriguing concepts illustrated by her study of a single patient during treatment. Individuals regulate their affect, she said, by evoking through their own behavior specific reactions, emotions, and fantasies in the persons with whom they are interacting. In correspondence she told me this idea was first forwarded in another paper (Baenninger-Huber, Moser, & Steiner, 1990), and is similar to ideas forwarded by Krause. In German, she wrote, the word for this is *Ubertragungsangebot*, which comes from psychoanalysis and can be translated as a transference offer.

This formulation provides an interpretation of *why* individuals display a particular array of emotional behavior—it is to reenact with another an particular interaction pattern, presumable one that repeats elements of their own interaction pattern with their parents. Although her data cannot prove this interpretation, her work and other papers by the Krause group importantly attempt to explain individual differences in the pattern of emotional behavior.

Baenninger-Huber's formulation is consistent with how Keltner and Moffit interpret their finding that externalizing adolescents show more anger. They point out that the high display of anger expressions is likely to evoke negative emotions in others, which in turn contributes to the social rejection and hostility that such adolescents experience from others. They do not, however, go as far as Baenninger-Huber. They do not say that these adolescents are motivated to act this way because they need to cause others to reject them, repeating presumable traumatic or unresolved relationships with their parents.

Clearly an explanation is needed for why people would act in a way that causes others to act unpleasantly toward them, whether adolescents, as in Keltner and Moffit's study or adults who glare, as in the study by Chesney et al. Other alternatives are that people who show a great deal of anger do so because earlier (traumatic?) experience has affected them in a way that: (1) has caused anger to dominate their affective system in a monopolistic fashion, generally being the first emotion to occur in response to a variety of appraisals; (2) has lowered the threshold for anger being expressed; (3) has damaged their capability to inhibit anger expressions; or (4) to use Lazarus's (1991) terminology, has caused the knowledge they draw upon in their primary appraisals to lead them to repeatedly interpret a variety of events as demeaning or personally assaultive.

These are not mutually exclusive explanations. Some may apply to one person, other explanations to other people. Or it may be that all of them apply to one person, but some of these explanations may be more relevant at one point in time than another. The important matter is that we are beginning now to establish marked individual differences in facial expressions of emotion, differences in the predominant emotion or emotions that are shown in certain circumstances, differences in the magnitude of the facial expressions, and perhaps also differences in the latency of the response. Much more work is needed to establish the stability of those individual differences, their developmental course, and how these differences in facial expression relate to differences in vocal expression. speech, and coincident physiological activity. Emotions are not just transient phenomena. There are stable individual differences in characteristic facial expressions of emotion. Now we can begin to design research not only to better document the nature of these differences but to begin to allow us to choose among various explanations of those differences.

Chesney et al. raise the interesting possibility that there may be signs of personality in facial activity, not just signs of emotion. The "glare" configuration, which they found more often in people presumed to be at risk for coronary artery disease than those presumed not to be at risk, *might* be such a sign. The actions that compose the "glare," they explain, could be controlled anger, low-intensity anger, or perhaps a marker of the personality trait of hostility, not the emotion anger. They cite indirect evidence that suggests it is most likely that glare is not an emotion sign but a sign of hostility, but the matter is far from settled. Ekman (1985) earlier suggested that accurate inferences about personality can be drawn by observing when specific emotions are shown, how often they are shown, and how strongly they are shown. So, for example, we think a person is hostile if that individual shows more anger than others, in circumstances others do not show anger, and when the person shows anger it is more intense and longer lasting than it is for others. But the Chesney et al. study raises an entirely different possibility—that there are direct signs of personality, perhaps related to emotion signs, but unique to personality.

Methodological Matters

The chapters in this book also illustrate a number of important methodological issues. As mentioned earlier, both the chapter by Rosenberg and Ekman and that of Ruch show that most prior research has probably underestimated the extent of the correspondence between facial expressions of emotion and subjective experience. Each of these chapters describes a very different methodological solution to the problems that have led to an underestimation of that correspondence. Although their solutions are not applicable in every research design, they should be considered by anyone intending to measure both expression and self-report of emotion.

In the study of smiles when lying, Ekman, Friesen, and O'Sullivan used EMFACS rather than FACS. By doing so, they reduced the scoring time, but because they used EMFACS they could not discover any other facial signs of lying or truthfulness that are not, strictly speaking, emotional behaviors. EMFACS focuses just on those facial actions for which there already is good evidence of their relevance to emotion. Other facial actions that might signal emotion, or other facial actions which are not emotional but might relate to the phenomena under study, are ignored by EMFACS. For example, the glare facial expression identified by Chesney et al. would not have been discovered if they had used EMFACS instead of FACS. While we have subsequently modified EMFACS to include the AUs relevant to glare as a result of this study, there may be other such expressions that will not be discovered if EMFACS is used rather than FACS. The use of EMFACS also makes it impossible to evaluate all of the other signs of emotional behavior apart from morphology listed above. Rosenstein and Oster's study is another case in which if an abbreviated a priori set of emotion categories had been scored, the differential responses to negative tastes they uncovered with Baby FACS would not have been found.

Ekman et al. showed that EMFACS misses some of the facial expressions that FACS is able to identify. This should not be a surprise, since to economize on time EMFACS does not allow slowed motion replaying. Again to economize on time, EMFACS does not score brow raises (AUs 1+2) and brow lowers (AU 4), when these occur alone. Often these actions are conversational signals, indicating emphasis, determination, or perplexity in the speaker, or an exclamation or perplexity in the listener. Two of the chapters reported differences between psychopathological groups and normals in these actions, and those findings would not have been obtained if EMFACS had been used.

To argue the opposite viewpoint, there is no reason to do a full FACS scoring unless there is a theoretical or methodological need to do so. In particular, the measurement of duration rather than frequency, which is very labor intensive, should be reserved for the following situations: when it is necessary to identify exactly places where emotion occurred so that other phenomena, such as physiological activity, can be examined at those moments (e.g., Davidson, Ekman, Saron, Senulis, & Friesen, 1990); when there is a hypothesis about duration itself, such as Frank et al. examined regarding the difference between enjoyment and nonenjoyment smiles; and when there is reason to believe that at least some subjects will show infrequent but long-duration facial expressions. This last reason for measuring duration refers to unusual occasions, for typically there is a very high correlation between frequency and duration.

To further measure the duration of onset to apex, the apex duration, and end of apex to offset takes additional time beyond simply getting the duration measure from onset to offset. Some of the chapters in this part, however, illustrate when precisely this type of information is needed (see Ekman, Friesens, and Simon; Frank et al.; Hess and Kleck; and Ruch's article on alcohol). Prkachin's study shows that duration and intensity measures were highly correlated; however, some of his findings were better revealed with one measure as compared to another. In the initial study of any phenomenon, it would appear wise to measure intensity, frequency, and duration, and perhaps some of the onset, apex, and offset measures. As more is known about a type of expression, it may become apparent, as it is now with the pain and startle expression, which of these indices can be eliminated.

Berenbaum and Oltmanns appear to have taken an opposite position, recommending the use of FACS only when the investigator has a very specific hypothesis to test. While I still maintain FACS is the technique to use rather than EMFACS when discovery is the object, and in the initial stage of research, perhaps Berenbaum and Oltmanns meant that FACS can be used selectively to test a hypothesis about a specific emotion. If, for example, one is only interested in assessing changes in fear, then FACS could be used to score just fear-relevant AUs, obtaining all of the timing measures that FACS entails but ignoring all AUs not relevant to fear.

If an investigator expects to collapse all of the FACS scoring into positive versus negative emotional expressions, as did Berenbaum and Oltmanns, then they might as well use EMFACS rather than FACS. Similarly, if all an investigator intends to do is to use a single summary score of the occurrence of each emotion in each subject or patient, then EMFACS may be preferable. If the signs of emotion are likely to be subtle, slight, fleeting, or masked, as commonly occurs in deception research, then again FACS is the method of choice.

Gosselin et al. utilized the tables published in FACS (Ekman & Friesen, 1978) to interpret which facial actions signify which emotions. Those tables were meant only as a beginning point to describe what we then thought were the prototypic combination of Action Units (AUs) for each emotion. They are by no means comprehensive and leave out many, perhaps the majority, of the combinations of AUs that, thought not prototypic, have been found to be signs of each emotion. Currently there are two methods for interpreting the emotional significance of AUs. Friesen and Ekman's (1989) "emotion dictionary" makes interpretations of AUs based on theory, findings, and intuitions. It was developed by specifying which AUs are required to signal a particular emotion, which other AUs are irrelevant, and which change the emotion interpretation. The dictionary then extrapolates logically to many other combinations of AUs. Ekman, Irwin, Rosenberg, and Hager's more recent FACS Affect Interpretation Data Base (FACSAID) accomplishes the same task in a different fashion. It was derived from the authors' examination of each of more than 5000 AU combinations that occurred in a large data set. Interpretations were based, again, on theory, findings, and intuitions. The database has grown as new AU combinations have been encountered in other data sets. It is likely that the interpretations made on the basis of the "emotion dictionary" and FACSAID would be the same, but there has as yet been no empirical test of that.

A number of chapters in this book illustrate the difference in the information obtained when results are analyzed on the purely descriptive AU level and when AUs are grouped on the basis of what emotion they signify. Heller and Haynal found nothing happened more than once when they performed their analysis just on the basis of AUs, but clear differences emerged when they analyzed their results in terms of the emotions signified by those various AUs. Steimer-Krause et al. provided an especially good illustration of analyses conducted at different levels, from the purely descriptive to the interpretative.

The studies by Frank et al., by Keltner, by Rosenstein and Oster, and by Prkachin illustrate the difference in the type of information that can be obtained by measuring the face as compared to having observers make judgments when viewing faces. They show also the value of using both approaches. The only way to test some of Ekman and Friesen's ideas about the characteristics that distinguish an emotional from a nonemotional smile was for Frank et al. to actually measure facial behavior. It is quite a separate question as to whether or not observers can accurately differentiate one smile from another. If they had just done a judgment study, they would have found that accuracy is possible, though meager, but they would not have been able to establish what are the actual signs in the face that distinguish one kind of smile from another, nor could they have discovered whether the differences between smiles are robust or modest.

Keltner's work to establish a signal for embarrassment meant that he had to do both a measurement study to discover what are the signs of embarrassment and a judgment study to find out whether people do recognize embarrassment and distinguish it from related states. It is conceivable that there could be a reliable sign of a state (such as the enjoyment smile versus nonenjoyment smile) that is not a very robust signal. Keltner's initial judgment study also obtained quite modest accuracy, but when he used his results from the measurement study to select expressions that had the various elements he had uncovered in the measurement study, he obtained higher agreement among observers in distinguishing embarrassment from other emotions.

Prkachin reports in his Afterword that facial measurement has outperformed naive observers' ratings of pain. He notes that the information is there in the face, but observers do not know what to attend to. He reports taking the obvious next step to train observers to be more accurate, but did not tell us the findings.

Rosenstein and Oster show that measurements could discriminate which stimuli the infants were responding to, while observers could not make some of these same discriminations. If an investigator were to only use observers' ratings as the tool for measuring the face, the investigator might well think that differences that Rosenstein and Oster found do not exist. Whenever observers fail to make a discrimination, it does not mean that the difference is not there, only that the observers don't recognize it. Similarly, as described earlier, both Berenbaum and Oltmanns and Ekman, Matsumoto, and Friesen found differences in studies of psychiatric groups that ratings made by observers did not distinguish. To show that a difference is or is not present requires the use of FACS (or if it is infants, Baby FACS).

This is an appropriate place to applaud Oster for her work in developing and promulgating this adaptation of FACS. It is true to the spirit of FACS in providing a means of closely describing facial activity, taking account of anatomical differences between the infant and adult behavior. It is consistent with FACS, and unlike MAX and Affex, in separating description from inference about emotion and in being comprehensive and not selective. Oster also provides descriptive codes for a variety of facial actions encountered in the infants. And she has separated brow lowering from bringing the brows together, utilizing AU 3 as well as AU 4. We originally had provided AU 3 for just that purpose, but dropped the distinction worried that it would not be reliable. I am convinced now, from Oster's work and our own observations, that the distinction can be made reliably.

In her Afterword Hess described a subsequent study in which she and Kleck had observers judge the different kinds of facial expressions she had measured in her chapter of this book. Noting the modest level of accuracy achieved by judges in Frank et al. and in her follow-up study, she raised the question as to why observers are not more accurate than they are. She suggested that observers follow a decoding display rule, trying to interpret the situation in the way it is intended and, presumably because of this, disattending to the clues that would allow them to better identify enjoyment from nonenjoyment smiles. We (Ekman, 1985/1992; Ekman, Friesen, & O'Sullivan, chapter 9) suggested that this is characteristic of deceptive encounters. Lies often succeed because the target of the lie is collusively involved, supporting the lie and ignoring discrepant information.

Ekman, Friesen and O'Sullivan's chapter raises the question of whether highly motivated people might be more accurate than others in distinguishing emotional from masking smiles. Ekman and O'Sullivan's (1991) subsequent study of such motivated people (law enforcement and national security personnel) examined accuracy in detecting deceit, not just accuracy in differentiating two types of smiles. They found that even such highly motivated people are not very accurate in judging who is lying and who is truthful. It remains to be known whether it is possible to train people to make these judgments more accurately.

Prkachin's article is notable for the excellent use of graphic displays to help in understanding the occurrence of particular AUs in the different types of pain stimulation. Baenninger-Huber also used graphic displays in an interesting way. Prkachin's work is also notable in the use of factor analysis to aid in identifying which AUs are consistently displayed with pain. The use of a drawing to illustrate the pain face is quite successful also, as were the photographic illustrations Keltner used for embarrassment.

Ellgring pointed out the need to develop better training materials for FACS. We wrote the training manual and materials nearly 20 years ago. We have changed how we use FACS, but those changes are provided to those who have learned FACS in a separate document, only after they have learned FACS. If we (Friesen and myself) do not rewrite the manual to incorporate those changes, the next generaton of facial researchers certainly should do so. They should consider making use of the new developments in interactive video, which could well speed up how long it takes to learn FACS.

Another important matter is to provide the person who has learned FACS additional training in its use. Rosenberg is working, with my advice, on this. And, on the horizon, perhaps less than five years away, are automated techniques for measuring visible facial movement, which may not totally eliminate the human who scores the face but will significantly reduce the time it takes (for a recent review of such work, see Ekman, Huang, Sejnowski, & Hager, 1994).

Conclusion

There can be no single conclusion from this set of very interesting studies beyond the very simple and dramatically illustrated fact that measurement of facial behavior reveals unique and important information about a wide variety of psychological phenomena. The richness and complexity of facial behavior cannot be captured by a still photograph, nor can the information that facial activity reveals be assayed by asking an observer to chose one from a short list of emotions or to use a rating scale. The tools for mining the flow of facial activity are available; the work required is arduous but not overwhelming; and as these chapters show, the rewards can be very high.

Acknowledgment

My preparation of this chapter was supported by a Research Scientist Award from NIMH (MH06092).

Notes

1. I might note that some authors (e.g., Hess and Kleck; chapter 12) use the term "posing" to describe trying to mislead another person, but I think we should reserve that term for when people respond to an investigator's request to produce on command a facial expression. For this reason I do not call the technique that I have used in my joint research with Levenson (Ekman, Levenson, & Friesen, 19834) posing, since in our directed facial action task we gave the subjects muscle-by-muscle instructions to construct an expression without ever mentioning the emotion itself. This is certainly not real life, any more than posing is, but it is a different instructional task than posing.

2. Many adults, especially women, show some signs of wrinkling along the sides of the nose when there is a moderate to strong AU 12, especially if the muscle orbiting the eyes (AU 6) is involved. I do not believe that this is actually due to the action of levator labii superioris, alaquae nasi, which is what AU 9 is supposed to measure. In my observation when this nose wrinkling occurs with a 6+12, it is not accompanied by changes in the upper lip, nostrils, or tip of the nose, which are marks of the action of this muscle. Often this wrinkling occurs as a momentary action, emphasizing the enjoyment signaled by AU 12. Sometimes it appears throughout the AU 12. My observations suggest that it is a consistent feature in some people; they will either never or always show this nose wrinkling with AU 6+12. I recommend, therefore, that we no longer score AU 9 if there is only wrinkling on the sides of the nose without the accompanying changes in the upper lip, tip of the nose, and nostrils. This is a change from the FACS manual, which allows the scoring a AU 9 if the only change observed is more than surface wrinkling on the sides of the nose. I believe this is consistent with how Oster scores 9 in the presence of 6+12 in infants. One more matter: when AU 9 does actually occur with AUs 6+12, should we interpret that as a blend of disgust and enjoyment, as we have been doing in the past? I have my doubts about that; certainly I think one can enjoy the feeling of disgust, but the occasions in which I saw a strong 9 with a strong 6+12 I do not think disgust was being experienced. I have nothing to recommend other than caution in interpreting this combination of AUs.

References

Baenninger-Huber, E., Moser, U., & Steiner, F. (1990). Mikroanalytische Untersuchung affectiver Regulierungsprozesse in Paar-Interaktionen. *Zietschrift fuer Klinische Psychologie, 19*, 123–143.

Davidson, R. J., Ekman, P., Saron, C., Senulis, J., & Friesen, W. V. (1990). Emotional expression and brain physiology I: Approach/withdrawal and cerebral asymmetry. *Journal of Personality Social Psychology, 58,* 330–341.

Ekman, P. (1972). Universals and cultural differences in facial expressins of emotion. In J. Cole (Ed.), *Nebraska Symposium on Motivation, 1971* (pp. 207–283). Lincoln, NE: University of Nebraska Press.

Ekman. P. (1979). About brows: Emotional and conversational signals. In *Human Ethology,* M. von Cranach, K. Foppa, W. Lepenies, & D. Ploog, (Eds.) Cambridge: Cambridge University Press, pp. 169–248.

Ekman, P. (1985/1992). *Telling lies: Clues to Deceit in the Marketplace, Marriage, and Politics, Second edition.* New York, W. W. Norton. (2nd Edition 1992)

Ekman, P. (1989). The argument and evidence about universals in facial expressions of emotion. In H. Wagner & A. Manstead (Eds.), *Handbook of social psychophysiology* (pp. 143–164). Chichester, England: Wiley.

Ekman, P. (1992). An argument for basic emotions. *Cognition and Emotion, 6,* 169–200.

Ekman, P. (1993). Facial expression of emotion. *American Psychologist, 48,* 384–392.

Ekman, P. (in press). Expression or communication about emotion. In N. Segal, G. E. Weisfeld, C. C. Weisfeld (Eds) *Genetic, ethological, and evolutionary perspectives on human development.* Washington DC: APA Books.

Ekman, P., & Friesen, W. V. (1978). *Facial action coding system: A technique for the measurement of facial movement.* Palo Alto, CA: Consulting Psychologists Press.

Ekman, P., & Friesen, W. V. (1982). Felt, false, and miserable smiles. *Journal of Nonverbal Behavior, 6* (4), 238–252.

Ekman, P., & Friesen, W. V. (1989). *Emotion dictionary.* Unpublished manuscript, University of California, San Francisco.

Ekman, P., Huang, T. S. , Sejnowski, T., and Hager, J. C. (1993). Final report to NSF of the planning workshop on facial expression understanding, July 30 to August 1.

Ekman, P., Irwin, W., Rosenberg, E. R. , & Hager, J. C. (1995). *FACS Affect Interpretation Data Base.* Computer data base, University of California, San Francisco.

Ekman, P., Levenson, R. W., & Friesen, W. V. (1983). Autonomic nervous system activity distinguishes between emotions. *Science, 221,* 1208–1210.

Ekman. P., & O'Sullivan, M. (1991). Who can catch a liar. *American Psychologist, 46,* 913–920.

Fridlund, A. J. (1991). Sociality of solitary smiling: potentiation by an implicit audience. *Journal of Personality and Social Psychology, 60,* 229–240.

Fridlund, A. J. (1992). The behavioral ecology and sociality of human faces. In M. S. Clark (Ed.), *Review of personality and social psychology* (Vol 13; pp. 90–121). Newbury Park, CA: Sage.

Fridlund, A. J. (1994). *Human facial expression.* San Diego, CA: Academic Press.

Izard, C. E. (1979). *The maximally discriminative facial movement coding system (MAX).* Unpublished manuscript. Available from Instructional Resource Center, University of Delaware, Newark, DE.

Lazarus, R. S. (1991). *Emotion and adaptation.* New York: Oxford University Press.

Index

Achenbach Child Behavior Checklist (CBCL), 437, 442–443
action units (AU), in FACS, 12–13, 44, 481–482
actors
  encoding and decoding of facial expression of emotions portrayed by, 6, 243–270, 473–474
  Stanislawski technique used by, 244–245, 258, 262, 264, 269
adolescent boys, facial expression of emotion and psychopathology in, 8, 434–449, 479
  anger in externalizers and, 434, 435, 440, 441, 442–444, 445, 446
  embarrassment in nondisordered boys and, 434, 436–437, 440, 441, 442–443, 444, 446
  fear and sadness in internalizers and, 434, 436, 440, 441, 442–443, 444, 445
Affective Communication Task (ACT), 143
affective disorders, facial expression in, 331–341
  adolescent boys and, 434–449
  diagnostic capability of facial measurement and, 331–342
  dissociation between verbal communication and facial expression and, 386–397, 477
  personality and, 450–452
  psychosomatic patients and, 361–385, 478
  suicidal depressed patients and, 398–407
  See also depression, facial expression of

emotion in; psychotherapeutic interaction, facial expression in; schizophrenia, facial expression of emotion in
affective flattening, in schizophrenia, 343–359
affective intensity, measures of, 143
Affective Intensity Measure (AIM), 143
affective regulation process, model of, 416–418
AFFEX system, 294
African Americans, embarrassment and shame in, 149–153
age differences, in infants' emotional expression, 289–301
aggressiveness, in Type A individuals, 455
agreeableness, facial expressions of emotion and, 450, 451
alcohol
  cognitive ability and, 120
  enjoyment and, 113–114, 115, 120, 121–123, 125–128
  exhilaration and, 96, 97, 99–101, 102, 105, 106
  extraversion and enjoyment and, 5, 112–130
  funniness and, 99, 100–101, 102, 105
  humor-induced positive and negative affect and, 123–124
  laughter and, 114–115
  mood state and, 120
  smiling and, 114–115
American infants
  Chinese infants compared to, 300–301, 325
  Japanese infants compared to, 6, 289–301, 325, 476

487

Printed in the United Kingdom
by Lightning Source UK Ltd.
103291UKS00001B/52